Clinical
Decision Making
in Fluency Disorders

FIFTH EDITION

Walter Harne Manning
October 8, 1942–September 12, 2023

"What you do for yourself dies with you when you leave this world, what you do for others lives on forever."

—Ken Robinson, British author and orator

The first time I met Walt, he made a comment about my Australian accent, punched me (hard) in the shoulder, and let out his loud, nasal laugh that anyone who knew him would instantly recognize! Not the image of the "highly respected fluency professor" that I was expecting! But that was Walt—always real, always himself, and always inviting you to do the same! Walt was a larger-than-life character who always filled any room he was in with his presence and laughter, which is not bad for a stutterer who grew up playing verbal gymnastics with people just to avoid stuttering on the name of the town he was from! He loved life, loved people, and was a natural scholar, teacher, and mentor.

Of course, Walt knew a lot about stuttering—he was the ultimate expert, with knowledge built from years of study as well as his own personal experiences with stuttering. But Walt's greatest gift was that he cared deeply and passionately for the people he worked with, both clients and students alike. He had a way of making you feel at ease, whether through careful, empathic listening, engaging conversation, or by being a crazy goofball, which he was very good at!! You just simply could not help but love this man!

Clinical Decision Making in Fluency Disorders was Walt's baby and he poured himself into the book. As Walt's PhD student, I worked with him on the third edition of the book, and then I was honored when he invited me to collaborate as a co-author on the fourth edition. As I completed the revisions for the fifth edition, my goal was to maintain Walt's voice throughout the book—a goal that I hope I have accomplished. This will always be Walt Manning's textbook and his influence will live on through the many students and individuals who stutter and who were touched by his words contained in this text!

And now I have to say "farewell," my friend! I can't believe that I will never again feel the strength of your hug, hear the sound of that laugh, or enjoy the counsel of your words. I am forever changed for the better having known you, Walt, my dear friend and mentor!

—Anthony DiLollo

Clinical Decision Making in Fluency Disorders

FIFTH EDITION

Walter H. Manning, PhD, CCC-SLP

Anthony DiLollo, PhD, CCC-SLP

PLURAL PUBLISHING INC.

9177 Aero Drive, Suite B
San Diego, CA 92123

email: information@pluralpublishing.com
website: https://www.pluralpublishing.com

Typeset in 10.5/13 Palatino by Achorn International Inc.
Printed in the United States of America by Bradford & Bigelow, Inc.

Library of Congress Cataloging-in-Publication Data

Names: Manning, Walter H., author. | DiLollo, Anthony, author.
Title: Clinical decision making in fluency disorders / Walter H. Manning,
    Anthony DiLollo.
Description: Fifth edition. | San Diego, CA : Plural Publishing, Inc., [2025] |
    Includes bibliographical references and indexes.
Identifiers: LCCN 2023024988 (print) | LCCN 2023024989 (ebook) |
    ISBN 9781635506334 (paperback) | ISBN 9781635504453 (ebook)
Subjects: MESH: Stuttering—therapy | Stuttering—etiology | Speech-Language
    Pathology—methods
Classification: LCC RC424 (print) | LCC RC424 (ebook) | NLM WM 475.7 |
    DDC 616.85/54—dc23/eng/20230907
LC record available at https://lccn.loc.gov/2023024988
LC ebook record available at https://lccn.loc.gov/2023024989

CONTENTS

PREFACE

A book is made from a tree. It is an assemblage of flat, flexible parts (still called "leaves") imprinted with dark pigmented squiggles. One glance at it and you hear the voice of another person, perhaps someone dead for thousands of years. Across the millennia, the author is speaking, clearly and silently, inside your head, directly to you. Writing is perhaps the greatest of human inventions, binding together people, citizens of distant epochs, who never knew one another. Books break the shackles of time—proof that humans can work magic.

—Carl Sagan

Having the opportunity to write a fifth edition of this book is a privilege and a labor of love—love for a profession that has provided us with the opportunity to meet and work with some of the most amazing people, from colleagues to clients, who have inspired and challenged us in ways we could not have imagined; love for a career in which we get paid to study the complexity and beauty of the human experience through the lens of communication; and love for a friendship that began with a shared interest in stuttering and has now spanned a quarter of a century!

As with previous editions, a primary goal of this book is to convey to the reader the enthusiasm and creativity associated with assisting people who stutter. Our hope is, as Carl Sagan poetically states in the opening quote, to be "speaking clearly and silently, inside your head, directly to you" as you encounter and work with the diverse and wonderful cohort of per-

sons who stutter and their families. We also want to provide the reader with the principles and clinical insights that enable those who stutter to improve their ability to communicate and enhance their quality of life. Although increasing fluency might be, for some, a high priority during treatment, the therapeutic journey is far more expansive and interesting. Throughout the book we emphasize the primary goals of enhancing communication and empowering clients to create an autonomous and agentic lifestyle.

The readers we have in mind as we write are graduate students who are beginning their first in-depth experience in fluency disorders. We hope this book launches them into a career-long interest in stuttering and the diverse, fascinating, and courageous people who deal with stuttering daily. We also hope that professional clinicians who want to learn more about this specialty area will find this book to be a useful and educational resource. The information and ideas discussed in these pages might also be useful for individuals who stutter (and the parents or spouses of people who stutter), as another purpose of this book is to make stuttering less of a mystery and to provide a sense of direction for the process of therapeutic as well as self-directed change.

During the formulation and development of the profession of speech pathology, particularly during the decades from the late 1920s through the 1960s, the area of fluency disorders was a major area of interest in our professional journals and texts. A review of the early issues of the *Journal of Speech Disorders* (published from 1936–1946) or the initial volumes of the *Journal of Speech and Hearing Disorders* (published through 1990) confirms that a large proportion of the articles addressed the nature and treatment of stuttering. As the scope of practice continues to expand in the field of communication disorders, fluency and fluency disorders have become but one of many areas that students are expected to learn about during their academic and clinical programs. Graduate students in speech-language pathology are expected to become generalists across the wide range of human communication and related problems. Because clinicians are asked to become knowledgeable about so many different communication disorders and related areas, there is concern that the qualifications of professionals for serving any one disorder are being compromised. One response to this concern, driven in part by consumer demand for better services, is the development of Special Interest Groups (SIGs) by the American Speech-Language-Hearing Association that provide enhanced professional qualifications and continuing education opportunities. One of these groups, SIG 4,

focuses on fluency and fluency disorders. Other SIGs that might be of interest to those working with persons who stutter include SIG 14, which is focused on cultural and linguistic diversity, and a recently added group, SIG 20, that focuses on counseling. Interacting with colleagues in such groups is a highly effective way to grow your applied knowledge and skills about stuttering and people who stutter.

The depth of the field is also changing. Reading the volumes of literature associated with but one specialty area of the field can be intimidating, even for someone who has been a clinician and researcher for many years. It is difficult to negotiate the amount of (sometimes conflicting) information that has become available about the many aspects of stuttering. But, reading through the thoughtful and often elegant comments of those who have spent a lifetime trying to understand and explain the nature of stuttering onset and development can be an enjoyable experience. One of the most difficult choices in preparing a text is not what to include but, given the space limitations, what to omit. The citations in this text are intended not only to provide support for the ideas that are offered but also to furnish readers additional, more detailed, sources of information about a topic. There is also the desire to pay homage to the people who have preceded us—to connect to the "citizens of distant epochs" and "break the shackles of time" as Carl Sagan put it—and credit coworkers in the field for their creative and insightful clinical and research ideas.

We would like to comment on the writing style of this book. We have used the active voice throughout, with the intention of engaging the reader. The "editorial we" has been used for the main body of the text and the first person for boxes titled *Clinical Decision Making* and *Clinical Insight*. Clinical Decision Making boxes are designed to address some of the options a clinician is likely to consider during the assessment and treatment processes. Clinical Insight boxes reflect a particular philosophical view about aspects of therapeutic change for individuals who stutter. On other occasions a third type of (untitled) box is used to provide information that in other ways supplements the text.

Some features in this edition have been revised and added to assist both instructors and clinicians. The total number of chapters in this fifth edition has increased to 15, with two new chapters, one on working with clients who are from cultural and linguistic environments different from one's own, and one on general principles of assessment that sets the

foundation for the more specific assessment chapters that focus on children and adults. All chapters were revised, with new material added and some older material removed or summarized where needed. We refined and expanded the Clinical Decision Making and Clinical Insight boxes and revised the discussion questions at the end of each chapter to correspond with the new organization of the book and the fresh information included in each of the chapters. Finally, an online companion website has been (and will continue to be) developed that provides the reader with a variety of materials, including video comments by the authors, PowerPoint slides that coincide with the chapters, a test bank for instructors, and video and audio examples of various fluency problems and therapeutic approaches.

ACKNOWLEDGMENTS

There are several people who played an important role in the creation of this, the fifth edition of this book. The constant support, understanding, and encouragement of our wives, Cheryl and Lara, were essential during the many months of ups and downs that typically accompany such a project. We also want to express our thanks to the staff at Plural Publishing—especially Valerie Johns—for their patience and guidance throughout this process. Finally, we want to express our admiration to the people whose journeys we have been able to share during many therapy sessions over the years. Their courage and persistence—and frequently good humor—has inspired us and helped to carry us through long and rewarding careers.

CONTRIBUTOR

Jean Franco Rivera Pérez, PhD, CCC-SLP
Associate Professor
Department of Communication Sciences and Disorders
Texas Christian University
Fort Worth, Texas
Chapter 9

REVIEWERS OF THE FIFTH EDITION

Plural Publishing, Inc. and the authors would like to thank the following reviewers for taking the time to provide their valuable feedback during the development process:

Katharine A. Blaker, MS, CCC-SLP
Clinical Instructor/Lecturer II
Department of Speech and Hearing
  Sciences
University of New Mexico
Albuquerque, New Mexico

Farzan Irani, PhD, CCC-SLP
Associate Professor
Department of Communication
  Disorders
Texas State University
San Marcos, Texas

Deanna M. Hughes, PhD, CCC-SLP
Assistant Professor
Department of Communication Sciences
  and Disorders
Chapman University
Irvine, California

James M. Mancinelli, PhD, CCC-SLP
Director of Clinical Education
Department of Communication Sciences
  and Disorders
La Salle University
Philadelphia, Pennsylvania

We would like to dedicate the fifth edition of this book to
Cheryl Manning and Lara DiLollo,
our partners and our inspiration

Nothing is more dangerous than a dogmatic worldview—nothing more constraining, more binding to innovation, more destructive of openness to novelty.

—Steven J. Gould (1995)
Dinosaur in a Haystack, Crown Paperbacks, New York, NY

Perhaps the hardest of all the things a clinician must learn is how to live well. You cannot heal a person's wound if you are a dirty bandage. Unless you are a healthy, strong person, your impact will be minimal, no matter what methods you use. There have been times when I resented my clients' expectations of what I should be, but I have noticed that over the years I have become a much better man than I hoped (or desired) to be. I have found that therapy is a two-edged chisel; it shapes the therapist as well as the client.

—Charles Van Riper (1979, p. 140)
A Career in Speech Pathology, Prentice Hall
Englewood Cliffs, NJ

The Effective Clinician

CHAPTER OBJECTIVES

- To describe the importance of the clinician in the therapeutic process
- To examine the characteristics of an effective clinician
- To discuss the use of humor in the therapeutic process

THE IMPORTANCE OF THE CLINICIAN

Beginning a book on fluency disorders by discussing the characteristics of the effective clinician is unusual. Typically, the first chapter describes the nature of stuttering, or provides the reader with historical or theoretical views of the problem—and these topics are presented in the early chapters of this book—but, because a primary goal of this book is to emphasize the ability of the clinician to make wise clinical decisions during assessment and treatment, we decided that discussing the "clinician" is the best place to begin. In earlier editions of this book, we proposed that as much as, or perhaps even more than, any other component, the clinician is central to the success of the treatment process. Clinical research in a variety of fields has continued to provide support for this idea. Not all clinicians—even those who are clinically certified, specialty certified, or have years of experience—are equally effective in assisting children and adults to address their stuttering or other fluency disorders. Having said that, we firmly believe that individuals can become effective clinicians by embracing the traits, skills, and attitudes discussed in this chapter and focusing on the person in front of them and not just the stuttering problem.

Having indicated in the Preface that another primary goal of this book is to convey the enthusiasm and excitement of working with people who stutter, we now step back a bit and place the learning process into a wider perspective. Following the intense years of formal education, you

1

will soon be on your own. Your role will no longer be that of a graduate student who is continually challenged by your instructors to demonstrate your knowledge and clinical skills. You will be a professional who is likely to be considered the resident expert on the topic of communication disorders in general and stuttering in particular. This change in roles may be difficult because during the years of graduate school, many student clinicians have relatively little exposure to the field of fluency disorders. Most students have the opportunity to take, at most, one (three-credit, we hope) course in stuttering and obtain clinical experience with relatively few individuals. Student clinicians typically observe the progress made by individuals for only a few weeks or months. When clients achieve success, it is often difficult for student clinicians to appreciate how much of a role they played in promoting change. Even if students are fortunate enough to take a course on stuttering that is an especially good one and the clinical experiences are instructive, it is only the beginning of learning about the experience of stuttering.

You may occasionally find yourself exhausted as you successfully negotiate the rigors of a good graduate program. Nevertheless, in order to become an effective professional, your learning must continue long after graduation. Think about it—the clinical decisions you will be making one or two decades after graduation will have little to do with much of the information you are currently learning! Reinterpretation of old data, as well as ongoing basic and applied research, continually lead to new constructs and ways of making informed clinical decisions. When people of earlier generations were students, many things they were taught—including the role of parents in the onset

and development of stuttering, the linear development of stuttering through primary and secondary stages, the likelihood of spontaneous recovery in young children, the possibility of relapse following treatment, and the role of genetics in the etiology and epidemiology of stuttering—have since been shown to be partially or completely inaccurate. The evolution of information occurs in all scientific fields, and the shelf lives of textbooks are not nearly as long as authors would like them to be. Of course, your instructors are not intentionally providing information that is incorrect. It is just that the profession is still climbing the hills and mountains necessary to allow us a more accurate view of the phenomena we are investigating and the people we are attempting to assist.

Carl Sagan's (1996) caution that "One of the great commandments of science is to mistrust arguments from authority" (p. 28) is probably good advice for many aspects of life. It is also good advice for consumers of all information, including the information discussed in this text! As you expand your knowledge through years of clinical experience with many different people and your participation in continuing educational activities, you will begin to create your own style of doing things. You will choose new ideas and approaches that will spring from basic and applied research yet to be conceived or conducted. Moreover, as you continue to be a student of your field, you will achieve additional insight, wisdom, and enthusiasm for your work.

Experienced clinicians, and—perhaps more important—clients who have experienced treatment for stuttering that was more or less successful, have suggested certain clinician characteristics that are more desirable than others. If this is your first exposure to the field of fluency disorders, this initial chapter may help you to determine the strengths that you bring to the clinical encounter, as well as those areas that you can work on to become the best clinician you can be.

The Critical Importance of the Clinician

First, let us re-emphasize that the clinician plays a vital role in a successful therapeutic process. A number of authors have considered this concept specifically in the area of fluency disorders (e.g., Cooper & Cooper, 1985c; Emerick, 1974; Guitar, 2006; Hood, 1974; Plexico, Manning, & DiLollo, 2005, 2010; Shapiro, 1999; Van Riper, 1975) and provide convincing arguments indicating that the clinician is a critical part of the therapeutic process. For example, regardless of the treatment strategy and the associated techniques, Cooper and Cooper (1985c) maintained that the person who is administering the treatment is the most important variable in creating the process of change. Murphy and Fitzsimons (1960) contended that during counseling, the "most important single variable affecting the success in the treatment of stutterers is—the clinician" (p. 27). Even if treatment takes the form of an archetypal program of behavioral modification, Cooper and Cooper (1985b) proposed that "it does matter who is doing the conditioning" (p. 21). Regardless of the treatment strategy, authors have consistently found that the clinician plays a critical role in orchestrating a successful treatment program (Emerick, 1974; Hood, 1974; Reeves, 2006; Shapiro, 1999; Van Riper, 1975; Yaruss, Quesal, & Murphy, 2002). In Chapters 8 and 10 we discuss empirical evidence supporting the importance of the clinician in the therapeutic process, not only for our field, but also in related fields such as counseling and psychotherapy.

Clinician Attributes

Although there is no exclusive set of attributes that define the ideal clinician, many authors have attempted to define such a set, with at least some level of agreement across the varied opinions. For example, Crowe (1997c) cited the American Psychological Association (1947) as recommending the following personal attributes for counselors and psychotherapists: resourcefulness, versatility, curiosity, respect for the integrity of others, awareness of one's own personality traits, humor, tolerance, ability to relate warmly to others, industry, responsibility, integrity, stability, and ethics. Similarly, Van Riper (1975) provided the first comprehensive description of the desirable attributes of clinicians who help children and adults who stutter. He described personality characteristics of *empathy*, an authentic sensitivity for the client; *warmth*, a respect or positive regard for the client; *genuineness*, openness, and the ability to disclose oneself as a real person; and *charisma* (perhaps the most enigmatic one), an ability to arouse hope, appearing confident yet humble, frank yet tactful. As Van Riper (1973) wrote, "Like fishermen, good therapists are optimists. Most of them have come to have profound respect for the latent potential for self-healing that exists in all troubled souls" (p. 230).

Another description of desirable clinician characteristics was proposed by Zinker (1977), who considered therapy a creative process of changing awareness and behavior. He suggested that a common malady among therapists is that they fail to see themselves as artists involved in a creative process. As the clinician becomes involved in the dynamic and shared process of change, the opportunity for creativity becomes more apparent. The experienced clinician can be seen as a guide who has a map of the territory. The clinician has a sense of direction about where the client may benefit from traveling and a notion of when it might be appropriate to initiate an exploratory trip off the main path. The challenge for the clinician is to "establish an adequate cognitive map which includes the client's experience of himself and then to point to action steps to make the solution possible for the client" (Zinker, 1977, p. 11).

In order to guide a person through successful therapy, Zinker proposed that the clinician possess several thought-provoking characteristics that nurture the creative process:

1. Creativity that is facilitated by a child-like wonderment and excitement
2. Patience for change without forcing
3. A love of play
4. A sense of humor
5. A positive attitude about risk taking
6. Willingness to experiment with different approaches and techniques
7. The ability to distinguish the boundaries between the clinician and a client
8. Willingness to push, confront, persuade, and energize another person to accomplish the work that needs to be done
9. A lifestyle that promotes a rich background with a range of life experiences

Zinker proposed that blocks to creativity lead to the clinician becoming stuck in a particular theoretical or professional stance or holding to the view that science and art do not mix (a science vs.

art dichotomy). Other blocks to creativity include a fear of failure (playing it safe and not taking risks), a reluctance to play (fear of experimenting with ideas and techniques and of looking silly), over-certainty concerning a particular school of thought (a rigidity concerning the nature of the problem-solving approach), giving up too soon when an approach or a technique does not appear to be "working," a reluctance to push hard enough to help others, or an inability to accept contrasting ways of interpreting things and events (believing that there is only one way or a single best way to define success during therapy). It is also worth considering that clinicians should not be exhibiting these blocks to creativity to their clients, who might already be experiencing them. Zinker's views are similar to those of David Luterman, an experienced counselor and author in the field of communication disorders. Luterman (2001) suggested that professional growth is severely limited by the clinician's fear of making mistakes and an unwillingness to assume risks during the therapeutic or counseling process.

Cooper and Cooper (1985b) also provided a description of several desirable attributes of the effective clinician. Many of the attributes described by these authors coincide with their view of fluency treatment as an interpersonal (communication) experience. The Coopers suggested that, especially during the early stages of treatment, the client–clinician relationship should be a major focus. They stated that the clinician should be *genuine* and able to openly express both negative and positive feelings to the client. However, as the clinician is expressing these feelings, it is important that she also indicate a belief in the worth and potential of the client (what Carl Rogers

CLINICAL INSIGHT

On a few occasions throughout this book, we will include comments from Daniel Goleman's (2006) book, *Social Intelligence*. Goleman provides a wealth of supporting data from studies in neuroscience when discussing the concept of *primal empathy*, the ability of individuals to unconsciously employ a "low road" to rapidly scan and interpret another individual for such issues as safety and trust. Neural circuitry connecting such areas as the sensory cortices, thalamus, and amygdala, as well as multiple systems of mirror neurons, allow some individuals to "bridge brains" (p. 43). The "high road," which involves the prefrontal cortex (the brain's executive center) is not involved. Goleman describes how mirror neurons fire in such a way that observing someone else being hurt also feels like being hurt to the observer. People develop an emotional contagion and synchrony as they resonate with another. As the synchrony occurs, individuals' moods begin to match, the timing of verbal and nonverbal communication becomes more coordinated, and participants become more comfortable with silences. The process must be spontaneous and unconscious rather than preplanned and intentional. Fortunately, as Goleman explained, the process is described as "eminently trainable" (p. 99).

[1957] termed "unconditional positive regard"). As treatment becomes challenging and the client is asked to make behavioral, attitudinal, and cognitive changes, the clinician should be continually *honest* in reinforcing the client's feelings of self-worth. Such honesty, the Coopers noted, is much easier to manifest when the clinician enjoys working with the client, something that might not always be the case. They warned that the clinician also needs to resist the urge to tell clients how they should feel. As Luterman (2001) cautioned, there is a great temptation to try to get the client to feel as we do—something to be avoided if we are to be helpful.

Importantly, Cooper and Cooper (1985b) also suggested that the clinician should be "devoid of dogma" and have the ability to adapt the therapeutic approach to the client's uniqueness and needs. This is a good way of saying that good clinicians are client directed rather than treatment directed. The clinician must be able to recognize subtle client responses that provide cues for direction and indicate progress. Effective clinicians are not daunted by a client's negative response to the suggestions and challenges of the therapeutic process. They are, in short, able to be a constant ally and to persevere along with the client when the process of change slows or becomes difficult. Effective clinicians inform the client by providing information about the client's progress and direction of treatment.

Undoubtedly, the characteristics we have discussed would be desirable for any clinician working with a person for any reason. And, of course, they would be valuable characteristics to have in a friend or colleague. Moreover, just as it is possible to be successful as a friend or colleague without being adept at all of these attributes, it is possible to be a successful clinician without possessing a high level of skill at each. Personal and professional growth, however, is something all clinicians should strive for—at all levels of experience and expertise—and can lead to increased skill in both areas of strength and relative weakness. Clinicians are encouraged to engage with workshops, journal articles, books, conference sessions, and other development activities to enhance your knowledge and skill in the various attributes described in this chapter, and thereby increase your effectiveness in treating clients.

Clinician Attitudes About Stuttering and People Who Stutter

Our attitude about those who come to us for help and our understanding of their communication problems have a fundamental influence on how we approach them as people during both assessment and treatment. What the clinician has learned and understood about the stuttering experience and what he or she has been able to observe about people who stutter will determine whether he or she will even have the desire to work with such clients.

One unique characteristic of the field of fluency disorders is that a substantial number of people who stutter (or have a history of having stuttered) have gone on to become professional clinicians, often specializing in stuttering and related fluency disorders. Assuming that clinicians with a history of stuttering have also acquired the necessary academic and clinical knowledge, their life experiences may provide some understanding about a client. The experience of having traveled within the culture of stuttering and survived the many tribulations along the way tends to promote the insight and empathy necessary for guiding others through the process of therapeutic change. It is generally easier to understand and relate to another's situation if we have shared the same or a similar experience (e.g., undergoing surgery, losing and searching for a job, loss of a loved one, experiencing a divorce). There are many examples of this understanding in the helping professions. For example, people with a history of substance abuse are often extremely effective therapists in alcohol and drug rehabilitation programs. They understand from their experience the nature of the problem and the many tricks that people use to deny the problem or avoid change.

This does not mean, however, that people who stutter or who have stuttered in the past will be more effective as clinicians or will necessarily have a greater understanding of the stuttering experience. With good preparation and experience, clinicians without a history of stuttering can have equal understanding and do not have to acquiesce when individuals who stutter offer the challenge, "How can you understand? You don't stutter!"

CLINICAL INSIGHT

One summer, I was contacted by a colleague from the Psychology Department at the university at which I was working. He had a 14-year-old nephew, Luke, coming to town for the summer and was hoping to get some help with Luke's stuttering. I agreed to see Luke at his house, and was then told that Luke was not a big fan of speech therapy and would not be told I was coming. When I arrived, Luke and I met in the basement of the house and I could tell from the start that Luke was not happy to meet me! His first words to me were, "I don't need any help with my speech, so you are wasting your time!" I responded, "Well, I promised your uncle that I would come and see you, so would it be okay if we just hung out for an hour, so I can at least say that I tried?" Luke agreed, so we just hung out and talked about what he liked and what life was like in his hometown. I didn't try to do any "treatment," but I did ask Luke about how he handled his stuttering, and I suggested a few things he could read if he wanted to (he was an avid reader). At the end of the hour, as I was preparing to leave, Luke said, "So, maybe you could come back a few times while I am here." I told him that if I did, we would need to do some work on his speech, but that we would do it in a way that would be more like the conversations that we had just had and less like his school experiences of speech therapy (which involved primarily naming pictures). I saw Luke a number of times over that summer and the subsequent two summers. The important aspect here is that, rather than pushing my agenda as the speech pathologist or the agenda of Luke's uncle, I was able to engage Luke where he was at and build a relationship that then allowed us to move forward in working on his stuttering. (AD)

(Manning, 2004b). It may be that one day a client will challenge you by asking such a question. If a client does, will he or she be correct and how will you respond?

HIGHLIGHTS

You don't have to be a person who stutters to appreciate the experience of stuttering—but you do need to learn to not be afraid of stuttering, be willing to engage in challenging behaviors (e.g., pseudostuttering, making difficult phone calls, etc.) with your clients, and seek out stories that elaborate on the experience of stuttering.

How Clinicians Interpret the Disorder

If stuttering is presented to students as a mysterious disorder, when those students become clinicians, they will naturally be wary about treating these clients. Stuttering may indeed be an enigma, for, as we describe in succeeding chapters, the problem is complex and many of the features lie under the surface. When responding to the suggestion that stuttering is like a riddle, Van Riper (1982) stated that "[it] is more than a riddle. It is at least a complicated, multidimensional jigsaw puzzle, with many pieces still missing" (p. 1). Sheehan (1970) frequently argued that stuttering is like an iceberg, with only small portions of the problem visible to

CLINICAL INSIGHT

Speaking as a person with a history of stuttering, I believe that there are many experienced clinicians who, although they have never stuttered, unmistakably understand the experience of those who do. These individuals demonstrate their understanding in the diagnostic procedures they use and create, the way they measure the success of their interventions, and the research questions they ask. They further their understanding by attending local and national meetings of stuttering support groups (see Appendix A) and by listening attentively to understand the essential themes of their clients' stories (see Chapter 8). Although we can never know every aspect of another's experience, we can learn enough so that we can provide accurate and timely help that enables our clients to more effectively cope with their situation. (WM)

On the other hand, speaking as a person who does not have a history of stuttering, I, too, believe that clinicians who do not stutter can understand the experiences of their clients who do. My personal journey in this regard started with a willingness to engage in pseudostuttering as a student clinician—to throw myself into a role that was unfamiliar to me and try to experience some of what my future clients were living every day. Reflecting on those experiences, and comparing those feelings to experiences in my own life from times I had to deal with some form of challenge, enabled me to start to develop a deeper understanding of the experiences of my clients. Also, seeking out the stories of persons who stutter—not just about therapy but about living with stuttering—became a passion that led me to seek out books and movies about living with stuttering, and to take every opportunity to engage in conversations and build relationships with persons who stutter. (AD)

those who are unwilling to look below the surface, where 90% of the iceberg is found (Figure 1–1). Sheehan (1980) also offered the pointed comment that "defining stuttering as [only] a fluency problem borders on professional irresponsibility. It ignores the person. It ignores his feelings about himself" (p. 392).

On the other hand, Ham (1993) argued that stuttering is not significantly more complex than many other human problems. Much of stuttering behavior is rule governed with cause-and-effect relationships that are understood. Many of the factors that precipitate and maintain stuttering are well known, and many children and adults achieve extraordinary success in modifying both their speech and their handicap as a result of treatment. As students have the opportunity to observe clinicians who understand stuttering and begin to experience success assisting people who stutter, they are likely to become enthusiastic about the assessment and treatment of the problem. Experienced clinicians know what success looks and sounds like, and these changes can be shown to the new clinician. As with most things in life, there is no substitute for experience. Only continual practice of your craft will enable you to learn by your successes as well as your failures. For those who are curious and excited by learning, the process is never complete.

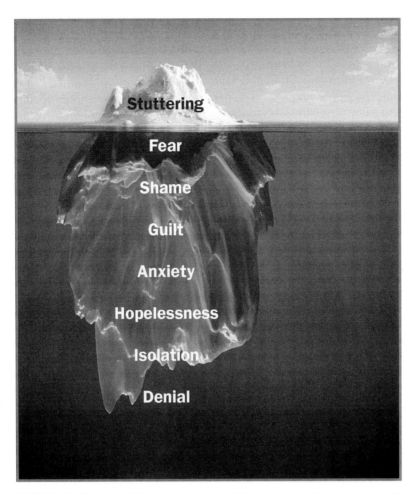

FIGURE 1–1. Sheehan (1970) frequently argued that stuttering is like an iceberg, with only small portions of the problem visible to those who were unwilling to look below the surface, where 90% of the iceberg is found.

One of the substantial problems faced by students taking part in any clinical experience is that they are not likely to see a long view of progress. This is due, in part, to not being able to follow clients throughout the continuum of change during and following structured therapeutic change. For many practical reasons it is rare, even for a professional clinician, to follow a client for more than a few months or years, particularly following dismissal from treatment. Most students lack the chance to observe and work with clients for a substantial portion of their formal treatment, the time during which the client pays a professional for services, let alone informal treatment, the much longer period when the client gradually develops the "response-ability" required for self-treatment. The window available to student clinicians in graduate programs for observing therapeutic change is a small one. In most instances, student clinicians are just beginning to understand the client and the nature of his or her stuttering as the semester comes to a close. When the global picture of behavioral, affective, and cognitive change is unavailable, it is understandable that the treatment process will appear enigmatic. Then again, if student clinicians know what to look for and can be shown indicators of progress during treatment (both for behavioral as well as cognitive–affective change), helping these speakers will be more likely to be viewed as a positive rather than an aversive experience. A central principle is indicated in the comments of Daly (1988), who noted that the better clinicians tend to be those who hold a belief that their clients have the capacity for success as a result of treatment. Such conviction by the clinician is essential, according to Van Riper (1973), who stated the belief that "out of the therapist's faith can come the stutterer's hope" (p. 230).

CLINICIAN INTERVENTION SKILLS

Given the aforementioned attitudes and personality attributes, we now discuss several intervention skills that can be acquired and developed by the student. There is, of course, considerable overlap across each of these abilities.

Critical Thinking

A question that we often get asked at conferences and presentations, and sometimes from our own beginning students, is, "How do I know what therapeutic approach to use with a given client?" The answer that we give when asked this type of question is, "It depends"—which, on the surface, does not appear to be a very helpful response. What we are trying to convey in that short answer, however, is that, as a clinician, you need to *think* and not just react.

Unfortunately, the default for many clinicians is to cling tightly to one therapeutic approach—one that appears to have "evidence" and that they can feel safe applying without needing to think too deeply. In contrast, effective clinicians engage in something called *critical thinking* as an integral part of their clinical decision-making process. This is how clinicians can be "devoid of dogma" (i.e., not hold tightly to one approach) and be able to adapt their therapeutic approach to the client's unique needs (Cooper & Cooper, 1985b).

A Definition of Critical Thinking

Wade et al. (2014) defined critical thinking as "the ability and willingness to assess claims and make objective judgments on the basis of well-supported reasons and evidence rather than emotion and anecdote" (p. 6). Significantly, this definition implies that there are two important aspects of being a critical thinker—"ability" and "willingness." Individuals need both critical thinking skills and the disposition, or willingness, to apply those skills to events and information that are read, observed, or discussed with others. Wade et al. further described critical thinkers as those able to look for and identify flaws in arguments, and to resist claims that have no evidence. Importantly, critical thinkers are described as being creative and constructive; identifying alternative explanations for events, thinking of implications for statements and beliefs, and applying knowledge in novel ways and situations.

Critical Thinking in Health Professions

The need for critical thinking in the health professions has received a great deal of attention. Every day, health professionals gather information from a multitude of sources and must process it in order to make sound clinical decisions that are often complex and carry significant consequences (Sharp et al., 2013). It has been widely recognized that the quality of clinicians' decision-making skills is the foundation for evidence-based practice, requiring the integration of best evidence, clinician expertise, and client preference for the delivery of person-centered care. Critical thinking—rather than depth of technical knowledge—has been identified as the most relevant knowledge and skill for helping to ensure quality clinical decision making (DiLollo, 2010; Finn, 2011; Gambrill, 2012; Gupta, 2011; Huang et al., 2014; Kamhi, 2011; Rousseau & Gunia, 2016).

Critical Thinking in Speech-Language Pathology

Mok et al. (2008) noted that graduate courses in speech-language pathology training programs often place an emphasis on "dispensing knowledge" (p. 439). As a result, students tend to focus on facts rather than learning how to integrate knowledge, which implies the need for something more in the training of future clinicians. Indeed, referring to the education of speech-language pathologists, Harris et al. (1998) suggested that there are

> . . . skills and attributes, beyond a body of knowledge in the field and appropriate discipline specific techniques, that must be fostered by institutions of higher education if graduates are to be equipped for the needs of a rapidly changing workplace. (p. 221)

Critical thinking encompasses many of the "skills and attributes" referred to by Harris et al.

The American Speech-Language-Hearing Association's (ASHA) guiding documents on preferred practice patterns in speech-language pathology (ASHA, 2004) suggest that clinical practice by speech-language pathologists should be both person centered and evidence based. Finn (2011) and Kamhi (2011) made the case that critical thinking underlies both of these practice endeavors, forming the base of knowledge and skills that allow for rational clinical decision making in the face of the complexity of human communication. Further, critical thinking has been highlighted as an essential knowledge and skill in several policy documents related to education in speech-language pathology, including the guidelines for the clinical doctorate in speech-language pathology (ASHA, 2015a), and the Academic Affairs Board report on the role of the undergraduate curriculum in communication sciences and disorders (ASHA, 2015b). Finally, critical thinking has also been identified as a core competency for implementing interprofessional education and practice (Interprofessional Education Collaborative Expert Panel, 2011), an endeavor that has been promoted as a practice priority by ASHA (2015c).

Not surprisingly, Finn (2011) suggested that critical thinking should be considered a "core skill" of a 21st-century education and recommended that we "require it of all of our training programs" (p. 71). Building on this foundation, a number of authors have reported on the importance of, and approaches to, training speech-language pathology students to use critical thinking in their clinical interactions (e.g., Coutts & Pillay, 2021; Ellis, 2017; Masuku & Mupawose, 2022).

Despite this, training programs for speech-language pathologists have been slow to incorporate specific critical thinking training as part of their graduate

CLINICAL INSIGHT

Using Socratic Questions to promote critical thinking. In many ways, Socrates is considered the father of critical thinking. In ancient Athens, Socrates would engage his students in a process that has become known as "Socratic questioning" by asking a series of questions that encouraged his students to question assumptions, look for evidence, consider alternative explanations and perspectives, and contemplate implications and consequences. We present here a few examples of Socratic questions from a more extensive list by Paul (1992, pp. 367–368). Students and clinicians can use these types of questions when discussing clinical topics with clients and colleagues, and when researching clinical information in books, in journals, and on the Internet.

Questions for Clarification
- What do you mean by _____?
- What is your main point?
- What do you think is the main issue here?
- Could you give me an example?

Questions About the Initial Question or Issue
- Would_____ put the question differently?
- Can we break this question down at all?
- Does this question lead to other questions or issues?

Questions That Probe Assumptions
- What are you assuming?
- What could we assume instead?
- Is this always the case? Why do you think the assumption holds here?

Questions That Probe Reasons and Evidence
- Could you explain your reasons to us?
- Are those reasons adequate?
- Do you have any evidence for that?

Questions That Probe Origin or Source Questions
- Where did you get this idea?
- What caused you to feel this way?

Questions That Probe Implications and Consequences
- What are you implying by that?
- What effect would that have?
- What is an alternative?
- If this is the case, then what else must be true?

Questions About Viewpoints or Perspectives
- How would other groups of people respond? Why?
- Can anyone see this another way?
- What would someone who disagrees say?

curriculum. A useful resource for students and clinicians looking for introductory material on critical thinking is *Asking the Right Questions: A Guide to Critical Thinking* by Browne and Keeley (2015), now in its 11th edition.

With critical thinking as our foundation for clinical decision making and driving the application of evidence-based practice and client-centered care, let us proceed with some other aspects of clinical intervention that are the hallmarks of effective clinicians.

Becoming Less Inhibited

Becoming desensitized to stuttering is an important first step in understanding the behavior and decisions of the person we are seeing. Only after the clinician is able to become uninhibited and fearless about stuttering in general will treatment proceed (Van Riper, 1982). In addition, when clinicians experience fear and anxiety in response to stuttering, they are more likely to react by limiting their treatment options to focus on familiar, safe procedures (e.g., strictly behavioral approaches), rather than being open to thinking critically and experimenting with adapting their therapeutic approach to the client's unique needs.

To be effective, the clinician must become progressively less inhibited about many aspects of stuttering. To start with, clinicians often need to overcome their concern about doing something "wrong" in therapy that will hurt the speaker and somehow make things worse. This common perspective is most likely related to the notion that there is something psychologically amiss or fragile about the person who stutters and that such individuals are unstable or especially susceptible to emotional trauma. In part, this attitude might be a result of the diagnosogenic view of stuttering etiology advocated during the period from the early 1950s through the late 1960s, which held that stuttering onset was the result of inappropriate listener reactions to the fluency breaks of young children (see Chapter 3). Alternatively, such a cautious approach could be related to the idea that any increase in the frequency of stuttering is necessarily bad. As we discuss in later chapters, for a number of reasons, an increase in the frequency of stuttering could be an important indicator of progress, particularly early in treatment. In addition, stuttering is highly variable, and changes in the frequency of the overt behaviors can be attributable to many, sometimes unknown, factors, only one of which is the clinician.

In extreme instances, of course, it is possible to make the stuttering, or even the person who is stuttering, in some sense worse. If, for example, the clinician is truly an unqualified, uncaring, and insensitive person, the client's struggle with stuttering could become worse. However, a qualified clinician who is inhibited about making a decision during treatment for fear of somehow injuring a client most likely possesses a naive view of the person. Most people who stutter are not emotionally unstable or fragile. To the contrary, many people who stutter are highly functional and emotionally resilient. Clinicians with training and experience should not exercise any more caution about doing something "wrong" when assisting a child or adult who stutters than they would with a client with any other communication problem.

The therapeutic alliance between clinician and client is an important aspect of the process of change during treatment. There is no question, especially with

CLINICAL INSIGHT

At the outset of my career, I had the opportunity to correspond with the charismatic and prolific Dr. Charles Van Riper, clearly a master clinician. I did not have the opportunity to know him well, but on one occasion we met in his office at Western Michigan University. I remember his primary comment about clinicians. Paraphrasing (for reasons those who knew him well will understand), he said that many clinicians are far too inhibited to be effective with people who stutter. They are afraid of eliciting even a moment of stuttering. They are afraid of joining in the process of touching, exploring, experimenting, and playing with the stuttering. They view stuttering as something to be suppressed and avoided. Likewise, we are intrigued when we ask students in class to follow our lead and voluntarily produce mild to moderate (or severe if they are brave enough) stuttering in front of their peers. Their reaction to the activity indicates the degree to which stuttering is stigmatized in society and the extent to which we must go to decrease our natural inhibitions about approaching and exploring the experience of stuttering. (WM)

adolescents and adults who stutter, that there is a strong counseling or psychotherapeutic component at the center of the process. As suggested by the quote by Van Riper at the outset of this chapter, there are aspects of this process of change and growth that impact the clinician as well as the client. It is rare that only one person grows within a dynamic, interactive treatment environment.

Nevertheless, because the process of change and growth is dynamic, it is not necessarily something that all clinicians are initially comfortable about entering. One alluring aspect of the behavior modification programs that became popular during the late 1950s, 1960s, and 1970s was the belief that the role of the clinician could be limited to the identification and modification of overt stuttering behaviors. The behaviors that were audible and visible on the surface were the major focus of treatment. Frequency counts were made, contingencies were agreed on or at least implied, and rewards and punishments were dispensed by the clinician

based on the client's behavior and performance. The often manualized treatment process was clear, goals were explicit, and fluency was charted and altered. The approach was relatively easy to teach to students as well as clients. Some clients did well, as some clients will do in nearly all reasonable treatment approaches (see Chapter 7). Some even stayed well. The point is not whether behavior modification approaches are effective, for they can be. A particular treatment strategy can only be evaluated based on the needs and response of the client. The point is that when using any treatment, including current behavioral modification programs (which tend to encompass more broad-based and multifactorial philosophies and approaches than in the past), the clinician needs to be uninhibited. The clinician needs to be uninhibited about stuttering and the people who are doing the stuttering if he or she expects the client, parents, teacher, or spouse to also approach, understand, and alter the problem.

One of the unique aspects about the series of treatment sessions featuring Charles Van Riper that is produced by the Stuttering Foundation is that the clinician (Van Riper) demonstrates an uninhibited and interactive therapeutic style with his young adult client Jeff (Van Riper, 1977, Video #1080, Therapy in Action). Van Riper models attributes of empathy, genuineness, warmth, charisma, and particularly frankness throughout the treatment sessions with Jeff. Because the tapes were made in the 1970s, the approaches, technology, and attitudes that Van Riper employs in his interactions with Jeff can be somewhat distracting to contemporary observers, making it necessary for new clinicians to view the tapes several times in order to fully appreciate the nature of the therapeutic interaction. After viewing the tapes a few times, observers are able to detect the genuine, humanistic, and supportive nature of Van Riper's therapeutic interaction. It becomes clear that Van Riper is obviously unafraid of stuttering. As documented by the analysis of the verbal patterns during the therapy sessions by Blood et al. (2001), Van Riper simultaneously challenges and supports Jeff and modifies his approach based on Jeff's response as therapy progresses. He imparts to Jeff a distinct sense of direction as he helps him to move forward in treatment. There are moments of spontaneous humor on the part of both participants that indicate their synchrony. The tapes also provide a good illustration of how a productive therapeutic relationship is like many successful relationships—they are not always idyllic or characterized by what has been described as "good rapport."

Another beneficial aspect of this video series is that the student has the opportunity to see an extended window of change as Jeff progresses through treatment. Although the observer is not assisting in the process, it is encouraging to see that dramatic success is possible during a relatively brief period of therapy. There is some indication that students can increase their level of self-efficacy about clinical performance with fluency clients as a function of academic training (Rudolf et al., 1983). There is, however, no substitute for a successful hands-on clinical experience.

Avoiding Dogmatic Decisions

Being able to see beyond the dogma of one particular treatment strategy is a sign of clinical wisdom and maturity. Making use of the oft-quoted adage, Egan (1990) cautioned that we should "beware the person of one book" (p. 26). The message of a single book or single author can too easily become a calling and exclude other beneficial possibilities. It is true that the discovery of *the* method can be empowering and give a sense of direction to the clinician and, therefore, to the client. However, as Egan pointed out, such devotion to a single treatment path can also lead to a closing down of new ideas and new growth—a sign of a lack of *critical thinking* on the part of the clinician. It is also a path that is likely to lead to boredom. Egan recommended that, for a professional, the foundation for choosing a strategy or technique should not be the treatment protocol, but the nature and needs of the client. As we suggest throughout this book, clinical decisions should be driven by critical thinking, with primary focus on the goals and values of the client and the therapeutic context rather than dogma. A technician, particularly an inexperienced one, is likely to make decisions according to the guidelines of the treatment manual, without questioning assumptions, evidence, implications, or other perspectives. Although this approach is nearly always less thoughtful and creative, it can be much easier and even comforting. It is likely to require less thinking and responsibility and fewer decisions on the part of the clinician. As we see later in this chapter, professionals are more likely to make decisions based on a critical analysis of the contextual cues of the dynamic therapeutic situation. It might be instructive to consider that the most proficient and creative professional chefs rarely follow a cookbook.

Opening Your Treatment Focus

One of the characteristics of learning a new activity is the amount of attention required to focus on the techniques. When first learning a sport such as soccer, for example, it is necessary to learn such techniques as passing, receiving, and shooting the ball. Later, with more experience, one moves beyond the techniques. The accomplished player has a broader, less technical view of the game. With experience, the view includes the strategies of the event and, particularly, an analysis of the other team's strengths and weaknesses. The player's focus begins to expand, allowing a focus on the movements and anticipated actions of the person's own teammates as well as the players on the opposing team. Although the techniques remain essential to the accomplishment of the overall strategy, the most important aspect of the process is not so much what to do or how to do it, but when to do it and why. Similar to inexperienced players or coaches, new clinicians tend to focus on mastering the techniques rather than the overall long-term strategies and goals. Even more to the point, new clinicians are more likely to focus on the techniques rather than

CLINICAL DECISION MAKING

Several years ago, at a professional meeting of speech-language pathologists, I was a member of a panel that was asked, along with the audience, to view a series of videotapes of children and adults with fluency disorders. The panel's task was to react to these hypothetical clients and speculate about the various strategies and techniques that might be appropriate for treating them. As we took our turns offering suggestions about each speaker, it became embarrassingly apparent that one member of the panel was giving the identical response each time. Regardless of the client's characteristics such as age and severity and nature of the stuttering, this clinician would take her turn at the microphone and say something such as, "I believe strongly in the 'X' method and feel that this approach would be ideal for this client. I have seen this method work for many clients and would prefer to use this approach with this person." Beyond the highly questionable efficacy and research outcomes for this particular method, the audience witnessed a clear example of a "one book" approach to treatment. The clinician was familiar with a particular approach and this was the approach she believed in. It was apparent that the dogma of the approach mattered more than her clients. (WM) the people they are trying to help. In part because they know relatively few techniques at the beginning of their career, new clinicians are apt to think to themselves, "What can I do in the therapy session today?" rather than the more Socratic question, "What does my client need from me now, and how does that fit with our long-term goals of treatment?"

We are not suggesting that specific treatment techniques are unimportant, for we discuss many of them in succeeding chapters. They are, of course, every bit as essential to treating clients as knowing how to pass, receive, and control the ball is to playing soccer. You cannot participate in the game well if you are not adept at the techniques. Techniques are unquestionably important, and the professional clinician must know many of them and know them well. However, they are not the most important aspect of the process. The ability to look beyond the techniques—even beyond the treatment program—and see the client is something that distinguishes the experienced clinician from the novice, the technician from the professional, and the critical thinker from the dogmatist.

Just as the new instructor is less likely to vary from prepared notes or stray more than a few steps away from the podium, the less experienced player is more likely to have a rigid, preplanned attack. A preplanned strategy may work for a while, particularly with an easy opponent. However, the plan is not likely to work indefinitely and for everyone, especially with a challenging student or opponent. The accomplished participant is flexible; she or he can see what is occurring on the field in a broader sense. The accomplished athlete (or coach) is more likely to be aware of and willing to change strategy based on the circumstances and the level of competition. Decisions and actions are primar-

ily dictated by strengths and weakness of the other players or team. They most certainly are not dictated by a textbook or by dogma.

For decades, Van Riper stated that, "the client, not the clinician, is the guide," and certainly not the text or the treatment techniques. There are many paths up the mountain and the path is likely to be different for each person, in part because everyone is beginning the journey from a different place, with a different history and a different set of skills. This seems rather complicated—and sometimes it can be. However, before we throw up our hands at the unique challenges presented to us by each client, it is important to realize that many individuals who stutter have some similar cognitive and behavioral responses to stuttering. Moreover, there are basic goals (Chapter 10) and principles of change (Chapter 12) that contribute to success.

Calibrating to the Client

At the outset of the first several treatment sessions, it is not unusual for clinicians to find that they are presented with a wide range of information by clients. Not only are we introduced to expected overt or surface behaviors that we have seen before in other speakers who stutter, but we might also observe some new behaviors that are unique to this person. Some of these behaviors may be obvious and explicit. Other behaviors may occur rarely or not at all during the initial sessions. Some of the coping behaviors learned long ago have become part of this person's response to stuttering and might become apparent only during more stressful speaking situations; they are seen only rarely, if at all, during treatment sessions.

We are likely to see these behaviors only when we accompany the person into daily speaking situations beyond the treatment setting. We may also observe these behaviors if we call clients unexpectedly or meet them by chance in a social situation. In any case, there are apt to be many surface behaviors that are unique to each speaker, and it will take even experienced clinicians some time to become attuned to them.

In order to fully appreciate the nature of the client's stuttered speech, it could be useful to also consider the quality of the person's speech when they are not stuttering. What is it about the subtle surface behaviors of this speaker that indicates to us that the speaker is fluent? Is the client producing truly fluent speech that, as Starkweather (1987) indicated, is characterized by an easy, smooth, relatively effortless flow of information? Or, is their nonstuttered speech characterized by something less than a spontaneous, effortless quality? It could be that the speaker is hesitating, possibly avoiding or exchanging words, sometimes making it difficult for the listener to understand the information the speaker is trying to communicate. It can be useful in calibrating yourself to the client to differentiate at least three levels of fluency: stuttered speech, careful and unstable speech, and effortless, spontaneous speech.

One procedure that aids in the calibration process, especially during the first several meetings, is to shadow or pantomime the client's speech (Van Riper, 1973). In this way the clinician is able to get a feel (literally) for how the client might, for example, slightly slow his or her speech before a feared sound or word. The clinician can begin to determine whether the speaker scans ahead and "pre-tastes" words while considering whether to try

moving through them. Using audio or video recordings at the outset of treatment can assist clinicians in tuning in to their new client. The clinician can become calibrated to the client's speech patterns by pantomiming the tapes at the office, at home, or, if not distracting, while driving in the car. Although on the surface, the client might appear to be fluent, with time the clinician will be able to detect instances when the client is speaking carefully and making a concerted effort not to stutter. The speech will be unstable, and the clinician will get the sensation that the client is "talking on thin ice." The client is not stuttering in a technical sense, yet seems as though he or she could fall through the surface of fluency at any moment.

As we become calibrated to the new client, we will begin to notice how the client's speech looks, as well as how it sounds. We can begin to tune in not only to the surface structure, but perhaps even more important, to the covert, or deep structure of the person. What are the cues signaling that this speaker might be experiencing some loss of control, fear, or helplessness, as he approaches, and moves through, moments where stuttering is expected? Although the speaker might not have overtly stuttered on a word, she was not completely in control of her speech. It is as though the stuttering was just under the surface. Until we become calibrated to that person, we are not likely to detect such occurrences. Detecting this loss of control, a key feature of the stuttering experience, is discussed in greater detail in Chapters 2 and 6.

Observing Silence

In observing both the surface and deep structures of the client's speech, experi-

CLINICAL INSIGHT

When I introduce the concept of pantomiming the client's stuttering to my students (usually early in their first semester in grad school), I invariably get nervous, anxious, or sometimes even hostile reactions! I believe that this happens for a number of reasons: First, for many of these students, the clinical interaction is still something new and anxiety provoking, and the thought of doing something as "unusual" as mimicking their client's speech disorder simply horrifies them! Second, many of these inexperienced clinicians have yet to desensitize to stuttering, so producing disfluencies in front of their client provokes anxiety. Finally, many students simply think that pantomiming a client's stuttering will offend the client and/or the parents of the client. This fear can be mostly overcome by explaining the purpose of pantomiming to the client and parents ahead of engaging in the activity. I must point out, however, on the few occasions where I have forgotten to alert clients or parents ahead of time, I have never received a negative reaction when doing this activity. (AD)

enced clinicians are apt to minimize their own talk and maximize observation. This is more likely to occur as the therapeutic alliance matures. One helpful way to tune in to someone is to stop talking. Rather than fill in the silent pauses or provide answers to questions, clinicians use the silence as a time for reflecting on what the client has said. Communication does not cease during silence. Body language, eye contact, and facial expressions tell much about the status of what has been said—and left unsaid. Silence on the part of the clinician may even be thought of as providing the client with a degree of independence. Van Riper (1975) suggested that when the clinician finds himself or herself uttering more than four or five sentences in a row, "warning lights should go off." This is especially true, he suggested, if the sentences contain many I's and we's. Silence on the part of the clinician (or instructor) can force action and response on the part of the client (or students). During the silences by the clinician not only do clients have

the opportunity to achieve greater independence, they also have the chance to take responsibility for the pace and direction of treatment. In fact, Luterman (2001) suggested that allowing silence is a hallmark of a client-centered approach, and provides clients with a message that they are responsible for doing the hard work of change. Similarly, DiLollo and Neimeyer (2022) stated that, during an extended period of silence, if the clinician "rescues" the client by anxiously jumping in with a rephrased or follow-up question, then the clinician has taken over the responsibility of the session and cast himself or herself in the role of "fixing" the client's problem.

Modeling Risk-Taking

On occasion, as clinicians we must be prepared to take the lead and demonstrate our willingness to take risks. Sheehan (1970) made the insightful comment that "the Achilles heel of most normal speaking

CLINICAL INSIGHT

Perhaps more than any other event, one of my experiences during a therapy session has remained with me over the years. As a recent college graduate, I had been in therapy for a few months. Although he was not a person who stuttered, the clinician who was seeing me that day (Eugene Cooper) was the first who conveyed to me a real understanding of my plight. The therapy session turned out to be a particularly demanding one. I was being challenged to be introspective and candid about my experience with stuttering and my many patterns of avoidance behavior. There were many long and (for me at least) frustrating silences. It was a difficult but productive session. As we neared the end of our time together that day with another moment of silence, he quoted a line that went something like this: "I knew we were friends when we could share the silence." As it turned out, over the next many years he was to become my professional mentor, colleague, and close personal friend. (WM)

therapists who try to work with stutterers is simply that they are not willing to do what they ask their stutterers to do" (p. 283). If we convey anxiety about stuttering and the tasks that await our clients on the road to change, how can we expect them to follow our recommendations and to move forward? We do not have to do so often, but occasionally we will be called on to demonstrate our willingness to take risks and to lead the way into speaking situations. Each situation is an opportunity for us to demonstrate that it is possible to be reasonably calm in the midst of stuttering and to openly and easily stutter. Alternatively, depending on how difficult a speaking experience may be for the clinician, it is a chance for the clinician to demonstrate that, despite some obvious anxiety, he or she is committed to the client. For example, the clinician may voluntarily stutter to a stranger on the street as the client observes. The clinician can openly stutter on the question, "Pardon me, do you have the ta . . . ta . . . ta . . . ," until the listener provides the time of day. It is one thing to tell the client that you

are committed to helping him or her, but showing the client is far better.

It is easy to discuss the variety of therapeutic tasks that can be accomplished. It is another thing to take action, particularly action beyond the relatively secure walls of the clinic environment. As difficult as it can be because of logistical and time issues, the ability of the clinician to accompany clients into some of their daily speaking situations can be critical for functional change. As Peck (1978) suggested, the cornerstone of any clinical relationship is the commitment on the part of the clinician, who must be willing to join in the struggle rather than sitting back and playing the role of a professional. There will be times during successful treatment when the clinician will be asked to take the field and join in the struggle; not to talk about commitment, but to demonstrate it (see Manning, 1991b, 2004). As proposed by others in this chapter, the clinician should indicate a positive attitude about risk-taking and both encourage and challenge the client to go beyond his or her previously established boundaries. If

CLINICAL DECISION MAKING

Several years ago when I was a doctoral student conducting therapy with a young man in his 20s, we left the safety of the clinic in order to obtain some realistic examples of his stuttering behavior as well as typical listener reactions. As we walked across the campus of a large Midwestern university, his task was to stop people and inquire about the location of various buildings. Although it was early in the treatment process and he was stuttering severely at this point, he was, nevertheless, willing to take part in the activity. Following a particularly difficult speaking situation, where he found himself completely stuck and unable to say anything, his listener, not knowing what else to do, apologized and walked away. I could see that the young man was devastated and was unable to continue. Perhaps I had asked too much of him. Perhaps I should have done what I was asking him to do. So I took my turn. I asked him what I should say and how I should stutter to the next person we would meet. His task was to verify that I stuttered in the preplanned way and to identify specific listener responses. After we had successfully done this with several strangers, he was more than willing to take the lead in gathering the information we had set out to find. (WM)

the clinician can show that he or she is a stable and understanding ally, clients will be much more likely to go beyond their previously established boundaries.

Challenging the Client

Assuming that we are able to provide the security of a committed therapeutic alliance and a strategy for change with the client, we then must begin assisting the person to move forward. However, change is often difficult even when the motivation exists. Changing the surface characteristics and, especially, the deep structure of stuttering can be difficult, particularly with adolescent and adult speakers. If it were easy, anyone could do it and there would be far fewer people handicapped by the problem of stuttering. However, it is difficult to alter the equilibrium that has been established in one's psyche and in the roles that stutterers and their listeners

have developed over many years. Change involves work; it is time consuming, and it can be expensive. At the very least, it is an inconvenience.

Because of the difficulties involved, change is not apt to occur without some applied force. The current ways of speaking and thinking about speaking must be moved off-center. There will be times during treatment when the clinician will have to push hard and indicate that specific, concrete tasks must be accomplished. Moreover, on more than a few of those occasions, even the most motivated of our clients will not comply. They may be unable to comply because they do not understand the task, because we ask them to move too quickly, because the task seems too difficult, or simply because they do not have the energy to do what needs to be done. Still, on occasion challenging the client—just as in parenting, teaching, or coaching—to go beyond his or her previous comfort levels of performance also shows our respect for the client's potential. Most adult clients come to us knowing that the task is likely to be challenging. They often want us to push them harder, but we are fearful of eliciting a negative reaction. There is, however, some evidence that greater progress in fluency treatment is made when the client is pushed to the point of eliciting negative affective feelings toward the clinician (Cooper & Cooper, 1965; Manning & Cooper, 1969). As Cooper and his associates suggested, the dynamic process of change is not likely to yield a consistently positive client–clinician relationship. Just as change is a function of a teacher–student, parent–child, or coach–player relationship, there may be times when progress is especially difficult and the mentor must do what is necessary. Thus, there will be times during treatment when the effective clinician will say and demand things that the client does not want to hear or do. Moreover, there will be periods when, based on our clinical experience and our long-range view of the treatment process, we will have to stand firm in our clinical decisions and demonstrate our allegiance to the therapy protocol. It might not be our basic nature and it could feel uncomfortable, but temporarily being perceived as the "bad guy" can sometimes be good, especially when it promotes long-term success for our clients.

CLINICAL INSIGHT

Most of the readers of this book are graduate or undergraduate students who are at the outset of their journey to understanding the nature of stuttering and how to help people who do it. But all of us, no matter how many years we have been at this, must continue to be students of our field. Regardless of whether or not continued study and learning are mandated by our professional association, it is essential that we constantly acquire new information and perspectives about our areas of expertise. The accuracy of the information in any field that is moving forward is characterized by a remarkably brief half-life. Over several years I surveyed the faculty at my program about the things they were taught during their many years of schooling that were later shown to be wrong. They always responded with an extensive and fascinating list of things that they, in turn, taught their students until new and more accurate information was discovered.

It is a daunting responsibility to become astute consumers of the new information in your field. The recent emphasis on evidence-based practice offers some help in this process, but it is far from being the answer. Throughout your career you will face the continual goal of sifting the wheat from the chaff as you hear presentations and read professional journals. It is a lifelong adventure to work toward expertise in your areas of interest. Success in any field of endeavor often requires a philosophy that balances enthusiastic curiosity with careful skepticism, a task that is both demanding and intrepid. As we suggested at the outset of this chapter, the clinician is a critical variable in the success of any therapeutic intervention. How is it that some individuals are able to develop exceptional levels of performance? (WM)

Clinician Mindfulness

In Chapter 12 we discuss the value of mindfulness as a facilitator of client change during the therapeutic process. In this chapter we briefly introduce another clinical characteristic that has been shown to improve therapeutic outcomes, clinician mindfulness. There is evidence that greater clinician mindfulness improves treatment outcomes in a variety of areas. Beach et al. (2013) found that increased physician mindfulness improved health care quality. Mindfulness has traditionally been trained through meditation practice and is made up of a composite of skills including attentive observation (Brown & Ryan, 2003; Kabat-Zinn, 2003; Leclercq, 2002), empathy (Rogers, 1957), curiosity, and presence (Epstein, 2003a, 2003b).

In spite of the common view, there is nothing especially exceptional or mystical about meditation. It is simply time spent paying attention to your inner thoughts while not passing judgment on them. It is especially helpful when encountering something difficult by accepting and allowing the experience rather than trying to direct and change it. Rather than attempting to control the experience, one accepts and allows the experience.

Epstein (2003b) suggested that journaling is a good way to become intimate with your own thoughts and feelings. He suggested, for example, writing down thoughts about clients you have seen on a particular day and how you reacted to those clients. Early the next day read what you wrote, doing your best to read with an accepting and empathetic view toward yourself.

The benefit to you and your client is seen in increased therapeutic presence (Geller et al., 2010), attentiveness, and deeper listening to the client's concerns.

HIGHLIGHTS

Clinician intervention skills are NOT the specific techniques that target the disfluencies or concomitant behaviors, but, rather, are a set of skills that help the clinician engage with the client and make effective clinical decisions. These skills include:

- Critical thinking
- Becoming less inhibited
- Avoiding dogmatic decisions
- Opening therapeutic focus
- Calibrating to the client
- Observing silence
- Modeling risk-taking
- Challenging the client
- Client mindfulness

The experience can also reduce psychological stress as well as burnout (Krasner et al., 2009). Another result for the clinician may be the increased belief that he or she can effectively counsel a client and receive constructive criticism (Larson & Daniels, 1998).

DEVELOPING EXPERTISE: IMPLICATIONS FOR CLINICIANS

The literature describing the ability of individuals to achieve expert performance encompasses a wide variety of human activity, including athletics, dance, chess, and a variety of other domains across the arts and sciences. In general, the research indicates that a minimum of 10 years of intensive preparation is necessary to attain the highest level of performance (Ericsson & Smith, 1991; Simon & Chase, 1973). Berliner (1994) summarized the literature on expertise and found agreement with the opinion that 10,000 to 20,000 hours of practice are required in order to perform an activity appropriately and effortlessly, two hallmarks of exemplary performance. Although natural aptitude certainly plays a part, empirical evidence indicates that training and preparation are prerequisites for achieving superior performance (Ericsson & Smith, 1991). Berliner (1994) provided a useful explanation of expert performance in his description of a five-stage model proposed by Dreyfus and Dreyfus (1986). Note the increasing application of critical thinking from novice to expert.

Novices, who are new to an activity, spend much of their time labeling their activities. They tend to act deliberately and pay close attention to context-free rules concerning how things are to be done. Novices tend to be relatively inflexible and are likely to closely follow such context-free rules and protocols. These attributes are characteristic of students and first-year professionals.

Advanced beginners are similar to novices in that they are likely to follow rules. Although they may learn the rules, they are unsure what to do or not to do when new or unusual circumstances occur (e.g., being uncertain about how fast to drive or when to shift gears when driving on ice or snow). Eventually, advanced beginners begin to understand when to ignore or break the rules when that would be the better thing to do. However, because advanced beginners are often unsure of the appropriate indicators and patterns to guide them in their decision making, they are likely to respond to new situations by following the rules. Because of their relative lack of experience, the advanced beginner will tend to react to new situations by classifying and describing events rather than responding creatively or problem solving. Another interesting sign of the advanced beginner is the tendency to set up barriers to help keep authority in his or her own hands. These attributes are characteristic of second- and third-year professionals.

Competent individuals (and not everyone achieves this level) are those who possess more than the usual motivation required for gaining additional experience. An important change takes place as competent performers begin making their own choices and developing their own priorities and strategies. Because they are making more of their own decisions, competent individuals tend to have a greater appreciation of the resulting success or failure of their choices and take more responsibility for the outcome of their actions. With continued experience, they further refine and focus their understanding concerning the important indicators and patterns that enable them to make the best decisions. An important hallmark of the competent individual is the ability to develop a better sense of timing and know not only *what* to do but *when* to do it. These attributes are characteristic of professionals with 3 to 4 years of experience.

Proficient performers begin to develop what seems to be an intuitive sense of situation. They are able to make micro-adjustments (as when making small balancing adjustments while riding a bike) that less proficient individuals are unlikely to notice. Importantly, they begin to take a holistic approach to their performance. This holistic view allows the proficient performer to recognize expansive, reoccurring patterns that others are unlikely to see. As a result, they can anticipate events with greater precision. These attributes are characteristic of professionals with more than 5 years of experience.

In order to become an *expert*, it is usually necessary for the person to focus on one or a very few specific domains with great dedication and persistence. This has some implications for our field in general, for one might ask, given the ever-expanding scope of practice for speech-language pathologists, whether or not it is possible for one to become truly competent in more than one or perhaps a few specialty areas. As we discussed earlier, it takes many thousands of practice hours (10,000–20,000 hours for chess players; 10,000–15,000 hours of teaching; reading more than 100,000 x-rays) to approach this level of expertise in a given area. Following years of such focused learning, experts appear to develop an intuitive grasp of the situation and seemingly perform effortlessly, "becoming one" with an activity (the car they are driving, the instrument they are playing, the tools or techniques they are using). Experts often appear to be nonanalytic and nondeliberative, as vividly demonstrated by the pianist or the accomplished martial artist; the individual parts of the activity are not easily described as deductive or analytical behavior, and performers are able to respond in a rapid and fluid manner. Berliner (1994) cited the vivid example of Wayne Gretzky, often considered the best hockey player in the history of the sport, who when asked to explain his extraordinary success on the ice, responded by saying, "I don't know; I just go to where the puck is going to be" (p. 9).

Although Berliner (1994) was interested in understanding expert performance as it applied to exceptionally adept teachers, his work closely parallels the work of clinicians in our field and includes many of the concepts discussed in the section on critical thinking. He found that expert instructors are flexible in their approach, apt to consider alternative responses to a situation, unlikely to follow a manual, opportunistic about ways to connect with their students (rather than following a preplanned approach), and often follow the lead of the student. These experts become integrated individuals who focus less on themselves and more on the student. Additionally, they are unusually sensitive to the affective concerns of their students. We refer to many of these same characteristics on several occasions throughout this book as we describe the nature of the therapeutic process for individuals who stutter.

We now move to the final section of this chapter to discuss a variable that, perhaps to the surprise of some, has been associated with successful therapy and exceptional clinicians. In this section we are suggesting that the recognition of humor provides an overarching indicator of many successful clinicians as well as a sensitive metric of successful therapeutic change for many individuals undergoing therapy for stuttering.

HUMOR AND THE CLINICIAN

As indicated throughout the earlier sections of this chapter, many experienced professionals suggest that humor is a valuable characteristic of clinicians and a natural part of a dynamic therapeutic process. The primary focus of our discussion about humor in the following paragraphs concerns a range of clinician attributes that have frequently been associated with a successful therapy outcome. However, our discussion also relates to how our clients interpret themselves and their circumstances and how humor both affects and reflects therapeutic change. It is clear that a sense of humor is helpful, sometimes even essential, for coping with life on a daily basis. For example, Brissette et al. (2002) found humor, acceptance, and positive reframing to be three functional coping responses. This can be true for the clinician who is working to help people with serious communication problems as well as the speaker who, at least at the outset of treatment, is often overwhelmed with his or her problem.

A Historical Perspective

In order to advocate for the importance of humor in the process of change, we place the discussion of this uniquely human characteristic into historical perspective. Kuhlman (1984) reported that during the first two decades of behavior therapy (1950–1970) there was not a single reference to humor in the literature. Beginning in the early 1970s, there was a substantial and progressive increase in the therapeutic use of humor, particularly in the professional fields of clinical psychology, counseling, and allied health. McGhee and Goldstein (1977) reported that humor began to be recognized as a legitimate part of the human healing process—a way to maintain both physical and psychological health. These authors found that humor was positively correlated with such personality characteristics as enthusiasm, playfulness, hopefulness, excitement, and vigorousness; it was negatively correlated with fear, depression, anger, indifference, and aloofness (McGhee & Goldstein, 1977). Subsequent research by Thorson and Powell (1993b) confirmed many of these relationships and added a few more. Using the Multidimensional Sense of Humor Scale (MSHS) developed by the authors, Thorson and Powell (1993a) found that MSHS

scores positively correlated with exhibition, dominance, warmth, gregariousness, assertiveness, excitement seeking, creativity, intrinsic religiosity, arousability, positive emotions, extraversion, and cheerfulness. Humor scores correlated negatively with neuroticism, pessimism, avoidance, negative self-esteem, deference, order, endurance, aggression, depression, death anxiety, seriousness, perception of daily hassles, and bad mood.

Clearly, there are some valuable concepts for the speech-language pathologist with regard to the use of humor in therapy. Kfrerer et al. (2023) performed a comprehensive scoping review of humor in rehabilitation that included the fields of audiology and speech-language pathology. They found that humor is used primarily in a positive way in rehabilitation and concluded that it can be an important tool for the rehabilitation professions. These authors found that humor contributed to a sense of belonging for clients, improved client–clinician relationships, and improved group cohesion. They also noted that nonverbal humor cues were often important in cases where communication was difficult or impaired for clients.

In the field of fluency disorders, there has been limited academic interest in the therapeutic value of humor. Van Riper (1973) commented briefly about the significance of humor for the person who stutters, describing it in terms of an antiexpectancy device used to lessen the severity of stuttering. He referred to Bryngelson (1935), as well as Luper and Mulder (1964), who recommended that people who stutter learn to joke about their stuttering in order to help others feel more at ease and to help themselves develop more optimistic attitudes about their problem. There are also several examples of humor occurring throughout the series of videos of Dr. Van Riper's therapy sessions with Jeff mentioned earlier. In the final episode in the series, filmed some 20 years after the final therapy session, Jeff was interviewed by Dr. Barry Guitar and asked to reflect on his successful therapeutic experience. One of his recollections was the importance of Van Riper's ability to help him "play with his stuttering" and take a humorous perspective about aspects of his stuttering experience. Based on a review of the literature on therapeutic humor, Manning and Beachy (1995) proposed that humor should be taken seriously as a variable in the therapeutic process for individuals who stutter. Guitar (1997) provided an example of this, suggesting the use of humor during the transfer stage of treatment with children as a way of showing them how to open up about their stuttering.

Acknowledging Humor During Therapeutic Change

To some clinicians, treatment is "serious business," an unlikely place to find humor. One can imagine people reacting to the suggestion of acknowledging humor during the treatment of a serious and handicapping problem by questioning how one could possibly imply that there is something humorous about such a condition. Not surprisingly, clients also might have this initial question about the appropriateness of humor during treatment. However, there are clinicians who argue that a humorous view of the circumstances presented to us by life could be considered an appropriate issue for the process of treatment (Schimel, 1978).

It is important, therefore, to consider the way we think about humor in a therapeutic sense. The phrase "using humor" might give the impression that a clinician will arrive at the treatment session with a well-rehearsed series of jokes (Kuhlman, 1984) or perhaps wearing a red nose. Rather than thinking of incorporating humor in this sense, Kuhlman (1984) proposed that humor is more appropriately viewed as an integral part of the interactional aspects of treatment. Rather than considering humor as a technique or tool, humor is best conceived as a characteristic of a successful therapeutic alliance and a sense of timing during conversations. Kuhlman suggested that *spontaneity* is the essence of all effective humor, and certainly this can be true of the therapeutic alliance. Accordingly, until the clinician is calibrated to the client and until some level of trust and intimacy has been established, humor is less likely to serve a beneficial purpose. This perspective was also taken by Simmons-Mackie and Schultz (2003) based on their analysis of both verbal and nonverbal therapeutic interactions with adults with aphasia. These authors found that humor effectively enhanced the interpersonal interaction between clinician and client. These authors also made the important distinction that spontaneous, rather than preplanned humor is most effective in promoting and managing therapy interactions.

Humor and laughter frequently take place during successful treatment, including treatment for fluency disorders. There is, during effective treatment, the enthusiasm and excitement of exploration. The resulting change in insight often leads to an expression of humor, and conversely, humor can lead to insight. The author E. B. White (1954/1960) wrote that "humor at its best is a kind of heightened truth—a super truth." Therapeutic protocols seek to expand the client's awareness of and

CLINICAL INSIGHT

On many occasions we have asked the members of a group therapy session to see if they can recall instances when their stuttering has resulted in a humorous experience. The newer members of the group typically respond with some strange looks, and it's not unusual for a participant to question the appropriateness of such a request. The more experienced group members, however, are more than happy to tell what often have become their favorite stories, stories that are unique and truly humorous. These are individuals who have clearly achieved some distance from the original experience and have achieved a conceptual shift concerning their previously embarrassing circumstances. They typically have also achieved a good deal of mastery over their speech. (WM)

insight about the problem that brought him or her to treatment. Allport (1961) demonstrated the close relationship between insight and humor, finding a positive correlation of .88 between the two. He further noted that insight and humor were related to an individual's capacity for self-objectification and the ability to construe oneself as both subject and object (Kuhlman, 1984). That is, humor reflects a person's ability to step away and distance himself or herself from the situation in order to gain a degree of insight. The distance provides for a degree of objectivity that allows us to see ourselves from a new angle or with a "God's eye" view. As a result of three basic characteristics (conceptual shift, distancing, and mastery), humor can be an effective facilitator of therapeutic change.

The Conceptual Shift

Two similar views of humor provide a good beginning for appreciating the possibilities for intervention with individuals who stutter. Morreall (1982) suggested that laughter is the natural expression of the feeling of amusement in response to a sudden conceptual shift. He suggested that the essence of humor is found in the enjoyment of incongruity. Associated with an appreciation of incongruity is a conceptual shift (not necessarily an emotional one) in the way we consider an event. For maximum effectiveness, the conceptual shift must be immediate and the change relatively large. When the shift is predictable or anticipated, the degree of humor decreases accordingly.

Davis and Farina (1970) advanced a similar explanation for a humorous event. They included as basic features of humor the sense of contradiction or incongruity, as well as the sudden integration of contradictory ideas or concepts. Furthermore, this new insight often results in an objective—in contrast to an emotional—experience of the concepts. As Davis and Farina (1970) explained, "We may say that on the cognitive side, laughter results from the sudden insightful integration of contradictory or incongruous ideas, attitudes, or sentiments which are experienced objectively" (p. 307).

Such conceptual shifts are not likely to take place early in the therapeutic relationship. The initial treatment sessions often are spent gathering information such as acquiring baseline performance, obtaining demographic data, developing procedural guidelines, and becoming calibrated to the client. During these initial stages, the clinician is becoming attuned to the client and his or her story. Once the therapeutic relationship matures and the client begins to understand that the clinician is capable of providing a secure and supportive environment, humor is more likely to become a feature of the dialogue. As the sessions continue, an interactional environment will begin to be established in which spontaneity and expressions of concepts beyond the preliminary aspects of the relationship begin to occur. As more intimacy is established in the relationship, the limits of appropriate humor can expand, as well as the number and severity of the taboos that may be violated in safety (Kuhlman, 1984). Accordingly, humor leads to a relaxed atmosphere that encourages communication, particularly on sensitive matters (McGhee & Goldstein, 1977). Although humor is but one dynamic in the process of promoting clients' conceptual shifts about themselves and their situation, it can play an important role in that process.

As humor facilitates insights about an old problem, the client might respond with pleasure or laughter. A kind of catharsis may take place, and for the first time, a new way of looking at the problem may result. Kuhlman (1984) suggested that the client's laughter, if spontaneous and genuine, can be taken as a sign of validation of a change in insight. On occasion, a client's initial reaction to a new view of the problem or the situation could be one of anger. She might not like the view that the new insight provides, especially if the old, habitual view is more comforting. Consequently, the appropriateness of a humorous interpretation of an event must be judged within the context of the therapeutic relationship at a particular moment. To be appropriate as well as effective, the timing of the humorous response must be both accurate and spontaneous.

It has often been suggested that an integral part of a comprehensive behavioral treatment strategy involves the client's development of a new belief system—a paradigm shift—about himself or herself and the problem (e.g., Botterill & Cook, 1987; Cooper, 1993; Covey, 1989; DiLollo, Neimeyer, & Manning, 2002; Fransella, 1972; Fransella & Dalton, 1990; Hayhow & Levy, 1989; Kuhlman, 1984; Peck, 1978; Plexico et al., 2005; Van Riper, 1973). Changing perspective may be difficult, and the client might tend to deflect the clinician's alternative views of the problem. As Kuhlman (1984) suggested, although people seek treatment in order to feel better, they are often less than enthusiastic about the behavioral and cognitive changes necessary to achieve the goals of treatment. It is common for the client to cling to established perspectives and belief patterns because they are familiar, comfortable, and self-protective. The client is often too close to the situation—especially a threatening or emotionally laden one—to see it any other way. He or she might have viewed the situation for so long from a particular perspective that no other view seems possible. As Kuhlman (1984) stated, before clients are able to adopt a new belief system, they must acknowledge and dismiss the old one as being in error in some way. Although humor does not have to be a part of the process, it can be an effective and pleasurable way to facilitate and share the beneficial changes that are occurring.

Distancing With Humor

To facilitate the development of a new cognitive perspective and begin to form a new belief system about both oneself and the problem, it is often helpful to step away from the situation somewhat

(Kuhlman, 1984). It is not necessary to step back a great distance, only far enough to see its paradoxical aspects. Until the person is able to move back somewhat, especially from a threatening experience or a problem that creates anxiety, the paradoxical aspects of the situation will not be readily apparent. However, as the client, with the clinician's assistance, is able to achieve greater distance, it will be possible to gradually gain objectivity by viewing the problem with the "third eye" of humor. Rather than endlessly reliving earlier experiences with the old view, new interpretations will become possible. Humor promotes the possibility that the client will begin to play with the possibilities and enjoy considering a variety of new interpretations of the experience.

Morreall (1982) also discussed the role of distancing in humor. He suggested that humor has a liberating effect. Often something is funny because it violates what is supposed to be sacrosanct; it goes against the rational or accepted order of things. Morreall made the observation that humor enables us to achieve some distance and perspective. This occurs not only in situations where we are failing, but also in situations where we are succeeding, for humor can prevent us from overrating our achievements. The more developed a person's sense of humor, the wider the range of situations in which the clinician can achieve the distance required to promote laughter. For the clinician, and certainly for the client, it is important to appreciate that to the extent that we can achieve this distance from the practical aspects of a situation, we will be free from being dominated by it. Moreover, to the degree that a person can appreciate the humor in his or her own personal situation, that person will be liberated from the

dominance of emotions and more likely to develop a more objective view.

Mastery and Humor

Lefcourt and Martin (1989) found that the expression of humor is also related to a feeling of mastery and self-efficacy (see Chapter 14) of a task or situation. Their interpretation of this relationship relates to the view of humor as a reducer of stress. As Kuhlman (1984) pointed out, the relationship between mastery and humor is readily observed in children as they face problem-solving situations. Laughter is often a byproduct of children's shifts from one cognitive stage to another as they master a new problem. Problem solving, especially when the experience is a new one, is exhilarating (Levine, 1977). The client's subsequent behavior change suggests that some reorganization of internal reality (insight) has been achieved, which allowed the problem to be solved.

This perspective of humor and mastery also coincides with the view of humor suggested by Freud (1928). That is, the humor process includes a cognitive reorientation in the face of stress (Martin & Lefcourt, 1983; Nezu et al., 1988). The ability to recognize and appreciate humor has been shown to be related to a person's internal locus of control, which provides an indication of how much the individual perceives events as a consequence of his or her own behavior (Craig et al., 1984). Subjects who hold an internal locus of control were found to smile and laugh more in the face of stress (Lefcourt et al., 1974). Martin and Lefcourt (1984) found that people with better internal locus of control scores demonstrate greater ability to take multiple perspectives when problem solving as well as to resist the

CLINICAL INSIGHT

One afternoon during our group therapy session, Marcy was reporting to the others that she had finally, after many failures, willed herself to order something at a drive-through restaurant. Since we were at the early stages of treatment, the goal of this activity was simply to do the task regardless of any stuttering that might occur. In vivid detail, Marcy described her fear as she approached the enclosed microphone-speaker and her attempt to place her order. The typical semi-intelligible voice asked for her order, and she promptly responded by saying, "I would like an order of fries, a Coke, and a ham-ham-ham-bur-hambur-hamburger." The group responded with applause at her courage for taking such a risk and carrying out an action that she had rigorously avoided for many years. She thanked us all, but added that the only real problem she had was when she pulled around to receive her lunch. The cashier handed her an order of fries, a Coke, and five hamburgers. The laughter of Marcy along with the other members of the group suggested that she had achieved some distance from an event that had always been thought of as an absolutely dreadful experience. (WM)

effects of persuasion. People whose locus of control is more internally based are better able to consider alternative constructions for their experiences. Although having multiple perspectives regarding an issue does not necessarily lead to humor, the experience of humor is believed to require a person's ability to view a situation or event from multiple perspectives (Lefcourt & Martin, 1989).

Lefcourt and Martin (1989) suggested that to have a greater ability to entertain alternative interpretations for experiences, one must perceive oneself as an actor, a determiner of one's fate, and an active maker of choices. In the absence of choice, one is more likely to feel controlled and constrained. Only by making choices among available options can one be free. Thus, in the exercise of choice and the ability to consider alternative interpretations, there is a connection between a sense of mastery and the potential for humor (Lefcourt & Martin, 1989).

Everyone has experienced relief following the successful completion of a particularly daunting activity. Sometimes with adults (and even more so with children) accomplishment and the associated relief are often accompanied by laughter. Laughter is also frequently present in

HIGHLIGHTS

The use of humor in therapy has a long, well-established history in counseling and psychotherapy. Although not well researched in the treatment of stuttering, a number of prominent clinicians such as Charles Van Riper, Bryng Bryngelson, and Barry Guitar have advocated for its use in stuttering treatment. Humor can also be a signal of therapeutic change as a sign of a conceptual shift for clients, a sign that they can distance themselves from the effects of the problem, and as an indicator of mastery over a perceived problem.

the retelling of the experience. As people who stutter achieve the ability to vary and change their behavior they are likely to report humorous reactions and experiences that would not have been regarded as humorous only a short time earlier.

CONCLUSION

In this chapter, we have addressed a critical component of the treatment process for people who stutter—the understanding and expertise of the clinician. We have considered the impact of the clinician's personal characteristics, attitudes, and skills on the treatment process and described the characteristics of the experienced and effective clinician. We found that experts in many areas tend to be guided by principles rather than sharp-edged rules. Experts are less likely to follow a preplanned strategy or a manually driven approach. Rather, they were more likely to employ critical thinking and follow the lead of the individual they are assisting. They are flexible and opportunistic in considering alternative responses, and they are sensitive to that person's affective and cognitive response. Table 1–1 provides a summary of several

continuums that help to distinguish the technician from the professional.

Along with these clinician characteristics, we also introduced the variable of humor, as both a characteristic of the effective clinician as well as an indication of cognitive change as people achieve a conceptual shift, mastery, and distance concerning their situation. The clinician's ability to recognize and respond to humor could be an overarching indicator of a clinician's ability to lead the way in viewing the client's current circumstances from different perspectives. The results of many investigations provide convincing evidence of the relationship of humor to many personality characteristics (e.g., creativity, risk taking, intimacy, empathy, trust) that positively influence the therapeutic alliance and the ability of the clinician to affect a successful therapeutic outcome.

It is good to have a guide when beginning a new adventure. The effective guide is able to provide help that is both timely and insightful. It takes energy and optimism on the part of the clinician, as the work is sometimes demanding. Each client provides a challenge that may test us, and it is necessary and appropriate that we ask ourselves if we are up to the

TABLE 1–1. Continuums That Distinguish Clinical Decision Making By a Less Experienced Technician and By a More Experienced, Professional Clinician

Technician	Professional
Narrow focus on problem	Open focus on problem
Guided by rules	Guided by principles
Preplanned procedures	Flexible procedures
Dogmatic treatment	Treatment alternatives
Technique directed	Client directed
Intolerant of ambiguity	Tolerant of ambiguity

task. Burnout is a frequent problem in the helping professions. However, if we view our journey with each client as a new adventure and as an opportunity for continual learning and growth, we renew ourselves with continuing opportunities for personal enrichment. Much of our growth comes from the people we are trying to assist. The best clinicians recognize that clients have much to teach us and that we often benefit nearly as much from the treatment process as they do. Although we have traveled along paths of therapeutic change before, the territory and timing of the steps will be new for our companion, to whom we must attend closely with both determination and esteem.

❓ TOPICS FOR DISCUSSION

1. Why start a book on stuttering with a chapter about the clinician?

2. What are some of the reasons many clinicians are resistant to providing treatment for people who stutter?

3. Aside from a graduate course, where can one obtain information and insight about the nature and treatment of stuttering?

4. Which of the personality characteristics of clinicians described in this chapter do you feel that you possess? Which characteristics would you like to enhance and why?

5. Which of the clinician intervention skills described do you feel are the most challenging for you?

6. How do you rate yourself on critical thinking? What evidence do you have to support this belief?

7. Given each of the talents and skills you have achieved, where would you place yourself on the novice–expert continuum described in this chapter?

8. Using a variety of everyday or clinical circumstances, consider whether rules or principles may result in better problem-solving strategies.

9. What, in your opinion, are the most convincing arguments that the ability to construct a humorous interpretation of an event is an indication of cognitive change?

10. Rather than thinking in terms of "using humor" as a technique, describe how you might integrate a humorous perspective into the therapeutic setting.

11. Provide at least two examples of experiences in your past that were embarrassing or frightening at the time but have since become some of your favorite humorous stories.

📖 RECOMMENDED READINGS

Browne, M. N., & Keeley, S. M. (2017). *Asking the right questions: A guide to critical thinking* (12th ed.). Pearson.

Cousins, N. (1979). *Anatomy of an illness.* Norton.

Mahoney, M. J. (2000). Training future psychotherapists. In C. R. Snyder & R. E. Ingham (Eds.), *Handbook of psychological change* (pp. 272–735). Wiley.

Manning, W. (2004). "How can you understand? You don't stutter!" *Contemporary Issues in Communication Science and Disorders, 31,* 58–68.

Van Riper, C. (1979). *A career in speech pathology.* Prentice Hall. (See the chapters titled, "The Clinician's Skill" [pp. 103–114]; "The Rewards of Therapy" [pp. 115–138].)

> When I asked my mother what she thought caused me to stutter, she told me about my Aunt Helen and about everything the psychologists and therapists she and my father consulted had told them, and then added, "You know, when you were very little, still a toddler, and were living on 178th Street in the Bronx, you were playing on the floor in the living room, and this mouse ran right past you. I had the superintendent come and plug up the hole, and it never happened again, but I always wondered."
>
> —Marty Jezer (1997, p. 32), *Stuttering: A Life Bound Up in Words*, Basic Books, New York, NY

The Nature of Fluent and Nonfluent Speech: The Onset of Stuttering

CHAPTER OBJECTIVES

- To answer the following questions:
  - What is stuttering?
  - How do we know when we see and hear it?
  - Who stutters?
  - What do we know about it?
  - How and when does it start?

WHAT IS STUTTERING?

Stuttering and Related Terminology

Prior to offering generally accepted definitions of stuttering, we introduce some of the related terms and concepts (Table 2–1). For example, the term *stammering* can be found in some early literature in this country, where it tended to be used interchangeably with stuttering. Currently the term *stuttering* is used in the United States, but *stammering* is often used in Europe to mean the same thing. The major self-help group in Great Britain, for example, is called the British Stammering Association.

The term *disfluent* is often used in the literature to indicate the fluency breaks of normal speakers, whereas the term *dysfluent* is used to describe the abnormal fluency breaks of people who stutter. According to a variety of medical dictionaries, the prefix *dis* means reversal, separation, or duplication. The prefix *dys*, on the other hand, means difficult, impaired, painful, bad, or disordered. Because of the potential confusion of the words and because of a degree of overlap in the fluency breaks found in stuttered and normally fluent speech, the majority of authors are content to use the term *disfluent*.

TABLE 2–1. Equivalent Terms Commonly Used for Describing Stuttering and Associated Behaviors

Stuttering	Stammering	
Fluency	Normal speech	
Disfluency	Dysfluency	
Primary behaviors	Core behaviors	Alpha behaviors
Secondary behaviors	Accessory behaviors	Coping behaviors

Person-First Terminology

"Stutterer" or "person who stutters"? This is a dilemma faced by researchers, authors, and clinicians—with no clear answer coming from the literature or guiding professional bodies such as the American Speech-Language-Hearing Association (ASHA) or the American Psychological Association (APA). Research has suggested that some speakers prefer to be called "people who stutter" (in part because it highlights the fact that stuttering is only a part of them), others prefer the identity-first term, "stutterer," and still others remain indifferent to the topic (St. Louis, 1999). ASHA adheres to the style guidelines of the APA (2019), which suggest using person-first language unless those being discussed have a different preference, in which case their preference should be honored. When no clear preference is discernable, authors may choose to reflect both perspectives in their writing. Given that some people seem to be uncomfortable with the term *stutterer*, we will continue to use "person who stutters" or "child who stutters" in this book.

But what does this mean for clinicians? Since there are many differing opinions on this topic, we feel that it should be up to each individual, rather than society or the clinician, to determine which term they are most comfortable with. This means that clinicians should ask clients if they have a preference and then follow whatever terminology each client prefers.

Defining Stuttering

The variety of definitions of stuttering that have been offered over the years indicate the many ways of viewing this problem. Sometimes the definitions reflect the author's view of etiology rather than actually defining the problem. Wendell Johnson's 1946 definition, for example, reflected his view of etiology when he argued that stuttering was what the person who stutters does to avoid stuttering (Johnson, 1946). During the 1940s and 1950s, Johnson and his associates came to define stuttering as an *anticipatory, apprehensive, hypertonic avoidance reaction*. This view held that stuttering was a learned response to environmental events and was something that the person (a) does, rather than something that happens to him or her; (b) anticipates will occur; (c) is fearful or apprehensive about doing; (d) is tense (hypertonic) about; and (e) and tries to keep from happening again (avoidance). This was a somewhat restrictive definition, as stuttering can occur in the absence of some or even many of these attributes.

Views of stuttering as classical or operant conditioned behavior are reflected in Brutten and Shoemaker's (1967) definition that "stuttering is that form of fluency failure that results from conditioned negative emotion" (p. 61). Conversely, for those who view stuttering as a type of primary neurosis, a symptom of a basic emotional or psychological conflict, there is a tendency to define stuttering by citing the presumed source of the conflict (cause) rather than describing the stuttering behavior (symptom). Coriat (1943), for example, described stuttering as a psychoneurosis characterized by the persistence of early, pregenital oral nursing, oral sadistic, and anal sadistic elements. Taking a similar approach, Glauber (1958) described stuttering as "a symptom in a psychopathological condition classified as a pregenital conversion neurosis" (p. 78). Perhaps the most extraordinary explanation was offered by Fenichel (1945), who stated, "Stuttering is a pregenital conversion neurosis in that the early problems of dealing with retention and expulsion of feces have been displaced upwards into the sphincters of the mouth" (cited in Van Riper, 1982, p. 264).

Alternatively, other researchers have defined stuttering in reference to the observable features and the listener's experience of stuttering. For example, Guitar (2014) defined stuttering as "an abnormally high frequency and/or duration of stoppages in the forward flow of speech" (p. 7). One of the most frequently cited definitions of stuttering comes from Wingate (1964), who also defined stuttering in terms of its observable features but added that the disruptions are "not readily controllable" (p. 488). He stated that "the term stuttering means (a) disruption in the fluency of verbal expression, which is (b) characterized by involuntary, audible or silent, repetitions or prolongations in the utterance of short speech elements,

namely, sounds, syllables and words of one syllable. These disruptions (c) usually occur frequently or are marked in character and (d) are not readily controllable" (p. 488). Similarly, Perkins (1983) defined stuttering with the speaker's loss of control in mind, stating that stuttering may be defined as a "temporary overt or covert loss of control of the ability to move forward fluently in the execution of linguistically formulated speech" (p. 431). Van Riper's (1971) definition of stuttering also focused on the interruption of the forward flow of speech but added that the disruption could be caused by a motor problem or by the speaker's reactions to the disfluencies. He stated that "stuttering occurs when a forward flow of speech is interrupted by a motorically disrupted sound, syllable, or word or the speaker's reactions thereto" (p. 15).

The World Health Organization (WHO) provided a definition of stuttering in 1977 that took a slightly different angle. This definition points out, in contrast to the perception of many nonprofessionals, that the person who stutters knows what he or she wants to say. Although we all experience word-finding problems on occasion, telling a person who stutters to "stop and think what it is you want to say" indicates a substantial lack of understanding about the nature of the problem. The WHO (1977) stated that stuttering includes "disorders in the rhythm of speech in which the individual knows precisely what he wishes to say, but at the time is unable to say it because of an involuntary, repetitive prolongation or cessation of a sound" (p. 202).

In 2001, the WHO provided a revised framework for describing the consequences of disorders, which resulted in the *International Classification of Functioning, Disability, and Health* (*ICF*; WHO, 2001).

The new *ICF* framework acknowledges that all disabilities involve more than the observable behaviors. An important difference in this revision is that no distinction is made between the concept of the "disability" (the difficulty performing tasks) and the "handicap" (disadvantages experienced in the ability to achieve life goals). Furthermore, the revision construes both environmental and personal factors as central to the disorder. Yaruss and Quesal (2004) interpreted this revision and its implications for the experience of stuttering. They described how, in this latest WHO model, environmental influences (e.g., support from others, attitudes of society, communication services, support organizations, educational services) and the individual's response to his or her ability to participate across many aspects of life (e.g., social, education, work, employment, civic involvement) are important aspects of stuttering beyond the observable features of the problem (e.g., repetitions, prolongations, blocking of airflow and voicing).

Along with the WHO definitions and criteria for health disorders, the American Psychiatric Association publishes the *Diagnostic and Statistical Manual of Mental Disorders* (5th ed., Text revision; *DSM-5-TR*; American Psychiatric Association, 2022), a formal classification of mental health disorders, which serves as a reference and diagnostic tool for mental health and other clinicians. The *DSM-5-TR* no longer uses the term "stuttering," using "childhood-onset fluency disorder" as the preferred term and differentiating it from adult-onset acquired forms of disfluency (see Chapter 11).

The Speaker's Loss of Control

It is unfortunate that many definitions of stuttering include the perceptual effect of the stuttering on a listener but fail to consider the reaction of the speaker that occurs before, during, and following the most obvious aspect of the stuttering moment. Van Riper (1982) acknowledged this when he stated that "stuttering occurs when the forward flow of speech is interrupted by a motorically disrupted sound, syllable, or word, *or by the speaker's reactions thereto* [emphasis added]" (p. 15).

Several authors agree that the involuntary nature of the problem and the associated loss of control and helplessness felt by the speaker are crucial features at the core of the stuttering experience (Bloodstein, 1987; Cooper, 1968; Manning, 1977; Manning & Shrum, 1973; Perkins, 1983; Van Riper, 1937). Van Riper (1937) stated that "the stutterer feels he has no control over his stuttering performance" (p. 151). Bloodstein (1987) felt that for the person who stutters, the fundamental difference between real and fake stuttering is the awareness of tension and being out of control associated with real stuttering. Perkins (1983) also argued that the involuntary nature of stuttering is at the core of any definition of the stuttering experience. It is this loss of control that makes stuttering categorically different from more typical fluency breaks. He pointed out the shortcomings of definitions that depend exclusively on listener perception. Although the listener might be able to identify the acoustic features of the fluency break, he or she is not likely to distinguish this core cognitive-affective experience of the event.

When discussing the handicapping effects of stuttering, Silverman (1996) suggested that how speakers react—what they tell themselves about their stuttering experience (or the possibility of stuttering)—helps to define themselves and their speech. Silverman maintained that the number of choices and activities that stuttering prevents the person from doing defines the degree of handicap. Citing several personal accounts (Attanasio, 1987; Carlisle, 1985; Johnson, 1930; Murray & Edwards, 1980; Shields, 1989; Sugarman, 1980; Van Riper, 1984), Silverman pointed out that the actual handicap that can result from being a person who stutters can be considerably different (often much greater) than the surface features of the stuttering would indicate. It is not uncommon for the handicapping effects associated with stuttering to result from speakers' reactions to their situation and their attempts to alter or adapt to the problem, often in less than effectual ways. Although the idea of losing control of one's speech can be difficult for the observing clinician or researcher to identify and quantify (Martin & Haroldson, 1986; Moore & Perkins, 1990), Manning and Shrum (1973) argued that such a loss of control is identifiable. The client is able to know whether he or she or the stuttering is "in charge" of his or her speech. Many people who stutter are able to consistently indicate whether or not they have achieved control of their speech. The experience is somewhat analogous to tipping back and forth between losing and regaining one's balance. Once calibrated to a speaker, the experienced clinician can become adept at identifying the degree of the speaker's control or the lack of it.

Recently, Tichenor and Yaruss (2019) advocated for redefining stuttering from the perspective of the person who stutters. They conducted a qualitative study to explore how adults who stutter define stuttering. The study involved interviewing 22 adults who stutter about their personal experiences with stuttering and how they define the condition. Results suggested that, for persons who stutter, the primary impairment in stuttering is not the overt, observable behaviors (i.e., repetitions, blocks, prolongations) that are prominent in other definitions, but rather "an internal sensation of being stuck or losing control" (p. 4363). These authors framed their definition as an update of the *ICF* model of stuttering proposed by Yaruss and Quesal (2004):

> For underlying genetic and neurological reasons (etiology), people who stutter experience a disruption in planning and/or executing what they want to say (primary impairment in body function or structure). They experience this as a sensation of losing control or of being unable to move forward in their speech (primary symptom). This sensation may lead them to experience and exhibit certain personal reactions. These can be described as (a) affective reactions, including emotions such as embarrassment, anxiety, and shame; (b) behavioral reactions, including covert and overt behaviors such as disruptions in speech (i.e., speech disfluencies), as well as tension and struggle, or avoidance; and (c) cognitive reactions, including a sense of anticipation and feelings of low self-confidence or self-esteem. These personal reactions often interact and co-occur with one another and ultimately lead to limitations in performing daily activities that involve talking, as well as restrictions in the ability to participate in life areas, such as social interaction, education, or employment. Environmental influences, including listener reactions, may also negatively affect all of these factors. (Tichenor & Yaruss, 2019, p. 4364)

In summary, although the surface features of stuttering are often obvious and quantifiable, it would appear that some of the most telling features lie under the surface and reside in the more subtle cognitive and affective layers of the experience of stuttering. In fact, according to the persons who stutter (PWS) from the Tichenor and Yaruss (2019) study, the observable, surface features of stuttering might be reactions to an awareness on the part of the PWS that a loss of control is imminent.

HOW DO WE KNOW WHEN WE SEE AND HEAR IT?

Core Behaviors

Van Riper (1971) used the term "core behaviors" to describe the basic, observable behaviors of stuttering: repetitions, prolongations, and blocks. These behaviors appear to be involuntary, characterized by persons who stutter as a feeling of being out of control. They differ from "secondary behaviors" that the person who stutters acquires as learned reactions to the basic core behaviors. *A repetition* is when a sound, syllable, or single-syllable word is repeated several times. Repetitions are the core behavior observed most frequently among children who are just beginning to stutter. *A prolongation* is when the sound or air flow continues, but movement of the articulators is stopped. Prolongations as short as half a second could still be perceived as abnormal; in rare cases they might last as long as several minutes (Van Riper, 1982). *A blocks* is when a person inappropriately stops the flow of air or voicing, often combined with stopping the movement of the articulators as well. Blocks may appear at any level of the speech mechanism—respiratory, laryngeal, or articulatory. As stuttering persists, blocks often grow longer and more tense. Ambrose and Yairi (1999) also added "broken words" to the list of stuttering-like disfluencies. *Broken words* are when a block or pause occurs within a word at a non-syllable boundary. These stuttering-like disfluencies are qualitatively different from the typical disfluencies that occur in the speech of both persons who stutter and those who do not (Table 2–2). There is some disagreement on whether repetitions of single-syllable words should be counted as a stuttering-like disfluency or a typical disfluency (Ambrose & Yairi, 1999). The clinician will ultimately have to decide if such repetitions occur with tension and struggle (more stuttering-like) or with ease and lack of tension (more formulative), and if a specific occurrence of the disfluency is typical for that individual or looks or sounds different. It is also important to note that in developmental stuttering, disfluencies typically occur at the start of a syntactic unit (i.e., the first word in a sentence or clause). Similarly, at the word level, disfluencies typically occur on the first sound or syllable of the word.

People who stutter vary considerably in how frequently they are disfluent and the duration of disfluencies. On average, a person who stutters does so on about 10% of words while speaking or reading aloud, although individuals vary greatly, with some disfluent on as few as 5% of words, whereas others can be disfluent on 50% to 70% of words. Similarly, the duration of disfluencies can range from a few milliseconds to several seconds (or even minutes in an extreme case). However, most disfluencies typically last around 1 to 5 seconds.

Although it is important to recognize the variability across individuals who stutter, it is equally important to recognize that variability occurs within each person who stutters as well. All individuals who stutter report that the frequency and duration of their disfluencies varies significantly day-to-day and even hour-to-hour. Environmental and interpersonal factors often play a role in this variability, but just as

TABLE 2–2. Core Behaviors of Stuttering

Stuttering-Like Disfluencies	Example
Part-word repetitions	"li-li-li-like"
Single-syllable word repetitions*	"We-we-we-we went to the game"
Prolongations	"lllllllllike"
Blocks (fixed posture then release)	"We went to the ^^^game"
Broken words (pause or block at nonsyllable boundary)	"I was g-(pause)-oing to the game"
Typical Disfluencies	**Example**
Whole-word repetitions (multisyllable)	"Open-open-open the door"
Phrase repetitions	"I want-I want-I want to go to the game"
Interjections	"um" "er" "uh" "like"
Revision/incomplete phrase	"We went – The game was fun"

Note. *Could be classified as either stuttering-like or typical.

frequently, individuals can find no explanation for why their stuttering varies.

Secondary Behaviors

PWS react to repetitions, prolongations, and blocks by trying to end them quickly if they cannot avoid them altogether. Such reaction is random struggle but soon turns into well-learned patterns. We can divide secondary behaviors into two broad classes: escape behaviors and avoidance behaviors. *Escape behaviors* occur when speakers get stuck in a disfluency and attempt to terminate it and finish the word. Examples of escape behaviors include eye blinks, head nods, or interjections of extra sounds. Often, especially when first using a specific escape behavior, it will succeed in terminating the disfluency, thus rewarding (and strengthening) that behavior. Over time, however, the effectiveness of that behavior to terminate the disfluency will decrease, and, often, a different behavior will be added. This is how some PWS end up with several escape behaviors that have been learned over the course of many years.

Avoidance behaviors, on the other hand, are learned when speakers anticipate a disfluency and recall the negative experiences they have had when stuttering. To avoid stuttering again, they might resort to behaviors used previously to escape from moments of stuttering, such as eye blinks or added sounds. Alternatively, speakers might try something new, such as changing the word that was planned. In many cases, especially at first, the avoidance behavior prevents the disfluency from occurring and provides emotional relief that is highly rewarding. Soon the avoidance behavior becomes a strong habit and is resistant to change.

Distinguishing Stuttering From Normal Fluency Breaks

The fact that all speakers experience disruptions in their fluency brings up the question of whether it is possible to accurately distinguish between the fluency breaks of normally fluent speakers and those who stutter (see Table 2–2 for types of stuttering-like and typical disfluencies). Whether or not the fluency breaks of stuttered and nonstuttered speech are categorically different or can be thought of as being on the same continuum has long been a historical point of contention in the field. Even the semantics of what to call the fluency breaks of typical and stuttering speakers has created difficulty. At the center of the controversy is whether the fluency breaks of nonstuttering speakers are qualitatively different than those of stuttering speakers. It is also important to understand that most of the early research was conducted with older speakers. Until recently, little information about the features of stuttering in children at the point of, or shortly following, onset was available. We first provide an overview of what have been considered the distinguishing characteristics of both fluent and stuttered speech in adolescent and adult speakers. We then consider the nature of these characteristics in young, preschool-age children, who provide an understanding of the situation near the onset of stuttering.

Distinguishing adults who stutter from those who do not is not as easy as it might appear. Some people who stutter do not do so in any easily observable way; at least, they do not do so by producing the repetitions, prolongations, or blocking behavior of traditional stuttering. They might speak very carefully, avoiding sounds, words, or people, or, in some instances,

cease speaking altogether by pretending to be deaf or choosing to be electively mute (as described by James Earl Jones in his book *Voices and Silences* [Jones & Nivens, 1993]). As we will see in succeeding chapters, it is clear that during both our assessment and treatment we must go beneath the surface and consider not only the more obvious behavior characteristics of the person's speech but also the affective and cognitive features of how the person is coping with his or her problem.

Some authors have suggested that it is best to consider the fluency breaks of all speakers as falling along the same continuum (Bloodstein, 1992; Starkweather, 1992). After all, it has been suggested that people who stutter are making use of essentially the same speech-production system as normal speakers. Even given some difficulties at one or more levels of the language and speech production system, one might expect that there would be considerable overlap in the nature of the speech produced by stutters and nonstutterers alike. Others have suggested that the fluency breaks of those who stutter and those who are normally fluent are categorically different (Hamre, 1992; Yairi, 2004; Yairi & Ambrose, 2005).

Van Riper (1982) suggested criteria for differentiating the fluency breaks of typically fluent speakers from those who stutter. Table 2–3 provides a summary of the more prominent features that help to distinguish stuttering and normal disfluency on the basis of the overt (extrinsic) speech characteristics. Of course, it is important to recognize that the covert (intrinsic) features of the stuttering experience must also be considered when differentiating between a typically fluent speaker and someone who is stuttering.

From a historical perspective and for our subsequent comments about assess-

TABLE 2–3. Guidelines for Differentiating the Fluency Breaks of Typically Fluent Speakers and Those Who Stutter

	Stuttered Speech	Fluent Speech
Repetitions	More than two per word More than 2/100 words	Less than two per word Less than 2/100 words
Prolongations	Greater than 1 second	Less than 1 second
Airflow	Frequently disrupted	Consistent airflow
Tension	Effortful speech with potential rise in pitch	Effortless and spontaneous
Phonation	Monotone or unusual inflection pattern	Normal inflection
Articulation	Inappropriate placement, schwa vowel in place of correct vowel	Appropriate articulatory placement
Awareness	Frustration, avoidance, shame, lack of eye contact	Absent

Source: Adapted from Van Riper, 1982.

ment, it is important to understand that many of the categories used by Van Riper were influenced by the work of others who developed one of the first systems for categorizing fluency breaks, and one that was used for many years (Johnson, 1961; Johnson & Associates, 1959; Williams et al., 1968). This scheme placed some of the surface behaviors of stuttering into the seven categories of part-word repetition, single and multisyllabic word repetition, phrase repetition, interjections, revision-incomplete phrase, disrhythmic phonation (sound prolongations within words, unusual stress or broken words), and tense pause (barely audible heavy breathing and other tense sounds between words). When repetitions occur it is nearly always the first sound or syllable of the word that is repeated one or more times.

For the large majority of fluent as well as nonfluent speakers, part-word repetitions occur at the outset of the word. Although word-medial (*ha-a-a-a-as*) or word-final (*smile-ile-ile, like-ike-ike*) repetitions are

not characteristic of child-onset stuttering, they have been reported for typically developing children (Van Borsel et al., 2005), and are characteristics reported in individuals with disorders of executive function such as traumatic brain injury (Lebrun & Leleux, 1985), developmental delay (Stansfield, 1995), and Asperger's syndrome (Plexico, Cleary, et al., 2010; Scott & Sisskin, 2007; Sisskin & Wasilus, 2014). Additional details concerning these atypical fluency disorders and treatment options are discussed in Chapter 13.

Yaruss (1997a) also provided a summary of terms that have more recently been used to categorize the fluency breaks of individuals who do stutter and those who do not (Table 2–4). The fluency breaks of speakers who stutter tend to be characterized by *within*-word motoric breakdowns in producing syllable and word-size units. The breaks of normally fluent speakers tend to reflect difficulty in formulating the content of the message. These breaks tend to occur *between* larger word and phrase

TABLE 2–4. Ways of Categorizing Disfluencies

Within-Word Disfluencies	Between-Word Disfluencies
Monosyllabic whole-word repetition	Phrase repetition
Sound/syllable repetition	Polysyllabic whole-word repetition
Audible prolongation	Interjection
Inaudible prolongation	Revision
Stuttering-Like Disfluencies (SLD)	**Other Disfluencies**
Part-word repetition	Interjection
Monosyllabic word repetition	Phrase repetition
Disrhythmic phonation	Revision/incomplete phrase
Stutter-Type Disfluencies	**Normal-Type Disfluencies**
Part-word repetition	Whole-word repetition
Prolongation	Phrase repetition
Broken word	Revision
Tense pause	Incomplete phrase
	Interjection
Less Typical Disfluencies	**More Typical Disfluencies**
Monosyllabic word repetition (three or more repetitions)	Hesitation
	Interjection
Part-word syllable repetition (three or more repetitions)	Revision
	Phrase repetition
Sound repetition	Monosyllabic word repetition (two or fewer repetitions: no tension)
Prolongation	
Block	Part-word syllable repetition (two or fewer repetitions: no tension)

Note. Fluency breaks characteristic of individuals who do stutter are listed in the first column. Fluency breaks characteristic of individuals who do not stutter are listed in the second column.

Source: Used with permission of the American Speech-Language-Hearing Association, from Yaruss, J. S. (1997). Clinical measurement of stuttering behaviors. *Contemporary Issues in Communication Science and Disorders, 24*, 27–38; permission conveyed through Copyright Clearance Center, Inc.

units of language production. The other basic characteristic is the extent of both the duration and tension of the break, with both being noticeably greater during stuttered speech. Throughout this text we adopt the terminology used by Yairi and his colleagues of *stuttering-like disfluencies* (SLDs) and *other disfluencies* (ODs).

As the preceding attempts to differentiate the nature of stuttered and normally disfluent speech indicate, there appears to be some influence of motoric and formulative factors in the inability of humans to generate completely fluent speech. Van Riper (1982) and Perkins (1983) suggested, for example, that a fluency break is more likely to be considered normal or nonstuttered if it is the result of "linguistic uncertainty." That is, the speaker is hesitating because he or she has not yet formulated how to express himself or herself. Stuttering is more likely to be occurring when formulation is not the major issue and if there is a physical constriction or closure of the vocal tract. Drawing from comments of these authors as well as the writings of Starkweather (1987), Bloodstein (1974), Yairi and Clifton (1972), Gordon et al. (1976), and Manning and Shirkey (1981) suggests the use of two categories for describing the continuum of fluency breaks among speakers: motoric and formulative fluency breaks.

Motoric fluency breaks are characterized by (a) breaks between sounds or syllables (part-word breaks), (b) obvious effort or tension (often focused in but not limited to the vocal tract), (c) pauses with a possible cessation of airflow and voicing, and (d) an excessive prolongation of sounds or syllables. These breaks are more typical of speakers who stutter but might occur in normally fluent speakers during conditions of communicative or emotional stress.

Formulative fluency breaks are characterized by (a) breaks (usually in the form of repetitions) between whole words, phrases, and larger syntactic units; and (b) interjections between whole-word or larger syntactic units. Formulative fluency breaks are the result of linguistic planning or uncertainty and may provide the speaker time to organize the remainder of the sentence. These fluency breaks are characterized by little or no effort or tension and are typical of normally fluent speakers. Not surprisingly, formulative fluency breaks can also show up in the speech of adults who stutter, although with less frequency than the motoric fluency breaks that are more often associated with stuttering.

Significantly, the fluency breaks of young adults who stutter are made up almost entirely of motoric fluency breaks. In fact, there appears to be a notable absence of formulative fluency breaks, a characteristic that can be used to distinguish adults who stutter from normally fluent speakers (Manning & Shirkey, 1981). Although there is little research on how the quality of a speaker's fluency changes during and following treatment, it could be that progress in treatment is sometimes signaled by an increase in the frequency of formulative fluency breaks to levels typical of normal speakers. That is, as the person who stutters begins to consider the variety of ways of expressing a thought rather than dealing with the short-term problems inherent in avoiding or struggling through a motoric fluency break, formulative breaks could increase in frequency to normal or near-normal levels. The relatively few studies conducted with older, typically fluent speakers provide preliminary evidence suggesting that formulative fluency breaks tend to increase somewhat during late adulthood, and that motoric fluency breaks continue to be infrequent (Gordon et al., 1976; Manning & Monte, 1981; Yairi & Clifton, 1972). Although there is considerable overlap in the surface features of adult stuttered and nonstuttered speech (e.g., the frequency and type of breaks), the core feature of helplessness and lack of control is generally absent from the experience of fluency disruptions of typically fluent speakers.

WHO STUTTERS?

Stereotypes of People Who Stutter

A wide variety of groups, including speech-language clinicians, teachers, and naïve listeners, have consistently assigned negative stereotypical attributes to persons who stutter (Boyle, 2015; Boyle et al., 2016;; Cooper & Cooper, 1996; Crowe & Walton, 1981; Doopdy et al., 1993; Lass et al., 1989; Lass et al., 1994; Logan et al., 2011; Ruscello et al., 1994; Turnbaugh et al., 1979; Walden & Lesner, 2018; Woods & Williams, 1976). Several reasons have been suggested for the formation of these negative stereotypes. One possibility is that typically fluent speakers have limited personal experience with individuals who stutter. Their views of a person who stutters might be influenced by the way these individuals are portrayed in books, movies, television, and news media. Benecken (1995) suggested that these sources of information often depict those who stutter as possessing neurotic or even psychopathic characteristics. Benecken's suggestion was supported by Evans and Williams (2015), who conducted a qualitative analysis of 40 feature-length films that portrayed stuttering. These researchers found that only three of the films sampled gave a positive portrayal of stuttering, and the remaining films portrayed PWS as socially, mentally, or morally flawed, with poor relationships, and low life satisfaction. Recent media attention on the speech of President Joe Biden, who has publicly disclosed his history and struggles with stuttering, also reinforce the negative impact of media on the public perception of stuttering through the propagation of harmful myths and stereotypes. Farzan and Tetnowski (2022) described how some media outlets reported a moment of stuttering by President Biden as a "vocal flub," suggesting that his "brain just broke" and calling for him to undergo cognitive evaluations. In addition to the traditional media outlets referred to by Benecken (1995), the rise of social media (e.g., Facebook, Instagram, Twitter) now provides additional sources of information for typically fluent speakers to form views of stuttering and PWS. Azios et al. (2022) suggested that accessibility to information through social media might contribute to the continued transmission of a "stuttering stereotype" and fuel stigma associated with stuttering. The impact of social media is not, however, all negative. For example, Raj et al. (2023) reported that Facebook groups for PWS can provide an extension of in-person support groups for PWS and can help share more accurate information with the general public.

It has also been suggested that the greater mental effort required by listeners to both recall and comprehend information from stuttered speech could elicit a negative behavioral response from listeners (Panico & Healey, 2009). Another possibility for the often negative characteristics attributed to PWS by typically fluent speakers was proposed by White and Collins (1984) and subsequently by Doopdy et al. (1993) and Guntupalli et al. (2006). These authors suggested that normally fluent speakers interpret stuttering in terms of the negative internal states (e.g., self-consciousness, anxiety, and stress) that might accompany their own (formulative) speech disfluencies. That is, fluent speakers infer from their own experiences of disrupted fluency that people who stutter are chronically anxious or nervous.

This view is supported by the findings of Mackinnon et al. (2007), who used an anchoring and adjustment model (Epley et al., 2004; Tversky & Kahneman, 1974) to explain how listeners tend to make such inferences about people who stutter. Mackinnon et al. (2007) had 183 male and female participants use a 25-item semantic differential scale (Woods & Williams, 1976) to rate two hypothetical adult male speakers. One speaker was described as an "uncontrollable trait stutterer" and one a normally fluent speaker who "temporarily stutters." The results coincided with the anchoring-adjustment model, which suggests that when people must make a rapid judgment about another person, they begin by anchoring their understanding from an egocentric perspective. The researchers found that the observers interpreted stuttering by relating the behavior to their own disfluent experiences and associating the experience with emotions of being nervous, fearful, tense, and anxious. The results also indicated an adjustment process as the participants altered their understanding until a plausible (but typically insufficient) explanation was achieved. That is, there was small but significant adjustment resulting in a less negative and less emotionally extreme rating assigned to the temporarily disfluent speaker. The listeners, however, because of a lack of understanding about the nature of stuttering, failed to make a full adjustment in the case of the person with consistent stuttering. Mackinnon et al. (2007) suggested that providing listeners with a more accurate explanation of stuttering and the people who do it might help to further the adjustment process in order to understand that the speaker who stutters is basically no different than the typically fluent speaker. Baryshevtsev et al. (2020) replicated the findings of Mackinnon et al. that typically fluent speakers generalize their own disfluent speech experiences to persons who stutter when forming impressions, perpetuating the negative stereotypes of PWS as chronically anxious and nervous.

The Variety of the People We See

Not surprisingly, people who stutter seldom conform to any stereotype. In fact, one of the hallmarks of "stuttering" is that the people it affects present with an incredibly diverse combination of speech and nonspeech behaviors. Although there are likely to be some cognitive, emotional, and behavioral characteristics that commonly occur across our clients, most people who stutter are vastly more different than they are the same. Some have one or more obvious or perhaps subclinical problems that can make successful treatment more difficult. Others have many talents and abilities (see Chapter 14) and are very likely to find success with many forms of intervention, or even perhaps on their own or as a member of a support group as described in Chapter 15. It is important to enjoy this diversity and to appreciate the context of our clients' histories and their stories so that we can help to create a match between what they need and what we are able to provide.

WHAT DO WE KNOW ABOUT IT?

Prevalence

Prevalence is the frequency with which a condition is observed in a population at any given point in time. As might be expected, estimates of prevalence vary considerably across studies and across geographical locations. In general, however, the prevalence of stuttering worldwide is around 1%, with some European countries reporting slightly higher prevalence numbers, and the United States reporting slightly less than 1% prevalence (Bloodstein et al., 2021). Therefore, based on an estimate of the population of the United States in 2023 of 334.5 million (U.S. Census Bureau, 2023) and the prevalence of stuttering ranging from 0.07% to 1% of the population, the estimated number of individuals who stutter in the United States ranges from 2.3 to 3.3 million. When considering the world's current population of 7.9 billion (U.S. Census Bureau, 2023) and

1% prevalence, there are approximately 79 million persons who stutter in the world.

Incidence

Incidence is defined as the proportion of the population who have experienced a condition at any time in their lives. Again, variability exists in data collected around the world for measures of the incidence of stuttering. Bloodstein et al. (2021) reported figures ranging from 5% to 15% but suggested that a "plausible" figure for lifetime incidence of stuttering is 8% to 10%.

Curiously, stuttering has been described as a relatively low-incidence communication problem. It should be noted that although low-incidence is commonly used in this context, what is typically meant is that stuttering is a low-prevalence problem, suggesting a relatively low number of persons identified as a PWS (or child who stutters) at any given point in time. As demonstrated by the numbers cited earlier, stuttering is neither a low-incidence or low-prevalence disorder, with millions of individuals worldwide who either consider themselves or are considered by their parents to be persons who stutter.

HOW AND WHEN DOES IT START?

Age at Onset

Andrews (1984) suggested that the risk of developing stuttering drops by 50% after age 4, 75% after age 6, and is virtually nil by age 12. A different assessment was noted by Yairi and Ambrose (2005), who studied a younger sample of children and found that 60% of the children began to stutter prior to age 3 and more than 85%

by 3½ years of age. They noted that stuttering onset was unlikely after age 4 and especially unlikely after age 6. Bloodstein et al. (2021) reviewed a number of studies that examined the onset of stuttering in young children and concluded that there is general consensus that the mean age at onset of developmental stuttering is 30 to 33 months, with few cases occurring prior to 24 months or after 42 months of age. They also indicated, however, that a number of studies have reported stuttering onset occurring during early adolescence. Plexico et al. (2005) found that it is not usual for adolescents and adults to report that the first time they realized that they stuttered was just prior to or during their early teenage years. In some instances, it could be that although the actual onset took place during the preschool years, the stuttering was present in a mild and less handicapping fashion. It was not until the speaker experienced the public societal penalties and associated social and educational disadvantages associated with stuttering that it became a problem. As described in Chapter 13, the onset of acquired stuttering during the middle or late adult years is likely to occur in cases of neurological or psychological origin. An epidemiological study of stuttering across the entire life span by Craig et al. (2003) found the lowest prevalence (0.37%) for the group of individuals who were 51 years of age and older.

Conditions Contributing to Onset

This section considers two sets of conditions that have been related to the onset of stuttering. These are issues that clinicians are frequently questioned about by clients and parents. The wide diversity of conditions at onset argues against a unitary or simple explanation for the etiology of stuttering (see also Chapter 3). The many conditions that have been associated with stuttering onset could complicate the task of diagnostic decision making for the clinician. Furthermore, many of these conditions interact with one another (e.g., age and gender), and it is difficult to categorically suggest that some factors are more influential than others. Given that caveat, we first describe a set of conditions that appear to have a greater influence on onset. The second set of conditions, less frequently mentioned in the literature, have comparatively less influence. Although these factors might be prominent aspects of the child's life, they are more likely to simply temporally coincide with the initial observation that the child is beginning to stutter. It is also important to understand that many investigations of young children who stutter are descriptive in nature and do not allow an assumption of cause-and-effect relationships between the speaker or environmental characteristics and the onset of stuttering. Although there might be a relationship between these factors, the fact that they are interrelated in some manner might only signify that one or more other factors are causing this relationship. Many of these factors, particularly the more influential ones, are discussed in considerably more detail in succeeding chapters.

More Influential Factors

Although these factors appear to have somewhat greater influence on the likelihood of stuttering, in many instances their precise impact remains unclear. In some cases, it might be best to think of some of these conditions as predisposing factors that can place a child at greater risk for both precipitating and maintaining stuttering (Silverman, 1992).

Age

Age can be considered a strong risk factor for stuttering for two primary reasons. First, as described earlier, the onset of developmental stuttering is typically in the range of 30 to 33 months, with few cases reported after 42 months. Accordingly, onset is very unlikely for children beyond the age of 5 years (Bloodstein et al., 2021). Second, natural recovery, which we cover in more detail in Chapter 4, occurs for up to 80% of children, usually within 3 years of diagnosis. Consequently, young children from 2 to 5 years old appear to be at the greatest risk of developing stuttering.

Gender

Kent (1983) pointed out that the higher occurrence of stuttering in adult males is one of the few consistencies about the disorder. The male/female ratios of school-age children and adults who stutter have been estimated to range from 3:1 to as high as 6:1. Interestingly, however, at ages around the time of onset, stuttering has been found to occur with approximately equal frequency for males and females, with ratios ranging from 1:1 to 2:1 (Kloth et al., 1999; Yairi, 1983). Recently, Yairi and Seery (2023) reported on data collected by the Stuttering Foundation of America for more than 18,000 children, between the ages of 2 and 5, who began stuttering. These data confirmed the roughly equal frequency of stuttering for males and females in very young children, with that ratio increasing with the age of the children to almost 3:1 (male:female) by age 4. This disparity across gender and age can be accounted for by the fact that females are more likely than males to experience a natural recovery from stuttering (Yairi & Ambrose, 2005). In addition, there are gender-related genetic influences that could result in males being more susceptible to stuttering and females having a higher threshold, with more factors required for stuttering onset (Kidd, 1984). Based on the results of several studies, Yairi and Ambrose (1999a) suggested that gender and genetics interact in such a way that young females who stutter are much less likely than boys to persist in stuttering.

Genetic Factors

There is a long history of research documenting that stuttering occurs with greater frequency in some families. Bloodstein et al.'s (2021) review indicates that the percentage of people who have relatives on the maternal or paternal side of the family who stuttered ranges from 30% to 69%. Studies concerning the genetics of stuttering have focused on the occurrence of stuttering in families, particularly in instances where there is a high density of stuttering in the first- and second-degree relatives. Research during the past few decades has indicated a genetic component in selected groups of people who stutter (Cox et al., 1984; Felsenfeld, 1997; Frigerio-Domingues & Drayna, 2017; Johnson & Associates, 1959; Kidd, 1977, 1984; Kidd et al., 1980; Pauls, 1990; Poulos & Webster, 1991; Sheehan & Costley, 1977; Yairi, 1983). As Ambrose (2004) pointed out, however, if stuttering onset is completely determined by genetics, when one identical twin stuttered the other would also, which is not always the case. It is apparent, therefore, that environmental factors are also influential. At this point it is reasonably certain that the onset as well as the persistence of (and recovery from) stuttering have strong

genetic components and that environmental factors also play an important role (see also Chapter 3).

Twinning

Approximately one third of all twin pairs are monozygotic and are genetically identical. The remaining twin pairs are dizygotic, or fraternal, and share about half of their polymorphic genes. A child is more likely to stutter if he or she is a member of a twin pair in which the other twin also stutters (Howie, 1981). This is especially true if the twins are monozygotic. It is less likely that both members of a fraternal twin pair will stutter (Howie, 1981). These findings seem to be explained by a genetic predisposition to stuttering (Howie, 1981; West & Ansberry, 1968) but family and environmental factors also have an influence.

Cognitive Abilities

The general cognitive abilities of children who stutter are similar to and perhaps somewhat better than those of their nonstuttering peers (Yairi & Ambrose, 2005). It is well documented, however, that individuals who possess less than normal cognitive abilities tend to have more issues of many varieties, including fluency problems (Andrews & Harris, 1964; Otto & Yairi, 1976). Van Riper (1982) summarized the results of seven independent studies indicating prevalence figures ranging from a low of 7% (Schaeffer & Shearer, 1968) to a high of 60% for clients with Down syndrome (Preus, 1972). Averaging across all seven studies, Van Riper (1982) found a prevalence figure of 24% ($SD = 18.1$). Of course, with this population there is also a much higher occurrence of many speech and language problems, including cluttering (see Chapter 13). In addition, it can be difficult to distinguish motor speech and language problems (particularly word finding) from fluency breaks, and developmental delays can mask the identification of fluency disorders.

Motor Abilities

Because the production of fluent speech requires complex motor skills, any delay or lack of coordination among the various levels of the speech production system is likely to adversely affect the development of normal fluency. The majority of the research concerning motor function of individuals who stutter has focused on adults (e.g., De Nil, 1999; Robb & Blomgren, 1997; Robb et al., 1998; Sussman et al., 2010). Research with children has indicated subtle differences in laryngeal function, speaking rate, and articulatory movement (e.g., Hall et al., 1999; Hall & Yairi, 1992; Riley & Riley, 2000; Zebrowski et al., 1985).

Speech and Language Development

Traditionally, there has been general agreement that children who stutter typically achieve lower scores than their peers on measures of receptive vocabulary, the age of speech and language onset, mean length of utterance, and expressive and receptive syntax (Andrews & Harris, 1964; Berry, 1938; Guitar, 1998; Kline & Starkweather, 1979; Murray & Reed, 1977; Peters & Guitar, 1991; Wall, 1980). More recent investigations suggest that the relationship of stuttering and expressive language and phonological abilities is far from simple. Watkins et al. (1999) studied 62 preschool children who recovered from stuttering and 22 who persisted in stuttering. Spontaneous language samples of 250 to 300 utterances were used to examine the children's expressive language skills (lexical, morphological, and syntactic measures). Both groups of children (those who recovered from and those who persisted in stuttering) displayed expressive language abilities near or above developmental expectations. For both groups of children, those who were the youngest when entering the investigation (2–3 years old) had expressive language scores well above normative values.

Yairi and Ambrose (2005) summarized their findings on the language abilities of children who were seen shortly after the onset of stuttering by stating that many such children have average or above-average expressive language skills. They also conclude that many of these children who have begun to stutter appear to have language skills that exceed their capabilities for producing fluent speech. As described in greater detail in Chapter 5, these expressive language skills tend to lessen to more age-appropriate levels as a consequence of natural recovery as well as successful therapy. Yairi and Ambrose further indicated that the likelihood of the recovery from or persistence of stuttering appears to have little to do with a child's language ability. However, linguistic variables such as grammatical complexity and loci of stuttering events (especially as related to language planning units) do appear to be important factors for understanding the occurrence of disfluencies for all speakers, regardless of whether they stutter or not.

For several years the co-occurrence of delayed phonological development and stuttering in children has been noted by many authors. A review of the literature on phonological development (and articulation disorders when including investigations conducted prior to the 1970s) and stuttering by Yairi and Ambrose (2005) indicates that co-occurrence is approximately

30% to 35% for children seen in clinical settings and less than 30% for the general population (Throneberg et al., 1994). Yairi and Ambrose (2005) pointed out issues to consider when interpreting the phonology–stuttering connection. Boys are more likely to stutter than girls and boys are also more likely to exhibit phonological deficits. Studies of relatively young children who stutter are likely to miss children who stuttered for a few months and then recovered. In spite of a number of well-constructed investigations, there is no strong evidence that there is any relationship between the production of phonologically difficult words and the occurrence of stuttering. Yairi and Ambrose (2005) also pointed out that the stuttering–phonology connection is not necessarily linear in that there is no clear relationship between stuttering severity and the level of phonological skills. Yairi and Ambrose summarized their findings about the connection between phonological development and the onset and development of (including recovery from) stuttering for preschool children by stating the following:

- Soon after onset, children who stutter tend to be behind normally fluent children in phonological development.
- Children who will eventually persist in stuttering are apt to be slower in phonological development than those who will eventually recover.
- In spite of this delay, phonological skills alone are insufficient to predict the further course of stuttering.
- The difference in level of phonological acquisition seen near stuttering onset between children whose stuttering will be persistent and those for whom it will be transient will probably have disappeared within 2 years.

- The phonological delay that is associated with stuttering will be overcome much sooner than earlier research would have predicted.
- The phonological development of children who stutter is similar in order of progression and strategies used to those of normally fluent children.

Response to Emotional Events

There are several interesting reports associating the rapid onset of stuttering (within 1–2 days) with unusual and possibly traumatic emotional events (see Mower, 1998). Although this is not generally viewed as a common occurrence, there is some justification for considering this form of onset as a subtype of stuttering. Yairi and Ambrose (2005) found that over 40% of the parents in their early experimental group indicated that their child experienced events that emotionally upset the child shortly before onset. In addition, more than 50% of the parents indicated that their children appeared to be undergoing some stress as a consequence of their rapidly developing language skills. Nevertheless, Yairi and Ambrose found no significant differences between the persistent, recovered, and control groups on anxiety scales designed for children—although the children in the persistent group had the higher mean scores (greater anxiety).

Guitar (2014) provided a particularly interesting interpretation of the research on the temperamental characteristics of children and the possible interaction with the regulation of emotion in the two cerebral hemispheres as it might relate to children who stutter. Guitar cited research by Davidson (1984), Kinsbourne (1989), and Kinsbourne and Bemporad (1984) indicating hemispheric specialization for emotions.

The left hemisphere is involved with regulating emotions associated with approaching, exploring, and taking action, and the right hemisphere is specialized for emotions that accompany avoidance, withdrawal, and arrest of action. Furthermore, Calkins and Fox (1994) and Davidson (1995) found that sensitive children are right hemisphere dominant for emotion. Combined with the information presented in Chapter 3 indicating an overactive right hemisphere for at least some individuals who stutter (albeit adults), this suggests that at least some individuals who stutter might be more temperamentally reactive. Kagan, Reznick, and Snidman (1987) found that more sensitive children react to novel or threatening stimuli by generating higher levels of physical tension, especially in laryngeal muscles. Of course, not all children who are sensitive or reactive turn out to be children who stutter. If a child also possesses familial characteristics leading to an unstable speech production system, however, this combination of factors might result in the onset of stuttering. Guitar, as well as Yairi and Ambrose (2005), considered the possibility that the presence of higher levels of anxiety might be associated with children who persist in their stuttering.

There are, of course, many forms of both emotional and communicative stress for families and children. However, there is no indication that children who stutter have a greater number of emotional conflicts than their normally speaking counterparts (Adams, 1993; Andrews & Harris, 1964; Bloch & Goodstein, 1971; Bloodstein, 1987; Johnson & Associates, 1959; Van Riper, 1982). Various forms of communicative stress, such as time pressure and verbal competition, undoubtedly enhance the possibility of breakdowns in the motor sequencing of speech. This could be particularly true if the temperamental nature of some children who stutter results in their being more susceptible to these forms of stress (Anderson et al., 2003). It can be difficult to connect a stressful event with the onset of stuttering, for as both Van Riper (1982) and Silverman (1996) pointed out, in many cases the initial signs of stuttering often precede the suspected event. Rather than being a cause of the stuttering, an event that happens to occur at approximately the same time as the stuttering was first observed might serve as a marker of that time period. Parents might report the onset of stuttering associated with an event without knowing that their child had been stuttering for some time in school and other locations outside the home. Examples of events that have been mentioned in the literature as being associated with stuttering onset include parental divorce, moving, separation from the mother, birth of a sibling, attending daycare centers, and imitating stuttering (Glasner & Rosenthal, 1957; Mower, 1998; Yairi et al., 1993). Mower's (1998) case study of sudden onset and subsequent remission in a young boy (age 30 months) provides a detailed example that seems to be best explained by factors of insecurity and sensitivity to environmental changes. As Bloodstein et al. (2021) explained, what is known about stuttering onset does not coincide with a form of trauma resulting in a conversion or somaticizing disorder (a physical problem resulting from psychological stress). A more likely possibility is that although the causes of stuttering are likely due to many genetic and neurological features, a "trigger" might set off or allow an underlying condition to emerge for people who are genetically predisposed to a condition.

Less Influential Factors

Physical Development and Illness

Children who stutter have the same general physical makeup as normally fluent children. There is no evidence that children who stutter are distinctive in terms of general developmental milestones such as ages of teething and weaning, or in developing the ability to dress and feed themselves, acquire bowel and bladder control, sit, creep, stand, and walk (Andrews & Harris, 1964; Cox et al., 1984). Yairi and Ambrose (2005) did note that 14% of the parents in their early experimental group reported that their children experienced illness or excessive fatigue just prior to stuttering.

On occasion, parents will indicate that stuttering began following an illness. However, children who stutter do not appear to have more illnesses than those who do not (Andrews & Harris, 1964; Johnson & Associates, 1959). Illness could, however, influence the nature and severity of stuttering in those who already stutter. It is difficult for children to maintain the energy to monitor speech production and use fluency-enhancing techniques when they are sick and their resistance and energy are low (Luchsinger & Arnold, 1965; C. Van Riper, personal communication, July 1, 1978).

Culture, Nationality, and Socioeconomic Status

Some descriptive research has found a higher occurrence of stuttering in African American than White populations (Dykes & Pindzola, 1995; Gillespie & Cooper, 1973). However, Proctor et al. (2001) surveyed 3,404 preschoolers, including 2,223 African Americans, 943 European Americans, and 239 others. Using individual speech screenings and teacher reports, they found prevalence figures of 2.46% overall with no group differences for African American and European American or other minorities. A comprehensive review describing the relative occurrence of stuttering according to both culture and race was provided by Van Riper (1982).

The relatively scarce data that are available concerning the possible effect of a child's socioeconomic status suggest that stuttering is present at the same frequency of occurrence in all socioeconomic groups. Undoubtedly, factors of socioeconomic level and race interact with   and cloud—this issue. The lack of diagnostic and treatment services for individuals in lower socioeconomic categories is likely to result in an underestimation of the occurrence of stuttering for these populations. It could also be that those in upper socioeconomic categories are more informed about and economically capable of obtaining assistance. At this point, there appears to be no convincing evidence of socioeconomic influences.

Bilingualism

The research on possible associations of bilingualism and the development of stuttering are both interesting and diverse. The findings of the early research suggested that the process of learning more than one language could result in stuttering onset. Travis et al. (1937) analyzed reading and conversational speech samples of 4,827 public school children (2,405 boys, 2,422 girls; average age of 8.5 years) in East Chicago, Indiana. The researchers found a higher occurrence of stuttering in both bilingual (2.8%) and trilingual (2.4%) speakers compared to monolingual (English-speaking) children (1.8%). Likewise, Stern (1948; cited in Bloodstein and Bernstein Ratner, 2008) surveyed 1,861 children and also found a higher occurrence of stuttering in bilingual children (2.16%) than monolinguals (1.66%).

Au-Yeung et al. (2000) used a self-report procedure on the Internet, and among 656 respondents (82.6% bilinguals, 17.4% monolinguals), they found exceptionally similar incidence figures among monolingual (21.74%) and bilingual (21.65%) respondents. However, Van Borsel et al. (2001) pointed out several methodological problems with the Au-Yeung study, including the lack of a definition of stuttering, which might have led to the inclusion of many other types of typical formulative or common disfluencies, as well as the possibility that many respondents were individuals with other fluency problems who were attracted to a website having to do with stuttering or stammering. There was also a possible bias introduced as the majority of those who responded were females.

A review of the literature by Van Borsel et al. (2001) cited studies that estimate that 50% of the world's population is (at the very least) bilingual. Given that incidence and prevalence figures are consistently reported across cultures and countries to be from 1% to 5%, respectively, it does not appear that learning to speak two or more languages is likely to dramatically increase the possibility of stuttering. Nevertheless, based on their review, Van Borsel et al. concluded that stuttering is probably more prevalent in bilingual than in monolingual speakers. Bloodstein (1995) cited a study by Stern (1948), who studied 1,861 children under age 6, finding a prevalence of 1.80% for monolingual children and 2.16% for bilingual children. Van Borsel et al. (2001) found no reports of stuttering when adults learned a second language. Bilingualism can take place simultaneously when a child learns two languages from birth or consecutively when learning another language following mastery of the first. The authors summarized the results of their literature review with the following points:

- Except for the results reported by Au-Yeung et al. (2000), the available findings indicate that stuttering is more prevalent among bilingual speakers.
- Stuttering could be present in one or both languages of bilinguals, although stuttering in only one language is rare. When stuttering is present in both languages they can be equally affected; however, it is more common for one language to be more affected.
- Many other factors might be operating for bilingual children, including the child being exposed to mixed linguistic input or being placed in a new cultural or living situation that requires learning a new language.
- Many of the disfluencies observed in bilingual children could be a function of language formulation issues and not true stuttering.
- Diagnostic criteria should include the presence of secondary behavior, negative feelings and attitudes about communication, and a family history of stuttering.

Recommendations for therapy for those speaking more than one language include acquiring the assistance of a native speaker of the language that the clinician has not mastered in order to distinguish stuttering from more typical or formulative disfluencies. Treatment might be more effective if it is initiated in the speaker's predominant or most proficiently mastered language (Scott Trautman & Keller, 2000; Shenker et al., 1998). Finally, Van Borsel et al. (2001) concluded that there is inconclusive evidence that a successful therapy outcome is more or less likely for bilingual speakers who stutter than for monolingual speakers. Given the equivocal results and the methodological problems of the relatively few published investigations on this issue, Bloodstein and Bernstein Ratner (2008) concluded that there was no solid indication that being a bilingual speaker is a risk factor for stuttering.

Imitation

Although it is not unusual for clinicians to be asked if their child could be stuttering as a result of hearing a playmate who also stutters, there is little evidence to support this possibility. In his review of clinical cases, Van Riper (1982) indicated that although there were several instances where imitation appeared to be involved in the onset of stuttering, only one case appeared to be finally attributed to this cause. Otsuki (1958), as cited by Silverman (1992), reported that in Japan, imitation was viewed as a major causal factor in 70% of his cases. The strongest arguments against imitation are the unique characteristics of each individual's pattern of stuttering and that the early forms of stuttering are frequently dissimilar from the more advanced forms.

CONCLUSION

The many attempts to provide a definition of stuttering can provide a confusing picture to students and professionals alike. For individuals seeking information so that they can help themselves or their children in dealing with the problem, the search is even more daunting and often frustrating. The different interpretations of what stuttering is (and is not) indicate the complexity of the problem. The stereotypes assigned to people who stutter, as with most stereotypes, might convey some elements of truth, but are generally inaccurate and naïve concerning the nature of the problem. More holistic descriptions by such organizations as the WHO provide more comprehensive and accurate explanations of stuttering by incorporating the cognitive and affective features of the problem. In addition, recent attempts to define stuttering from the perspective of those who stutter, rather than from the perspective of the listener or observer (e.g., Tichenour & Yaruss, 2019), help us to understand the complex nature of this disorder that spans almost all aspects of the person (i.e., speech, motor, cognitive, emotional, behavioral, identity).

Many factors have been associated with both onset and development that appear to have little influence on the development of stuttering. Other factors, particularly those of speaker gender, age, familial genetic factors, speech-motor abilities, and speech and language skills, appear to play a stronger role in influencing the nature of how the problem develops. As we see in the following chapters, as stuttering continues to evolve, the speaker's manner of coping with the problem can have an extensive and sometimes negative impact on the individual's self-interpretation and quality of life. Having begun to describe some of the basic concepts and terminology, we now begin to consider models of etiology in more detail.

? TOPICS FOR DISCUSSION

1. Describe some common stereotypes that listeners often have about people who stutter. Based on your experience, how well do these views describe people that you know who stutter?

2. Develop a response about the nature of stereotypes about stuttering to an adolescent who tells you, "Everyone thinks I'm stupid!"

3. What are the primary categories that help to distinguish stuttering from more usual fluency breaks in young children?

4. What nonverbal behaviors might be useful for distinguishing between children who are stuttering and those with more usual fluency breaks?

5. What conditions or events might be associated with stuttering onset by parents? Why do you think these are important to parents, even if they are not well supported by research?

6. Give several examples of times when you experienced a "loss of control." Describe the emotional and cognitive characteristics of each experience.

7. Select a definition of stuttering and describe why you think it would be the best one to use when explaining stuttering to the parents of a stuttering child.

8. Develop two brief definitions of stuttering based on (a) your understanding prior to reading this chapter, and (b) your understanding having considered the explanations provided in this chapter.

📖 RECOMMENDED READINGS

Bloodstein, O., Bernstein Ratner, N., & Brundage, S. B. (2021). *A handbook on stuttering* (7th ed.). Plural Publishing.

Yairi, E., & Ambrose, N. G. (2005). The onset of stuttering. In E. Yairi & N. G. Ambrose (Eds.), *Early childhood stuttering: For clinicians by clinicians* (pp. 141–195). Pro-Ed.

Scientists often strive for special status by claiming a unique form of "objectivity" inherent in a supposedly universal procedure called the scientific method.... This image may be beguiling, but the claim is chimerical, and ultimately haughty and divisive. For the myth of pure perception raises scientists to a pinnacle above all other struggling intellectuals, who must remain mired in constraints of culture and psyche.

—Stephen Jay Gould (1995, p. 148)

Slavish adherence to a theoretical protocol and maniacal promotion of a single theoretical approach are utterly in opposition to science.

—Bruce Wampold (2001, p. 217)

... no model or theory will get it right all the time, and in practice, often a single theory (approach) explains only a small amount of the variance in targeted behaviors.

—Jill Cockburn (2004, p. 66)

A Historical Perspective on Etiologies and the Development of Stuttering

CHAPTER OBJECTIVES

- To provide a historical context for the evolution of the many theoretical perspectives of stuttering
- To provide a range of different theories of stuttering etiology that reflect the breadth of thought on the onset and development of stuttering
- To describe the most recent empirical advances that inform current theories of stuttering
- To describe similarities and differences across the various theories of etiology
- To suggest, as many have, that stuttering onset and development are best understood from a multifactorial perspective

THE IMPORTANCE OF A HISTORICAL PERSPECTIVE

Often the first and most frequently asked question of the clinician by clients, parents, and other professionals is, "What causes stuttering?" The clinician's response to this question will be the first opportunity to demonstrate his or her competence and understanding concerning the problem. The clinician's response will set the stage for the client's interpretation of himself or herself and his or her speaking ability. Informing the speaker (and his or her spouse or parents) that stuttering is a symptom of a psychological conflict resulting from a pregenital conversion neurosis is likely to have a considerably different effect than explaining that stuttering is likely the result of a combination of genetic and neuro-physiological influences. The clinician's understanding about the possible etiologies of the problem will also have an influence on the his or her treatment decisions. If the clinician believes that fluency failure is a result of excessive communication demands that exceed the speaker's capacity for speech and language production, some treatment recommendations will be judged more appropriate than others. The clinician's explanations concerning etiology will also influence the parents' response to their child, including how they deal with any guilt or shame they associate with their child's speech and how they respond when their child speaks fluently or stutters.

As we noted in Chapter 2, stuttering is complex and difficult to define. Perhaps no other disorder of human communication has been described in so many different ways. Stuttering has been called, among other things, a mystery, an enigma, a puzzle, and a riddle (Bluemel, 1957).

Stuttering can look, sound, and feel very different depending on one's experience, perspective, and particularly whether one is a person who stutters—reminiscent of the often-cited analogy by Wendell Johnson (1958) about a group of blind men describing an elephant. Each arrived at a very different conclusion because they were examining a different aspect and were unable to see the entire structure of the animal. Sheehan's (1970) iceberg analogy described in Chapter 1 illuminates the enigma somewhat by recognizing that many of the core emotional experiences of stuttering are not readily apparent to most observers. Both characterizations suggest that stuttering is a complex disorder composed of many levels and factors. The etiologies of the various forms of child-onset stuttering and related fluency problems that humans manifest continue to be an appealing mystery as well as an attractive challenge for dedicated researchers.

The uncertainties concerning the etiology of stuttering are such that it could

CLINICAL INSIGHT: A COMMENT ABOUT EVIDENCE

After many years of evaluating and reviewing manuscripts submitted to a variety of professional journals it becomes clear that there are many equivocal and contradictory findings concerning many issues. This inconsistency is the result of several factors, including sample size, inclusion and exclusion criteria for participants, validity, reliability of the procedures and measures used to determine the dependent variables, and the choice and interpretation of the various statistical analyses. On occasion it becomes apparent that the results and their meaning could be influenced by the authors' unintended or intended research agenda—the reason for the initial quotes at the outset of this chapter. It is the responsibility of the authors to conduct accurate research and the reviewers to conduct a rigorous and fair evaluation of the work. It is also up to the reader, the consumer of the information, to exercise a healthy level of skepticism when reading the articles in professional journals. As Gould (1997) stated, "Skepticism is the agent of reason against organized irrationalism—and is therefore one of the keys to human social and civic decency" (pp. ix–xii).

be argued that one sign of competent clinicians is that they do not casually provide an answer to the question of etiology. Glib and evasive answers about such a dynamic and complex problem could be one sign of a less than knowledgeable (or ethical) professional. Throughout history, there has been no shortage of people who offered simplistic explanations concerning the etiology and treatment of stuttering. One does not have to travel far on the Internet before finding uninformed and inaccurate statements, particularly about naïve and guaranteed cures. These are typically accompanied by testimonials from former clients who now profess to be as fluent as those who anchor the national news. Silverman (1996) made the barbed—but accurate—comment that should any so-called authority propose to understand the cause, let alone a cure for those who stutter, all but the most naïve clinicians should be highly suspicious of anything else the person might say. Some of the best experts in the field have reflected on the ambiguity of this multidimensional human problem that can so dramatically detract from one's ability to communicate with others. For example, on two occasions, renowned stuttering clinician and researcher Conture commented about this issue:

> I don't know what causes stuttering. I also don't know the best way to treat it. I don't even know if there is one way. I'm not sure if anyone else does either. Of one thing I am sure, however: The history of stuttering reflects a multidimensional problem that has repeatedly and successfully defied unidimensional solutions. (Conture, 1990, p. 1)

> . . . stuttering is a multidimensional problem that has defied a variety of unidimensional explanations. . . . It would certainly be nice to say, for example, that we will tell our readers what causes stuttering. Yes, that would be comforting, reassuring, and a minimally ambiguous thing to say. However, to suggest that we know, in any absolute or certain fashion, what causes stuttering would be intellectually, ethically, and professionally dishonest. (Conture, 2001, p. 2)

Although clinicians and researchers might not yet have a completely satisfactory answer about the etiologies of the problem, it is important for clinicians to have an opinion. The clinician should, at the very least, have a reasonable response to the questions of causation and development. In a few select cases we are able to identify, with reasonable certainty, a likely cause. For example, as described in Chapter 13, there are instances of adult sudden onset, such as acquired stuttering, where it is possible to identify specific environmental (e.g., posttraumatic stress disorder [PTSD]) or neurologic (e.g., traumatic brain injury [TBI]) events that appear to have precipitated the problem. Even then, though, we do not fully understand the precise cause-and-effect relationships between these events and the onset of the speaker's fluency problems. The possible reasons for the onset of developmental (child-onset) stuttering are even less certain, for there appear to be combinations of several factors that come together within a requisite time interval during the early phases of speech and language acquisition that contribute to the etiology of stuttering. Furthermore, the combination of factors that precipitate stuttering, as well as the individual's emotional reaction to the situation, vary for different people and subgroups of people who

CLINICAL INSIGHT: A COMMENT ABOUT COMPLEXITY

The number of physiological and neurological systems that come together in precise synchrony to produce smooth, coherent, meaningful communication is astounding. In addition, there are the diverse contexts in which human communication occurs, the intended meanings, the unintended meanings, the meaning of changes in tone and inflection, and so on. The point is that human communication is an exceptionally complex phenomenon. Given this, it is not unreasonable to think that a disorder that disrupts human communication in the variety of ways that stuttering appears to do is also highly complex.

A complex problem impacting a complex system

It is unlikely, then, that there will be a single, simple explanation, or a single, simple solution or treatment. This is exactly what we see with stuttering!

stutter. The problem, especially for adolescents and adults, is plainly not a simple one. If there were a single or obvious reason why people stutter, the answer would have been found long ago. Many intelligent and dedicated people have spent lifetimes (e.g., Van Riper, 1979, 1990) searching for a cause.

Fortunately, in most cases, it is not necessary for the clinician to know the precise cause of the problem in order to provide the speaker with substantial help. Fish (1995) suggested that efforts to determine the causes of many current human problems might be unnecessary, misguided, or even counterproductive. As Guitar (2019) indicated, although one could spend a lifetime and not know all there is to know about stuttering, it is not necessary to understand everything in order to be of assistance to people who stutter. Moreover, although explanations about etiology vary, there are seeds of truth in many of them.

Although stuttering is a complex phenomenon, it nevertheless holds a fas-

cination for most people. Students of the field only have to mention to one or more people that they are taking a course on the topic in order to elicit a flood of inquiries. The initial questions often center on etiology, the psychological components of the problem, and the possibilities of treatment. Much of the interest about stuttering centers on the mystery of the etiology and the unique, sometimes humorous, situations that stuttering can create.

THEORIES OF ETIOLOGY

Bloodstein and Bernstein Ratner (2008) pointed out that whereas some theories focus on the onset or etiology of stuttering, others attempt to explain the nature of the stuttering event. Many more recent theories are similar to earlier theories with a new conceptual framework. Some readers might not value the historical context provided by earlier theoretical perspectives of stuttering etiology.

Another factor that tends to influence the nature of theories is the notion of what is currently popular. Wingate (1968) suggested that the questions that are asked in a field are influenced by the *zeitgeist* (the spirit of the times). What is published is driven, to some degree, by what is fashionable as much as it is by the decisions of reviewers and editors. Those issues that are considered important enough to be supported by available funds are influenced by the zeitgeist. Questions are researched, and the results of investigations generate further considerations along a line of inquiry. The zeitgeist gradually changes and the pendulum swings back and forth, often returning to views that were thought to have outlived their usefulness. Sometimes the published articles—particularly review articles—summarize research that has pursued a particular direction for a time. These review articles, in turn, have their own influence on the zeitgeist. However, review articles might simply reflect and document changes in the zeitgeist that have already occurred. For example, views of stuttering as a neurophysiological problem that were popular during the first third of the 20th century have again achieved favor as a result of new understanding concerning normal speech and language acquisition, as well as technological advances. New research methods such as qualitative research and rapidly advancing technologies such as neuroimaging and genetic engineering provide new ways of asking old questions that advance our understanding of the stuttering experience and anatomical and physiological characteristics that could explain the onset and development of stuttering.

There is some measure of support as well as conflicting evidence for nearly all attempts to explain the onset of stuttering. The many attempts to formulate models that explain stuttering suggest that we are investigating a multidimensional problem. Understanding the impediments that humans encounter when attempting to produce speech fluently is complicated by the fact that fluency problems take many forms, most of which are often highly variable. There are no absolute criteria for differentiating stuttered speech from fluent speech. Conture (1990) compared stuttering to the common cold. Despite years of trying, no one has come up with a simple cause or solution to the problem, although there are variety of explanations and remedies. For some people, sometimes, a remedy will work. In other instances, possibly because of the interaction of the remedy and the person—or the timing of this interaction—the remedy is less effective. Each theoretical viewpoint and resulting treatment recommendation comes with its own cadre of supporters. There is one major difference, however, between the common cold and stuttering. The likelihood of successfully treating a relatively brief cold is considerably better than altering an often well-established network of behaviors and attitudes that are united by the helplessness and fear found in stuttering. Other comprehensive descriptions of the long and fascinating history of proposed stuttering causation are provided by Bloodstein et al. (2021), Van Riper (1982), and Silverman (2004).

A Historical Perspective on Stuttering Etiology

Perhaps the oldest view is that stuttering is a form of punishment for wrongdoing

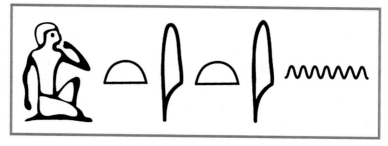

FIGURE 3–1. From right to left, the symbols represent the concept of "impediment" or "to impede," and the final portion, the figure to the left with one hand pointing to the mouth and the other to the ground along with the other symbols represents a reduplicated verb root *nitnit* or *njtjt*, which is interpreted as "to talk hesitantly" or "to stutter" (Faulkner, 1962). (From L. H. Corcoran and A. Webb, Institute of Egyptian Art and Archaeology, University of Memphis. Reprinted with permission.)

or sin on the part of the child or the parent. Undoubtedly this view continues to be held today in some cultures and socioeconomic groups throughout the world. Stuttering has been around for a long time throughout human history (see "Evidence from the Human Genome" later in this chapter). There have been, for example, several discussions about the possibility that Moses was a person who stuttered (Attanasio, 1997; Bobrick, 1995; Fibiger, 1994; Goldberg, 1989; Silverman, 2004). The earliest recorded mention of stuttering is provided by the Egyptians of the Middle Kingdom some 4,000 years ago, indicating that the problem has been present for at least as long as human civilization has been documented. A sequence of hieroglyphics on a papyrus discovered by W. Golenischeff included a narrative dating from 2000 BCE (Figure 3–1). As reported by Shapiro (1999), the original copy (Labeled P. Leningrad 1115) is preserved in Moscow (Lichtheim, 1973).

Many anatomical structures of the body, particularly those associated with speech production, have been implicated as a cause of stuttering. Examples include—but are not limited to—dryness of the tongue or problems in the hyoid bone, the hard palate, the uvula, the root of the tongue, and the larynx; various aspects of the hearing mechanism including the higher auditory pathway; assorted bones of the head; the endocrine and autonomic nervous systems; and the central nervous system. The tongue, as a primary articulator and often involved during moments of stuttering, has often been implicated. According to Silverman (2004), the belief that stuttering results from an abnormality in the tongue's structure, function, or both, appears to have been the most widely held view between the time of Aristotle and the Renaissance, approximately 1500 CE.

Because many anatomical structures used in speech were thought to be the source of the problem, it was not uncommon to recommend various forms of surgery for those who stuttered. Believing a spasm of the glottis to be responsible for stuttering, Johann Dieffenbach, a German surgeon, performed more than 250 operations on the tongues of people who stuttered in France and Germany in 1841. Performed without anesthesia, the operation involved making a horizontal incision at the base of the tongue and excising a triangular wedge. As self-proclaimed experts in stuttering are fond of doing, Dieffenbach claimed that his technique was highly successful—except, of course, for those who died as a result of infection. As his claims failed to be confirmed by others, the technique was abandoned by the end of the same year (Hunt, 1861/1967). (Interestingly, the common houseplant dieffenbachia, known for its bitter-tasting leaves, is named after this infamous surgeon.)

Other "cures" for offending parts of the anatomy included severing the hypoglossal nerve, piercing the tongue with hot needles or blistering it with fluids, encouraging smoking as a sedative for the vocal folds, and both tonsillectomy and adenoidectomy. According to Blanton and Blanton (1936), such procedures continued in the United States through the first few decades of the 20th century. There is also a long history of placing objects in the mouth or next to a variety of locations in the vocal tract (both externally and internally) in order to elicit fluency. The first reported example of such an approach may be that of Demosthenes, who was told to place pebbles under his tongue and practice speaking loudly to the sea. During the past several centuries there have been a multitude of devices (see Silverman, 2004; Van Riper, 1982) that facilitated fluency by both distracting the speaker from his or her habitual method of speech production and creating altered forms of phonation, articulation, timing, and proprioception. With few exceptions,

however, these devices provide, at best, only temporary fluency.

At the most basic level, models of stuttering can be separated into (a) psychological theories, suggesting that stuttering behaviors are a symptom indicative of an underlying psychological or neurotic conflict; (b) learning theories, proposing that at or near the onset of stuttering the speaker realizes that speaking is difficult and subsequently learns to anticipate stuttering and struggles when attempting to produce fluent speech; (c) physiological theories, proposing that the speaker's ability to produce fluent speech breaks down, particularly in response to various forms of stress; and (d) multifactorial views that consider combinations of neurophysiological, epigenetic, and linguistic factors that result in the onset and development of stuttering (Table 3–1). There is considerable overlap between many of the theoretical perspectives, with some providing better explanations of the onset of stuttering and others providing explanations of the subsequent development as speakers cope with the problem. Some explanations are not fully developed and do not provide relationships among variables and make predictions and are therefore difficult to test. We discuss the basic ideas of each view in the next section followed, in turn, by examples of investigations that speak to the veracity of each viewpoint.

PSYCHOLOGICAL THEORIES

Stuttering as a Symptom of Repressed Internal Conflict

Van Riper, after many decades of treating thousands of children and adults who stuttered, wrote an engaging article in

TABLE 3–1. Summary of Theories Explaining the Onset and Development of Stuttering

Category	Theory	Summary
Psychological Theories	Repressed-Need/ Internal Conflict Hypotheses	Psychoanalytic theory of stuttering. Disfluent behavior is seen as a psychopathologic symptom of repressed internal conflict. Multiple possible sources of the conflict have been proposed, such as fixation at oral or anal stage of psychosexual development or inadequate interpersonal relationships. Little success has been reported for the psychoanalytic treatment of stuttering. Research has not supported the presence of psychological problems for children who stutter. While adults who stutter may experience social anxiety as a result of stuttering, they have psychological issues at rates comparable to the general population.
	Influence of Parents	Psychological characteristics of the parents of children who stutter have been extensively investigated. Overall, there is little to no evidence to indicate that parents of children who stutter are any different, as a group, compared to parents of children who do not stutter.
	Personality Disorders and Stuttering	Some researchers have suggested that adults who stutter present with a personality disorder (PD). This suggestion, however, has been challenged by other researchers. In general, no consistent evidence has been found for PWS having a personality disorder at rates greater than the general population.
Learning Theories	Anticipatory- Struggle Model	This perspective suggests that stuttering is a learned behavior. As a result of normal disfluencies the child believes that speech/communication is difficult and fearful. The child learns to anticipate disfluencies and struggles to avoid or escape the disfluency. Research has suggested that, although stuttering is not caused by the anticipatory-struggle mechanism, learning to fear disfluencies and struggling to avoid them can play a significant role in the way children and adults cope with and manage their stuttering.
	Diagnosogenic Theory	Wendell Johnson (1930) suggested that stuttering is the result of normal disfluencies being labeled (by parents, teachers, or others in the child's life) as stuttering. As the child becomes aware of the disfluencies, fear, avoidance, and struggle increase along with negative reactions by parents, teachers, etc. Although no evidence to support this theory has been found, it is one of the more well-known theories of stuttering and has led to many recommendations from teachers, physicians, and SLPs to simply ignore a child's disfluencies and to never use the "S-word"! Clinicians may encounter parents who want "indirect therapy" for their child as a result of the (incorrect) belief that talking about "stuttering" is likely to make the problem worse or contribute to it becoming a chronic condition.

TABLE 3–1. *continued*

Category	Theory	Summary
Learning Theories *continued*	Continuity Hypothesis	Bloodstein (1950) suggested that stuttering results from the tension and fragmentation of the fluency breaks in the normal disfluencies of young children. He believed that the tension and fragmentation increased as a result of communicative pressure. There is no specific evidence supporting this hypothesis.
	Operant Conditioning Models	Operant conditioning models of stuttering propose that the fluency breaks of young children are shaped by the response they elicit. In other words, listeners' often negative responses to the child's fluency breaks reinforce their occurrence. The moments of disrupted fluency are then gradually shaped into greater abnormality, with associated struggle and secondary characteristics. These models, although providing some insight into how stuttering behaviors might be therapeutically manipulated, have not been successful in explaining the etiology of stuttering.
	Two-Factor Approach	Brutten and Shoemaker (1967) attempted to combine classical-conditioning and operant-conditioning models in the *two-factor approach*. They suggested that the initial fluency breaks occur as a result of classical conditioning, with negative emotion (and the response of the autonomic nervous system) being associated with the act of speaking. The emotional reaction of the child results in a disruption of the cognitive and motor sequencing of speech production, resulting in disfluencies. The secondary responses that enable the speaker to avoid and escape from stuttering are the result of operant conditioning and increase the overt, secondary characteristics of the problem. Research has failed to support such behavioral factors as the original cause of stuttering, although there is evidence that observable stuttering behaviors can be shaped in this way.
Physiological Theories	Cerebral Dominance/ Cerebral Asymmetry	Stuttering is a result of a lack of dominance of the left hemisphere for the organization and management of language and speech production. Early studies focused on the peripheral functions (handedness, vision, listening, etc.). Studies make use of a wide variety of speech perception and production of individuals who stutter and fluent peers. Results were often inconsistent and conflicting in supporting mixed or heightened right hemisphere activity for adults who stutter. The few studies done with children did not support mixed or a lack of left hemispheric dominance.

continues

TABLE 3–1. *continued*

Category	Theory	Summary
Physiological Theories *continued*	Structural and Functional Neurological Differences	In the last few decades technology in neuroimaging (e.g., CT, rCBF MRI, PET, fMRI, etc.) has yielded many intriguing results about both structural and functional differences in children and adults who stutter. Many more studies were conducted with adults than children. Many regions of the brain have been associated with stuttering (left and right superior temporal gyrus, inferior frontal gyrus, basal ganglia, thalamus, premotor cortex, motor cortex, just to name a few). Results generally indicated atypical structural and functional features in the left hemisphere and excessive activity (most likely compensatory in nature) in the right hemisphere. Research has identified several examples of anomalous structural features and reduced integrity of white matter (myelinated) neural transmission functioning, particularly for adults who stutter. Recent research has also found evidence of reduced integrity of white matter fiber density axonal diameter, and myelination for children as young as 2–3 years of age. Overall, research suggests that there is some neurological component to the etiology of developmental stuttering but no single structural or functional cause has been isolated.
	Genetics	Recent investigations have implicated several genetic sites on different chromosomes that are associated with stuttering. Studies with identical (monozygotic) twins have demonstrated the potential combined role of genetics with other factors, as concordance for stuttering was observed for some twins but not for others. Overall, there is clear evidence that genetics plays an important role in the etiology of stuttering for some PWS (i.e., we know stuttering tends to run in families) but it remains unclear how genetic components combine with other factors to cause stuttering.
	Cognitive/ Linguistic and Motor Sequencing	Several investigators have proposed that stuttering is the result of a combination of inefficient higher level linguistic processing and lower level production of language and speech. As a result of structural and functional anomalies in the cortical and subcortical systems, individuals have difficulty generating temporal motor patterns necessary for sequencing speech. Related studies have found inefficient timing for other, nonspeech motor activities for those who stutter. Research on these theories demonstrates a potential mechanism for some aspects of stuttering.

TABLE 3–1. *continued*

Category	Theory	Summary
Physiological Theories *continued*	Covert Repair Hypothesis	The model proposes that all speakers have the ability to internally (covertly) monitor and detect errors in phonological encoding just prior to the creation of articulatory commands. When errors are detected, phonological planning is interrupted, followed by covert repairing of the speech plan. For individuals who stutter, phonological encoding is slower and requires more time to activate a target. The extra time taken for detection and repair along with the less efficient selection of phonological targets results in stuttering. Again, research on this hypothesis demonstrates a potential mechanism for some aspects of stuttering.
	EXPLAN Model	Much like the Covert Repair Hypothesis, this model suggests that production is not associated with internal or external monitoring. The cognitive-linguistic plans (PLAN) and the motor system receive and execute (EX) the linguistic sequences. When the linguistic (syntactic, lexical, phonetic) plan is not accurate, the motor system is unable to produce speech, and breakdowns occur at the language-speech interface. Speakers respond by stalling or repeating.
	Cybernetic and Feedback Models	The role of feedback during speech production is similar to the self-regulation designs in many mechanical and biological systems where the goal is to match the intended and actual output of the system. When a disruption to the accuracy of the feedback occurs, the system tends to oscillate similar to stuttering. These models help to explain the mechanism of stuttering without necessarily explaining the specific etiology of the problem.
Multifactorial Models	Demands and Capacities Model	The complex nature of stuttering has led researchers to develop many multidimensional models that incorporate the many extrinsic and intrinsic features of stuttering. Because of their complexity, these models can be difficult to test. The Demands and Capacities Model (DCM) provides a straightforward explanation to parents of children stutter. The model considers both the capacities of the speaker and the effect of both internal and environmental "demands" placed on the child for producing fluent speech.
		The goals of therapy are to find a balance between the demands placed on the child for fluency and the child's abilities that enhance the likelihood of fluent speech.

continues

TABLE 3–1. *continued*

Category	Theory	Summary
Multifactorial Models *continued*	Multifactorial Dynamic Pathways (MDP) Theory	Emphasizes the dynamic developmental context in which stuttering emerges and in which the trajectory to persistence or recovery occurs. Smith and Weber suggest that multiple factors contribute to the onset and persistence of stuttering, including motor, linguistic, emotional, and central neural aspects, and emphasized that these factors have varying weights in different individuals who stutter. As a consequence, each child who begins to stutter will experience a unique, dynamic pathway into the diagnosis of stuttering, that will ultimately lead to recovery or persistence. The MDP theory provides an explanation of the large percentage of children who recover from stuttering, suggesting that in these children, brain adaptations occur that successfully compensate for the atypical neural activity underlying the stuttering disfluencies, leading to more stable speech production networks. For the remaining children who begin to stutter, brain adaptations are inadequate to compensate for the atypical neural activity, and stuttering becomes a long-term, chronic problem. The speech motor systems of these children remain vulnerable to breakdowns in the face of increasingly complex language demands and psychosocial pressures. As the child matures and if stuttering persists, the complex sequences of central neural activity that drive the speech motor and other behaviors characteristic of that child's stuttering become overlearned patterns, interfering with fluent speech production into adolescence and adulthood.
	Neurophysiological Model	Similar to the Demands and Capacities model, this model emphasizes the dynamic interplay among the: (a) processing: central neurophysiological processing; (b) output: motor, cognitive, language, social, and emotional processes; and (c) contextual, environmental influences. The model emphasizes that the neurological and physiological features of the stuttering experience occur long before and long after an overt stuttering event. This view is also optimistic in that the mammalian brain is continually changing throughout life and amenable to adaptive change as a result of successful therapy.

what was then called the *Western Michigan University Journal of Speech Therapy*. Written in 1974, the article was titled "A Handful of Nuts" (see also Van Riper, 1979). Among the many hundreds of clients he had seen up to that point in his career, Van Riper found only a very few who had severe emotional problems. Although his description of these clients makes for some interesting reading, as we shall see, there are relatively few people who stutter who have such deep-seated emotional problems.

Through the first several decades of this century, many people who treated stuttering in this country were physicians, and some of these individuals held a psychoanalytic view of the problem. This perspective was that stuttering is a psychopathology and that the overt stuttering behaviors are symptomatic of a deep-seated psychological disorder. Bannister (1966) described this point of view in the following manner:

> . . . psychoanalytic theories seem to suggest that man is basically a battlefield. He is in a dark cellar in which a well-bred spinster lady and a sex crazed monkey are forever engaged in mortal combat, the struggle being refereed by a rather nervous bank clerk. (p. 21)

The neurotic or psychoanalytic explanation of stuttering also has been termed the repressed-need hypothesis (Bloodstein & Bernstein Ratner, 2008; Silverman, 2004). That is, stuttering is seen as a neurosis, and individuals who stutter do so as a result of a repressed, neurotic, unconscious conflict. Stuttering behavior is seen as a symptom that is symbolic of this conflict. The origin of the conflict is a central question, and there has been no shortage of suggestions about the possible source. Some theorized that the source was psychosexual, a fixation of psychological development at an oral or anal stage of infant sexual development (Glauber, 1982). It was proposed, for example, that one who stuttered had not experienced oral erotic gratification as an infant, possibly due to a disturbance in the mother–child relationship. Others proposed a neo-Freudian view that the source of conflict

was the result of inadequate interpersonal relationships (Barbara, 1965, 1982; Wyatt, 1969). Other unconscious and repressed needs that have been suggested take the form of stuttering to gain attention or sympathy, or to avoid responsibilities. Many of these opinions sound strange and even preposterous to current speech-language pathologists. The chapter by Travis, "The Unspeakable Feelings of People With Special Reference to Stuttering," that appears in the two editions of his *Handbook of Speech Pathology* (Travis, 1957, 1971) provide lurid examples of this viewpoint. Although it is unlikely that a client or parent will have knowledge of many of these psychoanalytic opinions about stuttering etiology, given current accessibility of knowledge via online sources—which can often be inaccurate or, at best, presented without context or evidence—clinicians should be aware of these views and be able to respond to this manner of conceptualizing stuttering.

American physician Edward Scripture (1931) was one of the first to combine psychotherapy and speech treatment that focused on changing specific speech habits. This combined approach was also taken up by other clinicians who are psychoanalytically based (e.g., Barbara, 1982; Freund, 1966; Glauber, 1982).

Evidence From Empirical Investigations

According to Silverman (2004), there has been relatively little success reported by those using a psychoanalytic approach for treating stuttering. Brill (1923) indicated that after 11 years of treating a total of 69 individuals who stuttered through psychoanalysis, he was able to claim only five persons who were cured, one of whom subsequently relapsed. There is a suggestion that even Freud himself (Freund,

1966) did not believe that psychoanalytic techniques were particularly helpful in treating stuttering.

Adams (1993) reviewed 35 articles that investigated the psychological characteristics of the parents of children who stutter. He found that the vast majority of investigations indicated no differences between the parents of children who stutter and the parents of typically fluent children. Other authors have found similar results. An extensive review of the literature concerning the role of parents of young children who stutter by Nippold and Rudzinski (1995) found little evidence that parents of children who stutter differ in the ways they respond to their children. In a review of studies that have investigated the influence of both home environment and parent–child interaction, Yairi (1997b) also found that the evidence failed to support the view that parents of children who stutter have abnormal personalities and emotional or adjustment problems. Yairi concluded that, "it is clearly time to declare that the belief that parents' personalities or attitudes are causally related to stuttering is null and void for purposes of counseling and treatment" (p. 44). More recently, based on many years of longitudinal data, Yairi and Ambrose (2005) concluded that parents of stuttering children do not perceive their children appreciably differently than the parents of fluent children.

Finally, Yairi and Ambrose (2005) suggested that as part of the information provided to parents about their child who is stuttering, clinicians may consider the following:

The best research has failed to show that people who stutter, as a group, are more neurotic or have more other psychological disorders than those who do not stutter. We do not think that your child began stuttering because of any serious emotional difficulties. (p. 387)

With the development of university speech and hearing centers and the creation of the National Association of Teachers of Speech in 1925 (the precursor of the American Speech-Language-Hearing Association; Paden, 1970), fewer physicians provided treatment. The new clinicians, who were trained in the behavioral sciences, were less likely to hold a psychoanalytic view of stuttering.

LEARNING THEORIES

Stuttering as a Learned Anticipatory Struggle

This view of stuttering onset has been termed the anticipatory-struggle model (Bloodstein & Bernstein Ratner, 2008; Silverman, 2004). The essence of this model is that stuttering is a learned behavior. This view, at least in an informal sense, also has a long history. Van Riper (1982) indicated that Amman (1700/1965) was one of the first to state that stuttering was, in fact, a learned, bad habit. In a precursor to the learning theories of the 20th century, in the 1800s, Erasmus Darwin (grandfather of Charles Darwin) attributed stuttering to emotionally conditioned interruptions of motoric speech. Arnott (1928) believed that stuttering resulted from a learned "spasm of the glottis." According to Van Riper (1982), this was the most popular view of stuttering onset and development in both the United States and Great Britain from the middle to the end of the 19th century. For example, during this time, Alexander Melville Bell (grandfather of Alexander Graham Bell) wrote a number of books suggesting that stuttering was learned. One important implication of this view was to place the problem within the arena of the educator rather than the medical professional (Bell, 1853). Dunlap (1932) also considered much of stuttering to be learned and recommended weakening the behavior by having the speaker purposely or voluntarily stutter. However, these views of stuttering as a learned behavior were the exception during the early part of the 20th century.

After several decades in which the zeitgeist favored physical and psychoanalytical views of stuttering etiology, during the middle third of the 20th century (beginning approximately in 1930) there began a gradual change toward viewing stuttering as learned behavior. Many people were entering the field at this time with backgrounds in psychology, and the majority had received their training at the University of Iowa. Many of these scholars had a profound influence on the general field of communication disorders. This concentration of researchers, clinicians, and authors led to what has been termed the "Iowa Development" (Bloodstein, 1995). A second generation of clinicians included such individuals as Hugo Gregory, Joseph Sheehan, David Williams, and Dean Williams.

The Diagnosogenic Theory

A most influential result of the Iowa development was the diagnosogenic theory of stuttering onset as proposed by Wendell Johnson. At the time, this was one of the most comprehensive theories of stuttering onset and development. Having been influenced by the writings of Korzybski (1941) in his book *Science and Sanity* and his work in general semantics,

Johnson developed a "semantic theory" of stuttering. General semantics is the study of the ways in which people use words to explain their lives and solve problems. Johnson's theory also became known as the semantogenic or interactional theory (Perkins, 1990), and it had both a profound and lengthy impact in the area of fluency disorders. A key aspect of a general semantic approach to events and behavior is our interpretation of the events and our choice of labels for these occurrences. The theory held that stuttering evolves from normal fluency breaks to which parents (or other significant people in the child's environment) overreact and mislabel as "stuttering." Two sentences contained in Johnson's (1962) *An Open Letter to the Mother of a Stuttering Child* state the essence of this view:

> The diagnosis of stuttering—that is, the decision made by someone that a child is beginning to stutter—is one of the causes of the stuttering problem, and apparently one of the most potent causes. Having labeled the child's hesitations and repetitions as "stuttering," the listener—somewhat more often the mother than the father—reacts to them as if they were all that the label implies. (p. 2)

The theory assumed that many children, including those who eventually stutter, experience a period of typical and effortless fluency breaks. Additionally, when children are penalized (typically by their parents) for producing these normal disfluencies, the result is increased anticipation and struggle behavior. Stuttering, therefore, is created by the listener as normal breaks in fluency are shaped into stuttering. Eventually, the speaker "learns" to stutter in his or her unique manner and the problem becomes self-reinforcing.

Evidence From Empirical Investigations

As with other explanations of stuttering onset and development, there are several studies that provide support and several that do not. That is, typically speaking, preschool children do tend to repeat and hesitate (Johnson & Associates, 1959; Yairi, 1981, 1982). A central question, however, is whether these early fluency breaks are normal or the stuttering-like disfluencies (SLDs) described in the previous chapter. Although Johnson and Associates (1959) tried to make the case that the initial fluency breaks are essentially normal, the majority of subsequent researchers and authors (Ambrose & Yairi, 1999; Bloodstein, 1958; McDearmon, 1968; Throneberg & Yairi, 1994; Van Riper, 1982; Wingate, 1988; Yairi, 1997a; Yairi & Ambrose, 1999a; Yairi et al., 1993; Yairi & Lewis, 1984) indicate that at the onset of stuttering, the original fluency breaks are far from normal, both in terms of quantity and quality.

One of the more compelling attempts to determine if stuttering could be created by labeling normal fluency breaks as "stuttering" was an unpublished master's thesis by a student, Mary Tudor, at the University of Iowa in 1939. The investigation, titled "An Experimental Study of the Effects of Evaluative Labeling on Speech Fluency," was conducted under the direction of Wendell Johnson. It is important to emphasize that the investigation was conducted some 3 years prior to the initial development of the diagnosogenic theory and was not, therefore, an attempt to provide support for the theory. The goal of the study was simply to see if labeling someone as a person who stutters would temporarily alter a young speaker's fluency. Although available at the University of Iowa library to anyone, it was generally unknown until described by Silverman (1988b) as "The Monster Study.". In response to the reaction created by the publication in 2001 of a newspaper article describing the study and the alleged long-term effects on some of the children who participated, a thorough re-analysis of the design and analysis of the data was conducted by Ambrose and Yairi (2002).

Tudor's (1939) subjective analysis of the results of the study suggested that, by the end of the investigation, all six children in her experimental group (i.e., typically fluent children labeled as "stutterers") showed varying degrees of speech disruptions and concern about their speech. According to Tudor,

> They were reluctant to speak and spoke only when they were urged to. . . . [T]heir rate of speaking was decreased. They spoke more slowly and with greater exactness. They had a tendency to weigh each word before they said it. . . . [T]he length of response was shortened. . . . [T]hey became more self-conscious. They appeared shy and embarrassed in many situations. . . . They accepted the fact that there was something definitely wrong with their speech. Some hung their heads—others gasped and covered their mouths with their hands. (pp. 147–148)

The reanalysis by Ambrose and Yairi (2002) of the original study, however, indicates a very different understanding of both the nature and the results of the study. In their concluding comments, Ambrose and Yairi suggested that the investigation provides a good example of how the quality of an investigation must be considered when interpreting and accepting the results. Ambrose and Yairi pointed out the many fatal flaws in both the design and interpretation of the original data, including poorly controlled participant selection and assignment to groups, imprecise analysis of data, and inaccurate interpretation of results.

Ambrose and Yairi (2002) pointed out that the investigation was not published, not because of any attempt to conceal the obvious ethical issues, but because it failed to confirm any of the research questions. Furthermore, the issues that today would be seen as inappropriate and deceptive and that would clearly fail to meet the current standards of internal review boards for conducting research are best placed in the context of the research community in the 1930s. The development of recent standards for the protection of human participants began in the years following World War II and, in spite of valiant efforts, did not become mandated until the early 1990s in the United States. Finally, it is clear that the investigators, Tudor and Johnson, did not intend to cause harm. As Ambrose and Yairi explained, the investigators attempted to induce a temporary disruption in fluency rather than a long-term effect. The study did demonstrate that labeling someone as a "stutterer" does not have a long-term influence.

The Continuity Hypothesis

Another explanation of stuttering as learned behavior is the continuity hypothesis as described by Bloodstein (1961, 1993, 1995) and by Shames and Sherrick (1965) in their explanation of normal disfluencies increasing as a result of reinforcement. Like the diagnosogenic theory, this view also proposes that stuttering develops from the normal fluency breaks produced by young children. Bloodstein suggested that both the tension and the fragmentation of fluency breaks increase as a result of communicative pressure. The development of stuttering is not a consequence of the child's trying to avoid normal fluency breaks that have been mislabeled, but as tension and fragmentation increase, especially for part-word repetitions, the pattern becomes chronic and the child is more likely to be identified as someone who stutters.

Models of Stuttering as an Operant Behavior

During the late 1950s and early 1960s, there was increasing interest in conceptualizing stuttering in terms of classical (respondent) conditioning or operant (instrumental) conditioning. Both approaches hold that the speaker gradually learns to stutter, but for slightly different reasons. With classical conditioning, the speaker learns to associate speaking with emotional arousal and the involvement of the autonomic nervous system (just as a dog salivates having learned that a ringing bell is associated with the dispensing of food). That is, through a reinforcement schedule, a previously neutral stimulus (a bell) is associated with the food. Just how negative emotion might be associated with speaking is unclear, although some children—not necessarily those who are eventually diagnosed as stuttering— might have physical or personality characteristics that make it more difficult for them to achieve fluency. In addition, as discussed in Chapter 5, some children could have a reactive personality that sensitizes them to stressful environmental events. In any case, the child learns that speaking is often difficult and begins to both anticipate fluency disruptions and struggle during fluency breaks in the manner of classical conditioning. Whether or not the initial fluency breaks are normal has been a major issue. If the initial breaks are normal, then the argument that stuttering is principally a learned behavior is strengthened. If the initial or core breaks in fluency are not normal, learning would be of less importance suggesting that—at least at the outset—one or more aspects of the child's speech production system is not functioning normally. As we discussed, the investigations of Yairi and his associates indicates that the initial fluency breaks (the SLDs) are distinctly different from the usual disfluencies of young children.

Models of operant conditioning are based on Skinner's (1953) concepts of experimental analysis of behavior. The primary association in operant models is between a behavior and the consequence of the behavior. A reinforcement is seen as positive when the occurrence of the behavior (the operant) increases and negative when the behavior decreases. Operant models of stuttering propose that the fluency breaks of young children are shaped by the response they elicit. These theories propose that listener responses to the child's fluency breaks reinforce their occurrence. The moments of disrupted fluency are then gradually shaped into greater abnormality, with associated struggle and secondary characteristics. Operant models do better in accounting for the evolution of stuttering and the great variety of avoidance and escape behaviors that often develop than they do in explaining the onset of the problem. Individual speaker responses to listener reactions tend to shape somewhat distinctive coping behaviors. The fact that these coping or secondary behaviors are not regularly reinforced makes them particularly resistant to change, as an intermittent schedule of reinforcement tends to strengthen behaviors, making them more difficult to extinguish. Over time, the learned or secondary behaviors such as eye blinks, head movements, tongue protrusion, or gasping for air become part of an integrated and tightly bound pattern of behavior.

Brutten and Shoemaker (1967) attempted to combine classical conditioning and operant conditioning models in what they termed a two-factor approach. They suggested that the initial fluency breaks occur as a result of classically conditioned negative emotion being associated with the act of speaking (and the participation of the autonomic nervous system). The negative emotion results in a disruption of the cognitive and motor sequencing of speech production. The secondary responses that help the speaker to avoid and escape from stuttering are the result of operant conditioning and soon become part of the problem.

Evidence From Empirical Investigations

The early work of researchers provided encouraging results indicating that stuttering was an operant behavior, and that stuttering could be unlearned based on positive or negative consequences. For example, Flanagan et al. (1958, 1959) and Martin and Siegel (1966a, 1966b) found that stuttering could be reduced when immediately followed by punishing loud noises or electric shocks. However, there were also many investigations showing inconsistent results that did not follow the outcomes predicted by the operant model (e.g., Martin et al., 1975; Williams & Martin, 1974). No acceptable explanation has been offered for why stuttering behavior increases or decreases as a result of contingent responses. This is most likely due to the complex interaction of the speaker's many possible reactions to the wide variety of factors present in most speaking situations. Several researchers have found that responses contingent on stuttering serve to distract the speaker or highlight the occurrence of stuttering, resulting in a decrease in stuttering (Cooper et al., 1970; Daly & Kimbarow, 1978; Siegel & Martin, 1966). Siegel (1970), at the time one of the foremost researchers in the field of behavioral science and fluency disorders, published a review of traditional learning theories of stuttering. Siegel pointed out that operant conditioning models fail to adequately explain stuttering behavior in the laboratory, let alone in the real world. Although research has shown that it was clearly possible to manipulate the secondary behaviors of stuttering, researchers and clinicians had much less success in explaining the development of the core behavior of the problem—that is, the cause of the fluency breaks in the first place.

PHYSIOLOGICAL THEORIES

Cerebral Dominance Theory

In the 1920s, a number of anecdotal reports suggested that individuals who stutter are more likely to be left-handed or ambidextrous than nonstutterers and that the onset of stuttering had occurred in conjunction with attempts to change their handedness in some way (Bloodstein et al., 2021). In response to this concept and the early understanding that, for most individuals, speech and language appeared to be associated with left-hemisphere dominance (Geschwind & Galaburda, 1985), Samuel T. Orton proposed a theory of stuttering that would become known as the "Cerebral Dominance" theory (Orton, 1927). Subsequent publications including a text by one of his students, Lee Edward Travis, popularized Orton's theory (Travis, 1929, 1931).

Orton and Travis theorized that because the muscles of the speech mechanism receive nerve impulses from both the left and right hemispheres of the brain, it is necessary for one hemisphere to be dominant over the other in order for speech movements to be properly synchronized. They proposed that the left hemisphere was the more dominant in this process. They suggested that the nervous system of people who stutter had not matured sufficiently to achieve left hemispheric dominance over speech movements, and that this maturational failure resulted from hereditary influences, disease, injury, or even emotional arousal and fatigue.

Evidence From Empirical Investigations

Initially, research on the theory focused on investigating the handedness of individuals who stutter, and the results were encouraging. By the 1940s, as investigations yielded inconsistent findings, interest in the cerebral dominance theory subsided because there was little support for the idea that people who stutter as a group differed from nonstuttering speakers on measures of handedness or sidedness. The inconsistent results prompted researchers to develop new ways of studying the innate "sidedness"—rather than simply the handedness—of individuals.

Dichotic Listening Procedures

Dichotic listening tasks involve the simultaneous (competing) presentation of two different signals to opposite ears, with subjects being required to repeat back what was heard in one or both ears (Mueller & Bright, 1994). As the auditory-cortical system is taxed by the simultaneous presentation, auditory processing via the primary (contralateral) pathways indicates accuracy and response time advantages for stimuli presented to right-ear–left hemisphere or left-ear–right-hemisphere pathways. Studies employing this technique with individuals who are fluent speakers have reported a significant right ear advantage (REA) in the recognition of linguistic stimuli (e.g., Broadbent & Gregory, 1964; Kimura, 1961; Lowe-Bell et al., 1970), whereas other studies (e.g., Kimura, 1964) have reported a left-ear advantage (LEA) for the recognition of dichotically presented melodic tones. These findings have suggested hemispheric dominance for certain psychological phenomena, such as speech and language, which have been associated with left-hemisphere processing (Kimura, 1961; Studdert-Kennedy & Shankweiler, 1970) for most right-handed individuals. Furthermore, numerous studies have found REAs for both right- and left-handed subjects (e.g., Berlin et al., 1973; Kimura, 1961; Studdert-Kennedy & Shankweiler, 1970).

The cerebral dominance theory of stuttering (Orton, 1927; Travis, 1931) suggests that due to lack of a dominant hemisphere for language in the person who stutters, his or her performance on a dichotic listening task should demonstrate a reduced or nonexistent REA or perhaps an LEA. Curry and Gregory (1969) presented both verbal and nonverbal dichotic stimuli to adults who stuttered and a group of fluent speakers and found that on a verbal task 75% of the nonstutterers demonstrated an REA, whereas 55% of the participants who stuttered demonstrated a LEA. They reported that no differences were found between the two groups on the nonverbal tasks. Similar results were found by other researchers (Brady & Berson, 1975; Cerf & Prins, 1974; Curry & Gregory, 1969; Moore, 1984; Moore & Haynes, 1980; Sommers et al., 1975) using meaningful words as stimuli.

However, conflicting evidence regarding the performance of persons who stutter relative to typically fluent individuals on dichotic listening tasks has been found by a number of researchers (e.g., Dorman & Porter, 1975; Liebetrau & Daly, 1981; Pinsky & McAdam, 1980; Sussman, MacNeilage, & Lumbley, 1975). These authors failed to find differences in performance on dichotic listening tasks between speakers who stuttered and those who did not.

One possible explanation for these discrepancies was presented by Moore (1976, 1984). Moore suggested that differences in the dichotic verbal stimuli (e.g., syllables, digits, words) between the various studies might have influenced the results. He stated that studies that employed meaningful linguistic stimuli rather than syllables in their dichotic listening tasks (e.g., Curry & Gregory, 1969; Sommers et al., 1975) did indicate that persons who stutter as a group failed to demonstrate an REA.

Similarly, Molt and Brading (1994) questioned the accuracy of dichotic listening measures of hemispheric specialization that used consonant-vowel (CV) syllables. They compared the performance of a group of persons who stutter to a group of fluent speakers on a dichotic listening task that used CV syllables, while also measuring hemispheric activity via recording of event-related potentials (ERPs). They found no significant differences between the groups on the dichotic listening measure, but they did note laterality differences between the groups based on the ERP recordings, a finding that they suggested was "especially notable in that the scalp-recorded electroencephalographic activity should reflect actual hemispheric patterns to a greater extent than dichotic ear advantage measures" (p. 149).

Electroencephalography (EEG) and Event-Related Potentials (ERPs)

In order to provide support for his theory, Travis and his colleagues conducted a number of investigations using *electroen-cephalographic* (EEG) studies (see Bloodstein & Bernstein Ratner, 2008, pp. 128–132) to compare the cortical potentials of individuals who stuttered with those of typically fluent speakers (e.g., Travis & Knott, 1936, 1937; Travis & Malamud, 1937). These authors used what became the first of many techniques that represent the characteristics of neurological systems. EEG indicates neurological activity as reflected in the waxing and waning of electrical signals from tens of thousands of neurons in the cerebral cortex (Guenther, 2008). The alpha wave (8–10 Hz) is one of many EEG waveforms obtained from the cerebral cortex that indicate changes in ERPs between separated points on the scalp (Bhatnagar & Andy, 1995). Neural activity following the presentation of a stimulus is indicated by a suppression of the rhythmic activity of the waveforms. For example, the rhythmic activity alpha potentials disappear or are greatly attenuated in the presence of active cognitive processes. *Magnetoencephalography* (MEG) also measures many neurons in the cortex by employing *superconducting quantum interference devices* (SQUIDs) that provide sensitive readings of magnetic fields produced by neuronal activity (Guenther, 2008).

Several investigators have consistently found asymmetry of EEG patterns with greater suppression of alpha waves in the right hemisphere of adults who stutter (Boberg et al., 1983; Moore & Haynes, 1980; Moore & Lang, 1977). Although many studies have indicated increased activity of the right hemisphere for adults, there have been few investigations of younger speakers who stutter. Fitch and Batson (1989) used EEG to investigate alpha-wave suppression with young (ages 10–15) stuttering speakers during auditory-verbal, auditory-nonverbal, visual-verbal, and visual-nonverbal tasks. Whereas the 12 fluent male participants indicated no evidence of hemispheric asymmetry, the 12 young men who stuttered (with Stuttering Severity Instrument [SSI; Riley, 1972] ratings ranging from moderate to severe) showed small but significant right-hemisphere asymmetry. In another investigation of younger speakers who stuttered, Khedr et al. (2000) found evidence of both slower and more asymmetric EEG rhythms for individuals aged 6 to 25.

Evidence of Cerebral Asymmetry From Neuroimaging Techniques

Guenther (2008) pointed out that the generation of language and speech is one of the most complex of all cognitive and motor tasks and that many cortical and subcortical portions of the brain are active during even the smallest of speech activities. Areas of the cerebral cortex in the temporal, parietal, and frontal lobes are involved in auditory, somatosensory, and motor activities. In addition, many subcortical portions (the cerebellum, basal ganglia, thalamus, and brain stem) of the brain contribute to the neural control of speech. Determining the precise contribution of any one area is confounded by the variability in the location of specific brain functions, the anatomical variability between subjects (brain size, shape, and gyral patterns), and the adaptability of the brain, as well as the data averaging and spatial smoothing procedures often necessary when analyzing images.

Structural and Functional Neuroimaging

In order to understand the results of investigations using the various technologies, it is necessary to appreciate the basic terminology of the various techniques for viewing the structure and functions of the brain. *Structural* neuroimaging studies identify anatomical structures of the brain using *computed tomography* (CT) and *magnetic resonance imaging* (MRI) techniques. CT (originally called *computed axial tomography* or CAT) uses a narrow x-ray beam and computerized reconstruction to create "thin-slice" images of cross-sections of the body. Structures that are denser (e.g., bones of the skull) result in lighter images than softer tissues (e.g., the brain and muscles), resulting in absorption maps of the structures (Bhatnagar & Andy, 1995; Guenther, 2008). CT scanning indicates the structural characteristics of cortical and subcortical regions indicating lesions and cerebrovascular disease. MRI creates brain images by using the magnetic properties of hydrogen atomic nuclei. Because water contributes approximately two thirds of human body weight, it contains a large number of hydrogen atoms. The structure(s) to be imaged are placed into a strong magnetic field and short-wave radio-frequency pulses are directed toward it. Transmission of these pulses temporarily aligns the normal random polarity of the hydrogen atoms. When the pulses cease, the atoms return to their previous alignment, and in doing so discharge electromagnetic signals. These signals are converted by a computer into shades of black, gray, and white. Because of the varying water (and therefore hydrogen) content of brain structures, MRI provides greater resolution of brain tissue than does CT scanning (Bhatnagar & Andy, 1995; Kertesz, 1989).

Functional brain imaging includes radiographic techniques that investigate the physiological and biochemical properties of the brain and include *functional magnetic resonance imaging* (fMRI), *regional cerebral blood flow* (rCBF), *positron emission tomography* (PET), and *single photon emission computed tomography* (SPECT). Functional imaging allows for better spatial resolution for cortical as well as subcortical areas; however, temporal resolution is not as good as the previously described ERPs.

Based on the brain's uptake of oxygen leading to increased blood flow during activity of a region (the hemodynamic response), PET scanning, like rCBF, uses a radioactive isotope to measure physiological events in the brain (Guenther, 2008). PET uses a positron-emitting isotope "tagged" to a natural body substance (e.g., water or glucose) that will be metabolized by cells in the brain. Brain activity and metabolism occurs in response to stimuli or tasks. As radiation is released, changes in blood flow are associated with particular areas or regions of interest (ROIs) of the brain (Bhatnagar & Andy, 1995). According to Bhatnagar and Andy (1995) and Kertesz (1989), PET scans allow the study of physiological activity within the brain that directly reflects cognitive functioning. SPECT also makes use of radioactive tracers (Bhatnagar & Andy, 1995) and is functionally similar to PET, although not providing as much detail. SPECT has been used to determine dopamine transport and therefore has been used to study motor function in the basal ganglia in individuals who stutter (Guenther, 2008). Recordings provide images of thin cross-sections of the brain from multiple directions and indicate biochemical and physiologic properties. Radioactive isotopes can only be used with adults and allow for a limited number of scans. In addition, the resulting low-level signal requires averaging of responses over tasks and individuals.

fMRI combines the structural imaging techniques described previously with real-time representation of physiological activity in the brain (Bhatnagar & Andy, 1995), but the scanning process involves the generation of loud noises that can be disturbing to the client. This form of imaging provides better spatial resolution than PET. There is also less risk to participants because the injection of radioactive isotopes is not necessary. Both PET and fMRI make use of subtraction analysis whereby levels of brain activity recorded during the participant's performance of a task are compared to those during a resting state or baseline task (Guenther, 2008). The results from the fMRI can be combined with MEG to improve the temporal resolution of fMRI. However, the fMRI procedure can easily be influenced by minimal movements of the participant. Summaries of these functional imaging techniques are provided by Bloodstein et al. (2021), De Nil (2004), Guenther (2008), and Ingham (2004). De Nil explained that the objectives of investigations using these imaging technologies involve (a) detecting differences in brain activity during speech and language perception and production in normally fluent and stuttering speakers, and (b) identifying cortical patterns characteristic of stuttered versus fluent speech.

Indications of Structural and Functional Differences

It appears that Travis and his colleagues were on the right track in their investigations. Unfortunately, they lacked the technology that has been developed in recent years (and is rapidly advancing) that provides greater precision in understanding the structural and functional characteristics of the human brain, particularly as it relates to the production of language and speech. Neuroimaging studies of adults who stutter have consistently found right

hemisphere differences in the form of larger regional volume or thickness and higher white matter integrity (Jäncke et al., 2004; Neef et al., 2017). In addition, Belyk et al. (2014) reviewed a number of studies that demonstrated smaller volume or thickness and decreased integrity of white matter tracts in the left hemisphere of children who stutter compared to age-matched typically fluent peers.

Aligning with these structural findings, studies have found differences in brain function during tasks that involve speech that support the concept that the right hemisphere might be over activated in adults who stutter. For example, Rastatter et al. (1998) found increased beta oscillations in the right temporoparietal lobe during a reading task, and Salmelin et al. (2000) found greater right-lateralized suppression of beta power in the mouth motor cortex for adults who stutter during single-word reading.

Chang et al. (2019) reviewed the findings from both structural and functional studies with both adults and children who stutter and concluded that "the core deficit in stuttering is an impairment of the left hemisphere feedforward control system (and thus left hemisphere anomalies are found in both adults and children who stutter), and this deficit forces over-reliance on right hemisphere feedback control mechanisms, eventually leading to right hemisphere morphological changes seen in adults who stutter" (p. 573). Following up on this work, Chang and Guenther (2020) proposed that the primary impairment underlying stuttering is malfunction in the *cortico-basal ganglia-thalamocortical loop* that is responsible for initiating speech motor programs. They suggested three possible loci of impaired neural processing within the cortico-basal ganglia-thalamocortical loop that could lead to stuttering behaviors: (a) impairment within the basal ganglia proper; (b) impairment of axonal projections between cerebral cortex, basal ganglia, and thalamus; and (c) impairment in cortical processing. Chang and Guenther suggested further research is needed to refine their proposal and identify neural deficits involved in stuttering.

Changes in Asymmetry as a Result of Fluency-Inducing Activities and Treatment

An especially intriguing finding from a number of investigations is that as a result of fluency-inducing activities or effective treatment, speakers who stutter show a change from prominent right-hemisphere asymmetry to the more typical left-hemisphere asymmetry noted in fluent speakers (e.g., DeNil et al., 2000; DeNil et al., 2003; Ingham et al., 1994; Kell et al., 2009; Neumann et al., 2018; Wood et al., 1980). Recently, Korzeczek et al. (2021) conducted resting-state fMRI scans of 22 persons who stutter following 1 year of fluency shaping treatment. They reported observing a strengthening of two connections important to motor control of speech as a result of the fluency shaping treatment: the left inferior gyrus connection with the precentral gyrus at the representation of the left laryngeal motor cortex, and the left inferior frontal gyrus with the right superior temporal gyrus.

Conclusion

Based on the enormous amount of data that have been accumulated on the brains of persons who stutter, the consensus must be that Orton and Travis were on the right track—although, perhaps, for the wrong reasons—in suggesting that stuttering has at least some foundation in the brain of the person who stutters and that it might be related to both structural and functional differences compared to the brains of typically fluent speakers.

EVIDENCE FROM THE HUMAN GENOME

The Human Genome Project

In 1990, the Human Genome Project was initiated with the goal of mapping the human genome. The project was sponsored by the U.S. Department of Energy and the National Institutes of Health (NIH) and was conceived as a 15-year project. The involvement of 18 countries resulted in unexpected progress and in the spring of 2003, on the 50th anniversary of the fundamental description of the structure of DNA by James Watson and Francis Crick, the human DNA sequence was completed. (For further information, see the website for the Human Genome Project: https://www.genome.gov/human-genome-project).

The genome is an organism's complete set of DNA, from the smallest organism (about 600,000 base pairs) to the largest (humans have about 3 billion base pairs—although so do mice). The human genome is arranged into 23 pairs of chromosomes (including a pair of sex chromosomes), physically discrete molecules of varying sizes. Each chromosome contains many genes, each with specific sequences that encode instructions for making proteins. The genes are individual units that code for specific products that comprise the structure and functions of the body. A major research goal is to understand how the genes interact with one another and the environment. The human genome is estimated to have 20,000 to 30,000 genes. For more than 50% of the genes that have been discovered, the functions are unknown.

One of the many research sections of the Human Genome Project is found within the NIH National Institute on Deafness and Other Communication Disorders (NIDCD). The Family Research Project on Stuttering, a part of the NIDCD's Genetics of Communication Disorders Section, was coordinated by Dr. Dennis Drayna until his retirement in 2019. The goal of the Family Research Project on Stuttering is to identify regions of the human genome using linkage analysis. Linkage analysis utilizes DNA samples to determine which variants of known markers are co-inherited with stuttering within a family. These markers are typically single nucleotide polymorphisms (SNPs). SNPs are variations that occur when a single nucleotide (A, T, C, or G) in a sequence is altered. For example, an SNP might change the DNA sequence AAGGCTAA to ATGGCTAA. For a variation to be considered an SNP, it must occur in at least 1% of the population. Linkage analysis determines the genes that are in proximity to one another on a chromosome. Genes found to be close to one another are more likely to be inherited together (or linked). The threshold of a good load score is 3.0 (indicating odds of 1,000 to 1). A number of single-gene disorders (e.g., cystic fibrosis, Huntington's disease, muscular dystrophy) have been identified. This process is now being used with more complex genetic disorders such as stuttering.

Complex disorders are the result of both genetic and nongenetic factors and include cardiovascular disease, psychiatric disorders, and metabolic disorders. Linkage studies of these disorders have resulted in many possible locations of genes associated with the disorder and tend to have low load scores. Again, the strategy for these studies is to find markers that are common to identify family members with the problem and those who are not affected. This strategy is termed a genome-wide association study (GWAS), which often results in identifying variants that explain a small fraction of a disorder with load scores of <1.5. Future studies that await advances in information analysis are intended to provide whole-genome sequencing that might be able to identify all of the genetic variants in a single individual. As Drayna suggested, it might not be necessary to identify all of the gene variants that cause stuttering.

Understanding how inherited *genotypic* traits (the fundamental heredity of an individual) are manifested in behavioral *phenotypic* responses (the outward, visible expression of a person) as a result of the individual's environment (*epigenesis*) is a primary goal of the project. In addition, scientists have begun to address the ongoing discussion of the role of the nature–nurture continuum as it applies to the onset and development of stuttering. In order to identify a disorder, families with many cases of a problem are identified. Linkage studies are performed with the goal of finding a location of the causative gene(s) along the length of each chromosome that is co-inherited or linked with the disorder in the family. Researchers then search for the location of a genetic variant that is carried by the affected members of the family compared to those who are unaffected. To date, suggestive evidence of linkage for causative genes for stuttering has been found on chromosomes 2, 3, 5, 7, 9, 12, 13, 15, and 21 (Drayna, 2016).

In his book *Social Intelligence,* Goleman (2006) described the nature of epigenetics, or the understanding of how our experiences with our environment influence how genes function. Genes "express" themselves via their signature proteins only through interplay with the environment. This interaction results in the activity of genes being sped up or slowed down or even in genes being turned on or off. Citing the work of Plomin and Crabbe (2002), who described how genes affect behavior (behavioral genomics), Goleman stated that, in fact, "It is biologically impossible for a gene to operate independently from its environment: genes are designed to be regulated by signals from their immediate surround, including hormones from the endocrine system and neurotransmitters in the brain—some of which, in turn, are profoundly influenced by our social interaction" (p. 151).

Studies of Twins

For many years, it has been noted that stuttering tends to run in families, suggesting a genetic link for the disorder. Drayna (2016) indicated that the incidence of stuttering in first-degree relatives is 20% to 74%. Investigators of patterns of expression of stuttering in families, particularly in twin pairs, suggest that there are genetic influences that at least predispose a person to develop stuttering. *Concordance* is the occurrence of a trait in both members of a pair of twins. When this is not the case, the twins are said to be *discordant.*

Several investigators have studied the occurrence of stuttering in identical twins (monozygotic with identical genetic makeup) and fraternal twins (dizygotic, sharing only about half of their genes). Although concordance occurred more often in monozygotic twins than in dizygotic twins, some identical twins were discordant, suggesting the influence of environmental factors (Andrews et al., 1991; Dworzynski et al., 2007; Howie, 1981). Howie (1981), for example, found that 6 out of 16 identical twin pairs did not

result in concordance for stuttering. In a series of investigations, Kidd and his associates (Kidd, 1977, 1984; Kidd et al., 1981; Kidd et al., 1980; Kidd et al., 1973) found convincing evidence that the occurrence of stuttering follows familial patterns, which the authors suggested can be explained by a combination of both genetic and environmental factors. Studies of children who have been adopted indicate that stuttering is more closely related to whether or not a child's biological parents stutter than whether the adoptive parents stutter (Felsenfeld, 1996). From a large population of twins in Australia, Felsenfeld et al. (2000) identified 91 twin pairs in which one or both members stuttered. Diagnostic information obtained via telephone for 457 of these individuals verified self-reporting of stuttering. Monozygotic twins were concordant for stuttering 45% of the time, and dizygotic twins were concordant 15% of the time. The authors determined that approximately 70% of the variance-associated liability for stuttering was attributable to additive genetic effects, with the remainder (30%) due to nonshared environmental factors. More recently, Drayna (2016) reported that concordance in studies of identical twins ranges from 20% to 63% and of fraternal twins from 3% to 19%, and that modeling using twin data estimates that 80% of stuttering is the result of genetic effects.

Studies in Families With a High Occurrence of Stuttering

Studying the pattern of occurrence of stuttering in families over generations provides a way to indicate the form of genetic transmission. Non-sex chromosomes are referred to as autosomes. Many genetic diseases and other problems are transmitted as single gene autosomal traits, which can be either dominant (e.g., Huntington's disease) or recessive (e.g., cystic fibrosis) in their mode of inheritance. Some disorders such as hereditary deafness can be caused by mutations in many different genes, some inherited as dominant and some inherited as recessive. Andrews and Harris (1964) traced the family history of 80 stuttering children. They found that males were more likely to stutter than females, that females were more likely to have relatives who stuttered than males, and that those who stuttered were more likely than fluent speakers to have stuttering relatives. Several experimenters found that the risk to first-degree male relatives of an individual who stutters is about fivefold greater than in the general population (Ambrose et al., 1993; Kidd, 1984). A model based on the results of Ambrose et al. (1997) indicated that females who stuttered were likely to have a parent who stuttered 19% of the time, whereas males who stuttered were likely to have a parent who stuttered 67% of the time.

Pedigree analysis makes use of family tree diagrams across several generations to determine genetic relationships and modes of inheritance. Diagrams are created using symbols to indicate family members (boxes for males, circles for females), and vertical lines extend down to children and subsequent generations. Individuals possessing a trait in question are indicated by shaded symbols. The pedigree is drawn from the point of view of the person who first called the family to the researcher's attention—referred to as the *proband*. *Segregation analysis* is a statistical method for determining whether an observed trait is compatible with a particular mode of inheritance. In an analysis of the familial distribution of stuttering in the relatives of 69 school-age children who stuttered, Ambrose et al. (1993) found evidence suggesting a single major gene locus for the familial transmission of stuttering (see also Ambrose et al., 1997).

Using data from a previous multigenerational pedigree analysis of 56 adult probands of European origin with persistent child-onset stuttering, Viswanath et al. (2004) used complex segregation analysis to determine a model that would provide a best fit for the original data. The authors reasoned that because stuttering appears to be the result of complex genetic traits rather than a simple mode of inheritance, a possible mutation in the major gene is expressed in the phenotype only when certain combinations of environmental and other polygenic factors are present. This combination of factors might obscure the disease penetrance of the mutation and introduce non-Mendelian disease-transmission probabilities. Based on their statistical modeling, they found that the most parsimonious model for explaining the earlier pedigree results was an autosomal dominant Mendelian transmission where the penetrance of the dominant *allele* (one of the genes from the two parents) is influenced by two covariates:

sex and the affection status of the parents. In addition, complex segregation analysis indicated that, "When there is no affected parent the disease penetrance for the carrier is 38% for males and 7% for females. With the addition of an affected parent, the male and female risk becomes 67% and 19% [respectively]" (Viswanath et al., 2004, p. 408). A power calculation based on linkage simulation resulted in a LOD score of 6.8 for 10 cM density genome scan markers when the model was applied to 47 pedigrees. An LOD score (a logarithm of the odds to the base 10) is a statistical estimate of the probability that two genetic loci are physically near each other on a chromosome and thus likely to be linked (inherited together). A desirable threshold for LOD scores is 3 (indicating odds of 1,000 to 1) and is considered to indicate linkage. These findings of a significant major gene combined with multifactorial polygenic effects (a mixed model) agree with those of Ambrose et al. (1993); however, this might only be the case for the phenotype used in this study, persistent child-onset persons who stutter.

Recent studies have taken advantage of unique populations with an unusual (social/family) structure. For example, in Pakistan 70% of all marriages are between first or second cousins, a pattern that has persisted over centuries. This results in a population structure with greatly increased incidence of genetic disorders. Riaz et al. (2005) investigated 46 Pakistani families where stuttering was identified across two or more generations. The investigators performed a genome-wide linkage analysis on 144 probands. The results indicated significant linkage to chromosome 12q (LOD = 4.61) as well as indication of linkage to chromosome 1q

(LOD = 2.93). No evidence of linkage was obtained for chromosome 18 as noted in other studies (e.g., Shugart et al., 2004), leading the authors to suggest that "stuttering, like numerous Mendelian and non-Mendelian genetic disorders, can be caused by mutations at many different loci" (Riaz et al., 2005, pp. 649–651).

Similarly, Raza et al. (2013) performed genome-wide linkage scans with a 33-member family from Cameroon who had a history of persistent developmental stuttering. After dividing the large family into five subfamilies, significant linkage was found in the subfamily named 1E to the markers on chromosomes 2p and 15q, with LOD scores ranging from 4.7 to 6.6. Further analyses discovered two heterozygous mutations in the AP4E1 gene, which is known to be involved in protein trafficking in the trans-Golgi complex. The authors concluded that their findings provide evidence that trafficking of acidic hydrolases from the trans-Golgi network to the lysosomes is associated with persistent stuttering.

A number of other studies (e.g., Kang et al., 2010; Suresh et al., 2006; Wittke-Thompson et al., 2007) have implicated chromosomes 7 (males), 9, 13, 15, and 21 (females) as potentially being involved in developmental stuttering. Furthermore, Frigerio-Domingues et al. (2019) summarized gene-finding research related to stuttering and stated that mutations in the GNPTAB, GNPTG, NAGPA, and AP4E1 genes have been associated with the disorder. They described how these four genes are all are involved in the process of intracellular trafficking, an important process for optimum cell functioning, and noted that deficits in this cellular function are associated with a wide range of neurological disorders.

Evidence From Genetic Studies With Mice

Another approach for understanding the role of various genetic mutations in humans is to use genetic engineering and place homozygous equivalents of gene mutations into mice (a knock-in), a procedure that has been used in the study of several human disorders. Although vocal behavior of mice is not a model for human speech, it could serve as a model for volitional control of the vocalizations. Mice display rich vocal (mostly ultrasonic) communication in the form of syllable repetitions in the form of doublets (two of the same syllable types in a row) and complex structures that are characterized as "songs." This is especially true when young mice (pups) are separated from their mother during the first few weeks. Barnes et al. (2016) placed a homozygous equivalent of the GNPTAB Glu1200 Lys mutation into a group of mouse pups and compared their vocalizations to a group of control pups. Although there were no significant changes in the frequency of doublets, the mice exhibited a greater percentage of syllables of a single type, suggesting that they might be more stereotyped in their vocalizations. The experimental pups produced significantly fewer vocalizations in comparison to their littermates. Although the duration of the experimental pups' vocalizations remained unaltered, the duration of the pauses increased. The authors compared the vocalizations of the experimental mice to 500-word recordings of adults who stuttered. Using acoustic analyses similar to those used with the mouse recordings, Barnes et al. found similar alterations seen in the speech of humans who carry

this mutation. Similarly, Han et al. (2019) introduced GNPTAB Ser321Gly and Ala-455Ser mutations into mice and reported that these mice showed altered ultrasonic vocalizations but were normal in nonvocal behaviors.

Genetic Factors in Treatment and Recovery

Despite the relatively large number of studies investigating genetic links to stuttering, very few studies have examined genetic factors related to treatment and recovery from stuttering. Frigerio-Domingues et al. (2019) investigated genetic influences on therapy outcomes in a study with 101 persons who stutter, 51 of whom also carried a mutation in one of the GNPTAB, GNPTG, NAGPA, or AP4E1 genes. All participants engaged in an intensive fluency shaping program. Results indicated that carrying a mutation in one of the stuttering genes can impact therapy outcomes, with mutation carriers achieving less therapeutic success than those without a mutation. The authors noted that stuttering treatment outcomes can be influenced by many factors, of which genetics is only one, but that the observed effects of genetic factors suggest that it might play a role in stuttering treatment plans in the future.

The behavioral studies of Yairi and Ambrose (2005) described in Chapter 2, along with the most recent genetic studies, indicate that a strong family history is the most reliable predictor of persistence or recovery. However, the issue of what is being genetically transmitted is complex and compounded by the variety of technical approaches that are used, subtle and inconsistent findings of genetic influence, interaction with possible gender effects for those who stutter (e.g., Suresh et al., 2006; Viswanath et al., 2004), and the issue of whether or not speakers who experience transient and persistent stuttering represent the same or different genetic conditions (Ambrose, 2004; Ambrose et al., 1997; Viswanath et al., 2004).

Researchers have found that the disproportionate ratio of males who stutter indicates a genetic loading for the likelihood of onset as well as recovery (Yairi & Ambrose, 1999). The skewed male sex bias in the prevalence of stuttering suggests that males are more susceptible to stuttering, females are more resistant to it, or both. It could be that females will stutter only with a higher degree of genetic loading and will also be more likely to pass it on to their offspring. Similar findings have been noted in the familial history of cluttering (Weiss, 1964), and the co-occurrence of stuttering and other related speech and language problems (e.g., cluttering) has often been noted. People who stutter are far from a homogeneous population, and it appears that some, particularly those with a strong familial history of stuttering, might possess a strong neurophysiological loading for the disruption of speech fluency. As noted in subsequent chapters, these findings have strong implications for treatment and posttreatment success as well as the possibility of relapse.

The Possibility of Genetic Engineering for Those Who Stutter

As described in a number of sources including the August 2016 issue of *National Geographic* (Specter, 2016), the rapidly advancing technology associated with understanding the human genome has led to an understanding of how to make changes in the DNA of human cells. Researchers are able to use the gene editing technique called CRISPR to genetically engineer plants and animals to become resistant to disease or environmental conditions. For example, the DNA of mosquitoes can be altered to yield sterile offspring to prevent the spread of deadly diseases. The process is a replication of one that naturally occurs in nature and makes use of an enzyme called Cas9. The enzyme acts like a scalpel to snip out an unwanted DNA sequence followed by an insertion of nucleotides provided in the CRISPR package. As the author of the *National Geographic* article stated, "No discovery of the past century holds more promise—or raises more troubling ethical questions" (p. 40).

Although stuttering can be extremely detrimental and handicapping to one's life, it would be difficult to equate it to conditions that are life-threatening where genetic engineering has been used to correct significant genetic problems including one type of hepatitis, muscular dystrophy, leukemia, and cystic fibrosis. However, if it eventually becomes possible to specifically identify the gene variants that are linked to child-onset stuttering, it is not difficult to imagine that individuals would choose to do just that.

Given these and other possibilities for a technological understanding of the etiology and treatment of stuttering, it would seem worthwhile to offer a word of caution as expressed by Christopher Constantino, a speech-language pathologist, stuttering researcher, and person who stutters (in Manning & Quesal, 2016). He expressed the need for prudence in balancing the promise of technology that attempts "to understand stuttering from the inside" (p. 149) by studying the brains, cells, and genes of PWS, and thus "concentrating power in the hands of researchers" (p. 149), as opposed to a more experiential, holistic understanding of stuttering that values the person and impacts social discourses (about stuttering and disability) as "a valued form of human variation. . . . I truly value my experiences with stuttering. I hope someday we will no longer speak of cure but rather of healing and agency" (p. 149).

Conclusion

Let us end this section with, first, a comment from Frigerio-Domingues and Drayna (2017), followed by a brief reflection on the philosophical and ethical considerations related to genetics and genetic engineering.

> Finally, next generation DNA sequencing technologies represent the new standard in human genetic and genomic analyses. While linkage, population based association, and gene identification studies in stuttering have made gradual progress, the ability to assay all the genetic variation in individual exomes and genomes presents improved prospects for identifying more of the genes that underlie stuttering. Knowledge of how these gene defects can, individually or acting together, lead to the observed pathology provides the prospect for improving our understanding and treatment of this long enigmatic disorder. (Frigerio-Domingues & Drayna, 2017, p. 100)

DISRUPTION OF COGNITIVE-LINGUISTIC AND MOTOR-SEQUENCING PROCESSES

Some investigators have suggested that people who stutter experience somewhat more specific problems in processing the various features of higher level organization and lower level implementation of language and speech. Some models incorporate internal or external loops for monitoring speech and language output. In addition, most models relate the variety of difficulties that could impact the ability of humans to fluently express themselves to suspected anomalies in the structure and function of the cortical and subcortical neural system. Or as Bannister (1966) whimsically explained, some models of the many problems that humans experience are those of "a digital computer constructed by someone who had run out of insulating tape" (p. 22).

Kent (1983) proposed that stuttering originates in a central nervous system disturbance that results in a "reduced ability to generate temporal patterns, whether for sensory or motor purposes, but especially the latter" (p. 252). Speakers who stutter appear to lack the ability to smoothly sequence the movements or gestures of speech. There is some indication that people who stutter perform less well than fluent controls on tasks requiring the discrimination of subtle temporal differences in signals (Hall & Jerger, 1978; Kramer et al., 1987; Toscher & Rupp, 1978). Individuals who stutter might be demonstrating a lack of central nervous function that allows for the control of both incoming and outgoing signals.

Other investigators have considered the abilities of individuals who stutter on nonspeech activities such as auditory and visual tracking, finger tapping, and reaction time. Several researchers have found that subjects who stutter perform less accurately or slower on these activities than those who do not. Related to this general line of thinking is the fact mentioned earlier that many more males than females are found to stutter, with ratios from 3:1 to 5:1 often cited (American Psychiatric Association, 1994; Andrews & Harris, 1964; Beech & Fransella, 1968; Bloodstein, 1987; Van Riper, 1982). The findings of Geschwind and Galaburda (1985) suggest the possibility that because of the secretion of testosterone during fetal development, males have more disorders involving less-than-ideal development in the left hemisphere. The result is less obvious hemispheric dominance for speech activities, and a central nervous system that is more vulnerable to fluency disruptions.

Evidence From Empirical Investigations

Individuals who stutter have been found to be somewhat slower in starting and stopping a sound when they hear a buzzer (Adams & Hayden, 1976; Freeman & Ushijima, 1974, 1978; Starkweather et al., 1976). Individuals who stutter also have been found to be somewhat slower when reacting to respiration (during exhalation) and articulation (lip-closing) movements. The results of a number of studies (see Bloodstein et al., 2021; Silverman, 2004) consistently indicate that people who stutter have slower phonatory reaction times (the time it takes to initiate or terminate phonation in response to a signal). In addition to the many experimenters who have reported slower responses for speech and nonspeech tasks, there are also reports of decreased accuracy for achieving articulatory targets. There have also been many investigations suggesting that adults who stutter have a neurophysiological deficit that results in an inability to achieve accurate articulatory targets or move their articulators as quickly as their nonstuttering counterparts (e.g., Alfonso et al., 1987; Caruso et al., 1988; De Nil &

Abbs, 1990; Zimmerman, 1980, 1981). This seems especially to be the case for people who stutter more severely.

The Covert Repair Hypothesis

The covert repair hypothesis (CRH; Kolk & Postma, 1997; Postma & Kolk, 1993; Postma et al., 1990) proposes a psycholinguistic perspective involving both production and perception to account for fluency breaks. The model proposes that internal or covert monitoring allows speakers to detect errors in phonological encoding prior to the implementation of articulatory commands. As errors are detected, the planning of the phonetic sequence is interrupted, and the correct plan is reinitiated. As a result of this error detection and subsequent covert repair (editing) of the speech plan, fluency breaks occur. This internal monitoring and repair occurs for all speakers, but Kolk and Postma proposed that individuals who stutter possess an abnormally slow rate of phonological encoding, requiring more time to activate a target and resulting in a greater chance of error. Furthermore, individuals who stutter tend to begin speech rapidly, not allowing time for their slowed phonological encoding system to select phonological targets. The process of detection and repair, in combination with a system that is not adept in selecting the correct phonological target before it, produces stuttering behavior.

Kolk and Postma (1997) suggested that this covert process could be thought of in much the same way as overt self-repairing. That is, the process involves an interruption of speech production and a revising of the necessary movements, followed by a new attempt with a revised plan. This hypothesis nicely explains many of the disfluencies of normal speakers and has been extended to explain the fluency breaks in stuttering speakers, for both loci (the beginning of words and syllables) and type of intrasyllabic disfluencies (part-word repetitions and pauses). It also coincides well with a number of reports of phonological-processing abilities of individuals who stutter (Bosshardt, 1990; Bosshardt & Nandyal, 1988; Postma, Kolk, & Povel, 1990; Wingate, 1988).

Evidence From Empirical Investigations

The CRH appears to offer a number of testable ideas and has generated a good deal of research. However, as with other models, the reasoning is somewhat circular (Yaruss, 2000) in that the CRH assumes that individuals who stutter put demands on their phonological encoding mechanism that exceed their (assumedly diminished) ability to rapidly and precisely select correct phonological units. Nevertheless, some studies and clinical observations have provided partial support for the CRH. Louko et al. (1990) found that children who stutter also produced a greater number and variety of phonological processes (systematic or rule-governed sound changes). Authors have found that some children show an increase in speech disfluencies when undergoing treatment for articulation and phonological disorders (Hall, 1977; Ratner, 1995). LaSalle and Conture (1995) and Yaruss and Conture (1996) found preliminary support for the notion that both overt and covert self-repairs could interact with a child's ability to perform phonological encoding in a timely manner. In contrast, Brocklehurst (2008) reported that although the rate of phonological encoding is similar for stuttering and nonstuttering children, there are differences in the way that children

who stutter organize lexical information that might contribute to some occurrences of stuttering. Brocklehurst concluded that although there is not strong support for the CRH, error repair requiring monitoring and restarting of encoding sequences might play a role for speakers with persistent child-onset stuttering. Eichorn et al. (2016) investigated the effect of engaging working memory on the fluency of 19 adults who stuttered and 20 adults who did not. Following baseline tasks that required spontaneous speech for 60 seconds for each of four topics, participants were given a series of dual tasks that required both spontaneous speaking and secondary tasks that placed demands on auditory or visual-spatial working memory. In contrast to the predictions of the CRH, the results indicated no change in error frequency under the dual task conditions compared to baseline conditions.

The Execution and Planning (EXPLAN) Model

In many ways, the EXPLAN model (Howell, 2004; Howell & Au-Yeung, 2002) elaborates the CRH by suggesting independent linguistic and motor processes. However, EXPLAN is presented as an autonomous model in that this sequence of production is not linked to internal or external monitoring. Speech is initiated by an internal cognitive-linguistic system that covertly plans (PLAN) the syntactic, lexical, phonetic features in serial order. The motor process organizes and executes (EX) the output. Fluent speech occurs when the motor system receives and executes the linguistic sequences in order. If the linguistic system experiences difficulty in generating a linguistic (syntactic, lexical, and phonetic) sequence, the motor system is unable to execute fluent speech. As a result—and this is the case for all speakers—breakdowns in fluency occur at the language–speech interface; although one linguistic plan is completed, the next plan is not ready for execution. Speakers might respond by stalling and either repeating speech already produced (whole words) or pausing, allowing time for the completion of the linguistic plan. Speakers might also continue with the linguistic sequence that is available and attempt to advance forward. However, without sufficient time, speakers are likely to prolong the first part of the word (e.g., "ssssister"), repeat the first syllable (as in "suh-suh-sister"), or insert a pause (as in "s-ister"; Watkins et al., 2008).

Howell and his colleagues argued that although children who stutter are similar to controls in syntactic ability (Howell et al., 2003; Nippold, 1990, 2001), there are several studies suggesting that speakers who stutter have difficulties with motor timing (Caruso et al., 1988; Max et al., 2003; Smith & Kleinow, 2000; van Lieshout et al., 1996), a problem that is exacerbated as linguistic complexity increases. As with several of the models discussed in this section, the results of recent neuroimaging studies provide support in the form of structural and functional differences found in adults and children who stutter (e.g., anomalous white matter tracts in the ventral premotor cortex and functional difficulties in cerebellum).

Evidence From Empirical Investigations

Anderson and her colleagues devised novel procedures to consider the possibility that young children who stutter experience slowness, inefficiencies, or dyssynchronies with lexical phonological and syntactic encoding (Anderson & Conture, 2000, 2004; Anderson et al., 2005; Anderson et al., 2006). For example, Anderson and Conture (2000) found that children who stutter might have disparities in their lexical and syntactic abilities, suggesting an imbalance among different language formulation processes.

Anderson and Conture (2004) used a computer-based sentence-structure priming task with simple active affirmative declarative (SAAD) sentences along with a speech reaction time measure. The procedure determined the time from the onset of a picture to the onset of a child's verbal response in the absence and presence of semantically unrelated SAAD priming sentences. Children who stutter not only exhibited slower speech reaction times in the absence of the sentence priming task, but also tended to benefit more from the syntactic primes than the children who did not stutter. Although Anderson (2008) found some evidence indicating that the semantic-phonological connections of children who stutter are not as strong as those of the nonstuttering peers, she suggests that any problems that they have with speech-language production might be more likely related to lexical or phonological encoding, morphosyntactic construction, or a combination of processes.

Cuadrado and Weber-Fox (2003), Salmelin et al. (2000), Watson et al. (1994), and Weber-Fox (2001) used a variety of approaches and brain imaging technologies to investigate the performance of persons who stutter on linguistic processing tasks. Their findings provided partial support for the EXPLAN model.

CYBERNETIC AND FEEDBACK MODELS

The nature of auditory feedback in those who stutter is another feature that has been the subject of research. Cybernetic theory has to do with the automatic control inherent in many mechanical and biological systems. Many such systems incorporate various forms of feedback that are used to regulate the output of a system—similar, for example, to a thermostat that is part of a closed-loop arrangement that controls the temperature of a building. The goal of such a system, termed a *servosystem*, is to match the intended output to the actual output and reduce any differences that are detected between the two—the error signal—to zero. If for some reason there is a distortion of the information arriving via the feedback loop, the error signal will be incorrect. When this occurs, the system tends to go into oscillation. Fairbanks (1954) and Mysak (1960) described the nature of such systems and interpreted many aspects of speech production in this manner. The basic idea was that for speakers who stutter, the distorted feedback creates the misconception that an error has occurred in the flow of speech. Stuttering occurs when the speaker attempts to correct an error that has, in fact, not occurred.

Evidence From Empirical Investigations

A number of studies (e.g., Black, 1951; Lee, 1951; Neeley, 1961; Yates, 1963) provided some indication that what was occurring for speakers who stuttered was a distorted auditory feedback signal. They noted that for normal speakers, altering the auditory feedback by delaying the signal tended to produce stuttering-like behavior. For example, it was generally agreed that fluent speakers who stutter speak under conditions of delayed auditory feedback (DAF) in much the same way people do when they stutter. That is, the effect of DAF on normal speakers is to produce repetitions and prolongations of sounds, slowing of speech, pitch increases, and greater vocal intensity. In order to "beat" the effect of the delayed feedback, the speaker must disregard that signal, slow his or her speech, and focus attention on the undistorted tactile and proprioceptive feedback that is available from articulatory movements. When speakers who stutter respond (with or without DAF) in this manner, there tends to be a reduction in the severity of stuttering. Depending on how these fluency breaks are considered, there might also be a reduction in the frequency of stuttering (Hayden et al., 1977). Because of these effects of DAF, some treatment programs have employed it as a way to establish fluency in some speakers (Ryan & Van Kirk, 1974; Shames & Florance, 1980). Once the speaker learns to maintain improved fluency under the distorted feedback, the delay intervals are varied in the direction of instantaneous or normal feedback, and the speaker, although now weaned from the device, continues to use the slow speech along with emphasizing proprioceptive feedback.

MULTIFACTORIAL MODELS

As suggested earlier in this chapter, simplistic and unidimensional approaches to understanding stuttering onset and development, although they might be easy to explain and understand, are far from adequate. As authors and researchers have increasingly appreciated the multidimensional nature of stuttering, there has been an increase of such models that describe the many intrinsic and extrinsic factors that influence one's ability to produce fluent speech (Andrews et al., 1983; Andrews & Neilson, 1981; Cooper & Cooper, 1985c;

De Nil, 1999; Neilson & Neilson, 1987; Riley & Riley, 1979, 1984; Smith, 1990, 1999; Smith & Kelly, 1997; Wall & Myers, 1995). Multifactorial models by their nature involve many factors, are complex, and are therefore more difficult to understand and to test than simple models. However, they have led to many empirical investigations as well as clinical techniques. It seems reasonable to heed Cockburn's (2004) view that:

No single theory dominates behavioral change and health promotion. Many concepts in different models overlap, and some aspects of behavioral change models have a stronger evidence base than others. The most useful approach is to combine concepts from more than one theory to address a problem . . . no model or theory will get it right all the time, and in practice, often a single theory (approach) explains only a small amount of the variance in targeted behaviors. (p. 66)

The Demands and Capacities Model

The demands and capacities model (DCM) is appealing, particularly for clinicians, because it includes many of the factors that seem to influence fluent and nonfluent speech. From a clinical standpoint, it provides a straightforward explanation for parents of children who might be stuttering (see Curlee, 2000; Gottwald & Starkweather, 1999). Variants of this model were first proposed by Andrews and colleagues (Andrews et al., 1983; Andrews & Neilson, 1981; Neilson & Neilson, 1987; Riley & Riley, 1979, 1984). For example, based on their accumulated diagnostic data, Riley and Riley proposed

a component model that describes factors that distinguished the ability of children to produce fluent speech. These components include attending, auditory processing, sentence formulation, and oral motor ability. Their assessment and treatment approaches concentrate on enhancing a child's ability to improve performance in one or more of these components rather than altering environmental demands (see Chapter 5). Other authors (Adams, 1990; Gottwald, 1999; Gottwald & Starkweather, 1999; Starkweather, 1987; Starkweather & Gottwald, 1990) have provided theoretical elaboration.

The DCM considers both the capacities of the individual and the effects of both internal and environmental "demands" in the development of stuttering. The model proposes that children who stutter possess genetically influenced tendencies for fluency breakdown that interact with environmental factors to both originate and maintain the problem. The model also addresses, in a preliminary way, how human genotypes interact with the environment to create what we observe as individual phenotypes of a specific person. Recent understanding of epigenesis has resulted in explanations of the multiple interactions influencing this process (see Kelly, 2000; Smith, 1999; Smith & Kelly, 1997).

In the DCM the deterioration of fluency is viewed as reflecting an imbalance between the child's current capacities or abilities for producing fluent speech and the demands placed on the child. Capacities are viewed as inherited tendencies, strengths, weaknesses, and perceptions, which could influence a child's ability to speak fluently. They are dynamic and changing rather than static. Capacities include—but might not be limited to—the general categories of motoric (the ability to initiate and control coarticulatory movements smoothly, rapidly, and with minimal effort), linguistic (the ability to formulate sentences), socioemotional (the ability to produce smooth movements when under communicative or emotional stress), and cognitive (the ability to use metalinguistic skills).

Demands take the form not only of environmental demands (external) but also self-imposed demands (internal). Examples of external demands are fast speaking rates used by parents and other adults, time pressure to respond quickly, and competition and lack of turn-taking by other speakers. Examples of internal demands include overstimulation of language centers and demand for language performance, including the need to formulate complex sentences; excitement and anxiety; and cognitive requirements for expressing complicated thoughts. If the internal or external demands exceed the capacities of a particular child, stuttering is more likely to occur. The model is dynamic in that internal or external demands interact with the speaker's skills at a given moment. Although the child is not viewed as possessing a disorder or deficit, the skills that allow fluent speech production change as the child grows both physically and cognitively, just as internal and external demands change over time. As Starkweather and Gottwald (2000) described, when the positive forces (either environmental or internal) outweigh the negative ones, the person will be fluent; when the negative forces outweigh the positive ones, fluency will break down. Because these internal and environmental variables have been identified in the literature as making it more or less likely that a person will speak fluently, it is reasonable to suggest that a threshold might be present that varies for different speakers.

Evidence From Empirical Investigations

The DCM, despite its intuitive appeal, has received criticism from those who suggest that, for a variety of reasons, it is not possible to test the model (Ingham & Cordes, 1997; Siegel, 2000). That is, the capacities that are suggested as being necessary for producing fluent speech are not directly measurable, and specific requirements for mismatches between demands and capacities are not defined. In addition, no thresholds are indicated for when mismatches may lead to the disruption of fluency. Finally, these authors suggest that the model invites circular reasoning: Stuttering occurs when demands exceed capacities indicating that demands are too great for the child (Ingham & Cordes, 1997).

Siegel (2000) suggested that reconfiguring the model as a "demands and performance model" would lead to empirical testing of the proposed relationships of a child's ability and behavior. However, others have questioned the necessity or value of such a change (Curlee, 2000; Kelly, 2000; Ratner, 2000; Starkweather & Gottwald, 2000; Yaruss, 2000). As Kelly (2000) indicated, performance (the execution of an action or a reaction to stimuli) might be more measurable than capacities (faculties or potential), but the interaction of the two is clear and has been inferred in many areas of scientific study, including the behavioral sciences. The DCM brings together many of the complexities that have been observed about stuttering and the people who speak in this fashion.

Ratner (1995, 1997, 2000) described support for the model in the form of a trading relationship between fluency and associated speech and language capacities in children. She noted that a proportion of children's fluency breaks evolve from linguistic pressures that exceed their productive capacities. That is, a fluent child sometimes begins to "stutter" following intervention to enhance expressive language or phonological skills (Hall, 1977; Meyers, Ghatak, & Woodford, 1990). Furthermore, Winslow and Guitar (1994) demonstrated a relationship between conversational turn-taking and fluency for a 5-year-old child during family dinnertime interaction. Fluency increased when conversational demands were lessened with turn-taking, and stuttering increased when turn-taking rules were withdrawn. Yaruss and Conture (1995) found that nonstuttering children exhibited a strong positive correlation between their articulatory speaking rate and their diadochokinetic (DDK) rate, indicating that these children speak at rates in line with their abilities. The children who stuttered in their study, however, showed a mild negative correlation between speaking rate and DDK, suggesting that children who stutter might attempt to use speaking rates that exceed their ability to rapidly and precisely move their articulators. Yaruss (1997b) also found a trade-off between production rate and DDK accuracy. Children exhibiting faster DDK rates also produced more errors than children with slower DDK rates, again suggesting that children who produced more errors were actually exceeding their ability to rapidly and precisely move their articulators in a speech-related task.

Additional investigations might help to specify the relationships between a child's capacities (e.g., DDK ability) for responding to demands of rapid speech. Of course, understanding the relationships between capacities and demands and determining thresholds for fluency disruption might be particularly difficult for socioemotional and cognitive domains.

Likewise, specifying and quantifying self-imposed demands will require creative research designs. Defining and testing the model will likely lead to capacity–demand relationships that are unique to particular children at different points in their development.

The Dynamic-Multifactorial Model

In an attempt to create a unified strategy for communicating about the disorder, Smith (1990, 1999) and Smith and Kelly (1997) provided a novel way of describing the multifactorial nature of stuttering within a nonlinear, dynamic framework. They suggested that viewing stuttering by tabulating a linear sequence of disfluency units provides only a record of the surface events. Although tidy and simplistic in nature, the problem with this approach is that stuttering is a complex and dynamic disorder with many processes that underlie the surface behaviors. Using an analogy from the scientific study of volcanoes that fits nicely with stuttering, the authors explained that early volcanologists concentrated on the surface characteristics of volcanoes. That is, they counted and classified volcanoes based on the shape of the landform and type of eruptive materials. After decades of this approach, researchers began to understand that classifying volcanoes by their surface characteristics failed to explain the dynamic nature of the phenomena. A true understanding of volcano activity only began once the volcanologists began to apply the theory of plate tectonics to the problem. This explanation of what was occurring under the surface provided a unified framework for studying the many aspects of volcanic activity. Likewise, Smith and Kelly (1997) suggested that a major impediment to developing a global theory of stuttering is the belief in the "reality of the units of stuttering" (p. 29). These surface units of stuttering are akin to the smoke of the volcano and fail to provide insight into the true dynamic nature of the phenomenon. Moreover, concentrating on the surface behaviors of stuttering will continue to obscure our understanding of the multifactorial nature of the disorder.

Perhaps the best argument in favor of this view is the fact that the stuttering experience occurs for the speaker even when a listener is unable to perceive the surface behaviors in the form of a traditional moment of stuttering. As we discuss at several points in this book, it is possible for profound stuttering events to take place in the complete absence of any observable stuttering events. As Smith and Kelly pointed out, even though stuttering "events" might appear to be highly specific on the surface of the speaker's behavior, the dynamic processes influencing the relative level of fluency–disfluency are distant in time and space from the event that is perceived as stuttering. That is, there are many neurological and physiological events that occur long before the placement of some arbitrary timing mark suggesting the onset or termination of the stuttering event. Even though precise identification of those stuttering events on the surface might be possible, at best it provides an artificial boundary for segmenting the dynamic process of speech production. Additionally, there is no one-to-one relationship between traditional classifications of fluency breaks and many of the underlying events. Commenting on the use of traditional fluency form types in analyzing stuttering, Smith (1999) stated:

Requiring researchers to use these units, to use "reliable means" of classification, and to interpret their data in relation to these units is analogous to asking the scientist who is recording seismic activity around volcanoes to interpret the data in relation to the pattern of smoke rising from the surface of the volcano. (p. 30)

For those who live with it, the notion that stuttering is a multifactorial problem is clear, and it has frequently been compared to the many layers of an onion. During treatment (or self-directed change) the many layers must be peeled away in order to get at the core characteristics of the problem.

Smith also provided other important insights that impact the way we look at theories of stuttering onset and development. She attempted to integrate the nature and nurture views of onset. Although the genetic and physiological aspects of the central nervous system are being implicated in the etiology of stuttering, no single gene locus has been identified. Smith pointed out that the mammalian brain is constantly changing in response to environmental stimuli. Both the structure and the function of the brain are remodeled not only during the early years of development, but also as a result of experience and learning, throughout all stages of life. Nearly all the recent neurological and genetic research suggests the interactive and dynamic nature of the organism with the environment, supporting Smith's premise that understanding the onset and development is not a nature versus nurture issue. The two perspectives are essentially the same, an organic–learning combination.

Smith also employed the concept of "attractor states" from dynamic systems theory to understand the development of both normal nonfluency and stuttering in children. Attractor states are observed when systems self-organize into models of behavior that are preferred, even though they might be very complex or even undesirable. Once the system is in a deep or stable attractor state, it takes more energy to move away from that state. Although during childhood the skills necessary for producing fluent speech are developing and are influenced by both nature and nurture, instability of speech is predictable. Children move between fluent and nonfluent attractors during development. Following years of development, the fluent young adult demonstrates a highly stable attractor for fluent speech and few unstable or disfluent attractors. For those who stutter, however, there is a combination of both fluent and disfluent attractors, resulting in instability and perpetuating a breakdown in speech motor control. Furthermore, adults who stutter could have stable patterns of neuromuscular activity during stuttering (as in a tremor). The ultimate goal of this modeling is to study the factors that influence speech motor performance and "to understand the dynamic interplay of these factors as the developing brain seeks the stable, adaptive models of interaction among neural networks that generate . . . fluent speech" (Smith, 1999, p. 42).

Finally, as Smith (1999) explained, "Successful behavioral therapy essentially helps the child to establish adaptive, stable patterns of operation and interaction among the widely distributed neural networks involved in language production" (p. 37). Fortunately, the mammalian brain is plastic and continually changing. Although the structure and cortical functioning of the brain are rapidly changing during early development, when children are more responsive to therapy that might facilitate this remodeling, this pro-

cess continues throughout life, resulting in an experience-determined plasticity in the adult brain. This view of therapeutic change is similar to the neurological findings resulting from successful therapy described earlier in this chapter by Boberg et al. (1983), De Nil et al. (2003), Foundas et al. (2001), Giraud et al. (2008), Kroll et al. (1997), and Neumann et al. (2005).

Building off the dynamic-multifactorial model, Smith and Weber (2017) proposed a *multifactorial, dynamic pathways* (MDP) theory of stuttering that emphasizes the multilevel events occurring at the time when childhood-onset (developmental) stuttering emerges, and recovery or persistence occurs. Smith and Weber described the factors that contribute to the onset and persistence of stuttering, including motor, linguistic, emotional, and central neural aspects, and emphasized that these factors have varying weights in different individuals who stutter. As a consequence, each child who begins to stutter will experience a unique, dynamic pathway into the diagnosis of stuttering, that will ultimately lead to recovery or persistence.

More specifically, Smith and Weber (2017) described stuttering as follows:

a neurodevelopmental disorder that begins during the preschool years when emerging neural networks critical for speech motor development produce unstable, aberrant control signals that give rise to SLDs. The occurrences of involuntary disruptions in speech, in turn, produce responses in the child's internal and external milieu at both behavioral and physiological levels. These processes then may have epigenetic influences on the expression of genes involved in the development of speech motor systems. (p. 2495)

The MDP theory also provides an explanation of the large percentage of children who recover from stuttering, suggesting that in these children, brain adaptations, in the form of neural growth and connectivity changes, occur that successfully compensate for the atypical neural activity underlying the stuttering disfluencies, leading to more stable speech production networks. For the remaining children who begin to stutter, brain adaptations are inadequate to compensate for the atypical neural activity, and stuttering becomes a long-term, chronic problem. The speech motor systems of these children remain vulnerable to breakdowns in the face of increasingly complex language demands and psychosocial pressures. As the child matures and if stuttering persists, the complex sequences of central neural activity that drive the speech motor and other behaviors characteristic of that child's stuttering become overlearned patterns, interfering with fluent speech production into adolescence and adulthood.

Smith and Weber (2017) pointed out that central to their account of stuttering, and what sets it apart from mechanistic explanations, is the emphasis on the dynamic developmental context in which stuttering emerges and in which the trajectory to persistence or recovery occurs. Several studies have found support for the MDP theory of stuttering by demonstrating how using multiple risk factors to assess children yields more accurate predictions of stuttering persistence and recovery compared to using factors in isolation (Walsh et al., 2021) and by identifying neurophysiological risk factors for stuttering persistence such as trajectories of neuroanatomical development (Chow & Chang, 2017; Garnett et al., 2018), patterns of neural activation during speech (Hosseini et al., 2018), articulatory kinematics (Usler et al., 2017), and sympathetic nervous system arousal (Zengin-Bolatkale et al., 2018).

The Neurophysiological Model

De Nil and his colleagues described a model that provides a comprehensive and unifying model of stuttering (De Nil, 1999). This model also includes capacities or skills similar to those noted in the DCM. In addition, De Nil proposed that just as nature and nurture are not separate phenomena, psychological and neurophysiological processes are not independent entities. This model emphasizes the dynamic interplay among three levels of influence on human behavior and on stuttering in particular: processing (central neurophysiological processes), output (motor, cognitive, language, social, and emotional processes), and contextual (environmental influences). Bidirectional dynamic feedback takes place across all levels and continually influences output. That is, environmental stimuli and behavioral consequences are filtered through neurophysiological processes and vary both between individuals and within individuals. Long-term modification of behavior necessitates the modification of how information is processed centrally.

CONCLUSION

We have considered several perspectives about why it is that some speakers have more difficulty than others producing fluent verbal communication. It seems best to view those who have such problems on a continuum with their fluent peers rather than categorizing them into distinctly different stereotypes. On several occasions throughout this book, we note that there are many more similarities between fluent and nonfluent speakers than there are differences. Playing the role of a person who stutters in daily speaking situations illustrates this to even the most fluent speakers by bringing forth natural coping responses common to everyone. It is also clear that people who stutter are far from a homogeneous group. This could be one reason there have been so many explanations for stuttering onset throughout history. It also might help to explain why some speakers are more apt to recover than others, why treatment techniques that work well with one person do not work as well with another, and why relapse is an especially important issue for some people.

The wise clinician should have an understanding for many views concerning etiology that have been proposed in the past as well as the more current models. Certainly, the experienced clinician should have an appreciation for the lack of support for certain perspectives and understand, for example, that individuals who stutter are no more neurotic than their typically fluent peers. The ebb and flow of theories reflects an interaction between the current zeitgeist and the published research, and the process moves forward in directions that are sometimes unpredictable. The long history of viewing stuttering as a combination of learned behaviors has helped to explain many of the responses that can be more (and often less) helpful for those who stutter. The once-influential diagnosogenic theory found little support in subsequent empirical literature. Incorporation of classical (respondent) conditioning and operant (instrumental) conditioning models began to inform the decision making of clinicians, particularly in the 1960s and 1970s.

In this chapter, we have selected relatively few investigations from the long list of studies indicating that adults who stutter demonstrate many unique speech- and nonspeech-related characteristics. Many experimenters have identified subtle motoric and temporal characteristics suggesting variability or instability for those who stutter. Ever more technologically sophisticated investigations continue to identify unique structural and functional differences in cortical and subcortical neural systems of these speakers. Reading through the literature, one can easily begin to wonder how adults who stutter can function at all during daily activities. Until recently, the majority of these investigations have been conducted with adults, and many have suggested that the findings indicate the effects of years or decades of compensating for and adjusting to one's stuttering. More recent studies have begun to use children, with results suggesting that some of the anatomical–physiological and motoric–acoustic characteristics might also be present shortly following the onset of stuttering.

Early conjectures and evidence of anomalies in the central nervous system of those who stutter, especially in the form of cerebral asymmetry, have received continued support in recent research employing advanced technologies. These investigations are increasingly informing our understanding of both structural and functional characteristics that distinguish individuals who stutter from their fluent peers, even during the earlier years of language and speech development. Indications of normalization of brain asymmetry as a result of treatment are particularly intriguing and could eventually prove helpful in assisting the speaker to alter his or her neurological functioning (brain plasticity). Studies using advancing techniques of neuroimaging, neural modeling, and genetic linkage, along with investigations of cognitive and behavioral factors, provide support for the utility of multifactorial models for developing a broad and deep perspective about the nature of stuttering. It might be that the successful outcome of research in the areas of neuroscience and genetics will go a long way toward building a consensus about the etiology of the problem.

Some might be frustrated by the complexity of stuttering and would like to have a clear, unequivocal answer as to how and why stuttering has such a long history as a universal characteristic of human communication. As we suggested in Chapter 1, it is probably best for the clinician to cultivate a tolerance for ambiguity and espouse a broad perspective for the many accounts of stuttering. Having many views for what seems on the surface to be essentially the same problem would seem to detract from our credibility as a profession. Although we do not know all that we need to know, we have good information about what to do when faced with children or adults who stutter. A variety of assessment and treatment protocols and techniques have been shown to be effective and, as a profession, we have been and will continue to be of great assistance to children and adults who stutter. Even so, the obvious complexity of the problem we call stuttering requires that the clinician approach the problem with a Swiss army knife rather than a hammer in hand.

TOPICS FOR DISCUSSION

1. How will you respond when you are asked by the parents of a young stuttering child the inevitable question, "Why is my child stuttering?"

2. Why is it useful for clinicians to know about theories of stuttering etiology that we now know do not fully explain stuttering?

3. Why do you think there are so many different theories of the etiology of stuttering?

4. How can you demonstrate your competence as a clinician given the multiple explanations and current status of the research on stuttering etiology?

5. Of the various etiological theories discussed in this chapter, which one is most appealing to you?

6. How would you respond if a friend commented, "Stuttering is mostly a psychological problem, isn't it?"

7. Which investigations described in this chapter do you feel provide the strongest support for the idea that stuttering has a neurophysiological basis?

8. What are the basic similarities and differences in the three examples of multifactorial models presented in this chapter (the DCM, the MDP model, and the neurophysiological model)?

9. Discuss why it is important to have a historical context for understanding the various theoretical perspectives of stuttering etiology. What factors appear to influence current perspectives?

RECOMMENDED READINGS

Ambrose, N. G., & Yairi, E. (2002). The Tudor study: Data and ethics. *American Journal of Speech-Language Pathology, 11,* 1190–1203.

Conture, E. G. (2001). Conclusions. In E. G. Conture (Ed.), *Stuttering: Its nature, diagnosis and treatment* (pp. 327–378). Allyn & Bacon.

Ingham, R. J., Cykowski, M., Ingham J. C., & Fox, P. T. (2007). Neuroimaging contributions to developmental stuttering theory and treatment. In R. J. Ingham (Ed.), *Neuroimaging in communication sciences* (pp. 53–85). Plural Publishing.

Manning, W. H. (1995, September/October). *Paddling in the stream of speech: Letting GO.* The National Stuttering Project.

Smith, A., & Kelly, E. (1997). Stuttering: A dynamic, multifactoral model. In R. F. Curlee & G. M. Siegel (Eds.), *The nature and treatment of stuttering: New directions* (2nd ed., pp. 204–217). Allyn & Bacon.

Van Riper, C. (1974). A handful of nuts. *Western Michigan Journal of Speech Therapy, 11*(2), 1–3.

Van Riper, C. (1990). Final thoughts about stuttering. *Journal of Fluency Disorders, 15,* 317–318.

In my early professional years, I was asking the question: How can I treat, or cure, or change this person? Now I would phrase the question in this way: How can I provide a relationship which this person may use for his own personal growth?

—Carl Rogers

Principles of Assessment

CHAPTER OBJECTIVES

■ To explain the importance of a person-centered approach to the assessment of stuttering
■ To describe ways for clinicians to engage in collaborative goal setting with clients
■ To describe general guidelines for the assessment of individuals who stutter

Good treatment begins with good assessment. The purpose of assessment includes describing what clients' stuttering looks and sounds like; assessing how clients are currently functioning, including the areas where stuttering has its greatest impact on their life and how context influences performance; describing how clients and others in their environment react to the stuttering; and making recommendations related to treatment. In this chapter we discuss some general principles of assessment for persons who stutter. Then, in the next two chapters, we

look at specific aspects of assessment for preschool and school-age children who stutter (Chapter 5) and adolescents and adults who stutter (Chapter 6).

Bloodstein et al. (2021) outlined some guiding principles of assessment with persons who stutter. These include that the person who stutters and their family are central to the assessment process, that shared goal setting and pretreatment assessments are important, and that the relationship between the clinician and the client influences assessment. These principles all point to the critical importance of a person-centered approach to assessment.

Person-centered assessment of stuttering assumes that PWS are the experts on their lived experiences with stuttering (Botterill, 2011; DiLollo & Neimeyer, 2022), and it is important for the clinician to create a collaborative and supportive relationship that allows for a deeper understanding of the PWS's experiences. Effective communication, especially empathic listening (see Chapter 8), is central to person-centered assessment and treatment (DiLollo & Neimeyer, 2022; Luterman, 2017) and has been associated with increased engagement in treatment and improved outcomes (Stanhope et al., 2013).

Determining what aspects of their experience of stuttering the client deems important to target in treatment is a critical characteristic of effective assessment. Sønsterud et al. (2020) reported on a mixed-methods study of adults who stutter and their preferences for stuttering treatment goals. They found that the majority of participants wanted to improve in the areas of speech fluency, emotional functioning, life participation, and understanding of stuttering. What is important from these findings is that participants had a number of areas that they wanted to target that related to their quality of life (i.e., not simply increased speech fluency). As described earlier, clinicians should recognize their clients to be the experts on their stuttering and work with them in deciding what changes they want to make and then work collaboratively toward that outcome (DiLollo & Neimeyer, 2022; Leahy & Walsh, 2010).

This person-centered approach to stuttering assessment is built on a strong therapeutic alliance between the client and the clinician, which itself is founded on the clinician's effective use of empathic listening and the counseling mindset discussed in Chapter 8. It has been noted that the therapeutic alliance is a key element of assessment and treatment (Duncan et al., 2010; Wampold & Imel, 2015) and that it might be particularly important in stuttering assessment and treatment, given the relatively common reports of less-than-satisfactory prior therapy described in the literature (Bloodstein et al., 2021). Consequently, clinicians must find a way to engage clients (and their families) in collaborative goal setting that suits their individual needs and preferences. For some, this might be an unstructured brainstorming session, with ideas proposed and adjusted collaboratively, whereas for others it might involve the clinician providing textbooks and other materials to help the client build knowledge about his or her options prior to coming up with potential goals.

THE POSSIBLE SELVES MAPPING INTERVIEW

For clinicians looking for a semistructured way of approaching collaborative goal setting, DiLollo and Neimeyer (2022) described a process called the Possible Selves Mapping Interview (PSMI). The PSMI is a hands-on, visual strategy that can be used with both individual clients and small groups. It is a way of helping individuals map out their hoped-for and feared possible selves in a variety of domains and can lead to collaborative discussions on setting goals related to their hoped-for and feared possible selves.

Possible selves are hypothetical images about one's future, including the ideal selves that we would like to become (e.g., a successful author), as well as the selves that we are afraid of becoming (e.g., a lonely hermit). Essentially, they are the future-oriented components of the self-identity involved in goal setting and motivation (Markus & Nurius, 1986). *Hoped-for possible selves* focus on the hopes, dreams, and aspirations of the individual and consist of images and visions of the individual in desired end states. *Feared possible selves*, on the other hand, are the possible selves that an individual fears becoming and wants to avoid. Instead of influencing an individual's movement toward a goal, the feared possible self plays an important role in the self-concept by acting as a motivator so that actions are taken to avoid that future possible self (Markus & Nurius, 1986).

The Possible Selves Mapping Interview Process

For a full description of the PSMI process, see DiLollo and Neimeyer (2022, Chapter 25). The following is the basic process for a PSMI with a client who stutters:

1. Explain the concept of possible selves to the client.
2. Set the domain of interest for the possible selves—in this case speech and fluency.
3. Elicit hoped-for possible selves and write them on separate note cards, note expectancy (i.e., how likely it is to be achieved) and anything done recently to try to achieve these possible selves, and organize them from short term to long term.
4. Elicit feared possible selves and write them on separate note cards, note expectancy and anything done recently to try to avoid these possible selves, and organize them chronologically.
5. Debrief.
6. This process can be repeated to create possible selves maps for other domains such as social and relationships, self-image, job and career, school, and so on.

Figure 4–1 shows a visual summary of this process as it would look on green and yellow note cards.

Debriefing and Goal Setting

In the Debriefing section, the possible selves map (or maps, if multiple are cre-ated) is reviewed with the client. In some cases, clients can be asked to summarize their map "as if they were talking to someone who knew nothing about them" (Shepard & Marshall, 1999). In return, the clinician then resummarizes the map and checks for accuracy.

Identifying clients' hoped-for and feared possible selves can provide the clinician with useful information for planning both short-term and long-term treatment goals, as well as providing insight into how clients perceive various aspects of their stuttering and its impact on different parts of their lives. DiLollo and Neimeyer (2022) used an example case to illustrate the application of the PSMI process with a client who stutters. In this case, the client, Ted, was a 16-year-old male who was diagnosed with stuttering at age 6 and had been in school-based speech therapy for 10 years. Figure 4–2 illustrates Ted's possible selves map for the domain of speech/fluency.

Using this map, the clinician and Ted could discuss the first three possible selves—on both the hoped-for and feared tracks. Ted could describe why those are important to him, and then he and the clinician could brainstorm about setting goals to (a) achieve the hoped-for possible selves, and (b) prevent the feared possible selves. For example, they might set a short-term goal to *use pull-outs successfully on 80% of opportunities while practicing his class presentation.* They might also agree on a longer term goal to *use pull-outs and preparatory sets on 90% of opportunities in a 10-minute conversation (a) with the clinician in the therapy room, and (b) with a stranger in a setting outside the therapy room.*

Similarly, the clinician and Ted could discuss the last two possible selves that relate to more adaptive aspects of Ted's communication and come up with goals designed to encourage Ted to experiment

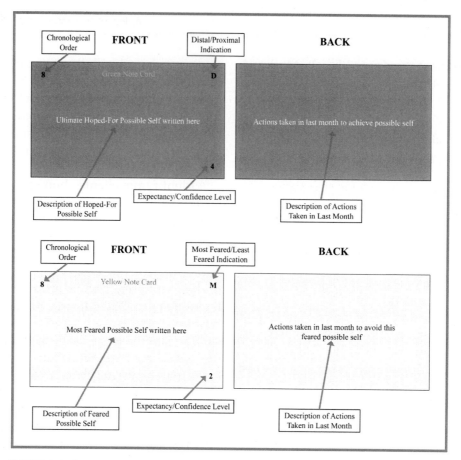

FIGURE 4–1. Green and yellow note cards showing hoped-for and feared possible selves. *Source*: From *Counseling in Speech-Language Pathology and Audiology: Reconstructing Personal Narratives, Second Edition* (p. 332) by DiLollo, A., & Neimeyer, R. Copyright © 2022 Plural Publishing, Inc. All rights reserved. Used with permission.

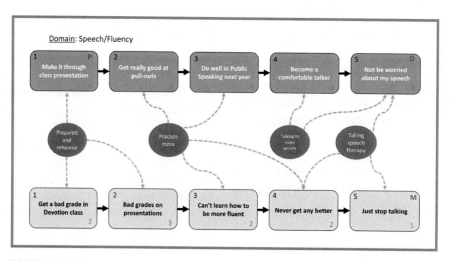

FIGURE 4–2. Ted's possible selves map for the speech/fluency domain. *Source*: From *Counseling in Speech-Language Pathology and Audiology: Reconstructing Personal Narratives, Second Edition* (p. 336) by DiLollo, A., & Neimeyer, R. Copyright © 2022 Plural Publishing, Inc. All rights reserved. Used with permission.

with different attitudes toward his speech and communication. For example, Ted and the clinicians might design a goal to *challenge himself to participate in three separate novel social events before the end of the semester.* They might also set a goal to *achieve a self-rating of 4/5 (on a 5-point comfort scale, with 5 being the most comfortable) in at least one of those social events.*

CONSENSUS GUIDELINES FOR THE ASSESSMENT OF INDIVIDUALS WHO STUTTER ACROSS THE LIFE SPAN

A team of 12 expert clinicians and researchers who average more than 28 years of experience working with persons who stutter and have written extensively about stuttering came together to develop consensus guidelines for the assessment of individuals who stutter across the life span (Brundage et al., 2021). These experts, from Australia, Belgium, the Netherlands, the United Kingdom, and the United States, each provided detailed descriptions of the type of data that they routinely collect during diagnostic evaluations of preschool children, school-age children, adolescents, and adults who stutter. They then used an iterative content analysis process to identify core areas that reflected common domains that they judged to be important for evaluating stuttering for varying age groups. As a result, they identified six core areas that should be addressed in any assessment for individuals who stutter.

Area 1: Stuttering-Related Background Information

The first core area is what most clinicians would recognize as a case history where extensive stuttering-related background information is gathered. This is usually information about the person who stutters and his or her experiences related to stuttering, major concerns, and goals for treatment. Case histories and interviews should be conducted with the client and other relevant individuals, who could include parents, teachers, and other caregivers and significant others. Although there are many different case history forms available, particularly online and in various textbooks, many clinics have their own proprietary forms that are required. It is important to remember, however, that no form, no matter how comprehensive, can capture everything clinicians need to know about their clients. Try to use forms as a starting point for your conversations with the client and significant others, inviting them to clarify and elaborate on answers provided and to express their own opinions and ask their own questions. Similarly, lists of questions should be used to guide conversations rather than replace them—we have seen many novice students wield their list of questions like a hammer, bludgeoning clients with a new question before they can take a breath. Engaging in a conversation and placing clients in the role of expert on their own stuttering gives the client and family members the opportunity to describe their own unique story of the problems that they might be experiencing and to explore what they would like to gain from the assessment and subsequent treatment.

Area 2: Speech, Language, Temperament, and Related Background Information

The second core area is the assessment of various aspects of speech, language, and temperament development. Brundage et al. (2021) suggested that these assessments should be routinely done with preschool and school-age children who stutter but only "as needed" in adolescent and adult clients. Such assessments are typically done through standardized tests of speech sound development, expressive and receptive language, and temperament questionnaires for different age groups. Much of this information can also be obtained through direct observation of the client, and interviews with parents and the child, adolescent, or adult.

Area 3: Speech Fluency and Stuttering Behavior

The third core assessment area is speech fluency and stuttering behavior. The goal of this aspect of assessment is to determine (a) if the client is demonstrating observable stuttering behavior, and (b) what the client does when he or she stutters. This involves collecting speech samples, counting and classifying disfluencies, and determining severity. As mentioned in Chapter 2, one of the hallmarks of developmental stuttering is that it is highly variable, meaning that it is important to collect speech samples across multiple speaking tasks and settings. In the past, this could be quite challenging for some clients, but with the almost universal ownership of cell phones that have the capability of recording audio and video, clients and their families can easily record speech samples in multiple settings with little intrusion on their daily tasks.

In addition to the stuttering behaviors that the clinician observes from the various speech samples, the client, caregivers, and family members should be provided the opportunity to describe their own perceptions of how stuttering presents and varies across situations. Clients can also be asked to rate their severity of stuttering across different situations and settings.

Area 4: Speakers' Reactions to Stuttering

The fourth core area is the client's reactions to stuttering and how those reactions influence communication and quality of life. Consequently, it is important for the clinician to include ways of exploring clients' awareness and anticipation of stuttering, and how these impact their participation, with particular interest in avoidance behaviors and coping strategies that have proven successful or unsuccessful. This type of information can be obtained through published self-report measures as well as interviews and observations.

Area 5: Reactions to Stuttering Within the Environment

The fifth core area relates to gaining understanding about the speaker's environment and how it impacts stuttering behavior and the client's experience of stuttering. Taking a person-centered approach to assessment as described earlier in this chapter, it is important to understand clients within the context of the environment in which they function. This will include learning who the significant people in the client's life are, how they react to the client's stuttering, and how they have attempted to help when stuttering occurs. This might include discussions of bullying for school-age and adolescent clients, although it should be remembered that adult clients can also experience bullying in various forms. In addition to the people in the client's life, assessment in this area should also explore the various environments in which the client typically functions (e.g., home, work, school, etc.) and examine situations in which speaking is more or less difficult, or where stuttering severity is greater or reduced.

Area 6: Adverse Impact Associated With Stuttering

The sixth core area of assessment involves identifying any adverse impacts that stuttering has on the client's communication, education, employment, and quality of life. There is likely some crossover between this area and some of what is explored in Areas 4 and 5, but the focus here is to examine closely "the consequences of living with stuttering" (Brundage et al., 2021, p. 2383). This includes exploring how stuttering impacts the choices and decisions that the client makes, and those made or not made in the past. This information can be accessed through interviews and conversations with the client, as well as via standardized assessments.

DiLollo and Neimeyer (2022) suggested a novel approach that can help clients take a different perspective on how stuttering is impacting their choices. They suggested taking a narrative therapy approach, externalizing stuttering and examining the relationship that the client has with stuttering. In this context, the clinician can ask the client questions like, "What decisions has stuttering made for you recently?" and "What was stuttering telling you that made you decide not to go to the party yesterday?" Through these types of questions, as well as other creative activities such as having the client write an autobiography of stuttering (see DiLollo & Neimeyer, 2022, Chapter 14), the client and clinician can explore the relationship between stuttering and

the client to build a better understanding of the impact that stuttering has in the life of the client.

CONCLUSION

This chapter has outlined a person-centered approach to the assessment of stuttering for clients of any age or background, emphasizing that people who stutter and their significant others must be critical contributors to the assessment and goal-setting processes. Individuals who stutter know themselves and their stuttering best and have important insights about their stuttering that must be taken into account in gathering assessment data, the analysis of assessment results, and the development of intervention plans. Importantly, this chapter sets out the broad range of information that is needed to conduct a comprehensive assessment of stuttering, moving beyond a simple evaluation of speech fluency or observable stuttering behaviors. Finally, in keeping with this person-centered approach, it should also be noted that the selection of specific assessment areas and tools or procedures must be individualized and tailored to each client's or family's unique needs.

In the next two chapters, we discuss the processes related to the assessment of preschool and school-age children and then adolescents and adults to examine some of the issues and concepts associated with assessing stuttering at these different stages.

? TOPICS FOR DISCUSSION

1. Which definitions of stuttering described in Chapter 2 fit with the assessment process described in this chapter?

2. Why is simply evaluating the frequency and type of disfluencies that a client produces not sufficient as an assessment of stuttering?

3. Why is it so important to include families and significant others in the assessment process?

4. Why is there nothing in this assessment process that tries to identify the cause of the client's stuttering?

5. In pairs, do a PSMI with your partner using a domain (e.g., social or relationships, school, job or career, self-image) of interest to you and discuss the results and what you learned about the process.

6. Write an autobiography of a problem that you live with—it could be something small or big, but one you are willing to talk about with others—and share it with others in a small group. Then discuss what you learned from the process of both writing and sharing the autobiography.

📖 RECOMMENDED READINGS

Bloodstein, O., Bernstein Ratner, N., & Brundage, S. B. (2021). *A handbook on stuttering* (7th ed.). Plural Publishing.

Brundage, S. B., Bernstein Ratner, N., Boyle, M. P., Eggers, K., Everard, R., Franken, M., . . . Yaruss, J. S. (2021). Consensus guidelines for the assessments of individuals who stutter across the lifespan. *American Journal of Speech-Language Pathology, 30,* 2379–2393.

DiLollo, A., & Neimeyer, R. A. (2022). Autobiography of the problem. In *Counseling in speech-language pathology and audiology: Reconstructing personal narratives* (2nd ed., pp. 215–220). Plural Publishing.

DiLollo, A., & Neimeyer, R. A. (2022). Possible Selves Mapping Interview. In *Counseling in speech-language pathology and audiology: Reconstructing personal narratives* (2nd ed., pp. 325–342). Plural Publishing.

It's not enough to know what type of fluency problem the child has. We need to know what type of child has the problem.

—Charles Van Riper (1965)

I think that inside my mouth there is something wrong with me. And that is why I'm going to speech therapy to help my speaking. I have to take my time and be brave. I think my body is ready to talk but my mouth isn't. If I take my time I think I will be all right. But it is very hard because I want to be like everybody else. It's hard being different from everyone else. I'm lucky that I have such supportive parents and friends to help me get through my problem. I've learned that real friends do listen and I love them for it.

—Lester L., 10 (nearly 11), Philadelphia, PA

The Assessment Process With Young Speakers: Preschool and School-Age Children

CHAPTER OBJECTIVES

- To provide a discussion of the broad issues that clinicians must consider when planning and engaging in assessment with preschool and school-age children
- To describe the process for determining whether or not the child is stuttering (Decision 1)
- To describe the process for determining the course of stuttering— persistence versus recovery (Decision 2)
- To describe how assessment data can provide guidance for intervention
- To describe the potential educational impact of stuttering and the responsibilities of the individualized education program (IEP) team

- To provide descriptions of frequently used assessment measures for preschool and school-age children

The emphasis of this chapter concerns two primary decisions that the clinician will need to make when evaluating the possibility of stuttering in young children. Considering the suggested criteria for distinguishing unusual from usual fluency breaks described in Chapter 2, the clinician must first make a judgment about the nature of the child's fluency and whether or not it is within reasonably normal limits.

Guidelines discussed earlier including the occurrence of stuttering-like disfluencies (SLDs) at a rate of more than three SLDs per 100 syllables, the number and rate of repetitions, the clustering of SLDs, the child's reaction to his or her fluency disruptions, and the concern of the parents will help to inform the clinician about whether the child is stuttering or not. Nevertheless, because of the variability in the fluency of young children, the clinician will need to obtain samples of the child's speech in a variety of speaking conditions.

Once the clinician concludes that the child's fluency breaks are characteristic of stuttering, she will then need to make a second, more difficult decision—are the stuttering-like disfluencies likely to be a temporary or a permanent characteristic of the child's speech? As Yairi and his colleagues have pointed out, remission following the onset of stuttering is generally gradual, with most children recovering within 3 to 4 years following onset. Remission from stuttering with young speakers was suggested many years ago, with estimates of this phenomenon varying widely from approximately 32% to more than 80% (Andrews & Harris, 1964; Bryngelson, 1938; Cooper, 1972; Curlee & Yairi, 1997; Kloth et al., 1999; Panelli et al., 1978; Starkweather, 1987; Van Riper, 1982; Yairi & Ambrose, 1992a; Young, 1975).

Yairi and Ambrose (2005) suggested that the often-cited recovery rate of 75% for younger speakers who stutter could be an underestimate. They argued that because some children who continue to stutter show only traces of stuttering and many who recover on their own go unreported, they proposed a rate of recovery that is closer to 85%.

It is also noteworthy that the nature of the remission is typically complete, for once these young children recover there is little or no chance of relapse and the quality of their speech appears to be identical to typically fluent children (Finn et al., 1997). In part because there are so many variables involved, not to mention that it requires the clinician to predict the future,

making the decision about whether or not a young child will continue to stutter is problematic. Conture (1997) concluded that although clinicians might be reasonably good at identifying stuttering-like fluency breaks, they are not particularly good at predicting whether or not a child will continue to stutter or benefit from intervention. Given the uncertainty about the chronicity of stuttering, the clinician will need to consider a response that—depending on such factors as the child's age, length of time since onset, family history of stuttering, language and speech characteristics, cognitive development, and temperamental nature—can range from informal monitoring of the child's speech to direct therapeutic intervention.

THE CONCERNS AND QUESTIONS OF PARENTS: THE INITIAL STAGES OF COPING WITH A CHILD WHO MAY BE STUTTERING

In Chapter 11, we describe the role of the entire family in a comprehensive therapeutic approach with children as well as adults. During our first contact with the family the parents have several concerns and questions about the disfluencies of their child. Plexico and Burrus (2012) provided a thorough description of how parents attempt to cope with the many issues created by having a child who stutters. Based on a detailed phenomenological analysis of 12 parents, these authors identified feelings of uncertainty and concern about the onset of stuttering in their child. The primary concerns of the parents included the following:

- Was their child really stuttering, and if so, would it persist?
- What is the possible cause, and what treatments options are available?

- Should they discuss the problem in the home (10 of the 12 participants thought it should not be discussed)?
- When should they seek professional help, and how long should the therapy last?
- What is the possibility that their child would have a restricted lifestyle and suffer socially?
- Would their child experience bullying and fail to have a productive life?

The parents also reported a variety of initial responses to their children's stuttering, including the most frequent response of asking their children to slow their rate of speech and to think about what they were going to say. More appropriate and helpful responses included actively listening to their child, reducing time pressure, maintaining eye contact, not speaking for them, attempting to instill confidence and self-esteem, and letting their child know that they would be there for them and that they would not have to face any problem alone. Professional help for the child was most often received in the child's school. Parents reported examples of clinician recommendations, which included less appropriate suggestions such as asking the child to slow down, think of what they were going to say, and repeat the word following a disfluency, as well as more appropriate suggestions such as using smooth and easy speech and drawing out disfluent sounds. Parents also reported that they were typically unsatisfied with the level of services that were provided in the school setting and felt uninformed and uninvolved in their child's therapy. Alternatively, the parents indicated that opportunities to observe therapy resulted in greater understanding and assistance for working with their child at home.

As others have done, Plexico and Burrus (2012) recommended a family systems approach that included the parents as an important component of the therapeutic process. That is, the clinician should value the development of a strong therapeutic alliance between the clinician and the family, not just with the child. They summarized their recommendations in the following quote:

> In order to relieve the many forms of stress experienced by parents of children who stutter, clinicians need to provide information that will help parents more effectively cope with their situation. This includes providing information on the nature of stuttering, the cause of stuttering, teasing and bullying, support groups, and involving parents in the therapeutic process so that they can understand and facilitate the desired therapeutic changes beyond the clinic environment. (Plexico & Burrus, 2012, p. 287)

In an effort to provide clinicians with an understanding of the impact of stuttering on children and their parents, Langevin et al. (2015) developed a 20-item survey, Impact of Stuttering on Preschool Children and Parents (ISPP). The survey was designed to elicit both quantitative and qualitative information including the parents' perceptions of how a child's stuttering could influence the child's self-confidence, emotional response to stuttering, interaction with peers, and quality of life. Other questions focused on the reaction of the child's playmates and how the parents were affected emotionally by their child's struggle to communicate. Langevin et al. found that 89.6% of the 77 parents who completed the ISPP reported that their children showed a range (1–13, median = 2) of negative reactions, including frustration, withdrawal, decreased self-confidence and assertiveness, reduced or changed verbal output, comments about their inability to talk, mood changes, and avoidance behavior. Teasing and walking away were common reactions by the child's peers. Nearly all of the parents (90.9%) indicated that they were negatively affected by their child's stuttering in the form of worry, anxiety, concern, frustration, being upset, and self-blame about the possibility that they might have caused the stuttering. Parents reported that they responded by taking time to listen to their child, waiting for the child to finish talking, modifying their own speech, and asking their child to modify their speech.

THE IMPORTANCE OF THE INITIAL MEETING: TWO PRIMARY DECISIONS

It is important to realize that the initial assessment meeting with the child and the parents is the first opportunity for the clinician to show his or her understanding about both the nature of stuttering and the impact it can have on the child and the family. This is the first chance for the clinician to begin making the problem less mysterious, alter some of the myths or misinformation that the family might associate with the problem, alleviate the feelings of guilt that often accompany stuttering, and begin to provide the parents with a sense of direction and control about the problem. As Conture (1997) suggested, the clinician's ability to orient the family to the true nature of the problem could be the main benefit that the child and the family receive from the diagnostic meeting(s). Another excellent comment by Yairi and Ambrose (2005) will echo throughout the following chapters on intervention: "It is also important for clinicians to understand, and to impart to parents, that *stuttering* is not a bad word" (p. 283).

DECISION 1: DETERMINING WHETHER OR NOT THE CHILD IS STUTTERING

The variability of stuttering for older speakers described in the previous chapter is even more apparent with young children, in part because children are rapidly maturing neurologically, physiologically, emotionally, and linguistically. Although some authors have found that nonstuttering children demonstrate relatively little variability in fluency across speaking situations (Martin, Haroldson, & Kuhl, 1972a, 1972b; Wexler, 1982), many others have noted the highly variable nature of fluency in young speakers who stutter (Bloodstein, 1995; Conture, 1990; Starkweather, 1987; Van Riper, 1982; Yaruss, 1997a). Such variability provides clinicians with both good and bad news. The good news is that it is generally easier to change behavior that is variable and relatively new, making treatment more likely to be successful (Starkweather, 1992, 1999; Starkweather et al., 1990). The bad news is that this same variability can make obtaining representative samples of a child's fluency more problematic than with older speakers.

The case history information that is available to the clinician prior to the first meeting with the family will often provide a variety of clues about the nature of the child and the potential for stuttering. For example, as noted in Chapter 3, it has long been recognized that stuttering tends to occur more often in some families than in others (Andrews & Harris, 1964; Bloodstein, 1995). Ambrose et al. (1993) found that for children who stutter there is a 42% chance that someone in the nuclear family also stutters and a 71% chance that there is someone in the extended family who stutters. Many other factors such as

CLINICAL INSIGHT

Although authors now agree that many children recover from stuttering, few have investigated whether these same speakers are more likely to begin stuttering again later in their adult years. It is relatively rare to find speakers who begin to stutter as adults (see Chapter 13). It could be, however, that some people who begin stuttering later in life are those people who stuttered as children, more or less spontaneously recovered, and later—apparently in response to one or more sources of stress—again began to experience breaks in their fluency. We have seen a few such adults with whom a reoccurrence of stuttering seems to be a central component for what originally appeared to be a "late or adult onset" of stuttering. How this might happen is not well understood. If we consider this question from the perspective of the dynamic-multifactorial model (Smith & Kelly, 1997), a person who develops late-onset stuttering might be someone with a combination of factors that could have produced stuttering as a child but, because of some dynamic factor or weighting of factors (e.g., specific environmental factors), stuttering did not manifest or only did so briefly. In adulthood, if factors or weighting of factors changed for that person, the threshold for stuttering to manifest might be reached (or reached again).

the academic performance of school-age children, estimates of self-esteem, psychosocial functioning, and family structure and history could be influential in determining whether or not the child is stuttering. Of course, the assessment process provides a face-to-face opportunity to obtain the characteristics of the child and the nature of the fluency breaks that are of concern to the parents.

Eliciting Fluency Breaks

Assuming that the child will cooperate, conversational speech samples can be elicited and recorded during the initial clinical evaluation. Speech samples, video recorded by the parents from representative situations outside the clinic setting, typically at the child's home, can also be obtained either prior to or following the evaluation, and are often especially useful.

A 300- to 500-word sample produced in two or three settings is a reasonable goal. The frequency of SLDs can be obtained in either percent syllables stuttered (%SS) or percent words stuttered (%WS) and the types of fluency breaks analyzed. The frequency of %WS can be converted to %SS by multiplying %WS by 1.5 (Andrews & Ingham, 1971).

On the day of the evaluation, the child might fail to exhibit the behaviors that concern the parents (or teacher). Although this could occur during the assessment of adults who stutter, it is more often the case with younger speakers. One option beyond obtaining the typical conversational speech sample is to ask the child to create a narrative discourse. Byrd, Logan, and Gillam (2012) compared the frequency of SLDs for 22 children who stuttered and 22 children who did not matched for age and gender. Children were assigned to one of two age groups:

younger (mean age of 6;11) or older (mean age of 9;5). Both groups of children took part in two conditions: (a) a structured conversation where they were asked to respond to a series of 29 questions about eight picture cards resulting in a turn-taking conversational interaction between the child and an adult, and (b) a request to create a story based on the sequence of the same eight pictures. As the authors explained, because narrative discourse typically contains more complex language than conversation, it requires the child to create information about the characters in the story, the choices the characters make, and the actions that are taking place. The authors found that the narration task resulted in significantly more SLDs than the structured conversational interview and mean length of utterance (MLU) was significantly longer during the narration condition. The age of the children did not influence the frequency of the children's SLDs in either condition. Based on these results, the authors suggested that the many conceptual and linguistic complexities associated with the narrative task are more likely to elicit SLDs and that clinicians would acquire greater insight about the child's stuttering behavior by using both conversational and narrative speaking tasks.

If, after these activities, no SLDs are elicited, the clinician could consider introducing *mild* forms of communicative stress at various times during the assessment process. As indicated in Chapter 1, this requires a clinician who is uninhibited and unafraid of stuttering and one who understands that a momentary in-

CLINICAL INSIGHT

Today, almost everyone has a cell phone with the capability to record high-quality video and audio. This makes the task of getting speech samples from outside the clinic much easier and more likely. Consequently, this should be considered standard procedure for most client evaluations. Parents should be instructed (preferably ahead of the evaluation appointment) to record examples of their child in a variety of settings, being sure to capture the child's *typical* performance, as well as any specific or unique behaviors that they might feel the clinician needs to see and hear. Similar instructions can be given to adult clients, requesting that they bring to the evaluation appointment several videos of themselves speaking in a variety of settings. It is often difficult for nonclinicians to judge the length of samples in terms of words or syllables, so it is usually better to simply request at least two to three videos that are around 10 minutes or more in length, with the individual being evaluated doing most of the talking during that time. Additional shorter videos that show specific behaviors or reactions to disfluencies are also useful and should be encouraged. Ideally, the videos that are brought to the evaluation appointment can be transferred to the clinician's computer or mobile device for analysis.

Note: Clinicians must stay alert to the Health Insurance Portability and Accountability Act (HIPAA) regulations regarding any video transferred to their electronic devices and be sure to properly secure such information before leaving the clinic.

crease in stuttering will not only do no harm but could provide helpful information. Moreover, throughout both assessment and treatment it is constructive to communicate curiosity and interest rather than aversion about stuttered or "bumpy" speech. Minimal examples of such speech are all that are usually required in order for the clinician to obtain adequate samples. Of course, as it becomes necessary to elicit fluency breaks from children in this fashion, parents or others who might be observing the evaluation should be informed about the purpose of these activities.

There are many benign techniques the clinician can use to elicit fluency breaks in children. Essentially, what we are doing is creating a speaking situation where minimal temporary demands are placed on the child. As the demands exceed the child's ability to produce fluent speech, fluency breaks are likely to occur. Perhaps the most subtle form of disrupting a child's fluency is for the clinician to turn away as the child is describing an event or activity. Loss of the listener's attention has long been acknowledged as an effectual technique for eliciting fluency breaks in children (Johnson, 1962; Van Riper, 1982). Another strategy is to create some form of minimal time pressure for the child to speak. This can be accomplished by asking the child to name objects in a book or in the room as rapidly as possible, or to describe a series of pictures presented at a rapid rate. The clinician also could ask the child to respond to a series of questions or ask him or her to answer somewhat abstract or difficult-to-answer queries (Guitar & Peters, 1980), such as, "How far is it from here to your home and how do you get there?" or "What does your mother (or father) do when they go to work?" Depending on the age of the chil-

dren, they could be asked to read from books that are somewhat above grade level (Blood & Hood, 1978). Another option is to momentarily have other listeners come into the room. Typically, only one or a few of these activities are necessary to obtain examples of fluency breaks. Obviously, these techniques must be performed with appropriate understanding and sensitivity by the clinician as well as others who are involved. It is not necessary to elicit many of these breaks, and once a few examples have been obtained, the clinician can consult with the parents to determine if these behaviors are indeed the behaviors they have observed and are concerned about. The clinician cannot assume that the fluency breaks that occur during the assessment are of the same form and degree that the parents have previously observed.

As we described in Chapter 4, it is important to gather speech samples from a variety of settings. This is particularly important with young children. This was underscored by Yaruss (1997a) in a study of 45 preschool children undergoing diagnostic evaluations for stuttering. Frequency counts were obtained for both typical and SLDs for each of the children as they took part in three to five of the following situations during the evaluation session:

1. Parent/child interaction—The child interacts with the parents (usually the mother) while playing with figures or games.
2. Play—The child and the clinician play with objects in a natural, free-play situation.
3. Play with pressures imposed—The clinician gradually increases conversational pressure by asking questions, breaking eye contact, interrupting, or

increasing time pressure (e.g., speaking faster).

4. Story retell—The child retells a familiar story while using a picture book.
5. Picture description—The child describes pictures with minimal input from the clinician.

Yaruss (1997a) found that the children who stuttered showed significantly greater variability across the speaking situations than within any single situation. Notably, the "play with pressure" situation resulted in the greatest number of disfluencies, although this was not the case for all the participants, as many children exhibited highly individualized patterns.

Based on these results, Yaruss (1997a) suggested that sampling of a child's fluency in a single speaking situation is unlikely to result in a representative sample of behavior, particularly for children who exhibit a greater number of stuttering-like disfluencies. Indeed, he noted that approximately 19 of the children evaluated had fewer than 3% SLDs in at least one situation and 18 of the children produced more than 10% stuttering in another situation. In other words, if the common guideline of 3% disfluencies had been used as a threshold, approximately 40% of the children would not have been correctly identified as stuttering. Of course, as Yaruss pointed out, a single metric of stuttering frequency would not be used alone to indicate the presence of stuttering. The results also indicate the potential problem of placing too much importance on the frequency of stuttering, especially during a single speaking situation.

In some instances, in spite of our best attempts within several speaking situations and environments, we are unable to obtain samples of the fluency breaks that are of concern to the parents. It is usually possible to reschedule another assessment during a period when the child is experiencing more difficulty, or we might observe the child in a more natural setting at home or in school.

Another aspect of stuttering that has been shown to differ between children and adults who stutter is the frequency of stuttering on content and function words. As the name implies, content words are those that contain the content of the idea we want to convey (e.g., nouns, verbs, adjectives, and adverbs). Function words serve to make the sentence structure correct (e.g., pronouns, prepositions, and auxiliary verbs). Because the function words do not directly contribute to the message being expressed (or written), they are typically unstressed. Researchers have noted that function words are more likely to be disfluent for both fluent and younger speakers who stutter. For example, Howell, Au-Yeung, and Sackin (1999) found that 2- to 6-year-old speakers had a higher percentage of stuttering on initial function words than content words. For older age groups, ranging from age 7 to 40, stuttering decreased on function words and increased on content words. This pattern of disfluencies was also noted by Juste et al. (2012), who also found that as children become adolescents, those who stutter show no difference between the frequency of disfluencies on function and content words, whereas those who do not stutter continue to present with more disfluencies on function words. With increasing age, content word stuttering increased and function word disfluencies decreased for those who stutter. This phenomenon coincides to some degree with the EXPLAN theory (Howell & Au-Yeung, 2002) discussed in Chapter 3, which proposes that disfluencies are the result of an immature planning and execution process that is out of synchrony.

The Nature of Stuttering at Onset

In describing the onset and development of stuttering in Chapter 2, we discussed the overt behaviors that tend to differentiate the fluency breaks of children who stutter (CWS) from normally fluent children. In this section we present a variety of additional characteristics that help to make this distinction. As in Chapter 2, many of the comments in this section are taken from the work of Yairi and his colleagues at the University of Illinois Stuttering Research Program as discussed in the Yairi and Ambrose (2005) text *Early Childhood Stuttering, for Clinicians by Clinicians.* The highlights of their findings are briefly reviewed here.

A summary of findings by Yairi and Ambrose (2005) indicates that, at the onset of stuttering, the disfluencies are markedly different from those (normal disfluencies) of fluent children. In contrast to the widely held view from the middle decades of the 20th century, stuttering does not appear to arise from the normal disfluencies of young children. Yairi and Ambrose made the important point that parents who believe that their child has begun stuttering are often correct. These authors also state, "if it is unclear whether the disfluency is stuttering or not, there is no objective basis for great concern at that moment" (Yairi & Ambrose, 2005, p. 139). Although CWS do produce normal or typical fluency breaks, they are not prominent—two thirds of the disfluencies of CWS are composed of SLDs, whereas two thirds of the disfluencies of normally fluent children are normal or typical disfluencies.

According to Yairi and Ambrose (2005), parents commonly indicate some degree of physical, emotional, and language stress associated with stuttering onset, with only about 20% of onset occurring under unremarkable circumstances. Associated characteristics are often present at onset, with about half of the children showing tense movements in parts of the body, especially the head, face, or neck. Following onset, relatively few children show a linear progression of more severe and complex stuttering over time. For children who have begun to stutter, the rate of the repetitions is significantly faster, with shorter intervals between the repeated units than the repetitions of normally fluent children. Normally fluent children rarely, if ever, produce disrhythmic phonations (tense prolongations of sounds and cessation of airflow and voicing).

In order to increase diagnostic sensitivity, Ambrose and Yairi (1999; see also Yairi & Ambrose, 2005) developed a single score that combines three primary dimensions of disfluent speech (frequency, type, and extent of stuttering; Table 5–1). Ambrose and Yairi found that the *weighted SLD* score did a better job in distinguishing stuttering from normally fluent children than a basic count of SLDs. For example, a weighted SLD of 4 or above and associated nonspeech and psychosocial characteristics (e.g., awareness, negative attitude about communicating, struggle and escape behavior) are indicative of stuttering. The weighted SLD is tabulated using the following steps:

1. Add together the number of part-word and single-syllable word repetitions per 100 syllables (PW + SS).
2. Multiply that sum by the mean number of repetition units (RU). (RUs are

TABLE 5–1. Disfluency Criteria to Diagnose Mild Stuttering

Measure (Frequency per 100 Syllables)	Minimum Criteria for Stuttering
Part-word repetitions (PW)	≥1.5
Single-syllable word repetitions (SS)	≥2.5
Disrhythmic phonation	≥0.5
Repetition units	≥1.5
Stuttering-like disfluency (SLD)	≥3.0
Weighted SLD	≥4.0
Repetitions (PW + SS) with two or more *extra* units	≥1.0

Source: From *Early Childhood Stuttering* (p. 338), by E. Yairi and N. G. Ambrose, 2005, Austin, TX: Pro-Ed. Copyright 2005 by Pro-Ed, Inc. Reprinted with permission.

the number of times a sound, syllable, or word is repeated prior to saying the word, divided by the number of words where this occurred.)

3. Add to this total twice the number of disrhythmic phonations (DPs; blocks and prolongations) per 100 syllables. Ambrose and Yairi (1999) explained that because DPs are absent or rare in fluent speakers, they are a strong indicator of stuttering and are thus weighted. The resulting formula is [(PW + SS) × RU] + (2 × DP).

Conture (2001) provided a list of seven criteria to consider when making the decision whether to initiate treatment with young children. Treatment is recommended if children meet two or more of the following criteria: (a) the frequency of disfluencies is greater than 10%; (b) sound prolongations make up more than 30% of the within-word disfluencies; (c) a score of 19 or greater on the Stuttering Severity Instrument (SSI; Riley, 1994); (d) score of 17 or greater on the Stuttering Prediction Instrument (Riley, 1981); (e) the child's stuttering is associated with eyeball movements to the side, eyelid blinking, or both; (f) clusters of stuttering constitute 25% of the child's disfluencies; and (g) the child has been stuttering for 18 months or more.

Indicators of Awareness

Many years ago, Johnson and Associates (1959) noted that young children who stutter tend to display a variety of nonspeech reactions to their stuttering, such as tense body movements. These movements have often been referred to as secondary behaviors or secondary characteristics, and they might provide the clinician with an indication of the child's awareness about his or her stuttering. A number of studies by Conture and his associates (Conture & Kelly, 1991; Schwartz & Conture, 1988; Schwartz et al., 1990), as well as studies by Yairi et al. (1993), indicated that young children who stuttered exhibited many such behaviors—including head, eye, torso, and limb movements—during (or in anticipation of) stuttering. Children who stuttered averaged 1.48 movements during stuttered words and 0.63 movements during nonstuttered words (Conture & Kelly, 1991).

Conture (1990) suggested two categories of nonspeech behavior that should be considered: (a) body movement and tension, and (b) psychosocial discomfort and concern. These coping responses are likely a result of the child's awareness that speaking is difficult as well as the recognition of unfavorable reactions by listeners. Conture and Kelly (1991) observed more nonspeech movement and tension in 30 children 3 to 7 years old who stuttered than a matched group of fluent children during comparable sections of fluent speech. Specifically, the CWS (a) showed more frequent movement of their eyeballs to the left or right, (b) blinked their eyelids, and (c) raised their upper lip. Conture and Kelly theorized that these nonverbal responses were ways of coping with listener responses to their speech difficulty. Yairi et al. (1993) found that 16 young children who were within 3 months of stuttering onset averaged 3.18 (range = 0.8–5.9) head and neck movements per moment of stuttering. During follow-up testing, the authors found that as stuttering decreased, the frequency of the movements decreased. The awareness of young speakers who have begun to stutter might also be reflected by pitch rise; prolongations; schwa substitutions, or the substitution of the neutral schwa vowel for the appropriate vowel (ka, ka, keep; Manning et al., 1975); a high rate of part-word repetitions; and cessation of airflow and voicing (Adams, 1977a; Throneberg & Yairi, 1994; Van Riper, 1982; Walle, 1975).

With the presence of such behaviors, it can be assumed that the child is aware of the problem and is searching for ways of coping. Even at a young age, the child is attempting to cope with the helplessness inherent in the experience of stuttering.

In a classic study of this important issue, Ambrose and Yairi (1994) used a unique videotape of puppets, one of whom stuttered. Children were asked to "point to the puppet that talks the way you do" (p. 234). The researchers found that 20 CWS (age 2–5 years) were more likely to identify with the disfluent puppet, whereas normally fluent control children identified with the fluent puppet. Although the majority of the young children who stuttered were not overtly aware of their stuttering, the results indicated the presence of awareness at some level and increasing awareness with increasing age. They also noted that awareness of stuttering was not related to stuttering severity (as indicated by an 8-point stuttering severity scale).

Based on their experience with many young children at the Michael Palin Center in London, Rustin and Cook (1995) pointed out that some preschool children are able to be very clear about the difficulties they experience. There are ample investigations indicating that school-age children as young as 6 years old who stutter are not only aware of their stuttering, but quickly develop a negative attitude about their speech and communicating (De Nil & Brutten, 1991; Riley & Riley, 1979; Vanryckeghem & Brutten, 1996, 1997), as well as fears and avoidance behaviors (Conture, 1990; Peters & Guitar, 1991; Williams, 1985). Vanryckeghem et al. (2005), based on a study using a 12-item self-report measure, the Communication Attitude Test for Preschool and Kindergarten Children Who Stutter (KiddyCAT), extended the age of this negative self-response to the experience of stuttering to preschool and kindergarten children to as young as 3 years old, approximately the time when stuttering onset is observed.

Although the use of projective drawings has received limited attention, some clinicians (e.g., Chmela & Reardon, 2001) have found that drawings by children clearly reflect their interpretation of their circumstances and their perceived ability to communicate, including their frustration and anxiety about speaking. Compared to young children (5–10 years old) who stutter, DeVore et al. (1984) found that children who did not stutter drew significantly larger drawings that were placed nearer the center of the page. As a result of a 12-week program of individual therapy, the children who stuttered showed significant changes in position and size of their drawings. They created larger drawings and placed them nearer to the center of the page, and the figures were more likely to extend to all four quadrants of the sheet rather than only the lower left quadrant. After treatment there were no significant differences in the drawings by the CWS and those who did not stutter , and the A-19 Attitude Scale (Guitar & Grims, 1977) indicated no significant differences between the two groups of children.

When children reach school age and begin to experience the social penalties that are likely to occur around their speech difficulties (if they have not already occurred), they quickly become acutely aware of their stuttering. Depending on such factors as the nature and severity of the child's stuttering and the support from his or her family, teachers, and friends, the child's reactions to his or her fluency problem can vary widely. Some children are able to adjust and to some extent counter the negative effects of stuttering by developing their academic,

social, and athletic talents and abilities. In rare instances, a child who stutters might aggressively respond to his or her situation either by physically fighting those who tease or bully the child or by developing speaking skills and engaging in activities such as acting or debating. Others might be devastated by their inability to achieve fluency and withdraw into a restrictive lifestyle, as described by Rabinowitz (2001):

> At some point in my childhood, maybe the first time I tried to speak and the only sound out of my mouth was an unintelligible stutter, I lost the ability to laugh, even to smile, without conscious thought or effort. I was judged by my words or, rather by my inability to produce them in the way that others did. From then on, I learned to trust no one and to speak only when absolutely necessary. As far as I was concerned, trusting led to betrayal and pain, and speaking was an unbearable horror. Words were my enemy. (p. 189)

Anxiety Levels in Children Who Stutter

Research concerning anxiety in children who stutter began to occur in the 1990s. Two types of anxiety have been identified and have been the focus of this research. Measures of trait anxiety (indicated as A-Trait) are designed to indicate a person's general level of anxiety. Evidence of trait anxiety is obtained by having the individual respond to self-report scales containing questions about how he or she generally feels (e.g., I feel happy "hardly ever, sometimes, or often"). Measures of state anxiety (indicated as A-State) are designed to indicate a person's anxiety as he or she reacts to specific situational stimuli. A frequently used measure of anxiety is the State-Trait Anxiety Inventory for Children (STAIC) developed by Spielberger et al. (1972). Scores on both the State and Trait subscales of the STAIC range from 20 to 60, with higher scores representing greater anxiety. Using the STAIC, Craig and Hancock (1996) found no significant differences between 96 (untreated) children who stuttered and 104 children who did not stutter (age range = 9–14 years). This was the case for both State and Trait subscales. In addition, the authors found no significant association between stuttering frequency and state anxiety. Likewise, Yairi and Ambrose (2005), using the Revised Children's Manifest Anxiety Scale (RCMAS; Reynolds & Richmond, 1994), found no clear indications of higher anxiety on any of the subscales during the early stages of stuttering, but did note that anxiety tends to increase with time.

In a meta-analysis of studies that investigated anxiety in children and adolescents who stutter, Bernard et al. (2022) examined 11 cohort studies and found that some children presented with increased anxiety symptoms, and that this was true for even preschool-age children. These authors did, however, state that they could not determine if the elevated anxiety symptoms are associated with state or trait anxiety. They suggested longitudinal studies with children and adolescents who stutter to investigate how anxiety symptoms might develop over time.

Temperament and Reactive Characteristics of Children Who Stutter

It was common in the early and middle years of the 20th century to attribute the onset of stuttering to personality characteristics and unconscious conflicts over unsatisfied needs or neurotic parental personalities (see Chapter 3). However, few studies have supported the notion that children who stuttered, or their parents, displayed basic emotional maladjustments. More current models of stuttering onset and development (Conture, 2001; Riley & Riley, 2000; Smith & Kelly, 1997), as well as several investigations into the temperamental characteristics of children who stutter (Anderson et al., 2003; Embrechts et al., 2000; Ezrati-Vinacour et al., 2001; Glasner, 1949; Vanryckeghem & Brutten, 1997; Wakaba, 1998), indicate that many children who stutter might be more sensitive, inhibited, and reactive than their nonstuttering peers. As discussed briefly in Chapter 2, there is convincing research indicating that some children are more likely than others to be upset by changes in routine or inhibited with strangers (Calkins & Fox, 1994; Kagan et al., 1987). Yairi and Ambrose (2005) suggested that such personality and temperamental factors could play a role in determining speech fluency for some subtypes of individuals who stutter. They concluded that it is difficult to determine if the relationships of these perceived characteristics of young children who stutter are the result of inherent biological and personality characteristics, a consequence of early self-awareness of stuttering, or an interaction of several influences. The following studies, generally with younger participants, attempted to understand these relationships.

Temperament has to do with how an individual reacts and interacts with his or her environment in terms of flexibility, persistence, and approach behavior. Some children are more reactive and less adaptive and therefore likely to be sensitive to and distracted by environmental stimuli. They are less likely than other children to stay on task until completion. These children also tend to have lower levels of emotional regulation and are more likely to react negatively to changes in their environment. Several studies have found that children with these characteristics are more likely to be at risk for the onset of stuttering (e.g., Conture, 2001; Eggers et al., 2010; Riley & Riley, 1979, 2000; Smith & Kelly, 1997; Starkweather & Gottwald, 1990; Zebrowski & Conture, 1998).

Research by Conture and colleagues resulted in the creation of a communication-emotional model, the Dual Diathesis-Stressor Model (Conture et al., 2006; Walden et al., 2012). The model focuses on several characteristics of children that could help account for the onset of stuttering. The model proposes that children who stutter experience difficulty associated with the many skills required for speech planning and production including disassociations among the components of speech-language planning (e.g., Byrd, Vallely, et al., 2012; Melnick et al., 2003). Beyond having a vulnerable speech-planning and production system, and as a result of endogenous neural structures responsible for emotional reactions and emotional regulation, some of these children might be predisposed to experience greater levels of emotional reactivity in response to environmental (exogenous) stressors. Consequently, some children have greater difficulty regulating their emotional reactivity resulting in a diathesis—an unusual vulnerability or disposition of the body to respond to an external stressor that is characteristic (endogenous) for some individuals. Rocha et al. (2019) examined temperament dimensions, executive functioning ability, and anxiety levels in school-age children who stutter and their nonstuttering peers. Participants were 100 Portuguese children 7 to 12 years old, including 50 children who stutter and 50 children who do not stutter.

Temperament was measured through the parent report questionnaire, the Temperament in Middle Childhood Questionnaire (TMCQ). Executive functioning was evaluated through children's responses on the Children's Color Trails Test (CCTT), and anxiety level was assessed through the Multidimensional Scale for Children (MASC). Rocha et al. reported that older children who stutter exhibited significantly higher scores on the Anger/Frustration, Impulsivity, and Sadness subscales of the TMCQ, and lower averages on the Attention/Focusing, Perceptual Sensitivity, and Soothability/Falling Reactivity subscales. On the executive functioning task, the younger children who stutter exhibited significantly higher average execution times than their nonstuttering peers. These authors also noted that there were no statistically significant differences in anxiety between children who stutter and children who do not stutter, and no statistically significant correlations between temperament factors and measures of executive functioning. Overall, this study suggests that children who stutter might experience lower ability to orient attention and greater emotional reactivity compared with their nonstuttering peers, and it also provides support for a multidimensional view of stuttering.

Several studies of the temperamental characteristics of children who stutter made use of parent reports of their children's temperamental characteristics resulting in contradictory results. For example, Lewis and Goldberg (1997) found that CWS were more adaptable and less negative in their emotions. In an effort to provide greater accuracy in determining levels of reactivity for children who stutter, Arnold et al. (2011) studied nine preschool CWS and a control group of nine children who were fluent. Rather than relying on parent report, electroencephalograms (EEGs) indicating emotional reactivity and regulation were recorded as children listened to conversations that conveyed happy, neutral, and angry emotions. The results indicated that deceased use of emotional regulation strategies by the CWS was associated with increased stuttering. The authors proposed that, given a vulnerable speech planning and production system, the division of attentional resources needed to efficiently plan and produce speech and use regulatory strategies to decrease the emotion associated with this activity might be a problem for CWS. The problems associated with concurrently attending to these two ongoing processes could contribute to the challenges for CWS in maintaining fluent speech-language planning and production.

Noting that most studies of children's temperament have used clinical populations already in treatment, Kefalianos et al. (2014) used a prospective, longitudinal design to see when temperament differences emerge for young children who eventually begin to stutter and whether temperamental differences were accompanied by precursors of anxiety. Results support the possibility that differences in temperament, at least for somewhat older children who stutter, are a consequence of rather than a cause of stuttering. The authors interpreted the results to indicate that temperament is not necessarily associated with the onset of stuttering at least during ages 2 to 4. They did suggest that preschool children who stutter who are seen in clinical settings might have different temperamental characteristics.

Because speech production has been shown to increase autonomic arousal in adults, Arnold et al. (2014) attempted to determine the extent to which autonomic arousal would occur with speech and nonspeech tasks for children as well as adults. Results indicated that autonomic arousal was significantly higher for speech than the nonspeech tasks. The children had significantly greater arousal than adults on blood pressure variability (BPV) for nonspeech and similar arousal levels for speech tasks. Although there was no difference in arousal by gender for the adults for speech and nonspeech tasks, autonomic arousal remained high for the school-age boys when completing the second, more open-ended speaking task compared to the first simple sentence task. The school-age girls and young adults demonstrated lower autonomic arousal for the second, more demanding open-ended speech task. The authors concluded that the speech tasks promoted higher levels of autonomic arousal than nonspeech tasks and that children demonstrate greater autonomic arousal for nonspeech oral motor tasks than adults. The finding of greater levels of arousal for boys might relate to their increased likelihood of developing speech-language disorders such as specific language impairment and persistent child-onset stuttering. The authors cited studies suggesting that because girls seek out more opportunities to talk with others, they tend to have more experience with speech-language tasks. As a result, they might have demonstrated lower arousal to the successive speech tasks presented in the study due to this increased exposure in daily life. Boys, on the other hand, might have or seek out fewer opportunities to use their speech-language skills in daily life and could have less familiarity and comfort with a range of speech-language tasks.

Choi et al. (2016) investigated the emotional reactivity of 47 children (36 boys, 11 girls) who stuttered (mean age =

50.69 months). The results indicated an association between young children's positive emotional reactivity and stuttering, with negative reactivity seemingly more associated with the children's stuttering positive emotional stress (lesser degrees of emotional regulation). The results support the concept that emotional processes are associated with stuttering, at least for positive emotional reactivity.

Participation of the Parents in Assessment

In the sections of this book where we discuss the significance of counseling (Chapter 8) and the treatment of young children (Chapter 11), the importance of parent participation in the therapeutic process is emphasized. Unfortunately, in some cases parent involvement during assessment and especially treatment will be nonexistent. The motivation for initiating treatment could be minimal if the family physician or friends and family members suggest that the problem will likely go away by itself (Ramig, 1993b). In contrast to Rustin (1987; Rustin & Cook, 1995), who was reluctant to recommend treatment without parent involvement, Ramig

contended that even in cases where parents cannot or will not become involved in treatment, the clinician should enroll the child. In our experience, although some children might benefit from increased understanding about the nature of their problem and practice with basic therapeutic techniques, real long-term changes are less likely to occur without the involvement of at least one dedicated parent.

Rustin and Cook (1995) provided several questions the clinician can use to discover the nature of the family and of parent–child interaction. Although the questions themselves are important, the most important facet of the interview process is the clinician's style and ability to be flexible and creative as he or she interacts with the parents. As Caruso (1988) described, the intent is to follow the parents' lead, all the while probing for areas of interest and concern. As Rustin and Cook (1995) indicate,

> In the interview, we learn about the rules and regulations in the child's life, the parents' attitudes toward child rearing, pertinent issues within the parental relationship, the problem-solving strategies employed, and the place the disfluency problem holds

SPEECH AND NONSPEECH CHARACTERISTICS OF CHILDREN WHO STUTTER

- Occurrence of stuttering in nuclear or extended family
- Parents identify child as stuttering
- Weighted SLD score of 4 or greater
- SLDs increase when communicating under pressure
- SLDs accompanied by tense movements of head, face, and neck
- Behavioral or formal indicators of negative psychosocial reactions to stuttering
- Child self-restricts communication and social interaction
- Child might be easily upset by changes in routine or be inhibited with strangers

within the family. The interview is structured in such a way that the basic and non-contentious case details are gathered in the early stages of the process, with a gradual move toward more sensitive and emotional material as it progresses. (p. 129)

DECISION 2: DETERMINING THE COURSE OF STUTTERING

Once it is determined that a young speaker's fluency breaks are SLDs, the next clinical decision is whether this pattern is likely to continue and develop into a chronic problem. As Yairi and Ambrose (2005) commented, "as stuttering continues, the difficulty lies not in correct diagnosis of stuttering, but in correct diagnosis of its recovery" (p. 139). Although the nature of the fluency breaks (particularly SLDs) is important to consider, there are several factors that appear to influence whether the child is likely to continue stuttering.

The clinician will also need to consider a related decision about the extent and nature of the intervention that might be appropriate for the child and his or her family. This will involve factoring in the history of stuttering in the child's family, the response of the child to his or her speech problem, and the willingness of the parents to support and become actively involved in the therapeutic process. Because of the large proportion of children in whom stuttering will likely subside, the reasonably good probability that treatment will be successful with young children, and the likelihood that treatment will be more demanding for adolescents and adults, the issue has been hotly debated (Curlee & Yairi, 1997). Although the decision is a difficult one, an informed and wise decision at this point is critical.

The longitudinal data of Yairi and Ambrose (2005) indicate that there is no one factor that can be used to predict the course of stuttering and that the best we can do is determine those factors that are most likely to *suggest* the chances of recovery or persistence. However, there are several trends that have obvious clinical utility and allow the clinician to make informed predictions. Yairi and Ambrose (2005) indicated that a strong family history is one of the most reliable predictors of persistence. As described in Chapter 3, although we are currently uncertain about what is being transmitted, there appears to be a strong genetic component for both recovery and persistence of stuttering. Children who come from families where one or more family members stutter are less likely to recover; where stuttering has persisted for family members, the child is more likely to follow the same pattern. Although the outcome is far from certain, the majority of the time children are more likely to recover if the family member who has stuttered has recovered.

Gender is also a relatively strong indicator of the course of stuttering in that females are more likely to recover, and males are more likely to continue stuttering once they begin. Based on their longitudinal research over many years, Yairi and Ambrose (2005, p. 298) provided incidence figures indicating that for a boy, the risk of persistent stuttering is 1.5% and the risk of recovered stuttering is 5.3%, with a total risk of 6.8%. For a girl, the risk of persistent stuttering is 0.5% and the risk of recovered stuttering is 2.7% with a total risk of 3.2%. In addition, Yairi and Ambrose pointed out that recovery is more likely to take place sooner for girls than for boys. Whereas girls are more likely to recover within a year after the onset of stuttering, boys could take several years to recover. For girls, a pattern of stuttering for 12 months without improvement suggests the possibility of chronicity. Furthermore, those children who recovered early and maintained fluency for at least 12 months did not relapse.

Another trend that appears to be strongly predictive of recovery or persistence is the pattern of SLDs during the first year following onset (Figure 5–1). In contrast to the more traditional view of gradually increasing stuttering severity described at the outset of this chapter, in the majority of early childhood cases, stuttering starts out being readily obvious and after continuing for several weeks or months, gradually decreases. Yairi and Ambrose (2005) suggested that although a child might continue to stutter for several months, a downward pattern in the number of SLDs during the first year is a strong sign of eventual recovery. Particularly for children who are going to recover,

the frequency of SLDs and overall severity of stuttering is likely to decrease during the first 6 months following onset and nearly always begins to subside by the end of the first year. Although the overall level of severity at the outset is unrelated to whether the young child will persist or recover from stuttering, Yairi and Ambrose indicated that continued severity is a primary indication for concern. That is, when children continue to maintain a stable or escalating level of SLDs during the first year following onset, persistence of stuttering is more likely. That is, a stable or inclining pattern of SLDs is indicative of persistent stuttering.

In a related issue, for many children, the ratings of SLDs and stuttering severity by both the parents and clinicians also begin to decrease during the first year following onset. These findings indicate that parental judgment of their child's speech difficulty should be considered a funda-

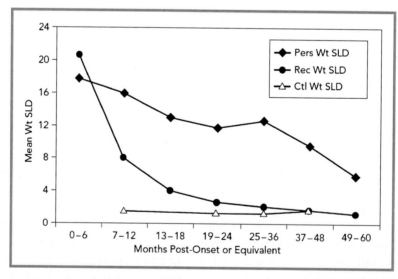

FIGURE 5–1. Mean weighted (Wt) stuttering-like disfluency (SLD) for persistent (Pers), recovered (Rec), and control (Ctl) groups over time. (From *Early Childhood Stuttering* (p. 177), by E. Yairi and N. G. Ambrose, 2005, Austin, TX: Pro-Ed. Copyright 2005 by Pro-Ed, Inc. Reprinted with permission.)

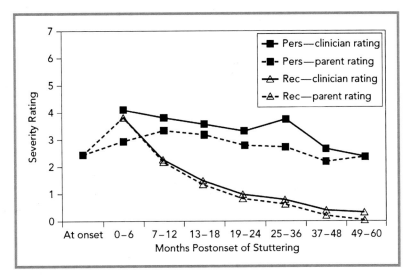

FIGURE 5–2. Mean parent and clinician severity ratings for persistent (Pers) and recovered (Rec) children over time. (From *Early Childhood Stuttering* (p. 184), by E. Yairi and N. G. Ambrose, 2005, Austin, TX: Pro-Ed. Copyright 2005 by Pro-Ed, Inc. Reprinted with permission.)

mental part of a diagnosis of stuttering (Conture & Caruso, 1987; Onslow, 1992; Riley & Riley, 1983) for, as presented in Figure 5–2, parental and clinician ratings tend to coincide (Yairi & Ambrose, 2005).

Yairi and Ambrose (2005) also noted that longer strings (iterations) of part-word repetitions (more than three but often much longer) were found to indicate persistence of stuttering. Conversely, recovery was indicated by a gradual decrease in the number of repetitions. In contrast to some suggestions in the literature, Yairi and Ambrose did not find the duration of individual stuttering events to be predictive of persistent stuttering. In fact, children who recovered showed an *increase* in the silent intervals between repetition units such that the resulting iterations were slower in tempo. Yairi and Ambrose interpreted this as a normalization process that clinicians can perceptually distinguish without the use of sophis-

ticated measuring equipment. Finally, Yairi and Ambrose found that although at the outset of stuttering there were no differences in the occurrences of head and facial movements for children who recovered or were persistent, a decline in secondary characteristics was predictive of recovery.

Yairi and Ambrose (2005) also reported a tendency for children who begin stuttering somewhat later (35 months rather than the typical onset of 33 months) to persist in stuttering. This factor might interact with the possibility that somewhat older children are more likely to be aware of the stuttering closer to the time of onset and might react to the unfavorable responses of others as they experience the effects of socialization during the early preschool years. A related factor is the duration of the child's stuttering following onset. As indicated earlier, Yairi and Ambrose found that a history of stuttering lasting beyond 1 year indicates the likelihood of persistence, particularly for females. Nevertheless, natural recovery can occur 3 years following onset, with some children taking as long as 4 years to recover. Given that the most common age of onset is 33 months (2 years, 9 months), the data from Yairi and Ambrose indicate that some children are still likely to recover through 6 or 7 years of age. Although, as we have seen, awareness by the child as well as negative affective reactions can occur shortly following onset, the older the child and the longer he or she experiences the frustration and communicative effort associated with stuttering, the more affective and cognitive coping responses will come into play.

It is important to note that expressive language skills are *not* predictive of recovery and, as indicated earlier, Yairi and Ambrose (2005) found that both persistent and recovered groups of CWS display expressive language ability at or above normative expectations. These findings are similar to those of Kloth et al. (1999), who, in a prospective study, found that children at risk for stuttering (as indicated by a parental history of stuttering) and who subsequently stuttered or were fluent followed the same patterns of articulatory rate and linguistic development. Yairi and Ambrose pointed out, however, that most language measures are general and suggested that a more detailed analysis of language skills might help to predict chronicity. Yairi and Ambrose (2005) suggested that their results provide initial empirical validation for the idea that "Many young children who begin stuttering seem to have language abilities that exceed their capabilities for fluent production of speech" (p. 251). However, these findings do not support reducing the child's language stimulation or suggest that adults simplify their language

when working with children who stutter (Bonelli et al., 2000). As mentioned previously, although at the outset of stuttering children who continue to stutter tend to be slower in phonological development, phonological skills alone are insufficient to predict the course of stuttering.

However, Ambrose et al. (2015) found unexpected results regarding the language–stuttering connection. The authors conducted a 5-year longitudinal study designed to determine patterns that coincided with persistence or recovery of young children (2–4 years old) who stutter. The 58 CWS were compared to a control group of 40 age- and gender-matched normally fluent children. Children in four Midwest sites were evaluated in four domains: epidemiology, motor, language, and temperament. Children were seen for seven visits over a period of 5 years. The initial visit occurred within 1 year of stuttering onset followed by visits at 6 months, 1 year, 18 months, 2 years, 3 years, and 4 years later. The study concluded with the children classified as persistent or recovered. The results indicated that the children in the persistent group achieved lower scores than those in the recovered group and the control groups on standardized language tests and in phonological accuracy. The persistent group also showed greater kinematic variability and were identified by their parents as being more negative in temperament.

Yairi and Ambrose did not design their longitudinal studies to directly consider the predictive value of concomitant learning and language-speech problems often present in children who stutter. However, they did agree with others that the presence of other problems is likely to degrade a child's ability to communicate, decreasing the possibility of remission. This could be an important consideration given that Blood and Seider (1981) found that 68% of 1,060 children being treated for stuttering in elementary schools had other speech, language, hearing, or learning problems, with speech sound disorders the most often reported. How these other communication problems might influence the possibility of natural remission, the likelihood of successful treatment, and the possibility of relapse following treatment is unclear.

One possibility for this type of interaction of speech and language domains is suggested by two investigations of the same children by Watkins et al. (1999) and Paden et al. (1999). Watkins et al. (1999) conducted an extensive evaluation of the expressive language abilities of 84 preschool children close to the onset of their stuttering. Both the children who recovered from stuttering ($n = 62$) and the children who persisted in stuttering ($n = 22$) were found to have similar expressive language abilities. Overall, and regardless of whether or not the children recovered, language abilities were near or above normative expectations. However, the extent of the children's language abilities varied according to age. Advanced language abilities were especially the case for those children who experienced an early onset of stuttering and therefore entered the study in the youngest age group (2–3 years old). These children were found to consistently demonstrate language skills that were well above age expectations, often meeting expectations for children a full year older. This was true for these younger children whether they recovered or not.

The children who experienced a later onset of stuttering and entered the study at 4 to 5 years of age and persisted in stuttering tended to show language skills that were slightly (but not significantly) below their peers of the same age who recovered. This finding, along with the results of the investigation of the same children by Paden et al. (1999) indicated that, regardless of age, all of the children who persisted in stuttering also scored lower on virtually every measure of phonological ability than the children who would recover. This combination of results led Watkins et al. (1999) to suggest, as Ratner (1997) had previously done, the possibility of an asynchronous or out-of-phase pattern of development, particularly for children who start to stutter prior to age 3. Based on the combined results of the investigations, Watkins et al. (1999) suggested the possibility of "developmental tradeoffs operating such that advanced proficiency in one domain requires sacrifice of performance in another domain" (p. 1133). The results of investigations by Watkins et al. (1999) and Paden et al. (1999) suggest a combination of language and phonological variables that could inform the possibility of stuttering onset and remission. That is, although precocious language might be a risk factor for stuttering for children with early onset, these children are also more likely to recover than children with somewhat later onset (and more age-appropriate language skills). The presence of a phonology–language gap, however, could suggest the possibility of stuttering chronicity.

Table 5–2 summarizes the indicators of remission (green flags) and persistence (red flags) based largely on the work of Yairi and Ambrose (2005). Indicators are listed in the probable order of their predictive ability.

Despite the valuable longitudinal information provided by Yairi and Ambrose as well as others, predicting the course of stuttering for young children is far from certain. Clinicians will want to develop and communicate to parents the possible indicators of remission and persistence discussed in this section and their philosophy concerning intervention.

Given the high recovery rate of stuttering for young children, therapy might simply facilitate what could be a natural process of recovery. Nonetheless, the clinician will want to consider the concern of parents as well as the child's struggle to speak. The experience can be a painful one for the parents and other members of the extended family. The child might indicate obvious frustration in his or her efforts to communicate, sometimes refusing to speak at all. Even without the presence of some or many of the red flags indicated in Table 5–2, a brief period of therapy might be a reasonable choice, particularly if this is the desire of the parents.

Recently, new studies are adding to our understanding of the multidimensional nature of stuttering and how that impacts our ability to determine if children who stutter will recover or if the stuttering will persist and be a lifelong issue. Walsh et al. (2021) conducted a longitudinal study to investigate how epidemiological and clinical factors collectively predict persistence of or recovery from stuttering. They collected epidemiological and clinical measures from 52 preschoolers diagnosed as stuttering and followed those children for more than 3 years to document whether they eventually recovered or persisted in stuttering. They used risk

TABLE 5–2. Indicators of Recovery From (Green Flags) and Persistent (Red Flags) Stuttering Based on Yairi and Ambrose (2005) and Others

Indicators of Remission—Green Flags	Indicators of Persistence—Red Flags
No relatives who stutter	Family history of persistent stuttering
Relatives who stuttered and recovered	Relatives continue to stutter
Female	Male
Decreasing pattern of SLDs within 1 year of onset	Stable or increasing number of SLDs within 1 year of onset
Decreasing severity ratings by clinicians and parents	Stable or increasing severity ratings by clinicians and parents
Child stuttering is within 1 year of onset	Child is stuttering more than 1 year following onset (especially females)
Decreasing secondary movements (e.g., head and eye movements)	Stable or increasing occurrence of secondary movements
Few repetitions	Many (>3) part-word repetitions
Slower rate of repetitions	Rapid rate of repetitions
Few reactions to stuttering by the child	Strong reactions to stuttering by the child
No concomitant learning or communication problems	Concomitant learning or communication problems
Onset of stuttering at ages 2–3	Later onset of stuttering at ages 3–4
No delays in phonological development	Delays in phonological development

CLINICAL DECISION MAKING

A telephone call or e-mail contact from a parent who is concerned about the onset of stuttering behavior in their child is a common occurrence for the clinician specializing in fluency disorders. Although the factors and trends described in this chapter are always considered, some period of informed observation is usually a reasonable course of action. The following two e-mail messages from a concerned mother provide a common example.

To begin with, the comments are especially interesting because the mother was a speech-language pathologist. Although she had relatively little experience with childhood fluency problems, she was able to provide an informed description about other related characteristics of her son's speech and language. Following the first e-mail message, I suggested that the mother obtain video examples of her son's fluency in a variety of speaking situations. I also assured her that, particularly with her experience, she was unlikely to complicate the problem as long as she (and her husband) responded in a natural way typical for any situation where their child was having a problem and was frustrated. As is often the case, the parents were extremely appreciative of the information and support and expressed a great decrease in their anxiety about the situation.

The first message received during the first week of November:

Alan is 2.5 years old, and his brother is 10 months old. He has had what I considered "normal disfluencies" for the past 3 to 4 months or so. It was not something I was concerned about. His language skills are very good, and I attributed the disfluencies to rapidly emerging language. Around 2 to 3 weeks ago, the stuttering really began to increase, both in number of occurrences and in severity. Within the past week it has become very concerning, not only to myself, but to other family members and his preschool teachers. Where he typically might repeat some initial sounds 3 to 4 times, he is now repeating up to 20 times, and now there are secondary behaviors—eye closing, grimacing. The prolongations are longer. A few times in the last few days he has sighed and just given up trying to get the message out. At these times when his awareness and frustration were evident, I acknowledged that "your words seem to be getting a little stuck" and offered reassurance that everyone has trouble with this from time to time. This did seem to make him feel better. The disfluency is worse in the first hour or so he is awake, and again at the end of the day, so fatigue does seem to be a factor. But it happens throughout the day, too. It happens not only when he is trying to express something a little more complicated or abstract (as was the case for the past few months) but also on very simple, straightforward messages. We have had nothing out of the ordinary happening at home. I cannot think of any new stressor. We are modeling slow speech and trying to make communication as well as other activities as unhurried as possible. We make eye contact when he gets really stuck, and try not to show any distress. My ultra laid back husband is worried . . . "It's getting worse

continues

each day!" His language and articulation are good. My father had a first cousin who "stuttered badly" but was "cured when he joined the army" and presumably had therapy for the first time (otherwise no family history).

The second message was received the second week of December:

Hi! I was just thinking this week that I wanted to e-mail you. We never got Alan's disfluencies recorded because they abruptly stopped! I don't know what happened, but we are so thankful that he is having an easier time talking! I know he may start having difficulty again, and if he does I will get back in touch with you. For now, though, things are going really well.

Thanks again for your help, enjoy your Holidays! [We never heard from the mother again.]

(WM)

factors found to be significantly associated with stuttering persistence to build single- and multiple-variable predictive statistical models and assessed each model's prediction capabilities by how accurately the model predicted a child's stuttering outcome. Results indicated that the following factors were significantly associated with an increased probability of persistence of stuttering: (a) a positive family history of stuttering, (b) poorer performance on a standardized articulation and phonological assessment, (c) higher frequency of SLDs during spontaneous speech, and (d) lower accuracy on a language (nonword repetition) task. They also found that the interaction between family history of stuttering and nonword repetition performance was also significant. Curiously, Walsh et al. did not find a relationship between sex and stuttering outcome (a common predictive factor cited in the literature) but did note that they had far fewer females in the study, including only four in the persistent group, giving them insufficient power to detect potential differences. In conclusion, Walsh

et al. proposed that using the full multiple regression model incorporating all the risk factors provides the best fitting model with the highest predictive accuracy and lowest error rate. They pointed out that these findings support the multifactorial dynamic pathways (MDP) theory of stuttering (Smith & Weber, 2017) that proposes that complex, nonlinear interactions among multiple factors contribute to the development of stuttering (see Chapter 3).

Similarly, Singer et al. (2022) set out to explore how well a cumulative risk approach, based on empirically supported predictive factors, predicts whether a young child who stutters is likely to develop persistent developmental stuttering. They used extant data on 67 3- to 5-year-old children who stutter (44 persisting, 23 recovered) from two longitudinal studies to identify cutoff values for continuous predictive factors and binary predictors. The optimal combination of predictive factors and the odds of a child developing persistent stuttering based on an increasing number of factors were calculated. Results indicated that the predictive factor model that yielded the best predictive validity was based on four factors: (a) time since onset (≥19 months), (b) speech sound skills (≤115 standard score), (c) expressive language skills (≤10 standard score), and (d) stuttering severity (≥17 SSI total score). When the presence of at least two of these predictive factors was used to confer elevated risk to develop persistent stuttering, the model identified that a child would have persistent stuttering with 93% accuracy (sensitivity) and was 65% accurate at predicting that a child would recover (specificity). As a child presented with a greater number of the four identified risk factors, the odds for persistent stuttering increased. The authors developed a screening tool based on their findings (see Figure 5–3) that could help speech-language pathologists evaluate a child's prognosis (if the child is similar to the children included in the study). To determine how many predictive factors indicate persistence, clinicians

need to assess the child's skills in the three factors identified in the author's model (i.e., speech sound accuracy, stuttering severity, and expressive language) and obtain the child's time since onset. Children who present with at least two factors indicating persistence are at greater risk for developing persistent stuttering.

CONSENSUS GUIDELINES FOR ASSESSMENT OF PRESCHOOL AND SCHOOL-AGE CHILDREN

In Chapter 4, we described the six core areas that Brundage et al. (2021) determined were components of a comprehensive stuttering evaluation. In the appendixes of their article, these authors provided examples of specific assessment tools or procedures that they use to assess each area. The appendixes for preschool children (Table 5–3) and school-age children (Table 5–4) are reproduced here (with

TABLE 5–3 Commonly Recommended Procedures and Sample Data That May Be Collected as Part of a Comprehensive Stuttering Assessment for Young Children

Early Childhood Stuttering Assessment (ages 2–6 years)
Evaluation Procedures
Case history forms for the caregivers, including parents, teachers, and other family members, as appropriate
Interviews with the child and caregivers
Observation of caregiver–child interaction
Observation of the child's speech in various speaking situations
Screening and testing, as needed, of the child's language, speech, temperament, hearing, and related abilities
Observation and testing of the child's speech fluency and stuttering behavior, reactions to stuttering, and impact of stuttering
Risk factor analysis (examining data from various aspects of the assessment to hypothesize about child's risk for continuing to stutter; Singer et al., 2020)

continues

TABLE 5–3. *continued*

Sample Data for Area 1: Stuttering-related background information
Caregivers' view of the problem in general and main concerns
Caregivers' report of concomitant concerns and other diagnoses
Caregivers' report about the development of stuttering, including family history of persistence and recovery, time since onset and developmental course, and other speech or language issues
Caregivers' perceptions of prior therapy for stuttering or other concerns
Caregivers' knowledge and experiences related to stuttering, including beliefs about causal, eliciting, and reinforcing factors for stuttering (e.g., Palin Parent Rating Scales [Palin PRS; Millard, & Davis, 2016])
Caregivers' goals for stuttering treatment (e.g., Solution-Focused Brief Therapy [SBFT] scaling; Nicholas, 2015)
Child's perceptions and current knowledge about stuttering
Child's readiness for change and goals for treatment (e.g., SBFT scaling)
Assessment and progress reports from prior treatment, if applicable
Sample data for Area 2: Speech, language, temperament, and related background information
Caregivers' views about the child's development, including cognitive and social-emotional development, behavior, self-regulation abilities, perfectionistic tendencies, and coping skills
Clinician's observations of the child's communication and related skills
Scores on screenings and tests, as needed, of child's language development, speech sound production skills, and temperament (e.g., Child Behavior Checklist [CBCL; Achenbach & Rescoria, 2000], Child Behavior Questionnaire [CBQ; Rothbart et al., 2001])
Scores on screenings and tests of related factors, including anxiety (e.g., Spence Children's Anxiety Scale; Spence, 1998), as appropriate
Sample Data for Area 3: Speech fluency and stuttering behavior
Caregivers' observations and perceptions of fluency and stuttering, including types of disfluencies, physical tension, secondary characteristics, and severity (e.g., Palin PRS, Severity Ratings [SR]; Yairi & Ambrose, 2005)
Caregivers' observations and perceptions of and factors that affect fluency and stuttering in various speaking situations
Child's perceptions and self-ratings of speech, fluency, and stuttering, including types of disfluencies, physical tension, secondary characteristics, and severity, in various speaking situations, as possible based on child's cognitive development
Clinician's data on speech, fluency, and stuttering (e.g., frequency/percent of syllables stuttered [%SS or words stuttered, %WS], type, duration, and severity [e.g.., SEV; O'Brian et al., 2004] of disfluencies; physical tension; speaking rate; naturalness [Martin & Haroldson, 1992]; other speech characteristics) in different situations
Scores on tests and measures of speech fluency and stuttering (e.g., Stuttering Severity Instrument [SSI; Riley, 2009], Test of Childhood Stuttering [TOCS; Gillam et al., 2009])

TABLE 5-3. *continued*

Sample data for Area 4: Child's reactions to stuttering
Caregiver's observations of child's affective, behavioral, and cognitive reactions to stuttering (e.g., embarrassment, anxiety, shame, fear, avoidance, word substitution)
Child's report of reactions to stuttering and coping responses
Scores on tests of child's reactions to stuttering and attitudes about communication (e.g., KiddyCAT; Vanryckeghem & Brutten, 2007)

Sample data for Area 5: Reactions to stuttering within the environment
Caregivers' reactions to stuttering, degree of concern about stuttering, satisfaction with the child's communication, perceptions of how stuttering impacts the caregivers and family (e.g., Palin PRS)
Caregivers' observations of the reactions of others, including peers and family members

Sample data for Area 6: Adverse impact associated with stuttering
Caregivers' perceptions of whether and how much stuttering affects the child's willingness or ability to speak, participation in social and educational activities, and quality of life (e.g., Palin PRS)
Child's perceptions of whether and how much stuttering affects willingness or ability to speak, participation in social and educational activities, and quality of life

Source: Reprinted with permission from Brundage, B. S., Bernstein Ratner, N., Boyle, M. P., Eggers, K., Everard, R., Franken, M.-C., Kefalianos, E., Marcotte, A. K., Millard, S., Packman, A., Vanryckeghem, M., & Yaruss, J. S. (2021). Consensus guidelines for the assessments of individuals who stutter across the lifespan. *American Journal of Speech-Language Pathology, 30*(6), 2379-2393. https://doi.org/10.1044/2021_AJSLP-21-00107

TABLE 5-4. Commonly Recommended Procedures and Sample Data That May Be Collected as Part of a Comprehensive Stuttering Assessment for School-Age Children

School-Age Stuttering Assessment (ages 6–12 years)
Evaluation Procedures
Case history forms for the child and caregivers, including parents, teachers, and other family members, as appropriate
Interviews with the child and caregivers
Observation of caregiver–child interaction
Observation of the child's speech in various speaking situations
Screening and testing, as needed, of the child's language, speech, temperament, hearing, and related abilities
Observation and testing of the child's speech fluency and stuttering behavior, reactions to stuttering, and impact of stuttering

continues

TABLE 5–4. *continued*

Sample data for Area 1: Stuttering-related background information
Caregivers' view of the problem in general and main concerns
Caregivers' report of concomitant concerns and other diagnoses
Caregivers' report about the development of stuttering, including family history of persistence and recovery, time since onset and developmental course, and other speech or language issues
Caregivers' perceptions of prior therapy for stuttering or other concerns
Caregivers' knowledge and experiences related to stuttering, including beliefs about causal, eliciting, and reinforcing factors for stuttering (e.g., Palin Parent Rating Scales [Palin PRS; Millard & Davis, 2016)
Caregivers' goals for stuttering treatment (e.g., Solution-Focused Brief Therapy [SBFT] scaling; Nicholas, 2015)
Child's perceptions and current knowledge about stuttering
Child's perceptions of prior therapy for stuttering or other concerns
Child's level of concern, readiness for change, and goals for treatment (e.g., SBFT scaling)
Assessment and progress reports from prior treatment, if applicable
Sample data for Area 2: Speech, language, temperament, and related background information
Caregivers' views about the child's development, including cognitive and social-emotional development, behavior, self-regulation abilities, perfectionistic tendencies, and coping skills
Clinician's observations of the child's communication and related skills
Scores on screenings and tests, as needed, of child's language development, speech motor skills, speech sound production skills, and temperament (e.g., Child Behavior Checklist [CBCL; Achenbach & Rescoria, 2000]
Scores on screenings and tests of related factors, including anxiety (e.g., Spence Children's Anxiety Scale; Spence, 1998), as appropriate
Sample Data for Area 3: Speech fluency and stuttering behavior
Caregivers' observations and perceptions of fluency and stuttering, including types of disfluencies, physical tension, secondary characteristics, and severity (e.g., Palin PRS; Millard & Davis, 2016)
Caregivers' observations and perceptions of and factors that affect fluency and stuttering in various speaking situations
Child's perceptions and self-ratings of speech, fluency, and stuttering, including types of disfluencies, physical tension, secondary characteristics, and severity, in various speaking situations
Clinician's data on speech, fluency, and stuttering (e.g., frequency/percent of syllables stuttered [%SS], type, duration, and severity [e.g.., SEV; O'Brian et al., 2004] of disfluencies; physical tension; speaking rate; naturalness [Martin & Haroldson, 1992]; other speech characteristics) in different situations
Scores on tests and measures of speech fluency and stuttering (e.g., Speech Situation Checklist-Speech Disruption [SSC-SD; Brutten & Vanryckeghem, 2007], Stuttering Severity Instrument [SSI; Riley, 2009], Test of Childhood Stuttering [TOCS; Gillam et al., 2009])

TABLE 5–4. *continued*

Sample data for Area 4: Child's reactions to stuttering
Caregiver's observations of child's affective, behavioral, and cognitive reactions to stuttering (e.g., embarrassment, anxiety, shame, fear, avoidance, word substitution)
Child's report of reactions to stuttering and coping responses
Child's use of speech and stuttering management strategies
Scores on tests of child's reactions to stuttering and attitudes about communication (e.g., Behavior Checklist [BCL; Brutten & Vanryckeghem, 2007], Communication Attitudes Test [CAT; Brutten & Vanryckeghem, 2007], Speech Situation Checklist-Emotional Response [SSC-ER; Brutten & Vanryckeghem, 2007], Overall Assessment of the Speaker's Experience of Stuttering-School-Age [OASES-S; Yaruss & Quesal, 2016]
Sample data for Area 5: Reactions to stuttering within the environment
Caregivers' reactions to stuttering, degree of concern about stuttering, satisfaction with the child's communication, perceptions of how stuttering impacts the caregivers and family (e.g., Palin PRS)
Caregivers' observations of the reactions of others, including peers and family members
Child's perception of the reactions of others (e.g., experience of bullying)
Sample data for Area 6: Adverse impact associated with stuttering
Caregivers' perceptions of whether and how much stuttering affects the child's willingness or ability to speak, participation in social and educational activities, and quality of life (e.g., Palin PRS)
Child's perceptions of whether and how much stuttering affects willingness or ability to speak, participation in social and educational activities, and quality of life
Scores on tests of adverse impact and quality of life (e.g., BCL, OASES-S)

Source: Reprinted with permission from Brundage, B. S., Bernstein Ratner, N., Boyle, M. P., Eggers, K., Everard, R., Franken, M.-C., Kefalianos, E., Marcotte, A. K., Millard, S., Packman, A., Vanryckeghem, M., & Yaruss, J. S. (2021). Consensus guidelines for the assessments of individuals who stutter across the lifespan. *American Journal of Speech-Language Pathology*, *30*(6), 2379-2393. https://doi.org/10.1044/2021_AJSLP-21-00107

permission). These examples provide clinicians with an excellent resource as a starting point for designing a treatment protocol. As we discussed in Chapter 4, and as Brundage et al. specifically pointed out, "selection of specific assessment areas and tools or procedures must be *individualized* and *tailored to each client's or family's unique needs*. Specific assessment plans must consider each client's experience with stuttering, and the weighting of each component of the assessment (and, if indicated, the resulting treatment) must be guided by information provided by speakers and their families" (p. 2384, emphases added).

GUIDELINES FOR INTERVENTION

Zebrowski (1997) pointed out that although we may discover many characteristics that appear to be related to the chronicity of stuttering, each child who comes to us for an evaluation is unique. Zebrowski suggested that, based on the likelihood of children recovering without therapy, the clinician might want to consider one of several "decision streams" according to the characteristics of the child and the family. As shown in Figure 5–3, children are placed in one of four streams based on the time interval since onset. Stream I contains five characteristics, Streams II and III contain seven characteristics, and Stream IV contains four characteristics. The clinician's decisions (Plans A–E) are based on characteristics that have been identified in the literature—particularly those described by Yairi and his colleagues earlier in this chapter. Points are assigned when children possess the characteristics listed within each stream. For example, children who have been stuttering for fewer than 6 months are placed in Stream I. Children demonstrating all five characteristics associated with this stream are assigned a score of five points, and the clinician would respond with Plan A as described next. Children with a score of 4 or less would undergo Plan B.

Plan A (Stream I for Children Who Have All Five Recovery Characteristics)

Children with all five recovery characteristics have a high probability of recovery. Treatment consists of information sharing and bibliotherapy. The clinician provides parents with information about (a) normal speech and language development, (b) their child's speech and language relative to a normally fluent child, (c) information about what we do and do not know about causal factors for stuttering in children, and (d) the prognosis for recov-

ery for their child given the information accumulated at that point. In addition, parents are provided with reading material. Clinicians are available for monthly contact with the parents via telephone or e-mail to further explain the information and answer questions. Parents can monitor changes in frequency or type of fluency breaks. Particular attention is given to whether there is a gradual decrease in the repetitions of SLDs. If there is a stable or increasing pattern of SLDs, a follow-up visit is indicated.

Plan B (Stream I for Children Who Have Four of Five Recovery Characteristics)

Children with four of the five recovery characteristics also have a high probability of recovery. Treatment consists of all the components of Plan A, with the addition of language intervention, phonological intervention, or both, if appropriate for the child. The degree of intervention will vary depending on the child's age and the severity of the problem(s). In addition, family members with a positive history of stuttering are provided with counseling, given the likelihood of greater concern about their child.

Plan C (Streams II and III for Children With a Score of Seven Recovery Characteristics)

Recovery is less likely for the child who has been stuttering longer. These children began stuttering before the age of 3 years and have been doing so for 6 months to 2 years. If these children are female, have no family history or a family history of recovery, have few or no associated

Stream I
Interval since onset:
0–6 months

Award 1 point for each:

- 18 months to 3 years at age of evaluation
- **NO** family history of stuttering **OR** relatively small number of affected family members who recovered in childhood.
- Female
- Few to no associated behaviors
- No coexisting phonological, or cognitive problems

Plan A: Score 5
Plan B: Score 4 or less

Stream II
Interval since onset:
6–12 months

Award 1 point for each:

- 2–4 years of age at evaluation
- Began stuttering prior to 3 years of age
- Parents report observable decrease in sound/syllable and word repetitions and prolonged sounds
- **NO** family history of stuttering **OR** relatively small number of affected family members who recovered in childhood.
- Female
- Few to no associated behaviors
- No coexisting phonological, or cognitive problems

Plan C: Score 7

Stream III
Interval since onset:
12–24 months

Award 1 point for each:

- 2–5 years of age at evaluation
- Began stuttering prior to 3 years of age
- Parents report observable decrease in sound/syllable and word repetitions and prolonged sounds
- **NO** family history of stuttering **OR** relatively small number of affected family members who recovered in childhood.
- Female
- Few to no associated behaviors
- No coexisting phonological, or cognitive problems

Plan D: Score 6 or less

Stream IV
Interval since onset:
24–36 months

Award 1 point for each:

- Parents report observable decrease in sound/syllable and word repetitions and prolonged sounds
- **NO** family history of stuttering **OR** relatively small number of affected family members who recovered in childhood.
- Few to no associated behaviors
- No coexisting phonological, or cognitive problems

Plan E: Score 4 or less

FIGURE 5–3. Decision streams for intervention. (With the permission of the original author [Zebrowski], this figure has been modified from the original published in 1997. Given the current information concerning the expressive language abilities of children who stutter, the word *language* has been deleted from the final bullet in each of the four streams. *Source:* Used with permission of the American Speech-Language-Hearing Association. modified from Zebrowski, P. M. Assisting young children who stutter and their families: Defining the role of the speech-language pathologist. *American Journal of Speech-Language Pathology, 6*(2), 19–28; permission conveyed through Copyright Clearance Center, Inc.)

141

behaviors or concomitant problems, and demonstrate a decrease in symptomatology, they are more likely to recover. As the child continues to stutter 2 years after onset (particularly if the child is female), recovery becomes less likely. Treatment consists of all the components of Plan B with the addition of counseling for parents about ways to indirectly enhance the fluency of their child by practicing such activities as speech-rate reduction, longer turn-switching pause durations, and avoiding interrupting. Parents could also enroll the child in a parent–child group designed to facilitate fluency.

Plan D (Streams II and III for Children With a Score of Six or Fewer Recovery Characteristics)

This plan contains all the components of Plan C that are applicable plus monthly visits to the clinic or the parent's home for monitoring. Taped speech samples are analyzed for the quality of the child's fluency (SLDs, speed of repetitions, and reactions of the child as well as associated behaviors). In addition, during the visits to the clinic or the home, parents can be counseled about the possibility that their child might not recover from stuttering and the possibilities for more direct intervention.

Plan E (Stream IV for Children With a Score of Four or Fewer Recovery Characteristics)

These children have been stuttering from 2 to 3 years since onset and are the least likely to recover. Treatment consists of all the factors included in the preceding plans plus direct intervention according to treatment protocols described in this and other texts.

Using At-Risk Registers

For decades, parents of children who stutter have been told to take a wait-and-*see* approach in the hope that the problem would go away. Such advice is a common response of pediatricians (Yairi & Carrico, 1992). Another possibility is more of a wait-and-*watch* strategy using an "at-risk" register (Adams, 1977b; Onslow, 1992) for reducing the occurrence of the false positive (a normally speaking child is incorrectly identified as a child who stutters) and the false negative (a child who stutters is incorrectly identified as a child who does not stutter). A false positive would result in a child receiving unnecessary assistance in producing fluent speech. Of course, a false-negative identification would be a more serious error in that a child who could benefit from treatment fails to receive assistance, especially considering the evidence that treatment for more advanced stuttering is considerably more time-consuming and prone to failure and relapse than treatment closer to onset (Bloodstein et al., 2021; Conture, 1996; Costello, 1983; Onslow, 1992). Thus, as Onslow (1992) recommended, the process leading to negative identification should be conservative, whereas the process resulting in positive identification should be relatively liberal. It has been suggested that the negative identification of communication disorders could result in the inefficient use of health care services (Andrews, 1984; Curlee & Yairi, 1997). However, Onslow commented that this view is not held for other communication disorders and questioned both the logic and the ethics of a decision process that could result in the withholding of treatment from young children who stutter. Onslow also suggested that because of the difficulties in treating cases of advanced stuttering, accurate early identification could actually improve the overall efficiency of service delivery.

Onslow's at-risk register is composed of both negative and positive identification components. When stuttering is suspected, the parents bring the child to a clinic for a formal evaluation. The parents are requested to bring audio or videotapes of their child's speech made in a natural environment, indicating the fluency characteristics of concern. The identification of a problem is based on the perception of stuttering by the clinician(s) and the parents. If a parent considers that a child is stuttering (an important factor, according to Yairi & Ambrose, 2005) but the clinician fails to perceive stuttered speech in the clinic or in the recording, the child is listed in the at-risk register. In the case where a clinician perceives stuttered speech but a parent does not, positive identification occurs if a second clinician perceives stuttered speech. If the second clinician does not perceive stuttered speech, then the child is placed in an at-risk register.

Those children listed in the at-risk register are observed on a regular basis for a period of months or years. Onslow suggested that ongoing evaluations can take a variety of forms, including telephone conversations, face-to-face interviews with parents, or questionnaires mailed to the home. Another tactic is to have the parents periodically call the clinic and respond to a series of questions that might indicate forms of speech fragmentation, tension, or struggle. Those children who pass the ongoing evaluations will continue being included on the register until a negative identification is made. How long this process should continue is a good question, but based on Bloodstein's (1987) literature review, Onslow suggested a possible upper limit of 12 years. A child is moved to the positive identification component if at any point a parent becomes concerned, and a formal evaluation is again scheduled.

The use of an at-risk strategy places no pressure on the clinician to make either a positive or a negative identification. If there is uncertainty concerning the diagnosis, the child is listed on the register and, if necessary, will remain there until a decision is made. The clinician should not necessarily feel pressured to make a decision concerning intervention, for as Curlee and Yairi (1997) explained, no evidence is available that indicates that postponing treatment for a year or more results in poorer treatment outcomes. However, if the clinician is in doubt and there are several factors suggesting the persistence of stuttering, a period of trial therapy might be the best decision. Curlee (2007) recommended that when faced with such a dilemma, it is often best to support the parents' choice of whether or not to initiate treatment.

EDUCATIONAL IMPACT

For some children the academic impact of stuttering is obvious. Teachers could recognize that a child will consistently refuse to participate in class discussions, consistently avoid oral presentations, or not respond to questions. Most experienced clinicians have heard many descriptions from school-age children and college students who coped with their stuttering by being absent on the first day of class to avoid the usual round of introductions. Later in the semester they might have feigned an illness on the day of a scheduled oral presentation. Often the coping strategies are much more subtle, as when a student pretends not to know the answer to a question or intentionally responds incorrectly in order to minimize verbal participation (Gregory, 2004). In many such cases the teacher is unlikely to be aware that the motivation for a student's response is the possibility of stuttering and might consider the student to be shy, aloof, withdrawn, or anxious. In other instances, the child could be classified as a "slow learner," and in some instances, placed in a class for such students. Because many children who stutter are adept at concealing their stuttering, they are less likely to be identified by teachers and clinicians than, for example, children with a variety of other communication problems.

For other children, particularly those who appear to be succeeding academically, school administrators frequently take the stance that the child is not experiencing any adverse effects as a result of his or her stuttering. However, as Ribbler (2006) counseled, a full appreciation of the multidimensional nature of the stuttering experience suggests several ways in which such children are likely to experience limitations. Ribbler pointed out the wide variety of adverse educational effects that children who stutter are likely to face, both within and beyond the communication domain. Even for the child who is able to achieve grades that are at or above the level of his or her peers, the child's awareness of his or her stuttering and the possibility of social penalty are likely to influence his or her choices across a broad range of areas, any of which can prevent the child from realizing his or her full potential.

Academic learning: Along with decreased participation in classroom activities, children experience difficulty reading aloud and giving oral presentations. They are unlikely to ask questions of the teacher or other children.

Social-emotional functioning: Children who stutter are apt to experience difficulty establishing interpersonal relationships, joining conversations, introducing themselves, and initiating friendships. Children who stutter are more likely to withdraw from social situations, choosing not to talk at lunch, recess, or field trips. It is not unusual for children to be absent on the day of a class presentation. In some instances, the child will respond to teasing and bullying with physical aggression, creating even more problems for the child.

Independent functioning: The child is apt to avoid asking directions when walking around the school or campus. The child is also unlikely to clarify information about assignments resulting in missed deadlines.

Communication: Many children who stutter are less likely to use the telephone to help clarify assignments, discuss upcoming quizzes or tests, and join others in preparing school projects.

Finally, there is the potential for an adverse impact on the social aspects of the academic experience, including quality of life issues. Students who stutter might be less able to function independently and resolve problems in a variety of circumstances, including obtaining help or assistance from teachers or peers. Something

CLINICAL INSIGHT

Several years ago, I worked with a college student who described a pattern of avoidance and word substitution. He was the starting running back for a highly ranked Division 1 football team. He had always been a good student and received an academic rather than a football scholarship to the university. During a group meeting, he described a speaking event that took place when he was in junior high school. Rob had completed a class quiz, which was then graded by a student in the adjoining aisle. His paper was returned, and he saw that he had received a score of 95. The teacher went up and down the rows of desks, asking each student in turn to report his or her grade. When it was his turn, Rob stood and attempted to say "Ninety-five." After enduring a speech block for several moments, he decided he would be less likely to stutter if he said "Eighty-five." Again, experiencing a block as he attempted to say that number, he quickly decided to say "Seventy-five" and this time was fluent. The teacher recorded that grade and Rob sat down. No one in the room, including the teacher, suspected he had stuttered. But of course, Rob had experienced a profound moment of stuttering. (WM)

as seemingly simple as asking for directions to find a classroom or dormitory could be a major challenge, even for a college student. The lack of social interaction and associated information about school relationships and activities decreases the speaker's participation and awareness. Some students who stutter are unwilling to participate or play positions on athletic teams if they are required to deliver plays from the sidelines or assume leadership roles.

The potential for adverse educational impact due to a child's stuttering is not necessarily indicated by passing grades or the ability of the child to score within the normal range on standardized tests. The more essential issue is whether or not the child will have the opportunity to reach his or her potential. What are the self-limiting choices the child is likely to make that will limit his or her participation within each of the domains described by Ribbler? It could be that such choices are more likely indicated using qualitative measures such as self-generated oral or written narratives by the child.

The following is the American Speech-Language-Hearing Association's position statement concerning eligibility for communication services.

It is the position of the National Joint Committee for the Communication Needs of Persons with Severe Disabilities that eligibility for communication services and supports should be based on individual communication needs. Communication services and supports should be evaluated, planned, and provided by an interdisciplinary team with expertise in communication and language form, content, and function, as well as in augmentative and alternative communication (AAC). Decisions regarding team composition, types, amounts, and duration of services provided, intervention setting, and service delivery models should be based on the individual's communication needs and preferences. Eligibility determinations based on a priori [3] criteria violate recommended practice principles by precluding consideration of individual needs. These a priori criteria include, but are not limited to: (a) discrepancies between cognitive and communication functioning; (b) chronological age; (c) diagnosis; (d) absence of cognitive or other skills purported to be prerequisites; (e) failure to benefit from previous communication services and supports; (f) restrictive interpretations of educational, vocational, and/ or medical necessity; (g) lack of appropriately trained personnel; and (h) lack of adequate funds or other resources. More information about eligibility may be found at: https://www.asha.org/slp/schools/prof-consult/eligibility/

It is important to recognize that inclusion criteria vary according to the guidelines in each state. Most criteria go beyond the basic academic measures such as grades and include the effect of self-limiting choices that limit a child's participation as described by Ribbler.

Responsibilities of the IEP Team

Following the guidelines mandated by the Individuals with Disabilities Education Act (IDEA), clinicians working in a school setting are required to work with a multidisciplinary team to develop an assessment plan for each child for whom intervention is desired. Based on the knowledge gathered from case history information, formal assessment measures, and observation of the child's speech and interactive behavior in a variety of communication situations, it is first necessary to document that the child meets the state and local eligibility criteria. Unfor-

tunately, eligibility guidelines are often considered only in terms of academic achievement (grades), a restrictive and often prejudicial perspective (Ramig & Dodge, 2005). It is important to emphasize that the clinician should take the widest possible perspective, which includes the areas of academic competency, academic learning, and social-emotional and independent functioning as described by Ribbler (2006). Ramig and Dodge (2005) recommended that the clinician go well beyond a detailed documentation of the child's overt stuttering behavior (both in frequency and form) by also documenting and explaining the occurrence of coping behaviors, which often result in a far greater impact on social interaction and restricted participation (e.g., avoidance or changing of words or communication situations, escape or struggle behaviors that draw attention to the speaker and invite teasing and bullying by others). Even when the child does make a choice to participate, the child's response is apt to give the listener the impression that the child is uncertain as he or she hesitates, carefully scans ahead for feared words, or selects syntax that is less appropriate and eloquent than it would otherwise be. As Ramig and Dodge explained, such coping responses often prevent others from observing the child's real personality and emotions when communicating.

Once the child is qualified to receive intervention, the clinician will then participate with the multidisciplinary team in the development of an individualized education program (IEP) designed to address the variety of ways that the child can be assisted in achieving his or her educational potential. As Ramig and Dodge (2005) noted, it will usually be necessary to argue for specific intervention beyond what would be available as a result of the opportunities afforded by the general education program. The individualized program must include measurable goals and short-term objectives broadly related to all aspects of the child's educational program. Narrow goals that focus on high levels of fluency, although often part of an IEP, are far too restrictive and sometimes counterproductive. In some instances, such goals could set up the child (and the IEP team) for failure. It is better to view the process of therapeutic change for these young speakers as one of ever more successful management of stuttering, often providing supportive counseling to reduce the shame and avoidance that can continue formally (or informally) through the upper grades.

Most people, including educators and administrators, have no idea of the depth and breadth of the impact that stuttering can have on the restrictive decision making that is a basic part of the coping responses by people who stutter. The challenge for the clinician is to make this clear to all concerned and to document the educational impact of these decisions. Ramig and Dodge (2005) suggested that the various versions of the OASES, particularly the OASES-S, which are based on the World Health Organization's *International Classification of Function, Disability and Health (ICF)* described in Chapter 2, may be of particular help to the clinician for documenting the many levels of impairments to education that a child is likely to face. Ramig and Dodge (2005) also provided a list of short-term instructional objectives for a child who stutters, along with a sample IEP goal (4–7) for these objectives.

SAMPLE IEP GOALS

Sample Short-Term Objective

Will increase the use of noticeable prolonged onsets to at least three per day when participating in class (or another situation, such as a reading group).

Method of Measurement

Teacher observation of general behavior; SLP observation and report; student report.

Schedule for Achieving Objective

Beginning date: January 12. Target completion date: May 25.

Levels of Progress and Date

In this case, care must be taken to eliminate online verbal prompts or cues that may interfere with communication and undermine the child's willingness to perform the speech modifications. The danger here is that classmates may pick up on these verbal commands and use them to ridicule or try to gain control over the child when he or she is stuttering outside the classroom. Instead, prompts and cues can consist of offline reminders made by the teacher or by the SLP. In some cases, the student and teacher or LP may want to develop a discreet nonverbal signaling system.

continues

Objective Will Be Completed or Continued

By setting stepwise, achievable objectives, the IEP can provide the child and SLP with a way of measuring progress through recovery. The recovery path for stuttering is different and in many cases somewhat slower than for other challenges, and this must be acknowledged. Continuing an objective for several semesters would not be unusual for stuttering therapy transfer, and this should not be seen as negative or a failure.

The instructional objectives to be addressed in the IEP goal include the following:

- Use of fluency-enhancing behaviors such as continuous voicing or gentle onset in specified situations
- Use of stuttering modification techniques such as initial sound stretches, pullouts, and cancellations in specified situations
- Reduced frequency or use of a secondary stuttering behavior
- Reduced use of a stuttering avoidance technique, such as interjections, word avoidance, pretending not to know an answer, or avoiding speech
- Measured stuttering severity in a therapy setting/class participation, such as asking questions and volunteering to answer questions posed by the teacher
- Participation in groups and extracurricular activities that require various speaking skills, such as music groups, choirs, sports, crafts, chess clubs, writing clubs, stage set preparation, and management groups
- Participation in activities that require speech, such as debating clubs or drama groups

"IEP goal and short-term objectives for a child who stutters." From P. R. Ramig and D. M. Dodge. (2005). *The Child and Adolescent Stuttering Treatment and Activity Resource Guide.* Thomson Delmar Learning.

EXAMPLES OF ASSESSMENT MEASURES

There are many inventories, scales, and procedures that have been developed for evaluating the quality of both the surface as well as the associated cognitive and affective features of stuttering. These measures are helpful for obtaining both data-based and criterion-referenced information for assessing fluency disorders. Although the descriptions, situations, and categories associated with any single measure do not always coincide within a particular child, these measures can provide helpful information that often proves useful for determining possible treatment strategies and indicating therapeutic progress. Of course, assessment must go beyond formal procedures and include daily observation of the child's ongoing cognitive change and behavioral adaptation to the therapy process. The data obtained by using assessment protocols are no substitute for the clinician's ongoing observation of the child's response in naturalistic settings. Examples of these measures can be found on the companion website.

A-19 Scale

A scale designed for use with young children is the A-19 Scale for Children Who

Stutter (Guitar & Grims, 1977). Guitar and his colleagues have found that once a secure and trusting relationship between clinician and child is established, this 19-item scale helps to distinguish between children who stutter and those who do not. Once the clinician is assured that the child understands the task, the scale is administered by the clinician, who asks the child a series of questions concerning speech and related general attitude. One point is assigned for each question that is answered as a child who stutters might respond. The authors found that the average scores of 28 kindergarten through fourth-grade children who stuttered was 9.07 (SD = 2.44), and a matched group of nonstuttering children averaged 8.17 (SD = 1.80) on the A-19 (Figure 5–4).

Behavior Assessment Battery (BAB) (Plural Publishing, Inc.)

Recommending that the assessment of a fluency problem should be multidimensional and go beyond the molar count of stuttering moments, Brutten and Vanryckeghem developed a series of assessment measures for preschool, kindergarten (Vanryckeghem & Brutten, 2007), and school-age children (Brutten & Vanryckeghem, 2003, 2007). Both the child and adult forms of the BAB are designed to provide the clinician with an "evidence-based approach to diagnostic and therapeutic decision making." The BAB has been translated into 15 languages with norms established for different countries (Brutten, 1973, 1975; Brutten & Vanryckeghem, 2003). Four self-report measures are designed for school-age children: the Communication Attitude Test (CAT), the Speech Situation Checklist—Emotional Reaction (SSC-ER), the Speech Situation Checklist—Speech Disruption (SSC-SD),

and the Behavior Checklist (BCL). The Communication Attitude Test for preschool and kindergarten children who stutter (KiddyCAT) is a measure intended for preschool and kindergarten children.

Communication Attitude Test (CAT) (Plural Publishing, Inc.)

The original version of the CAT was developed by Brutten (Brutten & Dunham, 1989) and revised by De Nil and Brutten (1991) and Vanryckeghem and Brutten (1997). This self-administered measure asks the child to indicate a "true" or "false" response to a series of statements (e.g., I like the way I talk, I don't talk like other children, Kids make fun of the way I talk). One point is scored for each response that corresponds to the way a child who stutters is apt to respond. The CAT significantly differentiates children who stutter from those who do not (effect size = 1.82) and has both good test–retest reliability (Vanryckeghem & Brutten, 1992) and internal reliability (Brutten & Vanryckeghem, 2007). The measure also appears to have good content and criterion-related validity for indicating a child's negative belief system about his or her speech compared to children who are fluent. The current updated version of the CAT (Brutten & Vanryckeghem, 2007) has 33 true–false items; two of the original 35 items were removed due to the lack of a significant correlation with the test's total score.

Speech Situation Checklist—Emotional Reaction (SSC-ER) (Plural Publishing, Inc.)

As with the adult version, this checklist has two components. The first portion determines a child's situation-specific emotional reactions (fear, anxiety, worry, concern) to 55 communication situations

A-19 Scale for Children Who Stutter

Susan Andre and Barry Guitar
University of Vermont

Establish rapport with the child, and make sure that he or she is physically comfortable before beginning administration. Explain the task to the child and make sure he or she understands what is required. Some simple directions might be used:

> I am going to ask you some questions. Listen carefully and then tell me what you think: Yes or No. There is no right or wrong answer. I just want to know what you think.

To begin the scale, ask the questions in a natural manner. Do not urge the child to respond before he or she is ready, and repeat the question if the child did not hear it or you feel that he or she did not understand it. Do not re-word the question unless you feel it is absolutely necessary, and then write the question you asked under that item.

Circle the answer that corresponds to the child's response. Be accepting of the child's response because there is no right or wrong answer. If all the child will say is "I don't know" even after prompting, record that response next to the question.

For the younger children (kindergarten and first grade), it might be necessary to give a few simple examples to ensure comprehension of the required task:

a. Are you a boy?	Yes	No
b. Do you have black hair?	Yes	No

Similar, obvious questions may be inserted, if necessary, to reassure the examiner that the child is <u>actively</u> cooperating at all times. Adequately praise the child for listening and assure him or her that a good job is being done.

It is important to be familiar with the questions so that they can be read in a natural manner.

The child is given 1 point for each answer that matches those given below. The higher a child's score, the more probable it is that he or she has developed negative attitudes toward communication. In our study, the mean score of the K through 4th grade stutterers ($N = 28$) was 9.07 (S.D. = 2.44), and for the 28 matched controls, it was 8.17 (S.D. = 1.80).

FIGURE 5–4. A-19 Scale. (Reprinted with permission from Susan Andre and Barry Guitar.) *continues*

Score 1 point for each answer that matches these:

1. Yes	11. No
2. Yes	12. No
3. No	13. Yes
4. No	14. Yes
5. No	15. Yes
6. Yes	16. No
7. No	17. No
8. Yes	18. Yes
9. Yes	19. Yes
10. No	

A-19 SCALE

Name _____   Date _____

1. Is it best to keep your mouth shut when you are in trouble?	Yes	No
2. When the teacher calls on you, do you get nervous?	Yes	No
3. Do you ask a lot of questions in class?	Yes	No
4. Do you like to talk on the phone?	Yes	No
5. If you did not know a person, would you tell your name?	Yes	No
6. Is it hard to talk to your teacher?	Yes	No
7. Would you go up to a new boy or girl in your class?	Yes	No
8. Is it hard to keep control of your voice when talking?	Yes	No
9. Even when you know the right answer, are you afraid to say it?	Yes	No
10. Do you like to tell other children what to do?	Yes	No
11. Is it fun to talk to your dad?	Yes	No
12. Do you like to tell stories to your classmates?	Yes	No
13. Do you wish you could say things as clearly as the other kids do?	Yes	No

FIGURE 5–4. *continues*

14. Would you rather look at a comic book than talk to a friend?	Yes	No
15. Are you upset when someone interrupts you?	Yes	No
16. When you want to say something, do you just say it?	Yes	No
17. Is talking to your friends more fun than playing by yourself?	Yes	No
18. Are you sometimes unhappy?	Yes	No
19. Are you a little afraid to talk on the phone?	Yes	No

FIGURE 5–4. *continued*

(e.g., giving your name, raising your hand to talk in class, talking on the telephone, reading aloud from a book). Children are asked to indicate their emotional response to each situation using a 5-point Likert-type scale ranging from 1 (*not afraid*) to 5 (*very much afraid*). The child's ratings are totaled and contrasted with the norms provided in order to determine how the scores compare to children who do or do not stutter.

Speech Situation Checklist— Speech Disruption (SSC-SD) (Plural Publishing, Inc.)

Children are also independently asked to respond to the same 55 communication situations as on the SSC-ER by indicating the amount of speech disruption (part-word repetitions, sound prolongations) they experience. In the SSC-SD, the children also indicate their perceived degree of speech disruption on a second 5-point Likert-type scale ranging from 1 (*no trouble*) to 5 (*very much trouble*). The authors suggested that the clinician develop therapy targets that focus on those speaking situations the child rates as 3, 4, or 5 in

order to highlight sounds and words, interpersonal situations, and school experiences that are especially difficult. On both sections of the SSC, children who stutter score statistically significantly higher than those who do not.

Behavior Checklist (BCL) (Plural Publishing, Inc.)

The BCL provides a way for the child to identify his or her style of coping with sounds, words, and situations by using avoidance and escape behaviors. The child is asked to indicate "yes" or "no" as to whether or not they use each of the 50 behaviors described by the clinician "to help the sounds or words come out." The list of behaviors includes categories of body movements (e.g., closing your eyes), breathing (e.g., letting some air out before starting to speak), or speech-specific behaviors (e.g., changing sounds or words). The 50 behaviors were derived by accumulating avoidance and escape behaviors reported by a large and diverse group of children who stutter. The total number of behaviors reported by a child is contrasted with the normative data provided for children who stutter and those who do not. Investigations with the BCL indicate that children who stutter use significantly more of these behaviors than those who do not (Brutten & Vanryckeghem, 2003, 2007; Vanryckeghem & Herder, 2004).

Communication Attitude Test for Preschool and Kindergarten Children Who Stutter (KiddyCAT) (Plural Publishing, Inc.)

Intended for use with children between 3 and 6 years old, the KiddyCAT was originally developed by Vanryckeghem and colleagues (Vanryckeghem & Brutten, 2007; Vanryckeghem et al., 2005). The brief and easily administered measure provides a way for the preschool child to respond to 12 statements verbally presented by the clinician (e.g., Do you think that you talk right? Is talking hard for you? Do mom and dad like the way you talk?). Children with a negative attitude about speaking are likely to answer six of the statements with a "yes" response and six with a "no," resulting in a possible score range of 0 to 12. The mode, median, and mean scores for children who do not stutter were 0, 1, and 1.79, respectively, and mode, median, and mean scores for children who stutter were 5, 5, and 4.36, respectively.

Overall Assessment of the Speaker's Experience of Stuttering (OASES) (Stuttering Therapy Resources)

Developed by Yaruss and Quesal (2006), the OASES is designed to obtain information about the totality of the stuttering experience as delineated by the World Health Organization's *ICF* (WHO, 2001).

The OASES is one of the more popular measures of stuttering because it provides a comprehensive perspective of the impact of stuttering, there are versions for three age groups, and it is available in both print and digital versions in many languages. There are three forms according to the age of the client: the OASES-S for School-Age Children (ages 7–12), the OASES-T for teenagers (ages 13–17), and the OASES-A for adults (ages 18+). All of these are available in digital format for English-speaking people. As of this writing there are digital versions for the following languages: German (S/T/A), French (S/T/A), Dutch (S/T/A), Finnish (S/T/A), Turkish (S/T/A), Hebrew (A), Swedish (S/T/A), Korean (A), Japanese (A), Arabic (A), Farsi (A), Portuguese (Brazil) (A), Portuguese (Europe) (S), Spanish (S/T/A), and Norwegian (S/T/A).

The broad impact of stuttering is assessed across four major sections: Section I (General Information) contains items indicating the speaker's self-assessment of his or her impairment as well as the speaker's knowledge about stuttering and stuttering therapy. Section II (Reactions to Stuttering) contains items providing information concerning the speaker's affective, behavioral, and cognitive reactions to stuttering. Section III (Communication in Daily Situations) contains items about the difficulty the speaker experiences when communicating in important speaking situations. Section IV (Quality of Life) contains items providing information about the overall impact of stuttering on the speaker's quality of life. Overall, the various items provide the clinician with information about such factors as how much stuttering interferes with the speaker's communication, relationships, sense of confidence, and well-being. The client responds to the individual items using a Likert-type scale ranging from 1 to 5, and the scores are then totaled for each of the four sections and the test as a whole. The points for each of the four sections (and overall) are totaled and divided by the number of items completed, resulting in impact scores. Impact ratings across five levels of severity are then determined based on the impact scores: mild (1.00–1.49), mild/moderate (1.50–2.24), moderate (2.25–2.99), moderate/severe (3.00–3.74), and severe (3.75–5.00).

CONCLUSION

In recent years, a number of important research findings have emerged that have expanded our understanding about the onset and development of early stuttering. These studies have shown that, in contrast to our understanding only a few decades ago, the fluency breaks of young children who stutter are distinctly different from those who are fluent, a distinction that is most clearly indicated by the occurrence of SLDs (part-word repetitions, single-syllable word repetitions, and DPs). Furthermore, stuttering does not appear to evolve from normal fluency breaks and become progressively more severe, a view that very likely continues to be held by some clinicians. In fact, particularly considering the remission of stuttering for the large majority of children who initially experience stuttering, the overall pattern of stuttering severity shows a decreasing, rather than an increasing, curve.

Of the two primary decisions the clinician must make during the assessment process, determining whether or not a child's disfluencies are typical of stuttering is not especially difficult. In fact, it seems that parents are more accurate than some clinicians have given them credit for in identifying stuttering behavior in their children. Accordingly, parents play an essential role in the assessment process, providing historical, developmental, and psychosocial information about their child. Because fluency is often highly variable for young children, clinicians might need to obtain examples of speech in a variety of conditions and, on some occasions, employ tactics that are likely to introduce a moderate level of stress (e.g., time pressure) in order to elicit from the child the fluency characteristics of concern. The presence of many factors, including the occurrence of SLDs and the child's behavioral and emotional response to their difficulties in producing fluent speech, provide important indicators.

The clinician's ability to predict whether or not a child who begins to stutter will continue to do so is usually more challenging. Fortunately, data from several researchers, including Yairi and Ambrose (2005), Walsh et al. (2021), and Singer et al. (2022) are providing information to help clinicians forecast the future course of stuttering. Although there are a number of factors to consider—and not all of the researchers agree on exactly which factors are most salient—the decision to intervene can be made with greater confidence than was possible only a few years ago. Future longitudinal and especially prospective investigations should further increase the accuracy of this decision. The improving ability to predict the likely persistence of a young child's stuttering will allow for early intervention before stuttering develops to the point where a successful therapeutic outcome becomes less likely.

It is especially important to emphasize that the initial assessment meeting with the clinician is often the first opportunity for the parents to acquire the information, support, and therapeutic options for their child. The depth and quality of the clinician's understanding and experience will set the stage for how the parents choose to respond to the problem. Whatever the parents' decision, it is the clinician's opportunity to provide basic take-home messages so that the parents are better able to begin coping with their circumstances and make the best possible choices. Suggested take-home messages can include concepts such as the following:

- Stuttering is no one's fault.
- Parent involvement and support are essential for therapeutic success.
- Good treatment is likely to result in therapeutic success.
- You are not alone! Although stuttering is not a frequently occurring problem, there are many other children and families in a similar situation.
- There are support groups that can be extremely helpful for children and their parents.

TOPICS FOR DISCUSSION

1. Describe several activities that would be likely to elicit fluency breaks in the speech of a young child.

2. What are both verbal and nonverbal behaviors indicating that young children are aware that they are having a difficult time communicating?

3. How might you respond to a parent who asks, "How long will it take to cure my child's stuttering?"

4. What are the "red and green flags" that indicate the likelihood of remis-

sion or recovery from stuttering for young children?

5. Depending on the age of a child, which combination of the assessment measures and procedures described in this chapter do you feel provides the best picture of a child's affective and cognitive response to the stuttering experience?

6. What are your views concerning the efficacy and the ethical issues associated with using "at-risk" registers?

7. Describe the procedures and measures you would use to answer the two major clinical decisions discussed in this chapter.

8. With one student taking the part of the clinician and one or two others the part(s) of the parent(s), role-play a discussion of the emotions parents are likely to experience following their child's diagnosis of stuttering (see Chapter 8).

RECOMMENDED READINGS

Chmela, K. A., & Reardon, N. (2002). *The school-age child who stutters: Working effectively with attitudes and emotions.* Publication No. 5. The Stuttering Foundation of America.

Ramig, P. R., & Dodge, D. M. (2005). Strategies for developing individualized education programs. In *The child and adolescent stuttering treatment and activity resource guide* (pp. 31–37). Thomson Delmar Learning.

Yairi, E., & Ambrose, N. G. (2005). Development of stuttering. In *Early childhood stuttering: For clinicians by clinicians.* Pro-Ed.

"When you stutter you are always in a country where you don't speak the language."

—Kevin, an adult who stutters

What Mr. Spiro couldn't have known was that asking me to say my name out loud was like asking me to recite the Gettysburg Address. My history teacher had tried to make me do that but he finally let me write it out in longhand after it took me about half the class to get out Four Score and Seven Years Ago and with all the kids snickering at every word I tried to say.

—Vince Vawter, *Paperboy* (2013, p. 27)

The Assessment Process With Adolescents and Adults

CHAPTER OBJECTIVES

- To provide a discussion of the broad issues that clinicians must consider when planning and engaging in assessment with adolescents and adults
- To describe how assessment data can provide guidance for intervention
- To describe the variability of fluency and stuttering
- To explore the concepts and processes involved in the initial meeting with clients
- To describe the two principles of assessment with adolescents and adults
- To explain processes involved in mapping the surface features of stuttering in adolescents and adults
- To describe processes for discovering the intrinsic features of stuttering in adolescents and adults

- To provide descriptions of frequently used assessment measures for adolescents and adults

This chapter on the assessment of stuttering describes the features of stuttering as manifested in a fully developed form in adolescents and adults. The nature of stuttering is more clearly manifested in older speakers who have traveled the often-bumpy road of stuttering for many years. Many studies over the years with adolescents and adults have documented the wide range of negative impacts that can result from being a person who stutters. Examples include the possibility of teasing and bullying, negative peer reactions, elevated anxiety, negative attitudes about communicating, decreased contact with teachers, lower educational attainment, underemployment, lower earnings, stigma and discrimination, low self-esteem, less satisfying personal relationships, a reduced quality of life, frustration, anger, the possibility of depression, unsettling effects on family dynamics, isolation, and difficulty with health-related issues.

FUNDAMENTAL CONSIDERATIONS OF ASSESSMENT: IS IT STUTTERING?

On occasion a person will seek our help and it might not be immediately apparent that the problem has anything to do with stuttering. In an attempt to lessen the impact of stuttering on their lives, adult speakers will sometimes shape their speech and overall behavior into a pattern of symptoms that resembles other problems, such as motor-speech disorders, voice disorders, language disorders, social anxiety, or even emotional disturbances. For example, because of tension in a speaker's voice or the fact that he or she is speaking in a careful, slow, labored, or rhythmic manner, it might appear as though the person has a voice or word-finding problem. In order to protect himself or herself from the social penalties associated with stuttering, the person might refuse to speak or choose to speak in a way such that, although it is obvious that something is amiss, it is not clear that stuttering is the problem. Clinicians faced with such clients need to be thorough in their assessment, making sure to assess all six core areas identified by Brundage et al. (2021) and discussed in Chapter 4. In particular, clinicians need to take a counseling approach with these clients, using empathic listening and placing them in the expert role where they can tell their story (see Chapter 8 for more on taking a counseling approach).

Of course, sometimes what might be taken for stuttering really is something else. Other fluency disorders, such as cluttering and acquired stuttering that might be neurogenic or psychogenic, are often mistaken for child-onset, developmental stuttering. These other atypical fluency disorders are discussed further in Chapter 13. In cases of acquired stuttering, the primary distinguishing feature that can help clinicians with differential diagnosis is time of onset, which will be in early childhood for developmental stuttering, whereas for acquired stuttering, it will be recent and typically associated with some type of neurological or psychological trauma.

The Unique Sample of Our Clients

The vast majority of people who stutter do not seek treatment. Rather, they make it through life coping with the problem in more or less effective ways. They might not be aware that help is available, and for many who are, the time and cost of treatment could be prohibitive. For others, the challenges of treatment are so unappealing that they refuse assistance even if they are able to afford it. For some it could be that although the problem is apparent, it does not sufficiently negatively impact their quality of life and promote action. Individuals are frequently motivated to enroll in therapy when the meanings they make of their lived experience are restrictive and constraining (White & Epston, 1990).

Although there are no data to indicate the proportion of individuals who stutter who never seek formal help, there is little doubt that the majority of individuals who stutter never make contact with professional treatment centers. Consequently, these people never serve as participants for the research on which we base our understanding of the problem and form the rationale for most of our clinical decisions. It seems reasonable to suggest that our knowledge about people who stutter is based on a nonrepresentative, perhaps even biased sample of the total community population of people who stutter. The sample we observe is most likely skewed in the direction of people who, for whatever reasons, come to recognize not only that they need help, but are also able to seek and obtain assistance.

As with many challenging human conditions, those who stutter are sometimes able to achieve successful change on their own. Still, some strategies and techniques are likely to be more effective than others, and an experienced guide or coach can show the way or, at the very least, make the journey more efficient and often more pleasant. There are useful strategies and techniques that, although helpful, are nevertheless counterintuitive and not something that most people who stutter would consider—voluntarily stuttering (see Chapter 12) being, perhaps, the best example. Without the assistance of a good instructor, the novice is apt to select less effective or even counterproductive options. Without good coaching, when caught in a rip current, swimmers will attempt to swim back to shore rather than parallel to the beach; soccer players will kick the ball with their toe rather than their instep; kayakers will pull away from a wave or rock rather than leaning into it. Likewise, most people who stutter instinctively make every effort not to stutter. When they do stutter, they tend to expend increasing amounts of effort attempting to push through a sound or word. Without an experienced coach, teacher, or clinician, few people will be aware of the best techniques or why, how, and when to use them.

The Variability of Fluency and Stuttering

Even for typically fluent speakers, fluency is a speech characteristic that varies greatly—perhaps more so than any other—depending on the communicative situation. Most speakers appear to speak with little effort, with words flowing smoothly and effortlessly. Even for accomplished speakers, though, particularly when communicative or emotional stress is introduced, the smoothness often begins to disappear and breaks in the smooth flow of speech are likely to occur. For those who stutter, the variability is often especially pronounced, because, given their past experiences with fluency failure, these speakers are apt to react sooner and to a greater degree to fluency-disrupting stimuli such as time pressure and difficult speaking situations than fluent speakers. In addition, people who stutter are sometimes able to "turn on their fluency." By avoiding feared sounds and words or—with heightened energy and emotion, momentarily "rising to the occasion"—it is not unusual for speakers who typically stutter to temporarily achieve uncharacteristically fluent speech.

The variability of both the frequency and quality of stuttering is one of the hallmarks of child-onset stuttering. In fact, as we will see in Chapter 13, some forms of "atypical" fluency disorders do not show such variability, a characteristic that helps to identify these problems. This variability, although typical and to be expected, contributes as much as anything else to the mystery of stuttering. It is difficult for many listeners to understand how people can be speaking fluently and a moment later struggle dramatically as they attempt to say a word they have already said fluently. The "natural" variability of stuttering

CLINICAL INSIGHT

At a reception, a woman I was speaking to introduced me to her husband. He was a young man in his early 30s who was a successful businessman. He was extremely pleasant and outgoing. He also appeared to be spontaneously fluent. As we discussed my field and my interest in stuttering, he volunteered that he, too, had stuttered as a child and, on occasion, still had difficulty with certain words. His brother had also stuttered, and his description of the impact his stuttering had on his life as a young child and teenager left no doubt that he truly was a member of the clan of the tangled tongue. Although he had experienced some teasing about his speech, his close friends had been understanding and supportive. During his elementary school years he had been seen for a brief time by a clinician who emphasized speaking slower, something he felt provided little help. Now, as a young adult, he explained that, for the most part, he had "gotten over it." He described that actually, rather than stuttering (repeating sounds and words), he stammered (blocking and "getting stuck" on words).

When I asked what he had done to cope with his stuttering, he informed me that he had several techniques that he used. He had learned to adeptly change words or topics as he anticipated stuttering on a feared sound or word. He had adopted an assertive approach and "went for it" in many aspects of his life, including all communication situations. It was clear that although stuttering had been a traumatic experience for him when was younger, he wasn't going to let something like that get in his way. He had been an outstanding athlete and had a broad circle of friends. By any standard he was successful. He explained that "everyone has their faults" and that he just happened to be someone who stuttered.

Not all speakers would be satisfied with this approach to their stuttering. This young man adjusted his approach and, with a history of success in other areas of his life and the support of others, was able to elaborate a confident and assertive approach to communication situations. However, it was apparent that his stuttering continued to impact his life. He chose to describe his fluency breaks as *stammering* because that term, at least in the United States, generally has less stigma associated with it than the word *stuttering*. His statement that "everyone has their faults," although an accurate and generally healthy comment, suggested that he viewed stuttering—to some degree at least—as a "fault." His strategy of changing words prevented him from being as spontaneous as he might have otherwise been and required that he scan ahead for feared stimuli that might result in stuttering. Word avoidance and substitutions detract from the precision of the message and for some speakers, as well as listeners, can be highly frustrating. It is possible that the quality of this man's life would have been enhanced by learning more about and becoming desensitized to stuttering. He might have experienced some relief from his goal of hiding his stuttering by giving himself permission to easily stutter on some occasions. (WM) can make it difficult for a listener to adapt to and become accustomed to a speaker. Such variability also presents a predicament for the person doing the stuttering. That is, the person who stutters cannot always be certain of the amount and degree of difficulty he or she will experience in a given speaking situation. This, of course, makes it difficult for the speaker to compensate for a problem that is inconsistent and unpredictable. Of the many communication problems that people might experience, perhaps none is more variable than stuttering.

This variability of fluency both within and between speakers can make the assessment of fluency more formidable than it might first appear. As Bloodstein (1987) stated, "The great variability of stuttering from time to time under different conditions is liable to result in assessments that are unrepresentative" (p. 386). A single assessment protocol obtained at a particular time will provide only a glimpse of the depth and breadth of the problem. As with younger speakers, many aspects of stuttering will go undetected unless the assessment process is conducted in a variety of speaking situations. We are not likely to observe the variety of overt behaviors and covert coping responses during one or even several meetings. The more these situations simulate the speaker's daily communication situations, the more apt we are to obtain a true indication of the problem.

Surface and Intrinsic Features

Another basic characteristic of stuttering is that most of the features that we see and hear indicate only the surface features of the problem, the upper 10% of the iceberg. The typical listener naturally tends to focus on the obvious characteristics such as the frequency, duration, tension, and effort associated with the stuttered moments, as well as the sometimes dramatic accessory features the speaker uses to postpone or escape from stuttering. Although there is usually some consistency in these features across speakers, the diversity and sometimes unique nature of obvious coping responses require some exploration. The clinician can identify and monitor both the quantity and quality of these surface features, for these behavioral characteristics provide an indication of the severity of the problem and evidence of behavioral change during treatment. Even with younger speakers, and certainly with adolescents and adults, we must look below the surface of the speaker's behavior in order to obtain a complete appreciation of the problem. As interesting, even fascinating, as some of the surface features might be, it is good to keep in mind that these behaviors also reveal the nature of the dynamics taking place beneath the surface. Although these are less apparent aspects of the stuttering experience, they are, to varying degrees, normal and expected components. A primary aspect of the assessment process is to begin to identify both the surface and intrinsic features that are unique to each speaker, something we describe in detail later in this chapter.

THE INITIAL MEETING

Just as the initial evaluation session provides the first opportunity for the clinician to find out about the person who has come for assistance, it is also the client's first opportunity to find out about the clinician. As discussed throughout the text, the quality of the therapeutic alliance will be a major factor in determining how treatment will proceed or whether it will take place at all.

The client might already have some insight about the therapeutic process, as it is not uncommon for older individuals to have experienced previous treatment and know something about basic terminology concerning stuttering. Of course, there are also individuals who have had a less than satisfactory therapy experience and are skeptical of our ability to provide effective help. Some people might express their justifiable anger because of the less than competent assistance they feel they have received. Others will know absolutely nothing about the nature of stuttering and, depending on their cultural background and educational experience, bring with them some of the numerous myths that have been associated with stuttering. Whereas some people have a degree of inquisitiveness and openness about themselves and their stuttering, the narratives of others are infused by embarrassment and shame. Our task at the outset is to find out where they are on their journey of understanding their situation and their willingness to enter into the work of developing alternative ways of coping.

With this in mind, the way we start this initial meeting can hold a great deal of significance for how the rest of our assessment—and possible treatment—with the client will unfold. Consequently, we want to start this initial meeting by inviting clients to share their story—not *stuttering's* story, but their own personal narrative (DiLollo & Neimeyer, 2022; Di-Lollo et al., 2002; Leahy et al., 2012) that includes all aspects of their life, such as their relationships, who they are, how they see themselves, what they like and dislike, how they spend their time, how they succeed and fail, and what they fear. This accomplishes three very important outcomes: (a) It provides us with a full account of the person who is seeking help rather than the limited version that focuses only on the stuttering, (b) it moves the status of "expert" from the clinician to the client and tells the client that we recognize them as the expert on their own story, and (c) it tells the client that we are interested in them as a person, not simply as a "problem" or as a "stutterer," which helps build trust and fosters the therapeutic alliance.

In Chapter 8, we describe in more detail the "counselor mindset" and how to use the skills of empathic listening to allow and encourage clients to tell their personal narratives. What is important is that the clinician provide an open invitation, something like "Tell me about yourself," and then follow up by listening intently and purposefully to the story, refraining from asking questions, tolerating extended periods of silence, and encouraging the client to keep talking by reflecting feelings and emotion (e.g., "That sounds very frustrating" or "That must be really hard for you"). Starting an evaluation in this way enables the client to direct the initial content and provides the clinician with insights into what the client views as the most important aspects of their story. This is why it is important for the clinician to ask as few questions as possible at this time: Asking questions takes control of the story away from the client, focusing instead on what the clinician believes to be important.

Substance Abuse and Stuttering

On occasion it becomes apparent, either during the initial assessment or early in the treatment process, that individuals who seek our help are addicted to alcohol, drugs, or both. The motivation, judgment, and general cognitive functioning of these individuals are likely to be inconsistent or impaired. Until the person has successfully completed a program of detoxification and rehabilitation, treatment for his or her fluency problem—particularly in the long term—is not likely to be beneficial. Given the association between anxiety and substance abuse (Bolton et al., 2006) it would not be surprising to consider the possibility of self-medication by adolescents and adults who stutter. Surprisingly, investigations have not found this to be the case for individuals who stutter. Iverach et al. (2010) compared the rate of abuse among 94 adults seeking treatment for stuttering to a group of 10,610 control participants. The adults who stuttered were not found to take part in substance abuse (including alcohol) at a greater rate than the controls. The authors suggested that the results might be due to the fact that the participants who stuttered were currently taking part in a treatment program, which might have decreased their level of anxiety. More recently, Heelan et al. (2016) found similar results with a community sample of individuals who stuttered who were not enrolled in treatment. Making use of a national database in the United Kingdom, a cohort of 10,491 participants were followed from age 16 to age 55. The results indicated no relationship between stuttering and high levels of alcohol consumption or smoking.

In spite of these results, it is possible that clinicians will encounter clients who have concomitant addiction problems. In such cases, it is important for the clinician to determine the role, if any, that stuttering plays in the individual's addiction problem. Providing clients with alternative coping strategies for their stuttering can help with addiction problems, but is likely not the only intervention needed. Referral to other professionals and organizations who specialize in treating addiction problems can be an important factor in helping the client. Other professionals, however, are unlikely to fully understand the impact of stuttering on the person, or the most appropriate ways to address the stuttering problem. Consequently, speech-language pathologists should work closely with other professionals in a coordinated approach to best help the client.

Determining the Speaker's Desire for Change

Virtually all clinical authorities agree that the motivation of the person who stutters is a key feature of a successful treatment outcome (Van Riper, 1973). Motivation can also be regarded as a covert aspect of stuttering and can be difficult to identify and quantify. The person's commitment to change and growth should be assessed prior to, as well as throughout, the therapeutic process. Depending on past successes and the client's response to new and sometimes difficult challenges, motivation will vary greatly between and within clients.

What does not accurately—or at least not completely—reflect a person's level of motivation are the statements made during assessment and the initial treatment sessions. It is not unusual for clients to make sincere and honest statements of commitment, saying things that lead us to believe they are highly motivated. These are similar to the comments we make when deciding to do things like diet or train for an event such as a marathon or triathlon. Although it might be pleasant to hear these declarations of commitment during the assessment interview, by placing too much importance on such statements, we are likely to be deceived. It is often best to be cautious of statements that indicate that the person is overly committed. It is one thing to plan and discuss an arduous journey and quite another to persistently take each step along the way.

It is both natural and necessary to be motivated at the outset of treatment. As the process gets underway, there are many interesting things to learn about the nature of stuttering and about the speaker's history of dealing with the problem. However, the initiation of treatment can be both exciting and anxiety producing, as it is whenever we challenge ourselves with a new task such as taking a class, starting a new job, learning new skills, or expanding the envelope of our lives in any sense. There is an element of risk as well as the possibility of partial or complete failure. It is good to enter the process with some level of self-esteem and energy. Nevertheless, when evaluating a potential client, it is useful to consider the client's degree of "mental toughness" or "psychic energy" (Cooper, 1977). This is not to suggest that we only enroll highly motivated people in treatment, but the client's true level of motivation—whatever that might be—provides an indication of the progress we can expect once treatment is initiated. As clinicians we can provide a measure of reassurance, security, and support, but it is the speaker's motivation and determination that decide the rate of change.

It is often helpful to take some time during the initial meeting to provide an overall picture of the treatment process to the speaker and interested others. Speakers might be overly enthusiastic, in part because they do not fully understand the nature of the journey. They might believe that it is the clinician's role to "fix" or provide a "cure" for the problem when, in reality, they must do the largest share of the work. As speakers begin to appreciate the focus and effort it will take to alter their response to the problem, the initial high level of motivation might fade somewhat (sometimes referred to as the "honeymoon effect"). Of course, we do not want to compromise their level of motivation, for they will need to draw on this reserve. We do, however, want to provide potential clients with a realistic view of the journey.

One practical suggestion for determining a person's level of motivation is to describe examples of the activities that will occur during treatment. Of course, we do not want to discourage potential clients or scare them off by overly emphasizing the rigors associated with therapeutic change. A cautious explanation or demonstration might be worthwhile, though, for a realistic estimate of the speaker's determination. In addition, there are questions that the clinician can ask in order to tap into a potential client's level of motivation, questions that will force a realistic consideration of his or her current priorities. For example, we can ask the person how much treatment is worth. Ignoring what might be the actual cost of therapy, what would it be worth to the potential client? Possibly $5, $25, $50, or $100 per hour? How far would the person be willing to drive to receive treatment—5, 50, or 100 miles each way? Such questions might at first appear to be contrived, or even possibly unethical, and the clinician will need to present them with appropriate timing and candor. We have found that experimenting with these thresholds of cost or distance often provide a surprisingly precise indication of the eventual level of motivation that clients demonstrate once treatment is underway.

As with many aspects of life, timing is crucial. Most of us realize that the moment when the path of another person's life intersects with ours can be decisive. Anyone who has attempted to convince a junior high or high school student who stutters to enroll in treatment knows that some people do not want our help—or at least they do not want it now. The moments when people choose to come to us for help can provide insight into their motivation and readiness for change. Where they are in the process of change is critical for successful intervention. Investigations into the process of assisted and self-directed change suggest that a person's location on a continuum from self-reevaluation and contemplation of change to action and maintenance of change is a powerful factor in predicting a successful treatment outcome (DiClemente, 1993; Prochaska et al., 1992).

It is often informative to ask the speaker questions such as these: Why are you here today and not 6 months ago? Why today and not next year? What is it that prompted you to seek out and meet with us today? The answers to such questions are important in the overall determination of motivation and especially the client's readiness for change. Sometimes people refer themselves for treatment because they realize that their speech is preventing them from career advancement. They might seek assistance when they are facing a major speaking event such as a presentation or a ceremony in which they must take part. On a more basic level, speakers sometimes come to us as they are about to experience landmark events during their life cycle. It is at such transitional periods or "nodes" in a person's

life that self-awareness and introspection could be heightened and when significant decision making and restructuring take place (Kimmel, 1974; Sheehy, 1974; Valiant, 1977). During these periods, people are frequently more likely to assume increased responsibility for their lives and begin postponed but necessary journeys. Although transitional periods occur throughout life, one major period for people who stutter is likely to be when they are in their early 20s (Plexico et al., 2005). During this decade, people are likely to complete formal schooling, change their living status and location, enter or leave military service, initiate careers, and get married or have children. It could be that missing the opportunity to obtain effective assistance at this stage of their lives will result in decades of less-than-satisfactory communication and quality of life. Plexico et al. (2009b) found that it was not until the completion of college that the majority of their participants began to see their stuttering as a substantial hindrance to their future. The prospects of employment often served as a primary impetus for change. For example, two participants stated:

> I didn't like it [stuttering] before. I didn't like that I stuttered. But it didn't really have an impact on what happened in my life. But then once I got out there [in the workforce] it felt to me like it was having an impact. I wasn't getting an equal chance for a job because of it. For the first time my stuttering was a hindrance to me advancing in life. So I needed to do something to fix that or at least get to a point where it wasn't a problem. (p. 114)

> I know that I can make progress and that I'm the only one holding myself

back. [I] won't be thirty and still working . . . at a place where I'm not challenged and I don't have to talk. I don't want that. (p. 215)

Opportunities for reassessment and change might also occur during middle age, when people sometimes take the opportunity to do something about a problem that they have put into the background for much of their lives. As Newgarten indicated, middle age is characterized by "self-awareness," "heightened introspection," and "restructuring of experience" (cited in Kimmel, 1974, p. 58). Moreover, as Sheehy (1974) suggested, midlife is often characterized by a reexamination, whereby people question many views of self and others. At this time, they are more likely to readjust old responses to lifelong problems (Sheehy, 1974; Valiant, 1977). Of course, adopting new approaches to old problems is possible at any time during the life cycle, but it seems to be most frequent during the decades of the 40s and 50s. It could be that if individuals in that age range are interested in treatment, significant progress can result. Or it might be that individuals are more likely to employ self-directed change, possibly with the support of a self-help group, rather than seek formal treatment (especially if past treatment has not been helpful).

Cost of Treatment

The cost of treatment is a major consideration for nearly every client. The cost for individual treatment sessions varies widely, based on many factors, such as location. Of course, university-related clinic services where students are receiving training and experience are typically less expensive and private therapy with professional clinicians is somewhat more expensive. Even if clients are attending only one individual and one group session per week, the cost can quickly become prohibitive for many people.

People who stutter often experience rapid change during an intensive, residential treatment program, and one reason for this could be the motivation required to enroll. Not only does the cost of these programs represent a reasonably large financial commitment, but the participants also must often make significant social, educational, or vocational adjustments in order to attend. If someone is determined enough to use vacation time, spend a portion of their savings, and temporarily move some or all of their family to the location of an intensive treatment program for several weeks, it is probably a good indication that the person is highly motivated.

Some adults who stutter (and parents of children who stutter) simply cannot afford professional help unless the services are covered by insurance, which is not typically the case for fluency disorders. Treatment, especially for adolescents and adults who stutter, might require several weeks or months for successful change. Whether the treatment program is an intensive program lasting several weeks or a less intensive program where the speaker attends once or twice a week, the total cost can easily approach or go beyond several hundreds or even thousands of dollars. This is a significant amount of money by any standard, but the impact of successful treatment on the lives of the client can be momentous, even life altering. It is interesting to note that some people (and insurance companies or state agencies) are willing to spend a one-time expense of thousands of dollars on various assistive devices that might or might not provide increased fluency.

TWO PRINCIPLES OF ASSESSMENT

Although the assessment process will often be comprehensive and multilayered, it is useful to appreciate that much of what is done during both the assessment and the treatment of stuttering can be reduced to two basic principles. Often, during both assessment and treatment, we find ourselves returning to these principles, particularly when we are uncertain of our next step. First, and perhaps most important, the more an individual who stutters alters the choices and narrows the options that are available in life, the greater the influence and handicapping effects of stuttering are likely to be. Assessment must focus on determining the extent of such altered decision making in all its forms. In turn, many treatment goals will focus on increasing the person's ability to make choices based on information beyond the fact that stuttering is a possibility. Later in this chapter we describe the rationale for asking the speaker to respond to the question, "What do you do *because* you stutter?" The speaker's response to this question will provide a preliminary indication of how the possibility of stuttering impacts his or her decision making. As the members of the National Stuttering Association proclaim in the title of their newsletter *Letting GO,* the person who stutters must learn to "let go" and live life as it can best be lived rather than base decisions on the fact that, among many other important characteristics, he or she happens to be someone who stutters.

The second basic principle of assessment has to do with the various forms of effort and struggle behavior. Everything else being equal, the more a speaker reacts to his or her stuttering by trying to prevent it from occurring or by struggling through a moment of stuttering, the greater the impact of the problem. In this case, the question we might ask is, "What does the speaker do *when* he or she stutters?" The clinician can determine how and to what degree the speaker is closing down or restricting the speech production system, especially the vocal tract. What is the speaker doing with the source of energy in the respiratory system and the vocal tract resonator or filter that prevents these systems from being used efficiently? How is the speaker inhibiting normal voicing and articulation? What is the speaker doing to prohibit the transition from one sound or syllable to another? What is the speaker doing to keep from speaking (or stuttering) easily, openly, and smoothly? Much of what influences the clinician's determination of the speaker's stuttering severity and subsequent treatment decisions can be based on these two principles: (a) To what degree is the person using open decision making about communicating? (b) To what degree is the person attempting to speak with an open and flexible vocal tract?

ESTIMATING SEVERITY

Assessing the severity of stuttering is not as straightforward as determining the frequency or even the form of the stuttering events. Regardless of the frequency and form of the stuttering, people's responses to the problem—what they tell themselves about their situation—is a critical indicator of severity (Emerick, 1988). As discussed in Chapter 2, the revised *International Classification of Functioning, Disability, and Health (ICF)* framework as described by Yaruss and Quesal (2004) recognizes that all disabilities involve more than observable behaviors and include the many disadvantages the person experiences as he or she attempts to achieve life goals. We have seen many people who would be judged as having a severe fluency problem based on the nature of the surface features. They have frequent moments of stuttering accompanied by obvious tension and struggle behavior. However, they are not inclined to be disadvantaged or handicapped by stuttering. This is apt to be the case for individuals who regularly attend meetings of the national support groups for individuals who stutter (see Chapter 15). They make all or the majority of their decisions based on information apart from the possibility of stuttering. It is probable that many people who respond to their stuttering in this fashion never seek professional help. At the other extreme, we have seen adults who stutter infrequently, with relatively little tension or obvious struggle. Their stuttering moments are exceedingly brief and hardly noticed by their listeners. Nevertheless, they are devastated by these experiences. Even though by any objective or external standard the problem seems a

minor one, the fact that he or she is a person who stutters is a prominent theme in the person's current life story. These two divergent examples of how speakers respond to stuttering are, of course, endpoints of a continuum, with most speakers falling somewhere between these extremes. A primary task for the clinician is to help the client create a map of the surface behaviors of stuttering as well as the intrinsic features of the problem.

The field of counseling also faces a similar dilemma for assigning a severity level to a client's problem. Mehrabian and Reed (1969) suggested the following formula for determining severity:

$$\text{Severity} = \text{Distress} \times \text{Uncontrollability} \times \text{Frequency}$$

This formula could be particularly appropriate for assessing the severity of stuttering, because the formula factors in the speaker's reaction in terms of the affective and cognitive features of the problem. In

CLINICAL INSIGHT

A number of years ago, I worked with a college-aged man who had a long history with stuttering. This young man had many years of stuttering therapy under his belt and could use a pull-out or prep set without blinking an eye. He could also control his stuttering using easy onsets and careful articulation whenever he needed. Most people in this person's life did not even know that he was a person who stutters. But to him, stuttering was devastating! He described himself as "subhuman"—because, he said, speech and communication are what make us human, and if you can't do that, well, then you are just not really human! One day while we were talking, he told me about a time in high school when he was desperate for help, even entertaining thoughts of suicide. He went to the school speech-language pathologist, who proceeded to administer an SSI test. On completion of the test, the speech pathologist told this individual that she could not put him on her caseload as, based on his scores, his stuttering was not severe enough. Fortunately, he survived through self-help and support groups and is currently doing very well in a professional field. (AD) addition, frequency of stuttering, although often a major contributor to severity, is not the only factor, and even a low rate of frequency, when the formula is multiplied out, can result in a high level of severity. Also note that the multiplication signs imply that even low levels of distress or lack of control can contribute to the effective severity of the stuttering problem, thereby preventing the client from fully taking part in life.

MAPPING THE SURFACE FEATURES

The surface features of adults who stutter are relatively easy to determine, for these are the features that can be seen and heard as well as audio and video recorded. Speakers who have been stuttering for some time might be unaware of many obvious behaviors that have become incorporated into their stuttering. For such people, responding to the question, "What do you do *when* you stutter?" will take some exploration. Some speakers might need to become desensitized to stuttering by observing stuttering behaviors in other speakers (or the clinician as he or she voluntarily produces various stuttering form types). At the most basic level, there are three basic categories of surface features—frequency, tension, and duration.

Frequency

The frequency of fluency breaks is often one of the most obvious aspects of the problem and to some degree it impacts the perception of severity, particularly by the listener. Although the frequency of the fluency breaks is relatively easy to tabulate, it is also a feature that can be the most deceiving. The frequency of stuttering is

not likely to correspond to the impact of stuttering on the speaker (Manning & Beck, 2013b). For some speakers, particularly very young speakers, the frequency of fluency breaks provides a reasonable way to conceptualize severity. For other speakers, however, tabulating the frequency of stuttering events might fail to indicate the essence of the stuttering experience. We also have people who come to us who have other requests, though, as described by Jezer (1997):

> Speaking slowly and with great expression she told how she grew from a "shy, lonely, isolated little girl who never fit in" into a confident woman who was not afraid to speak in public. "We all know what stuttering is," she said, "and the blocking is only a very, very minor part. Stuttering is the isolation, pain, fear, and low self-esteem that must be relieved. And when they are relieved, I will be cured of my stuttering." (p. 242)

As Brundage, Bothe, et al. (2006) pointed out, many researchers and clinicians agree that reliable and valid tabulation of stuttering frequency is an important part of assessment and outcome measurement. The most common way to tabulate the frequency of stuttering is to determine the percentage of stuttered syllables (%SS) or stuttered words (%SW). Counts can be obtained by shadowing the syllable production of the speaker and indicating those syllables on which stuttering occurs. Stuttered syllables can be indicated with a keyboard or by hand by marking dots and dashes for fluent and stuttered syllables, respectively. Tabulating the frequency of stuttered syllables is thought to be a reasonable approach to indicating fluency because it is generally agreed that the timing of speech movements is closely related to syllable-sized (as opposed to word-based) units (Allen, 1975; Starkweather, 1987; Stetson, 1951).

Nevertheless, a number of studies have pointed out difficulties in obtaining reliable frequency counts, particularly across clinics (Ham, 1989; Ingham & Cordes, 1992; Kully & Boberg, 1988). Rather than counting specific stuttering events or focusing on the particular form of stuttering taking place, some have advocated time-interval judgments, whereby observers indicate whether or not stuttering has taken place during short (e.g., 5-second) intervals. This procedure is found to result in increased inter- and intrajudge consistency and greater accuracy for inexperienced observers (Cordes & Ingham, 1994, 1996; Ingham et al., 1993). Brundage, Bothe, et al. (2006) investigated the ability of 41 university students with relatively little experience observing stuttering and 31 speech-language pathologists (averaging 11.1 years of clinical experience) to identify the presence of stuttering during an audiovisual presentation of 216 five-second intervals. The judgments by both groups were then contrasted to those of 10 highly experienced observers. Both students and clinicians demonstrated relatively high levels of agreement (average of 88.5% and 87.4%, respectively), results that coincided with several earlier investigations of student raters. However, although students accurately identified 98% of the intervals determined to be nonstuttered, they only identified 37.5% of the intervals determined to be stuttered by experienced judges. Similarly, the clinicians accurately identified 94.1% of the intervals determined to be nonstuttered but only 51.6% of the intervals determined to be stuttered by the experienced judges. The authors pointed out that greater familiarity with the speakers as well as speaker input about the occurrence of normal or stuttered fluency breaks could increase accuracy. The results of these and earlier investigations indicate the necessity of training students and clinicians in the accurate identification of both stuttered and nonstuttered events. Although it is advisable to tabulate %SS or %SW during both conversational speech and reading activities, it is good to remember that these values tend to be highly variable for a speaker, depending on the speaking situation and the reading material. Speakers who are adept at avoiding and substituting words might have a greater frequency of stuttering when reading aloud because they are less able to avoid or substitute sounds and words. For these speakers, conversely, conversational speech provides the opportunity to alter words, sometimes possibly yielding a smaller %SS value than would otherwise be the case.

Although the frequency of fluency breaks is often positively correlated with other estimates of stuttering severity, it is important to appreciate that the frequency of these breaks also could be negatively related to the actual severity of the problem. That is, speakers who are adept at substituting words or circumlocuting portions of sentences might have a severe problem, but overt stuttering will be infrequent. Although the individual might not be seen or heard as a person who stutters, his or her manner of communication could convey other perceptions. One adult client who was extremely good at hiding his stuttering by circumventing speaking situations and avoiding and substituting words said, "People never knew that I was stuttering. They just thought that I was weird."

Cooper (1985) referred to the hazards of viewing stuttering primarily in terms of the number of fluency breaks as the "frequency fallacy," a position that has been supported by many subsequent studies (e.g., Blumgart et al., 2010; Craig et al., 2003; Tran et al., 2011; Manning & Beck, 2013b). Persons who stutter and who choose not to raise their hand in the classroom in spite of knowing the answer, not to ask for directions or assistance, not to order a particular item in a restaurant, not to use their spouse's name during introductions, not to make or answer a telephone call (especially in a crowded room), or not to use a paging or intercom system at the office, are severely impacted by their stuttering. Unlike the tree falling in the forest, there is no sound. Nevertheless, such choices are examples of profound stuttering events. These events are insidious because they nearly always have a subtle—but powerful—influence on the person's quality of life.

Although it is not surprising that individuals who stutter are likely to hide their stuttering from everyday listeners, some might be surprised to find that it is not unusual for speakers to do the same when interacting with their clinician. This could result from the speaker's desire to please the clinician, particularly if the clinician overemphasizes or places a high value on the achievement of fluency as the ultimate or only goal of therapy. In other instances, a speaker who has yet to become desensitized to the experience of stuttering might take the easier path of avoidance. As Sarah, a woman in her mid-20s, described:

> When I was in therapy in junior high I would substitute and I would not stutter and she would think that I was making progress, but I was hiding it the whole time. I don't know why I would hide it from the speech pathologist, you know. But it was

CLINICAL DECISION MAKING

There are occasions during the assessment of adolescents and adults when little, if any, overt stuttering will occur. This could be the result of the speaker being able to temporarily will himself or herself to override (or possibly avoid) moments of stuttering. This atypical level of fluency might simply be the result of the speaker having a particularly fluent day. When this occurs during an evaluation we have often thought (and on occasions expressed to the speaker) how this situation is similar to taking your car to a mechanic only to find that it has stopped making that funny sound. Some clients, in frustration, will plead for the clinician to understand that despite the fact that they are speaking fluently at the moment, they really do stutter. An appreciation by the clinician for this situation can show the client your understanding about the nature of stuttering. The clinician can acknowledge the variability of stuttering and that often, especially where stuttering is permitted or even encouraged, stuttering is less likely to occur. Furthermore, a thorough diagnostic interview will confirm patterns of behavior and decision making that are consistent with what is known about people who stutter. If the clinician is interested in obtaining examples of overt stuttering, all that is usually necessary is to have the client make telephone calls or speak to strangers inside or outside of the building.

just that I was ashamed of it, so any chance I could dodge a block I took it. So she thought I was making so much progress.

Tension and Duration

The tension and duration of observable stuttering are closely related and therefore discussed here together. Generally, the greater the tension or effort associated with a moment of stuttering, the longer the duration of the event. Some speakers exhibit muscular tension throughout their entire body both during and in anticipation of stuttering. Even when the speaker exhibits a relatively low frequency of stuttering, if any one of the events lasts for several seconds and is associated with considerable muscular tension, the ability of the person to communicate is severely compromised. With high levels of tension, particularly if it is focused at a specific point in the vocal tract such as the lips, tongue, or velum, a tremor is likely to occur. Tremors are the rapid, involuntary, oscillatory movement of muscles of the neck and head—considerably faster than a voluntary movement. The effect is often dramatic and contributes to the cosmetic abnormality of the problem.

Another concept related to tension and one that is helpful to consider is the degree to which a word is fragmented. As described in Chapter 2, fragmentation of the word—particularly a monosyllabic word—is a fundamental feature of nonfluent speech. Bloodstein (1993) described stuttering in its most basic form as "speech transformed by tension and fragmentation." As Bloodstein pointed out, the fragmentation of movement tends to occur prior to—or early in the performance of—

a difficult motor task. Nearly all fragmentation during stuttering occurs during the initiation of a word or a syntactic unit of a sentence or phrase. Speakers who stutter appear to be doing, to a more extreme degree, what nonstuttering speakers do.

With greater levels of tension there is also the possibility of a stuttering "block," whereby the vocal tract becomes occluded and both airflow and voicing cease. Closure often occurs at the level of the vocal folds (a natural point of stricture), but obstruction could also occur at any supraglottal point, during, for example, the production of plosive sounds. A good way for the clinician to interpret what is taking place is to consider what is physically occurring in the vocal tract in terms of the source-filter model of speech production (Fant, 1960; Kent & Read, 1992; Pickett, 1980). That is, the clinician asks, "What is the speaker doing to disrupt the source of energy, the air supply from the lungs? How is the speaker preventing the modulation of the air flow at the level of the vocal folds? How is the person constricting or occluding his or her vocal tract so as to adversely affect the resonant characteristics of this system?" A basic understanding of the anatomy and physiology, as well as the acoustics, of the speech production system enables the clinician to appreciate what the speaker is doing to make the process of moving from one speech segment to another so difficult.

It is also important for the person who stutters to understand the structure and function of the speech production system. Most individuals are vaguely aware of how speech is produced, and it will be useful for the clinician to provide the speaker with some understanding about the basic anatomical and physiological aspects of speech production. Doing so makes speech production as well as stuttering less of a mystery, and speakers can begin to monitor what they are doing to make speaking so difficult and to make better decisions about using the system more effectively. Speakers come to realize that they are not as helpless as they might feel in the midst of a moment of stuttering. In addition, by understanding the nature of this system, speakers are able to develop a heightened sense of proprioceptive feedback concerning the respiratory, phonatory, and articulatory integration necessary for fluent speech production. They also begin to develop this understanding and, quite literally, a feel for what they are doing (or not doing) with their system, enabling them to begin making choices that will make the process of speaking (and stuttering) easier and smoother.

Measurement of tension has been accomplished using a variety of techniques, including galvanic skin response (GSR), electroencephalography (EEG), and, most often, electromyography (EMG; Van Riper, 1982). Most clinicians are not likely to have access to such equipment. Fortunately, it is not usually necessary to have a high level of precision when measuring tension in the clinical setting. Experienced clinicians are able to identify the sites and the degree of tension with reasonably good consistency. Because tension and duration are often closely related, easily made measures of duration can yield an indication of the tension that is occurring. As with tension, measures of duration, such as spectrographic or waveform analysis—although helpful—are not usually necessary for clinical evaluation. The degree of tension and the duration of the fluency breaks also might be reflected in the rate of speech in words or syllables per minute, with lower rates indicating greater severity.

When determining the severity of stuttering, no single measure will provide the broad-based assessment necessary to capture the complex nature of the problem. The tabulation of the most prominent behaviors, as well as frequency, tension, and duration, is a good start, but only a beginning. The degree of abnormality shown by the person as he or she struggles is indicated by both verbal and physical movements prior to and during a fluency break. As we discussed in Chapter 3, the multifactorial, dynamic pathways (MDP) theory of stuttering (Smith & Weber, 2017) and the earlier multifactorial-dynamic model (Smith, 1990, 1999; Smith & Kelly, 1997) suggest that the stuttering event extends

CLINICAL INSIGHT

Quesal (2006) provided an effective metaphor for understanding the tension associated with communication when you are a person who stutters. Just as it is natural for a person walking on an icy sidewalk to exercise caution and experience some tension, communicating with faulty speech production results in the speaker putting forth greater effort, resulting in heightened tension. As with stuttering, you never know for sure when you might slip and fall on the ice. When a fall occurs, you are unsure if you will be hurt and to what degree the reactions of others will cause embarrassment. As a result of the constant tension and the efforts to prevent a fall—especially during more extreme conditions—walking becomes even more difficult.

well beyond the most obvious features of the disfluency. Furthermore, the behaviors associated with stuttering, and especially those at the extreme of the person's inventory of overt behaviors, might only be apparent during the more difficult speaking situations. Any coping behavior that at one time or another has enabled the speaker to escape from a stuttering moment, including extreme or even bizarre movements of arms, hands, legs, or torso, could be incorporated into a coping response. Virtually nothing should be a surprise to the experienced clinician, and the presence of these behaviors should be part of the overall determination of severity.

Subtle Surface Features

There are surface features of stuttering that, although they are observable, are often extremely subtle, so much so that it might take even an experienced clinician some time to detect them. We can think of these as surface features that are closely associated with the cognitive decision-making process that speakers use to cope with stuttering.

Avoidance

For many reasons, avoidance of feared stimuli associated with past fluency failure—the people, sounds, words, time pressure, and environments—is a natural but unproductive strategy for people who stutter. The core issue is that avoidance dramatically reduces participation in daily activities and choices. On many occasions, avoidance can negatively impact the person's lifestyle more than the actual stuttering. For some people, switching to another word often results in stuttering on the new word. It is not surprising that speakers can be highly resistant to letting go of what has become a primary survival response. It takes time and energy for the

---

CLINICAL DECISION MAKING

Avoidance behavior can be insidious, often difficult to identify, and especially resistant to change. People who show a high degree of avoidance behavior, if they initiate treatment at all, often find treatment difficult until they begin to become desensitized to stuttering. They might resist any suggestion to "touch" stuttering and activities that require them to approach stuttering, such as stuttering on purpose. They recoil against techniques that ask them to stay in the moment and vary the ways they stutter. They are likely to resist revealing to others that they are attending treatment or telling anyone about their therapy activities or goals. Because patterns of avoidance are often so subtle, and because they are such an effective way of covering up the stuttering behavior, clients want to hold on to these highly self-reinforcing techniques. Once identified, avoidance behavior in all of its forms is a crucial target both during and following treatment. Unless clients understand the many hazards associated with avoidance, this response to the anticipation of stuttering is likely to persist. As clients achieve the ability to shape the features of their stuttering and use fluency-enhancing or modification techniques as described in later chapters, avoidance tends to lose its usefulness and appeal.

speaker to successfully change his or her response to feared stimuli. It takes effort to scan ahead for these stimuli, and it takes even more effort to elude or respond to them as they come along. Some clients come to us feeling tired and frustrated by the ordeal. These people often show obvious relief when we suggest that they "give themselves permission to stutter."

Substitution

Substitution of words is a most obvious form of avoidance. In this case, another word is substituted for the feared sound or word, often with a slight change in the meaning of the sentence. Sometimes the meaning changes only a little (dog/poodle, x-ray/radiology, or white/vanilla). Sometimes it changes a lot (tea/coffee, no/yes, a grade of C/A). At the very least, substitution often results in an utterance that is less precise or appropriate given the context of the communication.

To the unsophisticated listener, nothing abnormal has occurred when the speaker adeptly substitutes one word or idea for another—but again, the speaker has experienced stuttering. It appears to be a good prognostic sign when the substitution of words is frustrating to the speaker. When this is the case, the speaker might be more inclined to reduce his or her habitual avoidance of feared words and make the effort to select words that coincide with the intent. Some of the most frustrated (and sometimes depressed) individuals are those who are extremely eloquent as indicated by their writing and their periods of fluent speech but are unable to speak with the same precision and eloquence when avoiding or substituting words.

Postponement

As the person who stutters chooses to approach a feared word, there is often a moment of hesitation, similar to one's

---

CLINICAL INSIGHT

As a young man in college, on those occasions when someone would ask me where my hometown was, I would do nearly anything to avoid saying the name "Williamsport." Instead, I would often say, "Well, I'm from a small town in Pennsylvania." If they inquired further, as of course they often did, I would say, "Well, it's in central Pennsylvania," or "It's a city about 85 miles north of Harrisburg." "Lock Haven?" they would respond. And I would say, "Well, it's a little east of Lock Haven." "Bloomsburg?" they would query. And I would respond, "No, it's actually west of Bloomsburg." Sometimes we would go on for a while, gradually narrowing down the possibilities, until they were able to correctly guess the name of the city. I would do whatever it took, including acting as though I had no idea where I lived, in order to hide my stuttering. During these exchanges I certainly appeared to be, at the very least, a little strange or, at most, not very bright. I frequently did the same thing when asked about such things as the schools I attended, the names of my teachers or classes, or my street address. The problems presented by stuttering went far beyond my speech. Stuttering was a way of making choices and a way of living in ways that I thought were necessary to survive socially. (WM) preparation for leaping over an obstacle. Sometimes the hesitation is subtle, taking the form of a slight pause. The speaker could be considering alternative words or thinking of different ways to structure or restructure the sentence in order to avoid using the feared word. Other times, particularly before uttering words that previously resulted in stuttering, the speaker will use a series of sounds (e.g., "ah") or words (e.g., "you know, let me see") into the flow of speech to postpone or assist in the initiation of the word. Postponements are most likely to occur with words that cannot be easily avoided, such as names, addresses, schools, or places of employment, although it is not unusual for speakers to avoid or substitute even these words.

Listening to speakers who make frequent use of postponements can be extremely difficult and unpleasant. These extra sounds and words, although maintaining a continuous flow of sound, severely disrupt the flow of information. These postponements are justifiably called "junk words," for they can litter the speech of people who are using them to the point that listeners, if given the option, will flee. As a result of treatment, clients are able to decrease the use of such postponements and starters, greatly increasing the flow of information and effectiveness of their communication. Even if there is no change in the frequency of stuttering, the effect is one of enormous improvement in the ability to communicate.

THE EXPERIENCE OF COVERT STUTTERING

Some speakers who are particularly adept at avoiding feared sounds and words, specific people, or speaking situations, might rarely if ever be perceived as a person who stutters. The person could, however, be thought of as someone who is introverted, shy, lazy, or at the very least, somewhat peculiar. Often, such speakers have been referred to as covert (Starkweather, 1987) or internalized stutterers (Douglass & Quarrington, 1952). A review of the literature on covert (or interiorized) stuttering by Constantino et al. (2017) indicates that although these speakers have been mentioned in the literature for more than a century there has been very little research about the characteristics of these individuals and how they manage to pass as fluent (Denhardt, 1890; Freund, 1934; Froeschels, 1948; Ssikorsky, 1891). Until recently, the literature has tended to characterize these people who pass as fluent as suffering from antisocial behavior due to a dominant need to hide their stuttering (Hoepfner, 1922), having powerful feelings of inferiority and apprehension (Stein, 1942), holding excessively negative views toward stuttering, and having high levels of social anxiety (Douglass & Quarrington, 1952). Kroll (1978) similarly suggested that people who stutter but pass as fluent (a) valued maintaining their role as a fluent speaker over exchanging ideas via verbal communication, (b) were less aware of their speech than people who do not pass as fluent, and (c) were more interested in pleasing superiors than pleasing their peers.

The literature that exists on passing as fluent mirrors the greater narrative of people who pass in other contexts. That is, passing as fluent, and passing in general, is seen as an inherently negative pursuit (Douglass & Quarrington, 1952; Froeschels, 1948; Hoepfner, 1922; Stein, 1942). This discourse positions passing as a repression of one's true, authentic self (Brune & Wilson, 2013) due to either internal or external factors, or a combination of both. When due to internal factors, passing is seen as a pathology due to elevated levels of shame, social anxiety, and poor self-esteem (Cox, 2013; Paterson, 2009). When attributed to external factors, passing is seen as the unfortunate result of social oppression and stigma (Goffman, 1963).

More recently, researchers have tried to take a more neutral interpretation of covert stuttering, with attempts to try to allow the individuals experiencing covert stuttering to speak for themselves. For example, several published personal accounts of covert stuttering describe behaviors such as using made-up names during introductions (Olish, 2009), dealing with the silence that surrounds stuttering (Wesseling, 2011), and the physical toll the stress of passing can have on one's body (Dartnall, 2003; MacIntyre, 2012; Mertz, 2009; Reitzes, 2012). Likewise, two phenomenological explorations of the experience of passing as fluent (Douglass, 2011; Douglass & Tetnowski, 2009) identified a transitional process of coming out of the closet as a person who covertly stutters, a practice that is generally associated with resilience.

In an effort to provide a more nuanced understanding of the experience of passing as a speaker who is covertly stuttering, Constantino et al. (2017) undertook a qualitative study that used the ethical theories of philosopher Foucault (1983a, 1983b, 1984/1997a, 1988, 1997b). The primary purpose was to contextualize responses obtained from semistructured interviews with nine participants (three males, six females) who self-identified as individuals who covertly stutter. Rather than a repression of an authentic self as described in the literature, the results indicate that passing is better understood as a form of resistance by people who stutter to a hostile society.

Douglass et al. (2019) conducted a phenomenological study of the therapy experiences of six individuals who covertly stutter. Their findings indicated that early therapy experiences were often negative, focused on fluency techniques, with very little coconstruction of therapetic goals or processes. Participants identified fluency-focused goals as validating the shame they felt about stuttering and reinforced their decision to pass as fluent. Ironically, participants were dismissed from therapy when they could successfully hide their stuttering from their clinician. Overall, stuttering therapy was seen as irrelevant to the needs of the participants as people who pass as fluent. Douglass et al. identified four themes that suggested potentially beneficial therapeutic goals for individuals who are covertly stuttering: (a) Therapy should include explicit goals and activities that are relevant to the individual, (b) there needs to be personalized selection of therapy techniques or strategies, (c) self-education about stuttering should be encouraged, and (d) education about stuttering should be provided for those in the person's environment.

Finally, Freud and Amir (2020) examined the association between resilience and covert and overt stuttering. Resilience was measured using the Connor–Davidson Resilience Scale (CD-RISC; Connor & Davidson, 2003), the covert aspect of stuttering was measured using the Overall Assessment of Speaker's Experience of Stuttering–Adults (OASES-A; Yaruss & Quesal, 2006), and the overt aspect of stuttering was evaluated using the Stuttering Severity Instrument-4 (SSI-4; Riley, 2009). Freud and Amir (2020) reported finding a strong, significant association between resilience and covert stuttering but no association between resilience and the overt measure of stuttering. They interpreted these findings as demonstrating the role of resilience in the construction of the individual's experience with stuttering and suggested that therapy approaches that directly promote resilience skills should be incorporated into stuttering therapy programs.

THE SPEAKER'S SELF-ASSESSMENT

The perceptions of speakers about themselves and their circumstances are likely to be one of the most important aspects of any assessment process, particularly for the adolescent or adult. One of the simplest, yet potentially most useful procedures for obtaining the initial perspective of clients on their stuttering is to have them respond to a series of questions designed to survey the range of their stuttering. These questions provide an opportunity to sample behavior and to assess individuals' understanding of their stuttering. The process easily leads to a brief period of trial therapy, often an important aspect of the assessment process.

In preparation for asking the questions, the clinician draws a simple scale with equal-appearing intervals (Figure 6–1), with 0 to the left representing "no stuttering," 1 representing "mild stuttering," and so on, to 8 at the right representing "severe stuttering." The clinician places the scale in front of the person and asks him or her to indicate the point on the scale that best represents his or her overall, or average, stuttering. Once this point is identified, the clinician (or preferably the speaker) can place an "A" or "Average" at that location. The act of giving speakers the pencil and placing the scale in front of them is a first step toward assigning them responsibility for their speech. It could well be the first time speakers have directly addressed their stuttering in a concrete and objective manner.

Once the client marks the point on the scale associated with what he or she per-

CLINICAL INSIGHT

As a young adult, the often subtle aspects of avoidance, substitution, and postponement were some of the most frustrating aspects of stuttering. I would say things less precisely than I was capable of, and often my meaning was distorted. Sometimes my listener could sense that the words did not exactly match the situation or my affect. In addition, I eventually realized how my thought process was inhibited when speaking. When writing, I enjoyed the challenge of finding and using just the right word to convey my meaning. However, when I spoke, I was often limiting my choices. For many years I had things to say, yet I refused to try. On a more basic level, I had things to say and I didn't even know it. I later realized that it was much like entering words on a computer screen and not knowing what you think until you write it. The new sentences result in ideas that, in turn, lead to new thoughts that you wouldn't have had otherwise. I realized that for many years, the same thing was happening when I spoke. Not only was I screening out many feared sounds and words, I was discarding current thoughts and future ideas. As my speech became ever more spontaneous and uninhibited, so did my thinking, and I found myself being able to access ideas I had not had before. This freedom is what I wanted when I was speaking. I realized that I valued spontaneity even more than fluency. (WM)

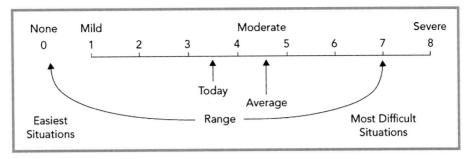

FIGURE 6–1. Equal-interval scale for determining the current, average, and range of stuttering behavior during the assessment of adolescents and adults.

ceives as his or her average level of severity, the clinician asks the client to indicate the point on the scale that best represents the sample of speech that we are hearing at the moment. Although these points can be identical, often they are not. For example, Silverman (1975) found that older children and adults judged the severity of their stuttering differently in a clinical environment than in daily beyond-treatment situations. By asking these two questions, the clinician is able to demonstrate an understanding of the variable nature of stuttering and that the behavior observed during the evaluation does not always represent the true nature and scope of the problem.

To take it a step further, the clinician can ask the client to indicate the extent of his or her stuttering behavior. How far toward either end of the scale does his or her stuttering range? What point on the scale indicates the quality of his or her speech in the best of speaking situations? For some speakers, this point represents no stuttering at all, or 0 on the scale. The speaker is then asked to indicate the point on the other end of the scale that represents his or her speech in his or her most difficult or feared speaking situations.

Once the speaker has identified a range of behavior, the clinician is able to make some observations about the person's speech and begin a short period of trial therapy. It will be possible for the clinician to determine, for example, whether his or her view of the surface features of the speaker's stuttering coincides with the client's own perception of severity. If it does not, and if the client perceives his or her stuttering very differently from the clinician, it could indicate that some time should be spent during treatment explaining the nature of stuttering and putting the client's stuttering into a broader perspective. Most individuals who stutter, unless they have attended group therapy or are a member of a stuttering support group, have not had the opportunity to observe a wide range of (particularly severe) stuttering behavior.

Assuming that the speaker has indicated a range of severity on the scale, the clinician can inform him or her that, in many ways at least, his or her stuttering is typical behavior for people who have this problem. That is, because of the variability and the nature of his or her stuttering, the speaker is not likely to be stuttering as the result of some neurological or deep-seated psychological problem. Of course, before issuing such a statement, the person's case history should be reviewed and the speaker's overall response to the examiner's evaluations should be considered. However, by explaining this to the client, the clinician provides an important service to someone who, for many years, might have regarded himself or herself as being far from normal physically or emotionally. Depending on what the client might have read or been told about stuttering as a physical or psychological and emotional problem, he or she might have concerns about these issues.

Next, the clinician can conduct some brief trial therapy by asking the person to stutter along with the clinician. This is likely to be the first time the speaker has been invited to purposely engage in this fearful behavior. The very act of asking the client to willingly stutter demonstrates an assertive, investigative, and alternative attitude on the part of the clinician. It models a willingness to lead the way that can be highly motivating to clients. It also provides the first opportunity to explore and vary a behavior that for too long has seemed fearful and uncontrollable. Although the speaker is likely to have provided an example of stuttering at the outset of the evaluation, we would also like to have an understanding of the person's mild stuttering. Many clients will initially respond to the request, "Show me what your mild stuttering looks and sounds like," by describing what they do when they stutter. Rather than a description of it, we want an example of the behavior they are concerned about and would rather avoid. Can the speaker willingly produce this behavior? Finally, can the person demonstrate, perhaps on his or her own or following our lead, examples of more moderate or possibly severe examples of his or her stuttering? If at any point in the procedure the person finds it difficult to voluntarily produce stuttering, the process can be facilitated by the clinician providing examples for the client to imitate. Both participants can then produce the examples together, followed by the client doing it on

his or her own. If, during this short period of trial therapy, speakers are able to become somewhat desensitized to their stuttering, it can be useful to ask them to replicate their stuttering to the point that voluntary stuttering changes to real, "out-of-control" stuttering. The physical and emotional features that distinguish both voluntary and real stuttering provide a starting point for experimenting with techniques that allow the speaker to achieve both variation and modification of behavior that was previously thought by the speaker to be entirely out of his or her control.

The degree to which the person can follow the clinician in experimenting with his or her stuttering tells us much about the person's levels of anxiety and motivation. These activities provide a preliminary indication of how much effort and time might be required for the person to approach, become desensitized to, and eventually alter his or her stuttering behavior. Can the person correctly identify occurrences and types of stuttering? Can he or she discriminate between the physical and emotional characteristics of real versus voluntary stuttering? Is the client willing to venture with us across the threshold of control to see that he or she is able to survive a deliberate moment of real stuttering? On the other hand, if the person is unable or unwilling to follow us in our attempts to experiment and vary his or her stuttering in this fashion, the process of treatment is likely to be more arduous.

DISCOVERING THE INTRINSIC FEATURES

Because of their very nature, the intrinsic or covert responses of the person to the experience of stuttering are somewhat more difficult to discover and quantify than the surface or overt speech characteristics. Because surface behaviors are more obvious, there is a tendency to spend the majority of the assessment time on these features. As suggested earlier, one of the ways to begin discovering intrinsic features is to ask the person, "What do you do *because* you stutter?" That is, what choices do you make—what do you do or not do—because of even the *possibility* of stuttering? This list is often considerably longer than the list of "things I do when I stutter," as the speaker gradually begins to understand how much even the possibility of stuttering has influenced the choices the speaker makes each day. Most of the choices are likely to be examples of avoidance in some form.

Identifying Speaker Loss of Control

As mentioned in Chapter 2, perhaps more than anything else, it is the speaker's feeling of losing control that differentiates people who stutter from those who experience the normal and usual fluency disruptions (Tichenor & Yaruss, 2019). Although normally fluent speakers rarely experience a profound loss of control while speaking, everyone has had a similar experience during an athletic or physical activity. There is an instant when you perceive that you are not in control of your body, a fleeting moment when you realize that you have lost your balance and might fall. It is at this moment that you recognize that you are helpless and are unable to determine the consequences of your experience. There is, at this moment, a level of anxiety and possibly fear. Such an experience is more likely to occur if you are taking part in activities that require a degree of precision, timing, and balance. Activities such as skiing, skating, paddling a canoe or kayak,

and wind surfing are good examples. However, it is also possible to encounter similar situations during more common activities such as riding a bike, climbing stairs, walking, or running. Another common example for adults is the feeling you have when sliding out of control in your car on an icy road. During these moments one can approach the level of fear and helplessness that occurs for a person who stutters during a moment of stuttering. This loss of control can be both profound and discreet. It has been suggested that it is measurable (Moore & Perkins, 1990), at least by the person doing the stuttering. Nevertheless, over the years authors have suggested that it is possible for experienced clinicians who become calibrated to their clients to be able to accurately identify such moments (Bloodstein & Shogun, 1972; Cooper, 1968; Manning & Shrum, 1973). For the nonstuttering clinician, these experiences provide an opportunity to connect to the person who stutters and demonstrate his or her understanding about this core aspect of the stuttering experience.

It will usually take several sessions before the clinician becomes calibrated to a new client and is able to recognize and verify the occurrence of some of these features. As we become attuned to the speaker, we can begin to identify the three levels of fluency: stuttered, unstable, and fluent. These levels of fluency tend to reflect the degree of control by the speaker. By pantomiming—imitating his or her speech production with our own mouths—we can begin to distinguish when the speaker is at each level of control. We can begin to sense when he or she is experiencing some lack of control over his or her fluency and identify those moments when stuttering does not quite reach the surface.

On other occasions, during what could initially appear to be seemingly fluent

CLINICAL INSIGHT

When taking a class on stuttering, students are often asked to take the part of a person who stutters in a series of daily speaking situations. On occasion, students completing this assignment report that they experience a distinct feeling of losing control as they are in the midst of stuttering. They describe having a feeling where, at least for a moment, they were uncertain about whether they would be able to stop voluntarily stuttering and continue on with what they intended to say. The experience is always described as unexpected and frightening. It can also provide some insight about why people who stutter, when they find themselves in such a condition, reflexively grasp for avoidance and escape behaviors (as irrational as they might appear to the observer) that have helped them cope with the situation in the past.

portions of speech, the person is, at best, on the edge of control. As discussed earlier, in order to prevent overt stuttering, the speaker might substitute and rearrange words. Although he or she may be producing "nonstuttered" speech, the speaker is not in control and is far from producing the effortless, smooth, and continuous speech that characterizes authentic fluency. It could also be that the perceptual effects of unstable speech indicate a lack of spontaneity and naturalness. The experienced listener—especially one who is familiar with how the speaker is capable of expressing himself or herself in terms of rate, tempo, and syntax—can detect this loss of control. The clinician might be able to sense the brief pauses or slightly sticky moments present in the unstable speech. There might be a slight hesitation prior to the onset of a word or a momentary prolongation or stickiness during the initial portion of a word or a retreating back to an earlier portion of the sentence. The speaker could slightly constrict the vocal tract, minimally slow articulatory movements, and use somewhat more effort to produce a word. The client selects a word that is close to—but does not quite provide—the mean-

ing the clinician has learned to anticipate. The client's body language (flaring of the nostrils, momentary loss of eye contact, and rapid eyelid movements) could indicate a brief moment of fear during the production of a word that is not smoothly produced. Without having awareness of this and by not responding to these cues, the clinician might believe that he or she is reinforcing fluent speech when, in reality, unstable speech, avoidance, and word substitutions are being rewarded. Of course, one of the best ways to identify or confirm these unstable events is to ask the speaker.

It could be that many of the characteristic differences that have been noted in the acoustics of the "nonstuttered" speech of people who stutter reflect this lack of control. Over the years, many researchers have observed a number of differences in the "fluent" speech of stutterers of various ages, including brief pauses (Love & Jefress, 1971); centralized formant frequencies (Klich & May, 1982); fundamental frequency variations (Healey, 1982); vocal shimmer (Bamberg et al., 1990; Hall & Yairi, 1992; Newman et al., 1989); voice reaction times (Cross et al., 1979; Reich et al., 1981); voice onset, initiation, and

CLINICAL INSIGHT

We have used two procedures to help students at least determine their level of anxiety about stuttering and self-efficacy regarding conducting treatment for individuals who stutter. The students listen to a progressively more severe series of audio and video examples of stuttering by adult speakers, and using a 1-to-10 scale where they self-indicate less to more anxiety, students rate their levels of anxiety as each sample is presented both at the outset and at the end of the semester. For several reasons, including a variety of class activities as well as the students' clinical experiences, self-ratings of anxiety routinely show consistent decreases, particularly with regard to speakers who are stuttering more severely. We also ask students to fill out a self-efficacy scale composed of 100 progressively more difficult clinical situations that they are likely to encounter when working with children or adults who stutter (Rudolf et al., 1983). Students' overall scores typically show large increases, indicating greater self-efficacy for entering into and conducting a wide variety of treatment activities. An example can be found on the companion website. (WM)

termination times (Adams & Hayden, 1976; Agnello, 1975; Hillman & Gilbert, 1977; Starkweather et al., 1976); and vocal tract instability as indicated by second formant frequency fluctuation compared to the control group of nonstuttering speakers (Robb et al., 1998). These acoustic characteristics could reflect brief moments where control was lost and unstable speech occurred. If investigators, rather than considering only the extremes of stuttered or nonstuttered speech, were to consider as a third category the nature of this perceptually unstable speech, these acoustic measures could yield even more distinctive results.

There is another important aspect of the relationship between control and fluency. Just as a stuttering speaker might feel wildly out of control as he or she circumvents possible stuttering moments and manages to sound fluent, it is also possible for him or her to speak in an overtly stuttered manner and be in complete control. In other words, the clinician can show the speaker that it is possible to stutter on pur-

pose in an open, effortless fashion while being completely in charge of his or her speech mechanism. Being able to purposely and realistically stutter with complete control helps the speaker to break the remarkably strong link between the stuttering and helplessness. The speaker begins to consider, often for the first time, that it is possible to stutter and not be helpless. It is even possible to stutter and not to be anxious or afraid. As we describe in more detail in subsequent chapters, it is possible to stutter in a different, easier, and more fluent manner.

Cognitive and Affective Factors

Closely related to the sensation of losing control of one's ability to speak are the related cognitive and affective features of stuttering. In an often-cited investigation, Corcoran and Stewart (1998) conducted one of the first qualitative studies of the experience of stuttering. The goal of their investigation was to discover consistent themes for eight adults (five men and three women ranging in age from 25–50 years) with a history of stuttering. The authors obtained narratives from the participants that were analyzed qualitatively in order to describe the core experiences of stuttering for the participants. The primary theme that Corcoran and Stewart noted was one of suffering that included elements of helplessness, shame, fear, and avoidance. Helplessness resulted from both the involuntary nature of their stuttering and the general lack of control in their lives. Participants described their core experience as a sense that their stuttering was beyond their control. Participants described shame and stigma that were experienced to a degree that other aspects of their selves were obscured or discounted. Because of the lack of an accepted explanation for stuttering, they tended to assign blame to themselves for their stuttering and the fact that they seemed to be unable to do anything about it. The feelings of helplessness and shame and fear of the stuttering experience in general and of listener reactions in particular was also a common theme. Last, concealment and avoidance of even the possibility of stuttering was a consistent pattern that often resulted in a dramatically constricted lifestyle. The authors proposed that the clinician is the major agent for assisting clients to transform the meaning of their stuttering, which, in turn, will provide a reduction in suffering and facilitate the modification of overt behaviors. The processes of understanding the client's story and allowing the client to begin to consider alternate views about the experience of stuttering can begin during the initial diagnostic interview. Subsequent investigations by Crichton-Smith (2002), Anderson and Felsenfeld (2003), and Plexico et al. (2005)

have confirmed and elaborated on these findings during the early or pretreatment stages of stuttering. In each of these investigations, individuals who stutter consistently describe themes of suffering, struggle, and restriction across many aspects of their lives. From the speaker's perspective, the impact of stuttering is represented by these intrinsic features as much or more than it is by the more obvious surface behaviors, such as the frequency of their stuttering.

The Presence of Anxiety

Beginning in the early 1900s, it was apparent to clinicians and researchers with an interest in fluency disorders that anxiety is a characteristic of adolescents and adults who stutter. As Guitar (2006) commented, "the experience of stuttering generates emotions, such as frustration, fear and anger in everyone who stutters" (p. 62). This perspective was noted in the *Diagnostic and Statistical Manual of Mental Disorders* (*DSM-IV-TR*; American Psychiatric Association, 2000), where stuttering was listed as a condition that is likely to cause excessive social anxiety and conceptualized as reactive to the stuttering (i.e., anxiety disorder not otherwise specified; see Morrison, 1995). That is, it was not appropriate to diagnose individuals with an anxiety disorder if they had already been diagnosed as stuttering. With the publication of the *DSM-V* (American Psychiatric Association, 2013), it became possible to determine a dual diagnosis if the anxiety disorder was seen as excessive or unrelated to stuttering. Of course, whether or not the level of anxiety for an individual who has stuttered into their adolescent and adult years is excessive (e.g., statistically or clinically significant) has been a

CLINICAL INSIGHT

Goleman's (2006) review of the literature on stress and health in his book *Social Intelligence* describes the effect of perceived stress on the sympathetic nervous system (SNS) and the hypothalamic–pituitary–adrenal (HPA) connections. Threatening reactions by others elicit an HPA response that produces the highest levels of cortisol (the stress hormone) of all laboratory conditions. The key factor in eliciting such high levels of stress appears to be the "judgmental scrutiny [which] delivers a particularly strong—and lingering—dose of shame" (p. 231). Furthermore, stress is further increased when the distress was not random but intended and when the person feels he or she is helpless to respond to the situation.

CLINICAL INSIGHT

It would be highly unusual for someone who stuttered to not have a heightened level of anxiety, for it is a natural response to a condition that often elicits unfavorable responses from listeners. Fluent students enrolled in a class on fluency disorders are often asked to take the role of a person who stutters while making a series of telephone calls and engaging in face-to-face communication situations. We then ask these students to rate their levels of anxiety during the activities by using two scales. The State Trait Anxiety Inventory (STAI; Spielberger et al., 1983) assesses general levels of anxiety and tension including a state scale (which assesses current levels of anxiety) and a trait scale (which measures typical levels of anxiety). The Social Interaction Anxiety Scale (SIAS; Mattick & Clarke, 1998) is designed to assess an individual's anxiety in social evaluative settings. For the majority of the students, the scales indicate extremely high anxiety ratings that are similar to people who stutter. An example from a fluent graduate student provides a vivid and poignant description of her experience:

> My degree of anxiousness surprises me as I loiter in the drive-thru line. For me, this is an assignment. I don't stutter. It's an experiment to see what it feels like, how other people react. And yet, I am terrified. Not of doing it wrong, not of being inauthentic or "found out." After all, I haven't been here often enough for someone to recognize me. But it's embarrassing. I don't want them to see me mess up.
>
> I already hate drive-thru lines, and ordering things in general. The assembly line's movement is highly regulated, and you must have your order ready to go, and your money in hand, and you will likely have to make decisions quickly, without being given time to think about them. Drive-thrus are notoriously bad places for communication, but at least I won't have to face someone directly. There's a sign posted at the menu board: "Please proceed to the second window." So much for

continues

that. Thankfully, I've had time to choose a Southwest Grilled Chicken Burger (which will go by "chicken burger" because that's enough to distinguish it) and chocolate turned-vanilla shake (because "chicken" already caused me trouble). I'll be using blocks and sound repetitions. Maybe I'll ask for a receipt.

She's waiting for me as I speak. It's hot. Her eyes are glazed. She doesn't want to be at work. As I begin talking, I find I've become angry at my steering wheel. The tense neck, furrowed brow, and averted eyes came without permission. When I think I have my words together, I face her again. But it doesn't always work. (In retrospect, she was good to me. She just waited. Perhaps I was no more disagreeable than any of her customers.) There are two or three cars behind me. Maybe more around the corner.

She missed what I said the first time. Are you kidding me? After all that? I'm panicking. But she remembers and I nod at her confirmation emphatically. I am reminded that I can nod and smile; I don't say another word. This solves the problem of cars behind me. What would I do with the receipt anyway?

I would never say to a person who stutters, "You are less than." But I found myself getting by with non-verbals, passiveness, and an ingratiating, apologetic demeanor. The stuttering was not real, but the shame was. I anticipated fear, and embarrassment, and vulnerability. Shame surprised me. Why shame? There's nothing to be ashamed of. Stuttering is a thing, and it happens, and people deal with it, like any number of things.

But I have to ask you, stranger, to make up for my deficits. And I have to ask all of you, guests, to wait a little longer for your food. I have to draw unwanted and unflattering attention to myself. I have to forgo the complexity of my desires, because they hold you up. I have to forgo everyday pleasantries and courtesies, because my participation in them interrupts their natural flow. In order to explain anything, I have to start talking—and the only way that works is if you are already willing to listen to me before I've said anything that you understand. I wish this was not how you knew me.

My gratitude is real. Still, I wish I didn't have to ask you to do this extra thing for me—this extra listening—because it puts pressure on the things I say to be things worth being said. A few times over. And it creates this imbalance in our relationship and I feel like I owe you.

Intellectually, I know that voice and identity are linked. And that relationships and communication are linked. But stuttering is a thing that people deal with in different ways. And it could be an informative part of how they perceive themselves, their place, their worth, and their relationships with others. Shame is not new for me, but this exercise brought it out. I can see why fluency issues, particularly in adolescents and adults, could have a serious psychological bent.

source of controversy as the decision has financial implications for service providers.

The possibility of anxiety has been documented using a variety of physiological measures such as heart rate, blood pressure, EEG, and skin conductance (Berlinsky, 1955; Brutten, 1963; Fletcher, 1914; Knott et al., 1959; Robbins, 1920; Travis et al., 1936) and self-report measures such as the Endler Multidimensional Scales (e.g., Messenger et al., 2004), the State and Trait Anxiety Inventory (e.g., Blood et al., 1994; Blumgart et al., 2010; Craig, 1990; Craig et al., 2003; Ezrati-Vinacour & Levin, 2004; Miller & Watson, 1992; Mulcahy et al., 2008), and the Taylor Manifest Anxiety Scale (e.g., Boland, 1953; Kraaimaat et al., 1991).

Some investigators found few significant differences in levels of anxiety when comparing individuals who stutter with fluent speakers (Andrews & Craig, 1988; Andrews & Harris, 1964; Andrews et al., 1983; Cox et al., 1984; Craig & Hancock, 1996; Hegde, 1972; Lanyon et al., 1978; Miller & Watson, 1992; Molt & Guilford, 1979; Peters & Hulstijn, 1984; Prins, 1972). For example, Molt and Guilford (1979) and Miller and Watson (1992) found no differences between adults who stutter and a group of controls on either state or trait anxiety. In commenting on the results of pharmacological treatment for stuttering, Bothe, Davidow, Bramlett, and Ingham (2006) stated that the lack of effectiveness for the use of anxiolytics (medications used for the treatment of anxiety) for the treatment of stuttering indicates "that stuttering is neither inextricably nor functionally related to anxiety" (p. 9).

Others, using different measures of anxiety, found significant levels of anxiety for those who had been dealing with stuttering for several years. Blumgart et al. (2010) used several measures of anxiety to compare 200 adults who stuttered and a control group of 200 fluent adults. The measures included the STAI and the SIAS. The results indicated that the adults who stuttered had significantly greater levels of state and trait anxiety as well as social anxiety. There were moderate to large effect sizes for all anxiety measures. Several studies by researchers in Sydney, Australia (e.g., Iverach et al., 2009a; Iverach et al., 2011) have also found significant levels of anxiety for adults, adolescents, and children who stutter.

Craig (1990) noted that most research on anxiety and related psychological processes among those who stutter has included only individuals who were seeking or receiving treatment. Craig and Hancock (1995) found that adults who experienced self-defined relapse were three times more likely to indicate higher trait anxiety levels. Craig et al. (2003) summarized the literature and concluded that those who seek treatment characteristically have greater levels of stuttering severity as well as higher levels of anxiety than their fluent peers. Notably, Craig et al. found that for those who successfully completed therapy, anxiety levels are often comparable to their fluent peers. They also found no significant differences in anxiety levels between individuals who stuttered who had received therapy and those who had not. Moreover, no significant differences in anxiety emerged when comparing individuals who stutter who had never received therapy with a group of nonstuttering controls. However, when comparing the nonstuttering controls with the individuals who had received therapy, a significant difference was found. In addition, no differences in anxiety levels were noted between those with a higher frequency (>6% SS) of stuttering and those with less frequent (<6% SS) stuttering. Finally, those who were seeking treatment had higher levels of anxiety.

Manning and Beck (2013b) examined 50 adults with a history of stuttering. Participant scores of trait anxiety (STAI), social anxiety (SIAS), depression (Beck Depression Inventory-II [BDI-II]; Beck et al., 1996), and personality features (The Assessment of *DSM-IV* Personality Disorders [ADP-IV]; Schotte & Doncker, 1994, 1996) were entered into a regression analysis with criterion variables (DVs; %SS, SSI-3 (Riley, 1994), and OASES (Yaruss & Quesal, 2006) total score. In order to explore the OASES further, each of the four OASES subscales was also examined. A separate regression was conducted for each dependent variable. The OASES total score model was significant and revealed that social anxiety and trait anxiety were the only significant predictors with medium effect sizes, respectively. In contrast, percent syllables stuttered and the SSI-3 were not significantly associated with psychological variables, suggesting that anxiety might not always be related to overt indicators of stuttering. Depression and personality dysfunction were not significantly associated with any measure of stuttering severity. The results indicated traditional procedures for assigning severity ratings to individuals who stutter based on percent syllables stuttered and the SSI are not significantly related to psychological processes central to the stuttering experience. That is, depression and personality characteristics do not meaningfully account for stuttering.

Assessing the Speaker's Decision Making

As a result of the cognitive and affective coping responses, speakers frequently make many of their daily decisions based on the possibility as well as the reality of stuttering. We want to examine the many examples of a speaker's narrowing of options that typically result from attempts to avoid stuttering. As with detecting loss of control, it will take several treatment sessions to become calibrated to the person's lifestyle and manner of expressing himself or herself before the clinician can begin to appreciate the client's decision-making paradigm (Hayhow & Levy, 1989). Even after becoming aware of these restricting choices, the person might not associate the choices with stuttering. The decisions have become a way of understanding oneself. The client might indicate, "This is just the way I am. I'm basically a shy person. I don't want to take part in class or speak in front of groups. I don't like to use the phone. I'd rather mind my own business and would prefer not to introduce myself to strangers." Indeed, some or all these things might be true, for not everyone who is free from stuttering is a highly verbal or interactive person. More frequently, though, for the person who stutters, many of these choices are informed by the probability of stuttering.

As the clinician is able to provide security and insight about the problem, the speaker is apt to become increasingly introspective about his or her patterns of responding to stuttering. It does little good at this point to ask the client to stop making what we see as poor choices, because these old responses are strong. Early on, the primary goal is to help the person to identify and acknowledge these choices, particularly those that foster denial or avoidance of stuttering. As people come to understand a wider range of options, they can begin to experiment with alternative choices in an ever-increasing range of communication situations. It is important to note, however, that as avoidance behaviors decrease, there is the possibility that the frequency of stuttering will increase. At this time, it is especially important to desensitize the speaker to the stuttering experience. Because the client is now taking part in speaking situations that he or she previously avoided (e.g., asking a question in class or the office, using the telephone, expressing an opinion during a discussion), there are more opportunities for stuttering to reach the surface. The choices the person is making are far better, but for the moment at least, listeners might hear more stuttering. In this instance at least, an increase in the frequency of stuttering can be appropriately interpreted as a sign of progress.

CONSENSUS GUIDELINES FOR ASSESSMENT OF ADOLESCENTS AND ADULTS

In Chapter 4, we described the six core areas that Brundage et al. (2021) determined were components of a comprehensive stuttering evaluation. In the appendixes of their article, these authors provided examples of specific assessment tools or procedures that they use to assess each area. The appendixes for adolescents (Table 6–1) and adults (Table 6–2) are reproduced here (with permission). These examples provide clinicians with an excellent resource as a starting point for designing

TABLE 6–1. Commonly Recommended Procedures and Sample Data That May Be Collected as Part of a Comprehensive Stuttering Assessment for Adolescents

Adolescent Stuttering Assessment (ages 13–18 years)
Evaluation Procedures
Case history forms for the adolescent and caregivers, including parents, teachers, and other family members, as appropriate
Interviews with the adolescent and caregivers
Observation of the adolescent's speech in various speaking situations
Screening and testing, as needed, of the adolescent's language, speech, temperament, hearing, and related abilities
Observation and testing of the adolescent's speech fluency and stuttering behavior, reactions to stuttering, and impact of stuttering
Sample data for Area 1: Stuttering-related background information
Caregivers' view of the problem in general and main concerns
Caregivers' report of concomitant concerns and other diagnoses
Caregivers' report about the development of stuttering, including family history of persistence and recovery, time since onset and developmental course, and other speech or language issues as relevant
Caregivers' perceptions of prior therapy for stuttering or other concerns

continues

TABLE 6–1. *continued*

Adolescent Stuttering Assessment (ages 13–18 years)
Caregivers' knowledge and experiences related to stuttering, including beliefs about causal, eliciting, and reinforcing factors for stuttering (Palin PRS; Millard & Davis, 2016)
Caregivers' goals for stuttering treatment (e.g., Solution-Focused Brief Therapy [SBFT] scaling; Nicholas, 2015)
Adolescent's perceptions and current knowledge about stuttering
Adolescent's perceptions of prior therapy for stuttering or other concerns
Adolescent's degree of concern, readiness for change, and goals for treatment (e.g., SBFT scaling)
Assessment and progress reports from prior treatment, if applicable
Sample data for Area 2: Speech, language, temperament, and related background information
Caregivers' views about the adolescent's development, including cognitive and social-emotional development, behavior, and coping skills
Clinician's observations of the adolescent's communication and related skills
Scores on screenings and tests, as needed, of adolescent's language development, speech sound production skills, and temperament (e.g., Child Behavior Checklist [CBCL]; Achenbach & Rescoria, 2000)
Scores on screenings and tests of related factors, including anxiety (e.g., Spence Children's Anxiety Scale; Spence, 1998), as appropriate
Sample data for Area 3: Speech fluency and stuttering behavior
Caregivers' observations and perceptions of fluency and stuttering, including types of disfluencies, physical tension, secondary characteristics, factors affecting variability and severity in different speaking situations (e.g., Palin PRS; Millard & Davis, 2016)
Adolescent's perceptions and self-ratings of speech, fluency, and stuttering, including types of disfluencies, physical tension, secondary characteristics, factors affecting variability and severity, in various speaking situations
Clinician's data on speech, fluency, and stuttering (e.g., frequency/percent of syllables stuttered [%SS], type, duration, and severity [e.g.., SEV; O'Brian et al., 2004] of disfluencies; physical tension; speaking rate; naturalness [Martin & Haroldson, 1992]; other speech characteristics) in different situations
Scores on tests and measures of speech fluency and stuttering (e.g., Speech Situation Checklist-Speech Disruption [SSC-SD; Brutten & Vanryckeghem, 2007], Stuttering Severity Instrument [SSI; Riley, 2009])
Sample data for Area 4: Adolescent's reactions to stuttering
Caregivers' observations of adolescent's affective, behavioral, and cognitive reactions to stuttering (e.g., embarrassment, anxiety, shame, fear, avoidance, word substitution)
Adolescent's report of reactions to stuttering and coping responses

TABLE 6–1. *continued*

Adolescent Stuttering Assessment (ages 13–18 years)
Adolescent's use of speech and stuttering management strategies
Situational speech-related anxiety hierarchy/avoidance hierarchy
Scores on tests of adolescent's reactions to stuttering and attitudes about communication (e.g., Behavior Checklist [BCL; Brutten & Vanryckeghem, 2007], Communication Attitudes Test [CAT; Brutten & Vanryckeghem, 2007], Speech Situation Checklist-Emotional Response [SSC-ER; Brutten & Vanryckeghem, 2007], Overall Assessment of the Speaker's Experience of Stuttering-Teen [OASES-T; Yaruss & Quesal, 2016])
Sample data for Area 5: Reactions to stuttering within the environment
Caregivers' reactions to stuttering, degree of concern about stuttering, satisfaction with the adolescent's communication, perceptions of how stuttering impacts the caregivers and family (e.g., Palin PRS)
Caregivers' observations of the reactions of others, including peers and family members
Adolescent's perception of the reactions of others (e.g., experience of bullying)
Sample data for Area 6: Adverse impact associated with stuttering
Caregivers' perceptions of whether and how much stuttering affects the adolescent's willingness or ability to speak, participation in social and educational activities, and adolescent's quality of life (e.g., Palin PRS)
Adolescent's perceptions of whether and how much stuttering affects willingness or ability to speak, participation in social and educational activities, and quality of life
Scores on tests of adverse impact and quality of life (e.g., BCL, OASES-T)

Source: Reprinted with permission from Brundage, B. S., Bernstein Ratner, N., Boyle, M. P., Eggers, K., Everard, R., Franken, M.-C., Kefalianos, E., Marcotte, A. K., Millard, S., Packman, A., Vanryckeghem, M., & Yaruss, J. S. (2021). Consensus guidelines for the assessments of individuals who stutter across the lifespan. *American Journal of Speech-Language Pathology, 30*(6), 2379–2393. https://doi.org/10.1044/2021_AJSLP-21-00107

TABLE 6–2. Commonly Recommended Procedures and Sample Data That May Be Collected as Part of a Comprehensive Stuttering Assessment for Adults

Adult Stuttering Assessment (ages 18 years and up)
Evaluation procedures
Case history forms for the adult and significant others, as appropriate
Interviews with the adolescent and significant others, as appropriate
Observation of the adult's speech in various speaking situations
Observation and testing of the adult's speech fluency and stuttering behavior, reactions to stuttering, and impact of stuttering

continues

TABLE 6–2. *continued*

Adult Stuttering Assessment (ages 18 years and up)
Sample data for Area 1: Stuttering-related background information
Adult's report of stuttering onset and relevant history
Adult's perceptions and current knowledge about stuttering
Adult's perceptions of prior therapy for stuttering or other concerns
Adult's readiness for change and goals for treatment (e.g., Solution-Focused Brief Therapy [SBFT] scaling; Nicholas, 2015)
Adult's current goals for therapy
Assessment and progress reports from prior treatment, if applicable
Sample data for Area 2: Speech, language, temperament, and related background information
Clinician's observations of the adult's communication and related skills
Scores on screenings and tests, of related factors, including Fear of Negative Evaluation (FNE; Watson & Friend, 1969), Self-Efficacy Scaling for Adults Who Stutter (SESAS; Ornstein & Manning, 1985) as appropriate
Sample Data for Area 3: Speech fluency and stuttering behavior
Adult's perceptions and self-ratings of speech, fluency, and stuttering, including types of disfluencies, physical tension, secondary characteristics, factors affecting variability, and severity in various speaking situations
Clinician's data on speech, fluency, and stuttering (e.g., frequency/percent of syllables stuttered [%SS], type, duration, and severity [e.g.., SEV; O'Brian et al., 2004] of disfluencies; physical tension; speaking rate; naturalness [Martin & Haroldson, 1992]; other speech characteristics) in different situations
Scores on tests and measures of speech fluency and stuttering (e.g., Speech Situation Checklist-Speech Disruption [SSC-SD; Brutten & Vanryckeghem, 2007], Stuttering Severity Instrument [SSI; Riley, 2009])
Sample data for Area 4: Adult's reactions to stuttering
Adult's report of reactions to stuttering and coping responses
Adult's use of speech and stuttering management strategies
Situational speech-related anxiety hierarchy/avoidance hierarchy
Scores on tests of adult's reactions to stuttering and attitudes about communication (e.g., Behavior Checklist [BCL; Vanryckeghem & Brutten, 2018], Communication Attitudes Test for Adults [BigCAT; Vanryckeghem & Brutten, 2018], Speech Situation Checklist-Emotional Response [SSC-ER; Vanryckeghem & Brutten, 2018], Overall Assessment of the Speaker's Experience of Stuttering-Teen [OASES-A; Yaruss & Quesal, 2016], Self-Stigmas of Stuttering Scale [4S; Boyle, 2013], Unhelpful Thoughts and Beliefs About Stuttering [UTBAS-6; Iverach et al., 2016], Wright-Ayer Stuttering Self-Rating Profile [WASSP; Wright & Ayre, 2000])

TABLE 6–2. *continued*

Adult Stuttering Assessment (ages 18 years and up)
Sample data for Area 5: Reactions to stuttering within the environment
Significant others' reactions to stuttering and perceptions about how stuttering affects both the speaker and themselves
Speaker's perception of the reactions of others (e.g., experience of discrimination)
Sample data for Area 6: Adverse impact associated with stuttering
Speaker's perceptions of whether and how much stuttering affects willingness or ability to speak, participation in social and educational activities, and quality of life
Scores on tests of adverse impact and quality of life (e.g., BCL, OASES-A, WASSP)

Source: Reprinted with permission from Brundage, B. S., Bernstein Ratner, N., Boyle, M. P., Eggers, K., Everard, R., Franken, M.-C., Kefalianos, E., Marcotte, A. K., Millard, S., Packman, A., Vanryckeghem, M., & Yaruss, J. S. (2021). Consensus guidelines for the assessments of individuals who stutter across the lifespan. *American Journal of Speech-Language Pathology, 30*(6), 2379–2393. https://doi.org/10.1044/2021_AJSLP-21-00107

a treatment protocol. As we discussed in Chapter 4, and as Brundage et al. specifically pointed out, "selection of specific assessment areas and tools or procedures must be *individualized* and *tailored to each client's or family's unique needs.* Specific assessment plans must consider each client's experience with stuttering, and the weighting of each component of the assessment (and, if indicated, the resulting treatment) must be guided by information provided by speakers and their families" (p. 2384, emphases added).

EXAMPLES OF ASSESSMENT MEASURES

Certainly, many speakers who stutter exhibit some common patterns of behavior and reactions to stuttering, but, as we indicated at the outset of this chapter, these can also be highly variable (and, on occasion, unusual) responses. There are many assessment devices that the clinician can use to obtain indications about the nature

and severity of stuttering. In the following section we describe some of the assessment instruments that we have found to be particularly useful. Importantly, many emphasize self-evaluation by the speaker (see Ingham & Cordes, 1997), particularly for indicating the intrinsic features of stuttering.

Locus of Control of Behavior (LCB)

The LCB scale, a 17-item Likert-type scale developed by Craig et al. (1984), is designed to indicate the degree to which a person perceives daily occurrences of stuttering to be a consequence of his or her own behavior. This scaling procedure is designed to indicate the ability of a person to take responsibility for maintaining new or desired behaviors. Subjects are asked to indicate their agreement or disagreement to each of the 17 statements about their personal beliefs using a 6-point bipolar Likert-type scale. The scores of the 17 statements are summed to yield a total LCB score, with items 1, 5, 7, 8, 13, and 16 scored in reverse order (e.g., a score of 4 is converted to a 1 and vice versa). Higher scores on this scale indicate a perception of external control or *externality* (the self-perception that their behavior is determined by forces beyond their control), whereas lower scores indicate the perception of greater internal control or *internality* (the self-perception that they are able to determine their own behavior).

Because all forms of intervention for stuttering promote the speaker's assumption of increased responsibility for changing his or her circumstances, the locus of control concept is intuitively appealing.

We have found that adults who would be regarded as severely stuttering often have LCB scores as high as 44 to 55. Nonstuttering speakers generally score in the high teens to low 20s. Craig and Andrews (1985) found that changes in LCB scores successfully predicted the outcome in 15 of 17 participants 10 months following treatment. However, De Nil and Kroll (1995) found LCB scores to be unrelated to a speaker's fluency and possibly influenced by whether or not increased assertiveness and responsibility are a focus of treatment (Ladouceur et al., 1989). An example of progressive improvement (decreases) in LCB scores for an adult with severe stuttering can be found in Chapter 14.

Stuttering Severity Instrument for Children and Adults (SSI-4) (Pro-Ed)

A frequently used instrument for determining stuttering severity, the SSI was originally developed in 1972 by Glyndon Riley for determining stuttering severity for both children and adults. The most recent (fourth edition) of this scale (SSI-4; Riley, 2009) includes several features designed to provide a more comprehensive perspective of stuttering severity compared to older versions of the scale. For example, it is recommended that the clinician (a) obtain speaking samples beyond the clinic environment, (b) acquire speech samples during a variety of telephone conversations, (c) use a 9-point naturalness rating scale, and (d) obtain self-reports of severity, locus of control, and avoidance of stuttering. These self-report processes are mentioned in the following sections describing the Clinical Use of Self-Reports (CUSR) and the Subjective Screening of Stuttering: Research edition (SSS-R). In addition, a computerized scoring system (CSSS-2) is available through the publisher.

When being administered the SSI-4, speakers who can read are asked to (a) describe their job or school, and (b) read a short passage (passages are provided). Nonreaders are given a picture task to which they respond. Scoring is accomplished across three areas. The frequency of the fluency breaks is tabulated and the percentage of stuttered syllables are converted to a task score (range = 2–18). The duration of the three longest stuttering moments (fleeting to more than 60 seconds) is tabulated and converted to a scale score (range = 2–18). Last, physical concomitants across four categories are rated on a scale ranging from 0 (*none*) to 5 (*severe and painful looking*) and totaled (range = 0–20). The total overall score is computed by adding the scores for the three areas. Percentile and severity equivalents are provided for preschool children, school-age children, and adults. The scale is commonly used because it can be used with virtually all age ranges, is easily and quickly administered and scored, and assigns a quantitative value to the individual's stuttering severity.

Subjective Screening of Stuttering Severity (SSS)

The SSI provides an indication of the speaker's overt stuttering features, but Riley et al. (2004) argued that the speaker's perception of his or her problem is at least as, and often more, important, than the frequency, duration, and struggle behaviors associated with stuttering. Although it is sometimes the case that ratings of overt stuttering by the clinician might coincide with the self-perceptions of severity by the speaker, it is not uncommon for this not to be the case. Furthermore, reductions of overt stuttering behaviors are clearly an important goal of treatment, but for many speakers, an internal locus of control and the freedom to communicate without avoidance are critical goals. The authors provided a convincing argument that the most important opinion concerning the speaker's ability to communicate is that of the speaker.

Over the last 35 years, J. Riley has developed questions to help her understand the attitudes and feelings of people who stutter. Chapter 4 of the manual for the SSI-4 (Riley, 2009) Clinical Use of Self-Reports (CUSR) outlines 16 questions to improve the communication between the speaker and the clinician. Three areas of the speaker's self-reported response to stuttering are covered by the CUSR: (a) perceived stuttering severity, (b) level of internal or external locus of control (effort to speak without stuttering), and (c) word or situation avoidance. Each item is self-rated for the experience of several speaking audiences such as a close friend, an authority figure, speaking to someone on the telephone, and others. Each item is rated on a 9-point semantic differential scale where 1 represents a normal speaking experience (target level) and 9 the most severe stuttering experience. Speakers use a series of 9-point scales to self-rate their perception of their stuttering experience by responding to the 16 questions. The selected item or items are rated in conversation with the clinician. The CUSR does not provide a standardized way to convert the item scores into subtest scores; rather, each item serves to measure a specific attitude or feeling. In this regard, each item is similar to those on the naturalness scale.

Each answer selected by the client provides an opportunity to explore an area that might need to be changed and that can become a therapy goal or objective. A change in rating from 8 to 6, for example, can communicate progress before it is obvious to the client. The examples that follow describe the use of three of the CUSR questions in therapy.

Item 1. How would you score your speech with the following audiences? (Severity)
A given client may score the speech as a 2 with a friend, a 6 with a stranger, and an 8 on the telephone. This awareness of variations in fluency during different speaking situations provides the clinician an opportunity to explore in depth what this variation in fluency means to the speaker and how to facilitate similar fluency with difficult audiences.

Item 4. How often do you change your words when you think you may stutter? (Avoidance)
This question provides a way to monitor the use of word or sound avoidance by a person who stutters. Everyday listeners cannot usually observe that a person is avoiding except that they might notice the

sentence sounds awkward. Treatment could require that the client and clinician become aware of avoidance and work toward modifying the behavior. Reduction in the score on this item indicates that avoidance of words, sounds, or both, is occurring less often.

Item 6. How much energy do you expend on how to speak rather than on what to say? (Locus of control) People who stutter often show emotion when faced with this question because they often expend so much energy trying to keep from stuttering or trying to cover it up that they do not realize that others might not notice or care if they stutter. They might even pass up or withdraw from a conversation because of the energy required to participate. When the clinician demonstrates an empathetic appreciation of the pain experienced by the person who stutters, the therapeutic relationship is enhanced. As the person shifts attention toward what is being said and away from the stuttering, the rating of this item should come down.

Four years of clinical trials by Riley et al. (2004) resulted in a research version that includes eight items within three subtests providing screening information about the speaker's self-perceived stuttering severity (two items), level of internal or external locus of control (three items), and word or situation avoidance (three items). Each item is rated on a 9-point semantic differential scale where 1 represents a normal speaking experience (target level) and 9 the most severe. All items are self-rated for the experience of speaking to each of three audiences: a close friend (these ratings are used for comparison but are not

included in the scoring), an authority figure, and use of the telephone.

The protocol for the research edition of the SSS, which is given using a pencil-and-paper instrument rather than an interview, can be used to obtain numerical scores. It has been used in several studies of the effects of medications on stuttering. Scores for the eight items just described and for the three speaking situations are used to compute a subtest score for Severity, Locus of Control, and Avoidance.

Riley et al. (2004) described how comparisons of the speaker's self-report responses to the preceding questions can be interpreted. For example, using one question having to do with severity could result in a low rating by the clinician on the SSI-4 in combination with a high rating by the speaker on the SSS-R. Such a discrepancy might indicate that even minimal stuttering is extremely painful to the speaker and that the person would benefit from activities involving desensitization to stuttering. A low SSS-R score in contrast to a high SSI-4 score might indicate denial, lack of awareness, or possibly some of the characteristics of cluttering (see Chapter 12).

Revised Communication Attitude Inventory (S-24)

The S-24 is an easy-to-administer 24-item inventory that continues to be used in many clinical studies. The S-24 was modified by Andrews and Cutler (1974) from the original 39-item Erickson S-Scale (1969). Clients respond to a series of 24 true–false statements according to whether or not the statements are characteristic of themselves. Designed for use with older adolescents and adults, the total score is obtained by tabulating one point for each item that is answered as a person who stutters would respond. Higher scores indicate a negative attitude about communicating. Individuals who stutter average a total of 19.22 (SD = 5.38) items scored in this manner, whereas nonstuttering individuals average a total score of 9.14 (SD = 4.24). Andrews and Cutler (1974) did not specify the reliability and validity processes but indicated that item analysis resulted in the deletion of items that resulted in poor test–retest reliability and validity. Mean scores on the S-24 discriminated between 36 individuals who stuttered and a control group of 25 fluent speakers, and pre–post treatment differences for the individuals who stuttered were significant.

Perceptions of Stuttering Inventory (PSI)

The PSI, developed by Woolf (1967), is designed to determine the speaker's self-rating of avoidance, struggle, and expectancy (of stuttering) for older adolescents and adults. The person responds to each of 60 statements according to whether or not he or she feels they are "characteristic of me." Statements that the person feels are not characteristic are left unmarked. Examples of inventory items include: "Avoiding talking to people in authority" (avoidance), "Having extra and unnecessary facial movement" (struggle), and "Adding an extra sound in order to get started" (expectancy).

Self-Efficacy Scaling for Adult Stutterers (SESAS) (see companion website)

Based on the work of Bandura (1977) with perceptual self-efficacy scaling, the SESAS (Ornstein & Manning, 1985) is designed to measure a speaker's confidence for entering into and achieving fluency in speaking situations beyond the treatment environ-ment. The first section of the scale (SESAS approach) asks speakers to indicate the likelihood that they could enter into each of 50 specific speaking situations by using a decile scale from 10 to 100 (higher scores indicate greater confidence). The speaking situations are ordered in a hierarchy from easy to more difficult. Speaker responses are averaged over the 50 situations to obtain the SESAS approach score.

The second section of the scale again asks the speaker to consider the same 50 speaking situations, this time indicating the speaker's confidence for maintaining a client-selected "level of fluency" based on the speaker's stage of treatment (SESAS performance). Speaker responses are averaged over the 50 speaking situations to obtain the SESAS performance score.

Ornstein and Manning (1985) found that 20 adults who stuttered (mean age = 26;11 years, range = 18–44 years) scored significantly lower on both the approach (M = 66.2) and performance (M = 55.8) portions of the SESAS than did a matched group of nonstuttering speakers. Interestingly, the mean scores of fluent speakers (94.2 and 98.0 for the approach and performance scales, respectively) indicated that they were less confident about approaching situations than about speaking fluently once they were in the situations. Conversely, the speakers who stuttered were more confident about approaching speaking situations than about maintaining fluency once they entered the situation.

Subsequent investigation (Manning, Perkins, et al., 1984) indicated that during treatment, adults who stutter demonstrate increasingly higher scores. In addition, the speakers began to normalize their approach and performance scores, in the sense that performance scores were slightly greater than approach scores. Several investigators have reported increases in SESAS scores as a result of treatment (Blood, 1995b;

Hillis, 1993; Manning, Perkins, et al., 1984; Langevin et al., 2006; Langevin & Kully, 2003). In some cases, adults who consider themselves recovered from stuttering have recorded SESAS scores that exceed those of nonstuttering adults (Hillis & Manning, 1996).

The SEA-Scale: Self-Efficacy for Adolescents Scale (see companion website)

Developed by Manning (1994), the SEA-Scale: Self-Efficacy for Adolescents, also based on the work of Bandura and his colleagues, is designed for older school-age children and adolescents. Clients are asked to assign a whole number value (1–10) to indicate their confidence for entering into and speaking in each of 100 progressively more difficult communication situations (higher scores indicate greater confidence). The procedure allows clients and clinicians to obtain a total average score for all 100 speaking situations and to map the speaker's predicted performance in 13 categories (Watson, 1988) of beyond-therapy speaking situations appropriate for younger speakers. The SEA-Scale was normed on 40 adolescent children who stuttered and a matched group of fluent children. The overall alpha level for the entire scale was 0.98, with subscale alphas ranging from 0.74 to 0.94. The children who stuttered scored significantly lower ($M = 7.21, SD = 1.8$) than a matched group of fluent speakers ($M = 8.65, SD = 1.2$).

Bray et al. (2003) investigated the relationship of self-efficacy to verbal fluency, academic self-efficacy, and depression for 21 adolescents who stuttered (13–19 years old) and a group of 21 adolescents matched for gender, age, grades, and academic achievement. The authors hypothesized that differences in each of these measures would be found between the two groups of speakers. The authors adapted the 100-item SEA-Scale as described earlier and created an abbreviated 39-item version of SEA-Scale, finding a Cronbach's coefficient alpha of .98 for the abbreviated version. The results of a discriminant function analysis indicated that speech self-efficacy in the form of the modified SEA-Scale was the only significant variable in the equation accounting for 61% of the variance in group status. A second discriminant function analysis that excluded the nonsignificant variables resulted in a single discriminant function that correctly classified 81% of the participants into their groups. The authors suggested that not only are adolescents able to use self-efficacy scaling as a measure of their confidence for verbal fluency but also that such change, in and of itself, is a viable target of treatment.

Adult Behavior Assessment Battery (BAB) (Plural Publishing, Inc.)

As part of the Behavioral Assessment Battery discussed in the previous chapter, Brutten and Vanryckeghem and their associates also created several self-report measures designed for adults (Brutten, 1973, 1975; Brutten & Vanryckeghem, 2003). The adult portion of the BAB includes three subscales as described in the following sections.

Speech Situation Checklist—Emotional Reaction (SSC-ER) (Plural Publishing, Inc.)

As with the earlier versions of the BAB, the current updated form of the Speech

Situations Checklist (SSC) has two components. The first component provides a way to identify the adult speaker's emotional reactions (anxiety, concern, worry) about entering situation-specific communication situations. Speakers respond to the question, "Are you anxious, concerned, or worried about your speech when you are entering . . . ?" that includes 51 communication situations (e.g., talking on the telephone, giving your name, ordering in a restaurant, talking with a sales clerk). Speakers are asked to indicate their emotional response to each situation by using a 5-point Likert-type scale ranging from 1 (*not anxious*) to 5 (*very anxious*). The ratings are totaled and compared with the norms that are provided.

Speech Situation Checklist— Speech Disruption (SSC-SD) (Plural Publishing, Inc.)

Adults also independently respond to the same 51 communication situations by indicating the extent of speech disruption (part-word repetitions and audible or silent prolongations) that they are likely to experience in each situation. This time the adult speaker rates the extent of the speech disruption they are likely to experience in each of the 51 speaking situations, making use of a second Likert-type scale from 1 (*no disruption*) to 5 (*great disruption*). Bakker (1995) found that the two components of the SSC were able to significantly discriminate adults who stutter from those who do not.

The Behavior Checklist (BCL) (Plural Publishing, Inc.)

The BCL provides a way for adults who stutter to indicate the avoidance and escape behaviors (e.g., substituting one word for another, pausing before trying to say a feared word, avoiding eye contact) that they typically use when anticipating or experiencing a moment of stuttering. Respondents first check whether or not they use a particular coping behavior and then indicate on a 5-point Likert-type scale ranging from 1 (*very infrequently*) to 5 (*very frequently*) the frequency with which they use a particular behavior. Investigations with the adult BCL indicate that adults who stutter are likely to employ significantly more of these behaviors than those who do not stutter (Vanryckeghem et al., 2004).

The Overall Assessment of the Speaker's Experience of Stuttering (OASES)

As described in Chapter 5, two forms of this comprehensive self-report measure are designed for teenage adolescents (OASES-T) and adults (OASES-A). It provides a comprehensive and consistent measure of the impact of stuttering (Constantino et al., 2016) and has been used in many investigations throughout the world.

The Ayre and Wright Stuttering Self-Rating Profile (WASSP) (see companion website)

Also based on the World Health Organization's *ICF* model and similar in many ways to the OASES, the WASSP is intended primarily as an efficient but comprehensive device for identifying behavioral and attitudinal features of stuttering for adolescents and adults (Ayre & Wright, 2009). Speakers are asked to respond to a series of 24 items, which are grouped into five sections: stuttering behaviors (8 items), thoughts about stuttering (3 items), feelings about stuttering (5 items), avoidance due to stuttering (4 items), and disadvantage due to stuttering (4 items). Self-ratings are indicated by the respondent circling a number on a 7-point Likert-type scale ranging from 1 (*none*) to 7 (*very severe*) that best describes their self-perceived severity. The results can be indicated using a summary profile, whereby two ratings (e.g., pre- and posttreatment) scores for each item can be graphically displayed according to perceived severity. Forms are provided for including summary comments by the clinician regarding client changes relating to each of the five sections on the response sheet and future treatment goals. Reliability was indicated by 32 individuals who stuttered but who were not presently receiving treatment.

CONCLUSION

Because most adolescents and adults who stutter choose not to seek professional help, our understanding of the problem is determined by what is certainly a nonrepresentative and possibly biased sample of all people who stutter. From the speakers we do see, it appears that developmental stuttering is a highly variable communication problem, a fact that can provide misleading information unless the speaker is seen in a variety of speaking tasks and environments. Because of this variability, as well as the ability of some speakers to mask the overt features of their stuttering by using a variety of coping behaviors, individuals who stutter are sometimes misdiagnosed as having expressive language, social anxiety disorders, voice disorders, neurological problems (e.g., Tourette's syndrome), or a variety of emotional problems. For many individuals who stutter, a thorough

assessment is ongoing and continues well into the early stages of treatment.

The severity of stuttering is indicated by many important surface features, including the frequency, duration, and tension associated with stuttering events as well as by the more subtle features such as the quality and stability of the individual's nonstuttered speech, avoidance and substitution of words, and postponement and escape behaviors. These surface features, as important as they are, fall short of indicating the full impact of the problem, particularly when the experience of the speaker is considered. The detection of the person's cognitive and affective responses (e.g., shame, fear, helplessness, and loss of control) to stuttering is especially relevant to understanding how stuttering impacts the speaker's daily functioning and quality of life. Much of the impact of stuttering is manifested by these cognitive and affective features. The continued development of both quantitative and qualitative tools has enhanced the ability of the clinician to discover and track these core features of the stuttering experience.

The assessment meeting provides the opportunity to establish the nature of the journey and the therapeutic alliance of the speaker and the clinician. It also provides the first opportunity for the clinician to demonstrate his or her understanding of stuttering. For adolescent and adult speakers, it can be helpful for understanding the individual's story to appreciate how and why they are seeking assistance at this particular moment. The initial meeting provides the clinician with the opportunity to determine the speaker's motivation and readiness for change. At the most basic level, the assessment process involves two primary issues: (a) to what extent the person is altering the choices and choosing to restrict the options that are available to him or her, and (b) how the person is using his or her vocal apparatus in ways that prevent the production of easy, open, and smooth speech.

Many assessment devices have been created that assist the clinician in determining the extent of the problem for the person who stutters. It is important to consider the speaker's self-perception of his or her situation. In many cases, qualitative measures of the speaker's narrative can provide valuable insight into the extent to which stuttering influences the person's ability to communicate and participate in daily activities. As we emphasize in subsequent chapters that address therapeutic procedures, the effective clinician not only tracks behavioral and cognitive change via formal assessment tools, but also pays close attention to the words speakers use to describe themselves and their situations.

❓ TOPICS FOR DISCUSSION

1. Although stuttering behavior might be apparent for an adolescent or adult speaker, describe how a person's coping responses sometimes mask many covert stuttering behaviors.

2. Explain to a family member or a friend who knows nothing about stuttering the nature of the cognitive and affective features of the problem.

3. Make a list of activities, people, and situations you have avoided or would like to avoid. Describe your motivation for and the impact of this coping strategy.

4. How would you go about determining a speaker's level of motivation for initiating treatment?

5. Produce a 300- to 500-word script that you can use to produce a short video recording that contains several normal and stuttered fluency breaks (moderate level of stuttering). Exchange the tape with a colleague who has made a similar tape. Practice with the tapes to establish both interrater and intrarater reliability (achieving at least .80) for identifying both normal and stuttered fluency breaks.

6. Describe to a colleague the steps for taking a client through the process of self-assessment and trial therapy as described in Figure 6–1.

7. Create a list of the basic take-home messages you would like to communicate to an adolescent or adult during the initial assessment meeting.

8. Describe in your own words the two fundamental principles of assessment discussed in this chapter.

9. Prepare a description of one or more situations where you have experienced a loss of control, emphasizing the cognitive (thought processes) and affective (anxiety, fear, embarrassment) nature of the experience.

10. Ask one or more friends to describe both a positive and enjoyable experience and a negative and anxiety-producing experience. Replay each tape two to three times while listening for quality words that indicate origin or pawn statements.

📖 RECOMMENDED READINGS

Anderson, T. K., & Felsenfeld, S. (2003). A thematic analysis of late recovery from stuttering. *American Journal of Speech-Language Pathology, 12,* 243–253.

Corcoran, J. A., & Stewart, M. (1998). Stories of stuttering: A qualitative analysis of interview narratives. *Journal of Fluency Disorders, 23,* 247–264.

Finn, P. (1997). Adults recovered from stuttering without formal treatment: Perceptual assessment of speech normalcy. *Journal of Speech, Language, and Hearing Research, 40,* 821–831.

Plexico, L., Manning, W., & DiLollo, A. (2005). A phenomenological understanding of successful stuttering management, *Journal of Fluency Disorders, 30*(1), 1–22.

We must let go of the life we have planned, so as to accept the one that is waiting for us.

—Joseph Campbell

Mandarin Chinese saying: 卜茹胡雪，闫胡泽 (Bu Ru Hu Xue, Yan De Hu Ze), which is literally, "How can (we) retrieve the baby tiger without going into the tiger's nest?" In other words, "Great rewards usually require a great degree of risk."

Understanding the Nature of Change

CHAPTER OBJECTIVES

- To examine the underlying features of therapeutic change
- To explore why change is difficult, even when it is a desired goal of therapy
- To explain factors that play a role in our ability to facilitate change in our clients

This chapter is intended as a prerequisite to the chapters that follow, where we discuss counseling with clients who stutter, the therapeutic process, and cultural considerations for fluency assessment and treatment.

As speech-language pathologists, we are in the business of change! Everything we do is related to change—either in terms of changes that we facilitate in clients' speech and language behaviors, changes in the affective and cognitive aspects of clients' lives, or helping them adapt to and compensate for physical and cognitive changes that have been thrust upon them due to injury, illness, or advancing age. For our clients who stutter, change can be happening on multiple levels, with rapid but fluctuating changes in their speech behaviors, changes in their fear and avoidance reactions to stuttering, and changes in how they think of themselves as communicators. Sometimes, change will even encompass more global issues of identity and social and familial roles. Strangely, as we discuss further in the section later on the *nature of change*, any type of change, no matter whether it is positive or negative, can be difficult and present an individual with significant challenges.

THE LIKELIHOOD OF SUCCESSFUL CHANGE

Successful treatment for stuttering and related fluency disorders must take place with an understanding on the part of the clinician that he or she is attempting to help people who have a multidimensional problem. It involves many layers, including—but not limited to—the quantity and quality of a person's speech. If the person has been stuttering for many years, patterns of behavior and thinking have become established. Helping people to move from their current state of speaking, thinking, and functioning with a communication problem that impacts virtually all aspects of life is no simple process. It should not be surprising, therefore, that stuttering, particularly for adults, is a communication problem that could take time—often years—to change (Manning, 1991a).

It is also important to appreciate, however, that stuttering is probably no more enigmatic than many other problems that humans experience. Andrews et al. (1980) commented that stuttering, although complex, is reasonably well understood and not terribly difficult to treat. Using meta-analysis, these authors compared the results of 42 treatment investigations and found treatment for stuttering to be effective and the results stable over time. Craig et al.'s (1996) 12-month posttreatment outcome data on children who were treated for stuttering with a smooth speech procedure indicated that 70% of the children maintained fluency levels of less than 2% syllables stuttered (%SS). Howie et al. (1981) followed 36 adults for up to 18 months posttreatment and found that adult clients have a 70% chance of gaining substantially improved speech as well as increased speaking confidence. Indeed, some adults who have experienced successful treatment for stuttering are able to achieve high levels of spontaneous fluency. Some speakers, even those who have experienced moderate to severe stuttering in their earlier years, are able,

as adults, to score higher than nonstuttering peers on measures of approach behavior in difficult speaking situations on the Self-Efficacy Scale for Adults who Stutter (SESAS; Hillis & Manning, 1996). As a result of treatment, they are likely to have learned much about the speech mechanism and the nature of speech and language. They are likely to have gained considerable experience when speaking in a large variety of individual and group situations. They might have taken an active role in a self-help organization. If clients continue expanding these experiences following treatment, it is not surprising that some of them are able to become better-than-average speakers.

Another note of optimism is that working with children and adults who stutter can be enormously enjoyable. As described in Chapter 1, as the client grows, often the clinician grows as well, for the most effective clinicians are always learning. They are making real-time decisions about the needs of the client as these needs become apparent. Although the treatment process for fluency disorders can be complex and even messy, it can also be dynamic and exciting.

If it is done well, fluency treatment can result in degrees of positive change in the speaker's perspective of the problem, level of fluency, and—in many cases—improvement in such areas as his or her relationships, problem-solving ability, self-esteem, assertiveness, and overall approach to life. To engage clients in such holistic growth (which is "change" that is deemed "positive"), clinicians must understand that the process of change goes well beyond the simple application of specific techniques and behavioral changes. Therapy involves helping to create a better future in addition to much improved communication for the person we are helping. Important cognitive and affective changes occur across the client's whole life experience. Just as most athletic activities are much more than the sum of many individual skills, the process of treatment is much more than the application of techniques to be mastered. In fact, as we see in succeeding chapters, it has frequently been argued that the consequences of overemphasizing therapeutic microskills rather than a holistic approach tend to lead to ineffective treatment.

THE NATURE OF CHANGE

On the surface of therapeutic success for individuals who stutter are the more apparent behavioral changes associated with increased speech fluency. By instruction and modeling we introduce and teach the techniques that are known to provide speakers with new ways of using their speech production system. This is an obvious response to the problem of stuttering, for as Yairi and Ambrose (2005) stated, "Speech disfluency lies at the core of the disorder of stuttering . . . disfluency is the essence of the disorder in its widely understood conventional sense" (p. 137). In addition, however, we also want people who come to us for help to develop new ways of considering themselves and their choices about communicating. In the previous chapter we noted some of the important affective and cognitive aspects of the stuttering experience that often impact even the youngest of speakers. The experience of stuttering often goes far beyond the overt surface features as children recognize and react with frustration and struggle as they try to cope with their inability to speak. For many of these children, modeling of fluency-enhancing techniques by the clinician along with

guidance and support by the parents can result in a relatively brief and successful intervention. As children begin formal schooling and experience the effects of socialization, there is the increasing possibility of a negative self-interpretation, lowered self-esteem, and the stigma associated with disfluent speech. As we describe, change for these older speakers is often more strenuous and complex. It is usually possible to assign a beginning to the change process, but—in most cases— there is not necessarily a clear ending point, because the adult speaker will continue to evolve for years both as a person and a speaker.

Hopefully, the reader of this chapter will see how information on the change process corresponds to the description of clinician characteristics found in Chapter 1, the principles of counseling found in Chapter 8, and the treatment approaches to be discussed in subsequent chapters. It should become clear that comprehensive treatment for adolescents and adults involves more than simply "fixing the stuttering" and making people fluent. The process of change for individuals who stutter is much bigger and far more exciting than the technical components of fluency. In many ways we are enabling people to live life in a broader and deeper manner as we help them to become "unstuck," not only from their speech but from a life of restricted decision making. In that sense doing therapy is, as Zinker (1977, p. 37) suggested, like making art, and the medium is a human life.

Technical and Adaptive Aspects of Change

To more easily conceptualize the challenges faced by clients as they undergo change during the therapeutic process, we start by borrowing concepts and terminology from the work of Heifetz and his colleagues on *adaptive leadership* (e.g., Heifetz et al., 2009; Heifetz & Laurie, 1997; Heifetz & Linsky, 2002). DiLollo and Neimeyer (2022) described how concepts of adaptive leadership map onto the therapeutic process and can be helpful in guiding clinicians in identifying needs and challenges associated with the specific speech, language, or hearing disorder, while also attending to the more affective and cognitive aspects of change. At the core of adaptive leadership lies the concept that any process of change will present challenges on two related aspects. *Technical challenges* tend to be the most obvious, surface issues faced by individuals or groups as they face change. Technical challenges arise from change in which the problem can be clearly defined by an expert and strategies are most effectively addressed through the application of expert knowledge to the intervention process. Changes related to technical challenges are typically well received, as they present a clear and relatively rapid solution to the problem. For a person who stutters, for example, a technical challenge might be the specific frequency of his or her disfluencies. The corresponding technical solution might be engaging in intensive fluency shaping therapy that eliminates or reduces the number of disfluencies. So, in a general sense, technical challenges tend to relate to the more extrinsic features of stuttering that we discussed in previous chapters.

On the other hand, more complex change issues, such as those related to an individual's cognitive and affective reactions to disfluencies, might be characterized as *adaptive challenges* (Heifetz & Laurie, 1997; Heifetz & Linsky, 2002). Adaptive challenges have no straightforward solutions and require changes in ways of thinking, as well as behaviors. Adaptive challenges, therefore, are sometimes difficult to identify and solutions often take considerable time to implement and produce observable results. Consequently, whereas technical challenges can frequently be addressed with a relatively simple solution, or by someone other than the person facing the issue (e.g., a professional or authority figure such as a speech-language pathologist), adaptive challenges must be addressed by those who are the "stakeholders"—that is, the ones who must make the changes to their thinking and behavior. In the case of persons who stutter, the technical solution of reducing the number of disfluencies might address the immediate needs or expectations of the client to reduce the overt signs of stuttering. However, addressing the adaptive challenge of changing thinking and feeling like "a stutterer" (i.e., changing identity) is a process that, with the support of a speech-language pathologist and an extended network of social supports, must be led by the person experiencing the stuttering.

DiLollo and Neimeyer (2022) noted that most clients come to us with communication problems that reflect elements of both technical and adaptive challenges. According to Heifetz et al. (2009), one of the most common mistakes in leadership is attempting to address adaptive challenges with technical solutions. Stuttering treatment provides an excellent example of this problem. Advocates of strictly behavioral treatments for stuttering treat stuttering only as a technical challenge. The behavioral treatments can be very effective at reducing the extrinsic (technical) aspects of the problem but fail to address the intrinsic (adaptive) aspects. In many cases, relapse from successful behavioral treatment, which, in some circumstances can be as high as 70% (e.g., Craig, 1998; Craig & Hancock, 1995), is related to the provision of only a technical solution to a problem that has both technical and adaptive challenges. In contrast, attempting to only address the adaptive aspects of stuttering, while ignoring the technical, is also likely to lead to long-term failure, as the person who stutters continues to struggle with his or her speech (L. M. Webster, 1977). As such, when considering the therapeutic process for persons who stutter, and the changes that such a process is designed to stimulate, it is important to distinguish between these two types of challenges—identifying aspects of the situation that are both technical and adaptive in nature—in order to design the most effective intervention.

PROCESSES UNDERLYING CHANGE

To begin our discussion of the process of change, let us first examine a perspective that can help us understand some of the processes that drive or regulate change. It should be noted that there are many ways a chapter such as this could approach the subject of processes underlying change, and it is beyond the scope of this textbook to examine and compare all such approaches. Consequently, to further explore this view of change, we have chosen to take a *constructivist* perspective, as this will also be the perspective that will frame much of our discussion related to counseling in Chapter 8.

At its most basic level, constructivism focuses on the active process of making meaning of life experiences. According to constructivist theory, an objective view of the world is not possible, as each individual will create his or her own version of reality, a perspective built out of each individual's unique life experiences. Constructivism also emphasizes that people strive to create order out of the complex stream of experience by identifying patterns and creating meanings to organize the world in an easily understandable way. Sometimes, the organization and meanings that individuals create can be problematic. Another basic tenet of constructivism, however, is that there are multiple ways in which individuals can create meaning from their experience. Constructivist therapists, who act as *facilitators of change* rather than directors, help clients recognize these problematic patterns and break free of them in order to create change.

Personal Construct Theory

The original constructivist perspective in clinical practice was formulated by psychologist George Kelly (1955/1991), who, interestingly for those interested in the history of stuttering therapy, studied psychology under Lee Edward Travis at the University of Iowa, alongside fellow student Wendell Johnson. Kelly viewed change as a part of the human condition, describing the human being as a "form of motion," intrinsically active and inquisitive, formulating his or her own "theory" of life, and testing out that theory in practical contexts. Landfield and Leitner (1980) described this process, stating,

> The person experiences his life by noting series of events from which he

abstracts the recurring themes and their contrasts. This dual process of abstracting and contrasting defines construing—a process which may encompass what we know as feelings, values, and behavior. (p. 5)

The result of construing leads to the development of personal constructs, defined as "personal dimensions of awareness anchored by contrasts in meaning" (Landfield & Leitner, 1980, p. 5).

Over time, this process of construing leads to the development of systems of constructs, the purpose of which Kelly (1955/1991) described as

. . . transparent patterns or templets which (man) creates and then attempts to fit over the realities of which the world is composed. The fit is not always very good. Yet without such patterns the world appears to be such an undifferentiated homogeneity that man is unable to make any sense out of it. Even a poor fit is more helpful to him than nothing at all. (pp. 8–9)

Kelly believed that the driving force behind this process of construing is *anticipation*. That is, through developing systems of constructs relative to a specific domain or set of circumstances, we strive to predict how events will unfold or how people, including ourselves, will react when faced with those circumstances. For example, a person who stutters might develop a system of constructs about himself that centers on his stuttering, ignoring other aspects of himself that could potentially contribute to his sense of self. In such a case, the "template" being used is a "poor fit," but it is still helpful for the individual in his attempts to anticipate

how events will unfold when he communicates with others.

Construct Systems and the Process of Change

Tight and Loose Construing. Kelly (1955/1991) discussed another aspect of the process of change by describing the way people construe in terms of a "tight/loose" dimension. A person employing tight construing might be rigid and highly organized and will have difficulty trying out new behaviors. Tight constructs lead to unvarying anticipations. Conversely, a person employing loose construing might be highly unpredictable, and could readily change his or her anticipations. Dalton (1987) suggested that people tend to "tighten up" their constructions around a problem area, and in response to a perceived "threat" to their construct system. This is important in relation to working with persons who stutter in that clinicians might observe clients "tightening" their constructs about themselves and their communication—always anticipating the presence of stuttering and the negative consequences associated with it and being resistant to trying out new behaviors.

The Experience Cycle. Generally, people move constructively between the extremes of tight and loose in terms of their constructions, in what Kelly (1955/1991) referred to as the "Experience Cycle" (Figure 7–1). The experience cycle, also sometimes referred to as the "creativity cycle," describes the primary mechanism underlying the process of change, and typically begins with loosened constructions and ends with tightened and validated constructions. Essentially, the creativity cycle is a way in which individuals update their

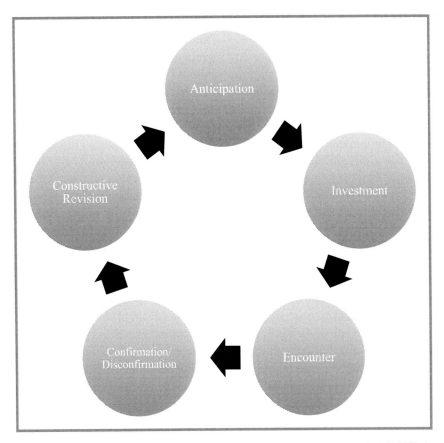

FIGURE 7–1. The experience cycle. (Adapted with permission from Neimeyer, R. A. [1987]. An orientation to personal construct therapy. In R. A. Neimeyer and G. J. Neimeyer [Eds.], *Personal construct theory casebook* [pp. 3–19]. New York, NY: Springer. Reprinted with permission.)

construct systems by allowing themselves first to be open to alternative constructions of events, then to test those alternative constructions against the established system, and finally to tighten up construing based on the new more facilitative system.

Kelly (1955/1991) used the metaphor of "people-as-scientists" to describe this view of the process of change, referring to the hypothesis testing used in the scientific method. In this sense, people form constructs about events, which they use as hypotheses to anticipate outcomes. They then test out the hypotheses through experiencing the event and either confirm or disconfirm the hypotheses. Adjustments can then be made to the constructs so that they provide more effective anticipations in the future. Kelly formalized his description of this process, suggesting that it is composed of five steps:

1. *Anticipation.* A construct or set of constructs provides the individual with some idea or expectation of what a given situation will hold.
2. *Investment.* Sometimes events or situations matter to us only a little,

whereas other times they matter a great deal.

3. *Encounter.* The individual engages in the event or experiences the situation. This is the test of the hypothesis or anticipation.

4. *Confirmation or disconfirmation.* The experience will either confirm or disconfirm the anticipations.

5. *Constructive revision.* Depending on the outcome (i.e., confirmation or disconfirmation), the constructs that led to the anticipation might be more strongly held or might be altered substantially.

Kelly (1955/1991) noted, however, that such change could, at times, be difficult. Given the organization of constructs into connected systems, changes to individual or sets of constructs must first be weighed against the damage to the overall system that could result from such changes. Frequently, the individual's personal investment in the larger system is so great that he or she will fail to adopt the more precise construct into his or her system. For example, John, an office worker who considers himself to be an honest person, is able to ignore his practice of stealing office supplies and selling them online by telling himself that he is very efficient at his job, and so probably saves his company more money than the cost of the supplies that he takes. In this case, for John to revise his constructs about himself would be too devastating to his entire system of constructs, so he simply finds a way to ignore the invalidating experiences. In contrast, Betsy, a colleague who has worked with John for a couple of years and has always thought of him as an honest person, sees John stealing office supplies on several occasions. For Betsy, changing her constructs about a colleague is not significantly damaging to her system, and so she changes her "opinion" of John (i.e., revises her constructs) and no longer sees him as an honest person.

CLINICAL INSIGHT

While working with Philip, a young man in his 20s who stuttered, I noticed that he was particularly unsettled during one of our sessions. When I asked him what was happening, he told me how he had been very fluent over the past week but that he had not enjoyed any of it because he knew it was simply due to him being better at his "techniques" and not because he was "really changing" in any way. In this case, Philip was unable to allow the experience of more fluent speech to impact his constructs of himself as a "stutterer"—and the consequential impact of that on his entire system of constructs—and so he found a way of dismissing that experience as essentially not meaningful. By doing this, however, Philip also robbed himself of the opportunity to start building new constructs about being a more fluent communicator. This was important for Philip as, by ignoring the meaningfulness of the behavioral changes he was experiencing, he continued to anticipate life as a "stutterer" and struggled with self-confidence and avoidance issues. By understanding the processes underlying Philip's resistance to change, I was able to work with him to overcome that resistance. (AD)

Emotional Responses to Change. A personal construct understanding of the process of change also provides us with a useful way of understanding the emotional responses to change that might occur for our clients. This is useful in that, by understanding the personal logic that is driving these emotions, clinicians will be better able to help clients formulate ways to successfully recognize and resist the impact of these emotional responses to change.

Kelly (1955/1991) described emotional responses to change by referring back to the concept of constructs and construct systems, and the impact that change has on those systems. His descriptions of these emotions are often quite different from the traditional definitions, so let's take a look at a few of the most common emotions seen in clinical situations.

1. *Fear.* Fear is defined as "the awareness of imminent incidental change in one's core structures" (Kelly, 1955/1991, p. 12). Such changes do not have to be negative, simply changes to the core structure of the person's system. Landfield and Leitner (1980) stated that, "if a person has defined his life-role in terms of sickness, the prospect of a successful therapy could be traumatizing" (p. 12). For persons who stutter engaging in successful therapy, fear might occur as they begin to experience greater levels of fluency and start to explore new roles that reduce or eliminate the "stutterer role" that has always dominated their identity.

2. *Threat.* Threat is defined as "an awareness of an imminent and comprehensive change in core structure" (Landfield & Leitner, 1980, p. 12). This would be when an individual believes that his or her core understanding of who they are as a person is being chal-

lenged. Fransella (1972) and DiLollo, Niemeyer, and Manning (2002), suggested that many persons who stutter struggle with successful, long-term therapeutic change in part because of the threat that successful therapy implies to their overall system of core constructs (i.e., their identity).

3. *Anxiety.* The personal construct definition of anxiety is an awareness that events that the person is experiencing lie mostly outside the range of relevant constructs in his or her construct system. In other words, the person does not have sufficient constructs to accurately anticipate the events in which he or she finds himself or herself. In such a case, the person has no way of understanding or anticipating the course of events. Again, Fransella (1972) and DiLollo, Manning, and Neimeyer (2002, 2003) demonstrated that persons who stutter tend to have a less developed system of constructs related to taking on the role of a fluent speaker (compared to a more elaborated system of constructs related to the role of a "stutterer"). This can lead to feelings of anxiety when the person is experimenting with the role of a more fluent speaker.

4. *Guilt.* Guilt is defined as occurring when a person acts in a way that is contradictory to his or her core role structure; that is, when the person does something that violates a strongly held belief about himself or herself as a person. For example, some of our clients who stutter, as they begin to use increased fluent speech in social situations, report feeling guilty—that they were not being true to who they are and that they were "deceiving" others (DiLollo, Niemeyer, & Manning, 2002).

CLINICAL INSIGHT

As is done in many courses on fluency disorders, I have the students in my course engage in pseudo-stuttering in public. At the start of each class, we spend time reporting on the various experiences that students have had and discussing the meaning of those experiences. One of the more profound learning experiences that students have reported appreciating is when we discuss their feelings of anxiety and guilt during their stuttering experiences. These discussions are framed around the constructivist concepts of anxiety and guilt, as described earlier. So, we talk about the students' inability to anticipate how the social interaction will unfold when stuttering, which leads to feelings of anxiety, and how that anxiety decreases slightly by the end of the assignment (one of the reasons that I have them engage in 10 interactions). I also wait for someone in the class to report feeling guilty about deceiving people when they are stuttering—which usually happens within the first couple of weeks—so that we can talk about the parallel between them taking on the "foreign" role of person who stutters and our clients being asked to take on the "foreign" role of fluent speaker. The understanding that their clients are having the same reactions as them when faced with similar change really helps to better prepare them to be empathetic and effective clinicians. (AD)

READINESS FOR CHANGE

Whereas Kelly (1955/1991) explored processes underlying change, Prochaska et al. (1992) examined the ways in which people move through the process of change. They proposed that individuals go through several stages as they change. Although their work generally focused on individuals with addictive behavior, their ideas have many applications to the treatment of other human conditions, including stuttering. Their stage model of change can be summarized as follows:

1. Change is cyclical through the stages.
2. There is a common set of processes that facilitate change.
3. It is possible to integrate the stages and processes of change.

Stages of Change

Successful treatment for stuttering can be closely tied to the ability of an experienced clinician to determine a client's readiness for change and to select treatment processes and techniques accordingly. Thus, the utility of the techniques depends on the clinician's ability to apply the right therapeutic technique(s) at the right time. The first part of the model suggested by Prochaska et al. (1992) is composed of the five stages of change (precontemplation, contemplation, preparation, action, and maintenance).

In the initial stage, *precontemplation,* the person is generally unaware of the problem and does not recognize the need for change. Awareness often develops gradually, along with a desire for change; however, at this stage the person has no intention of doing something about his or her situation in the immediate future (i.e., the next 6 months). When the issue comes to his or her attention, the individual might become defensive or deny that a problem exists, and he or she generally feels that the situation is under control.

The reader might recognize in the description of this stage signs of some of the underlying processes discussed earlier in this chapter. For example, denial of the problem, followed by a gradual development of awareness and desire for change, would suggest that the individual has been ignoring any invalidating experiences (i.e., to protect the integrity of her or his construct system) but is finding that position increasingly difficult to maintain.

As awareness of the problem increases, the individual begins to actively consider the possibility of change (i.e., during the next 6 months). As yet, there is no formal plan, but the person begins seeking information about the problem. This *contemplation* stage could extend for years, as the person weighs the pros and cons of his or her situation and the time, effort, and money it will take to change, as well as the likelihood of success. The characteristics of this stage would suggest that the person is experimenting with alternative possibilities to her or his current identity, but elaboration of the alternative is insufficient for the person to overcome the fear and threat associated with such changes to core constructs.

As a side note, it is important to appreciate that relatively few people who have a chronic or long-standing problem are actually ready to make changes. Summary data obtained on smoking cessation by Prochaska et al. (1992) illustrate this point. They noted that 50% to 60% of smokers are in the precontemplation

stage, with an additional 30% to 40% in the contemplation stage. Only 10% to 14% of this population can be categorized as being in the action stage.

As people move closer to the point of taking action about their situations (i.e., within the next few weeks), they reach the *preparation* stage by beginning to identify goals and priorities. At this point, they might begin to make some small (although not necessarily effective) changes. They are, nevertheless, moving in a new direction by making decisions in terms of specific goals. At this stage they are likely to seek information by reading, speaking with others, and searching on the Internet. In terms of underlying processes, this stage would represent an extension of the experimentation with an alternate identity and dealing with the fear and threat of substantial changes to the construct system.

As individuals reach the *action* stage, they begin to modify specific behaviors, their environment, or both. A key aspect of this stage is that people begin to use newly acquired skills to achieve specific goals. Importantly, these changes are apt to receive recognition and possibly support from others. The recognition and support from others is the key to this stage, as the more public trying-on of the alternative identity promotes a greater possibility for change.

In the *maintenance* stage, people begin to stabilize their behavioral and cognitive changes in order to prevent relapse or regression. This critical part of the process involves altering well-established behaviors, attitudes, and cognitions lasting from 6 months to an undetermined period of time. A marker of this final stage is the appearance of new and more effective behaviors and choices in daily situations beyond the treatment environment. The description of this stage encompasses the underlying process of constructive revision in which constructs are either confirmed and therefore strengthened or disconfirmed and then discarded or modified.

It is likely that the vast majority of all people who stutter are in the precontemplation stage. Those who seek our assistance are most likely in the preparation or action stages. Of course, our understanding of the person's stage of change will influence how we respond to those seeking our help. The situation for preschool and most school-age children (and to some degree adolescents) is somewhat different because they are more likely to be brought to us by their parents or referred by other professionals such as classroom teachers, physicians, or relatives. Depending on the age and maturity of the child, he or she will have varying degrees of awareness of his or her stuttering as well as varying degrees of motivation for taking part in treatment. Few of these younger individuals are likely to be in the action stage of change.

Floyd et al. (2007) found support for the stages of change model for determining a speaker's readiness for change with 44 adolescents and adults who stuttered (mean age of 34.9; range = 16–61 years). Using a modification of the Stages of Change Questionnaire (McConnaughy et al., 1983), the researchers found that confirmatory and exploratory factor analysis of participant responses indicated that the cognitive, affective, and behavioral factors that characterize stuttering discriminate stages of change for individuals moving through treatment. Of the 32 items on the questionnaire, 26 items were significantly related to their hypothesized stage. Floyd et al. (2007) also found some support for

the additive nature of the stages (people moving through the stages in sequence) in that the contemplation and action stages were positively correlated with their adjacent stages (action and maintenance, respectively). A goodness-of-fit test indicated that although the interpretive questionnaire structure that was used fit the data, it was not a perfect fit. The authors suggested that the questionnaire might be able to better discriminate between stages of change with the inclusion of items that provided a more sensitive indication of the unique characteristics of the stuttering experience. Future research with a larger and more diverse population of participants who are in differing stages of change should improve the ability of the test to determine where speakers are in the process of therapeutic and self-directed change.

The Cyclical Nature of Change

An important feature of the change model proposed by Prochaska et al. (1992) concerns the cyclical nature of the process. Prochaska et al. found that people often move from the action stage into maintenance and then back to precontemplation. As clients learn from their mistakes, they again advance to the next stage of change. Furthermore, relapse at any point in the change process is the rule rather than the exception, although in some cases, particularly if the circumstances are relatively uncomplicated, the process could indeed be thought of as a straight, smooth trajectory from beginning to end. Linear models of human adaptation to the loss of a loved one (e.g., Kübler-Ross, 1969) imply that people work through the various stages of grief, eventually reaching a stage called "acceptance." However, anyone who has worked through the arduous process of mastering a complicated athletic activity, obtaining an advanced degree, acclimating to a new city, or adjusting to the loss of a relationship or a job knows that the process of change is not usually linear. The process often requires revisiting the various stages of change, stages that you thought (and hoped) you were finished with. Things are never quite "back to normal" as a result of major change and, in some ways, the process continues for the rest of your life. This cyclical view of change also closely corresponds to findings by Neimeyer (2000) in his investigations about grief and loss.

Facilitating Change

Based on a comparative analysis of 29 major psychotherapeutic approaches, DiClemente (1993) described 10 categories of processes and associated techniques that facilitate change. These techniques are common to many therapeutic protocols (DiClemente, 1993; Prochaska et al., 1992).

1. Consciousness-raising helps individuals to increase information about themselves and their situation and employs techniques such as observation, confrontation, interpretation, and bibliotherapy (reading educational materials addressing the problem).

2. Self-reevaluation processes help individuals to assess how they feel and think about themselves with respect to their problem by using techniques of value clarification, imagery, and challenging beliefs and expectations.

3. Self-liberation processes help people to select goals, increase their belief in their ability to change, and commit to taking action. Techniques include decision-making therapy and developing resolutions.

4. Counterconditioning activities enable individuals to substitute alternatives for the anxiety associated with their condition and can be accomplished by techniques of relaxation, desensitization, assertion, and positive self-statements.

5. Stimulus-control processes help people to respond to aversive stimuli using techniques of restructuring the environment, avoiding high-risk cues, and fading or desensitization.

6. Reinforcement management helps people to reward themselves or create rewards from others using contingency contracts and overt and covert reinforcement for self-reward.

7. Helping relationships enable individuals to be open and trusting about problems with others who are supportive through the development of therapeutic alliances, increased social support, and association with support groups.

8. Emotional arousal and dramatic relief helps people to confront, experience, and express feelings about their problems and develop insight concerning possible solutions. Techniques involve role-playing and group therapy.

9. Environmental reevaluation helps individuals to assess how their problem impacts their personal and physical environment using techniques of empathy training and journaling.

10. Social liberation helps people to advocate for the rights and involvement of others by joining support groups and empowering policy changes.

Interestingly, referring back to Kelly's (1955/1991) personal constructs, the reader can see that these processes all involve identifying and examining the value of existing constructs, actively engaging in the experience cycle of encounter–confirmation–revision of existing constructs, or experimenting with new constructs and dealing with the associated emotional consequences.

Matching Stages and Processes

The third, and possibly most important, feature of Prochaska et al.'s (1992) stage model of change is the application of the various therapeutic processes during the appropriate stage of the client's process of change. Prochaska et al. proposed that mismatches in stage and process by clinicians often prevent or impede successful change by clients. This commonly occurs, for example, when clinicians select processes associated with the contemplation stage (e.g., consciousness-raising, self-evaluation) at a time when a client is ready to move into the action stage. Similarly, using action-oriented processes (e.g., behavioral changes, desensitization, and assertiveness training) with clients who are in the contemplation or preparation stages of change is likely to be unproductive.

Table 7–1 provides a summary of how the processes described by DiClemente (1993) map onto the stages of change described by Prochaska et al. (1992). Notice that processes can have potential application across more than one stage and that multiple processes might be applicable to a client in any given stage of change. It is important for clinicians to remember, however, that change seldom follows a simple linear path, and not all clients will necessarily follow the exact same progression through the stages of change (Neimeyer, 2000). As we discussed in the previous section on "the cyclical nature of

TABLE 7–1. Stages of Change, Characteristics, Therapy Goals, and Processes for Each Stage

Stage	Characteristic	Therapy Goal	Processes
Precontemplation	Unaware of problem; no intention to change	Increase awareness; get client to consider problem	• Consciousness raising • Self-reevaluation • Self-liberation
Contemplation	Aware of problem; considering change but no commitment to action	Raise awareness; facilitate specific plan for change	
Preparation	Intending to change; engaged in small changes	Encourage small steps already taken; increase commitment to change	• Counterconditioning • Stimulus control • Reinforcement management
Action	Decision to take decisive action	Make action plans; reinforce changes; provide support and guidance	• Helping relationships • Emotional and dramatic relief
Maintenance	Work to consolidate changes and prevent relapse	Support continued change and prevent relapse	• Environmental reevaluation • Social liberation

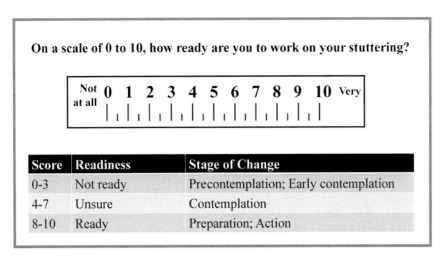

On a scale of 0 to 10, how ready are you to work on your stuttering?

Score	Readiness	Stage of Change
0-3	Not ready	Precontemplation; Early contemplation
4-7	Unsure	Contemplation
8-10	Ready	Preparation; Action

FIGURE 7–2. The readiness ruler.

change," Prochaska et al. (1992) noted that individuals frequently cycle through the stages, moving back to precontemplation after reaching maintenance.

Measuring Readiness for Change

So how can clinicians determine the readiness of a client for change? Several readiness for change questionnaires have been developed specifically related to alcohol use (e.g., Miller & Tonigan, 1996; Rollnick et al., 1992) and might be adapted for use with persons who stutter. An extremely simple yet effective tool that might be even more easily adapted for use by speech-language pathologists, however, is the *readiness ruler*. First developed by Biener and Abrams (1991) for measuring readiness for smoking cessation, readiness rulers have been demonstrated to be as or more effective compared to change questionnaires at measuring readiness for change for behaviors including alcohol consumption, tobacco use, and safer sex for both adult and adolescent clients (e.g., Heather et al., 2008; LaBrie et al., 2005; Maisto et al., 2011).

Bray et al. (n.d.) described the use of a readiness ruler as a part of a brief intervention for substance abuse training for physicians and related it to stages of change (Figure 7–2). This readiness ruler could be used by clinicians to gauge clients' readiness to work on their stuttering and to identify potential stages of change in order to engage in appropriately matched intervention processes. Using the standard question, "On a scale of 0 to 10, how ready are you to work on your stuttering?" the clinician can get an indication of clients' overall readiness for change. By framing different questions at appropriate times during the course of treatment, clinicians could also use the readiness ruler to explore clients' readiness to change specific aspects of their stuttering problem. For example, the clinician could ask, "On a scale of 0 to 10, how ready are you to change the avoidance behaviors you have been using?" The same types of questions could be framed to explore readiness to change aspects such as social roles, assertiveness, roles at work, self-expectations, and even issues related to self as a communicator.

THE SOCIAL CONTEXT OF CHANGE

In the previous sections of this chapter, we discussed processes underlying change, framed in terms of personal construct and construct systems, and the readiness for change, with reference to a stages of change model. As a final perspective on the process of change, let us now take a look at how change might impact individuals in a social context, and ways in which clinicians might help them adjust. Epston and White (1990) described the process of psychotherapy in terms of a change in life status for clients, as they leave behind their old ways and beliefs and move toward a preferred way of living and thinking. These authors emphasized, however, that change is difficult, and suggested using ceremonies based on the concept of "rites of passage" (van Gennep, 1960) as ways to facilitate the change process. So, let's take a look at what is meant by "rites of passage" and how this might help us understand the process of change for persons who stutter.

In his book *Rites of Passage*, French anthropologist van Gennep (1960) explored the fundamental process underlying the change of an individual's status in society. He observed that life is characterized by transitions from one social group or situation to another, such as individuals passing through various age ranges, school grades, social relationships, and occupations during their lifetime. All of these transitions, according to van Gennep, share a processual similarity that he called "rites of passage."

Van Gennep (1960) noted that almost all human societies use some form of ceremonial rites to mark these significant transitions in the social status of individuals. These rites of passage serve to ease the transition of individuals into new status or prestige roles, and to validate such changes, particularly on the occasion of life-transforming events such as birth, puberty, marriage, parenthood, and death, but also in other transitions related to social or professional roles. Comparing the structure of such rituals in diverse cultures, van Gennep (1960) noted that rites of passage often shared similar "ceremonial patterns" that included (a) rites of *separation*, (b), rites of *transition*, and (c) rites of *incorporation*.

Rites of Separation

Rites of separation set up the preparation for exit from the individual's current life and entrance into the new life. Van Gennep (1960) also referred to this as the "preliminal" stage, as it is a period of separation from everyday life that leads to a period of "liminality" or threshold existence. Persons who stutter might experience this stage in their attempts to leave their current life, dominated by stuttering, to experience a life where they have greater control, increased fluency, or reduced avoidance.

Rites occurring in this stage include forms of initiation activities that usher the individual out of the current life and into the next (Martinez, 2011). For persons who stutter, these might include the stuttering treatment or therapy sessions, self-help group activities, or other ways in which the client is actively working against his or her "old" way of living and thinking that is dominated by stuttering. Unfortunately, most speech-language pathologists place a great deal of focus on the "rites" involved with this stage—particularly rites that involve activities that promote behavioral change—often without recognizing the difficult, "transitional" nature of what they are engaging in with the client.

Rites of Transition

In this transition stage, individuals fully experience the process of change. Van Gennep (1960) referred to this as a "liminal" stage, literally meaning, "occupying a position at, or on, both sides of a boundary or threshold" (Oxford Dictionary, 2014). Turner (1969) elaborated on the concept of a liminal state, describing it as "a limbo between a past state and a coming one, a period of personal ambiguity, of non-status, and of unanchored identity" (p. 95). He further described individuals in this liminal state as being "betwixt and between the positions assigned and arrayed by law, custom, convention, and ceremony" (p. 95).

Not surprisingly, individuals in such a liminal state are considered to be exceptionally vulnerable. Schouten (1991) noted that individuals in a liminal state face the task of reconstructing congruous, integrated self-concepts; creating new roles; or emphasizing existing ones to fill the gaps left by roles they vacated in separating from their previous life. They might also engage in rejecting personal traits or aspects of self with which they are dissatisfied and work at replacing them with more desirable traits. Consequently, an important characteristic of liminoid states is the tendency to play and experiment with new categories of meaning (Turner, 1974) and to engage in "identity play" (Kelly, 1955/1991), to formulate, elaborate, and evaluate possible selves (Markus & Nurius, 1986) with an eye to self-change or self-completion (Wicklund & Gollwitzer, 1982).

In "trying on" these new possible selves, individuals in a liminal state might engage in rites that reflect various physical, emotional, and social changes from their past roles. Martinez (2011) described liminal rites that individuals engage in related to the reinventing of selves as reflected in the creation of avatars in Second World. These include physical characteristics, movement characteristics, profile, group membership, and conversation style. Interestingly, many of these categories would appear to fit well with the changes that persons who stutter might attempt during this transition or liminal stage. For example, clients experimenting with being more assertive, and engaging in fewer avoidance behaviors, might "try on" changes in physical appearance, such as a different hairstyle, different clothing styles, jewelry, and even body modifications (e.g., piercings, tattoos, etc.). They might also engage in changes in their "profile," or what they want people to know about them, changes in their group membership or social support structures that they rely on, and changes in their communication style that might include the words they use and attempts at being more fluent.

For speech-language pathologists working with persons who stutter, two primary concerns might emerge at this liminal stage. First, individuals could experience difficulty embracing the changes that occur during this time, despite such changes being in line with their goals for a new lifestyle. For example, recall from earlier in this chapter how Kelly (1955/1991) described emotional reactions to change—how acting in ways that do not match your constructs about who you are can generate feelings of anxiety, fear, and even guilt. Similarly, Markus (1977) described how "self-schemas" develop based on past experiences and tend to be "self-perpetuating" in that experiences that are inconsistent with self-schemas are resisted, manipulated, or ignored. As such, persons who stutter attempting to transform their lives could encounter significant emotional and cognitive barriers as they begin to test out new ways of behaving, thinking, and relating to others. As Fransella (1972) pointed out, if persons who stutter find the role of a (more) fluent speaker to be too "foreign," then they are likely to return to their previous life that, despite its deficiencies, is at least familiar. Second, there is some evidence that individuals can become "stuck" in this liminal stage if they appear to have no role in an alternative life. For example, Willett and Deegan (2001) suggested that some individuals with disabilities might perceive themselves as permanently suspended between the "sick role" and "normality" with no movement toward any type of incorporation rites. Willett and Deegan suggested that such "rolelessness" (Fine & Asch, 1985, p. 9) might produce an endless liminal state, resulting in difficulties with relationships and employment. This is similar to the argument proposed by Fransella (1972) and DiLollo and colleagues (DiLollo, Manning, & Neimeyer, 2003, 2005; DiLollo, Neimeyer, & Manning, 2002) regarding the lack of "meaningfulness" of the "fluent-speaker role" for most persons who stutter. As they engage in what appears to be "successful" treatment of their stuttering, persons who stutter might find themselves thrust into a new world in which they are essentially "roleless," caught between their prior role as a stutterer (that they know well) and a new role that promises to make them "normal" but is highly abstract and ethereal. The experience of such rolelessness for persons who stutter could, again, force

them back to their previous, known, stutterer role.

It is the responsibility of the clinician to be engaged with the client in such a way that he or she will recognize the potential problems associated with this liminal stage and be prepared to address these issues with the client through counseling (see Chapter 8 for more on counseling).

Rites of Incorporation

In this stage, also referred to as *"postliminal"* by van Gennep (1960), individuals move out of isolation and reincorporate into the social order with a new standing or new identity. Common rites observed in this stage include ceremonies, celebrations, dancing, exchange of gifts, and communal meals. Individuals might receive emblems of the new status, such as jewelry, new clothing, or new names, and rituals often involve the individual's immediate family, friends, or larger community.

Interestingly, there appear to be some formal "rites" associated with programs that attempt to increase the rate of fluent speech or seek to decrease avoidance behaviors and generate more acceptance of stuttering. For example, clients might receive a "certificate of completion" at the end of a structured fluency shaping program, or they might have a "graduation ceremony" at the conclusion of a stuttering modification program. These can be important events that mark for the clients a passage from one life to a new way of behaving and thinking. Such rites, however, are not always used in clinical settings or are frequently not taken seriously by clinicians as a useful tool in the process of change for their clients. Consequently, if no formal rites are used to mark their membership in this new life, clients can remain "roleless" in the vulnerable liminal state, increasing the chances of returning to their previous life (i.e., as a stutterer) in which they are sure of their membership. Clinicians are encouraged to include rites of incorporation into therapeutic processes. This might mean using a graduation ceremony or a certificate of completion as a way for family members and others in the client's social network to better understand and fully appreciate the client's journey through therapy and the preferred "story" that the client is now enacting (for more on personal "stories" or narratives, see Chapter 8).

CONCLUSION

The process of change is difficult, no matter whether it is change that accomplishes a long-sought goal or a change thrust upon someone as a result of injury or illness. All change presents individuals with both technical and adaptive challenges — both of which must be recognized and addressed if long-term effective change is to occur. As clinicians working with persons who stutter, we are privileged to play a role in the change process in which our clients engage. From relatively painless behavioral change that might result in increased fluency, to changes in assertiveness and avoidance behaviors that are more challenging, to far more difficult and profound changes to how the person thinks and feels about himself or herself as a person, as clinicians, our understanding of the process of change is critical to our clients' successes. As we have described in this chapter, clinicians need to be aware of the processes underlying change that relate to our clients' unique perspective on the world and their place in it. These

processes form not only the mechanisms for change but also the systems that resist change, even, paradoxically, change that is positive and wanted by the client. The information in the next chapter on counseling is designed to help clinicians address such issues through the use of a constructivist counseling framework.

Readiness for change is also a critical aspect of the therapeutic process that clinicians need to understand if they are to help their clients facilitate change. As we discussed in the chapter, it is important for clinicians to identify the stage of change that a client is in, and then to apply appropriate therapeutic processes that match that specific stage. The use of a readiness ruler can be helpful in accomplishing this task.

Similarly, clinicians should take advantage of rites of passage, or ways to help usher their clients into new, preferred lifestyles that might incorporate greater levels of fluency, more assertiveness, less avoidance, or greater acceptance of stuttering. The importance of rites of passage relates back to the processes underlying change in that successful therapy almost always involves more than simply changes in behavior—it involves change at multiple levels that sometimes extend to the very core of the person's identity.

❓ TOPICS FOR DISCUSSION

1. Describe a situation from your own experience that is an example of the *experience cycle* at work (i.e., a time when you confirmed or disconfirmed constructs).

2. Why is change difficult even if it is something that the individual wants

to change? Have you ever experienced this?

3. Discuss a time when you felt *guilty* for acting in a way that was in contrast to your constructs about yourself.

4. What assumptions does Prochaska et al.'s (1992) change model make about the process of change?

5. Considering Prochaska et al.'s (1992) model, explain some possible mismatches between *stages* and *processes* of therapeutic change. How would these create problems for clients?

6. Recall your coping response to a difficult or threatening experience and consider to what extent you responded in either a stepwise or cyclical manner.

7. Write down (for your eyes only) examples of various forms of denial that you have employed as a coping response about a difficult problem or relationship.

8. Explain some of the barriers to initiating and maintaining change.

9. Describe any *rites of passage* that you have experienced in your life.

10. How could you make a simple certificate of completion into a more meaningful rite of passage for a client?

📖 RECOMMENDED READINGS

DiLollo, A., & Neimeyer, R. A. (2022). The leadership of therapy: How to integrate counseling you're your clinical practice. In *Counseling in speech-language pathology and audiology: Reconstructing personal narratives* (2nd ed., pp. 57–70). Plural Publishing.

Floyd, J., Zebrowski, P. M., & Flamme, G. A. (2007). Stages of change and stuttering: A preliminary view. *Journal of Fluency Disorders, 32,* 95–120.

Prochaska, J. O., & DiClemente, C. C. (1992). Stages of change in the modification of problem behaviors. In M. Herson, R. Eisler, & P. Miller (Eds.), *Progress in behavior modification* (pp. 184–218). Sycamore.

van Gennep, A. (1960). *The rites of passage* (M. B. Vizedom & G. L. Caffee, Trans.). University of Chicago Press.

There is nothing of which we are more ashamed than of not being ourselves, and there is nothing which brings us greater joy and happiness than to think, to feel or to say what is ours.

—Erich Fromm

My feeling of success was fleeting, however, as at my Bar Mitzvah, I had somehow been fluent. But my fluency mystified me. There was no way to remember how I felt being fluent, because my fluency did not seem to come from me. I was beginning to fear fluency. I knew myself when I was stuttering. But I felt estranged from myself when I was fluent.

—Jezer (1997, p. 108)

Counseling Persons Who Stutter and Their Families

CHAPTER OBJECTIVES

- To explore how counseling is defined
- To discuss the reluctance of many clinicians to engage in counseling
- To describe some of the more recognizable counseling philosophies
- To describe a person-centered, constructivist-narrative approach to counseling
- To describe some of the basic clinical skills that underlie successful counseling

RELUCTANCE TO CONFRONT EMOTIONAL AND PERSONAL IDENTITY ISSUES

There is a notable history of counseling, in our field in general, and in the area of fluency disorders in particular. In fact, speech-language pathology as a discipline in the United States was founded in departments of psychology and psychiatry. Probably the most notable of these was at the University of Iowa, where first Carl Seashore and then Lee Edward Travis trained some of the founding fathers of our field—such names as Wendell Johnson, Charles Van Riper, Oliver Bloodstein, and Dean Williams—who were also primarily interested in the area of stuttering.

The increase during the late 1990s of the number of texts on stuttering that have included information on counseling indicates an increased appreciation of this aspect of treatment (e.g., Bloom & Cooperman, 1999; Crowe, 1997a; Manning, 1996; Shapiro, 1999). This trend has continued in the following decades, with multiple texts (and multiple editions of popular texts) related to counseling in communication sciences and disorders emerging on the market (e.g., DiLollo & Neimeyer, 2022; Flasher & Fogle, 2011; Holland & Nelson, 2018; Luterman, 2017;

Stein-Rubin & Adler, 2016). This also follows a general trend in health care toward increased provision of person-centered care (e.g., Bowers et al, 2001; O'Connell, 2008; Sumsion & Law, 2006) and an interest in patients' personal stories of illness, termed by Charon and others as "narrative medicine" (e.g., Charon, 2006, 2007; Curtis, 2013).

Despite this, however, it is not uncommon for clinicians to indicate their reluctance to confront aspects of treatment beyond those that they see as directly related to modifying fluency (e.g., Cooper & Cooper, 1985a, 1996; Kelly et al., 1997). To many clinicians, problems associated with bullying, low self-esteem, patterns of avoidance, frustration, depression, identity issues, and resistance to change seem mysterious and too far removed from the behavioral "speech therapy" that they are familiar with. As a result, some clinicians try to pass the responsibility for such cognitive and affective problems over to other professionals such as psychologists, school counselors, social workers, or physicians. A number of authors (e.g., DiLollo & Neimeyer, 2022; Holland, 2007; Silverman, 2011; Simmons-Mackie & Damico, 2011) have discussed the reluctance of speech-language pathologists (SLPs) to engage clients in a counseling relationship, pointing out that discomfort with engaging clients in counseling might be the product of a lack of adequate preparation of students in our training programs.

McCarthy et al. (1986) found that only one third of the programs in communication disorders offered or required a course in counseling. These authors noted that only 12% of clinicians who responded to their survey felt that they were adequately prepared to counsel their clients. A replication of this study 8 years later (Culpepper et al., 1994) noted almost no change in counseling training for SLPs and audiologists. Phillips and Lucks Mendel (2008) reported that 80% of clinical fellows in speech-language pathology and audiology indicated that they had received "no credit hours of counseling training" (p. 49). Unfortunately, this trend appears to be continuing as the percentage of communication sciences and disorders programs that offer a stand-alone course in counseling in 2017 had decreased even further to just 59% of all programs (Doud et al., 2020).

A MANDATE FOR COUNSELING

This reluctance to confront emotional and personal identity issues has led some SLPs to suggest that counseling is not part of their job and that it should be handled by counselors, psychologists, or even psychiatrists. The vast majority of the people who come to us, however, are ordinary people experiencing a *normal reaction* to a communication disorder (Luterman, 2017). As Luterman indicated, such people are generally experiencing normal emotions of stress and anxiety in the face of a serious problem. If our goal is to provide truly comprehensive treatment, we have no choice but to provide counseling to these clients and their families. In addition, as we indicated in Chapter 7, we are in the business of change, and facilitating effective, meaningful change frequently requires attention to more than simple motor behaviors. It is the responsibility of clinicians to provide whatever is needed for clients to improve not only their communication, but, ultimately, their quality of life.

As a discipline, we are guided by policies and procedures that have been documented by our national governing body, the American Speech-Language-Hearing

CLINICAL INSIGHT

When my students perform pseudo-stuttering in public as an assignment in my class, I ask them to try to take on the role for an extended interaction, not simply a brief exchange—and they have to do this 10 times! One of the reasons I have them do this is to help them experience the emotions associated with (a) being noticeably different than expected, and (b) acting in a way that is different from their core role or personal story. When students share their experiences in class, what we get are a lot of stories of fear, anxiety, shame, and even guilt, and very few stories of negative reactions from the public. I point this out here as an example of the "normal" reaction to a difficult situation referred to by Luterman. The emotions related to communication disorders—and those that are most obvious when dealing with stuttering—are not a part of the disorder and don't represent any personality defect on the part of the client. In fact, quite the opposite! The emotional reactions of clients to communication disorders tell us that they are quite "normal" and reacting in a very appropriate way. (AD)

Association (ASHA). These documents specifically describe the role of SLPs, preferred practice patterns, and ethical obligations that are deemed appropriate for working with clients, including persons who stutter.

Scope of Practice

In the recently revised *Scope of Practice in Speech-Language Pathology* (ASHA, 2016), the objective of speech-language pathology services is described as being to "optimize individuals' abilities to communicate and to swallow, thereby improving quality of life" (p. 5). In this document, *counseling* is listed as one of the eight service delivery domains for speech-language pathology, which were crafted to complement the *ICF* framework (WHO, 2014) that views body functions and structures, activity and participation, environmental factors, and personal factors as being important to optimal functioning and health.

The domain of counseling is described as providing "education, guidance, and support" to "individuals, their families, and their caregivers . . . regarding acceptance, adaptation, and decision making about communication, feeding and swallowing, and related disorders" (ASHA, 2016, p. 9). Throughout the document, words and phrases such as "empower," "educate," "provide support," and "address negative emotions and thoughts" are used to reflect the types of activities that SLPs are expected to engage in related to counseling. Knowing when to refer clients when counseling needs fall outside the areas of communication and feeding and swallowing is also emphasized. Importantly, clinicians must understand that counseling is a part of their scope of practice and that decisions to refer are made only if clients' counseling needs are unrelated to communication, feeding, or swallowing—or if clinical symptoms of depression or other mental health issues (including suicidal thoughts) are identified, even if related to communication, feeding, or swallowing.

Preferred Practice Patterns

In the document *Preferred Practice Patterns for the Profession of Speech-Language Pathology* (ASHA, 2004), it is noted that counseling should involve "providing timely information and guidance to patients/clients, families/caregivers, and other relevant persons about the nature of communication or swallowing disorders, the course of intervention, ways to enhance outcomes, coping with disorders, and prognosis" (p. 23). Such a description of counseling provides clinicians with an indication of the comprehensive nature of the counseling task. It is also pointed out in this document that counseling should be "conducted by appropriately credentialed and trained speech-language pathologists," again noting that this is a responsibility of the SLP and should not be referred to other professionals. It also implies that SLPs should be appropriately trained to engage clients in counseling, something, as we noted earlier, that is not always the case, even in ASHA-accredited programs.

Code of Ethics

In addition to scope of practice and preferred practice patterns, ASHA has published a *Code of Ethics* (ASHA, 2023) that guides clinicians in their practice of speech-language pathology. This document mandates that clinicians should engage in all aspects of the professions within the scope of practice and provide all services competently, using all available resources to provide high-quality service. This implies that clinicians should be using counseling (a resource and part of the scope of practice in SLP) to provide high-quality service.

DiLollo and Neimeyer (2022), after reviewing these and other documents, concluded that clinicians "have a mandate to provide clinical services beyond the simple teaching of behavioral techniques or use of technology" (p. 7), and that it is their "ethical responsibility" (p. 7) to become competent in all areas of practice, including counseling.

A DEFINITION OF COUNSELING

It is important to appreciate that, for most people, counseling is an everyday experience. Indeed, we counsel others in an informal manner as we help our family, friends, and colleagues deal with daily problems. Egan (2013) provided a particularly useful suggestion when he stated that the goal of professional counseling falls somewhere on a continuum between telling people what to do and leaving them to their own devices. The ideal location on the continuum is a point where we are "helping people make their own decisions and act on them" (p. 60). This concept is reflected in the consensus definition of counseling that emerged from the 20/20: A Vision for the Future of Counseling initiative that brought together 31 organizations engaged in professional counseling. This group defined counseling as "a professional relationship that empowers diverse individuals, families, and groups to accomplish mental health, wellness, education, and career goals" (Kaplan et al., 2014, p. 366).

Crowe (1997b) considered the definition of counseling in relation to speech-language pathology, and emphasized the differences between *counseling* and *psychotherapy*. He and others (e.g., DiLollo & Neimeyer, 2022; Rollin, 2000; Shames,

2006) agreed that counseling is seen as a type of psychotherapy for the purpose of support or (re)education for behavioral problems not associated with mental illness. As Crowe explained, counseling is intended for assisting those people with less severe interpersonal (as opposed to intrapersonal) problems. Psychotherapy, on the other hand, is intended for persons with mental illness related to basic problems in personality development and personal adjustment. Although communication disorders often result in serious problems on many levels, in most cases we are not working with people who have chronic life-adjustment problems. Luterman (2017), who for years has taken the lead in conceptualizing our intervention for communication problems as a humanistic and psychosocial process, also agreed with this view by indicating that our clients are experiencing a normal reaction to a very difficult problem.

DiLollo and Neimeyer (2022) provided a definition of counseling in speech-language pathology that applies to the counseling that clinicians will need to engage in when working with persons who stutter. They stated, "We define 'counseling' as those components of the clinician-client relationship that facilitate personal growth and empowerment for clients (and their families), with the goal of helping individuals and/or families manage, adjust to, and cope with communication and swallowing disorders and the treatments for those disorders" (p. 5).

Common Misconceptions

As a way to expand on our basic definition and develop some insight into the nature of counseling, let's consider some of the common misconceptions about the process. Understanding what not to do as a counselor can be as useful as appreciating what you can do. One of the most common misconceptions that many people have about counseling is that it is synonymous with "giving advice." Although there is no doubt that the clinician plays an important role in the direction and form that counseling takes, there is general consensus that simply giving advice is not the same as counseling (e.g., Anderson & Handelsman, 2010; Crowe, 1997b; Kaplan et al., 2014). As we discuss in more detail later in this chapter, engaging in effective counseling requires that the clinician recognizes the expertise, strengths, and resources that the client possesses and works to help the client bring those to bear on the problem to find his or her own best solutions. Such an approach encourages client "ownership" of solutions, an aspect that has been suggested as important in the process of change (Longenecker & Liverpool, 1987; Luterman, 2017; Yalom, 2002).

Another common misconception is that a primary goal of counseling is to *make people feel better*. Luterman (2017) and DiLollo and Neimeyer (2022), however, suggested that this is not the case. As Peck (1978) stated in the first sentence of his book, *The Road Less Traveled*, "Life is difficult" (p. 15). It is normal and acceptable for people to feel sad when undesirable or bad things happen to them. The problem and the pain associated with the problem might not go away (as with the loss of a loved one or the realization of a son's or daughter's speech, language, or hearing problem). With successful counseling, however, the client should be better able to manage the situation (Egan, 2013). As Egan (2013) stated: "Helpers are effective to the degree that their clients—through client–helper interactions—see the need to manage specific problem situations and develop specific unused resources and opportunities more effectively" (p. 9).

Similarly, it is not the task of the clinician to "rescue" clients (Luterman, 2017) by solving the problem for them. Accordingly, counseling is less about doing something to clients than it is about a collaborative process between the people involved. More important, rescuing people enables them to continue in the patterns they have established and negates their ability to problem solve and grow on their own. As Egan (1990) suggested, in many ways counselors stimulate clients to provide services to themselves, helping them to have "more degrees of freedom" in making choices in their lives

(p. 6). We take this approach in this and the following chapters as we describe the successful management of stuttering with adolescents and adults. Fortunately, it is not necessary to eradicate the last vestige of stuttering in order for individuals who stutter to achieve success.

WHEN TO "DO COUNSELING"

One of the most frequent questions we get from students is, "How do I know when I should be counseling?" Although it might seem a perplexing and daunting

CLINICAL INSIGHT

Responding to the inquiry, "How do you do counseling?" reminds me of questions I am sometimes asked when giving workshops on fluency disorders. Invariably someone in the audience will ask me how I would respond to one of his or her clients during a particular treatment situation. When that happened early in my career, I immediately became role-bound. I felt that I had to assume the role of the expert clinician who had come from another city with answers to all of the questions I would receive. For years I tirelessly tried to provide a worthy list of suggestions. On occasion, clinicians would later report that they found my suggestions to be helpful and sometimes they would let me know that the "techniques didn't work."

Now, rather than responding to such questions with ideas that might or might not work I immediately respond to such questions by sincerely saying, "You know, I have absolutely no idea!" My response often elicits a puzzled look from some in the audience and, of course, for the moment at least, I come across as something less than an expert (a liberating feeling!). The point I want to make with the audience is that there are many reasonable techniques that might or might not work depending on many factors. I am unable to know the likelihood of success of any technique until I spend time with the speaker and begin to comprehend how determined and resilient the person might be. I need to understand the speaker's history of success and failure in communicating within the context of the educational, vocational, and social aspects of their life. I need to appreciate the level of support the person is likely to have from his family and friends. I need to determine how willing the person is to experiment with different techniques and the extent of their persistence in applying the techniques across a range of speaking situations. For these reasons and more, because I know absolutely nothing about the child or adult being referred to, I don't believe that it's my role to suggest specific techniques. That adventure is the responsibility of the clinician and the speaker as they journey together. (WM) task for the novice clinician (and for some more experienced clinicians, as well), it turns out that this is really a very simple question. Before we answer this question, however, let's go back and review the concepts introduced in Chapter 7 on technical and adaptive challenges, as these provide us with useful terminology that can help with this dilemma.

Technical and Adaptive Challenges

Recall that *technical challenges* have a known solution, or, at least, a solution can be determined by an individual with "expert" knowledge. They relate to the more surface-level aspects of stuttering that are reflected in the speech behaviors and secondary behaviors that contribute to the way stuttering looks and sounds. As SLPs, we tend to be comfortable and adept at identifying and working on these surface behaviors—and the chapters that follow this one are full of techniques and strategies that clinicians can use in such endeavors. *Adaptive challenges*, on the other hand, involve the more subtle, intrinsic aspects of the problem that cannot be addressed by "experts" but must be worked on by the clients themselves (i.e., the stakeholders). When working with persons who stutter, adaptive challenges involve dealing with issues of change that generate significant emotional reactions. By conceptualizing clients' problems around technical and adaptive challenges, it becomes relatively easy to see the role of (and need for) counseling in the process of therapy.

So, getting back to the original question—"How do I know when I should be counseling?"—that answer is, *you are always counseling*, because technical and adaptive challenges are both parts of an integrated whole person, attempting to function in a complex and dynamic social environment. They tend to not only present simultaneously, but in a way that is inextricably woven together. Counseling, therefore, should be an integral part of how you interact with the client, and, for SLPs, should be *a way of thinking as much as a way of doing* (DiLollo & Neimeyer, 2022).

OVERVIEW OF COUNSELING PHILOSOPHIES

The goal of this chapter is to provide students and clinicians with a practical framework around which they might build their counseling practice with persons who stutter. To that end, we introduce in detail one specific framework that we have found useful. It should be noted, however, that we are not suggesting that this is the only way to approach counseling with persons who stutter. Indeed, there are literally hundreds of approaches to counseling in the psychology and counseling literature from which clinicians can choose. What we are recommending, however, is that clinicians adopt an organizing framework around which to build their approach to counseling, rather than randomly selecting and changing approaches, or having no systematic approach at all.

The Common Factors Model

Although we discuss the Common Factors model (Ahn & Wampold, 2001; Wampold, 2001) in more detail in Chapter 10, a brief introduction here is appropriate, as it can help explain our position that SLPs should choose a single, organizing framework for counseling. In the Common Factors model, psychotherapy (and, remember, most of speech-language pathology is a form of psychotherapy) is conceptualized as an activity that is socially constructed and mediated. Through extensive research that applied processes of meta-analysis and hierarchical linear modeling to an extensive range of therapy approaches, Wampold and colleagues determined a set of "common" factors that are both necessary and sufficient for change. These include (a) a bond between the clinician and client, often referred to as "therapeutic alliance" (also discussed in more detail in Chapter 10); (b) a setting for therapy in which the client feels safe and is willing to confide in the clinician; (c) a clinician who provides a psychologically derived (i.e., theory-driven) and culturally appropriate approach to therapy; (d) an explanation of the problem and treatment approach that is viable and believable, and is accepted by the client; and (e) a set of procedures, engaged by the client and clinician, that leads the client to enact something that is positive, helpful, or adaptive (Laska et al., 2014). Interestingly, Ahn and Wampold (2001) pointed out that clinicians' "allegiance" (or belief) in their chosen therapy approach, along with how well they administer that approach, have a far greater impact on the success of treatment than the choice of any specific therapeutic approach.

So, what the Common Factors model tells us about choosing an approach to therapy is that clinicians need to invest in a theory-driven approach to therapy that they believe in and can develop skill in administering. Consequently, we recommend that clinicians choose one theory-driven approach as a framework around which they can build their skills in counseling clients. As such, we devote most of our discussion in the remainder of this chapter to the *Constructivist-Narrative Therapy* approach described by DiLollo

and Neimeyer (2022). However, in order to provide some context and possible alternatives to this approach, let us first take a brief look at some other common counseling philosophies.

Behavioral Counseling

The original and strict version of the behavioral approach held that the individual has little or no choice and that all behavior is the result of environmental reinforcements (Skinner, 1953). Because of its structure, behavioral counseling provides an appealing strategy for engineering changes in the observable behaviors of speakers, especially for new clinicians. Structure is provided by a series of steps whereby behaviors are positively or negatively reinforced (or punished) in a precise and timely manner resulting in a series of successive approximations toward the desired goal. The concrete nature of the techniques and the specific, overt criteria for moving on to the next level make it relatively easy to teach and administer. The structured nature of the behavioral approach also lends itself to the creation of programmed or manualized therapeutic programs, a major reason why such approaches have achieved more empirical support in the form of randomized controlled trials. There is no question that reinforcement schedules can have an important therapeutic impact both within and beyond the therapeutic setting. Many investigations with persons who stutter have demonstrated that a speaker can be guided through a series of successful speaking experiences and achieve long-term success (Onslow et al., 2003). One of the limitations of strict behavioral approaches is a lack of emphasis on the "therapeutic alliance" that Wampold and colleagues identified as an important factor in the process of successful change.

Humanistic Counseling

Underlying the humanistic counseling approach, developed by Rogers (1951) and Maslow (1968), is the concept that humans have an innate drive toward self-actualization (i.e., the fulfillment of one's potential). The basic elements of this approach include the concepts of *congruence* (bringing into parallel the parts of the self, particularity the intellectual and emotional components), *empathy*, *self-actualization*, and *unconditional positive regard* for the client. The clinician's goal is to assist people in removing barriers to self-actualization and to help them to follow their innate drive toward growth. This form of counseling stresses the quality of the *therapetic alliance*, with little emphasis on diagnosis and testing. The clinician's role is primarily one of *unconditional positive regard* for the client and *empathetic listening*. These qualities, when combined with the *congruence* of the counselor (the coming together of the clinician's experience of the moment, the awareness of the experience, and the genuine communication of the experience) facilitate the client's "resources for self-understanding and growth" (Luterman, 2001, p. 14). Humanistic counseling and the critical nature of the therapeutic alliance have often been advocated for by clients and their families (Backus & Beasley, 1951; Cooper, 1966, 1968; E. Webster, 1966, 1968, 1977). However, as Luterman pointed out, the abstract nature of the basic concepts involved can be difficult both to teach and to understand. Furthermore, the unstructured approach places the responsibility for change almost completely on the client, and, for some clients, it is difficult to accept that the self-actualizing drive will come into effect. According to Luterman, this approach does not work well with children, severely self-involved adults, or those with limited abilities, or with novice or insecure clinicians.

Existential Counseling

The existential approach comes from the French intellectual movement of the mid-1800s and the work of the Danish philosopher Søren Kierkegaard. This view holds that many human problems are a result of anxiety due to the basic facts of our existence. That is, we must die, we have freedom to make choices, we are alone, and life is meaningless. This view is different from traditional psychoanalytic theory, where the source of anxiety results from the conflict between the *id* (the pleasure drive) and the *superego* (social restrictions). In existential theory, there is no clinical value in understanding the client's past history or behavior. For individuals whose response to life is to avoid the basic facts of human existence, there are some negative, sometimes neurotic results.

Death

Existentialists hold that anxiety resulting from our eventual death can result in the avoidance or postponement of activities or decisions. Furthermore, it can result in a decreased ability to appreciate our everyday existence. By not recognizing the boundaries of our existence, we are likely to miss the beauty of the commonplace. The greater this death anxiety, the more one is likely to experience a restricted and unfulfilled life. The recognition that nothing is permanent enables us to value what we have been given while we can.

Responsibility

Each of us is responsible for our own actions. Whether we admit it or not, in many respects, at least, we are in charge. Because of this, the clinician should not feel sorry for the client with a problem. There is no intention to blame clients or make them feel guilty, but rather a recognition that people have a choice about what to do about their situation and about what to tell themselves about their circumstances. If they choose, their problems can be approached as a series of challenges or opportunities to learn and grow. Virtually every writer in counseling agrees that the starting point of therapeutic change is the assumption of responsibility by the client and a decision to change (DiClemente, 1993). As Luterman (2001) pointed out, the assumption of responsibility coincides with his earlier comments that we ought not to play the role of the rescuer. To the degree that we attempt to fix or rescue clients, they will continue to feel powerless and rely on the clinician.

Loneliness

As Luterman (1991) stated, "We are alone and that crushing fact is central to existential thought" (p. 19). Of course, all of us are lonely at times, but clients with communication disorders are apt to be uncommonly so. By confronting our loneliness, we are able to generate an unconditional regard for humanity in general.

Meaninglessness

As if loneliness was not difficult enough to face, existentialists propose that there is no intrinsic meaning to the world; the cosmos is indifferent to our circumstances. This central aspect of existential thought cannot be judged as good or bad. Nevertheless, as Luterman (2001) pointed out, we are able to construct our interpretation of our purpose in life. For a clinician, this means that our basic task is not to judge clients but to understand their view of the world and to assist them in finding more appropriate and functional ways of managing life's circumstances.

Luterman explained that the existential approach lacks a unifying approach for confronting the various sources of anxiety. The approach offers more of a philosophy than a treatment protocol and goes beyond the accepted limits for most speech-language pathologists. Nevertheless, the concepts provided by this counseling philosophy could provide a way to understand the narratives of our clients, as well as our own.

Cognitive Counseling

This view of counseling holds that many human problems are, in many important ways, a function of how we think about the problem. The clinician helps clients to identify specific misconceptions and unrealistic expectations that underlie their situation and their behavior. This process can be highly confrontational, because the clinician challenges clients to examine the underlying irrational and inaccurate assumptions that are reflected in their language and their actions.

There is historical precedence for cognitive approaches in the area of fluency disorders. A number of authors advocate the use of some form of cognitive restructuring as a primary or supplemental approach to treatment, particularly for adolescents and adults (Bryngelson et al., 1944; Cook & Botterill, 2010; Emerick, 1988; Johnson, 1946; Maxwell, 1982; Menzies et al., 2009; Van Riper, 1947, 1982; Williams, 1979). Specific recommendations of several of these authors are described in later chapters.

Because speakers often indicate their cognitive positions through the language that they use, it is important to listen closely and consider what our clients (and others) are telling us, consciously or unconsciously. As Luterman and others explained, we can listen for "quality words" such as "can't," "should," "ought," and "but," as well as the ways in which people describe themselves and their circumstances: "I'm an idiot," or "I can't speak in front of a group." The point is that the language people use informs the clinician about the speakers' cognitive state. Alternatively, choosing language that more accurately reflects the situation can inform and alter the speakers' cognitive interpretations: "I am not an idiot but in that instance I did an idiotic thing," and "Although I am anxious I am capable of speaking in front of a group." As Luterman (2001) stated, "I find that when I listen to the irrational assumptions that are reflected in the language of the client, and when I gently change the language, there is often immense benefit to the client" (p. 28).

Luterman (2001) suggested that SLPs (and audiologists) unknowingly use this counseling approach as we frequently attempt to persuade our clients how they "ought" to be thinking and behaving. The problem is that a rigid cognitive approach risks such persuasion of the client to adopt what the clinician believes to be a more reality-based response to the problem. As described earlier, an approach that emphasizes the accuracy of the clinician's perceptions and authority usually results in a dependent client. Luterman also cautioned that the emphasis of some cognitive therapies prevents the expression of real and natural emotions that accompany communication problems. The emotions are an important component of the problem and, as we shall see, an important aspect of the inclusive process of therapeutic change.

POSTMODERN COUNSELING

Postmodernism is best seen as a broad cultural trend in many fields, including art, architecture, law, literary criticism, and philosophy (Neimeyer & Raskin, 2000). In contrast, the modern, objectivist orientation consists of "experts" telling the client what is "real" or "true" or "healthy." For modernists there is a single, knowable reality. Disorders are viewed in terms of the degree that an individual's cognitive distortions result in a deviation from reality as defined by what is considered by society as the norm. The focus of diagnosis and intervention is on "measuring essential structures and empirically establishing the efficacy of preferred interventions designed to correct such disorders" (Neimeyer & Raskin, 2000, p. 5).

The understanding proposed by those advocating postmodern approaches could appear as shocking or blatantly wrong to those raised and schooled in the modernist tradition. The postmodern view, rather than espousing a single reality, proposes that there are multiple realities that are created by individual, social, and temporal factors. There is both the recognition and a celebration of these multiple realities according to the contextual history of a person's life. With this view, treatment is not informed by a process of discovering the truth about a person and helping that person to adjust to the norm. Rather, the therapeutic process is centered on "an exploration of how people construct truths about themselves and their relationships" (Monk et al., 1997, p. 85). This approach to how individuals come to understand their world is reflected in the constructivist view that each individual creates his or her own story based on the experiential exploration of his or her intimate attachment relationships. Individual narratives are influenced by such primary factors as culture and gender. It is within this crucible that individual identity and disorder are constructed. The implications of this perspective provide optimistic and creative possibilities for liberating the individual from what has become a limiting and oppressive story (Neimeyer & Raskin, 2000).

A CONSTRUCTIVIST-NARRATIVE APPROACH TO COUNSELING

In Chapter 7, we introduced some basic concepts of personal construct theory (Kelly, 1955a, 1955b, 1991), a postmodern theory that emphasizes each individual's unique construction of reality based on her or his abstraction of repeated themes in her or his experiences. These abstracted themes (and their contrasts) form *personal constructs* that people use to anticipate how events will unfold. We also described how emotions such as fear and threat relate to an awareness of possible change to one's construct system, how anxiety is seen as when one's constructs are insufficient to adequately anticipate events being experienced, and how guilt is seen as acting in a way that is in contrast to strongly held constructs about the self.

The Constructivist-Narrative Approach

Although the term *narrative* is commonly used in speech-language pathology to refer to a type of discourse that has certain linguistic properties (McCabe & Bliss, 2003), in this context the term takes on a narrower focus. In this application the term *narrative* refers to an individual's personal story, which influences how events and experiences are interpreted, consolidates self-understanding, and guides behavior (DiLollo & Manning, 2007; DiLollo & Neimeyer, 2022; Monk et al., 1997; Parry & Doan, 1994; White, 2007).

The narrative therapy model (White & Epston, 1990) has several appealing features. It provides an optimistic orientation that assumes that people are able to take action and rewrite their stories in order to alter meaning in their lives. It allows the clinician and others to view the person as a "courageous victor rather than a pathologized victim" (Monk, 1997, p. 4). The emphasis of the therapeutic interaction is on the person and his or her story rather than specific therapeutic techniques or the clinician. The process does not require that the clinician know "the way" but emphasizes the client and clinician working together to discover the directions and techniques that are likely to be the most helpful for the client. It does not place the clinician in the role of an authority charged with solving people's problems (Leahy, 2004; Leahy & Warren, 2006; White, 2007).

Monk (1997) described the process of narrative therapy using the analogy of an archeologist uncovering remains:

With meticulous care and precision, the archeologist brushes ever so gently over the landscape with an instrument as small as a pastry brush. With these careful movements, she exposes a remnant, and with further exploration, others soon appear. Disconnected fragments are identified and pieced together as the search continues. With a careful eye for the partially visible, the archeologist begins to reassemble the pieces. An account of events in the life of the remains is constructed, and meaning emerges from what was otherwise a mere undulation in the landscape. (p. 3)

A narrative approach invites the clinician to take up an investigative, archeological position in order to discover the partially visible and often scattered fragments of a person's story. Like the archeologist, the clinician will need to have genuine curiosity, persistence, care, and sensitivity. Eventually, the clinician begins to assemble the fragments of the person's narrative in order to understand the person's story and the social and cultural context in which it was formed.

A Framework for Constructivist-Narrative–Based Counseling With Persons Who Stutter

DiLollo and Neimeyer (2022) combined aspects from constructivist theory and narrative therapy in a framework for audiologists and SLPs to use as a systematic approach to person-centered counseling (Figure 8–1). In this framework, DiLollo and Neimeyer described counseling as a way of thinking about and reacting to clients, as opposed to a more linear set of procedures or techniques that characterize most descriptions of counseling. This approach places clinicians in a role of *always counseling*, by reacting to client needs and modifying treatment to fit the social, emotional, and psychological aspects of the problem—aspects that

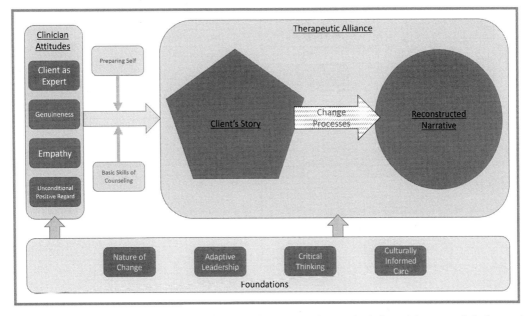

FIGURE 8–1. The constructivist counseling framework. *Source:* From *Counseling in Speech-Language Pathology and Audiology: Reconstructing Personal Narratives, Second Edition* (p. 35) by DiLollo, A., and Neimeyer, R. Copyright © 2022 Plural Publishing, Inc. All rights reserved. Used with permission.

are frequently ignored by clinicians who are focused on the technical aspects of the clinical problem.

This framework provides clinicians with a way to approach their clinical interactions with persons who stutter from a person-centered counseling perspective. Figure 8–2 provides a visual summary of how this framework might apply to working with a person who stutters. Starting with a "client who stutters," we see that there are both technical and adaptive challenges related to the problem. For clinicians, this is the beginning of the process, as identifying technical and adaptive challenges can help to conceptualize the

aspects of treatment that are needed. For example, technical challenges related to stuttering tend to be the specific reduction or modification of the client's disfluencies, and the teaching or learning of techniques to accomplish such behavioral changes. As indicated in Figure 8–2, the clinician's role in addressing technical challenges is typically as the "expert"—bringing the knowledge and experience to bear on the problem and applying evidence-based practice to achieve the desired behavioral changes. Interestingly, however, as we discussed in Chapter 7, change is difficult, and the behavioral changes associated with successful treatment of stuttering (i.e., fluent

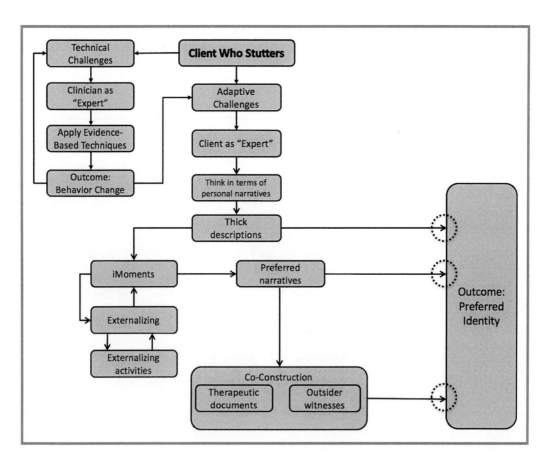

FIGURE 8–2. The process of constructivist-narrative based counseling with a client who stutters.

CLINICAL INSIGHT

Let's take a look at a couple of cases that we follow through the process outlined in Figure 8–2.

Case 1: Adam, a 22-year-old male, comes to a speech-language pathologist because he is struggling with his fluency in educational, work, and social settings. Adam is feeling distraught, as he now believes that he will never be able to control his speech, and he will never have the opportunity to become a math teacher, which is what he had always wanted to do. Although it might quickly be apparent to the clinician that Adam demonstrates relatively effective control of his disfluencies using a combination of fluency shaping and modification techniques, she should take a credulous approach and not simply listen to Adam's story but accept it as true and valid. By exploring Adam's story as if it were a true, full account of his experiences, the clinician can be alert to signs of parallel, alternative narratives that Adam is, at this time, unable to view as meaningful as they do not fit with his dominant narrative of being a "victim" of stuttering. The clinician taking this credulous approach is often very different from the typical way clients have interacted with clinicians in the past—when they are told that they are "doing a great job" and that they have the skills needed to be successful (almost implying that they could be successful if they really wanted to be). Being person centered in this way, rather than confronting Adam with the clinician's version of reality, opens the door for the possibility of getting Adam to explore some of the alternative stories that, at present, are not part of his awareness. It also helps to avoid the resistance that is often associated with clients like Adam, who are frequently labeled as "noncompliant" when they resist homework assignments or frequently miss therapy sessions.

Case 2: Sharon is a 7-year-old girl who has been stuttering for about 2 years. She is particularly troubled by her disfluencies and refuses to talk in class or mix with her peers during lunch breaks. Sharon's parents are very concerned, as she always seems to them to be withdrawn and not interested in making friends. When she met with the speech-language pathologist, Sharon was hesitant to talk at first but eventually opened up and told her story. She described how stuttering made her feel like she wasn't as smart as the rest of the kids, and how it made her shy and stopped her from making friends. She drew a picture of herself for the clinician and in the picture, Sharon depicted herself as much smaller than all the other children—even though she was relatively tall for her age. Taking the credulous approach, the clinician explored Sharon's story with her, initially accepting that her story was true—that stuttering really did make her "smaller" and not as smart as the rest of the kids. For Sharon, this was a new experience, and she felt like someone was finally taking her seriously rather than simply dismissing her fears and telling her how smart and beautiful she was. For the clinician, this approach helped to build rapport and trust with Sharon and helped her to be more open in sharing more details about her story, thus increasing the possibility of identifying those alternative narratives that were being ignored.

or modified speech, increased assertiveness, decreased avoidance, etc.) tend to generate their own set of adaptive challenges related to issues of identity, belonging, previous social roles, and even guilt. Consequently, as can be seen in Figure 8–2, outcomes from addressing technical aspects of stuttering tend to feed back into the need for additional adaptive work.

Adaptive challenges associated with stuttering include both those that relate to aspects of stuttering itself and those that relate to the successful behavioral treatment of the surface behaviors of the problem. In both cases, clinicians need to be engaged in counseling processes to help the client address these issues and work toward a preferred identity. As can be seen in Figure 8–2, there are three points at which clients might emerge from clinical interactions with preferred identity outcomes. Although the specifics of these preferred outcomes will differ from client to client, in all cases they would include technical "fixes" (e.g., fluent speech through application of fluency shaping techniques, more fluent stuttering through use of stuttering modification techniques, less avoidance through successful desensitization, etc.), as well as adaptive solutions (e.g., feeling more comfortable in a "fluent speaker" role, adjusting to living a more socially active life, accepting being more assertive, etc.) that contribute to their overall improvement in quality of life.

In the sections that follow, we describe the different processes that might occur at each level of the diagram in Figure 8–2. Note that there are three points at which clients might exit the process (see the circles in Figure 8–2). Some clients will exit at the first outcome level and need nothing more from the counseling process than a recognition of, and accounting for,

their personal story. Other clients, however, might need further help from the clinician to facilitate changes in the way they think of themselves before exiting the process at the second outcome level. These could be clients who, without counseling, might be likely to relapse from successful (technical) stuttering treatment. Such clients typically develop strong technical skills to manage their disfluencies, but struggle with changing the way that they think about themselves as communicators, generally feeling uncomfortable in the role of a more fluent or confident speaker. Finally, a few clients might need even further help from the clinician to reconstruct their personal narrative to allow them to benefit from the behavior changes they have learned. These might be clients who have recognized an alternative, preferred personal narrative but have difficulty incorporating this different story as a part of their identity.

Client as Expert

DiLollo and Neimeyer (2022) emphasized the person-centered stance of the clinician as the overarching basis of counseling. The difficulty for SLPs working with persons who stutter is that they have two primary roles to play in clinical interactions, and each of these roles requires a different stance. When working on the client's disfluencies and related behaviors (i.e., the technical aspects of the problem), the clinician must remain the expert and direct the course of treatment (although still remaining client centered). When helping the client to integrate these technical aspects into his or her life and identity, the clinician must relinquish the expert status and recognize that the client is the expert on his or her own life. This stance allows clinicians to focus on the person first, enabling them to better understand the stuttering problem within the context of the client's life.

Eliciting Personal Narratives

The central concept of the framework is *personal narratives* (DiLollo & Neimeyer, 2022). People develop personal narratives that both reflect and influence their behaviors, emotions, and self-image (Neimeyer, 2000; White & Epston, 1990). The stories that people tell themselves, along with the stories that others tell about them, and the stories that society tells about them, work together to create an individual's personal narrative. However, people can only "story" a part of their lived experience, meaning that there are many aspects of a person's experiences that are missed or ignored—leading to the possibility of parallel narratives that might be valid but remain unnoticed by the individual (Winslade & Monk, 1999).

Over time, these stories can become what White (1989) referred to as "dominant narratives"—narratives that, for the person, provide a fundamental understanding of who they are and how they interact with the world. For many reasons, however, these dominant narratives can be limiting, thereby preventing people from enacting their own *preferred identities* or narratives that lead them to more fulfilling and functional lives (DiLollo & Neimeyer, 2022; Neimeyer, 2000). For example, a man in his early 20s, who has stuttered since the age of 3 but has now learned the tools to smooth out his speech, feels that he is deceiving people by "pretending" to be a more fluent speaker.

Clinicians working from this framework, therefore, can take what Raskin and Morano (2004) referred to as a "credulous approach" to clients' stories. This involves the clinician adopting a stance of openness and acceptance in order to understand how the client is experiencing the world at the present time. The information the client shares is accepted at face value and presumed to be experientially true for that client, even if it does not fit with how the clinician might see things. The credulous approach, therefore, conveys respect for the client's reality, at the same time allowing the clinician to understand that it is not likely the whole or only story. The client thus feels that his or her dominant narrative has been heard and taken seriously, allowing for the possibility of therapeutic conversations that focus on alternative ways of construing the problem.

Thick Descriptions

The stories that are elicited through a credulous approach are typically what White (1989) referred to as "problem-saturated" descriptions or what Payne (2006) called "thin" descriptions. Such thin descriptions derive from a person's unexamined personal, social, and cultural beliefs, and are the descriptions that we get from clients when we ask about the problem. It is the description that extends from the person's dominant narrative and is usually limiting and imposed by role stereotypes, cultural or social expectations, and the stories that others tell about us. In Case 1, Adam's story reflected his dominant narrative of himself as a helpless victim of stuttering, unable to loosen stuttering's hold over his life—a narrative that many individuals who have lifelong experiences with some form of disability experience.

This might also be influenced by marginalizing narratives of "weakness" and "helplessness" imposed on many in our society who deal with chronic disability (Willett & Deegan, 2001). In Case 2, Sharon's story again reflected her dominant narrative of herself as less than the other children as a result of the various forms of penalty that those in society who are different tend to receive.

Thick descriptions, on the other hand, more closely correspond to the actual, complex experiences of life, and open space for a reexamination of some of the alternative stories that have been "glossed over" to protect the dominant narrative (Payne, 2006). Consequently, clinicians need to encourage thick descriptions by taking a genuine interest in their clients' stories (i.e., not just the problem's story), asking clarifying and extending questions. In the cases of Adam and Sharon, the clinicians invited a broader telling of each person's story, first by accepting their "problem-saturated" story, then by attending more to the person (as opposed to the problem) and showing interest in more details of their story—without reference to any specific "problem" (Payne, 2006).

Identifying Alternative Narratives

A basic tenet of both constructivist and narrative approaches is that there are always alternative ways of interpreting experiences. Typically, experiences that contrast with our dominant narratives are ignored or relegated to "footnotes" within the main text of our story—frequently mentioned only as brief passing comments. White and Epston (1990), however, believed that it is these very experiences that provide "a rich and fertile source for the generation, or re-generation, of alternative stories" (p. 15).

iMoments

As the person provides the more detailed "thick" description of his or her lived experience, the clinician listens for experiences that contrast with the dominant narrative. These will include occasions when the person has overcome the influence of the dominant narrative, even if only briefly, or found ways to creatively deal with it. These are the potential alternative storylines that can be explored by the client and clinician. DiLollo and Neimeyer (2022) labeled these events "iMoments," drawing from the work of Gonçalves et al. (2010), who defined various types of "innovative moments" during the process of therapeutic change.

The clinician's role is to identify these iMoments in their conversations (i.e., thick descriptions) with clients. Payne (2006) suggested listening for "clues" to potential iMoments, which he described as usually coming in brief, passing comments, that allude to some taken-for-granted reference of resistance to the dominant narrative. In our examples, Adam's dominant narrative, which had perhaps developed over the years to protect him from pushing himself to do things that were potentially painful and posed the risk of failure, was now becoming dissatisfying to him as he began to seriously contemplate his future. As the clinician engages him in a conversation about himself and his life, he is pressed into providing an expanded account of his thin story. In doing so, he might mention in passing how his desire to become a math teacher was recently rekindled by a successful class presentation that he made in a computer programming course—followed quickly by the "rationalization" that "by some fluke of nature, it went well, but even then, I screwed up the end by getting stuck answering the last question!" To Adam, such a passing comment does not register as meaningful, and the event does not counter his dominant narrative in any way. The clinician, however, noting the inconsistency between the dominant narrative and the detail of the story (i.e., as a clue to a potential iMoment) might invite Adam to talk more about that event, saying something like, "Tell me some more about this presentation. I am really interested in what you did to get through it successfully." In doing so, Adam might then talk about how well prepared he was for the presentation, how confident he was that he knew this material better than anyone else in the class, and that he really concentrated on keeping a slow rate and using his techniques to stay fluent. This provides the clinician with an opportunity to ask "curious questions" (DiLollo & Neimeyer, 2022) about the event. For example, in Adam's case, the clinician might ask, "It is interesting to me that you said earlier that it was a fluke of nature that the presentation went well. I wonder if there might be another explanation?" Similarly, the clinician might ask, "Can you think of any other times that this has happened—maybe even just small examples?" In these ways, the clinician encourages Adam to examine his dominant narrative and some potential exceptions to it that might open some space for alternative stories.

Similarly, Sharon's dominant narrative is providing her with an identity that will not lead to a satisfactory quality of life. As the clinician engages her in a conversation about herself and her life (as opposed to just her problem), she is pressed into providing an expanded account of her thin story. In doing so, she might mention in passing how even though she always does well on tests, she just doesn't feel

smart. The clinician, picking up on the potential clue, might ask Sharon to talk more about how well she does on tests, being careful not to fall into the trap of instructing her how to view the contrast (e.g., by saying, "See, if you do well on these tests, you really are smart!"—which is typically what everyone else is doing). This is important, as we want Sharon to "discover" the inconsistency herself, and to start seeing it for herself as a meaningful difference. This frequently takes a lot of restraint and patience on the part of the clinician. In following up, the clinician might ask Sharon if she can think of any other examples of things that she seems to do well. She might say something like, "Well, there was this time that they needed an extra girl to play soccer at lunch and they convinced me to play. When we finished, they all said I was really good and should join their team; but I think they were just being nice." This would be another opportunity for the clinician to suggest that Sharon expand on her story, asking her to, "Tell me more about when you played soccer," perhaps followed by, "You said you thought the girls were just being nice. I wonder if there might be another reason that they said what they did?" As with Adam, the clinician is encouraging Sharon to examine her dominant narrative and some potential exceptions to it that might open some space for alternative stories.

Externalizing and Externalizing Activities

Sometimes clients do not bring up clues to alternative narratives even when encouraged to provide thick descriptions of their experiences. When this happens, clinicians can use "externalizing" to help clients begin to think differently about their dominant story. White and Epston (1990) described externalizing as an approach that "encourages persons to objectify and, at times, to personify the problems that they experience as oppressive. In this process, the problem becomes a separate entity and thus external to the person or relationship that has been identified as the problem" (p. 38). In other words, as Michael White has been quoted as saying, "The person isn't the problem; the problem is the problem" (White & Epston, 1989). The intent of externalizing is to shift the focus of conversation from a "problem-person" to the relationship between the person and the problem. This enables the clinician and the client to work together to resist the effects of the problem.

For some clients, using a single word or short phrase to "name" the problem helps to create opportunities for "externalizing conversations" (White & Epston, 1990). For example, considering the first case that we have been following, Adam might decide to simply use the term *stuttering* to name the problem (i.e., names don't have to be creative, they just have to represent the problem for the client in a meaningful way). This would enable the use of externalizing language by Adam and the clinician in their conversations about the problem. The clinician might ask, "What did *stuttering* say to you that prevented you from attending that party last night?" Similarly, as Adam gets used to the concept, he might say, "I really intended to go and talk to my advisor yesterday about changing to a teaching major, but *stuttering* kept telling me how I'd just embarrass myself and I just couldn't do it."

As a 7-year-old girl, Sharon, from our second case, might have difficulty grasping the concept of externalizing. In such a case, clinicians can try using items such as puppets or other toys to represent differ-

ent characters. For example, with Sharon, the clinician might use a puppet and suggest that they are going to pretend that the puppet is Sharon's fear. Sharon then gets to name the puppet (she calls him Fred Fear—or just Fred for short!), and then she and the clinician can play out some scenarios with other toys taking on the roles of Sharon's family and friends. The goal in this type of play is to have Sharon talk about the things that Fred is doing and saying to her and to others to make himself strong, and to resist Fred's influence by having Sharon come up with ways that what he is saying is wrong.

Sometimes clients and clinicians might have difficulty spontaneously using externalizing language. DiLollo and Neimeyer (2022) described a number of "externalizing activities" that clinicians can use to help clients start to think differently about their dominant narrative. In "Autobiography of the Problem," for example, clients write about the history of their relationship with the problem—but from the problem's perspective—giving a voice to the problem and inviting the client to consider things from a different angle. Other activities, such as "Dear John Letter" and "Chair Work," provide similar opportunities for the client to consider the problem from a different perspective. Similarly, DiLollo and Neimeyer described a drawing activity in which clients first draw a picture of themselves *with* the problem, followed by drawing a picture of themselves *without* the problem. This activity opens up opportunities for the clinician to ask the client about the differences between the two drawings and what they represent.

Coconstruction of Preferred Narratives

As clients explore and experiment with alternative, preferred personal narratives, clinicians must also account for the role that outside sources play in our self-stories (Winslade & Monk, 1999). In this sense, there is always an element of "coconstruction" of personal narratives, as the clinician, family members, friends, coworkers, and even societal norms contribute to the stories people tell about themselves (DiLollo & Neimeyer, 2022).

Following the emergence of a possible alternative narrative that might be preferred by the client, the clinician's role is primarily that of retelling the emerging narrative in multiple ways and facilitating further retellings of the story by others (White, 2007). The clinician's retellings can be done verbally, through engaging clients in conversations about their emerging narrative and presenting them with reflections on the story. Alternatively, clinicians can use *therapeutic documents* (Payne, 2006) as a way of retelling the client's story. Therapeutic documents usually consist of simple, short emails, letters, certificates, or even short videos in which the clinician presents a retelling of the preferred narrative in some form that "encapsulates new knowledges, perspectives, and preferred changes which have become part of the person's enriched but still fragile" story (Payne, 2006, p. 127). Returning to our previous cases, Adam's clinician might use a simple email sent after a session in which Adam seemed to offer an emerging story that resisted his old dominant narrative. In part, this email might state something like, "You really caught my attention today when you described the successful presentation that you made and how it rekindled your desire to be a teacher. It was interesting how, as we talked, you identified other times when you have 'risen to the occasion,' as you put it, and been successful speaking in front of groups of people. I wonder what this says about you as a

communicator?" Similarly, Sharon's clinician might create a certificate for her that incorporates some of the externalizing language that they have been using in their sessions. For example, Sharon's certificate might say, "Awarded to Sharon, for being alert to the lies that Fred Fear tells Sharon and other people, to try to trick them into thinking that Sharon is not smart." Additionally, the clinician might give Sharon a second certificate that refers to her efforts at resisting the lies that Fred Fear tells her and others.

As a more comprehensive version of the client's preferred story emerges, the clinician might facilitate further construction of the story by organizing *outsider witnesses* (White, 2007) to listen and respond to the narrative. Outsider witnesses can be drawn from the clients' family and friends, other clients, or other clinicians. The important aspect of this process is the opportunity for the client to tell her or his preferred story publicly, and to then observe listeners reflecting on the story, making comments, drawing comparisons to their own experiences, and posing questions—all of which constitute a retelling of the client's narrative in a way that connects it with the outside world. Leahy and colleagues (Leahy et al., 2012; Logan, 2007) described the use of outsider witnesses with persons who stutter, reporting that the process aided their clients in supporting, expanding, and grounding their alternative, preferred story.

BASIC COUNSELING SKILLS

The essence of counseling, as well as therapy in general, is not about techniques. Indeed, Rogers (1980) spoke against the appalling consequences of overemphasizing technique during counseling; to be effective, the clinician must approach counseling as a fully human endeavor. As we indicated in our earlier discussion of expert performance (see Chapter 1), and as many experienced therapists recognize, good counseling technique flows from the clinician's personality and empathy (Luterman, 2017). If the clinician acts mechanically, the technique is likely to fail because it will be discontinuous with the authenticity of the relationship. As Luterman (2017) explained, "Technique should not be apparent to the person being counseled or to an observer. If people know they are being counseled, you are probably doing it wrong" (p. 89).

As we discussed earlier in this chapter, there are many different ways that the counseling process can be conceptualized and described, as evidenced by the myriad of different approaches described in the counseling and psychology literature. (We reviewed a few of the most common ones in an earlier section of this chapter.) Each different philosophical approach to counseling has its own specific set of techniques that are intended to move clients toward preferred outcomes. Underlying these techniques, however, are basic counseling skills that are common to all approaches. Having laid out a framework around which clinicians can conceptualize their attempts at counseling (which included some techniques that might be useful), let us now turn to some of those basic counseling skills that can make or break any counseling technique that clinicians attempt.

Listening

To be an effective counselor, the primary skill that clinicians need to develop is *listening*. Effective listening is central to any counseling approach, but more so as approaches move toward the more humanistic end of the spectrum. In fact, Rogers (1961) believed that simply listening to a client, especially to his or her emotions, could, by itself, lead to positive changes for the client. Of course, this concept of listening is not quite the same as what we all do on a daily basis. As a matter of fact, for the most part, people are not particularly good listeners (in the therapeutic sense). So, for SLPs, listening is actually a skill that needs to be shaped and worked on if it is to be used effectively to encourage our clients to provide the thick descriptions that we described earlier.

Inadequate Listening

As we move through our daily lives, there are a number of ways that we listen that are less than adequate. At this point, it is important to note that hearing and listening are not synonymous. Hearing is simply the act of perceiving sound, requires little to no effort to accomplish, and does not imply any level of comprehension. Listening, on the other hand, specifically implies that comprehension is occurring, and requires concentration and focus on the part of the listener. Egan (2013) described four types of "inadequate listening" that clinicians should pay attention to: (a) *nonlistening* or "tuning out"—hearing the sounds but not processing the meaning of the message; (b) *partial listening*—the listener is only partially engaged and concentrating on what the speaker is saying; this often happens to clinicians if something the client says triggers a thought or memory about something unrelated to the client's story; (c) *tape-recorder listening*—as we discuss shortly, simply hearing words but not connecting to meaning and emotions embedded within the message is not satisfying for clients; and (d) *rehearsing*—when the clinician stops listening and starts thinking about, and even rehearsing, how he or she is going to respond to the client and what questions he or she will ask. This is a common problem for inexperienced clinicians or those who are anxious about their role as a counselor.

Reflective Listening

Carl Rogers (1961) used the term *reflective listening* to refer to a type of listening in which an individual tries to understand what it is that the speaker is feeling as well as what the words of the message actually mean. This understanding is then reflected back to the speaker in the listener's own words. This type of listening has also been referred to as "empathic listening" (Egan, 2013), "active listening" (Gordon, 1970), and "empathetic listening" (Luterman, 2017), and forms the cornerstone of any humanistic form of counseling. If practiced correctly, this type of listening will encourage clients to talk more and share at a deeper level, as they will feel truly "heard"—something that seems to be all too rare in today's busy world.

Silence

Becoming comfortable with silence is a skill that is essential for encouraging the thick descriptions that we discussed earlier in the chapter. This is especially true when working with persons who stutter, as they might sometimes take longer to express their thoughts or respond to a question. Silence can be difficult for the clinician as well as the client, and its intensity will eventually force the inexperienced clinician to become role-bound

and act (Luterman, 2020). If the clinician "rescues" the client during an extended period of silence, then she has assumed responsibility for the session, casting herself in the power role of the expert (DiLollo & Neimeyer, 2022). If the clinician can maintain periods of extended silence, the client is forced to think and reflect, dig deeper, and examine previously ignored aspects of his or her story—possibly leading to clues to potential iMoments. As the clinician comes to appreciate how silence can serve many functions for promoting change, he or she is likely to become more comfortable with the pauses in the conversation. As Luterman (2017) stated, "It often shows a fine command of language to say nothing" (p. 96).

Silence is not a void, but a vital part of communication and the change process. As in Oriental ink drawings, the open spaces are an intentional and important part of the overall composition. The deepest feelings in a relationship can take place in silence, for there is companionship in thoughtful silence. When observing couples who are congruent it is possible to see that communication continues during moments of silence.

Empathy

The clinician who is able to express empathy is able to journey inside another's world. As Egan (2013) explained, "being with" the client is temporarily living another's life as a means to viewing the person without labels, interpretation, or categories. It is important to distinguish empathy from sympathy. Sympathy denotes agreement, whereas empathy denotes understanding and acceptance of the person. Rogers (1986) suggested that empathy is, in and of itself, a healing

CLINICAL INSIGHT

Engaging in reflective listening is a skill that, like any other skill, requires practice. Frequently, the emotions underlying speakers' messages have little to do with the words that they use, being revealed more in their tone of voice and body language. Clinicians need to "tune in both mentally and visibly" (Egan, 2013, p. 80) to clients in order to accomplish this. What is vitally important, however, is that reflective listening is practiced with genuineness and empathy—something new clinicians, who tend to be more *technique focused*, often struggle with.

During the early stages of practicing reflective listening in my counseling class, students will often go through the process correctly—listening intently to their partner, reflecting back the correct meaning, and accurately recognizing and reflecting back feelings embedded within the story told by their partner. Frequently, however, when we debrief after the activity, there will be a number of comments regarding how the practice felt "fake" or "condescending" to both the listener and the partner. We then discuss how, because this was an academic exercise to learn a "technique," there is a tendency for the listener to be focused on the technique itself rather than being psychologically and emotionally present for the partner. Usually, following this discussion, students make rapid progress with the "technique" primarily because—ironically—they start to focus on the person and *not* the technique! (AD)

agent: "It is one of the most potent aspects of therapy, because it releases, it confirms, it brings even the most frightened client into the human race. If a person is understood, he or she belongs" (p. 129).

Egan (2013) indicated that whereas listening to the client helps the clinician get in touch with the client's world, empathy helps the clinician to understand that world. He noted that clients rate understanding as the thing they find most helpful during counseling. Virtually all authorities agree that reflective listening and expressing empathy are affirming and highly therapeutic for the client. Listening with understanding allows the clinician to establish a cognitive map that describes the client's experience of himself or herself (Zinker, 1977). It is from this map—this understanding of the person—that the clinician can begin to formulate the direction(s) of change that will assist the client through the treatment process. Although the majority of clinicians who assist individuals who stutter do not themselves stutter, it is possible for the fluent clinician to understand and to fully empathize with their clients (see Manning, 2004b). It is also good to realize that it is not always necessary to say anything in order to demonstrate empathy. Empathy is indicated by the very act of spending time with and listening to someone, as well as a glance or a touch.

Asking Questions

Asking questions is an overrated aspect of clinical interaction. As speech-language pathologists, we are used to asking a lot of questions when taking a case history, for example, or when trying to determine the cause and nature of a specific speech, language, or swallowing disorder. Sometimes, however, our sessions can resemble an interrogation rather than a conversation. Let's take a look at the two different types of questions that clinicians can use to gain different types of information.

Open-ended questions are questions that have no correct answer and require an explanation. They are designed to encourage clients to provide a response based on their own knowledge, experiences, and feelings. In this way, open-ended questions reflect the "client as expert" stance that is part of the framework for counseling discussed earlier in the chapter. These types of questions frequently begin with words such as "Why," "What," and "How," or phrases such as "Tell me about . . . ." Clinicians should strive to use these types of questions when exploring the client's story and building rapport.

Closed-ended questions, on the other hand, are questions that can typically be answered with a "Yes" or "No" response or a brief statement of information. These types of questions are designed to gather specific information, usually related to the "technical" aspects of the client's problem. Problems arise, however, when clinicians ask closed-ended questions about topics that relate to the client's broader story.

Humor

As discussed in Chapter 1, humor can play an important role in a dynamic clinical relationship. Humor allows the clinician to challenge the client and to discuss things that would otherwise be too risky or even taboo. Humor involves aspects of distancing oneself from a problem, conceptually shifting one's view of the situation, and mastering events and situations that were previously avoided or anxiety producing. As Rusk (1989; cited in Egan, 1990) suggested, deliberate self-change requires a willingness to (a) stand back from yourself far enough to question your familiar beliefs and attitudes about yourself and others, and (b) persist at awkward and risky experiments designed to increase your self-respect and satisfy your needs. Not only can humor facilitate such self-change, but for the clinician, humor provides a window for viewing the cognitive changes associated with a problem.

CLINICAL INSIGHT

To help my students learn about asking questions, I have them do just the opposite—they have to spend 10 minutes talking with a partner (who has been given a communication disorder role to play) *without asking any questions.* At the end of the time, the student in the role of the clinician has to identify the communication problem as well as the social and emotional aspects of the problem. Needless to say, initially, most students are stumped as to how to proceed. Eventually, they realize that they can have a conversation with the client and use *reflective listening* to encourage the client to divulge and expand on basic information. During debriefing, students often comment on how they learned things that they would never have thought to ask about if they had been asking questions. The point of this activity is to demonstrate that we often rely too much on asking questions (especially closed-ended questions). (AD)

CLINICAL INSIGHT

In his book *Social Intelligence*, Daniel Goleman (2006) described the value of humor in the establishment and enhancement of the therapeutic alliance. Goleman explained that playfulness is a source of joy for all mammals, often beginning with tactile stimulations and visual–auditory interactions among parents and offspring. The strong neurological responses from the brain indicate that playfulness is a natural and often instantaneous response that fosters synchrony and resonance between two creatures.

As we discussed in earlier chapters, the playfulness and spontaneity of humor are not apt to characterize the therapeutic alliance until the child or adult feels secure and understood in the treatment environment. However, understanding and sensitivity to the other person and their story often create experiences where humorous connections can be made. The opportunities for shared understanding provided by the humorous interpretation of events often forge a powerful connection. As Goleman (2006) suggested, "Laughter may be the shortest distance between two brains" (p. 45).

CONCLUSION

Counseling is an essential part of the therapeutic change process for individuals who experience a communication problem, and this is certainly the case for people who stutter. Unfortunately, relatively little information is provided to our students concerning the principles of counseling in many of our academic programs, with even fewer programs providing specific skills training in counseling. The people who seek our help tend not to have serious psychological problems but normal reactions to the stress resulting from their communication problems. For some, emotions presented by the communication problems represent the most handicapping features of the problem, whereas for others, adjusting to the change that results from effective treatment presents the greatest challenge. These natural and expected challenges and emotions should not, however, represent an intimidating aspect of therapy for the clinician. It is

helpful to realize that our goal is not to "fix" these emotions but rather to help the person take action and function in spite of them.

Although there are a variety of counseling approaches, the Common Factors model suggests that it is useful for clinicians to find an approach that they believe in and can become proficient in administering. We presented details of a constructivist-narrative therapy framework around which clinicians can build their practice of counseling with persons who stutter. This framework emphasizes the distinction between technical and adaptive aspects of the problem, making the client the expert on adaptive issues, and focusing on eliciting personal narratives, identifying potential alternative storylines, and helping clients elaborate preferred narratives. It is hoped that by embracing such an organizing framework, clinicians can seamlessly integrate counseling with the more behavioral "speech therapy" that is, perhaps, the more familiar role to many speech-language pathologists.

Of course, even more fundamental to successful therapeutic interaction than the overall framework are basic skills that all counselors need. These include the use of reflective listening, avoiding the non-listening traps that all listeners frequently fall into, the effective use of silence to facilitate clients' depth of reflection, connecting empathically with clients, the appropriate (and, perhaps, minimal) use of open-ended and closed-ended questions, and the therapeutic use of humor to facilitate cognitive change. These basic counseling skills underlie virtually all approaches to counseling, particularly those toward the humanistic end of the spectrum.

We are likely to employ counseling in some form with most of the people we see, and everyone involved, including spouses and families, is part of the therapeutic process. To the extent that we can show them that we understand their plight and assist them in developing more degrees of freedom in dealing with their problem, our clients will be moving forward. On many occasions, our ability to truly understand and to provide timely support makes more difference to our clients than we realize.

❓ TOPICS FOR DISCUSSION

1. What are arguments for and against speech-language pathologists engaging clients in counseling?

2. Find other definitions of counseling and compare them to the one from DiLollo and Neimeyer (2022) described in this chapter. What are the similarities and differences? How does each one help you to understand the process of counseling with persons who stutter?

3. What are the primary problems with viewing counseling as a process of informing and persuading clients?

4. Considering the counseling philosophies described in the chapter, describe why one (or more) is more appealing to you than others.

5. What are some of the similarities and differences between the various counseling philosophies described in this chapter?

6. Try writing your narrative (not to share), then try to identify where some of the subplots of your story came from (e.g., a comment made by a teacher that changed the story of you as a student).

7. Describe the key components of the constructivist-narrative framework.

8. Try out the "autobiography of the problem" externalizing activity. Choose a problem in your life—a small one that you are willing to share with others —and write the problem's autobiography (e.g., Here the problem is "procrastination"—Tony and I are old friends. I always know just the right thing to say to him to convince him that everything will be fine if he just waits until a bit later to get started on that project. In many ways, I think he really likes me, even though at times I get him into a bit of trouble! . . .).

9. What basic counseling skills described in this chapter are you most (and least) comfortable with?

10. Try using reflective listening in a conversation with a partner and then

discuss how it felt for the listener and the speaker.

RECOMMENDED READINGS

DiLollo, A., & Neimeyer, R. A. (2022). *Counseling in speech-language pathology and audiology: Reconstructing personal narratives* (2nd ed.). Plural Publishing.

Egan, G. (2013). *The skilled helper: A problem management and opportunity development approach to helping* (10th ed.). Brooks/Cole Cengage Learning.

Luterman, D. M. (2017). *Counseling persons with communication disorders and their families* (6th ed.). Pro-Ed.

St. Louis, K. O. (2001). *Living with stuttering: Stories, resources, and hope.* Populore.

It is not our differences that divide us. It is our inability to recognize, accept, and celebrate those differences.

—Audre Lorde

Diversity is a fact, but inclusion is a choice we make every day. As leaders, we have to put out the message that we embrace and not just tolerate diversity.

—Nellie Borrero

Working With Individuals From Different Cultural and Linguistic Backgrounds

Anthony DiLollo and Jean Franco Rivera Pérez

CHAPTER OBJECTIVES

- To define diversity in terms of a broad range of dimensions
- To provide a broad understanding of the meaning of culture
- To explore the concepts of cultural responsiveness and cultural humility
- To describe a culturally responsive, person-centered model for working with persons who stutter

DIVERSITY

Data from the 2020 U.S. Census reflect a continued trend of the diversification of the U.S. population. Although "White alone" continues to represent the largest proportion of population at 61.6%, this represents an 8.6% decline since 2010. All other groups, including "White in combination with another race" and "Multiracial" (defined as two or more races), saw population gains in the past decade. Significantly, the "Some other race" population is now the second-largest non-White race group, comprising 15.1% of the total population compared to 18.7% for Hispanic or Latino, 12.4% for Black or African American, 10.2% for Multiracial, and 6% for Asian (Jones et al., 2021). These numbers tell us that more than 127 million people living in the United States identify as something other than White and that they represent a multitude of different ethnic origins and cultural systems—and, based on a prevalence rate for stuttering of approximately 1%, more than 1 million of them will identify as a person who stutters.

Racial and ethnic diversity, however, is just one dimension of a much larger picture of how the U.S. population is composed of different elements (LeBlanc et al., 2020). Diversity includes a variety of dimensions, including race and ethnicity, culture and language, age and generational differences, gender identity, sexual orientation, weight and body morphology, socioeconomic status, neurodiversity and cognitive abilities, religion, and differences in experiences and values. Given the racial and ethnic diversification of the U.S. population, and the numerous other categories recognized as part of our diverse society, it is inevitable that clinicians will encounter clients whose experiences, values, and beliefs are significantly different from their own. In fact, taken from a person-centered perspective, everyone has their own unique set of experiences, beliefs, and values that make up their personal identity, so, in many ways, we are always surrounded by people who are both different from us and different from each other.

Significantly, research suggests that despite being immersed in a diverse society, we are not very good at accurately recognizing the differences between us and others (Blaine & Brenchley, 2020). Our tendency is to project our own feelings, values, and expectations onto situations, sometimes assuming other people will be more different from us than they are, at other times underestimating the diversity around us. This means that clinicians, who are responsible for providing culturally responsive and clinically competent services during all clinical interactions, must be mindful and purposeful in how they approach the issue of diversity.

CULTURE, CULTURAL RESPONSIVENESS, AND CULTURAL HUMILITY

Hyter and Salas-Provance (2019) defined culture as "a set of factors from multiple dimensions that can describe how one person or a group of people experience life, and engage in daily practices" (p. 6). It includes factors such as problem-solving strategies, family roles, values, beliefs, symbols, attitudes, religion, artifacts, and communication. Culture binds people through shared norms, values, and beliefs. These definitions of culture, however, risk implying homogeneity within cultural groups, which is far from real experience. Epner and Baile (2012) pointed this out, stating, "Cultural processes frequently differ within the same ethnic or social group because of differences in age cohort, gender, political association, class, religion, ethnicity, and even personality. Culture is therefore a very elusive and nebulous concept, like art" (p. iii34). The definition of culture is further complicated when considering multicultural societies, where each cultural group is constantly undergoing modifications and mixtures that make it different from the cultural group of origin (Epner & Baile, 2012). As individuals, we typically fit into a variety of cultures, some of which fit us more comfortably than others, and we encounter cultures different than our own on multiple occasions every day. This places us in a position, according to Hyter and Salas-Provance (2019), to decide who and what to accept or reject, how we will address our own biases, and how we value cultural diversity. Our level of cultural responsiveness and humility will shape the choices we make.

Cultural Responsiveness

Cultural responsiveness involves an ability to comprehend and appreciate cultural differences, examine one's unconscious biases, and move beyond differences to work productively with individuals and families whose cultural contexts are different from your own. Being culturally responsive means valuing cultural diversity, seeking knowledge of different cultural perspectives, and creating work and community spaces where cultural diversity is respected and valued (Azul et al., 2022). Cultural responsiveness is an ongoing, developmental process that involves lifelong learning and a commitment to being reflective and introspective. As Hyter and Salas-Provance (2019) pointed out, "there is not one point in time when we can say that we are safely culturally responsive in every one of our interactions. It is, so to speak, always a work in progress" (p. 7). To be culturally responsive, one must practice cultural humility by engaging in a self-evaluation that involves acknowledging and challenging our personal unconscious biases and power dynamics. This process also entails recognizing the limitations of one's own cultural perspective and prioritizing the lived experiences and perspectives of individuals from other cultural backgrounds.

Cultural Humility

Defined as an ongoing commitment by clinicians to self-reflection and self-critique, person-centeredness, and mutual respect with all clients and colleagues, cultural humility is conceptually very similar to cultural responsiveness. Cultural humility emphasizes self-awareness on the part of clinicians and acknowledges the ways in which cultural values and sociopolitical forces shape client experiences and opportunities. In many ways, cultural humility, and the person-centered philosophy that underlies it, is part of what drives cultural responsiveness. For the remainder of the chapter, we use the term *cultural responsiveness*, with the understanding that the cultural humility aspects of self-reflection, self-critique, and mutual respect are subsumed into the definition of cultural responsiveness.

THE UNIVERSALITY OF STUTTERING

Bloodstein et al. (2021) provided a very interesting historical account of investigations into the cultural demography of stuttering. Despite many early claims that stuttering did not exist in some isolated indigenous communities in New Guinea, Australia, and North America—including Wendell Johnson's well-documented article titled "The Indians Have No Word for It" (Johnson, 1944)—the conclusion drawn by Bloodstein et al. (2021) is that stuttering is present across all cultures and languages in all parts of the world. They stated that although there have been reported differences in prevalence of stuttering across various cultural groups, these are most likely related to differences in the culture's identification of typical and impaired speakers or genetic differences, particularly for isolated communities that are more genetically homogeneous.

Robinson (2012) reported that stuttering has been studied in a range of cultural groups, including Native American, African American, Asian, Hispanic, and African. Robinson concluded that these studies suggest that cultural differences influence speech fluency and that there are differences in perceptions, beliefs, values, and norms about speech fluency and fluency disorders among these various cultural groups. He stated, "One possible significance of these suggestions is that cultural factors might appreciably affect the outcomes of clinical intervention with fluency disorders" (p. 165).

Bilingualism and Stuttering

Curiously, there is no consensus definition of bilingualism reported in the literature. For example, it has been defined as linguistic competence in more than one language (Shenker, 2011), the use of more than one language in everyday life (Grosjean, 2010), and the coexistence of more than one language system within an individual (Hakuta, 2009). This absence of a clear and accepted definition of bilingualism is a confounding factor that has made research related to bilingualism difficult to interpret (Choo & Smith, 2020; Mumy, 2023). Indeed, Van Borsel (2011) warned that reported data regarding bilingualism and stuttering should be interpreted with caution.

Although there is a significant and growing body of research on bilingualism and stuttering, there are differing opinions regarding the role that bilingualism plays in the development and course of stuttering (Gahl, 2020; Mumy, 2023). Some of this confusion could be related to an influential and frequently cited article by Travis et al. (1937) in which the authors reported a 1% higher prevalence rate for bilingual children compared to monolingual children. Despite repeated questioning of these findings by other researchers and demonstrations of a number of flaws in the study (Gahl, 2020), the Travis et al. article continues to be cited as evidence that bilingualism might have a causal relationship

with stuttering. A number of authors and researchers, however, agree that there is insufficient evidence to support the causative relations between bilingualism and stuttering (Bloodstein et al., 2021; Mumy, 2023; Yairi & Seery, 2023). Similarly, Choo and Smith (2020) conducted a comprehensive review of the literature on bilingualism and stuttering and concluded that speaking more than one language does not put a person at increased risk for stuttering.

There are a number of issues that clinicians need to consider when planning and conducting stuttering assessment and treatment with a bilingual child or adult. Byrd et al. (2015) argued that bilingual speakers are at a higher risk of a false positive identification of a stuttering disorder due to a lack of research and data to better understand the types, frequency, and patterns of disfluencies in bilingual children. Byrd (2018) suggested that without a point of reference for what is typical for speech disfluencies in the bilingual population and how those compare to what has been documented in the monolingual literature, it is impossible to determine what is atypical for a bilingual child. Byrd et al. (2015) suggested that current and relevant information regarding stuttering and bilingualism is critical to identification accuracy, but additional information could also be important. To that end, Byrd (2018) and Eggers et al. (2020) advised that characteristics other than the identification of type and frequency of disfluencies, such as parent concern, physical tension, and the rhythm or timing of disfluent speech, should be considered as primary evidence when determining the presence of a stuttering disorder in bilingual children.

There is some evidence that treatment of stuttering in one language can result in positive outcomes in the untreated language (Bloodstein et al., 2021; Choo &

Smith, 2020). This suggests that clinicians might be able to treat the stuttering of bilingual children in their own language, with the expectation that gains made will generalize to the child's home language. Of course, ongoing assessment will need to be conducted in both languages, with the use of an interpreter or clinician who speaks the child's home language.

A CULTURALLY RESPONSIVE, PERSON-CENTERED MODEL FOR WORKING WITH PERSONS WHO STUTTER

Culturally responsive practice is directly linked with the notion of person-centered care, although it cannot be assumed that a thoroughly person-centered approach, such as the one described throughout this book, will be sufficient to uncover all crucial dimensions of culture that might impact assessment and treatment of stuttering (Azul et al., 2022; Oelke et al., 2013). The impact of culture and social context should be explored in the clinical setting to clarify its relevance to the client's own perspectives and concerns and to ensure that cultural dimensions are not over-generalized by the clinician.

Robinson and Crowe (1998) presented a decision model for inclusion of multicultural variables in stuttering intervention. In this model, six levels are presented: preintervention, intake, evaluation, client counseling, treatment, and carryover or generalization. Decisions are made at each intervention level as to the relevance of cultural variables in the intervention process.

The model presented in Figure 9–1 is an adapted and updated version of the Robinson and Crowe (1998) model. In this model, there are seven levels: preintervention, a person-centered counseling approach, intake/the client's personal story, initial evaluation, treatment, change, and ongoing assessment.

Decision Level I: Preintervention

At this level, the client's cultural identification, age, gender identification, and basic case history information are gathered. Consideration of how this information might

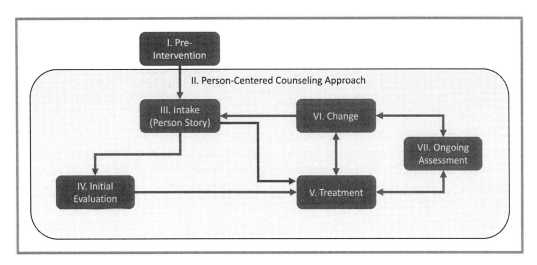

FIGURE 9–1. Decision model for culturally responsive practice. *Source:* Adapted from Robinson and Crowe (1998).

be obtained is important. For example, what is the client's or family's preferred language? Might the client or family be afraid or hesitant to complete a written case history questionnaire? Might the client or family withhold information because they don't think it is appropriate for them to provide their opinions to a professional? This information must be considered as preliminary and provisional, and care must be taken to avoid stereotyping a client based on this information.

It is also at this stage that clinicians should engage in an internal self-reflection to consider the influence of their own unconscious biases and beliefs and the potential impact they might have on service delivery. Similarly, clinicians should reflect on and acknowledge their limitations in education, training, and knowledge and seeking additional resources and education to develop cultural responsiveness.

Decision Level II: Person-Centered Counseling Approach

This is where the clinician sets the framework for the clinical interaction. A person-centered counseling approach places the client (and family) at the center of the clinical interaction, with a focus on the goals, values, and preferences of the client. Within the context of this person-centered approach, the clinician can demonstrate respect for each individual's ability, age, culture, dialect, disability, ethnicity, gender, gender identity or expression, language, national or regional origin, race, religion, sex, sexual orientation, socioeconomic status, and veteran status (ASHA, n.d.). All other decision levels operate within this framework and so will be extensions of this person-centered approach.

Decision Level III: Intake/Personal Story

At this level, the clinician uses person-centered and culturally responsive practices to learn about the client and their family. At this time, the clinician should concentrate on ways to learn about the client's personal story or narrative (DiLollo & Neimeyer, 2022) with little attention focused on the stuttering. This is an opportunity to demonstrate to clients and their family that you value them as people and you are interested in their values and beliefs and how they differ from your own.

Decision Level IV: Initial Evaluation

As described in Chapters 4, 5, and 6, a comprehensive assessment of stuttering includes evaluation of the surface stuttering behaviors (i.e., disfluencies, secondary physical behaviors) as well as the person's (and family's) reactions to stuttering and how stuttering impacts the person's self-image. When evaluating disfluencies with regard to frequency, type, and duration, clinicians should account for disfluencies in all languages that the person speaks (i.e., not just in English), as well as exploring with the client how their reactions and emotions related to stuttering might differ between languages. When using standardized tests, the clinician might find it necessary to modify test items or testing procedures to make them more inclusive of the values and experiences of the client. For example, if the pictures used in an instrument depict middle-class White America (which most do), the clinician might want to substitute those pictures with ones that reflect the client's specific culture and culturally relevant experiences. The clinician should also consider the differences in child-rearing practices and verbal expectations when observing parent–child interactions as part of an evaluation. Similarly, with adult clients, the clinician should note culture-specific pragmatic and social interaction styles, such as who is allowed to speak and when, the rules for interruptions, and how topics are introduced (Robinson, 2012). Conversational samples should reflect the experiences of clients and their cultures rather than the experiences and expectations of the clinician.

As part of a culturally responsive assessment, the clinician must be interested in the clients' interpretations of their own communication problems. Kleinman et al. (1978) proposed a series of questions that could help to provide insight into a client's personal meaning of illness or their "explanatory model." Kleinman et al. suggested that these questions could be an effective way for clinicians to learn about and better understand the client's experience of illness, whether asked specifically or used as a framework for conversations about culture. Within the context of a stuttering evaluation, clinicians could incorporate these questions as a part of an overall attempt to understand the client's story:

1. What do you think caused your stuttering?
2. What do you call it?
3. Why do you think your stuttering started when it did?
4. What do you think stuttering does to you? How does it work?
5. How severe (serious, terrible) is your stuttering? Will it have a short or long course?
6. What kind of treatment do you think would work?
7. What are the most important results you hope to get from this treatment?

8. What are the main (biggest) issues stuttering has caused you?
9. What do you fear most about your stuttering?
10. What do you fear most about the treatment for your stuttering?

Importantly, these questions also position clients in the role of the expert about their stuttering. As such, they can lead to the collaborative goal setting that was emphasized in Chapter 4. Asking clients questions about what kind of treatment might work and what results are most important to them can lead to understanding aspects of the client's stuttering that they deem important to target in treatment.

A culturally responsive clinician should be aware that, even when individuals share similar cultural backgrounds, their values are shaped by their own experiences and their interpretations of those experiences. Consequently, it is important that clinicians avoid using preconceptions of a particular population (i.e., stereotyping) and make efforts to understand each client's whole story. Through self-reflection on our unconscious biases and power dynamics, we can reduce the assumptions and stereotypes we have about groups of people. Kleinman et al. (1978) suggested that clinicians use an ethnography as a way of better understanding clients' personal stories. In an ethnography, importance is placed on understanding the individual's point of view and involves the client's description of what life is like in their world. It provides clients with an opportunity to describe the richness of their experience and embraces the complexity of culture and the mixing of ethnic groups in a way that is supportive of the goals of cultural responsiveness.

In addition, clinicians should try to assess the client's and family's health literacy to enable appropriate and effective communication. This is important so that information presented during assessment (and later during treatment) is provided in a format that clients and their families can understand and comprehend.

Decision Level V: Treatment

In Chapters 5 and 6 we discussed various approaches to treatment of stuttering for children through adults and emphasized that treatment should be individualized to suit the specific needs, values, and preferences of the specific client and that treatment goals should be the result of a collaborative effort between the client and clinician. Likewise, a culturally responsive approach to stuttering treatment should integrate the client's traditions, customs, values, beliefs, religion, and interaction styles into the treatment program through active collaboration with the client and their family and specific discussion of the goals of treatment.

The clinician should make an effort to modify any stimuli used in treatment so that they represent the client's experiences and cultural background, and strategies should be developed and incorporated to minimize conscious and unconscious cultural biases. For example, if the client has never experienced a traditional American birthday party, using that as a theme for eliciting treatment targets would be inappropriate. Similarly, Robinson (2012) suggested that if using a commercial fluency treatment program that involves specific activities and materials, clinicians might find that, rather than modifying materials, the program's concepts can be preserved and used with other activities that better fit with the client's experiences.

Clinicians should consider how clients and their families view the concept of treatment and how successful treatment (i.e., changes in behaviors) might be interpreted and accepted (or rejected). This might be related to the client's or family's beliefs about why the client stutters, how people might be "cured" of stuttering, or how the client's role in the family or community might change. Similarly, clinicians should consider how the client and their family might react if treatment does not produce the changes that they are expecting. Might the client be blamed? Might the clinician be blamed? Is there a possibility for additional shame and stigma if treatment is deemed "unsuccessful"? Although these are questions that might be asked when working with any client, clinicians often assume they know the answers to these questions when a client appears to have shared values and a shared cultural and linguistic background. It is easy for clinicians to then unconsciously extrapolate those assumptions to other clients who do not share their cultural background. In a culturally responsive approach to stuttering treatment, clinicians would be aware that making such assumptions could lead to problems during and after treatment.

Decision Level VI: Change

Change is hard. This is where the clinician involves the family, peers, and the client to ensure that the skills learned in therapy translate into meaningful changes in participation and the ways in which the client reacts to their stuttering. At this level, the clinician needs to consider questions about the consequences of changes that are happening with the client as a result of successful treatment of their stuttering.

For example, how will changes in stuttering behaviors be accepted by the client's family and others in their environment? How will changes impact the client's identity, including their cultural identity? How will changes in the way the client engages with others impact their role in the family or with their peers? How will changes impact the future that the client and others in the client's life had planned?

Decision Level VII: Ongoing Assessment

This level includes formal assessment of progress being made toward treatment goals as well as monitoring the clinical interaction itself and continued self-monitoring on the part of the clinician. Ongoing assessment of progress toward treatment goals should include the collaborative process between client and clinician in deciding if goals are being met and progression to new goals. The clinician should also find out from the client whether there is anything the clinician needs to change so that the client feels better supported. Any challenges to the client's well-being as a result of the clinical interaction are eliminated or reduced. If issues are identified, the clinician will take responsibility and explore ways to address the issues, which might include further professional development in diversity, equity, and inclusion. It is also important that clinicians continue to self-reflect and monitor their biases, cultural values, and assumptions related to the client and continue to look for ways to increase their cultural humility. This might include proactively seeking out a variety of sources of information on diversity in addition to specific speech-language pathology professional development courses. Sources of information on diversity could include talking with colleagues about their perspectives on diversity; reading books, poetry, or autobiographies related to issues of diversity and equity; listening to podcasts; and watching movies and documentaries on the topic of diversity.

CONCLUSION

When working with persons who stutter, clinicians will encounter clients with experiences, values, beliefs, and ways of life that are different from their own. It is important for clinicians to be mindful that diversity encompasses more than just racial and linguistic differences and might be obvious (e.g., when someone looks or sounds different) or more subtle (e.g., when someone has had very different life experiences). Similarly, the concept of "culture" is complex—elusive and nebulous according to Epner and Baile (2012)—in that it could refer to many different dimensions that bind people together. Importantly, it cannot be assumed that taking a person-centered approach as described in Chapter 8 will be sufficient for the clinician to adequately respond to clients whose cultural backgrounds are different from their own (Blaine & Brenchley, 2020). Cultural responsiveness combines a person-centered mindset with specific attitudes and practices that can help clinicians respond appropriately to clients who are different from them in both obvious and subtle ways. This involves a willingness and determination to be self-reflective and even self-critical in examining your own personal biases, to value cultural diversity, and to seek knowledge of different cultural perspectives and practices.

The culturally responsive, person-centered model for working with persons who stutter described in this chapter can help guide clinicians to consider ways of approaching their clinical interactions that promote identifying, accepting, and embracing diversity. Clinicians should view this as an opportunity to grow both professionally and personally as they open themselves to the different perspectives, beliefs, practices, values, and stories of the people with whom they work.

❓ DISCUSSION QUESTIONS

1. Make a list of different dimensions of your identity (e.g., female, athlete, father, Asian American, etc.). Compare your list with others in a small group. What are some similarities you share with others in the group? What are some differences?

2. Using the list you made for the first question, name a stereotype associated with one of your dimensions that is not consistent with who you are. Share with others in your group.

3. Define *culture* in your own words. Share your definition with others in a small group and discuss how and why they are different.

4. What are some of your cultural biases or stereotypes?

5. How can you improve your cultural responsiveness? Try to be very specific about exactly what you will do (e.g., don't say "read a book"; instead, say "Read Ibram Kendi's *How to Be an Anti Racist* book").

📖 ADDITIONAL RESOURCES

Hyter, Y. D., & Salas-Provance, M. B. (2019). *Culturally responsive practices in speech, language, and hearing sciences.* Plural Publishing.

Rivera Perez, J. F. (2020). Self-treatment in adult fluency disorders—The tip of the iceberg. In A. F. Hamilton (Ed.), *Exploring cultural responsiveness: Guided scenarios for communication sciences and disorders (CSD) professionals* (pp.165–171). ASHA Press.

All clinicians should also train themselves in the subtle skills that enable them to sense the hidden feelings of their clients. These are not to be found in textbooks or classrooms. They must be mastered in the situations of intimate human encounter. Some of my students and clients have felt that I had an uncanny ability to read their thoughts—and at times I have indeed experienced something akin to clairvoyance—but only after I had observed and identified closely with the person long enough. . . . It is the result of very careful observation, uninhibited inference making, and the calculation of probabilities. It comes through empathy.

—Charles Van Riper (1979, pp. 107–108),
A Career in Speech Pathology, Prentice Hall

The Therapeutic Process:
Facilitating a Journey of Change

CHAPTER OBJECTIVES

■ To bridge the gap between the person-centered, client-directed role of the counselor and the client-centered, clinician-directed role of the speech therapist

■ To provide information regarding the rationale for selection of therapeutic approaches

■ To discuss the importance of the therapeutic alliance (i.e., this is *not* just a "counseling" concept)

■ To outline some basic principles of stuttering therapy as a foundation for the approaches discussed in subsequent chapters

In previous chapters, we examined the process of change and determined that, regardless of whether the change is considered to be positive or negative, it will be difficult for the client. We also discussed the need for counseling, both for the emotional responses to stuttering, as well as for the emotional responses to the changes that occur in stuttering treatment. The constructivist-narrative framework for counseling is one way that clinicians can construct a systematic approach to counseling that is integrated into their overall practice and not viewed as an "add-on" to traditional therapy. This point is important in the context of this chapter, in which we explore the *therapeutic process*, which incorporates counseling and traditional speech therapy under one conceptual umbrella—we are, after all, treating a whole person, not simply a speech-generating machine that is somehow broken. Therefore, we must understand the therapeutic process in the context of that whole person.

In upcoming chapters, we discuss processes and techniques for working directly with the problem of stuttering, not only in terms of eliminating or modifying the speech disfluencies, but also in terms of addressing secondary physical behaviors and avoidance behaviors that form part of the overall impact of stuttering on the person.

A ROAD MAP FOR CHANGE

The term *therapeutic process* is frequently used to refer to the overall course or progression of treatment within a specific domain—such as treating stuttering—and incorporates aspects such as how treatment approaches are selected, how technical and adaptive aspects of the problem are addressed, and how different aspects of treatment are integrated into the process. In this way, it might be considered a "road map" to facilitating client change, not through the sheer skill and expertise of the clinician, but through a collaborative, relational process that incorporates humanistic, cognitive, and behavioral treatment approaches.

Selecting a Route

Stuttering therapy has been compared to a "journey" by various authors (e.g., Plexico et al., 2005; Shapiro, 2011), as well as in previous editions of this book, so we decided to stay with the "road map" analogy as a way of framing this chapter—the goal of which is to look at how we facilitate the therapeutic process. First, however, a word of warning. Some younger readers might have some difficulty understanding certain aspects of this analogy, as the recent widespread availability and use of GPS navigation devices and apps has all but made traditional paper maps

disappear. Despite this, the analogy fits well and even this shift to a technological solution can help us better understand some aspects of the therapeutic process. For example, GPS systems are extremely useful in places where the driver has no *local knowledge*. They select a route and you (the driver) follow it, turn by turn, to the destination. It even gets you back on course if you make a wrong turn, and it will choose the same route to the destination every time. No decision making is needed by the driver. This is kind of like "manualized" stuttering treatment programs—a predetermined route that must be followed exactly that will be the same for every client, with no decision making needed by the clinician, or even, for that matter, any real (local) knowledge of stuttering. But have you ever used a GPS system in a location where you *do* have local knowledge? If so, what you find is that, frequently, the GPS system does not take you the optimal or most efficient route, does not account for local traffic patterns or temporary roadblocks, and does not know which roads to avoid because they have large potholes. And, sometimes, you and your passengers simply have preferred roads that you like to use—for any number of idiosyncratic reasons. Local knowledge—knowledge of the nature of stuttering and possible treatment options—is vital for optimizing and individualizing the therapeutic process.

Planning the Journey

When we used to use paper maps, before heading out on a journey, we had to plan out the route that we would take. This is like planning out a course of treatment. Decisions need to be made: Is the clinician doing all of the driving, or will the driving be shared with the client? What is going to be the final destination? Will this be the client's decision, the clinician's decision, or a collaborative decision? What route will you take to get to the final destination? As with any plan, flexibility is important, as there might be detours and delays, unanticipated stops, and even changes to the final destination as the journey progresses.

Assuming that some of these clinical decisions have been made—that the client and clinician will work collaboratively in a client-centered model to agree on long-term outcomes—selecting a treatment approach or philosophy might be the next step. As we discuss in detail in the chapters that follow, there are a number of different roads that lead to the same destination, with fluency shaping and stuttering modification approaches as the dominant broad categories, but also a number of specific manualized programs of treatment (e.g., Breitenfeldt & Lorenz, 1999; Roseman & Johnson, 1998), hybrid or integrated approaches (e.g., Guitar, 2014), and even technological approaches (e.g., the SpeechEasy device) also available. Clinicians frequently have preferences for treatment approaches, often based on philosophical position, past experience and training, or personal comfort level. It is important to remember, however, that the decision regarding the selection of a treatment approach is not made solely based on clinician preferences, but in collaboration with the client. Consequently, clinicians need to be competent in a variety of approaches, and approach clinical decisions regarding treatment with an open mind. It is important to remember that there are many roads that lead to the destination—finding the right road for your client's particular journey can prevent him or her from losing his or her way and avoid unnecessary delays and detours.

REFLECTIONS ON EVIDENCE-BASED PRACTICE

When planning a journey, it is usually a good idea to see what others who have made the same journey have to say about the various routes that are available. One of the primary decision-making processes available to clinicians who are planning treatment is *evidence-based practice* (EBP). In recent years, our field, along with many other health and behavioral sciences, began to embrace the concept of EBP. This means that as clinicians we should be able to provide evidence that the treatment protocols and associated techniques we select truly make a difference to the people we intend to help. Of course, the people we are helping would like to know this also, as do parents, spouses, and certainly the agencies that are financially supporting the treatment. It is this latter group of funding agencies that has driven this process as much as anything.

One of the regularly cited articles on the topic of EBP is that of Sackett et al. (2000), who described it as "the conscientious, explicit, and judicious use of current best evidence in making decisions about the care of individual patients" (p. 1). The practice also incorporates "the integration of best research evidence with clinical experience and patient values" (p. 1). A position statement by the American Speech-Language-Hearing Association (2005) indicates a nearly identical description: "The term *evidence-based practice* refers to an approach in which current, high-quality research evidence is integrated with practitioner expertise and client preferences and values into the process of making clinical decisions" (p. 1).

Returning to our journey analogy, then, EBP is akin to reading recommended reviews on the possible route to take to find out which ones will actually get you to the destination, how long they might take, what pitfalls might be encountered, and what added benefits certain routes might offer, and then using that information to decide which route best fits the driving experience, needs, and preferences of both the client and the clinician.

Unfortunately, many student clinicians, supervisors, and even some experienced clinicians fixate on the "high-quality research evidence" aspect of the definition of EBP (which might not be surprising given the EBP label), and frequently forget about the integration of "practitioner expertise and client preferences and values." This narrowing of the understanding of EBP is problematic for a number of reasons:

1. It takes the client and his or her preferences and values out of the equation, making it impossible for the process to be "client centered" or for intervention to be individualized for the client's specific needs.
2. It undervalues the expertise and creativity of the clinician, reducing her or him essentially to a technician.
3. It fails to consider important differences between the goals and procedures that are followed by clinical researchers and practicing clinicians.

The first two points relate to aspects of the therapeutic process that we have already discussed in previous chapters. First, the importance of being client-centered and giving up the "expert" role were discussed in Chapters 7 and 8 and

relate to the understanding that clients have knowledge and expertise about their problem that clinicians can never directly know. Consequently, clinicians must respect this expertise and allow clients to take the lead in many aspects of the treatment process, thereby individualizing the process based on the clients' unique needs and preferences.

Second, in Chapter 1 we discussed the meaning and importance of being a "professional" rather than a "technician" and how this distinction has its roots in the level of flexibility, creativity, and critical thinking employed by the clinician. Similarly, the Common Factors model, which we introduced in Chapter 8 and discuss in more detail later in this chapter, indicates that the "quality of the clinician" accounts for a significant proportion of the change that occurs in treatment (Ahn & Wampold, 2001). Given this, it would seem unwise to marginalize the impact that clinicians can have on the therapeutic process by essentially removing them from a decision-making role by overemphasizing empirical research findings.

Finally, when attempting to apply research findings to clinical interactions, differences between the goals and procedures that are followed by clinical researchers and practicing clinicians need to be taken into account. In order to demonstrate the often subtle cause-and-effect relationships of our clinical procedures, considerable rigor and control are exercised by clinical researchers. Participants are included (or excluded) with the goal of maximizing the homogeneity of those participating in the investigation. Individuals with cooccurring conditions are typically excluded because that could make the results difficult to interpret. Specific protocols are followed, and treatment techniques are prescribed. Typically, the protocols are manualized in order to ensure adherence and consistency (treatment fidelity) to the associated therapeutic ingredients and maintain control of possible contaminating factors. Ideally, as in randomized controlled trials (RCTs; or meta-analysis of several RCTs), participants are randomly assigned to the groups. The results of rigorous testing during these well-controlled conditions are designed to lead to outcomes demonstrating the *efficacy* of treatment protocols.

Practicing clinicians also want to demonstrate that what they are doing on a daily basis to assist their clients is likely to be helpful and result in successful therapeutic outcomes. However, clinicians see their clients under circumstances that are far less ideal and less well controlled than those found in research laboratories. Professional clinicians are responding to individuals who have not been randomly assigned to various treatment protocols. Clinicians are likely to be helping people who are highly heterogeneous and present with a variety of other, sometimes related, communication problems. There are likely to be uncontrolled (and often unknown) environmental factors that could be impacting the influence of the treatment procedures being implemented. The results of these clinical investigations are intended to result in outcomes demonstrating the *effectiveness* of treatment protocols.

THE MEDICAL MODEL

So why is there an apparent mismatch between a broader understanding of the therapeutic process—and, inherently, the process of change—and this narrow view of EBP taken by some clinicians?

Evidence-based clinical practice is based on the medical model, which stipulates that there are specific ingredients that account for and are necessary for the remediation of a medical disorder. Because of the specificity of the (theoretically effective) ingredients that are administered to the experimental group(s) of participants (vs. the theoretically inert placebo administered to the control participants), the researchers and their assistants follow procedural manuals in order to assure adherence to the treatment protocols. Although this model has obviously resulted in important, often critical, advances in the development of medications and procedures in the field of medicine, this model (and associated research protocols) might not be the best, or certainly not the only, model for explaining the ability of humans to change as a function of treatment (or on their own beyond the scope of formal treatment).

It has also been suggested that the traditional medical model has other disadvantages for conceptualizing the human change process. For example, the model has been described as an illness-based model that too easily dichotomizes individuals as being either normal or abnormal (Raskin & Lewandowski, 2000). It also tends to situate the person administering the treatment as an extraspective observer of objective medical "facts." In addition, the medical model of disability tends to foster a disease-entity approach that all too easily pathologizes people and casts them in a passive role, with the inference that experts are needed to cure or "fix" them (Monk et al., 1997). Finally, others suggest that the medical model of mental health, along with the *Diagnostic and Statistical Manual of Mental Disorders* (5th ed., Text revision; *DSM-5-TR*) of the American Psychiatric Association (APA, 2022) fosters the use of terms that, although we are accustomed

CLINICAL DECISION MAKING

Assigning clients to different forms of treatment and then asking which program might, by some criteria, be the best one might be the wrong question. In many ways, such a question is analogous to questions about which car, religion, or political party is the best. Prochaska and DiClemente (1992) referred to research in behavioral therapy that attempted to determine which treatment is best for a particular problem as "horse race research." In some cases, a particular approach won, whereas in other investigations, other methods finished first. Most cases, however, produced "a disappointing abundance of ties" (p. 204). In addition, they proposed that one of the major research issues for the future is how those interested in modifying human behavior can more effectively match treatment strategies and techniques to people. Thus, a better question to ask is this: What behavioral processes are best for whom, and when?

to using them, might not provide the most accurate or facilitative view of the person we are attempting to help (e.g., disorder, pathology, symptoms, patient, recovery, cure; Monk et al., 1997; Raskin & Lewandowski, 2000).

THE COMMON FACTORS MODEL

In order to make a journey successful, there are a number of things that need to happen regardless of the route taken. For example, the planned route needs to be accessible and have roads that can be verified as real roads and not simply dirt tracks. There will be many hours of driving involved. All drivers will need to trust the map and the planned route, and trust each other as competent drivers. Numerous authors, starting as far back as Rosenzweig (1936), followed by Frank (1974), and more recently Wampold and his associates (e.g., Ahn & Wampold, 2001; Laska et al., 2014; Wampold, 2001, 2015; Wampold et al., 1997) have described a similar set of "common factors" related to

psychotherapy, suggesting that such factors are common to almost all therapeutic approaches and, even more significantly, account for far more of the change that occurs during therapy than the specific techniques specified by the approach itself.

Wampold and his colleagues used the statistical techniques of meta-analysis and *hierarchical linear modeling* (HLM) to determine the factors that account for the variance in treatment outcomes. Using these procedures, they were able to determine effect sizes—an index of how much the dependent variable (treatment outcome) can be controlled, predicted, or explained by an independent variable such as the type of treatment administered. According to Cohen (1988), who developed the mathematical concept of effect size (d), a d of .20 might be considered a small effect size, .50 medium, and .80 large. When Wampold et al. considered the issue of *absolute efficacy* (whether or not individuals received treatment), they found that effect sizes averaged .80. This large effect size (particularly for the social sciences) observed across studies using many different treatment approaches indicated that treatment was remarkably efficacious. When they considered the issue of *relative efficacy* where all individuals received different treatments, they found that effect sizes reached a maximum of .20, a difference that is considered inconsequential both clinically and theoretically.

The fact that Wampold and his associates observed consistently uniform efficacy across treatments suggested that the specific ingredients associated with the various treatments were not responsible for treatment benefits. Drawing on meta-analyses of large numbers of primary studies, Wampold (2015) compared the effect sizes for several common factors to specific effects for psychotherapy. His findings are summarized in Table 10–1. The effect sizes for the *common factors* range from .24 to .72, with a number (i.e., Goal consensus/collaboration, alliance, empathy, and positive regard/affirmation) reaching Cohen's (1988) medium category, and one further factor (i.e., Congruence/Genuineness) just .01 below the medium category. In contrast, the *specific effects* reported by Wampold ranged from .01 to .20, with none rising above Cohen's small category. Wampold (2015) concluded that the common factors are a real

TABLE 10–1. Effect Size for Common Factors and Specific Effects of Psychotherapy

Common Factors*	Effect Size (*d*)
Goal consensus/collaboration	0.72
Alliance	0.57
Empathy	0.63
Positive regard/affirmation	0.56
Congruence/genuineness	0.49
Expectations	0.24
Cultural adaptation of evidence-based treatments	0.32
Therapist effects—in clinical trials	0.35
Therapist effects—in naturalistic settings	0.55
Specific Effects of Psychotherapy*	
Treatment differences	0.20
Adherence to protocol	0.04
Competence—at providing elements of treatment protocol	0.14
Specific ingredients—difference if subtracting a key ingredient from a treatment	0.01

*Adapted from Wampold (2015).

therapeutic aspect of psychotherapy and "attention must be given to them, in terms of theory, research and practice" (p. 276).

Herder et al. (2006) also found similar results in a meta-analysis of behavioral treatment for stuttering. From a total of 1,798 manuscripts identified through electronic and hand searches, 12 articles met the inclusion criteria, which included random assignment of participants to an experimental and a control (or comparison/alternative treatment) condition prior to intervention. Herder et al. found an overall (absolute efficacy) effect size of .91 in favor of the participants who received treatment. Analysis of the studies that compared one treatment group to another had an effect size of .21, indicating that no one treatment demonstrated a significant effect over another. It is interesting to note that, independent of the work of Wampold and his colleagues, Herder et al. (2006) came to the conclusion that "the critical element(s) for successful intervention might not lie with the intervention itself" (p. 70), but in the common element(s) found in many treatment approaches. Like Wampold and his colleagues, they further suggested that the knowledge and skills of the clinician who is providing the treatment could be a critical element influencing the success of treatment.

The evidence for the Common Factors model from Herder et al. (2006) and Wampold and colleagues has significant implications for SLPs engaging in therapeutic endeavors. Several authors have indicated that SLPs tend to provide highly structured services that are focused on specific techniques (e.g., DiLollo & Favreau, 2010; Leahy, 2004; Panagos & Bliss, 1990). The evidence from Wampold (2015), summarized in Table 10–1, would suggest that adherence to a specific protocol, the specific ingredients or techniques of a treatment approach, and even the competence of the clinician to use such techniques—all aspects of the highly structured, technique-driven approach reportedly taken by many SLPs—are likely to have minimal impact in terms of the process of therapeutic change. Alternatively, Wampold's findings point us in the direction of a collaborative, person-centered approach that emphasizes attributes such as empathy, positive regard, affirmation, and genuineness—all elements of a broader concept frequently referred to as "therapeutic alliance"—as a more effective therapeutic process to stimulate client changes.

CO-DRIVERS ON THE JOURNEY: THE THERAPEUTIC ALLIANCE

Therapeutic alliance is the most researched common factor (Wampold, 2015). Indeed, there is a large body of work in the field of clinical psychology supporting the idea that the quality of the therapeutic alliance is of primary importance to the successful outcome of therapy (e.g., Bachelor & Horvath, 1999; Blatt et al., 1966; Brown, 2004; Burns & Nolen-Hoeksema, 1992; Connors et al., 1997; Del Re et al., 2012; Horvath & Symonds, 1991; Krupnick et al., 1996; Martin et al., 2000). According to Bordin (1979), therapeutic alliance is composed of the bond between clinician and client, their agreement about the goals of therapy, and their agreement regarding the tasks of therapy. Feller and Cottone (2003) argued that empathy, which is related to positive regard and genuineness (Wampold, 2015), is also an important component of therapeutic alliance. Quesal (2010), in proposing that "loss of control" be considered the "critical factor" in stuttering (as opposed to surface behaviors), suggested empathy, or viewing stuttering from the perspective of the client, as an important aspect of therapy with persons who stutter. Clearly, such client-centered perspective taking is likely to engender a stronger bond between clinician and client and generate agreement regarding the goals and tasks of therapy (i.e., therapeutic alliance).

Plexico, Manning, and DiLollo (2010) conducted a phenomenological study in order to understand, from the perspective of clients who had received therapy for stuttering, the characteristics of clinicians who are effective or ineffective in promoting a successful change in the client's ability to communicate and how these characteristics relate to the constructs of the therapeutic alliance and clinician competence. Twenty-eight adults (19 male, 9 female) who had taken part in therapy for 6 months to more than 12 years with one or more clinicians served as participants. Participants were asked to write responses to four prompts:

1. Describe the characteristics of a clinician you felt was *effective* in promoting a successful change in your ability to communicate.
2. Describe how you felt in that interaction.
3 and 4. Respond to the same two prompts about an *ineffective* clinician.

The phenomenological analyses resulted in 750 meaning units and 50 categories that were distilled into 15 primary categories. The results provided a summarization in the form of an essential structure of both ineffective and effective clinicians.

The essential structure of an ineffective clinician: Ineffective clinicians are perceived as not being knowledgeable about the nature and depth of the stuttering experience, lacking in interest in the nuances of therapeutic change, and inattentive to the client. They are unlikely to actively listen and attend to their clients' capabilities and goals resulting in a failure to establish a beneficial therapeutic alliance, thus hindering client motivation and the desire to attend therapy. Their dogmatic adherence to a particular therapeutic protocol and associated techniques leaves the client feeling misunderstood, inadequate, shameful, discouraged, and without hope. As a result, the client leaves the therapeutic process experiencing negative emotions of frustration, anger, embarrassment, and guilt.

The essential structure of an effective clinician: Effective clinicians are professional, passionate, committed, and confident individuals who understand the nature and depth of the stuttering experience and its treatment. They believe in the therapeutic process and in the client's ability to accomplish therapeutic change. They are client driven and employ clinical decision making that accounts for the client's needs, capabilities, and personal goals. As a result, clients experience increased desire and motivation to attend therapy. They actively listen to their clients with a patient and caring demeanor, building feelings of confidence, acceptance, understanding, and trust. This, in turn, leads to a therapeutic alliance from which they empower the client's autonomy, agentic behavior, and cognitive change. As a result, the client becomes a more effective communicator with greater fluency.

These descriptions emphasize the importance of the therapeutic alliance to clients' perceptions of success, as well as highlighting specific clinician characteristics and behaviors that promote the development of the therapeutic alliance. Many of these characteristics and behaviors match those listed under "common factors" in Table 10–1 and have been shown to account for a significant proportion of the change that occurs during treatment.

Leahy (2004) examined therapeutic discourse with the purpose of better understanding how traditional approaches to clinician–client communication inhibit the therapeutic alliance. She pointed out the many word choices by the clinician that promote an asymmetrical interaction. For example, therapeutic discourse is often characterized by a three-step process of the clinician making a *request* (or asking a question), the person *responding*, followed by the clinician *evaluating* the person's response (RRE). When evaluating the client's response, the clinician often provides markers of authority and compliance such as "mmm," "good," "right," or "OK." The clinician often follows the client's response with another request. Leahy provided several examples of the RRE pattern with discourse examples from clinicians and clients presenting with several communication problems, including fluency. Many of Leahy's suggestions are similar to Luterman's admonitions concerning the ineffectiveness of counseling based on informing or persuading.

As Leahy (2004) also pointed out, an asymmetrical relationship is also enhanced by the environmental context of the encounter and the framing of the participants' social and speaking roles. Leahy quoted Simmons-Mackie and Damico (1999), who described the "routinized therapeutic context, with its well defined and expected roles" and "standard features which served to reinforce the underlying social contract and therapeutic goals" (p. 315). Most people recognize these verbal and nonverbal cues as we seek the services of, for example, a physician or a dentist. From the outset we find ourselves in a subordinate position, coming to the provider's location at the appointed time, sitting in a reception area (often for a lengthy interval), responding to a series of instructions (typically followed by additional waiting), being seen for a specific period of time, and eventually being told that we can leave.

Of course, this standardized procedure or script (see Panagos & Bliss, 1990) and the common sequence of the RRE discourse could be driven by the clinician's concept of his or her role and the pursuit of the session objectives. As Leahy (2004) pointed out, when demonstrating a therapy technique, the clinician's role is to keep the person "on task" and "to model, monitor, encourage self-monitoring, and evaluate progress" (p. 78). This can occur, for example, when clinicians seem to be in "mad pursuit of fluency" rather than attending to the contextual characteristics of the message or the individual. Leahy suggested that this "institutional pattern" of discourse conceptualizes and promotes the client as an "error-maker." As the client assumes this role it results in limited engagement by the client and minimal exchange of information. These patterns typically promote an asymmetrical relationship, with the clinician in the authoritative role of the expert and the client in the subordinate role (Leahy, 2004).

Leahy (2004) invited the clinician to consider moving away from this style of interaction and increasing the symmetrical features of the therapeutic discourse.

This is accomplished by the clinician following the speaker's lead and engaging in a sociorelational rather than an institutional frame, which focuses on the person rather than the problem. As we begin to frame the interaction in a sociorelational context, the participants are able to adjust their roles to promote the development of the speaker's communicative competence. Leahy provided examples of how the participants' roles can be negotiated in ways that elaborate the client's role as a competent communicator. The clinician can, for example, reduce his or her institutional and authoritative stance by decreasing his or her role as an evaluator and frequently using authoritative markers. In behavioral techniques, the clinician can become sensitive in the use of pronouns (e.g., I, you, we) when requesting (rather than directing) actions of the speaker. The clinician can follow the conversational lead of the client and summarize the speaker's comments as a way of recognizing the speaker's contributions.

In conclusion, let us state that this discussion is not intended to suggest that the medical model is not useful in many ways, both in general and in the area of fluency and fluency disorders in particular.

CLINICAL INSIGHT

Placebo effects have long been considered unwanted and confounding influences during the process of medical intervention. When controlled trials are conducted, the experimental participants receive the true or active medication and the control participants receive the inactive substitute. The success of the active intervention is determined by comparing the response of the people who receive the medication to those who receive the placebo. More recently, however, researchers are finding that placebos are not necessarily inactive. For example, Groopman (2004) in his book *The Anatomy of Hope*, described the biological effects of a person's emotions. Just as with negative emotions such as anxiety and fear, there are physical consequences associated with positive emotions such as hope. Groopman provided convincing research linking a person's beliefs and expectations (key aspects of hope) with the release or inhibition of chemicals within the body. Groopman provided fascinating medical examples of this mind–body connection and how emotions directly influence the status of tissues and organs, including the autonomic nervous system. In fact, the environmental cues provided by the physician or counselor as part of the ritual of professional interaction help to reinforce the client's expectation of benefit from the medicine or technique. To the extent that people believe that they are being helped, they are likely to experience decreased levels of anxiety and despair. Groopman described how the "spark of hope" can break the cycle of pain and hopelessness and set off a chain reaction that facilitates healing. It is likely that such mind–body connections play an active role during intervention for cognitive and behavioral concerns. As we understand more about and appreciate the true nature of placebo effects, it could be that we will begin to consider some of them as an important part of comprehensive therapeutic and self-directed change. Considering placebo effects in this way might indicate that good intervention is even more effective than we previously realized.

However, a hallmark of the scientific approach is being open to alternative explanations. To date, most of our investigations about why people stutter have been informed by the modern Western medical models of human health and development. It has been commonly assumed that, as a profession, we should follow this same (medical) model in our approach to understanding and treating stuttering. Certainly this model has proven useful, and currently important progress is being made in areas such as genetics and neuroimaging. It could be, however, that our investigations about *how to help people* who stutter are less well informed by the medical model, and there are other ways of considering how it is that humans are able to successfully cope and respond to therapeutic intervention.

THINKING ABOUT EVIDENCE

As we mentioned earlier, when selecting a route for your journey, it is often a good idea to learn about the possible routes from others who have driven the routes before. Of course, you have to be mindful of who it is you are listening to. Is the person reliable? Has the person really driven the route or is he or she just "faking it"? What is the person's level of driving skill and experience? Is he or she likely to recommend a dangerous or risky shortcut, or some long, winding scenic route? In the same way, when examining research as part of our evidence-based practice, we have to examine the evidence critically, asking ourselves how reliable and valid it is, as well as how well it fits our own clinical skills and expertise, and the client's needs and preferences.

Authors have been responding to the need for obtaining evidence to support our diagnostic and treatment decisions. However, individuals in a number of fields have pointed out that good evidence does not have to come in the form of RCTs. Rosenbek's (2016) article "Tyranny of the Randomized Clinical Trial" points out that RCTs are not the only way to provide guidance for treatment options and decisions and that, "The absence of the results of an RCT is not absence of evidence" (p. 242). Rosenbek, an experienced researcher and clinician, argued that including the perspective of clinical experience with the research data has several advantages. He cited the paper by Sackett et al. (1996) on evidence-based medicine, which maintained that, "Clinical expertise is as critical as the data because it enhances diagnosis and leads to more thoughtful identification and compassionate use of individual patients' rights and preferences" (Rosenbek, 2016, p. 71).

Ratner (2005) explained the limitations of RCTs for the field of speech-language pathology. The control groups called for during RCTs are a particular problem, not only because of the ethical issues of withholding treatment from individuals who would likely benefit from assistance but also because it is not possible to "wash out" the effect of learning as a result of previous treatment(s). Withdrawing treatment from people who have experienced it is not likely to undo the learning and cognitive changes that have taken place. As mentioned earlier, the positive placebo effects experienced by individuals who are selected for a control group might well result in some improvement, moderating the true effects of the treatment. In addition, there is the possibility for EBP to provide compelling but superficial evidence for selected "brands" of treatments. It is also possible that an overemphasis on EBP could result in the endorsement of questionable treatments that do not make use of conceptually or empirically sound principles of change. This is more likely to occur with "brands" of treatment, in which a group of individuals is involved in training and franchising (Ratner, 2005).

Ratner (2005) made the essential point that our choice should not be between treatment protocols that advocates indicate have received the necessary levels of empirical support and what these same authors deem as nonefficacious treatments. This, however, is the only choice that is sometimes offered. As Sackett et al. (2000) cautioned at the outset of their article on EBP, we need to be careful not to be "tyrannized by evidence . . . for even excellent evidence may be inapplicable and inappropriate for an individual patient" (p. 1). More to the point, we need to be careful of those who would choose to use EBP as a "club" to force others to use particular treatment protocols, especially while discrediting what others are doing. In fact, some treatments that might be found to be efficacious could also be unacceptable to people for a variety of reasons. It is not unusual, for example, for autonomous people to decline participation at the outset. Others fail to comply with the protocol or withdraw from the study. Researchers who are conducting efficacy or effectiveness studies should not exclude participants who were in some way noncompliant with the treatment protocol—although they often do (Hollis & Campbell, 1999). Excluding individuals who are noncompliant risks biasing the results in favor of the treatment. LaValley (2003) explained how intention-to-treat (ITT) analysis shows that those who are compliant with a treatment protocol (regardless of the treatment) often have better outcomes than those who are non-compliant. In fact, this is also the case for those receiving a placebo (Coronary Drug Project Research Group, 1980).

Finally, as Ratner (2005) pointed out, we should not confuse the concept "currently without substantial evidence" with the concept "without substantial value." As Westen and Morrison (2001) stated, "To infer that one treatment is more efficacious than another because one has been subjected to empirical scrutiny using a particular set of procedures and the other . . . has not is a logical error" (p. 878). In other words, we need to be careful to distinguish the notion of empirically *unvalidated* from empirically *invalidated* treatments. Furthermore, as several authors (Ratner, 2005; Siegel, 1993; Westen & Morrison, 2001; Zebrowski, 2007) have pointed out, it is not enough to show that a treatment "works." We also need to understand the underlying principles that enable us to understand *why* it works. As Ratner suggested, people are not likely to use a program if it does not make sense to them, no matter how many RCTs have been conducted. Only by understanding what principles and cause-and-effect relationships are operating can the clinician adjust a treatment protocol when necessary to the unique characteristics of his or her clients.

Fortunately, investigators are beginning to find evidence for the usefulness of the Common Factors model in comparing the effectiveness of empirically informed treatments of stuttering. Following earlier reports of similar results for three treatment protocols during 3-month treatment programs and up to 1 year posttreatment (Craig et al., 1996), Hancock et al. (1998) conducted a 2- to 6-year follow-up of 62 children ages 11 to 18 who had received one of the three stuttering treatments used in the study (intensive smooth speech, parent-home smooth speech, and intensive electromyography feedback). Using several indicators of stuttering behavior, speech naturalness, communication attitudes, and anxiety, the authors found no differences in long-term effectiveness among the three programs. More recently, in a small RCT, Franken et al. (2005) compared the Lidcombe Program and the demands and capacities protocol. Again, stuttering frequencies and severity ratings significantly decreased and were similar for the children in both programs. Likewise, Huinck and Peters (2004) compared the outcome of three treatment programs for adults—two intensive programs (one focusing on fluency shaping and one on stuttering modification) and a third highly individualized treatment program. Subjective and objective posttreatment and follow-up measures both 1 and 2 years later demonstrated dramatic improvement for all programs with only subtle differences between programs long term. All programs resulted in substantial improvements in fluency and self-concept, lowered anxiety, and speech motor control. The previously described investigation by Herder et al. (2006) also provides support for the equivalence of empirically informed behavioral treatments for stuttering.

Given this information concerning EBP, what is a clinician to do when faced with the obvious need for evidence to support his or her clinical decisions? Some of the possible responses are informed by our comments in Chapter 1 about the characteristics of effective clinicians and the development of expertise. The Common Factors model also provides some good news. The research consistently indicates that the clinician is the most important factor in accounting for therapeutic success, much more so than the specific techniques associated with any particular treatment protocol. Of course, this also places con-

siderable responsibility on the clinician to develop a high level of competency by continuing to be a student of the field and continuing to refine his or her understanding and skills—and committing to the therapeutic alliance with every client. Indeed, as Brown (2006) suggested, clinicians have an ethical responsibility to assess and improve their personal effectiveness; they cannot rely on treatments alone.

TAKING A CLOSER LOOK AT THE MAP: THE TOPOGRAPHY OF STUTTERING THERAPY

Goals of Treatment

One of the first objectives during the initial treatment sessions is to demonstrate our sense of direction to the client by providing a map of the journey. For excellent examples of pretreatment orientation statements see Cooper (1985), Guitar (2006), and Maxwell (1982). It is important for the client to have a clear understanding of the treatment process, and success could be more likely to occur if both the client and the clinician share a similar view (Ahn & Wampold, 2001; Wampold, 2015). At the outset of treatment, the client's concept of his or her fluency disorder itself is apt to be unclear. The clinician who is able to help the client decrease the mystery and understand what is known about the stuttering experience provides a valuable service to the speaker. Before speakers can begin to accurately monitor and self-manage themselves and their speech, they must begin to appreciate the nature of the problem in general and the dynamics of their own specific response to their situation.

There are three primary objectives when working with a person, regardless of age, who stutters: We would like to help

CLINICAL DECISION MAKING

By all accounts, Dean Williams was the embodiment of the expert clinician. His description of one of his "clinical failures" provides a comment on the principle of following the client's lead in the clinical process. On analysis of this case, Dean felt that this person was "helpable" but that he was unable to help her (Susan) because of his own errors in judgment. Here is Dean's description of one such error:

> Unfortunately, I began therapy with the preconceived idea of what it was I wanted her to accomplish. There was no attempt to first find out what she considered to be her problems and then to begin at this point. In other words, I did not bother to listen to what she was trying to tell me. I was too busy explaining the "stuttering problem" and the therapy procedures she was to follow. (D. E. Williams, 1995, p. 131)

See also Williams (2004, pp. 71–76).

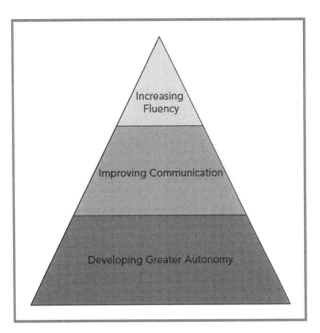

FIGURE 10–1. Three primary therapeutic objectives for assisting individuals who stutter.

them (a) increase their level of fluency, (b) improve their ability to communicate, and (c) develop greater autonomy. Although each of these objectives is important and, of course, highly related to the others, we can conceptualize them as being progressively more basic for long-term success, as expressed in Figure 10–1.

That is, although a clear goal of therapy for fluency problems is to assist the speaker in increasing his or her level of fluency, a more central goal is to help the speaker to develop his or her ability to communicate more effectively—perhaps by reducing the avoidance of feared words, producing easier and less effortful stuttering, maintaining appropriate eye contact, and turn taking. As people progress in therapy, they often realize that communication is more basic than fluency itself. Yes, fluency is important, but ideal fluency is not necessary for effective communication. Conture (1999) expressed this well by stating:

> The purpose of speaking is to communicate our ideas, feelings, thoughts, desires, and wants with others. When an individual cannot speak when, where, and with whom, and about what he or she wants, his speech is less usable, regardless of its fluency. . . . It is utility, not fluency of speech that is our ultimate goal. Fluency is a vehicle to obtain the goal; it is not the goal itself. (p. 24)

Most basic, however, is the clinician's ability to foster the speaker's development of an autonomous, agentic lifestyle, a therapeutic objective that is discussed in Chapter 12.

Levels of Fluency

Speakers who are regarded as normally fluent demonstrate a wide range of fluency across different situations. As discussed in Chapter 3, this range of fluency is greater in speakers who stutter. When considering the goals of treatment, authors have found it useful to distinguish at least three levels of fluency (see Guitar, 2014).

Spontaneous fluency can be thought of as ideal, normal speech. The speech is smooth and might contain only sporadic fluency breaks, which are primarily a function of formulating language and speech. Speech flows easily with little apparent effort, and virtually no attention is paid to how the speech is produced and fluency is achieved. Speakers, as well as the listener, are able to attend to the message, and the speaker's fluency does not detract from the information being delivered. It is important to recognize that, following successful treatment, some people who have stuttered for many years are able to achieve this level of spontaneous fluency in all speaking situations. The importance of spontaneity in speaking (for both fluent as well as stuttered speech) is elaborated in subsequent chapters and emphasized as one of the essential long-term goals of therapy.

Controlled fluency is normal or nearly normal speech production, but with the price of increased effort on the part of the speaker. Although the speaker must attend to his or her manner of speaking in order to achieve and maintain fluency, the speech moves forward with few, if any, obvious fluency breaks. There is a price to be paid in the form of vigilance and self-management of those fluency breaks. This management, to the degree that it is perceived by the listener, could detract somewhat from the message. On occasions, the method and the message of speaking might carry nearly equal weight. Depending on the ability of the speaker to apply techniques that facilitate the smooth coordination of respiration, phonation, and articulation, this type of fluency could be perceived as unstable speech. In many ways, this type of fluency is similar to that of a normal speaker who is placed in a speaking situation that contains a high level of communicative or emotional stress.

Acceptable fluency takes the level of self-monitoring and self-management of the speaker to another stage. Now the effort to manage fluency is increased, and the techniques being used to change the form of the stuttering might become more prominent than the content of the message. The speaker could be producing less than ideal fluency but still, speech that is much preferred to the client's old automatic, reflexive form of stuttering. Although stuttering is taking place, because these events are undergoing modification or smoothing, it is possible for the speaker and the listener to achieve a good level of communication.

THE IMPORTANCE OF MODELING

Although modeling of both attitudes and techniques by the clinician and others is discussed throughout this text, we take a moment to emphasize this important aspect of the change process. Modeling of different ways of considering stuttering attitudes and behaviors can have a profound impact for some speakers. Examples of alternative and possibly better ways of doing and thinking about things can be modeled by the clinician as well as other people in the client's environment. If we want our clients to give themselves permission to take risks and experiment with new ways of doing things, modeling is a good way to demonstrate this. Observing people as they successfully perform athletic, singing, writing, or speaking activities can be a critical and motivating influence for those who desire to perform these activities. The experience often helps to increase the observer's self-expectations and willingness to invest

the effort to undertake difficult tasks. Our expectation of our client's ability to change is confirmed by our willingness to lead the way by challenging ourselves and changing aspects of our own lives. Our modeling of attitudes and behaviors can provide a way to challenge, disrupt, and eventually alter the client's current belief system and behaviors. Furthermore, as discussed in Chapter 1, in order to provide a helpful model, the clinician will need to completely understand the stuttering experience and become desensitized to playing the role of a person who stutters.

VARIABLES IN CHOOSING A TREATMENT

There are several basic treatment considerations that are influenced by such things as the clinical setting and the client's needs and capabilities. These characteristics require the clinician to make decisions about the form that treatment will take. In some instances, the choices are already made for the clinician and the client according to the nature of the treatment setting or the options that are available because of such issues as time and expense (Starkweather et al., 1994).

The Timing and Duration of Treatment

There is considerable variation here, ranging from intensive, residential programs lasting 6 or more hours each day for 1 or more weeks to treatment in public schools, which could take place as little as 1 hour or less each week, often in a group session. Generally, adolescents and adults who have been stuttering for years require a longer time in treatment; preschool speakers often make faster progress and require much less time. Less intensive treatment disrupts the client's everyday life less, but changes could come slower, and the client might become discouraged. On the other hand, intensive treatments, particularly in settings away from the speaker's daily environment, often result in more rapid change (Prins, 1970) but with possible problems in transferring the gains to the speaker's more typical daily surroundings. The duration of treatment also can be influenced by such factors as the complexity of the fluency disorder, other coexisting communication problems, and the person's motivation. For adult speakers, formal treatment lasting 1 year with at least one individual and one group meeting each week has been suggested as a minimum requirement for success (Maxwell, 1982; Van Riper, 1973).

The Complexity of Treatment

A client's degree of handicap across the social, educational, and vocational aspects of his or her life will be a major factor in determining the course and length of intervention. Children and adults who come to us with a variety of linguistic, learning, social, emotional, and family issues are usually more likely to also have greater difficulty with the process of therapeutic change. On the other hand, those children with few other problems and qualities such as high self-esteem, good academic performance, high levels of family support, and social and athletic skills, generally are more likely to achieve success in therapy. Furthermore, the client's personality and emotional characteristics such as defensive behaviors, coping strategies, resistance to change, anxiety, inhibited behavior, or depression can also increase the length and complexity

of treatment. In such instances, treatment might require the use of many strategies and techniques as well as other professional clinicians in areas such as counseling, psychology, or psychiatry.

The Cost and Treatment Setting

This important aspect of treatment also varies widely. Undoubtedly many individuals do not seek treatment due to the cost. Because of the typical length of treatment and the lack of reimbursement by insurance companies, the cost of successful treatment can quickly become prohibitive for some people. Fees for diagnosis and treatment are generally lower in academic programs but scheduling and quality of service can sometimes be secondary to the academic and clinical training requirements of the program (semester breaks, changes in the consistency or availability of student clinicians). The level of service can also be compromised somewhat in public or private school settings, where availability of specialists, scheduling, and caseload requirements could vary widely.

The treatment that is provided is often determined in large measure by the setting. In this regard, St. Louis and Westbrook (1987) submitted that the choice of treatment might not always be made with the client as the primary consideration.

It seems plausible that typical delivery models for stuttering therapy evolved as much to suit clinicians' tastes; administrators' desires; school, university, or hospital schedules; or physicians' prescriptions as they did to provide the maximum benefit to stutterers. (p. 250)

The treatment strategies and techniques the clinician selects might or might not coincide with the available environment. That is, the clinician might want to schedule the client for several sessions each week, but multiple sessions might not be possible due to the logistics of the parents' or client's work schedule and distance from the treatment center. Although parent participation is important for success, some are unwilling to attend treatment sessions. Individual treatment might be necessary, yet the caseload in the clinical facility (particularly in the public schools) could only allow for group treatment, often including children who possess a variety of communication problems.

The opportunity for monitored practice outside the clinic or school setting is essential. Often, however, because of logistic, legal, insurance, or time constraints, the clinician is unable to go with the child or adult to more realistic speaking situations in offices, restaurants, or shopping malls. This is an important feature, as treatment settings that fail to create such experiences also might fail to provide realistic indications of change or progress. At the very least, the clinician should create opportunities to monitor the client's performance in the form of direct observation, interviews with the client following practice sessions, or monitoring with audio or video recordings of speech samples obtained beyond the treatment environment.

Cultural Considerations

When traveling, knowing and respecting the different road rules and driver expectations that exist in another country (or even city or rural area) is critical. Imagine, for example, the chaos and danger of ignoring the local road rules for an American driving in Australia, where they drive on the left side of the road. Families could demonstrate a range of cultural expectations and beliefs about stuttering itself and about therapeutic intervention in general. Interestingly, Wampold (2015) described how adapting an evidence-based treatment to incorporate cultural myths and traditions as part of the explanation (e.g., using the cultural "myth" as an explanation for stuttering) resulted in a more effective treatment compared to unadapted evidence-based treatments. Consequently, it is important for clinicians to learn about and be mindful of such beliefs and expectations by talking with clients and their families about such issues. Learning about cultural beliefs and practices from clients and their families is preferred to "textbook" learning that can lead clinicians to develop stereotyped views that might or might not apply to their specific client and his or her family. See Chapter 9 for further discussion on a culturally responsive approach to working with persons who stutter.

CONCLUSION

In Chapter 7, we discussed the process of change and the difficulties faced by clients when changing aspects of their life by engaging in therapy, with the goal of helping readers to begin conceptualizing their work with persons who stutter as a holistic process. Chapter 8 continued this goal, presenting a framework for counseling that focuses on empowering clients as the "experts" and listening to their personal story, with the understanding that stuttering is only one part of that story. In this chapter, we conclude our preparation for the upcoming focus on treatment by discussing how clinicians can conceptually "map out" the therapeutic process, and the roles that EBP, the medical model, and the Common Factors model can play in such conceptualization.

We reflected on the call for evidence-based research in our field and offered some alternative interpretations of this important concept. We suggested that, despite the important contributions of the medical model, there are other ways of conceptualizing therapeutic (and extra-therapeutic) change. We have argued that the Common Factors model provides an alternative way of considering the human change process and the critical factors that inform our clinical decision making. The factors of clinician expertise, the clinical alliance of the clinician and the client, and the clinician's allegiance to the chosen treatment protocol are critical and influential factors across treatment approaches that are empirically driven. Researchers are beginning to find evidence supporting the significance of these common factors across empirically informed treatments in the field of fluency disorders. The clinical decisions of proficient and expert clinicians are apt to be guided by theoretically motivated as well as empirically informed and validated information.

Beginning in Chapter 11, we discuss a variety of strategies and associated techniques that focus more specifically on changing the levels of the stuttering experience. The authors of a recent comprehensive review of many treatment approaches concluded by saying,

> . . . we are comfortable in saying that there are a large number of reasonably well-tested therapies for stuttering that have the good potential to help a large number of individuals. Some will work better for some than for others, and some clients may establish a better therapeutic alliance with some clinicians than others. In all this variety, there is continued hope for most people who stutter. (Bloodstein & Bernstein Ratner, 2008, p. 389)

? TOPICS FOR DISCUSSION

1. In this chapter, we used the analogy of the therapeutic process as a journey. Describe a different analogy for the therapeutic process.

2. To what degree do you believe that fluent speech is a necessary and sufficient indicator of successful therapeutic change?

3. How might you respond to a new adult PWS who, at the outset of therapy, asks you, "What are my chances of success?"

4. How does a clinician know that he or she has built a strong therapeutic alliance with his or her client?

5. Think of a time when someone displayed *empathy* toward you (you don't have to discuss the details). How did it feel for you to experience someone empathizing with you?

6. Distinguish between research intended to demonstrate treatment *efficacy* and research intended to demonstrate treatment *effectiveness*.

7. Compare and contrast the basic tenets of the medical model and the Common Factors model of therapeutic change.

8. What are some ways that a clinician who does not stutter can model risk-taking for his or her clients who stutter?

9. Why is learning about a client's "culture" by reading a textbook not recommended?

10. Describe three aspects from this chapter that surprised you, and explain why they were surprising to you.

RECOMMENDED READINGS

American Speech-Language-Hearing Association (ASHA). (2005). *Position statement on evidence-based practice.* https://www.asha.org/policy/PS2005-00221/

Bernstein Ratner, N. (2005). Evidenced-based practice in stuttering: Some questions to consider. *Journal of Fluency Disorders, 30*(1), 163–188.

Plexico, L. W., Manning, W. H., & DiLollo, A. (2010). Client perceptions of effective and ineffective therapeutic alliances during treatment for stuttering. *Journal of Fluency Disorders, 35*(4), 333–354.

Wampold, B. (2015). How important are the common factors in psychotherapy? An update. *World Psychiatry, 14,* 270–277.

Zebrowski, P. M. (2007). Treatment factors that influence therapy outcomes for children who stutter. In E. Conture & R. Curlee, *Stuttering and related disorders of fluency* (3rd ed., pp. 23–38). Thieme Medical.

A lot of times, after I'd been outside playing and had gotten real thirsty, I'd run into the kitchen and ask her to give me a glass of water. I was still stuttering badly, of course, so it took some time. And early on, she would stop washing dishes or whatever she was doing and just reach down, pat me on the back, and encourage me: "C'mon Robert Earl, spit it out now, son." After a while though, whenever I ran in there and started tripping over my words, she'd say the same thing, but instead of patting me on the back she'd take the dishrag and pop me upside my head with it. It didn't help me "spit it out" any quicker, but I learned to stop asking and get that water for myself, real quick.

—Bob Love (2000), *The Bob Love Story*, Chicago, IL: Contemporary Books

Facilitating Fluency for Preschool and School-Age Children

CHAPTER OBJECTIVES

■ To describe therapeutic approaches for assisting preschool and young school-age children who have been confirmed to be stuttering

■ To provide the clinician with examples of both indirect and direct forms of intervention that have been demonstrated to be effective with young speakers who stutter

CLINICAL INSIGHT

At the outset of this chapter, we would like to make a comment about how children who stutter might be viewed by others. Given the earlier descriptions of the difficulties associated with the stuttering experience, it is not unusual for these children to be perceived by others (including their parents) as shy, withdrawn, anxious, and possibly somewhat fragile. It is also possible to see them as heroic. On occasion it might be worth asking parents to temporarily take the role of a person who stutters at a mild to moderate level. For a few hours they can stutter on the telephone and in conversation with individuals in their community. They will soon see how daunting it can be to assume this role even for a brief period. It will help them to appreciate that, in spite of stuttering, their child has the determination, courage, and resilience to interact with others, play with friends, and go to school each day.

- To explore strategies to help the young speaker to enhance the amount and quality of fluent speech
- To explore strategies to help the young speaker to alter stuttering in the direction of effortless and smooth disfluencies
- To describe the essential role of the parents in the process of therapeutic change
- To provide counseling strategies that focus on desensitizing the child to the experience of stuttering
- To describe procedures for mitigating the impact of bullying
- To explore the possible effects of a variety of coexisting problems that are likely to impact the therapeutic process
- To provide recommendations for ways the classroom teacher could best respond when he or she discovers a child who stutters in the classroom

THE AGE OF THE STUTTERING AND THE LIKELIHOOD OF SUCCESS

The largest number of individuals who stutter are found among children in their preschool and early school years; there are far more children who stutter than adolescents or adults. Consequently, several authors have suggested that clinicians will have the greatest impact by providing service to this group of speakers. As described in Chapter 2, the literature strongly suggests that by the early teenage years, there is a notable decrease in the number of individuals who stutter. As Bloodstein et al.'s (2021) review of many prevalence studies indicates, the prevalence of stuttering remains consistent through the elementary grades and begins to gradually decline during the high school years. Al-

though a child's chronological age is a factor influencing the behavioral features and severity of stuttering, age is not as meaningful as the length of time stuttering has been taking place. As Conture (2001) put it, the age of the stuttering is usually more meaningful than the age of the child. Children as young as 2 or 3 years old can present with strikingly complex stuttering behaviors and with high levels of tension, struggle, and fear. As described in earlier chapters, the longer a child has been stuttering, the more likely it is that the problem will become chronic.

In contrast to the sometimes more demanding challenge of facilitating successful treatment for adolescents and adults who stutter, the literature consistently indicates that assisting preschool and early school-age children is often successful (Adams, 1984; Bloodstein et al., 2021; Conture, 1996; Conture & Guitar, 1993; Fosnot, 1993; Franken et al., 2005; Gottwald & Starkweather, 1995; Guitar et al., 2015; Lincoln et al., 1997; Miller & Guitar, 2009; Onslow et al., 2003; Starkweather, 1987; Starkweather et al., 1990). Interventions for young speakers typically make use of techniques that help the child to make slower and easier movements for voicing and articulation, decrease sensitivity to the stuttering event, increase self-confidence and problem solving as it relates to speech and communication, and promote an enjoyment of speaking. The reports of successful treatment for preschool children are undoubtedly aided (and confounded) by the fact that many children would have recovered on their own during the first months following onset. As a result, there has been some debate about the cost-effectiveness and ethical considerations of early intervention (Curlee & Yairi, 1997).

The literature indicates that treatment for somewhat older school-age children also is effective (Conture, 1997). However, as children experience the socialization process and the penalties associated with less than acceptable fluency during the early years of school, treatment tends to become more complex. Depending on the child and the coping behaviors that can rapidly evolve, clinicians might also make use of stuttering-modification procedures such as voluntary stuttering, cancellations, and pullout techniques (see Chapter 12). In other words, clinicians tend to employ a multifactorial approach whereby the clinician, often with the assistance of one or more parents, helps the child to improve skills or capacities in a number of areas that facilitate a smooth flow of language and speech.

Clinicians have also seen a history of increasingly direct forms of intervention with younger speakers during the last decades of the 20th century. According to Gottwald and Starkweather (1995), this is partially a result of the implementation of federal Public Law 94-142 in 1975, calling for the education of all handicapped children, and Public Law 99-457 in 1986, requiring early intervention for children 3 to 5 years old. Perhaps even more influential were the results of research findings with young children by Yairi and his associates described in Chapter 2 that documented the characteristics of very early childhood stuttering, indicating that 75% of the risk for stuttering onset occurs before the age of 3 years, 5 months (Yairi & Ambrose, 1992a, 1992b). The increased understanding of early childhood stuttering, in combination with successful intervention for children who are seen as soon as possible following stuttering onset, began to make it clear that such treatment offers the best chance for altering the development of the problem. As we see in the following pages, early intervention with young speakers

has been found to be both effective and long-lasting.

BASIC CONSIDERATIONS WHEN TREATING YOUNG CHILDREN

There are, of course, many salient distinctions between intervention with children and with older speakers. In earlier chapters, the natural variability of fluency was noted, and this is especially true for younger speakers. Variability in the frequency and form of early developmental stuttering makes both assessment and therapeutic change somewhat more difficult to determine for this age group. There is always the question of how much behavioral change is due to treatment and how much is due to the natural variability of the stuttering. In contrast to older speakers, there are several other important factors that are likely to influence how we assist young children who stutter.

- Children are functioning with conceptual, linguistic, affective, and neurophysiological systems that are far from adult-like and are still in the process of maturation.
- The clinician is more likely to place emphasis on the evaluation and possible treatment of other communication, learning, and behavioral problems.
- Teasing and bullying at school and in other social situations could occur.
- Depending on the child's level of awareness and reaction to the stuttering experience, the clinician could select treatment techniques that are less direct than those used with adults.
- Parents and a variety of other professionals, including the child's

classroom teacher, play essential roles in the treatment process.

■ There tends to be somewhat less effort needed for helping the child to transfer and maintain treatment gains into extra-treatment environments.

■ The likelihood of achieving natural and spontaneous fluency is much greater for young children than for adults.

■ Relapse following treatment is not as likely as with adults.

Another thing that is unique about children who stutter is the setting where they are likely to be receiving therapy. Most children are seen in a public-school setting under conditions that can limit the effectiveness of therapy. It is not unusual for clinicians to be responsible for double or triple the maximum caseload of 25 to 40 children recommended by the ASHA direct service itinerant model (ASHA, 1984; Kelly et al., 1997; Mallard & Westbrook, 1988). The lack of time available for individual treatment often results in children who stutter being seen along with children who have a variety of other communication problems. In most cases, children attend treatment, at most, twice a week for 20 to 30 minutes each session (Healey, 1995; Kelly et al., 1997). Finally, because children who stutter typically make up only 3% to 4% of a clinician's caseload (Blood & Seider, 1981; Kelly et al., 1997; Slater, 1992), it is usually difficult to organize group therapy for these children with distinctive problems and treatment goals. All these issues combine to create what are often obviously inadequate services for children who stutter. It is not unusual to hear public school clinicians express their frustrations concerning these and other conditions that hamper the delivery of quality services for children who

stutter. The frustration and anger expressed by persons attending local and national self-help meetings also reflect the less-than-adequate service delivery experienced by individuals who have attended school-based treatment programs. Clearly, this is not always the case, and there are examples of school systems that provide outstanding service to these children and their families, often made possible by clinicians specializing in fluency problems and the creation of after-school and summer programs.

An issue that is not unique to children has to do with how we, as clinicians, assign value to and describe both fluent and stuttered speech. That is, when we are speaking to younger as well as older individuals who stutter, how do we express ourselves about stuttering and the importance of fluency? Do we, by our verbal and nonverbal behavior, imply that fluency is "good" and stuttering is "bad" (or at least not as good as fluency)? If so, we could easily be engendering feelings of shame in the young speaker, who might already feel as though stuttering is his or her fault. Regardless of the overall treatment strategy, the effectiveness of many treatment techniques requires that the child be free to experiment with a variety of fluent and nonfluent speech behaviors. An overemphasis on fluent speech as the only valued goal of treatment can easily lead to the child trying not to stutter, something he or she is already likely to be doing. Although it is true that listeners react negatively to most forms of stuttered speech, one of the clinician's basic goals is to break up the simplistic, conceptual dichotomy that all fluent speech is good and that stuttered speech must always mean that the speaker is out of control and helpless. An important aspect of treatment is breaking the link between stuttering and being out of control. The speaker can, in fact, learn to tolerate "being in" the stuttering and choose from several responses that lead to a smooth and effortless form of stuttering. The speaker can understand that surface fluency, at the cost of many forms of avoidance and word substitution, is not control at all. All these aspects that are unique to the nature of stuttering in younger speakers combine to produce a number of clinical choices that the clinician must consider. One of these is the directness of the intervention process.

INDIRECT AND DIRECT TREATMENT STRATEGIES

In order to fully appreciate the current thinking regarding treatment for young children who stutter, it is useful to provide some historical context. Except for the latter years of the last century in the United States, the treatment for young children who stuttered was indirect. That is, the children themselves were not the recipients of the intervention activities, and few specific instructions were given to the child about modifying his or her fluency. Rather, the adults in the child's environment— the parents, family members, grandparents, and teachers—received advice concerning procedures for altering the child's environment. The choice of this general approach was due to the many cautions from authorities who, over the years, recommended that the clinician avoid making children aware of the problems they were having with their speech. Clinicians were advised not to bring the child's disrupted speech to his or her attention or to respond in ways that might associate negative emotion with speaking. This view was especially popular during the decades

of the 1940s through the 1960s and coincided with the prominence of the diagnosogenic theory of stuttering onset and development described in Chapter 3. The following series of quotes from a popular textbook of the time by Eisenson and Ogilvie (1963) reflects the then-current thinking about intervention for young children who were considered to be experiencing *primary* stuttering. Described by Bluemel (1932), primary stuttering is seen as a transient phenomenon during which the child does not yet show awareness of his or her problem or demonstrate struggle behavior while speaking:

> The emphasis of treatment for the primary stutterer was to prevent the child from becoming aware that his speech was in any way different from others and a cause for concern. . . .
>
> . . . Essentially, therefore, the primary stutterer is to be treated through his parents if he is not of school age. If he is of school age, teachers as well as parents become the recipients of direct treatment. (Bluemel, 1932, p. 318)

Parents were instructed to respond in the following ways:

> If the child is a primary stutterer or is showing any of the speech characteristics associated with stuttering, it is essential that signs of parental anxiety be kept from him. Do not permit the child to hear the word stuttering used about his speech. Do not . . . do anything that makes it necessary for him to think about speaking or to conclude that he is not speaking well. (Bluemel, 1932, p. 323)

Another good example of this indirect approach is seen in Johnson's (1962) *Open*

Letter to the Mother of a Stuttering Child, which contained this statement:

> Do nothing at any time, by word or deed or posture or facial expression, that would serve to call Fred's attention to the interruptions in his speech. Above all, do nothing that would make him regard them as abnormal or unacceptable. (p. 3)

Finally, Van Riper (1939), in the first edition of his popular text, *Speech Correction: Principles and Methods*, wrote, "The way to treat a young stutterer in the primary stage is to let him alone and treat his parents and teachers."

With such cautions, few clinicians and parents were likely to intervene directly to assist a young child with his or her communication problems. The thinking was that direct intervention could make the stuttering more severe, a fear that permeated the decision-making process for clinicians at the time. Although these views are not likely to be held today, there are undoubtedly many clinicians who are overly cautious about assisting young stuttering children and associate the natural variability and sometimes increased stuttering with greater severity.

Although there is considerable overlap between indirect and direct methods of treatment for children (Conture, 2001), an indirect approach might be appropriate for a child whose stuttering is characterized by relatively easy fluency breaks with little tension or struggle and who is generally unaware of any speaking difficulty. In such cases, the clinician is likely to model and encourage easier and perhaps slower ways (e.g., "turtle speech") of speaking but make little or no effort to directly modify specific features of the child's stuttered speech. The child's parents are provided with information concerning the developmental nature of language and fluency and encouraged to adjust the various environmental factors that tend to both disrupt and promote fluency. For example, decreasing demand speech; promoting turn-taking; desensitizing the child to fluency-disrupting stimuli; and rewarding open, easy, and forward-moving speech guides the child toward increased fluency.

Treatment is more likely to be direct if the child has been stuttering for several months and is experiencing tension and struggle behavior or fragmenting monosyllabic words. In addition, the child might be exhibiting the nonverbal characteristics of more developed stuttering such as breaking eye contact with the listener (Conture, 1990). If the child shows these reactions on measures of awareness and negative reactions to communicating described in Chapter 5, the clinician will be more likely to initiate activities directly with the child that are designed to enhance fluency and, in some cases, modify moments of stuttering. Fluency modification techniques are most likely to be used for such children (Gregory, 1995; Guitar, 2006; Healey & Scott, 1995). However, depending on the success of these techniques, stuttering modification techniques might also be employed. That is, rather than focusing solely on enhancing fluent speech, the child can follow the clinician's model in producing and contrasting both fluent and stuttered speech with the eventual goal of enabling the child to choose the easier and smoother form of speaking. Of course, the clinician can select the most appropriate activities along a continuum of directness according to the needs of the child and his or her response to treatment.

Regardless of how directly the clinician works to enhance the child's fluency, treatment for a young child who stutters should be characterized by a high degree of understanding, reassurance, and encouragement by the clinician. A major focus of both indirect and more direct approaches is to make speech enjoyable for the child. A highly supportive treatment environment enables the child to approach and explore the speaking experience and to enhance the ability to make choices about how speech is produced. Primary messages to the child via verbal and nonverbal modeling of both the parents and the clinician include such concepts as (a) stuttering is not the child's or the parents' fault, (b) speaking can be easy and enjoyable, and (c) the child is capable of selecting and producing forms of fluent speech.

THE IMPORTANCE OF PARENT PARTICIPATION IN TREATMENT: THE IMPACT ON THE FAMILY

There is a wealth of information supporting the idea that parents play an influential role in the successful management of communication problems, and this is certainly the case with stuttering. Beilby (2014) provided a comprehensive overview of the impact of stuttering on a child and his or her siblings and parents. Some of the highlights from one of their studies (Beilby, Byrnes, & Young, 2012) indicated that fluent siblings exhibited strong emotions regarding their sibling who stuttered. Fluent siblings reported being frustrated by the sibling who stuttered but being upset when their sibling was bullied or teased by others, and the majority of siblings wanted to be more involved in the therapy process than they currently were. Paraphrasing Botterill (2011), one

of the developers of Parent–Child Interaction Therapy (PCIT) at the Michael Palin Center in London, no single component of the family can be understood in isolation. The whole family, not just the child with the problem, should be viewed as "the client."

Understanding the impact of stuttering on family members and the concerns and questions that parents bring to the assessment and treatment sessions can be identified by an automated, online version of the Palin Parent Rating Scale (Palin PRS) designed for children up to 14½ years old (Millard & Davis, 2016). This scale provides clinicians and parents an efficient assessment of three important factors about younger speakers who stutter: (a) the impact of stuttering on the child, (b) the severity of stuttering and its impact on the parents, and (c) the parents' knowledge about stuttering and confidence in managing their child's stuttering. A free, online version of the 19-item questionnaire takes only a few minutes to complete and has high internal consistency and reliability. The information can assist clinicians in determining specific therapeutic needs of the children and parents and track therapeutic progress. Registration, instructions, and access to the Palin PRS are available at https://www.palinprs.org .uk/secure/pprs_connect.php

Because stuttering is typically a developmental problem beginning during childhood and parents are the most important models for their children, successful intervention requires the participation of the parents. Conture (2001) pointed out that parents need to be rewarded for their insight and courage when they ask for help for their nonfluent child. The last thing parents need is for the clinician to lecture or reprimand them for their previous patterns of parent–child interactions. Parents should be informed at the outset that they have not caused this problem to occur, nor do they bear the responsibility for eliminating it. However, parents can be shown how to assist in providing vital understanding and support. In some cases, parents will play a major role in administering and monitoring therapy techniques.

As influential as their participation in treatment for their child might be, on some occasions parents are unconcerned or uninterested in taking part in their child's treatment. Conture (2001, p. 154) provided a sensitive and insightful description of parents who, for a variety of reasons, are unable or unwilling to become involved. They might be unable to take part due to work, travel time, or financial concerns. They could feel that the child will outgrow the problem. In such cases simply observing the child or initiating individual treatment is likely to be counterproductive. However, if the child's pattern of stuttering as well as his or her emotional and social maturity warrant, Conture suggested intervention in the form of parent–child fluency groups or a period of trial therapy (p. 167).

Ramig (1993b) also acknowledged that parents have many priorities, including work schedules and financial survival, which are likely to be regarded as more important than the current status of their child's speech fluency. Additionally, in rural or poor urban areas, there might be no way to contact the parents by telephone or Internet, the parents might not be able to read or write, or English might be a second language. There might be only one parent in the home, making transportation of the child to treatment difficult or impossible.

Nevertheless, as we have indicated, it is the consensus of many experienced clinicians who have achieved therapeutic success with young children who stutter that parental involvement in treatment is crucial (Bluemel, 1957; Botterill et al., 1991; Brignell et al., 2021; Conture, 1990; Conture & Schwartz, 1984; Ham, 1986; Johnson et al., 1967; Peters & Guitar, 1991; Riley & Riley, 1983; Rustin, 1987; Starkweather et al., 1990; Wyatt, 1969). Rustin and Cook indicated that if there is going to be any realistic chance for therapeutic success, the parents must play a major role. She stated that "without the involvement of parents, clinicians become powerless to help the child beyond the confines of the clinic room" (Rustin & Cook, 1995, p. 125). Likewise, Ramig (1993b) and Bronfenbrenner (1976) stated that without the parents' developing ability to help their child, the effects of treatment will likely deteriorate. Our experiences in running summer programs for children who stutter consistently show that those children whose parents attend sessions make considerably more progress than children whose parents, for one reason or another, do not attend.

Parental involvement not only assists the child in making behavioral and cognitive changes, but also permits a form of mental hygiene to occur for the parents. Through counseling and parent group contact, the parents can accumulate the necessary information to become stronger and more confident about helping their child (Rustin & Cook, 1995). Although it might not be necessary for the clinician to spend a great amount of time desensitizing the young child to his or her fluency breaks, other people in the child's environment—including grandparents and teachers—often receive great benefit from these activities. It is also worth considering that increasing numbers of children from nontraditional families are being seen in clinical facilities. In such cases, the major caregiver might not be the child's parent.

Whoever takes on this role will play a central role during the stages of assessment, therapeutic change, and maintenance.

Ratner (1993) provided a helpful metaphor that clinicians can use to explain the nature of stuttering to parents. She pointed out the similarities of stuttering to allergies or juvenile diabetes. "Parental behaviors are not presumed to play a role in the onset of either allergies or juvenile diabetes. However, it is clear that the response of parents to these disorders can either mitigate or aggravate their consequences" (p. 238). To the degree that parents are able to adjust the child's environment in regard to such problems (e.g., exposure to allergens or adjustments in diet), the symptoms will become less severe. In the case of stuttering, parents can come to understand that although the etiology or the problem is unlikely to change, the maintenance of the symptoms can be significantly altered by the actions and support of the child's parents.

In order to assist the parents in understanding the problem and making good decisions on their own, the clinician can provide behavioral models as well as information. Still, the clinician needs to be cautioned to provide information in reasonable amounts. When counseling parents it is easy to provide too many recommendations too quickly (Conture, 1990; Luterman, 2017). As a result, parents can become overwhelmed and discouraged. Rather than lecturing the parents, it is more effective to follow their lead by listening to their questions and responding to—and expanding on—the issues they want to know about. Parents can select from a wide variety of helpful sources and obtain informative pamphlets, watch instructional videotapes, search the Internet, and observe treatment being conducted with their child. By taking such action they will be much more likely to provide the clinician with insightful ideas and suggestions.

One way to consider the levels of parental involvement throughout fluency therapy for their children was suggested by Ramig (1993b), who described three stages of parent involvement: (a) facilitating communicative interaction, (b) educational counseling, and (c) involving parents as observers and participants.

During the initial stage of *educational counseling*, a primary role of the clinician is to help demystify stuttering and increase the parents' understanding of their child's situation. The clinician explains the difference between normal breaks and stuttering-like disfluencies (SLDs), discussed in Chapter 2. Parents are informed that although the etiology of stuttering is not completely understood, a great deal is known about the dynamics of stuttering and much can be done to decrease the problem, especially in young speakers. With increased understanding, parents will become less anxious and inhibited about stuttering and see how their involvement in treatment will support rather than somehow hurt their child. As parents become more knowledgeable and desensitized, they will be better able to make intuitive and helpful responses to their child.

As Ramig (1993b) suggested, parents are likely to bring along many myths about stuttering including that as parents, by omission or commission, they have somehow caused the problem (Conture, 1990, 2001; Peters & Guitar, 1991; Rustin, 1987; Van Riper, 1982). Ramig (1993b) suggested that clinicians should see the reduction of possible feelings of guilt in the parents as a major achievement. Group meetings of parents provide an invaluable forum for dealing with these frustrations as parents begin to realize that they are not alone. Used in a variety of settings, including public schools and support groups, the meetings provide an opportunity for more seasoned parents to provide the support and insight that are especially helpful to other parents who are new to the experience (Berkowitz et al., 1994; Ramig, 1993b. Detailed descriptions of parent–child fluency group dynamics can be found in Conture (2001, pp. 167–177).

It is also helpful for parents to understand that, as a group, parents of stuttering children behave no differently than those of normally speaking children. As Ratner (1993) pointed out, there is no evidence for the view that parental interaction style is related to the severity of a fluency disorder. Furthermore, no correlations were noted between stuttering severity at initial assessment and parental conversational behaviors of speech rate, frequency of questions, and interruptions. In addition, Weiss and Zebrowski (Weiss, 1993; Weiss & Zebrowski, 1992) found that parents of children who stutter do not produce significantly more requests for verbal responses than parents of nonstutterers. Furthermore, the parents of children who stutter show no psychological differences when compared to the parents of fluent children (Adams, 1993).

Lau et al. (2012) found no significant differences in parenting styles for parents of children who stutter and parents of fluent children. According to Ramig (1993b), a second stage of parent involvement involves the *facilitation of communicative interaction* with the child. The goal of the clinician is to model for the parents the interpersonal styles that facilitate fluency during parent–child interactions. The overall communication and interpersonal characteristics of the child, as well as the child–parent interaction style, should be continuously evaluated. These character-

istics include linguistic as well as paralinguistic variables, many of which have been studied in recent years in an attempt to determine their effect on children's fluency (see Kelly, 1994, for a summary). Such studies have investigated the rate of the speech (Conture & Caruso, 1987; Kelly, 1994; Meyers & Freeman, 1985), parent verbal and nonverbal responses to the child's fluency breaks (LaSalle & Conture, 1991), the amount and type of interruptions of the child's speech by the parents (Meyers & Freeman, 1985), turn-taking behaviors and response-time latency (Kelly, 1994), the complexity of the questions posed to the child (Stocker & Usprich, 1976), and the tendency for the parent to provide verbal and nonverbal corrections to the child as he or she is speaking (Gregory & Hill, 1980). As these features are identified, the parents can be shown how to alter some aspects of their interactive style. For example, the mother can be shown how to slow her speech, provide more time for turn-taking, interrupt the child's speech less, and positively reinforce the child for using fluency-enhancing techniques.

Silverman (1996) suggested having the parents view videotapes of themselves and their child while the clinician points out both the less and more desirable ways they are responding to their child's fluency breaks. For example, the parents might be speaking rapidly and frequently interrupting or indicating by their body language (e.g., breaking eye contact) that they are not interested in what their child is saying. Recall, for example, the study by Winslow and Guitar (1994) mentioned in Chapter 3, which found that the fluency of a 5-year-old child increased when conversational demands were lessened by the implementation of turn-taking rules, whereas stuttering increased when these rules were withdrawn. During an obvious or severe stuttering moment, parents might unconsciously freeze or show anxiety or concern. They might have a pattern of asking their child difficult or abstract questions that require complex responses. On the other hand, of course, the parents could also be doing many appropriate things, including modeling slow, easy speech and responding with an unafraid attitude to stuttering behavior. Videotapes of clinician–child interactions also can be used to demonstrate desirable parent behavior.

A third and final stage of parental involvement places the parents in the role of *observers and participants* in the process of therapeutic change. The participation of both parents is often the ideal situation, although there is minimal research on the role of the father in this process. Ramig (1993b) indicated that even if only one parent is able to take part, the result is still likely to be beneficial for the child. Initially the parent's role is to observe the interaction of the child and clinician as the clinician models changes in the previously described interactive style. The clinician also demonstrates strategies for expanding the child's fluency and modifying moments of stuttering, using techniques described in the previous chapter as well as in later sections of this chapter. Parents gradually join in this process with the clinician and the child and eventually interact with the child on their own.

Current Treatment Programs That Involve Parents

The Lidcombe Program

A treatment strategy that places the parents in a central role is illustrated by the Lidcombe Program (Onslow et al., 2003; Onslow et al., 2023). Responding to the need to treat children who stutter at a community health center in a suburb of Sydney, Australia, the developers of the program were influenced by the success shown in a series of direct, response-contingent treatments for young stuttering children conducted in the United States in the 1970s (e.g., Martin, Haroldson, & Kuhl, 1972a; Martin, Kuhl, & Haroldson, 1972; Siegel, 1970).

At the outset of the Lidcombe Program (Stage I), parents attend weekly 45- to 60-minute sessions in the clinic and observe the clinician's use of verbal contingencies in response to the child's fluent and stuttered utterances. Following the clinician's model, parents learn to administer verbal response-contingent stimulation. Fluent responses are acknowledged with what is termed a neutral response (e.g., "That was good talking. Those words were smooth.") or praised (e.g., "Wow, good smooth talking!"). Unambiguous stuttering is highlighted by the clinician with responses such as, "That was bumpy speech," or "That was a bump there." The clinician is continually supportive, responding to the child's examples of stuttering intermittently in order not to overwhelm the child. The clinician (and eventually the parent) responds to fluent and stuttered events on a 5:1 ratio. Two "nonessential" child responses include self-evaluation of stutter-free speech (e.g., "Was that smooth?" or "Were there any bumps there?") and self-correction of stuttering (e.g., "Can you say 'orange' again smoothly?"). Self-corrections are praised (e.g., "Great talking, you smoothed out that bumpy word by yourself!"). As the parents learn to administer the verbal contingencies during structured activities, they begin to assume the role of the clinician, conducting the program at home during short (10–15 minutes) structured sessions, often using games. As the parents and the child adapt to the nature of the activities, the parents begin providing verbal contingencies during unstructured, everyday activities.

Because of the methodical, manualized nature of the approach and the focus on the child's frequency of stuttering, the program facilitates the ability of researchers to conduct controlled research. As a result, the Lidcombe Program has received extensive documentation in the literature. The investigators have demonstrated consistent and impressive efforts to show the efficacy of the approach. However, although many of the initial investigations showed high levels of treatment efficacy with well-trained clinicians, there was little control for natural recovery. Fortunately, more recent investigations controlled for natural recovery and continued to show impressive results. Phase III randomized controlled trial data controlling for natural recovery demonstrated large effect sizes for children who received the Lidcombe Program versus preschoolers who received no treatment for a 9-month period (Jones et al., 2005).

RESTART-DCM

RESTART-DCM (Franken & Laroes, 2021) is based on the demands and capacities model (DCM; Starkweather et al., 1990) and addresses four dimensions (motor, linguistic, socioemotional, and cognitive) that are theorized to contribute to developing stuttering. The program aims to diminish the environmental and self-imposed demands and enhance the child's capacities to speak more fluently.

A multifactorial assessment is conducted to examine the communication demands being placed on the child, as well as their capacities for fluent speech. The program involves three stages. In Stage 1, there is an effort to decrease linguistic and emotional demands (either self-imposed or generated by people in the child's communicative environment) to match the child's capacities for fluent speech. The focus of the training is with the parents' interaction style, implementing changes first in the clinic and then at home. If necessary, Stage 2 aims to increase the child's speech motor, language, and emotional capacities, while still diminishing the communicative demands addressed in Stage 1. Finally, if needed, Stage 3 focuses directly on improving speech fluency. Parents are instructed to do the tasks at home 15 minutes a day, for at least 5 days a week. de Sonneville-Koedoot et al. (2015) reported a range of positive outcomes for the RESTART-DCM program, including reduced stuttering frequency and improved attitudes.

Palin Parent–Child Interaction Therapy (Palin PCI)

Palin Parent–Child Interaction Therapy (Palin PCI; Kelman & Nicholas, 2020) is grounded in a multifactorial model of stuttering and aims to reduce stuttering frequency, struggle, or both. It involves a detailed assessment designed to identify factors that impact fluent speech, stuttering, and confident communication. Therapy involves developing a customized plan to promote the child's fluency that considers environmental and emotional linguistic strengths and needs. The program consists of *interaction*, *family*, and *child* strategies. Parents play a central role in in the intervention. The therapy is made up of the initial (interaction) stage, in which parent–child interaction strategies are practiced in short 5-minute periods referred

CLINICAL INSIGHT

Some of the most poignant comments by adults who stutter, including those who have successfully managed their stuttering, describe the silence that surrounded the topic of stuttering when they were children. They describe the frustration and shame that were heightened by the unwillingness of their parents to address a problem that was so obvious. Most parents are willing to address and try to help their child with other problems they might have, but stuttering is too often viewed as an embarrassing and taboo topic, and the silence is easily interpreted by the child to mean that stuttering is something that is plainly too shameful to mention. Dr. Alan Rabinowitz, in his 2005 keynote address to the Stuttering Foundation (Speech Foundation CD # 8500), recalled that, "My parents never knew what to do with me. . . . I loved my parents but their greatest mistake was their denial of my stuttering and their belief that to talk about the problem with me or in front of me would only hurt me more." Clinicians play a valuable role in helping parents to bring stuttering out of the closet and making it an acceptable topic of conversation. Clinicians can model an enlightened approach to an issue that is fascinating, help to alter the myths about stuttering, and mitigate the pain and humiliation so often and so unnecessarily experienced by young children and adolescents who stutter.

to as "special moments." After finishing the initial stage, the child's progress is assessed. If stuttering has not diminished, the more direct intervention components (interaction and family) are introduced over six sessions. Millard et al. (2009) and Millard et al. (2018) reported effective outcomes for the Palin PCI program, with reduced stuttering and increased parental knowledge and confidence, maintained up to 1 year posttherapy.

GOALS OF TREATMENT FOR YOUNGER SPEAKERS

A realistic goal of treatment, particularly with preschool-age children, is a high level of spontaneous or normal fluency (Conture, 2001; Guitar, 2006; Healey & Scott, 1995). The future for fluency is bright for such children who receive good, early

intervention. Of course, it is possible that some children could recover on their own without intervention. Depending on the weight the clinician places on the factors related to chronicity of stuttering described in Chapters 2 and 5, clinicians and parents might or might not opt for some formal assistance in facilitating fluency for these young speakers. The child's familial history of stuttering, as well as indications of the child's awareness and negative reactions toward his or her fluency breaks, will need to be considered. For preschool-age speakers it is reasonable to consider the frequency and quality of the child's disfluent speech as a primary indicator of successful change.

For the child who is somewhat older and undergoing the early stages of school and the socialization process, issues beyond basic measures of fluency are more likely to come into play. A short quote from Healey and Scott (1995) provides a broader view of the situation for these children:

> We are reluctant to base treatment effectiveness exclusively on pre and post-treatment fluency data. This seems to be a rather narrow definition of "success." Some children in our program have demonstrated increased levels of fluency but were unable to achieve a positive attitude about themselves as fluent speakers. (p. 153)

As with adolescents and adults, focusing on the child's fluency could provide the clinician with both a restricted view of the problem and a narrow definition of progress. However, there is little question that, even for young children, both affective and cognitive changes take place during effective therapy. It is not uncommon to encounter children who have stuttered for only a few weeks or months who demonstrate reactions of frustration, anger, and avoidance in response to their inability to easily produce speech. In any case, the monitoring of changes in these intrinsic features will provide the clinician with a broader view of progress and long-term success.

Other experienced researcher-clinicians (Conture, 2001; Guitar, 2006) also express the same comprehensive therapeutic view when assisting young children who are at the outset of stuttering. That is, along with a focus on reducing the frequency and form of stuttering, intervention also includes the goals of reducing negative feelings and thoughts about stuttering, decreasing avoidance, involving the parents in altering the child's environment, and enhancing the child's abilities and enjoyment associated with communicating.

Conture (2001) suggested that most children will take approximately 20 weeks (with a range of 10–30) of weekly therapy before they are ready for dismissal. He also advised, however, that clinicians should be careful not to force treatment into a family's busy schedule. The clinician should be prepared to give both the parents and the child an intermission from weekly treatment sessions and be available for consultation with the parents during such intervals. These children might be more likely to have a family history of fluency disorders or one or more other problems that make communicating or learning more complicated. In such cases, treatment could take somewhat longer.

A CONSIDERATION OF TREATMENT STRATEGIES

Although most current authors writing about treatment for young children recommend reasonably direct treatment, there is some question as to whether many practicing clinicians feel the same way. Based on several recent surveys of professional clinicians (see Chapter 1), some clinicians continue to be hesitant—or at least highly cautious—about working directly with young children who stutter. Whether the clinician chooses to work more or less directly with the younger child, the essence of treatment consists of some combination of both facilitating the child's capacities to produce effortless fluent speech and reducing the demands placed on the child that result in fluency disruption. As Starkweather (1999) suggested, "We can prevent the complexity of stuttering from developing, or if it has developed, we can undo it, untie the knots of frustration and struggle. And the younger the child is, the easier the knots are to untie" (p. 233). Certainly there will also be several associated goals, including desensitizing the child to the experience of stuttering, and increasing the child's resistance to fluency-disrupting stimuli.

It is also worth noting that many of the strategies and techniques used with adolescents and adults can be applied, in many cases with only minor alterations, to older school-age children. Of the two major strategies, various versions of fluency-enhancement approaches are most often used with younger speakers. Many stuttering modification techniques might also be appropriate depending on the level of struggle and emotional reactivity indicated by the child. Particularly with younger clients, the techniques associated with fluency enhancement and stuttering modification strategies become quite similar. Both strategies emphasize easy, often slowed, and smooth articulatory movements; light articulatory contacts; and attention to monitoring and producing consistent airflow and voicing. Perhaps most important, underlying these behavioral techniques is the cognitive set that the child is able to make choices and be in charge of his or her speaking mechanism.

Assisting the Child in Responding to Stuttering

For many children, particularly if they have been stuttering for a short time and have yet to incorporate high levels of avoidance behavior, modeling and instruction of fluency-enhancing techniques might be all that is needed to promote fluency. In other instances, the clinician might decide to also provide the child with strategies for helping him or her respond to stuttering in more positive ways. In order for the child to learn ways of changing the form

of his or her stuttering, it is essential to identify both the desirable and the less desirable characteristics of the fluency breaks. Some clinicians are undoubtedly concerned about using the "S" word (stuttering), and it is not uncommon for parents to avoid using the word *stuttering* in front of their children. Most clinicians and authors believe that referring to what the child is doing as stuttering is not a major issue with young children. Assigning unnecessary power to the word *stuttering* and making great effort to avoid its use is unnecessary (see Conture, 2001, p. 141). As Murphy (1999) suggested in his discussion of shame as it relates to stuttering, it is good for everyone to talk openly and forthrightly about stuttering. To the extent that we assign positive or negative value to any word, the word tends to become more powerful. However, using the word *stuttering* in a normal conversational manner is not, in and of itself, likely to make the situation worse. Whether the word *stuttering* is used or avoided, contrasting descriptors such as easy–difficult, slow–fast, gentle–hard, and smooth–bumpy are likely to be much more meaningful to a young child. These are also words that others (teachers, relatives, and friends) are less likely to interpret in a negative fashion.

One of the most efficient ways to identify and discriminate between different forms of fluency–disfluency is for the clinician to produce examples for the child. The style of the clinician when demonstrating these examples is important, and doing it in a matter-of-fact manner, with enthusiasm, curiosity, and a sense of fun is apt to be the best approach. Underlying these activities is the child's appreciation that he or she has the power to produce speech in a variety of forms. The contrasts between bumpy and fast versus easy and slow speech can be illustrated with body movements and toys. The clinician and the child can, for example, alternately tighten and relax various parts of their bodies (including the speech mechanisms), helping the child to differentiate between tightness and relaxation and giving the child a sense of control when using his or her "speech helpers." Both the clinician and the child can introduce intentional brief and easy stutters into their speech, experimenting and playing with alternative ways of easing or smoothing through them. It is not necessary to demonstrate extreme forms of stuttering—only a degree of mild tension and fragmentation is necessary to make the point. It is often especially instructive for the child to take the role of the "teacher" and direct the clinician (or the parents) as the adult speaker makes the suggested adjustments.

Of course, the primary goal of these activities is not fluency per se (although that is often the result) but the child's ability to vary and purposely control and vary his or her speech production (Williams, 1971). The child learns that he or she is not helpless and, in fact, has many choices about how to produce sounds and words. Once children are able to consistently alter their stuttering moments into easy, effortless productions, they will become able to revise real moments of stuttering in a similar fashion. The point is to assist the child in making the experience of speaking enjoyable while giving the child a sense of power over his or her speech, concepts that are emphasized by virtually all writers on the topic of treatment for young children.

Of course, it is important that parents understand the importance of highlighting their child's moments of difficult speech in a sensitive way and reward smooth and easy speech as it occurs. Parents can note such speech and respond with verbal praise, "Ah, that was easy (or smooth)!" or nonverbally, with a smile or eye contact, when they notice the child changing a bumpy form of speech into a smoother and easier version. However, Conture (2001) cautioned that not all parents will be able to do this without some observation and practice. He noted that some parents tend to reprimand, correct, nag, or badger the child regarding his or her speech. If this occurs it is best to demonstrate a better response by assisting the child in a gentle and appropriate manner. Without practice, some parents are likely to be inhibited about mentioning their child's stuttering or afraid of doing something wrong. Until they become desensitized, some parents will resist intentionally producing anything that resembles even easy and smooth stuttering in their own speech. The success of these experiences depends on the sensitivity of the clinician in guiding the parents toward a less reticent response when experimenting and "playing" with different forms of fluency.

Analogies that are appropriate for children can assist them in producing speech with an open and flowing vocal tract, often facilitating fluency and helping to alter the form of stuttering. As Conture explained, the creation of airflow in garden hose and balloon analogies (alternately constricting and releasing the flow of water or air) and lily pad analogy (lightly touching each sound or word while "talking across" the lily pads) enables the child to visualize the necessary flow of air and voicing as well as smooth and effortless speech production. For somewhat older children, it can be useful to use finger tapping (lightly touching the thumb and fingers while producing the sounds or syllables of a word) and gradually changing a tightly closed fist to an open hand corresponding to changing a voluntary (or real) moment of stuttering to effortless and forward-moving speech. A particularly appealing example of the closed fist to open hand example is demonstrated by Barry Guitar in the Stuttering Foundation video (#47), *The School-Age Child Who Stutters*. Williams's (1971) technique of instructing the child to momentarily "freeze" the stuttering for a moment followed by "moving on" into the following sequence of sounds and Conture's (2001) recommendations to the child to "change and move forward" are useful adaptations of stuttering-modification procedures suggested by Van Riper (1973) for older speakers. The many suggestions found in textbooks, pamphlets, and videos focus on suggesting and modeling for the young speaker ways to achieve airflow, voicing, and gentle, effortless movement of the articulators.

Also noteworthy is the concept of negative practice, whereby the child is asked to produce the very behavior we wish to alter. That is, rather than constantly urging the child to produce fluent speech, we are also requesting (and rewarding) examples of voluntary disruptions of fluency, and, importantly, showing the child that he or she has the ability to change the situation. The child, by using such suggestions, can become adept at releasing the struggled speech behavior and make the necessary transitional gestures that enable movement to subsequent sounds and syllables. As the clinician comes to know a child, terminology and analogies appropriate for the child's maturity can be selected to most effectively convey these principles.

Guitar (2006) suggested that young speakers who have been coping with stuttering for many years are likely to have incorporated responses that are characterized by avoidance and motivated by shame and embarrassment. Because of this possibility and depending on a variety of other factors including the age and maturity of the child, the severity of the stuttering, and the child's reaction to the experience of stuttering, therapeutic activities that address desensitization and cognitive restructuring about stuttering are likely to be important features of intervention. The case

CLINICAL INSIGHT

Although the clinician will be able to detect the many successes that the child is achieving as he or she is able to change his or her habitual forms of stuttering into less effortful and smoother forms, less sophisticated listeners are unlikely to take note of such success. Parents and teachers (and perhaps other family members and friends) can be taught that, although the child might continue to stutter for a time following the initiation of treatment, there are other indicators that provide evidence of important victories in the development of effortless stuttering and improved fluency, such as a slight slowing in the rate of repetitions, a continuation of airflow and voicing, an easy articulatory contact, and smooth transitioning through the sounds and syllables. To the extent that these important people in the child's life are able to appropriately respond to the child's increasing ability to make these changes during daily speaking situations, further success is enhanced.

study of a 9-year-old boy by Murphy et al. (2007a) provides a good example of ways to incorporate these features.

Noah, age 9, had a history of intermittent therapy, his score of 28 on the SSI-3 (Riley, 1994) was *severe*, his frequency of stuttering was 11 SLDs per 100 words, and his CAT-R (De Nil & Brutten, 1991) score (negative responses on 21 of 32 items) indicated strongly negative attitudes about communicating. Noah was coping with his stuttering by using many avoidance behaviors and was distraught as a result of being bullied by others at his school (a topic addressed later in this chapter). Murphy et al. described activities designed to assist Noah in becoming desensitized to stuttering and to cognitively restructure his response to his stuttering in order to use stuttering and fluency-modification techniques. Because Noah had been unwilling to use these behavioral techniques in the past, goals were designed to help him in becoming less sensitive to stuttering and to consider alternative responses to his experience with stuttering. The techniques were guided by the principle of approaching the problem and involved (a) learning key facts about stuttering in order to reduce Noah's uncertainty and increase his understanding; (b) learning about other people who stutter; (c) exploring and learning to tolerate his moments of stuttering (e.g., freezing and experimenting with variations of effort and movement as modeled by the clinician, including pseudo-stuttering with examples that were sillier and more extreme than those produced by the clinician); (d) changing negative to positive self-talk; and (e) self-acknowledgment to friends, his teacher, and his classmates. Noah brought several classmates to therapy to help them learn about stuttering and what he was doing to improve his speech. As a result of these activities, Noah was able to employ his speech management techniques in daily speaking situations beyond the treatment setting. Following these experiences, his scores on the SSI-3 were within the mild range, his frequency of stuttering decreased to 2% syllables stuttered, and his commu-

CLINICAL INSIGHT

In earlier chapters, we discussed the value of "using silence" and "leading from behind" in order to promote creativity and problem solving on the part of the speaker. There is real value in using similar strategies with younger speakers. For example, clinicians can ask the child to instruct them about how to do various techniques, often feigning misunderstanding ("You want me to do what?" or "Why do you want me to say it like that?") in order to encourage the child to demonstrate and expand his or her understanding of a technique. The clinician could pause, not responding immediately to a client's statement, encouraging the child to take action by reinterpreting or elaborating his or her question. Or the clinician might ask the parent or the child a question such as, "What do you think we should do next?" Such actions by the clinician, even early in the treatment process, set the tone for the transference of problem solving by the parents and the child beyond the treatment setting and facilitate the eventual maintenance of behavioral and cognitive changes following formal treatment.

nication attitudes approached those of normally fluent children of his age on the CAT-R. Noah's satisfaction with his speech was self-evaluated as an 8 on a scale ranging from 1 to 10 (in contrast to ratings of 1 and 3 prior to the initiation of therapy). Finally, his teacher reported that Noah was talking more in class (even if he did not choose to use his management techniques) and no longer using avoidance behaviors.

Ramig and Bennett (1995) provided a list of suggestions for the clinician, parents, and teachers when using a stuttering modification approach with younger children. They indicated that the clinician can do the following:

1. Explain the nature of the speech production system to the child and the parents, providing the child with understanding and the means of manipulating fluency.
2. Illustrate the physical behaviors associated with the child's smooth and bumpy fluency, using terms that the child can understand.
3. Show the child how to vary his or her speaking behaviors by adjusting his or her levels of effort. Making use of modeling (including bumpy fluency), the clinician and the child can explore ways of altering the features affiliated with effortful and disrupted fluency, gradually working in the direction of easier, forward-moving fluency breaks. The child's speech does not have to become completely fluent, but simply easier and smoother. Gregory (1989), for example, suggested that after a child experiences a difficult and tense moment of stuttering, the clinician should direct the child to produce the word again, this time reducing the tension by half. The incorporation of fluency initiating gestures at this point is

a good example of how the two general strategies can be intertwined during treatment with young children.
4. Discuss, with the child leading the way, strategies for responding to people and situations that arise in the child's world. Together, the clinician and the child (as well as parents and teachers) can role-play responding to teasing, participating in social and class activities, relaxing in preparation for stressful situations, changing negative into positive self-talk, using visualizations and positive affirmations, and responding to time pressures.
5. Help the child and his or her parents to prepare for the possibility of relapse by considering responses to possible increases in fear, avoidance behavior, struggle behavior, and fluency breaks. The clinician, the child, and his or her parents can discuss self-assessment procedures as well as prescribe possible responses.
6. Develop a schedule for the maintenance and use of both stuttering modification and fluency-maintaining skills in real-world contexts.

Assisting the Child in Producing Fluent Speech

Techniques for creating and promoting fluency go by several names. These techniques have been called fluency-initiating gestures (FIGs), fluency-enhancing techniques, fluency-facilitating movements, and easy speech. Regardless of the names for these techniques, they consist of procedures described in the previous chapter concerning older speakers that also assist the child in more efficiently managing fluent speech production (e.g., efficiently using the breath stream and vocal folds, creating lighter articulatory contact and movement, smoothing the transitions from one sound or syllable to another). Conture (2001, pp. 193–210) provided a variety of useful suggestions for explaining the nature of constricted versus open and smooth production in ways that children will understand, including the use of cursive writing as an analogy for slow and easy speech production. The child is shown how to smoothly make writing movements transitioning between letters at the same time that he or she is saying the sounds or syllables of the word. Not only is the clinician able to demonstrate the value of easy and flowing (vs. hard and erratic) movement during serial motor tasks, but the activity also provides an opportunity to show the child that speech is something he or she is producing rather than something that is happening to him or her. Of course, in order to make the activities enjoyable for the child, the clinician can incorporate puppets, games, or cartoon pictures with these activities. The clinician can choose from a wide variety of therapy techniques designed for children found in many sources, including Guitar (2006), Ramig and Dodge (2005), and Reitzes (2006).

One way to provide the child with a sense of his or her ability to create the necessary ingredients for fluency could be a sequence of solo, tangential, and interactive forms of play combined with sound production. For example, as the clinician and the child play separately with their own sets of toys (solo play), the clinician begins to model nonspeech sounds associated with the toys (sounds of animals, trains, and airplanes). Gradually, the clinician moves to producing one-word utterances to describe the movements. Little or no emphasis is placed on the child com-

municating; the focus is on the child's enjoyment when producing sounds and one- and two-syllable utterances. The clinician next begins to create minimal interactions with the child, briefly commenting on the child's activities with the toys. As the child becomes increasingly interactive, the activities become more cooperative, allowing for the playing of games. Still, the emphasis is on having fun and enjoying the experience of producing speech. This sequence of activities was originally presented by Van Riper (1973), and various interpretations were also presented by Conture (1990) and Shapiro (1999). As Conture suggested, games provide the opportunity to move into cooperative play and experience turn-taking during verbalization. The clinician can then begin to direct the level of communicative demand and model a variety of other interactive activities. Guitar (2006) suggested that this form of gradually increased interaction can be particularly helpful for children who are reluctant to separate from their parents or who refuse to talk with the clinician.

It is interesting to note that although children usually respond with greater fluency to slower and less complex speech produced by the parent or the clinician, the reasons for this effect are not well understood. Although there are a few investigations (each with relatively few participants) suggesting that modeling of slower speech by a parent is likely to result in greater fluency by children, Bernstein Ratner (1993, 2004) noted that such advice is universal and often suggested in the major training texts. Although slower speech by the parent might result in the child becoming somewhat more fluent, it is not understood why this is often the case. Bernstein Ratner suggested that it could be that a request to slow speech production assists in the motor planning and motor sequencing of sounds and syllables as well as decreasing self-imposed time pressure to complete the utterance.

It also could be that the pragmatic aspects of communication come into play more than the actual complexity of language. For example, Weiss and Zebrowski (1992) found that responsive utterances were significantly more likely to be produced fluently than assertive utterances. Although it is commonly suggested to parents that they model less complex speech and language for their nonfluent child, this has received little empirical support. Bernstein Ratner (2004) suggested that because the sophistication of linguistic input by the parents is a strong predictor of the child's subsequent language profiles, such modeling should not be recommended. More general approaches for both increasing the child's tolerance for and modifying communicative disruptors (interruptions, aggressive overtalking by others, lack of patient interest in the child when he or she is talking, overstimulation—particularly when the child is tired) might be more helpful components of successful intervention with young children who stutter.

Finally, Bloodstein et al. (2021) emphasized that the clinician should make it clear to the parents that recommendations for altering their communication style do not suggest that they are the source of the child's fluency problem. However, as with many other physical, academic, or social issues their child will encounter, the parents' thoughtful and supportive response to stuttering will improve the situation.

Another way to conceptualize treatment for a young speaker in the early stages of stuttering is to consider the demands and capacities (Starkweather & Gottwald, 1990) described earlier. That is, the clinician can determine what capaci-

ties are likely to increase the child's ability to produce fluent speech and facilitate the child's ability to achieve a sense of mastery over a speech-production system that is still in the process of maturation. In some cases, an initial response could involve adjusting communicative and environmental patterns in the home. Many of these behaviors (slow rate, more leisurely turn-taking, shorter utterances, and more frequent use of paraphrase) are already characteristic of parental- or child-directed speech (Bernstein Ratner, 1993). Gottwald and Starkweather (1995) provided a succinct description of this combined approach, including the goals of fluency enhancement, reduction of demands, and desensitization of the child to normal fluency breaks:

Depending on the child's specific needs, the clinician may use a reduced speech rate, many silent periods and pause times, and the language stimulation techniques of self-talk and parallel talk, but at a slow rate. Also, the clinician may reduce the number of language demands made on the child, including limiting questions requiring omplex answers and reducing implied expectations for ongoing oral communication. Finally, the clinician will use normal disfluencies, such as whole word and phrase repetitions. (p. 122)

Fluency-enhancing procedures provide the child with techniques for creating and expanding fluency. Ideally, the speech that is to be expanded and rewarded should have high-quality fluency that is characterized by smooth and effortless production rather than unstable movements. As with adults, it is good to keep in mind that the achievement of fluency should be enjoyable and empowering. The videos produced by the Stuttering Foundation provide concrete examples of how to implement many useful fluency-enhancing techniques. Underlying the documented success of therapy for younger speakers are the same principles that inform successful therapy for adolescents and adults. A successful therapeutic experience for younger speakers is enhanced to an extent by the clinician who:

1. understands the nature of stuttering and is willing to help the young speaker to experiment with and vary forms of nonfluent speech;
2. provides a supportive therapeutic experience that allows the child to become desensitized to and explore the characteristics of his or her stuttering;
3. enables the child to understand the basic features of speech production and promotes the child's ability to control these features, resulting in effortless and forward-flowing speech; and
4. elicits the understanding and support of parents and other important individuals in the child's daily environment.

Guitar (2006) described the concept of *superfluency*, an idea that seems particularly useful with older children who have been stuttering continuously into early adolescence. This idea involves four basic skills that parallel the fluency-shaping targets for older speakers described in Chapter 12. The skills are first modeled by the clinician, who then refines the child's responses. Guitar suggested that these skills can be introduced in any sequence, although, depending on the child, they are usually introduced according to those that are easiest for the child. *Flexible rate* involves showing the child how to slow the production of the initial syllables of a word or syllable on which the child expects to stutter (rather than slowing down all words in the utterance). All of the sounds in the word or syllable are slowed and lengthened, as is the transition to the subsequent sounds. *Easy onsets* emphasize the gradual onset of voicing (and the necessary airflow) rather than a sudden glottal attack. Physical movements with toys or bodily movements are often helpful to convey the concept. *Light contacts* for modeling easy articulatory postures (rather than pushing through an effortful stuck position) can be practiced on all types of sounds, many of which require a slightly distorted (but desired) production to create and maintain the light contact (particularly for plosives). *Proprioception* and heightened feedback for the locations and degree of contact and associated articulatory movements are used for both nonspeech and speech sounds. The sensory feedback can be heightened with exaggerated or slowed movements, closing the eyes, or using masking noise. The components of superfluency are gradually expanded, initially using three-word sentences with considerable modeling by the clinician and then with longer sentences and progressively less modeling by the clinician. Although the purpose is to use superfluency as stuttered words are anticipated, the child might also want to use these techniques on words where stuttering is not anticipated. The final goal is to increase the child's confidence in his or her ability to replace reflexive patterns of stuttering with these superfluent responses in progressively more difficult speaking situations beyond the therapy setting.

By using fluency-facilitating activities, the clinician assists the child in reaching a basal level of fluency in the treatment setting. Fluency-disrupting activities are then gradually introduced (e.g., listener loss, time pressure, and greater linguistic demands). As the child's fluency becomes unstable—but prior to the point at which a child will produce fluency breaks—the clinician minimizes the disrupting activities. As a result of these procedures, the child will gradually be able to increase his or her tolerance and will become "toughened" to various forms of demands, including communicative stress (Van Riper, 1973).

Beyond the specific techniques used, Ramig and Bennett (1995) provided a list of suggestions for the clinician, parents, and teachers when using a fluency-modification approach with younger school-age children. The clinician, parents, and teachers who are assisting the child can do the following:

1. Use basic and understandable terms when explaining and demonstrating what they want the child to do. Whatever terms are selected by the clinician (or better yet, the child) for describing the quality of the child's fluency (e.g., "easy" or "turtle speech," or "bumpy" or "rabbit speech"), they should be used consistently when identifying and rewarding target behaviors.
2. Regardless of the methods used, children need to have terms and concepts that enable them to conceptualize their ability to produce speech and language (Cooper & Cooper, 1991).
3. Model (rather than instruct) the child about how to perform target behaviors.
4. Model slow and easy speech when interacting with the child in a variety of treatment and extra-treatment settings.
5. Model slow and easy body movements when interacting with the child, again in a variety of treatment and extra-treatment settings. These movements can be coordinated with easy, slow, and smooth speech movements. Such activities are especially good to

use at the outset and end of treatment sessions.
6. Reinforce the child's accomplishments and feelings of self-worth in the context of as many experiences as possible.

COUNSELING RECOMMENDATIONS FOR PARENTS AND CHILDREN

Parents of children who stutter receive great benefit from counseling that emphasizes an understanding and a corresponding reduction of their anxiety concerning stuttering. During treatment sessions the clinician can provide the parents with valuable models, not only for facilitating behavioral change but also for creating an open, uninhibited style of addressing the cognitive and affective experiences of stuttering with their child. One primary goal is to help the parents make stuttering a topic that can be tolerated and discussed. Small group meetings of parents of children who are attending treatment provide a forum for developing an uninhibited attitude about discussing their child's stuttering and for providing supportive reassurance for the parents' active participation in therapy. In a related matter, it is important to appreciate that children are apt to feel pressure to speak fluently when talking to their parents. Older children, in particular, are apt to recognize that parents are anticipating a successful result from the effort and cost of therapy. Although spontaneous and effortless fluency is a realistic outcome, parents can also learn to recognize and appreciate easy and smoother forms of stuttering. Such understanding and attitudes about stuttering as modeled by the clinician and adopted by the parents are infinitely better than the "conspiracy of silence" recommended in the past.

For children who have been stuttering for a year or two, and especially those children who have experienced the socialization process associated with attending school, counseling is likely to be helpful and possibly essential. The relatively lack of sources that specifically describe counseling with young children who stutter (rather than their parents) could be due to the view that children are too young to benefit from counseling or the acknowledged discomfort that many speech-language pathologists have with regard to conducting counseling activities with children who stutter (DiLollo & Manning, 2007; Luterman, 2017; Shames, 2006). Although children might be aware of the breaks in their fluency and, in fact, associate negative feelings with that difficulty (Vanryckeghem et al., 2005), these emotions are not likely to be well developed or firmly established. This could help to explain the natural recovery for many young speakers as well as the success of treatment approaches intended to modify the speaking patterns of preschool children.

To one degree or another, most older children and adolescents are in the process of attaching negative feelings of shame and fear to their attempts to communicate. They are apt to be adjusting to their predicament by elaborating ever more sophisticated coping behaviors manifested by an overall pattern of avoidance and a restricted lifestyle. This is not to say that all children who stutter experience unhappy or unaccomplished lives. Their daily activities, though, particularly as they relate to verbally connecting with others and establishing themselves as autonomous individuals, are apt to be considerably more difficult than they would otherwise be.

Logan and Yaruss (1999) provided a comprehensive approach for helping clinicians and parents respond to the cognitive and affective features of stuttering in young children. They described modeling and listening activities that help parents respond to their children's stuttering that not only facilitate fluency but also an improved response to the emotional and attitudinal features of the stuttering experience.

With the clinician leading the way, parents can become truly desensitized to stuttering behavior in general and their child's pattern of stuttering in particular. Following the principle of approaching rather than avoiding the occurrences of stuttering as described in Chapter 10, parents can become comfortable enough to begin showing interest and curiosity about their child's stuttering behaviors. Examples of modeling behaviors by the parents include practice (by role-playing with the clinician) of a calm, objective, and interested response to their child's stuttering. As parents become aware of their feelings about stuttering, they are better able to stay in the moment and openly discuss possible responses to their child's speech, such as experimenting with purposely producing a variety of hard or easy fluency breaks as described earlier by Murphy et al. (2007a).

With experience, parents can evaluate and monitor their nonverbal responses to stuttering. The parents' mindset about what stuttering is and what it is not will begin to change for the better. They will be able to model easy, open, and relaxed fluency breaks in their own speech. They will be able to show their child that it is possible to discuss stuttering and speaking in general in an open and matter-of-fact manner rather than taking an all-or-none view about fluency and stuttering. Daily ratings of their child's fluency enable the parents to play an active role in documenting changes in the frequency and quality of their child's speech. Parents can become better listeners and learn to affirm their child regardless of whether or not stuttering is occurring; they can reassure and encourage their child regardless of their child's level of fluency. Parent support groups (either via meetings or a telephone network) are extremely useful in helping parents to understand that they are not alone and that their feelings about their child's stuttering are both natural and acceptable. Although there are many options for parents who want to help their child, often only a few of these will be necessary.

Another important feature of programs designed for children who stutter is the development of problem-solving skills (Gregory, 1986; Riley & Riley, 2000). With the clinician as a model, children are shown how to evaluate their usual ways of thinking about themselves and their problems, including, of course, their stuttering. As a result of the therapy experience, children should be able to provide more objective descriptions of their speech behavior and, depending on the age of the child, listener reactions. Beyond the achievement of increased fluency, are there indications that the child is experiencing a sense of command or power as he or she plays and experiments with different forms of fluency? Can the clinician find indicators that the child is beginning to change the interpretation of himself or herself and his or her overall problem-solving abilities? Such indicators could take the form of comments to the clinician, parents, or teachers. The child might demonstrate increased participation in class and social activities. Subtle changes might appear in drawings or comments recorded in a journal. The clinician or the parents might be able to identify in the

child an increase in positive rather than negative self-talk related to many activities, as well as a more agentic view about his or her behavior and choices. As Logan and Yaruss (1999) reported, as a result of therapeutic change, children also show more sophisticated coping reactions to other forms of adversity and stress, a response we have also noted with adults.

It is worth noting the comments about the development of expertise in Chapter 1, as well as Ham's (1999) advice that the accomplished clinician needs to be aware of many approaches. Children as well as adults will respond in unique ways to different therapeutic approaches. Furthermore, as we discussed in earlier chapters, the influence of any approach will always be somewhat different because of the characteristics of the clinician who is delivering the treatment as well as the child receiving it. As Starkweather (1999) stated,

> The technique that works so dramatically for one child does not necessarily work dramatically, or at all, for other children. Stuttering is so variable and so highly individualized that, few would disagree, no one method works for all children. (p. 235)

Clinicians who employ fluency-shaping strategies are likely to tabulate the resulting decrease in %SS or corresponding increase in fluent utterances. For some approaches, these tabulations are often the major (or only) criteria for moving a child from one step of the program to another. The emphasis in most fluency-shaping strategies is to reward periods of fluency and (less frequently) comment on or highlight instances of stuttering. As we have seen, however, analysis of these programs indicates that there are critical elements of support and reassurance taking place by

CLINICAL DECISION MAKING

How is the clinician to know whether or not to ask children about their concerns regarding their speech? As described in Chapter 2, children are not as likely as adults to describe their frustrations and fear related to the experience of stuttering but rather to show it in other ways (pitch rise; cessation of airflow or voicing; substitution of the schwa vowel; or avoidance of sound, words, and speaking situations). A few years ago, a friend of mine, who is an accomplished clinician, told me of a telephone call she received from another speech-language pathologist who worked with children who stutter. The caller explained that she had worked for several months with a young child who stuttered and had been able to teach him several techniques for achieving fluency. However, despite the child's ability to understand and use the fluency-enhancing techniques, he continued to be anxious about speaking and stuttered on many occasions both in and out of the clinical setting. Her question to my friend was whether or not it might be a good idea to "do emotions" with this child. Chances are that to some degree at least, all children who stutter are bothered by the experience. If the child is not highly reactive to the stuttering experience, the clinician might not need to spend much time "doing emotions." In most cases, however, spending time on the affective and cognitive aspects of the stuttering experience is an essential part of the treatment process from the outset and will be well worth the effort.

the clinician and the parent. In a straightforward and uninhibited manner, the adult helps the child to objectively identify the features of both stuttered and fluent speech. The child begins to understand that he or she has a choice about ways of speaking.

Some clinicians emphasize a stuttering-modification approach, which is characterized by a less structured interaction between the clinician and the child. This approach tends to place somewhat less emphasis on tabulating percentages of stuttering and greater emphasis on the child's cognitive and affective response to speaking. Depending on the age, maturity, and temperament of the child; the nature of the stuttering; the extent of parental participation; and the child's response to treatment, many clinicians use a combination of both fluency-enhancing and stuttering-modification strategies often employed with older speakers. The therapeutic approach selected for a particular child is also apt to be influenced by the clinicians' academic and clinical background as well as their clinical experience and interactive style. Certainly, it is appropriate for clinicians to have allegiance to a particular protocol, but, in fact, experienced clinicians are likely to adapt protocols, sometimes providing a direct instruction for rewarding fluency and highlighting moments of stuttering while at other times providing indirect modeling and suggestions for promoting fluency and cognitive and affective change. Undoubtedly, the enthusiasm and optimism of the clinician also plays a critical role when implementing any empirically informed (or validated) treatment.

Treatment approaches for preschool children who stutter contain several common factors that clinicians can draw from in planning treatment strategies for individual children. Although there are exceptions, clinicians using virtually all programs include activities designed to achieve the following goals:

- Enhancing the child's enjoyment of speaking
- Improving the child's self-confidence as a communicator
- Facilitating an active role for the parents
- Making certain that the child enjoys the therapy activities
- Providing the child with verbal praise or tangible rewards for success (easier forms of stuttering or fluency)
- Modeling easier forms of speech with good airflow, an open vocal tract, and light articulatory contacts
- Moving from less to more complex utterances (both motorically and linguistically)
- Altering fluency-disrupting factors in the child's environment (time pressure, overtalking by others, self-imposed demands for fluency)
- Desensitizing the child to fluency-disrupting factors (including teasing and bullying)

RESPONDING TO TEASING AND BULLYING

For some younger speakers, and certainly for older individuals, *shame* is one of the major affective features of the stuttering experience that influence their overall self-interpretation (Bloodstein et al., 2021; Cor-

coran & Stewart, 1998; Murphy, 1999; Plexico et al., 2005). As Murphy (1999) pointed out, teasing is one of the ways that the emotion of shame becomes attached to stuttering. A major aspect of shame is our interpretation of how we are viewed by others. A feeling of shame can pervade the individual's self-concept and typically results in a high degree of social inhibition and the desire to avoid or hide from others. In contrast, the feeling of *guilt* is generally associated with a particular behavior or act and is less apt to influence a person's self-concept (Murphy, 1999). Shame typically originates in the reactions of others in a child's environment, including parents, classmates, and teachers.

Comprehensive reviews of investigations by Boyle and Blood (2015) and Blood and Blood (2016) indicate that individuals with disabilities—including those who stutter—are more likely to experience victimization than their peers. Blood and Blood (2016) surveyed 36 adults who stuttered in order to determine the extent that recalled childhood victimization could be associated with psychosocial problems later in life. The Retrospective Bully Questionnaire (RBQ; Schafer et al., 2004) was completed by the people who stuttered and a matched group (gender, race, age, socioeconomic status) of 36 adults who did not stutter. Both groups were made up of 31 males.

Participants in the control group indicated no personal history or family history of stuttering. Participants were asked to indicate when the bullying took place (primary, secondary, university school years), whether they were bullied in one or more ways (physical, verbal, relational, or cyber), and the frequency and intensity of the bullying. Respondents also indicated their role in the bullying experience across five categories (bullied others, victim, bully-victim, bystander, uninvolved) as well as the frequency of the events. All participants also completed four psychosocial scales, the Social Interaction Anxiety Scale (SIAS; Mattick & Clarke, 1998), the Brief Fear of Negative Evaluation-S scale (BNFE; Watson & Friend, 1969), the Rosenberg Self-Esteem Scale (RSES; Rosenberg, 1965, 1979), and the Satisfaction With Life Scale (SWLS; Diener et al., 1985).

The results yielded several interesting outcomes. Regardless of whether they stuttered or not, the adults who recalled being victims of bullying scored the highest (poorer psychosocial scores) on all four scales. Nearly 88% of the nonstutterers and 100% of the people who stuttered with higher anxiety scores were determined to be victims based on their recollection of bullying incidences during their schooling. Those who stuttered scored significantly higher than those who did not on the SIAS, significantly higher on the BFNE, and significantly higher on the SWLS. No significant difference was found between the two groups for the RSES.

The majority of participants were in the bystanders' category (55.6% for those who stuttered and 66.7% for those who did not), a category that increased with age from primary school through university environments. Only 2.8% of those who stuttered were in the bully category, whereas 11.0% of the people who did not stutter were in the bully category, indicating that those who stuttered were less likely to bully others than the fluent individuals. Accordingly, 30.6% of the people who stuttered were in the victim category, with only 13.9% of those who did not in this category. The category of victim status for the persons who stuttered did show decreases from primary school (30.6%), to secondary school (27.8%), to the university setting (11.1%). The authors summarized their findings by saying that childhood victimization, certainly common for children who stutter, could result in an enduring effect for both groups of participants. Beyond having to cope with their communication problems, the stuttering children also have to deal with stigmatization and are also likely to have to deal with being targeted by bullies, possibilities that professionals who interact with the children should understand.

Murphy et al. (2007b) suggested the utility of making a distinction between teasing and bullying. Citing Tattum (1989) and Coloroso (2003), Murphy et al. (2007b) defined bullying as the conscious effort of someone to hurt or control another person. Teasing, on the other hand, is described as "an enjoyable, often good-natured exchange between friends, without the intention of being hurtful" (p. 140). Murphy et al. also described the many negative emotional effects of bullying that could include emotional (lowered self-esteem, depression, loneliness, anxiousness, and insecurities), academic (negative feelings about school, school dropout, social failure), and physical problems. Of course, children are likely to be bullied about a variety of physical or personal characteristics. Nonetheless, for the child who stutters, the behaviors associated with the struggle to speak provide an obvious and sensitive target. The child who stutters could also be a relatively safe target, as disfluent children might be unable to provide a verbal retort to the bully. In fact, taunting often results in increased stuttering (Blood & Blood, 2004).

Murphy et al.'s (2007b) case study of a young boy, Noah, described earlier in this chapter indicates that the primary impetus for his return to treatment was his experience of being bullied by his peers at school and on the school bus. The authors described an intervention strategy designed to assist Noah in developing effective responses to those who bullied him, at the same time educating others about stuttering and the consequences of bullying. With the clinician's help, Noah first learned to distinguish between statements that were clearly intended to be hurtful ("Hey, stutterhead!") and normal inquisitive comments ("Why do you talk that way?"). As the clinician validated Noah's concerns and at the same time indicated empathy for his experiences, Noah learned to assess what the children were actually saying and to differentiate statements that were intended as hurtful from those that indicated a natural curiosity. Noah was instructed about the nature of bullying and the nature of those who tend to do it; although some might be well liked, many children who bully others have low self-esteem, insecurity, and low self-confidence. As Murphy et al. pointed out, it is not unusual for bullies to come from hostile environments or homes where they are neglected (Olweus, 1993).

Because role-playing activities can be especially useful for approaching and becoming desensitized to particularly aversive situations, this was a major part of the program described by Murphy et al. (2007b). Noah and the clinician alternately took both sides of a bullying situation, and a wide range of possible responses were brainstormed and practiced. Primary goals were to create coping responses that Noah could rely on and to assist him in achieving a sense of control over the situation. Although all possible responses were considered, several that have been shown to be less effective for bullies were discouraged. For example, crying or ignoring the situation might escalate the bully's attempts to get a reaction. Although it is an instinctive response for some children, for many reasons physically fighting back is not likely to be helpful in the long run. For some children, clever or humorous retorts might be effective, but for the child who experiences considerable disfluency when being ridiculed, this, too, is unlikely to be helpful.

Role-playing activities also provide the child with the opportunity to vent his or her frustration and anger. For example, the clinician and the child can take turns giving and receiving specific taunts. The child is usually then able to become desensitized to the expected comments and to discuss alternative responses. The child also might be able to diffuse or redirect the sting of the comments by overt acceptance of his or her stuttering (Guitar, 2006; Van Riper, 1973) and acknowledging the obvious, thereby diffusing the situation. Guitar (2006) suggested that a forthright statement such as, "I know I stutter, but I'm working on it" (p. 367) could disarm the bully. Murphy et al. (2007b) cited the work of Cooper (2000), who provided a variety of possible responses to hurtful comments such as the "shrug" response (the child with an accompanying shrug says, "I don't care" or "So what?"), a "broken record" response (consistent repetitions of "Because I want to"), or the "mighty might" response (consistent responses of "You might be right"). Murphy (1999), citing Crosby (1997), suggested that for a child who is likely to be disfluent in such a situation, a consistent response of "So?" might be particularly fitting. If children are mature enough and reasonably fluent, they could respond to imitations of their stuttering by saying something such as, "Look, if you're going to stutter you ought to learn how to do it correctly. Prolong the first sound like this and add a little more tension. If you get really good at it and you're brave enough, see if you can do it with me at school tomorrow."

The second major goal of the strategy designed by Murphy et al. (2007b) was to assist Noah in educating his classmates and others about stuttering and the effects of bullying. The major focus was on the development of a classroom presentation to Noah's classmates. The activity has many advantages, including putting the child in the position of an expert (Blood & Blood, 2004; Murphy, 1998, 1999), and accomplishing self-acknowledgment of stuttering and desensitization (Dell, 1993; Ramig & Dodge, 2005; Reardon & Yaruss, 2004). Murphy et al. (2007b) suggested that the response of most individuals to those who stutter will improve as the nature of stuttering becomes less mysterious and better understood.

The rationale and advantages of a class presentation will need to be explained to the child's parents and teachers, who will, of course, be closely involved in the stages leading up to the presentation. Although for some children the challenge might be daunting, the process is broken into steps that are incorporated in the treatment sessions (e.g., presentations to the clinician, the child's parents, the teacher, groups of selected students). As described in detail by Murphy et al. (2007b), the clinician and child can make a series of videos of experimenting with different versions of the presentation. Murphy et al. provided an extensive sequence of topics that can be included in the presentation. Describing the heroic life stories of famous people who stutter and have achieved great success (see the Stuttering Home Page for links: http://www.mnsu.edu/comdis/kuster/stutter.html) is a good place to begin. Other topics include the nature of stuttering, examples of therapy

CLINICAL DECISION MAKING

A few years ago, a 13-year-old girl whose speech was characterized by both stuttering and cluttering sought our help. Like Noah, the primary reason she asked her parents to seek a clinician was her profoundly negative reaction to the bullying of others (primarily two boys at her school). For the most part, she was unwilling to discuss her experiences of being bullied and on those occasions when she did, she would begin to cry. Following some minimally successful attempts to role-play her experiences, I suggested that she try to write about one or more of her experiences and her reactions to what had occurred. I stipulated, however, that whatever she wrote was "for your eyes only"; there was no suggestion that she show her thoughts to her parents or to me. I was hoping that the experience of journaling would help to organize her thoughts about her experience. I was especially hopeful that the act of putting her thoughts on paper would help her to externalize, objectify, and achieve some distance from her experience. Not only was she able to create a written description of and begin to reinterpret the events but also, within a few weeks, took pride in showing her parents and me what she had written. We still had some work to do on her fluency, but a major barrier to progress had been diminished. (WM) techniques, ways to respond to stuttering, the experience of being bullied, and how to handle bullying.

Obviously, the classroom teacher should ensure that bullying in the classroom is off-limits. However, there will be situations where the teacher will be unable to prevent this behavior by other children. Certainly, the teacher or parent could discuss the injustice of such behavior with those involved. Of course, this is not always helpful and, in some instances, might increase the problem. Another possibility is to ask an adult who has undergone successful treatment to speak to the class. Volunteers for interesting and informative explanations about stuttering can be found through nearby clinics or local chapters of self-help groups. Such speaking opportunities are often welcomed by these individuals, who are often more than pleased to practice their public-speaking skills.

There is a wealth of good information and suggestions contained in several publications that have been designed specifically for assisting with problems created by children who stutter being bullied (Cooper, 2000; Dell, 1993; Langevin, 2000; Langevin et al., 2007; Reardon & Yaruss, 2004; Yaruss et al., 2004).

Based on empirically supported antistigma procedures in the psychology literature that have been employed for individuals with mental illness, Boyle et al. (2016) were the first to evaluate and compare validated antistigma approaches for persons who stutter. The authors randomly assigned 212 adults to one of three antistigma conditions and a control condition. The majority of the participants (69%) were White women ranging in age from 18 to 78. Prior to and after experiencing one of four 4- to 5-minute Internet-based videos, the participants completed a survey about stereotypes, negative emotional reactions, social distance, discriminatory intentions, and empowerment concerning people who stutter. A portion of the participants (132) also completed the survey again 1 week following the posttest. The survey categories and questions were derived from empirically validated antistigma strategies and socially valid outcome measures. The four conditions were categorized as follows:

1. *Contact:* An adult who stuttered (14% stuttered words) described his personal story composed of four components—a discussion of past and current struggles due to stuttering; an "on-the-way-up story" that included successful outcomes; an affirming, goal statement for what the audience should take away from the presentation; and an overall respectful tone.

2. *Education:* The speaker contrasted seven myths about stuttering (e.g., less intelligent or capable, more nervous, best to think about what you want to say, take a breath).

3. *Protest:* The speaker condemned a variety of inappropriate responses to stuttering (mocking, inappropriate media characterizations, stereotyping of those who stutter).

4. *Control:* The speaker provided information about famous artists of the 20th century with no information about stuttering or other communication disorders.

Each of the three antistigma conditions were significantly more effective than the control condition for decreasing negative emotions, negative stereotypes, discriminatory intentions, and increasing empowerment. Changes in social distance were not significant. Contact had the greatest positive effect for increasing affirming attitudes about people who stutter from pretest to posttest and pretest to follow-up. Post hoc testing indicated that contact, education, and protest resulted in significantly greater reduction in negative stereotypes versus the control condition. Education resulted in significantly greater reduction in negative stereotypes than contact or protest. The authors suggested that in vivo contact would further increase the effect of the antistigma experience by providing the participants the opportunity to ask questions and interact with the speaker, an outcome found by Flynn and St. Louis (2011). The authors concluded that contact is the optimal approach for increasing affirming and empowering attitudes about those who stutter. The four components of this approach also provide a strategy for individuals who stutter to disclose and discuss their stuttering with others, possibly resulting in decreased public stigma associated with stuttering.

CHILDREN WITH COEXISTING PROBLEMS

Although it has often been noted that children with fluency disorders tend to have other communication problems, both Nippold (1990) and Bernstein Ratner (1997) suggested that it is best to think of children who have cooccurring problems (particularly language and phonological or articulatory problems) as subgroups of children who stutter. Blood and Seider (1981) reported that 68% of 1,060 children being treated for stuttering in elementary schools had other speech, language, hearing, or learning problems. Most often noted is the frequent cooccurrence of articulation and phonological problems (Blood & Seider, 1981; Bloodstein & Bernstein Ratner, 2008;

Conture, 2001; Daly, 1981; Louko et al., 1990; Paden et al., 1999; Riley & Riley, 1979; Schwartz & Conture, 1988; St. Louis & Hinzman, 1986; Thompson, 1983; Williams & Silverman, 1968; Yairi et al., 1996). Daly (1981) also found that more than half of children being seen for fluency intervention also have articulation disorders. Just how these other communication problems relate to the onset or maintenance of stuttering is unclear. It is clear that the experience of communicating with others is apt to be a challenge for these children. Depending on the reactivity of a child faced with this situation, it is not surprising that the stuttering could be more severe, and that remediation could be somewhat more complex for these speakers.

The cooccurrence of fluency disorders and language impairment is less well documented but also has been noted (Blood & Seider, 1981; Louko et al., 1990; St. Louis & Hinzman, 1986; St. Louis et al., 1991). More recent studies have indicated subtle or nonclinical differences (Bloodstein et al., 2021) or that young children who stutter are no more likely to also have depressed language abilities than their fluent peers (Bonelli et al., 2000; Watkins et al., 1999). Furthermore, the presence of coexisting disorders might not always be apparent at the outset of treatment. For example, a child's language impairment might only become evident after fluency has improved (Merits-Patterson & Reed, 1981).

TWO EFFECTS OF COEXISTING PROBLEMS

There are two basic issues the clinician will want to consider with coexisting communication problems. First, it has been observed by some clinical researchers that, on occasion, children who are being treated for language disorders become more disfluent as a consequence of treatment (Conture, 1990; Merits-Patterson & Reed, 1981; Meyers et al., 1990). They also suggest that if a child is receiving treatment for severe articulation problems or unusual phonological problems, the possibility of stuttering onset could be increased. Treatment for articulation or language impairments also might precipitate fluency breaks if children are placed in treatment too early. That is, premature treatment might require the child to improve his or her articulation before he or she is capable of producing sounds correctly with relative ease and without excessive scanning or effort. As a result, treatment demands could exceed the child's still-limited capacities for producing speech fluently, something Conture (1990) suggested is more likely to occur for children who are approximately 5 to 6 years old:

> We are inclined to speculate that increases in the length and complexity of verbally expressed languages increases the opportunities for instances of disfluency to emerge and is probably a natural byproduct of improved but still unstable expressive language skills. (p. 105)

A related therapeutic issue for children who are being treated for fluency and other impairments is the "trading" relationships among the fluency, language, and phonological capabilities of the child. Such reciprocal interactions have been suggested between fluency disorders and both language and phonological capacities (Crystal, 1987; Masterson & Kamhi, 1992; Ratner, 1995, 1997; Ratner & Sih, 1987; Stocker & Gerstman, 1983; Stocker & Usprich, 1976; Watkins et al., 1999). This

relationship has been particularly well documented for expressive syntax and fluency (Gaines et al., 1991; Gordon, 1991; Gordon et al., 1986; Ratner & Sih, 1987; Stocker, 1980). The affiliation of a child's expressive and receptive capabilities is a major influence on clinical decision making for young children who stutter. That is, the clinician should introduce fluency skills at carefully graded levels of linguistic demand (Ratner, 1995; Stocker, 1980). According to Ratner (1995),

> Imitation and modeling tasks designed to address syntactic or morphological deficits, shown to be most efficient clinically in inducing changes in expressive language performance[,] . . . may evoke fluency failure. Similarly, fluency practice, if structured in such a way that it does not address the demand it poses on a child's expressive language capacity, may not produce desired changes in fluency. (p. 183)

As discussed in Chapter 3, such trading relationships and their resulting effect on a child's ability to produce fluent speech provide clinical support for a Demands and Capacities Model (Adams, 1990; Starkweather & Gottwald, 1990). That is, at least for some young stuttering children, any task that requires a child to formulate complex ideas with greater levels of language demand could result in decreased fluency. In fact, that is what Weiss and Zebrowski (1992) found with eight child–parent pairs. When these young stuttering children (average age 6 years, 11 months) were asked to respond to questions requiring greater linguistic sophistication, there was a greater occurrence of fluency breaks. That is, higher levels of language demand (Stocker & Usprich, 1976) resulted in significantly more disfluencies than lower level parent requests. In addition, disfluent utterances were significantly longer and more complex than those produced fluently.

Although clinical decisions are made more complex with the presence of multiple problems, the answer to the question of whether to initiate treatment of a child who is disfluent and has other concomitant communication problems or disorders is usually "yes." Articulation and language problems require long-term treatment, and the clinician is unlikely to be able to wait until these problems are resolved before initiating treatment for fluency problems. Given the success that is likely for early intervention of fluency disorders, waiting might only aggravate the problem. Many clinical researchers support the view of focusing on the combination of communication problems the child might have (Conture et al., 1993; Gregory & Hill, 1980; Guitar, 1998; Wall & Myers, 1995). Guitar (2006) did not find that treating other speech or language problems exacerbates the child's stuttering. Guitar provided some particularly good examples of how the clinician could adapt clinical activities to a child with multiple problems. For example, if the clinician is using the Lidcombe Program in order to facilitate fluency, Guitar indicated that other communication problems could be addressed prior to or (more typically) following Stage I of treatment.

Depending on the nature and extent of other associated problems, the clinician will have to decide whether the problems should be addressed sequentially or concurrently. Conture et al. (1993) advocated a concurrent approach for children with both fluency and phonological problems, making use of a fluency-shaping protocol along with indirect phonological intervention. These authors, however, advised

clinicians to avoid any overt correction of the child's speech. It is agreed by most authors that children should not receive any direct feedback concerning the accuracy of their articulation, to prevent possible communicative or emotional stress from impacting the child's capacities. Obviously, the response of each child to feedback will be different, with each one's unique capacities and responses to communication demands. For example, Conture (2001) recommended that the clinician assist the child to develop a "more physically easy, less hurried, less hesitant or rushed means of initiating and manipulating speech rather than an over careful, cautious, physically precise, and overarticulated productions of sounds" (p. 161). Ratner (1993) indicated that subtle forms of feedback in the form of imitation, recasts, and selective emphasis on language structures that children are finding difficult might facilitate overall communication development. The clinician should feel free to model fluency-enhancing gestures in his or her own speech. Certainly, the child's distinctive response to linguistic as well as emotional demands must be carefully considered, both within and beyond the treatment environment.

Ratner (1995) suggested that the blending of treatments (e.g., phonology and fluency) during a treatment session might work well for those children whose fluency system does not appear to be stressed by the requirements of feedback monitoring. However, if the clinician determines that working on one aspect of speech or language production places stress on the child's ability to produce fluent speech, it might be better to sequence treatment, achieving a stable level in one area before tackling the other. Whether or not to sequence treatment is a good example of the kind of clinical decision the experienced clinician must be entrusted to make. If, for a particular child, fluency problems appear to be related to expressive language formulation, the clinician might choose to emphasize language intervention skills prior to fluency treatment. Obviously, as Ratner (1995) pointed out, an inappropriate justification for targeting language prior to—or in place of—fluency is the lack of confidence a clinician might have for conducting fluency therapy. Given the evidence concerning clinician attitudes about people who stutter and about treatment with this population of clients (see Chapter 1), this is a valid concern.

Finally, Ratner (1995) suggested some principles that clinicians can use for making clinical decisions for children with fluency and other concomitant problems:

- The clinician should recognize that demands for phonological and grammatical processing compete with resources that permit fluent speech production.
- The clinician should organize treatment hierarchically, proceeding from language and articulation activities that the child has established and stabilized to tasks that involve greater demands.
- Even though it might slow progress in articulatory and linguistic growth, the clinician should structure interventions for children who stutter with minimum overt feedback.
- The clinician, based on the child's individual capacities and responses to communicative demands, should determine whether a child's multiple impairments should be treated concurrently, sequentially, or cyclically. Furthermore, this strategy should be subject to change in the event that

progress in one domain comes at the expense of regression in another.

Intervention for all clients is likely to be most efficient when a careful analysis of the speaker's capacities and responses to demands are factored into the treatment strategy. Clients can—and should—be pushed to the upper ranges of their ability in order to help them to change the many features of their fluency disorder. The clinician working with young children who stutter should be able to help them learn to easily produce difficult sounds or new grammatical structures without introducing the idea that they need be concerned or frightened or should struggle with their speech. It is possible to model a smooth and flowing manner of speech production while also giving the child a real sense of command over himself or herself.

TRANSFER AND TERMINATION ISSUES

Throughout treatment and certainly prior to the child's dismissal from formal treatment, the clinician will want to determine how well the child has been able to transfer new capabilities and techniques to the world beyond the treatment setting. Of course, the understanding and motivation of the parents will be the major factor in facilitating transference. Fortunately, as Conture (2001) pointed out, for many children the skills learned in the treatment setting transfer quite easily. Guitar (2006) noted that progress with younger children can be determined by such accomplishments as improved use of techniques, decreased reliance on cueing by the clinician, increased control of fluency, decreased avoidance of speaking and speaking situations, and increased risk-taking in speaking situations.

CLINICAL DECISION MAKING

The participation of the clinician in providing modeling and support for the child when practicing beyond the treatment environment cannot be overemphasized. As described in Chapter 1, the willingness to do yourself what you ask the speaker to do is critical. Guitar (2006) provided vivid examples of "scaffolding" the child's ability to use the techniques associated with the fluency-enhancing skills described earlier in this chapter. When making telephone calls and seeking out face-to-face speaking situations of gradually increasing difficulty, the clinician takes the first turn when speaking with others. During telephone calls the child and clinician can signal each other or the clinician coaches the child in freezing the stuttering and then gently moving through or sliding out of a moment of stuttering. As the child indicates the onset of fear or a moment of stuttering, the clinician might touch the arm of the child to cue the use of the skills. Continued desensitization and assertiveness are often necessary for expanding the child's confidence and success in daily speaking situations.

Criteria that the clinician might consider for the termination of formal treatment are provided by Gottwald and Starkweather (1995). Parents and teachers should feel confident about their ability to manage the child's improving fluency. These adults can assess the child's progress and make independent decisions concerning how to alter fluency-disrupting stimuli such as time pressure and linguistic demands across a variety of social and educational settings. Parents can create an environment that corresponds to the child's capacity to maintain fluency. In addition, the young child should be normally fluent for his or her age; some mild fluency breaks, particularly whole-word and phrase repetitions produced without effort, are unexceptional for 3- to 4-year-old children. Even fluency breaks produced with mild levels of tension could be acceptable if the clinician anticipates that the child will make continued improvement. Of course, termination is also facilitated by a gradual phase-out of treatment that provides the clinician with the op-

portunity to monitor the child's progress. Ideally, such monitoring should take place through age 7 or 8, when basic skills underlying fluency are thought to be internalized. Finally, parents and teachers should be informed about the characteristics of relapse, made aware of the signs of incipient stuttering, and encouraged to contact the clinician if such indicators occur.

THE POSSIBILITY OF RELAPSE WITH CHILDREN

In contrast to the situation for older speakers, the maintenance of the gains made during formal intervention is far more common with children (Bloodstein et al., 2021). Several investigators indicate that once formal treatment has been successfully completed, the chance of regression is much less likely with children than it is with adolescents and adults who have been stuttering for many years (Gottwald & Starkweather, 1995; Hancock et al., 1998;

Starkweather, 1999; Starkweather et al., 1990). However, a comprehensive treatment program will include periodic checks for as long as 2 years following the conclusion of formal treatment. As with older speakers, follow-up or refresher sessions of fluency-facilitating skills might be necessary for some children if fear, avoidance, or increased stuttering reoccur.

C.W. Starkweather (personal communication, July 8, 1995) estimated that the relapse rate following successful treatment for young children is approximately 2%. In a summary of the families seen from 1981 through 1990 at the Temple University Stuttering Prevention Center in Philadelphia, Gottwald and Starkweather (1995) indicated the following:

> Forty-eight of these families received individualized intervention services, ranging from parent counseling only to family counseling and direct therapy for the child. At the time these results were reported, three children and their families were still in therapy, and seven families had withdrawn from the program for a variety of reasons. The remaining 45 youngsters and their families completed the program. All 45 children were speaking normally at the time of discharge. Follow-up telephone calls to each of the families 2 years following program completion revealed that fluency had been maintained according to parent report. (p. 124)

Partial or even complete relapse can occur, of course, and one procedure that might prevent such regression is the use of a "buddy system." This could be especially helpful for the child who is having difficulty with motivation, carryover, or maintenance. When entering into new and difficult speaking situations outside the treatment setting, the presence of someone who understands the dynamics of the situation can have a powerful supporting effect. If the clinician or parent is not there, the presence of a speech buddy could be extremely beneficial. This strategy might be particularly useful with preadolescent or adolescent clients, who tend to spend the vast majority of their time with their peers rather than their parents or clinicians.

Hancock et al. (1998) conducted a 2- to 6-year follow-up of 62 children who had received one of three stuttering treatments (intensive smooth speech, parent-home smooth speech, and intensive electromyography feedback). These children, age 11 to 18 years, were older than those followed by Gottwald and Starkweather (1995). Children were assessed overtly during a clinic conversation with the clinician, while speaking on the clinic telephone talking to a family member or friend, and while talking at home. The authors found that most of the children had maintained the gains they had achieved 1 year posttreatment. About half of the children had less than 1% syllables stuttered across the three speaking contexts, and nearly 70% of the children achieved less than 2% syllables stuttered 2 to 6 years following treatment. From a parent's perspective, eight of the parents (13%) believed that their child had relapsed to pretreatment levels and 33 parents (53%) felt that their child's speech had deteriorated but not to pretreatment levels.

SUGGESTIONS FOR THE CLASSROOM TEACHER

For school-age children, classroom teachers can play a major role in facilitating therapeutic change. In some instances, the child's classroom teacher will have as much influence on a successful therapeutic outcome as the child's parents. However, in order for teachers to have a positive influence, they must have some understanding of the nature of stuttering and the objectives and rationale of treatment. Many authors provide a variety of suggestions for the classroom teacher who finds a child who stutters in his or her class (Conture, 2001; Cooper, 1979; Dell, 1970; Guitar, 2006; Van Riper, 1973, pp. 446–450). Of course, the character of the clinician–teacher relationship will depend on the model used for service delivery in the school. One possibility is a consultative model, where the clinician works through the teacher and parents to help the child. A collaborative-consultative model has the clinician working with the child on an individual basis but also collaborating with the teacher and parents in planning appropriate activities in the child's daily world. According to Gregory (1995), a pull-out model, where the children are taken out of the classroom and seen individually or in small groups by the clinician, is probably the strategy that is least apt to create meaningful professional interaction or long-term change for the child.

An efficient first step for involving classroom teachers is for the clinician to present a workshop for teachers and related school personnel. For many reasons, it is preferable for the clinician to be proactive in explaining the nature of stuttering to classroom teachers rather than waiting for them to one day discover such a child in one of their classes. Perhaps the most important reason is that many children who stutter can go undetected or be misunderstood. Some children who stutter will refuse to answer, intentionally saying, "I don't know" despite knowing the correct answer to the teacher's question.

They might also give the wrong answer due to the fear of stuttering on the correct answer. The story of the former football player (see Chapter 5) and the following examples are particularly effective stories to relate to classroom teachers.

Highly effective presentations can result from discussing the informative videotapes and pamphlets available through such groups as the Stuttering Foundation or the National Stuttering Association. Nearly everyone is interested in stuttering, and it is usually easy to draw an appreciative audience for such presentations. One good possibility is to show the 20-minute DVD (#0126) and accompanying handbook (#0125) available from the Stuttering Foundation titled *Stuttering: Straight Talk for Teachers*. The materials, presented by both young students who stutter and experienced clinicians, provide the audience with essential information about stuttering. Topics include information about responding to the child who stutters in the classroom, the basic principles of treatment, recommendations for teasing and bullying, and suggestions for assisting the child who stutters with oral presentations. Reardon (2000) provided a helpful checklist for helping classroom teachers identify students who stutter and for following their progress as they receive treatment (Figure 11–1). The reader is also referred to a Stuttering Foundation workbook designed for speech-language pathologists working in a school, titled *The School-aged Child Who Stutters: Practical Ideas for Working With Feelings and Beliefs About Stuttering* (Publication No. 5) by Chmela and Reardon (2001).

As the goals and techniques of treatment are explained to the child's teacher, he or she is more likely to become involved in treatment. As with parents, it is often better to show, rather than tell, colleagues what takes place during the treat-

Teacher Checklist—Fluency

Student: _____ Birthdate: _____ C.A.: _____ Grade: _____

School: _____ Teacher: _____ Section: _____ Date: _____

Speech/Language Pathologist: _____

The child above has been referred for or is receiving services regarding fluency skills. Please help me gain a better overall view of this student's speech skills by completing the following information.

Informational Checklists:

1. This student: (check all that apply)

   ___ doesn't mind talking in class.

   ___ seems to avoid speaking in class. (Does not volunteer, if called upon, may frequently not reply.)

   ___ speaks with little or no outward signs of frustration.

   ___ is difficult to understand in class.

   ___ demonstrates frustration when speaking (please describe): _____

   ___ performs average or above average academically.

2. This student is disfluent or stutters when he/she: (Check all that apply)

   ___ begins the first word of a sentence.

   ___ speaks to the class.

   ___ speaks an entire sentence.

   ___ gets upset.

FIGURE 11–1. A checklist to assist classroom teachers in identifying students who stutter and for following their progress as they receive treatment. *Source:* From Reardon, N. A., *Working with teachers.* Presentation to the Stuttering Foundation of America Conference, Stuttering therapy: Practical ideas for the school clinician. Charleston, SC, June, 10, 2000. Reprinted with permission.

ment sessions with the child. Live or taped demonstrations are especially important if the child is taken from the classroom for intervention. As the classroom teacher recognizes that a child is choosing to participate in class in spite of some stuttering, the teacher will be able to reward that response (either during or following the event, and either verbally or nonverbally).

When a child successfully uses a fluency- or stuttering-modification technique in the classroom, the teacher will be more likely to recognize what the child has done and know how to respond. When a

CLINICAL INSIGHT

Over the years, students have provided many examples of attempts to hide their stuttering from their teachers and classmates. More than one individual has reported piercing himself or herself with a pencil in order to be excused from speaking and be allowed to go the nurse's office with a bloody hand. Many have pretended to be sick on the day of a presentation or have feigned illness when faced with an unexpected assignment to speak in class. Others describe suffering the consequences of getting caught scribbling on or tearing out a page of a book in order to avoid taking their turn at reading in front of the class. One of the more poignant descriptions was that of a young boy who found himself frequently getting in trouble for talking during class, a boy the teacher viewed as an undisciplined student. The boy explained, however, that because he typically stuttered severely when called on by the teacher to speak before the entire class, he would fluently talk out of turn to a classmate in order to show his peers "that I really could talk."

child successfully alters his or her usual tense and fragmented speech into a more open and forward-moving pattern, the teacher has an opportunity to reward the accomplishment. Until the teacher is able to interpret these seemingly small events as victories, they will go unrecognized and unrewarded. As the teacher gains this brief experience with the child, the choice of how to respond in the classroom, playground, or the school lunchroom becomes apparent. With this understanding, the teacher will be much more likely to discuss the problem with the child and be another important source of support and encouragement in the child's daily school environment. The clinician might also want to consider communicating with the child's teachers via informal newsletters or email messages in order to document the nature of the progress the child is making.

The clinician should also alert classroom teachers that possible outcomes of successful treatment are increased participation, increased speaking, and possibly an increase in the occurrence of fluency breaks. As the child achieves success in diminishing his or her avoidance behaviors and increasing speech assertiveness, one possible result could be greater participation in the classroom. A child who might have chosen to sit quietly prior to treatment might begin to communicate more, begin to talk to friends, and on occasion, stutter more as a result of increased involvement in classroom activities.

Perhaps one of the most important concepts the clinician can impart to the classroom teacher is that unless he or she is a totally insensitive and uncaring person, he or she is not likely to harm the child who stutters. Yes, certainly it would be possible for an insensitive teacher to make things worse for the child. Clearly such people do exist, as reflected by reports in the newsletters of support groups. More often than not, however, classroom teachers are well intentioned and need to be given permission to respond naturally without fear of somehow damaging "this fragile child who stutters." As with parents, when the teacher understands the basic characteristics of stuttering behavior and avoidance responses, it becomes obvious that it is possible to discuss the topic of stuttering openly without hurting the child.

Many suggestions provided to parents can be applied, with slight modification, to the classroom teacher as well. For example, although there might be some exceptions, children who stutter should generally not be permitted to escape from school assignments and responsibilities. Just as the other children are required to take their turn, the child who happens to stutter must also take his or her turn in reciting, reading, and answering questions. To allow a child to escape these responsibilities could foster more harassment from peers than the fact that he or she occasionally stutters. If they could, some children who are fluent would also choose not to face the threat of class participation and public speaking. These decisions, of course, vary with the child and the circumstances, and it would be inappropriate to say that a child must always be required to take part in every speaking situation. However, the exceptions should be rare. Even children who stutter severely are able to take part in class presentations or plays. When the teacher understands that children who stutter are unlikely to stutter when playing a role—speaking with a dialect, singing, or speaking in unison with other children—the teacher is more likely to have the child participate. At the very least, the child could have a nonspeaking part or play a character that makes mechanical or animal sounds.

As the teacher begins to appreciate the effect of time pressure on fluency, he or she might decide, on occasion, to call on the child unexpectedly or early in the class, when he or she is less likely to stutter. The child can then relax a bit and attend to the rest of the class. By understanding the dynamics of fluency-enhancing or disrupting stimuli for a particular child, the teacher could choose to call on that child when the anticipated response is a short, perhaps one-word, answer. Of course, the teacher can reward the child for not avoiding and taking the opportunity to participate. With the assistance of the clinician, the teacher can talk privately with the child before or after class so there can be a mutual understanding about an anticipated or past speaking experience. Stuttering can be a serious topic, but with the assistance of the clinician, the teacher can become desensitized to it and show the child that it is possible to openly and easily discuss the problem.

Like parents, teachers can be shown the powerful effects of listener loss on the child's fluency. The ability of the teacher to remain calm, even during a moment of severe stuttering, communicates understanding and support to the child. Nonverbal indicators of anxiety and avoidance, such as becoming tense or rigid, turning away, or breaking eye contact, can be monitored and changed with some practice. Voluntary stuttering during role-playing activities with the clinician or other teachers and desensitization activities using videotapes also can be especially helpful. Generally, but again with some few exceptions, the teacher should not help the child say a word when he or she is experiencing an extended long block. There could be some occasions when there is no other choice but to help the child, but this should be infrequent.

Certainly, the teacher should not let other children interrupt a child while he or she is stuttering. Similarly, it is never beneficial for the teacher to suggest to the child that he or she stop and think about what he or she is going to say. Such comments simply indicate the naïvete of the

A SAMPLE LETTER FOR INFORMING CLASSROOM TEACHERS ABOUT HOW TO RESPOND TO A CHILD WHO STUTTERS

To the Teachers of Fred Smith at
South Park Elementary School

Date _____

Dear_____,

Fred has been attending the Speech and Hearing Center for the past few months in order to learn how to modify his stuttering and enhance his fluency. He has been doing well as he learns how to monitor and modify specific features of his speech, both in the clinic setting and at home with his family and friends. As he begins a new school year, it is important that his teachers have an understanding of the techniques he is using so that his efforts to smooth his speech and take part in speaking activities are rewarded. Here are some suggestions for helping Fred:

- Encourage Fred's participation in all speaking activities. Avoidance of speaking situations and specific words or sounds are a significant part of the daily impact created by stuttering.
- Of course, progress is indicated by decreased moments of stuttering. However, success is also indicated by Fred's ability to change his more typical stuttering moments into easier and smoother forms of stuttering; ask him to show you what this looks and sounds like.
- As Fred approaches an anticipated moment of stuttering, he will begin to slow his speech slightly and stretch out the initial sounds and syllables of the word he is going to say. Although his speech at this point may not always sound perfectly normal, his best response at this time is to move through the word with this "easy form of stuttering." Your recognition and positive response to his ability to do this are extremely helpful.
- You can find additional information about the nature of childhood stuttering and how to respond to a child who stutters in your classes by contacting any of the following groups via the Internet: The Stuttering Foundation; The National Stuttering Association; and Friends, The National Association of Young People Who Stutter. There is also a very informative website called the Stuttering Home Page that has a lot of good information for children and adults who stutter (as well as parents and teachers) and links to additional sites.

I would be happy to come to your school to speak with you and other teachers concerning these and other suggestions for Fred as well as other children in your school who stutter. Thank you for your help assisting Fred to increase his participation and his fluency. Please feel free to contact me if you have any questions concerning any of the recommendations I have suggested.

listener about the true nature of stuttering. A better response is for the teacher to restate to the class what the child has said. That is, even though the child might have struggled through his or her comments, the teacher can increase the value of the child's comments by paraphrasing his or her words. Such a restating of the child's words gives him or her increased importance and allows the other children in the class to appreciate the content of the child's response. It might take some practice to do this gracefully, but providing such a response is clearly much better than reacting with silence and pretending that no stuttering has occurred or unintentionally conveying the impression that what the child has said is unimportant. An open and forthright response by the teacher also carries a strong statement of unconditional acceptance of the child despite his or her manner of speaking.

CLINICAL DECISION MAKING

Throughout this text there are many examples of the countless decisions that clinicians need to make. Some children require more direct intervention than others. Some parents are willing participants in the process of therapeutic change, and others are not. Some children are especially sensitive or have experienced the added sense of shame brought about by bullying. Some classroom teachers are more adept than others at providing support and recognizing success. In many cases, the clinician will not know what the best decision might be until a choice is made and the outcome considered. With this in mind, consider the following circumstances and describe one or more possible choices or responses that could be made:

- A third-grade boy who has just begun treatment comes to a therapy session and states, "I feel really great. I haven't stuttered at all today!"
- A child tells you that the fluency-enhancing technique he learned and used perfectly in therapy last week "doesn't work at school."
- A child's teacher informs you that a child you are seeing for therapy refuses to take his turn presenting a report to the class.
- The parents of an 8-year-old child who stutters want their child to receive treatment, but the child refuses to attend individual or group treatment sessions.
- An elementary school student tells you that his preferred method of coping with his stuttering is to avoid words.
- A child tells you that his parents do not want to talk with him about what he is learning in treatment.
- The parents of a young client inform you that their child is being bullied by a child in the neighborhood because of his stuttering.
- The parents of an 8-year-old child are resistant to do easy voluntary stuttering during a treatment session.
- The parents of a child who is about to begin therapy ask you, "How long will it take for my child to stop stuttering?"

Perhaps most important, the classroom teacher can become an advocate for the child. By showing understanding, being available to the child, and rewarding what he or she recognizes as progress in the direction of behavioral and attitude change, the child's teacher, like the parent, can be a powerful force for decreasing the handicapping impact of stuttering and for preventing the maintenance and further development of the problem.

On those occasions when the clinician is working with a child privately or in a clinical setting outside of school, making contact with the school is an important part in helping the child to transfer his or her ability to modify his or her stuttering in this important setting. The sample letter (on p. 324) can serve as a model for informing teachers about how to respond to a child currently undergoing treatment.

CONCLUSION

In comparison to older speakers, treatment for young children who stutter is of much shorter duration and often more successful. Some of this success is undoubtedly the result of a natural process of recovery from stuttering during the preschool and early school-age years. In most cases, the length of the time that the child has been stuttering is liable to be more informative to the clinician than the chronological age of the child. Nevertheless, even for children who have been stuttering for as long as 6 to 12 months, the behavioral and cognitive patterns associated with stuttering are rarely embedded to the extent they are for older speakers. Nonetheless, many of the principles and techniques of change that allow older speakers to expand their fluency and modify their stuttering can be applied to children, keeping in mind, of course, that the young speaker's conceptual, linguistic, affective, and neurophysiological systems are still in the process of maturation. Regardless of the specific techniques used, children can learn how to more efficiently manage their breath stream, create a gentle onset of voicing, slow their articulatory rate, make easy transitions from one sound or word to another, and use light articulatory contacts. They can also become skilled at varying and changing the effort associated with the struggle responses they might have developed.

During recent decades, treatment for children has become increasingly direct. Clinicians are now more likely to model behavioral techniques that directly assist the young speaker in changing fluency rather than primarily focusing on altering the child's environment. Depending on the child, indirect techniques that help to alter the family's communicative style might also be useful for enhancing fluency. No matter the therapy approach, the involvement of parents and other family members is crucial for promoting and maintaining successful therapeutic change. The documented success of the Lidcombe Program provides support for such direct approaches and points to the importance of parental understanding and commitment for transferring and maintaining the fluency of young speakers in their daily environment. Recent research also indicates that the therapeutic success could be accounted for by important common factors that are found in several treatment protocols. Such factors as the active participation of the parents in the child's everyday environment, the reduction of parental anxiety, the acknowledgment of stuttering in an open and forthright manner, praise-giving by the parents conveying that the child has a choice about how he or she speaks, and the construction of a meaningful speaker role appear to play important roles in therapeutic success. Perhaps most essential, regardless of the particular treatment protocol and associated techniques, is the ability of the clinician and the parents to convey to the child that he or she is not helpless and has a choice about how to produce words and sounds.

As research increasingly points to both the awareness and reactive nature of some children to the experience of stuttering, counseling for children and their families has become even more vital. Consequently, the clinician, beyond modeling behavioral change, should also promote cognitive and affective change for the child as well as the parents. In cases where the child is particularly sensitive or experiencing the effects of bullying, understanding and support from the clinician become especially important. Activities that promote desensitization will allow the child to approach and explore his or her experience with stuttering, lessening shame and guilt. Related activities allow the child to vent their frustration and anger and become desensitized and knowledgeable about stuttering. Some children will become secure enough to acknowledge their stuttering to others, perhaps educating listeners concerning interesting facts about the topic. Parents are especially likely to benefit from counseling that emphasizes an understanding and a corresponding reduction of their own anxiety concerning stuttering. The clinician can play a key role in modeling an open, uninhibited style of addressing many stuttering-related issues, showing the parents that it is possible for stuttering to be an acceptable topic of discussion. A clinician's co-

ordination of informal group meetings of parents can be particularly helpful for becoming desensitized and exchanging helpful information about stuttering.

In contrast to their work with older speakers, clinicians are more likely to evaluate and determine the impact of cooccurring communication, learning, and behavioral problems on children. Although there are many children for whom stuttering is the only communication difficulty, there are most certainly subgroups of children who also have various degrees of phonological, language, and learning problems that impact fluency. The "trading" relationships across the various prerequisite abilities necessary for producing fluent, age-appropriate speech and language will need to be considered when selecting the sequence of intervention activities for such speakers.

Exchanging information with the classroom teacher of a child who is receiving fluency therapy is essential, but most teachers will appreciate knowing something about stuttering prior to discovering such a child in their classroom. The informed teacher can play an important role during transfer and maintenance of therapeutic successes. The presentation of a brief workshop with accompanying video and written materials is a highly efficient method of imparting key information. As classroom teachers achieve enhanced understanding about the basic characteristics of stuttering and the realization that a caring teacher is unlikely to harm the child, they are more likely to recognize and praise positive changes in the child's attitude and behavior. Working with clinicians, the classroom teacher can find many ways to include the child who stutters in class activities and can become an important advocate for the child.

The future for fluency is bright for young children who receive good, early intervention. Issues of transfer and maintenance are generally less difficult for younger speakers, particularly if the clinician, from the outset of treatment, works with the child's parents and teachers to promote these activities beyond the immediate treatment environment. Several investigators have demonstrated that regression and relapse to pretreatment levels following treatment is much less apt to occur with children than it is with adults. As described in Chapter 1, the clinician who models a confident, curious, and enthusiastic style can make the process of therapeutic change successful and enjoyable for the young child who stutters.

❓ TOPICS FOR DISCUSSION

1. What characteristics of younger children who stutter are likely to influence both your diagnostic and treatment decisions?

2. What were the views about direct intervention for young children who stuttered in the middle of the 20th century? How do these ideas contrast with current ideas?

3. How would you describe the primary goals and overall direction of therapy to the parents of a preschool child who is beginning treatment?

4. What are the basic principles and goals when providing counseling to the parents of a young child who stutters?

5. Describe the primary objectives and associated activities that are likely to be helpful for a school-age child who is experiencing bullying by peers.

6. Describe to a friend the techniques you would consider using to help children who stutter to deal with their fear and shame associated with stuttering.

7. What are the fluency-enhancing techniques you would consider using with a young child who stutters?

8. With a friend, model techniques that will assist a young child who stutters in varying and modifying his or her stuttering behavior.

9. What decisions will you need to make when deciding to treat a child who stutters and also exhibits one or more additional communication problems?

10. Prepare an outline of an in-service training for a group of 30 classroom teachers. What are the main points you want to make about the nature of stuttering, the nature of therapy, how they could help to identify a child who stutters in their class, and how they can assist in the treatment process? What pamphlets, videos, and Internet addresses would you make available to your audience?

📖 RECOMMENDED READINGS

Chmela, K. A., & Reardon, N. A. (2001). *The school-aged child who stutters: Practical ideas for working with feelings and beliefs about stuttering* (Publication No. 5). Stuttering Foundation of America.

DiLollo, A., & Manning, W. H. (2006). Counseling children who stutter and their parents, In E. Conture & R. Curlee (Eds.), *Stuttering and related disorders of fluency* (3rd ed., pp. 115–130). Thieme Medical.

Langevin, M., Kully, D., & Ross-Harold, B. (2007). Treatment of school-age children who stutter: A comprehensive approach with strategies for managing teasing and bullying. In E. Conture & R. Curlee (Eds.), *Stuttering and related disorders of fluency* (3rd ed., pp. 131–150). Thieme Medical.

Millard, S. K., Nicholas, A., & Cook, F. M. (2008). Is parent–child interaction therapy effective in reducing stuttering? *Journal of Speech, Language, and Hearing Research, 51,* 636–650.

Murphy, W. P., Yaruss, J. S., & Quesal, R. W. (2007). Enhancing treatment for school-age children who stutter I: Reducing negative reactions through desensitization and cognitive restructuring. *Journal of Fluency Disorders, 32,* 121–138.

Murphy, W. P., Yaruss, J. S., & Quesal, R. W. (2007). Enhancing treatment for school-age children who stutter II: Reducing bullying through role-playing and self-disclosure. *Journal of Fluency Disorders, 32,* 139–162.

Ramig, P. R., & Dodge, D. M. (2005). *The child and adolescent stuttering treatment and activity resource guide.* Thomson Delmar Learning.

We must do the thing we think we cannot do.

—Helen Keller

Nothing in this world can take the place of persistence.

Talent will not; nothing is more common than unsuccessful people with talent.

Genius will not; unrewarded genius is almost a proverb. Education will not; the world is full of educated derelicts. Persistence and determination alone are omnipotent.

The slogan "press on" has solved and always will solve the problems of the human race.

—Calvin Coolidge

Successful Management of Stuttering for Adolescents and Adults

CHAPTER OBJECTIVES

- To describe treatment options for individuals who have stuttered into adolescence and adulthood
- To describe the principles of change for individuals who stutter
- To provide a rationale for and description of the most frequently employed therapeutic protocols as well as some of the less commonly used approaches
- To examine the possibility of spontaneous speech
- To explore the process of choosing a treatment strategy
- To describe aspects of cognitive restructuring for adolescents and adults who stutter
- To discuss assistive devices and pharmacological treatments for stuttering
- To explore group treatment for adolescents and adults who stutter

In many instances, clinicians will take an eclectic approach and make use of more than one treatment protocol depending on the response of the speaker, often blending approaches and the associated techniques. Sheehan and Sisskin (2001) said it well by stating:

Individualized treatment requires flexibility on the part of the clinician to view the road to recovery from many angles. This requires a broad knowledge in basic research and clinical practice in the field of stuttering. Creativity can only operate in the context of a wide range of options. (p. 7)

As we discussed in Chapters 8 and 10, the issue is not that a particular approach is likely to be especially better than another. As long as the common factors that drive therapeutic change are present in a therapeutic protocol, the issue is more about the ability of the clinician to determine what is likely to be most beneficial for the speaker at a particular point in time. Regardless of the therapeutic protocol, we describe overarching basic principles that account for therapeutic success. As in the earlier chapters describing the diagnostic process, successful management of stuttering is viewed from a comprehensive and multidimensional perspective in that many aspects of both behavioral and cognitive/affective change are considered essential for success. The concluding portion of the chapter describes the unique characteristics of adolescents who stutter and the advantages of group therapy.

INFORMATION THAT INFORMS OUR TREATMENT DECISIONS

To this point in the text, we have developed several important themes that are essential for the successful therapeutic intervention for individuals who stutter. In the earlier chapters we intentionally avoided the discussion of specific treatment techniques in order to first provide the principles and conceptual framework that underlie the process of change. For example, we have argued that first and foremost it is important for the clinician to develop a thorough understanding of the stuttering experience and a speaker's suc-

cessful and unsuccessful efforts to cope with his or her communication problem. As Silverman (1996) advised, "The better able you are to understand the problems your clients will encounter as they try to change, the better able you will be to help them do so" (p. 170). In addition, we have suggested that as clinicians accumulate experience and continue to develop clinical expertise, they are more likely to make clinical decisions based on principles rather than rules. Experienced clinicians are apt to respond in nondogmatic and creative ways in response to the dynamic characteristics of the person and the situation. We have consistently indicated that, particularly for adolescents and adults who stutter, there are several interrelated goals of treatment for stuttering. Increasing the speaker's fluency is the most obvious goal. But as we indicated in Chapter 10, other, more fundamental, goals include increasing the person's ability to communicate more effectively (regardless of stuttering) and promoting an agentic lifestyle. Finally, even though the experienced clinician is apt to develop an empirically informed and theoretically based sense of direction about the therapeutic journey, we have maintained that, more than anything else, both the path and the pace of treatment should be set by the individuals we are trying to assist. The primary objectives of this chapter are to provide the reader with examples of treatment alternatives based both on the therapeutic philosophy of the clinician and the goals and abilities of the speaker. There are nearly infinite varieties of therapy techniques that the clinician can select, experiment with, and adapt to the therapeutic situation. People who take pride in doing a good job are constantly seeking new rationales and tools as well as adaptations of techniques that are useful to them and compatible with their approach to problem solving.

PERSPECTIVES ABOUT THERAPEUTIC TECHNIQUES

In Chapters 7 and 8, it was suggested that therapy and counseling are not about using techniques. Although specific therapeutic techniques are part of the treatment process, the *meaning* of the techniques is more important. Clients do not need to understand the theory behind our decisions during therapy, but they do need to understand the meaning of what they are doing.

Of course, clinicians should have a rationale for what they are doing (or not yet

---

CLINICAL INSIGHT

One summer, a colleague asked me if I would see his 14-year-old grandson, Sam, who was coming to stay with him for the summer break. Sam was being seen at his school for stuttering but didn't seem to be making any progress. I agreed to come to their house to see Sam and see if I could help. When I arrived, the first thing that Sam said once we were alone was, "I didn't want to see you and I am not interested in working on my speech!" It was said with a mild degree of disfluency, and a polite but very icy degree of certainty! My response was, "Well, everyone expects me to be here for an hour, so if I leave now, that would be kind of embarrassing! So how about if we just chat for a while—and I won't ask you to do anything with your speech—after all, you are on summer vacation and who wants to work on stuff when they are on vacation!" Sam and I spent the next hour talking about school, the town where he was from, Harry Potter, various books, more Harry Potter (he loved Harry Potter!), and a little about where I was from (I still have some of my Australian accent). As the hour wound down, Sam asked what kind of things I would want him to do if we worked on his stuttering. I told him that we would have to spend some time together figuring out what would be best, and threw out some possibilities that I thought he might like. At the end of the hour, I thanked Sam for chatting with me and, very genuinely, told him that I was glad that we'd had the opportunity to meet. As I was leaving, Sam asked, "Maybe you could come back tomorrow? I still don't want to work on my speech, but maybe we could talk about it like you said?" I worked with Sam several times that summer and more the following two summers. He made some progress, and we kept in touch, even after he stopped coming to stay with his grandfather over the summer.

The point of this story is that had I gone to meet Sam with my own agenda and focused on what I thought he needed, then our meeting would have lasted 5 minutes. Starting with Sam where he was at, and forging a relationship with him, allowed me to then play a role with him therapeutically. In one of our last face-to-face meetings, Sam told me that I was the first speech pathologist who actually seemed interested in him as a person rather than just as a "stutterer." All the technical skill in the world will benefit no one if we don't take the time to connect with people first. (AD) doing) in therapy, and it is often helpful to explain that rationale to the client. Without a shared meaning of what is taking place in therapy, the techniques are just techniques. It has often been suggested that a key trait of successful clinicians (and coaches and teachers) is their ability to motivate clients to practice between sessions. If clients understand the rationale for what they are doing in the therapy sessions, they are more likely to experiment with, and practice with, therapeutic ideas and techniques in their daily life.

Adolescents, and adults who have stuttered for several years, perhaps decades, are likely to have become sophisticated travelers within the culture of stuttering. By the time we are able to connect with them, they have a lengthy history of coping strategies that they have come to rely on. They have made many life choices and important decisions based on the fact that they are persons who stutter. To a greater or lesser degree, they have learned how to survive, and because of the shame and stigma associated with stuttering (Bennett & Chmela, 1998; Boyle, 2013, 2015; Murphy, 1999) they have learned subtle ways to hide and avoid revealing themselves as persons who stutter. It is not unusual for their fluency breaks to be so well disguised that the surface features of stuttering behavior are sometimes unapparent, even to the sophisticated observer.

It is good to begin this chapter with a note of optimism regarding treatment for adolescents and adults who stutter. Because of the volume of information and the many uncertainties about the important issues of etiology, treatment, and relapse, the literature can be discouraging for clinicians interested in helping older speakers with fluency problems. As described in Chapter 1, many clinicians are unsure of the strategies and specific techniques to employ with those who stutter. Fluency disorders, an area that for many years was at the core of the academic and clinical experience of students, is often omitted from the student's program or given less than adequate emphasis. As a result, many clinicians actively avoid—or at the very least are anxious about—the possibility of working with children and adults with fluency disorders. As we indicate throughout this book, though, there are many instances of highly successful management by adolescents and adults who have stuttered. Individuals who have stuttered for years are able to achieve high levels of spontaneous fluency and communicative skill (Anderson & Felsenfeld, 2003; Finn, 1997; Plexico et al., 2005). To be sure, some individuals continue to stutter to a degree but are able to manage their stuttering to the point that it has little or no effect on their ability to communicate and to enjoy a high-quality and autonomous lifestyle.

It might be helpful (as well as more realistic) for the clinician to conceptualize the therapy process for speakers who have been stuttering for several years as one of successful management rather than recovery. The term *recovery* implies that the primary goal of treatment is to cure the speaker and suggests that the speaker has moved from a pathologizing position to a symptom-free condition of normalcy. As we have indicated, such a view reflects a medical approach to therapeutic change. An alternative understanding of therapeutic or self-change for many individuals who stutter is one of successful management, whereby the person's history of being a person who stutters is incorporated into new and more effective ways of managing stuttering.

PRINCIPLES OF CHANGE FOR INDIVIDUALS WHO STUTTER

As we indicated at the outset of this chapter, one objective is to discuss basic principles, rather than specific rules, to be considered when assisting individuals who stutter to alter their situation as it relates to the therapeutic goals of fluency, communication, and agency. With this in mind, we begin to consider the principles of change that are present in a wide variety of treatment approaches and are consistently employed by experienced clinicians when assisting those who stutter. Pachankis and Goldfried (2007) suggested that principles of change are shared by all theoretical perspectives and lay "somewhere between the abstract level of theory and the more concrete level of technique" (p. 55).

A review of many current therapeutic approaches was assisted in large part by the comprehensive summary provided by Guitar (2006, 2014) in his text *Stuttering: An Integrated Approach to Its Nature and Treatment*. In addition, a review of additional manuscripts that investigated the ability of individuals to achieve successful management of their stuttering via therapeutic or self-directed change was conducted (Anderson & Felsenfeld, 2003; Conture, 2001; Finn, 1996; Onslow et al., 2003; Plexico et al., 2005; Ratner & Guitar, 2006). The principles associated with successful stuttering management also surface in detailed case histories, anecdotal reports, and presentations at professional and support-group meetings. Many of these same principles are reflected in the insightful comments by the 14-year-old Brad Sara appearing later in this chapter. There are, of course, variations and interactions of the common themes. Nevertheless, the common factors appear consistently in many treatment protocols within both our field and other related professions (Bachelor & Horvath, 1999; Hubble et al., 1999; Luborsky et al., 2002; Luborsky et al., 1975; Pachankis & Goldfried, 2007; Rosenzweig, 1936; Wampold, 2001; Wampold & Brown, 2005). The following are four basic principles that, as clinicians, we can reflect on as we make clinical decisions and assist our clients along their journey of successful therapeutic change.

Move Toward Rather Than Away From the Problem

Professionals are likely to refer to this as an approach–avoidance continuum. As most of us have experienced or at least witnessed on the news, often it is not the error or the crime, it is the cover-up that creates the greatest problem. Whatever the nature of the problem, moving away from the situation through denial or avoidance nearly always makes the situation worse. Experienced clinicians provide innumerable examples of activities that assist children and adults who stutter to move toward the problem, become desensitized, confront the situation, and take action (e.g., Chmela & Reardon, 2001; Guitar, 2006; Murphy et al., 2007a, 2007b; Reardon & Yaruss, 2004; Sheehan, 1970; Van Riper, 1973; Williams, 1971, 1983). Sheehan and Sisskin (2001) suggested that the speaker accept and embrace the stuttering in order to become desensitized to the stuttering experience and create options for change.

Assume Responsibility for Taking Action

Although specific techniques are an important part of a therapeutic program, the

CLINICAL INSIGHT

One of the common events when paddling in whitewater is the experience of encountering a large rock or a wave that rolls back on itself, called a hydraulic. If you are new to paddling, your instinct is to struggle against the often powerful flow of the river to avoid a threatening obstacle. Of course, as a novice, you are often unable to avoid the barriers to your progress as you flow down the river. As you approach obstacles your instinct is to lean back (upstream) away from the problem, but you quickly learn that when you respond in this way you will immediately find yourself upside-down. This is where a good coach can help. With proper instruction and experience, you'll discover something that's both subtle and amazing. You learn that, rather than expending so much effort trying to elude the obstacles, you'll have much better success by actively moving toward them! For example, as you approach a rock you will notice a pillow of water recoiling off the rock that will help you to move around it. You realize that the pillow of water wasn't detectable until you allowed yourself to get close to the rock. Furthermore, if you throw your upper body *into* the rock, you find increased stability and you will be able to use the rock for support. Similarly, if you lean into a hydraulic on the river or a wave on the ocean—not just tentatively reach for it with your paddle, but actively throw yourself into it with your paddle and entire upper body—you will achieve increased and dramatic stability as you use the energy of the water to support and right yourself. As you learn these techniques, paddling becomes much more dynamic and enjoyable and you begin to connect with the river. You can now begin to dramatically improve your paddling experience and enjoy the journey. (WM)

treatment process is far more comprehensive than any set of specific techniques. Clinicians are likely to use behavioral techniques that they have become comfortable with and that they feel have been useful to previous clients. Individuals, however, will not necessarily see these techniques in the same way. It is the speaker, who, based on such factors as his or her level of desensitization to stuttering, understanding of the technique(s), and ability in and motivation for using the techniques, will make the decision whether or not to use them, particularly in situations beyond the treatment setting.

Regardless of the treatment protocol, the speaker will need to take responsibility for identifying and developing his or her strengths. The speaker will need to take action by learning to self-monitor his or her performance and practice the techniques in daily communication situations. The behavioral techniques are not usually difficult to master within the safety and support of the therapeutic environment. The more difficult challenge is discovering ways to motivate the speaker to diligently practice the techniques in daily speaking situations, particularly situations that provide gradually increasing levels of communicative stress. As we emphasized earlier, to the extent that individuals are able to practice beyond the treatment environment and make use of the many important extratherapeutic factors, real progress takes place (Hubble et al., 1999; Lambert, 1992; Miller et al., 1997). Miller et al. (1997), for example, found that regardless of the therapeutic approach, participation in extratherapeutic activities and events accounted for approximately 40% of positive therapeutic outcome in psychotherapy, whereas specific methods or techniques accounted for only 15%.

Continual practice on a daily basis will result in a level of proficiency (and eventually expertise, as described in Chapter 1) whereby the speaker becomes one with the techniques. The techniques gradually begin to feel and sound more comfortable and habitual. Rather than consciously choosing to use a technique, the speaker immediately reacts to the impending or actual disruption of fluency with the new response and moves forward with the flow of speech. As the individual successfully employs the technique(s) on many occasions, the level of self-efficacy increases, which increases the likelihood of continued progress.

Restructure the Cognitive View of the Self and the Problem

When people come to us with a history of suffering, struggle, and a restricted lifestyle where stuttering is a dominant theme, some form of cognitive restructuring is required in order to achieve a successful therapeutic outcome. As noted throughout the previous chapters, particularly Chapter 8, the severity of the problem presented by stuttering is represented by these intrinsic features as much as or more than it is by the more obvious extrinsic or surface behaviors. Those who have studied the ability of individuals to make the transition to the successful manage-

ment of stuttering have found that cognitive restructuring is an important part of the process (Anderson & Felsenfeld, 2003; Corcoran & Stewart, 1998; Crichton-Smith, 2002; Finn, 1996; Plexico et al., 2005). Such cognitive changes are especially important for long-term success. As a result of speakers' ability to restructure their self-identity as well as the nature of the problem, they become increasingly assertive. They are more likely to take risks by acknowledging their stuttering and entering into difficult speaking situations—themes associated with successful change as reported by Anderson and Felsenfeld (2003) and Plexico et al. (2005). In addition, these authors found that participants indicated a reciprocal relationship in that cognitive changes facilitated the use of behavioral (speech) techniques and that the successful use of behavioral techniques led to further cognitive change. Strategies for facilitating cognitive restructuring are discussed later in this chapter.

Recruit the Support of Others

Closely related to the first three principles is the action required to identify individuals or groups who are able to provide mentorship and support. Mentors and support groups have been found to be important aids in the successful management of stuttering (Plexico et al., 2005). For those who stutter, mentors could be clinicians or other people who stutter who have achieved success. Members of support groups (see Chapter 15) can provide invaluable support and understanding, as the person is able to connect with others who share a similar story. Observing individuals who have achieved success on many levels can provide the encouragement to undertake a similar journey that will result in the creation of a new set of strategies for modifying the speaker's present situation. If possible, it is especially important to elicit the support and understanding of individuals who are part of the speaker's daily environment in order for them to recognize and reward the many indicators of successful change (see Chapters 14 and 15). Accordingly, as soon as possible, it is useful to have these individuals (e.g., parents, spouse, friends, coworkers) attend one or more treatment sessions so that they can appreciate what success looks and sounds like and so that they can acknowledge and verify it and help to place the changes into a historical context.

It is especially important to engage the client's spouse or partner in the therapeutic process. Boberg and Kully (1985) and Boberg and Boberg (1990) documented the critical role played by the client's partner in a successful therapeutic outcome. Boberg and Boberg recommended the participation of spouses in therapy and maintenance programs. They also encouraged the discussion between the partners, as well as others in their social life, about all aspects of the stuttering experience including current and accurate information concerning stuttering. More recently, Beilby et al. (2013) provided both qualitative and quantitative results for 10 couples where one member of each dyad experienced stuttering and 10 matched couples who were fluent. No significant differences were found between the two groups for perceived quality of life. The results supported and elaborated the work of the earlier studies that found that the fluent partner played a significant role in the therapeutic process. The individual who stuttered and his or her fluent partners experienced stuttering

and the resulting communication difficulties in a similar manner, experiencing social anxiety, negative reactions of listeners, and a cautious outlook about entering social situations. Among the many themes found in the qualitative analyses was strong support for the partner, patience, and acceptance of the spouse and his or her stuttering. The results support the inclusion of the fluent partner in the therapy process, as an agent of change in the treatment process.

THE GOAL OF FLUENCY

Even for the most severe clients, the quickest way to reduce the frequency of stuttering is to have the speaker use a number of fluency-enhancing techniques or electronic devices that result in nearly instantaneous fluency. It has been known for many years that immediate, if temporary, fluency can be achieved by having most speakers who stutter sing, read, or speak in unison with another person; speak in a loud or whispered voice; use a dialect or bouncy intonation; or speak while rhythmically moving a finger, arm, or leg (Bloodstein, 1949). The fluency-enhancing effects of these activities have been attributed to both the rhythmic effects (Van Riper, 1973) and the modification of phonation (Wingate, 1969). Some of the fluency-enhancing activities can provide highly dramatic results, and such instantaneous improvements in fluency tend to have the effect of making anyone who uses them an "expert" in helping those who stutter. Although many early stuttering and stammering schools were based on some of these activities, the effects on the speaker's fluency are short-lived (Silverman, 1976). In rare cases, at the initial assessment meeting or the first few therapy sessions, these activities can be used to temporarily enable communication with the client.

At the outset of treatment, fluent speech is often the primary (and frequently the only) outcome our clients ask of us. Elevated levels of fluency could also occur for adults after taking part in an intensive residential program. However, because of logistic or financial reasons, that is not where many clients are able to find help. In addition, the difficult transition from the focused and supportive clinical environment of an intensive program to the speaker's home and work environments often has an adverse effect on the gains made during treatment. It has been suggested that rapid and dramatic improvements that can occur in an intensive program might result in a fluent speaker who is unsure what he or she did to accomplish change (Boberg, 1986). Prins (1970) indicated that intensive residential programs might produce disfluency overkill and provide clients with the notion that stuttering will not occur as long as they follow the techniques they have begun to master. A similar comment was made by Kamhi (1982), who cautioned clinicians who suggest to clients that the use of fluency-enhancing techniques will result in fluent speech on all occasions. An insightful statement was also offered by Sheehan (1980), who commented that producing stutter-free speech is no more realistic than playing error-free baseball; just because a person possesses the capacity to function in an error-free manner, it does not follow that this will always be the case.

The extrinsic or surface features of stuttering will be the first to change as a result of treatment. In fact, a speaker might show rapid improvement in his or her level of fluency prior to initiating treatment (Andrews & Harvey, 1981). During the initial days or weeks of treatment, an improvement in fluency is likely to result from the speaker's acknowledgment of the problem as well as adaptation to the clinician, the treatment setting, and the client's understanding of his or her role in the treatment protocol. Certainly, an increase in fluency is reflective of change; however, it does not necessarily indicate progress. That is, the increased fluency in the treatment setting might have little relationship to the client's level of fluency beyond the treatment setting in his or her daily environment. It is one thing to hit 10 out of 10 shots when playing basketball alone. The real question is how many shots will be successful during competitive game conditions, when the pressure is great and there are clear penalties for failure.

With a multidimensional approach, the criterion of success in treatment is considerably broader and more inclusive of the many features of the stuttering experience than simply the number of fluency breaks expressed as a percentage of syllables or words stuttered. The descriptions provided by adult speakers who have accomplished successful management of their speech unmistakably indicate that absolute fluency is not a necessary or sufficient criterion for therapeutic success (Anderson & Felsenfeld, 2003; Krauss-Lehrman & Reeves, 1989; Plexico et al. 2005; Reeves, 2006; St. Louis, 2006; Yaruss & Quesal, 2002; Yaruss, Quesal, & Murphy, 2002). For many adults who have stuttered since childhood, it is not unusual for some fluency breaks to occur following successful treatment. The question is not so much whether the client will stutter, especially during unique, unexpected, or especially difficult communication situations. The more fundamental question is whether or not the person will choose to enter into the situation and take part in communicating and how he or she will manage possible stuttering events. As Sheehan stated in 1972 and others have often paraphrased, "Even though you may have no choice as to whether or not you will stutter, you do have a choice of how you stutter" (Sheehan, 2003, p. 33).

THE POSSIBILITY OF SPONTANEOUS SPEECH

In Chapter 2, we discussed the sensation of losing control of one's speech as a core experience of stuttering. The speaker feels that he or she has no choice but to abandon what he or she wants to say or put forth the effort to struggle with the sound or word and in the attempt to move forward. Many therapeutic approaches focus on techniques that are intended to provide a way of producing words fluently or to produce open and less effortful stuttering. Both approaches require considerable self-monitoring and careful management of how one is producing speech. A possible issue with both of these strategies is that the vigilance required for using the techniques results in speech that could be technically fluent but far from spontaneous.

A more effective and nuanced way of understanding this phenomenon is to consider the interplay of effort and fluency in terms of four categories: effortful disfluency, effortful fluency, spontaneous disfluency, and spontaneous fluency. Effortful disfluency is the typical experience of stuttering where the disfluencies are wrestled with as the speaker struggles for control of his or her speaking mechanism. Effortful fluency is the careful flu-

ency we characterized as "talking on thin ice." Spontaneous disfluency is when the speaker, although experiencing a stuttering event, does not need to do anything, as he or she never experiences a "loss of control." Although the stuttering occurs, the speaker continues to move forward as he or she produces effortless, open stuttering. Of course, spontaneous fluency, where speaking requires no monitoring or effort, is assumed by many to be the most desirable form of communicating.

At the outset of therapy, individuals are often speaking with both effortful stuttering and effortful fluency. Even when they are relatively fluent, they are cautious, scanning ahead for feared sounds or words and talking carefully in an effort to prevent stuttering. However, as therapy progresses it is not unusual for the clinician to detect "islands of spontaneous fluency," particularly in less stressful speaking situations. The individual is talking with a natural fluency without having to do anything and without having to exert any kind of control by self-monitoring and using behavioral "techniques." Over time, these moments of spontaneous fluency become longer and more frequent. The moments of stuttering require less and less effort to move through, as they less often cross the threshold that triggers a reaction. As the old ways of reacting to the moments of stuttering begin to diminish, speaking requires less and less control. That is, it is not only possible to achieve natural, spontaneous fluency, but where some stuttering still occurs, the disfluencies can also be spontaneous and not effortful or controlled.

Support for this suggestion is provided by Eichorn et al. (2016), who proposed that speaking during dual-task conditions that engaged working memory resources would result in enhanced fluency. Their results showed that engaging in working memory while producing speech resulted in significant reductions in disfluencies in both the adult participants who stuttered and adults who did not. The results coincided with the constrained action hypothesis (CAH; Vasic & Wijnen, 2005) that attributes disfluency to high levels of hypervigilance during the process of speaking. That is, conscious, explicit control of movements via working memory tends to constrain movement and disrupts automatization.

However, if working memory resources are engaged (as during the dual task conditions), it forces implicit processing that is efficient, resilient, and less vulnerable to distraction, resulting in effortless performance (Beilock et al., 2002). The implicit system is associated with well-practiced motor skills and facilitates effortless performance. For example, reducing the explicit monitoring and the penalty for errors or mistakes during many athletic activities such as skiing, shooting a basketball, or throwing a strike in a baseball game tends to enhance performance. Eichorn et al. (2016) suggested that the concept of "less is more" applies to the process of speech production and commented that, "Much like the axiomatic view that stuttering is essentially what a speaker does to avoid stuttering, the findings indicate that speech fluency is enhanced by less effort and compromised by more" (p. 427).

Constantino et al. (2020) took the concept of spontaneous speech in a different direction. They measured the spontaneous speech of 44 adults who stutter (20 women, 24 men), all of whom were native English speakers and had scores on the SSI-4, OASES, or both that indicated at least mild stuttering. The participants' spontaneous speech was measured in everyday speaking situations. Results indicated that spontaneity and fluency are independent, although correlated, constructs that vary with context. Most significant, however, was the finding that an increase in spontaneity significantly decreased the adverse impact of stuttering on people's lives, whereas fluency did not significantly impact the adverse life impact of stuttering.

ACHIEVING AGENCY

As we have seen, clinical researchers recognize that the speaker who stutters can provide highly relevant information about the nature and impact of the problem. Some researchers have suggested that it might be more appropriate to obtain this information using a format that elicits responses to open-ended questions rather than asking the individual to respond to a predetermined scale or questionnaire. For example, Westbrook and Viney (1980) suggested that a better way to determine the dynamic, multidimensional nature of a person's behavior and underlying psychological state is by eliciting a spontaneously produced narrative rather than a predetermined questionnaire such as the locus of control of behavior (LCB) described in Chapter 6. A construct that is similar to but distinct from locus of control in several important ways is *locus of causality* developed by psychologist DeCharms (1968, 1971). Locus of causality deals not with the control of events, but with the causation of behavior. DeCharms viewed human behavior as motivated by an individual's basic nature and temperament rather than responses to external stimuli. DeCharms called this innate characteristic of humans to make changes in their environment *personal causation*. He developed the concepts of origin and pawn to explain the motivation or causation of human behaviors. He also took into account that behaviors are influenced by an individual's social environment. That is, a person might choose to behave in a certain manner because the person "wants to" or "has to" depending on the circumstances. DeCharms termed these constructs origin and pawn, respectively. One behaves as an origin when he or she is the originator of his or her behavior. One behaves as a pawn when his or her behavior is caused by others or the environment.

Locus of causality is measured through a clause-by-clause content analysis of verbal or written narratives in response to an open-ended question (Westbrook & Viney, 1980). This procedure offers a number of advantages over the prearranged and fixed LCB questionnaire. Content analysis allows for the quantification of one's underlying psychological states (Gottschalk & Gleser, 1969). Although many psychological measures provide an indication of the individual's general traits, they are less likely to detect small changes. Greater sensitivity is obtained by the use of an open-ended procedure that elicits nonrestrained narratives rather than asking the participant to respond to a limited set of predetermined questions. Content analysis provides a participant with the freedom to respond in a way that is meaningful to them (DiLollo et al., 2003). In addition, rather than a one-dimensional *trait* construct (i.e., LCB), locus of causality is a two-dimensional *state* construct. That is, both origin and pawn measures are able to vary independently of one another; people with greater pawn perception do not necessarily have proportionally less origin perception. Content analysis procedures are also less reactive in that they

tap "into the flow of people's experience with interfering with it" (Viney, 1983, p. 553). Clauses are scored as descriptive or neutral statements, origin statements, or pawn statements. A clause is categorized as an origin statement if it expresses intention, effort, ability, overcoming the influence of others or the environment, or self-perception as a cause. A clause is categorized as a pawn if it expresses lack of intention, lack of effort or unintended outcome, lack of ability, being influenced by others and the environment, or self-perception as a pawn. All other clauses are scored as descriptive or neutral.

A pilot investigation by Manning et al. (2005) provided construct validity by indicating that locus of causality scoring was sensitive enough to demonstrate the expected changes in origin and pawn scores during therapy. Subsequent investigations have documented that adults who stutter experience a statistically significant increase in pre- to posttreatment origin scores and a statistically significant decrease in pawn scores (Lee et al., 2011). At the outset of treatment, adults who stutter showed significantly greater pawn scores than a control group of typically fluent adults and similar occurrences of origin statements. Following successful treatment, the adults who experienced therapy showed significantly greater origin scores than the fluent speakers and similar levels of pawn statements (Lee et al., 2015). Another difference between these two groups noted by Lee et al. (2015) was that typically fluent adults respond with significantly more neutral statements when describing a speaking experience than those who stutter. Fluent speakers do not typically describe a speaking experience in terms related to agency, a result that corresponds to the comments of Starkweather and Finn in Chapter 2 concerning the neutral feelings of fluent speakers about communication.

Despite the potential advantages that origin and pawn scaling could provide for predicting the development of agentic behavior during and following treatment, the time-intensive training and scoring necessary for obtaining acceptable levels of reliability limited use of the procedure with large-scale research projects and most clinical settings. An automated procedure, the Origin and Pawn Calculator (OPC), was developed using natural language processing and machine learning algorithms to automatically write narratives (Constantino et al., 2015). The software was able to identify written origin, pawn, and neutral statements with 77% accuracy and detect statistically significant changes in origin and pawn scores pre- to posttherapy. Unfortunately, the program is no longer available online.

CHOOSING A TREATMENT STRATEGY

Depending on how one conceptualizes the treatment strategies available for assisting those who stutter, there are several options open to the clinician. Therapy approaches vary according to such factors as the therapeutic philosophy, treatment goals and associated activities, duration and intensity of the sessions, and the age of the person who is receiving assistance. Although different treatment protocols might vary in one or more of these characteristics, for the most part, the four principles of change and common factors described earlier are common to each of them (see Chapter 7).

As discussed in Chapter 1, most recent graduates of an academic program are apt to adopt the treatment protocols they were taught and with which they are familiar. However, as professional clinicians achieve increased levels of experience and competency, they are less likely to employ a rigid, dogmatic, therapeutic approach. They begin to take greater responsibility for elaborating their clinical philosophy and adopting their clinical techniques to match their clinical style. As described in Chapter 1, experts develop a flexible and holistic approach where the focus is on the person they are helping.

Most treatment strategies for people who stutter are reasonably straightforward and easy to understand. However, it is one thing to be able to grasp the description of a technique in a textbook and quite another to know when and how to apply the technique when responding to a particular individual during the dynamic interaction of treatment. Despite what might be written in a text or treatment manual, the most appropriate clinical choice is not always obvious, even to the experienced clinician, and some experimentation might be required. Whatever the rationale and structure of the treatment program, the process of change is far more dynamic and interesting than the application of techniques. At its finest, effective intervention is the result of the clinician's astute and precise response to the person who has come for help. These responses become more likely as treatment progresses and the clinician becomes calibrated to the client. Depending on the client, the clinician could use a variety of techniques and possibly more than one overall treatment strategy. Even if a single overall strategy is used, the application will never be quite the same with each client. Our clients respond diversely to identical behavioral techniques, just as people do to identical dosages of the same medications.

When initiating treatment, the first decision for the clinician is the choice of a general intervention strategy. There are many paths for the clinician to follow, each with something to offer. We begin by simplifying the situation and discussing the most fundamental approaches: fluency modification and stuttering modification. We also discuss a third option, a strategy of cognitive restructuring that, although sometimes used independently, is more typically combined with the first two approaches. To take the possibilities further, ASHA's *Guidelines for Practice in Stuttering Treatment* (1995) describe a total of 10 treatment goals involving a variety of treatment choices.

The essential difference between fluency modification, stuttering modification, and cognitive reconstruction is best illustrated by considering the relative emphasis placed on the surface and intrinsic features of stuttering. Fluency modification approaches can be thought of as a form of physical therapy for the speech production system. The primary goal with this strategy is to enhance fluency by altering how the speaker uses his or her respiratory, phonatory, and articulatory systems. One assumption of the fluency modification strategy is that once the client has learned new ways of producing fluent speech, he or she will eventually show a corresponding change in the cognitive and affective features of his or her problem. Relatively little counseling in a traditional sense takes place. Fluency modification programs tend to be structured and often manualized. An extremely detailed description of such a program can be found in Ryan's (2001) text *Programmed Therapy for Stuttering in Children and Adults*. It is interesting to note, as have others (McFarlane & Goldberg, 1987; Ratner & Healey, 1999), that fluency modification approaches tend to be favored by clinicians who do not have a personal history of stuttering, whereas

CLINICAL INSIGHT

As we have mentioned previously, it is good to be wary of those who intensely advocate for a particular therapeutic approach, especially if at the same time they rage against the perceived inadequacies of others. On occasion, the literature concerning treatment strategies has taken on the flavor of the commentaries by zealous political or religious groups. In such instances, authors, who are certain of their virtue, invite the reader to take a stand concerning the treatment of the fluency problem, offering a sure road to success to the exclusion of other possibilities. In nearly all cases, such injunctions do more harm than good. In fact, there are many therapeutic approaches that have been shown to help people who stutter. To be sure, the logic and techniques associated with most intervention strategies provide the clinician with a framework and a sense of direction about treatment. Each strategy can provide something of value for the clinician and the client, depending on such variables as the abilities and needs of the client, the stage of treatment, and the expertise of the clinician. As Bloodstein (1999) commented, "Almost any therapy has the power to eliminate stuttering in someone, sometime, someplace."

stuttering modification approaches tend to be the treatment of choice among clinicians who have experienced stuttering.

The stuttering modification strategy, by nature, requires more cognitive intensity on the part of the clinician as well as the speaker. The speaker must not only evaluate and change his or her manner of speaking but must also attend to and alter his or her cognitive and affective responses. As a result, informal counseling in some form is typically an integral part of this approach. Stuttering modification programs are somewhat less structured and tend to take a more eclectic view of stuttering, involving layers of behavioral and cognitive change. As a result, stuttering modification is generally somewhat more difficult to teach and to learn, and it generally takes longer for the speaker to achieve fluency than with a fluency modification approach. Shapiro (1999, pp. 184–191) provided a succinct description comparing the rationale, goals, and procedures for fluency and stuttering modification approaches.

Citing Peters and Guitar (1991), Shapiro (1999, p. 191) provided suggestions for initiating therapy with a fluency or stuttering modification approach.

A stuttering modification approach might be indicated if the speaker:

- hides or disguises his or her stuttering,
- avoids speaking,
- perceives personal penalty as a consequence of stuttering,
- feels poorly about self as a communicator, and
- demonstrates a more positive response to stuttering modification trial therapy.

A fluency modification approach may be indicated if the speaker:

- stutters openly,
- does not avoid speaking,
- perceives annoyance or interference but no personal penalty from stuttering,
- feels positive about self as a communicator, and
- demonstrates a positive response to fluency shaping trial therapy.

With the third generic path, which we have termed cognitive restructuring, the cognitive and attitudinal features of the stuttering experience are the major focus of treatment. In a pure version of this approach, relatively little effort is directed toward the direct modification of speech or fluency. The primary goal is to change the way in which clients consider both themselves and their stuttering and interpret the responses of others. By decreasing avoidance behavior and becoming more assertive, the speaker is often able to make significant changes in the handicapping nature of stuttering. Rather than fighting speech blocks, the speaker is asked to stutter more openly and with less effort. Although the frequency of stuttering moments will stay the same or even increase, the quality of the fluency will improve. In addition, and most important, the quality of the client's communication style, as well as overall lifestyle, will often change for the better.

Although there are obvious differences between these three generic treatment strategies, they are far from mutually exclusive. For example, the consistent contact between the clinician and the client that is required during any treatment approach is, by nature, interpersonal and offers the likelihood of some form of supportive counseling. The very nature of a clinician working closely with an individual and guiding him or her through the many components of treatment provides the client with support and insight about the problem. Therapy, by definition, is always personal, for treatment involves one person assisting another in order to define and manage the problem (Emerick, 1988). Any systematic analysis and subsequent self-management of attitudes and speech behaviors will provide a degree of desensitization during treatment. Whether or not counseling is regarded as a basic or formal goal of treatment, counseling is occurring if a meaningful therapeutic alliance is occurring and the client is being listened to, encouraged, motivated, and challenged.

In addition, during the later stages of stuttering modification treatment, many of the fluency-initiating techniques (e.g., airflow, light articulatory contact, slow and effortless transitions from one sound or syllable to another) used during fluency modification coincide with and complement the stabilization and maintenance activities. Each strategy requires that the speaker monitor and practice techniques, and become more assertive, first within the treatment setting and then gradually beyond the security of the clinic, in daily speaking situations. Each method places great emphasis on the client taking primary responsibility for self-management. By beginning from somewhat different perspectives, each approach can result in increased fluency, as well as increased assertiveness and risk-taking behavior. Finally, each approach can result in a significant reduction of the client's handicap associated with his or her fluency disorder.

Fluency Modification Strategies

It is not usually difficult to invoke fluency even for individuals with the most severe stuttering. Bloodstein (1949, 1950) identified as many as 115 speaking activities or conditions where stuttering was reduced or absent. Such circumstances included activities such as speaking alone or during a relaxed state; speaking in unison with others; talking to a pet, an infant, or in time to a rhythmic stimulus; singing; speaking with a dialect; talking and simultaneously writing; speaking during auditory masking or delayed auditory feedback; shadowing another speaker; or speaking in a slow, prolonged manner. These fluency-enhancing activities also increase fluency for typically fluent speakers and involve combinations of altered vocalization (Wingate, 1969), enhancement of the speaking rhythm (Van Riper, 1973), distraction, and reduced communicative stress.

Many of the basic targets for achieving fluent speech described in fluency modification programs are analogous to the five parameters of forward-moving speech described by Williams (1957) in his classic 1957 article, "A Point of View About 'Stuttering.'" Williams described the following five basic things a speaker must do in order to achieve fluent speech: (a) generate a consistent flow of air from the lungs; (b) create movement of the rib cage and abdomen and articulators; (c) achieve timing and coordination for the onset and rate of movement for respiratory, phonatory, and articulatory activities; (d) initiate the onset of laryngeal movement for voicing and making the transition between voiceless to voiced sounds; and (e) produce appropriate levels of muscular tension required for moving the articulators. A basic aspect of Williams's view was that in order for those who stutter to be able to achieve fluency, speakers first must fully understand what they do to interfere with the achievement of these five parameters necessary for fluency. Williams suggested that because we are *doing* something when we speak, we can *do* something differently to promote forward-moving speech.

Fluency modification programs apply many of the principles discussed by Williams (1957) to help speakers make more efficient use of their speaking mechanisms. Fluency is created, often making use of slowed and prolonged speech segments to instate fluency with single words, gradually expanding to sentences and eventually conversational speech both within and beyond the clinical setting. The earliest versions of fluency-modification approaches were based on behavior modification paradigms and typically placed little or no emphasis on the intrinsic features of the stuttering experience (Cordes & Ingham, 1998; Costello, 1983; Ingham, 1984; Perkins, 1973; Ryan, 1980, 2001; Webster, 1974). No effort was made to deal directly with the speaker's cognitions concerning loss of control, fear, anxiety, and helplessness associated with stuttering. More recently, clinicians using a behavior modification approach have tended to broaden the focus of therapy to include cognitive and affective factors in the treatment process (e.g., Langevin et al., 2006; Langevin & Kully, 2003; Langevin et al., 2007).

An example of a fluency modification program that has been used for many years is the Precision Fluency Shaping Program (PFSP) developed by Webster (1975). With this program, stuttering is viewed as a physical phenomenon, and there is usually little or no discussion concerning the emotional or affective impact on the person who stutters. The premise is that if the speaker follows the rules of speech mechanics, the resulting speech will be fluent; if the rules are violated and the physical targets are not achieved, speech will not be fluent. With the assistance of a visual feedback system, the client is carefully taken through five gradations of muscle movements associated with the features of each sound class (e.g., vowels, glides, fricatives, plosives). Clients are informed about the vocal tract features associated with speech and learn the specific muscle movements associated with the fluent production of each class of sounds. The initial goal of the speaker is to achieve movement targets related to respiration, phonation, speech rate, voice onset, and articulation. Once the speaker consistently achieves these targets, the responses are then gradually transferred to longer and more complex speech sequences and ultimately to conversational speech. All the while, the ability of speakers to self-monitor the accuracy of their targets is emphasized, often with the use of software. Transfer activities are structured such that the speaker is able to gradually progress from simple, one-message questions to complex conversational dialogues in natural settings. Clients are provided with systematic opportunities to practice new speaking skills in a wide variety of treatment and, during the final stage of the program, beyond-treatment settings. Booster sessions are available to clients who desire them.

Bloodstein et al. (2021) provided a summary of a prolonged speech program for adults at the Australian Stuttering Research Centre. Known as the Camperdown Program (named for a neighborhood in Sydney), the approach avoids the problems that clinicians encounter when instructing and evaluating speakers as they attempt to achieve the various fluency targets. As Bloodstein et al. (2021) described:

Rather than detailed instruction in specific speech targets, participants in the program imitate a videotaped model of the desired speech pattern until clinicians agree that the speech pattern resembles that of the model. Then participants may adjust their speech pattern in any way that they wish to eliminate stuttering. Achievement of reduced stuttering using this model is then followed by an intensive group practice day, in which participants also learn to monitor their speech fluency and naturalness. Fluency instatement is then followed by weekly problem-solving sessions and patients move to a Performance Contingent Maintenance Phase after three weekly sessions in which within and beyond-clinic fluency and naturalness measures reach a set criterion. (pp. 433–444)

Because, as mentioned previously, fluency-modification treatments tend to be behavioral, highly structured, and sometimes manualized, they can be easier to teach than stuttering modification or—especially—cognitive restructuring strategies. However, as Conture (2001) pointed out, being able to modify aspects of fluent or stuttering behavior does not mean that we are necessarily changing all, or even the most critical, aspects of the problem. After many years of conducting behavioral studies in fluency disorders, Siegel (1970) provided a perceptive review of the problems and unresolved issues inherent in the behavioral modification approach. Prins and Hubbard (1988) also pointed out some of the potential problems associated with this therapeutic strategy. Nevertheless, behavior modification protocols have provided valuable information about the efficacy of procedures that clinicians can use to modify the surface features of stuttering.

Stuttering Modification Strategies

The stuttering modification strategy is also referred to as the traditional, Van Riperian, or nonavoidance treatment. One premise of this approach is that central to the problem is the speaker's fear, avoidance, and struggle to escape from stuttering. Thus, a primary focus of stuttering modification strategies is the desensitization to stuttering that leads to a reduction and management of fear, avoidance, and struggle. These goals are accomplished via a series of steps that help speakers to examine and identify their stuttering, achieve desensitization to the stuttering experience, and gradually alter their stuttering into intentional, open, smooth, and less effortful forms. A key part of the process is the speaker's ability to replace the old, out-of-control, reflexive stuttering with the new, more desirable, "easy stuttering." A common misconception of this treatment strategy is that it is designed to create "happy stutterers" who are content to stutter away merrily with no fear or avoidance. Although for some speakers such an outcome would represent a much improved situation, in fact, many speakers also achieve speech that is spontaneously fluent. Others who, following therapy, might continue to produce some obvious fluency breaks are able to successfully manage their previously uncontrolled stuttering moments and to make choices that are less influenced by the possibility of stuttering. Examples of this approach can be found in many sources, including Conture (2001), Guitar (2006), Luper and Mulder (1964), Shapiro (1999), Sheehan (1970), Van Riper (1973), and Williams (1971, 1983, 2004).

With this approach, along with the achievement of fluency, there is also a major emphasis on speakers' reinterpretations of themselves and the stuttering experience. Although the eventual achievement of fluency is obviously an indicator of progress, the quality of the stuttering is of primary concern. Progress is seen and heard as the speaker begins to be able to alter high levels of tension and fragmentation of an utterance into fluency breaks characterized by less effort, improved airflow, and increased smoothness. Moments of stuttering are systematically identified, and old patterns of stuttering are varied and formed into easier stuttering. The speaker eventually incorporates the new cognitive and behavioral responses to stuttering into conversational speech during treatment as well as daily speaking situations beyond the treatment environment.

In part, because the therapeutic alliance is a particularly important characteristic of the stuttering-modification approach, this strategy might be somewhat difficult for the new clinician to conceptualize. Observing a clinician demonstrate the various aspects of this approach is especially important when learning treatments that involve the important affective and cognitive features of stuttering. This approach requires the clinician to be particularly sensitive to the client's ability to move through the various stages of affective, behavioral, and cognitive change. The clinician will need to adjust the nature and timing of the activities and will be less able to "go by the book" or use a treatment manual. Although not always directly addressed, cognitive and affective changes could also occur during fluency-modification programs as clients begin to consider and construct new ways of thinking about themselves and their ability to communicate.

The stuttering-modification strategy, as described by Van Riper (1982), takes the client through the stages of identification, desensitization, variation, modification, and stabilization.

Identification

Speakers are first asked to identify both the surface and cognitive features of their stuttering. They are asked to identify, analyze, and confront the specifics of their individual patterns of stuttering. For example, with the assistance of the clinician, clients can make a list of "things I do when I stutter" to identify the surface features of their stuttering. These are behaviors that can be observed in a mirror, recorded, and identified on video and audiotapes. The identification of features that occur frequently during treatment is often a good place to begin simply because there are multiple occurrences. At this stage it is important to display an attitude of interest, curiosity, and enthusiasm for this first exploratory step. Some speakers, especially if they also have characteristics of cluttering (Chapter 13), will have difficulty identifying and monitoring overt behaviors that are obvious to the listener. They could also miss short but obvious fluency breaks. In such situations, the clinician can become a "human tape recorder." Rather than recording and replaying examples of stuttering on an audio or videotape (which, although somewhat cumbersome, might also help), the clinician can replicate what the speaker does on a real-time basis. By paying close attention to the speaker, the clinician can shadow the person's fluent speech and imitate the person's fluency breaks as they occur, immediately "playing them back" to the speaker. As

CLINICAL INSIGHT

On the afternoon of one of our first therapy sessions, I was helping Joyce, a woman in her 50s, to identify some of the characteristic behaviors that accompanied her moments of stuttering. As we worked together to identify and experiment with the various behaviors we were seeing and hearing, I commented on a particularly severe example. With a good deal of enthusiasm, I told her that what she had just done was "a really interesting way of stuttering." My interest and positive attitude about a behavior that had represented only embarrassment, shame, and misery for more than 50 years elicited surprise and spontaneous laughter from her and from me as well, as I experienced her delight. (WM)

the clinician closely follows the speaker and accurately imitates the physical and acoustic characteristics of the fluency break, the self-monitoring skills of the speaker improve. As described in a Clinical Insight box in Chapter 1, some students and clinicians who are not yet desensitized to stuttering are likely to be surprised and possibly distressed by this suggestion. It is, however, an effective way for the clinician to understand the overt aspects of the speaker's stuttering behavior.

In order to explore and identify the less obvious intrinsic features, the clinician can ask the speaker to make another list termed "things I do because I stutter," such as avoidances, anxieties, feelings of fear and helplessness, and the likely extensive number of decisions the speaker makes because of the possibility of stuttering. Some of these choices might not be obvious to the speaker and typically take longer to discover. For example, speakers might not associate many of their decisions to avoid certain words or activities with stuttering, thinking, "This is just who I am," or, "This is the way I have always talked." Depending on the age and maturity of the client, there are several ways for the clinician to describe this

process, including the approach similar to the process of creating a map described in Chapter 10:

Our goal at the outset is to create a map of the territory we will be traveling through. At the outset of our journey we want to understand the nature of the terrain and some of our options. In order to make the trip less mysterious and frightening, we want to understand the places that are likely to be particularly difficult. We want to know what skills and strengths we can bring along with us to help us respond to and perhaps change and respond more effectively to some of the things that we will encounter. As with any adventure, parts of the journey will be more difficult than others. But I want you to know that you are not alone and that together we will be able to make the choices that are best for you. We will know the direction we want to go, and there will be many interesting choices and victories that await you along the way.

Although the clinician will obviously lead the way during the initial stages of identifying the characteristics of the speaker and his or her stuttering, it is important for the client to take the lead in developing this list. This is likely to be the first time the person has been asked to assume this level of responsibility for the behavioral and cognitive features of his or her stuttering and the ability to communicate. By writing down and analyzing these surface and intrinsic features, the client is taking the first step toward self-management. In addition, this activity provides a way for the person to begin to externalize and objectify the features of the problem as described in the constructivist-narrative approach to therapy in Chapter 8.

At the outset of treatment, it can be helpful for the clinician to ask the client to prepare a written autobiography. The goal here is to understand the client's story and the influence that stuttering has played in the many facets of the person's life to this point. The assignment might also reveal something about how motivated the client is, his or her general intellectual and linguistic abilities, and his or her understanding about the nature of stuttering. After some training by the clinician, the speaker can also analyze tapes of himself or herself or other people who stutter in order to begin categorizing and understanding the different surface features of stuttering. A good place to begin is to identify examples of "good stuttering," the relatively brief and effortless examples of stuttering moments that most clients produce. These forms of relatively easy stuttering provide a good example of the less effortful stuttering we would like the speaker to eventually produce, and that are usually easier for the person to approach and analyze than the more effortful and complex forms of stuttering. Although we want to identify and demystify as many characteristics of

the speaker's stuttering as possible, some features might not be obvious until we become calibrated to the speaker and his or her cognitive and linguistic styles.

During this initial stage of therapy, the speaker is inclined to be highly motivated, for the speaker has reached the action stage of change described in Chapter 7. Clinicians can take this opportunity to demonstrate a genuine interest and curiosity as, along with the speaker, they begin to explore how the client manifests the problem in his or her own unique ways. The clinician has the opportunity to introduce information about what stuttering is and what it is not. To the extent that the speaker is able to understand and become desensitized to the stuttering experience, this initial stage of exploration will be a stimulating first step in the process of change.

Desensitization

As the speaker begins to appreciate that many of his or her responses to stuttering (or the possibility of stuttering) are understandable and natural, he or she will experience a degree of desensitization to both the overt (surface) and covert (intrinsic) features of the experience. For many people this is a critical step, because it will be difficult to critically identify, analyze, and vary behavior without achieving at least some distance and objectivity. For some clients who continue to be overwhelmed by their stuttering experience, identification and desensitization will take considerably longer. Eventually, the speaker will understand that it is possible to stay in the moment of stuttering and to reduce his or her fear to a manageable level. The person will begin to realize that he or she is not as helpless as in the past and appreciate that he or she has some options. Once the speaker is able to stay in the moment of stuttering with some level of objectivity, the stage is set for beginning to vary the surface features of stuttering.

If the clinician has not already done so, he or she might want to consider introducing the idea of stuttering on purpose, a technique often termed voluntary stuttering (also called pseudo-stuttering, negative practice, or bouncing). As we indicated in Chapter 6, the speaker's response to this activity provides the clinician with a clear indication of the fear associated with the stuttering experience. Until the speaker is able to decrease excessive levels of anxiety and fear to more manageable levels, he or she will have little success during the succeeding steps of treatment.

The clinician can introduce voluntary stuttering by asking the client to follow him or her in producing easy one- or two-unit repetitions and brief (1–2 second) prolongations. The clinician demonstrates to the client that it is possible to stutter and remain calm and completely in charge of his or her speaking. Some speakers who are quite desensitized might want to experiment with more elaborate stuttering, gradually incorporating the characteristics that are typical of their stuttered speech during more severe moments, including struggle behaviors such as the blocking of airflow and voicing. Speakers can voluntarily stutter in a variety of treatment (including telephone calls) and beyond-treatment settings in order to continually desensitize themselves, acknowledge their stuttering to others, and extend their levels of assertiveness. Although several experienced clinicians have advocated the use of this procedure (e.g., Grossman, 2008; Mayo et al., 2006; Sheehan & Voas, 1957), there has been relatively little empirical evidence for the practice. Plexico et al. (2005) found that seven adults who had successfully man-

aged their stuttering credited the use of voluntary stuttering beyond the clinic environment as critical to their therapeutic success, helping them achieve a personal sense of freedom. They described how it helped them to demonstrate their acknowledgment and acceptance of their stuttering. It was also a way to show the listener they were stuttering, thus minimizing the fear that a listener would suddenly discover that they were hiding their stuttering.

Of course, some speakers will initially resist the idea of stuttering on purpose. It seems counterintuitive to perform the very behavior they have come to us to help them prevent. Byrd et al. (2016) administered a 56-item survey to 206 adults (ages 18–85) in order to determine the affective, behavioral, and cognitive effects of voluntary stuttering. They also considered the effectiveness of three forms of voluntary stuttering: an imitation of the participant's real stuttering, sound and syllable repetitions with no tension (bouncing), and prolongations and blocks with no tension (slides). Although several participants indicated that voluntary stuttering was too "emotionally difficult" to do, following an initial experience of experimenting in speaking situations, the fear dissipated. Those who used voluntary stuttering in a manner similar to their real stuttering and did so beyond the therapy environment in daily communication situations reported significant reductions in avoidance behavior and decreased physical tension. They also reported experiencing reduced severity and an improved quality of life. Unfortunately, approximately one third of the participants reported no exposure to any form of voluntary stuttering during therapy, possibly because many clinicians are unfamiliar or (more likely) because many clinicians are inhibited and uncomfortable using or modeling voluntary stuttering for their clients.

With the clinician leading the way, voluntary stuttering opens the door for the speaker to experiment with other ways of stuttering and to become continually desensitized to the stuttering moment. After fighting for so many years to keep from stuttering, they can "let go" and (likely for the first time) give themselves "permission" to stutter. Many people find this to be a highly liberating experience that characteristically results in dramatically increased fluency. Perhaps most important, stuttering on purpose—particularly if it is done in an open and effortless manner—provides a way for the speaker to break the link between the experience of stuttering and being out of control. As the speaker learns to stay in the moment of stuttering, he or she will gradually see that instead of being helpless, he or she has some good options available for revising his or her fluency.

Variation

As the speaker becomes able to identify specific behaviors and attitudes and to decrease his or her reflexive reaction of anxiety and fear associated with the antici-pation or the onset of stuttering, he or she will slowly achieve the ability to make some changes. Instead of seeing stuttering as something that feels like it is "happening to" him or her, the speaker begins to recognize that much of his or her stuttering is a result of the decisions the speaker is making about speaking; things that he or she can identify and change. Coaching by the clinician during the moment of stuttering provides the speaker with a model for altering selected features of stuttering.

Of course, going from his or her old, reflexive, and automatic pattern of stuttering to fluent speech is an enormous leap and not one that a speaker should be expected to accomplish early in treatment. The speaker will have a much greater chance of success if he or she is asked to simply alter or vary some selected features of the stuttering. A small step forward is all that is necessary—or expected—at the outset. Moreover, success is apt to be intermittent. As during the identification stage, secondary or surface behaviors (eye blinks, junk words, postponement devices) that occur frequently, and are especially distracting or unappealing, are ideal features on which to concentrate. The speaker is not asked to stop performing these features, but rather to vary them

---

CLINICAL INSIGHT

In order to complete their assignment of posing as a moderately severe stutterer, two graduate students walked through a local mall and engaged in conversations with people at several stores. As they entered a bookstore, one of the students realistically stuttered as she asked for a book on the topic of physical therapy. The clerk checked her computer and indicated that no books on that topic were available. The student, still obviously stuttering, asked for something on the topic of occupational therapy. The clerk's search was unsuccessful yet again. After a brief pause, the clerk turned to the student and cautiously asked, "Would you be interested in something on speech therapy?"

CLINICAL INSIGHT

During the initial stages of acquiring a skill, many of the things we are asked to do seem counterintuitive. When we first learn to drive we are told that if the car goes into a skid, we should steer in the direction that our car is sliding. Of course, that seems nonsensical until we try it and it works. When traveling at even a moderate speed on a motorcycle, one way to turn to the *right* is to push on the *right* handgrip; when turning to the *left* you push on the *left* handgrip. It's called counter steering, and it allows the bike to lean and move in the direction you want to go. In various forms of karate, it is frequently best to step toward rather than away from your competitor. For most people, each of these choices would be the last response they would intuitively select. Similarly, to someone who has spent years hiding his or her stuttering, attending a support group with other people who stutter is not likely to be intuitive (Trichon & Tetnowski, 2006). Likewise, voluntarily stuttering is the last thing you would think of doing. It is counterintuitive to stutter in the moment that you would rather avoid or escape from the experience. Many treatment techniques require a different, often unique way of talking. The new way of speaking, although it might yield much sought-after fluency, is unstable, often sounds unnatural, and feels strange. Even with greater fluency, the new ways of talking are likely to be uncomfortable and different from the way of speaking that you have become used to. The new way of speaking might feel like a façade and not who you are. You feel like you are not being yourself and that adds to the anxiety when you try to communicate. However, with the courage and trust to face the very thing you wish to avoid, you could discover unexpected positive results.

in a preplanned and creative manner. That is, the person might select the behavior of postponing words by producing a series of "ahs" prior to the utterance of a feared word. Rather than attempting to cease production of the "ah" as a postponement or timing device, the speaker could begin to systematically vary the rate, intensity, number, or type of vowel segment (e.g., "eh," "oh," or "uh," instead of "ah"). As long as the speaker achieves some measure of control as evidenced by his or her ability to vary the old automatic utterance of "ah," a victory is achieved.

Another example might involve the slight variation of the especially difficult and scary blocks where airflow and voicing have stopped. At the initial stages of variation, a speaker might be able to move from being completely stuck to saying the word fluently. However, a more likely victory is for the speaker to let some air leak out in order to achieve airflow and possibly even voicing. Although some of these activities will detract from the speaker's overall fluency, the critical issue is the ability of the person to achieve a degree of control over his or her speech, a degree of control that he or she has never before experienced or appreciated. The variation of this previously uncontrolled behavior will set the stage for the speaker to modify his or her stuttering in more specific and refined ways.

A useful technique that has been advocated by many clinicians, including

Dean Williams, has been termed *freezing*. As the desensitized speaker willingly continues to stutter, the clinician explains and demonstrates how the stuttering can be systematically altered. The primary goal is to experiment and to "play" with the possibilities for stuttering in a different and easier manner. With this coaching by the clinician, the speaker continues to become desensitized and begins to recognize what he or she is doing to prevent the forward movement of speech and the transition to the next sound, syllable, or word. While following instructions by the clinician to slowly allow airflow and a gradual lessening of tension and struggle, the speaker attends to the physiological features necessary for making the transition to the next speech segment.

This form of coaching is vividly demonstrated on videos available through the Stuttering Foundation (see especially #76, Do You Stutter? Straight Talk for Teens; #79, Therapy in Action: The School-Age Child Who Stutters; and #83, If You Stutter: Advice for Adults). Such coaching might sound something like the following, in which a client is describing a conversation with his supervisor:

Client: "I was trying to tell my su, su, su . . ."

Clinician: (*reaching to touch the arm of the client*) "Good, OK get that one . . . stay with it. Keep stuttering just as you are.

Now see if you can gradually begin to slow the rate of your repetitions slightly."

Client: The client continues to repeat the syllable "su" and finds that he is able to continue stuttering while gradually slowing his rate of repetitions.

Clinician: "Now, produce the repetitions more rapidly. Now slowly again."

(*Client does so.*)

"Good, now slow down again and slowly move through the word by slowly stretching out the sounds and continue."

Modification

Now that speakers have become knowledgeable about their stuttering, they are somewhat desensitized, and they have experienced success in varying their typical pattern of stuttering, they are asked to develop more focused and specific responses. Again, the goal is to replace the habitual, reflexive, and out-of-control stuttering with a new, smoother (although not necessarily fluent) utterance.

It is important for both the clinician and client to appreciate that the old behavioral (and cognitive) responses to stuttering are well practiced and habitual. The old patterns of speaking are also comfortable, and on many occasions, what is expected by both the speaker and the listener. The new, albeit better, ways of speaking will feel awkward and will feel and sound strange until they are practiced enough and begin to become habituated. Smith and Kelly (1997) proposed a helpful theoretical explanation of what occurs as clinicians attempt to assist a person who has stuttered for many years. They suggested that stuttering behaviors could be best considered as hypercoordinated rather than discoordinated behaviors· That is, complex systems have a tendency to self-organize and settle into a mode of behavior that is preferred over other possible modes (attractor states). The more stable the attractor state is, the more effort or energy is required to move the system out of that condition. The process of change could involve helping the system (or person) to reorganize in order to move from a coordinated and stable mode of functioning to a different and unstable mode. Furthermore, because many systems are likely to function in a nonlinear and dynamic manner, it is unlikely that a single approach will facilitate the transition from one mode to another. That is, the process of change goes beyond simple cause-and-effect relationships, because there are many levels of functioning and many interactions occurring in complex and dynamic systems. Finally, there are no particular end-states to be defined for such systems. Rather, the properties of a complex and dynamic system interact and combine to produce new emergent properties that are likely to be unique to each system (Smith & Kelly, 1997).

What this model means for the process of therapeutic change is that established ways of thinking and behaving are usually stable. In a sense, the old behavioral and cognitive responses have built up a good deal of inertia that needs to be overcome if they are to be replaced with new and better responses. It is not surprising then that the process will often require discipline and practice in order to reorganize the system. Because people and the problem of stuttering are complex and dynamic, there is no single best strategy for assisting the person in accomplishing this reorganization. Finally, the end result of successful intervention and reorganization is not necessarily predictable or likely to be identical for every speaker. As the reader will note, many of these ideas coincide with the basic principles of change described at the outset of this chapter.

The first step in the modification techniques is called cancellation. This is some-times referred to as a postevent modification because the speaker changes the form of the stuttering after it occurs. Immediately after a stuttered word, the speaker stops and pauses for 2 to 3 seconds. The brief pause highlights the stuttering and could serve as a mild form of punishment for the speaker as his or her ability to communicate is terminated. Some people (including those who stutter) are somewhat determined to complete the message, and any stoppage both increases the time pressure to communicate and creates the hurdle of having to reinitiate speech. As easy as this task might seem, many individuals who stutter have some difficulty doing this during reading and more so during conversational speech. Those speakers who have not yet achieved a reasonable degree of desensitization often find this task especially difficult. However, the activities performed during this brief period provide the foundation of the stuttering-modification procedure.

As the client is able to detect his or her stuttering and consistently pause following the event, the client is asked to analyze the more obvious physiological features of his or her stuttering. Now, during the pause, the speaker slowly pantomimes his or her stuttering, examining the physical features of his or her behavior. As the speaker rehearses the physical patterns that correspond to his or her just-stuttered speech, he or she can begin to get a feel for his or her stuttering by considering such questions as, "Did I cut off my airflow and voicing? How and where am I constricting my vocal tract? What are the articulatory postures, respiratory, or phonatory movements I am doing that prevent me from saying the next sound or syllable?" At the outset this process will require a few moments, but with practice, it can be completed promptly. Once this analysis is accomplished, the speaker is rewarded by being able to continue with his or her message.

In the next step of the procedure, the clinician asks the speaker to use the pause following the stuttered word to silently pantomime a new, easy version of the stuttering. The speaker gradually includes both airflow and voicing and produces the word out loud. The speaker now reaches the final stage of this technique. Following each stuttered word, the speaker briefly pauses; quickly formulates the appropriate combinations of respiratory, articulatory, and phonatory patterns; and then produces the previously stuttered event with a slightly slower, effortless, and smooth form of "fluent stuttering." The new form of stuttering has the characteristics of fluency in terms of airflow, light contact of the articulators, gradual and continual voicing, and smooth transitional movements to the next sounds and syllables. It is important to note once again that although the speaker could likely say the stuttered word again fluently, the purpose at this point is not to achieve fluency. The goal is to replace (or cancel) the old, habitual stuttering response with a new and easier form of stuttering. The ability to use this technique is usually facilitated in a progression of reading, monologue, and conversation, both within and then beyond the treatment setting.

It is important to stress that the speaker is not canceling the stuttering event with the goal of achieving fluency. After all, the addition of yet another moment of easier and smooth stuttering following a real stuttering event will result in speech that is even more disrupted. However, the activity serves to break the link between stuttering and helplessness. Rather than reflexively fleeing from the event, the speaker is now able to stay in the moment, take charge of the experience, and select a new and better response. It is important for the speaker to appreciate the sense of agency that accompanies this experience. Each moment of stuttering, although it might be undesirable, is an opportunity to take charge of the stuttering—a chance at bat. At the outset of treatment, stuttering is scoring run after run while the speaker, although catching and systematically modifying the stuttering, has not rounded the bases once. Once the speaker begins to take charge of the large majority of the stuttering moments (something approaching 80%), there is often an increase in fluency and, more important, a dramatic increase in the speaker's confidence about their ability to repair the situation.

As a result of practice and persistence, persons who stutter can succeed both within and beyond the treatment environment. As individuals gain ability and confidence, the ability to successfully repair their situation in the stream of speech increases. The speaker begins to realize that he or she has a choice and that it is possible for him or her to be able to count on and successfully use well-practiced responses to previously feared situations; he or she is able to manipulate and play with possibilities within the turmoil of the stuttering moment. Moreover, the speaker is free to move ahead and achieve new success in increasingly more difficult speaking situations.

It might be obvious from the previous descriptions that cancellations are usually difficult to perform, particularly during the expectations and time pressure of daily speaking situations. Listeners tend to interrupt without waiting for the speaker to go back and modify the stuttered word. Because they are concentrating so closely on how they are speaking, speakers might lose their train of thought—although this

CLINICAL INSIGHT

Kayaking in whitewater requires a high level of skill and confidence. It is easy to lose control and find yourself under the surface of the water and in a threatening situation. Some anxiety is part of the experience. Complicating the situation is the fact that the novice tends to be rigid and inflexible. With increasing stress associated with the approach of a difficult section of the river, the likelihood of a mistake is high. Fortunately, with practice the novice becomes more proficient. Progress is seen as the paddler's strokes become more efficient and blended together. A crucial step takes place when the person learns to repair a mistake by rolling back to the surface.

Of course, this takes considerable practice. It is best to begin in the safe environment of a pool or lake. An experienced instructor explains the rationale and details of the rolling technique, and, together, the instructor and the paddler go over the sequence of events that must take place for the technique to be successful. The techniques are done deliberately and slowly, in a preplanned manner by setting up for the ideal roll position. The paddler learns to roll to both the left and the right, to roll with the kayak filled with water, and to roll without a paddle using only the arms and the associated hip snap. Eventually, the paddler learns to roll without first setting up in a roll position in order to approximate the unexpected situations found on the river. Finally, it is time to move from the safety of the flat water to the dynamic and unpredictable tumult of the river.

Depending on such factors as the water temperature, turbulence, and obstacles that appear in the boater's path, the first attempts of the paddler to roll in a moving stream are not likely to be successful. The likelihood of success decreases dramatically when the stresses of time pressure, distraction, and especially fear enter the picture. The paddler's initial reaction to being upside down for the first time in the river is apt to be one of fear or even panic. The techniques that worked so well in the secure environment of the pool are quickly forgotten, and the first reaction of the paddler is to exit the boat and swim to the surface. The paddler comes to the realization that his or her techniques must be practiced to the point that they are automatic and do not require thought. If the paddler takes time to think, what he or she will think about is fear.

As the paddler learns to habitually react to the situations on the river in this manner, positive things begin to occur. Confidence builds and paddling skills increase geometrically. The person becomes more flexible and begins to adopt a style of working with, rather than against, the power of the river. If a mistake is made, the person will repair it by getting back to the surface of the water and achieving control. Even better, the person will begin to experiment and play with different new techniques, intentionally entering more difficult sections of the river. The paddler gradually becomes less rigid, paddling with greater flexibility. Because he is more flexible, the paddler and his boat are able to absorb the impacts that previously had such a profound influence on his equilibrium. He or she gradually gains confidence in his or her ability to correct mistakes and, thus, is less concerned about making them. It's not long before the person begins to seek out more challenging rapids to paddle and new rivers to navigate.

Source: Adapted from "Paddling in Stream of Speech," *Letting GO*, National Stuttering Association, September/October, 1995.

will improve with practice. Most people who have undergone treatment will indicate that although they often become efficient in using cancellations in the treatment setting and outside of treatment while in the company of the clinician, they choose not to use this technique in most daily speaking situations. Nevertheless, it is an important technique to have available. The cancellation technique provides the speaker with the rationale and initial entry into a strategy for modifying the habitual stuttering the speaker had perceived as uncontrollable.

The next step in the modification of the stuttered event is the para-event modification, typically called a "pullout" or "slide out." Now, rather than waiting until he or she completes a stuttered word, the speaker will grab the word and begin to "slide out of it" by enhancing his or her airflow and voicing, altering his or her vocal tract with more appropriate articulatory postures, and gently stuttering smoothly through the word. Clients often find that pulling out of a stuttered moment is a natural progression evolving from the cancellation technique and might begin doing this spontaneously. The pullout is less obvious than the cancellation, communication is enhanced, and listener reactions might be more favorable. Nevertheless, it is important to continue practicing the postevent or cancellation technique as there will undoubtedly be stressful speaking situations when the speaker will be unable to catch his or her stuttering in time to use a pullout. On these occasions the last line of defense, the final opportunity to catch and take charge of a moment of stuttering, is the cancellation.

The final step in the modification sequence is the pre-event modification or preparatory set. As the speaker anticipates a moment of stuttering (and chooses not to avoid it), he or she begins the word with a smooth form of stuttering. With the "prep set," the speaker is preplanning, rather than reacting to, his or her stuttering. As with the preceding techniques, the targets incorporated in the fluency modification strategies (full breath, airflow, gradual onset of constant phonation, and

CLINICAL DECISION MAKING

The fluency that results from the cancellation repair technique is earned fluency to be sure, but it is extremely tenuous. On occasion, especially if a speaker requires additional desensitization, a speaker will be unable to successfully cancel the stuttered word. That is, as the speaker begins to replace the old stuttering with a smoother, controlled version of stuttering, he or she will lose control and revert back to his or her old, automatic, and helpless stuttering. If this happens, the client should attempt the cancellation of the stuttered word again until he or she regains control of the fluent stuttering. Success is defined by the client indicating that he or she is in charge of the word. The client can signal to the clinician with his or her finger whether he or she is in control of the stuttering. On occasion, it might take several cycles of losing and regaining control before he or she is able to be completely in charge of the stuttered word. In any case, it is best not to leave that word and go on to the next one until the speaker has taken charge of that word by successfully canceling it.

light articulatory contacts) are essential for achieving a smooth preparatory set. Furthermore, if a client's speech contains many very brief fluency breaks that he or she has difficulty identifying, the preparatory set provides a good way to eliminate them.

Perhaps the most difficult thing for both the clinician and especially the person who stutters to understand about these techniques is that the initial goal is not fluent speech. It is, however, the long-term goal. As the speaker begins to gradually modify the form of his or her stuttering and achieve a measure of command over his or her speech production system, fluency will follow. The process requires continued desensitization and experimentation with elements of the stuttering modification techniques that are found to be helpful for the speaker. The techniques will need to be overlearned and used in increasingly more difficult speaking situations beyond the clinic environment. The speaker will need to recruit the understanding and support of others, particularly friends and coworkers, so that they can facilitate the use of these techniques in the person's daily speaking situations. Listeners will need to understand the rationale and nature of the techniques so that they can recognize and reward what might first appear to be the speaker's somewhat unusual speaking patterns.

In order to be sure that the client understands both the rationale and the steps associated with each technique, it is often effective for the clinician to ask the client to explain and demonstrate it for the clinician. Of course, this can also be done with others present in the treatment setting or at home with a spouse or parent. Another related approach is for the clinician and client to switch roles, with the client guiding the clinician through the use of a technique. This can be enjoyable as well as instructive as the clinician makes intentional errors and feigns a misunderstanding concerning the technique or rationale for using the technique.

As we have stressed, in most cases it will take extensive and disciplined practice for the speaker to incorporate any technique into his or her habitual response during daily speaking situations. After learning a technique during a therapy session, it is not unusual for some people to come to the next session and inform the clinician that they were unable to use the technique:

> **Client:** "I tried the technique we practiced last time, and you know what? It didn't work."
>
> **Clinician:** "How many times did you try it?"
>
> **Client:** "Well, I attempted it yesterday, maybe 10 times!"

When we get that response, maybe we should respond by saying something like this:

> "Well, try it *300 times* and we'll see how you're doing then!"

Stabilization

From the outset of treatment, it will be essential for the speaker to transfer his or her new perceptions and abilities to situations beyond the treatment setting. During stabilization the speaker's performance in his or her daily world becomes the major focus. During this phase, the newly learned modification skills are practiced under increasingly more stressful conditions both within and beyond the treatment setting. The goal now is for the speaker to become resilient in responding to the variety of communicative pressures encountered in daily speaking situations. In order for the speaker to withstand these pressures, the various techniques must be overlearned. Unless such a level of performance is achieved the speaker will be unable to rely on his or her abilities when communicative demands are swift and intimidating. As we suggest many times throughout this text, speakers will have to practice techniques correctly hundreds or thousands of times in order to develop such a level of skill and confidence. This, of course, will take some time, but this is what is necessary for techniques to become an integral part of the person. Regardless of how many times it is done, successfully performing a technique within the safety of the clinic provides little indication about what will occur during the stressful speaking situations found in everyday life. Fortunately, as we mentioned in Chapter 2, humans have the opportunity to practice speech as much or more than any other activity.

It is also helpful for the speaker to test the new patterns of speaking and thinking in a systematic way. The clinician and client can develop and refine a continuum of easier to more difficult speaking situations. Some of the assessment devices described in Chapter 6 might help at this point. Of course, the ability of the person to develop expertise in monitoring and modifying stuttering will continue well beyond the period of formal treatment with the clinician. As described in more detail in Chapter 15, accomplished speakers will continually "push the envelope" and challenge themselves with new speaking adventures.

Stabilization activities also provide a good opportunity to heighten the ability of the speaker to monitor speech produc-

tion via proprioception. By using devices that provide auditory masking, delayed auditory feedback (DAF), or frequency altered feedback (FAF), the speaker can learn to focus on the feel and timing of his or her articulatory movements. Although such devices are not essential, they can be helpful in developing a heightened sense of the physical adjustments necessary for enhancing fluency.

At this time, it is also useful for the clinician to assist the speaker in bringing forth and revisiting fears and anxieties associated with especially difficult speaking situations. These could be experiences of fluency failure in the past as well as current or upcoming situations. As explained in the following section, with practice, the speaker can learn to withstand the negative emotions and counter the negative self-talk that often accompany these experiences.

LISTENER RESPONSE TO MANAGEMENT AND ACKNOWLEDGMENT TECHNIQUES

Kamhi (2003) suggested that most listeners respond in a generally appropriate and well-meaning manner when they encounter individuals who stutter. Of course, how a listener responds can be influenced by how the speaker is coping with his or her stuttering. On occasion, the avoidance and struggle behavior by the speaker creates confusion or even anxiety on the part of the listener. It is not unusual for listeners to be unaware that what they are witnessing is stuttering and not some other condition. To the extent that the speaker can indicate that he or she is stuttering, perhaps by stuttering in a manner that most everyday listeners associate with typical stuttering behavior (repetitions of sounds or words rather than blocking or extreme struggle behavior) or by acknowledging the fact that he or she is stuttering, listeners are apt to be more receptive to and understanding about the situation.

Kamhi (2003) also suggested that the high cognitive load experienced by the speaker (along with the stress of the communicative interaction) often results in gaze aversion by the speaker followed by a similar response by the listener. He suggested that this is what most listeners will naturally and instinctively do rather than following the "rules" suggested by professionals and support groups (e.g., maintain eye contact, wait patiently, not complete sentences or words, pay attention to the message rather than the manner of speaking, and not show discomfort, pity, or sympathy). For the most part, everyday listeners are unaware of these rules, and as Kamhi pointed out, clinicians should not suggest to their clients that most listeners will respond in an ideal manner.

A similar situation occurs as the speaker begins to consistently use fluency and stuttering modification techniques beyond the therapeutic setting. Listeners might not only fail to notice the often subtle improvements in the quality of fluency, but could also sense that something is different in the nature of the stuttering. Unless informed, the typical listener will not appreciate that the speaker is attempting to change his or her stuttering into easier forms or to use pullout and cancellation techniques. Unless the speaker or someone else explains what is occurring, the listener is likely to wonder if, beyond the stuttering, there is "something else wrong with this person." Manning et al. (1999) had groups of naïve listeners use a bipolar scale, a handicap scale, and open-ended questions to evaluate an adult male who simulated mild stuttering (SSI-3 score

of 17) or utilized stuttering-modification techniques (cancellations or pullouts). Listeners consistently preferred the condition where the speaker was stuttering over the condition when the speaker was stuttering and using stuttering-modification techniques. The results suggested that everyday listeners might be likely to react less favorably to a speaker with mild levels of stuttering who is modifying his or her stuttered speech than when the same speaker is simply stuttering.

People who stutter can lead the way in determining how listeners will react by informing their listeners. For example, Van Riper (1982) suggested that listeners are likely to think better of the speaker who acknowledges his or her stuttering and is able to convey to the listener that he or she is actively working on the problem. Many authors (Blood & Blood, 1982; Breitenfeldt & Lorenz, 1989; Collins & Blood, 1990; Hastorf et al., 1979; Silverman, 1988a) have suggested that acknowledgment of stuttering by the speaker could assist in improving the typically negative reaction of listeners.

By presenting listeners with videos of both an acknowledgment and a non-acknowledgment condition, Collins and Blood (1990) found support for Hastorf et al.'s (1979) suggestion that self-acknowledgment of a problem by an individual reduced listener uncertainty and promoted a more positive reaction. Collins and Blood (1990) also observed that the speaker's acknowledgment of his or her stuttering was particularly effective in eliciting a more positive response from listeners when the stuttering was rated as severe rather than mild.

Healey et al. (2007), however, found no effect for the strategy of speaker acknowledgment of their stuttering. Likert-type-scale data of five personality traits (sincerity, likability, trustworthiness, character, and emotional adjustment) indicated no differences in listener reactions to speakers who acknowledged their stuttering in one of three conditions—at the beginning, at the end, or not at all—during brief videotaped interviews. Healey et al. explained the contrasting results of their study and that of Collins and Blood (1990) in terms of a variety of differences in the research design, instructions, and stimuli conditions. For example, the listeners in the Healey et al. investigation took part in only one of the three acknowledgment conditions, whereas the participants in the Collins and Blood investigation observed speakers in both an acknowledgment and a nonacknowledgment condition. It appears to be that listeners are able to appreciate the potentially helpful effect of acknowledgment only when they have the opportunity to consider and contrast both conditions.

An investigation by Lee and Manning (2010) contrasting both research designs suggests that this is the case. The results indicated that unless listeners have the opportunity to directly compare (Collins & Blood, 1990) the self-acknowledgment of stuttering with a more common stuttering-only experience (Healey et al., 2007), self-acknowledgment by the speaker is not likely to be appreciated. It could be that as naïve listeners gain even minimal experience and understanding about the speaker's situation through a forthright and nonapologetic self-acknowledgment, they are better able to make an adjustment resulting in a more favorable evaluation of the speaker. The results provide support for the anchor adjustment model proposed by MacKinnon et al. (2007) suggesting that as listeners become more informed about the nature of stuttering, they are more likely to respond to the person in a positive manner. Furthermore, it has also been suggested that a more important aspect of self-acknowledgment lies in the ability of the speaker to decrease the avoidance behavior and achieve an agentic lifestyle (Bloodstein, 1995; Sheehan, 1975; Van Riper, 1982).

A study by Byrd et al. (2017) shed additional light on listener perceptions of self-acknowledgment of stuttering by controlling for a variety of variables: observer and speaker gender, and listener experience with stuttering. A total of 173 participants (ages 18–35) viewed two of four videos where a male (age 21) and female (age 24) read a version of the Rainbow Passage (Fairbanks, 1960). The self-disclosure videos contained a nonapologetic, neutral disclosure statement: "Just so you know, I sometimes stutter, so you might hear me repeat some words, sounds or phrases," a statement that has been shown to elicit more positive listener responses than an apologetic statement ("Please bear with me as speaking has always been difficult for me"; Byrd et al. 2016). As both speakers had a history of stuttering, the videos contained voluntary stuttering on 24% of the words with minimal variation due to the occurrence of some real stuttering moments. Participants saw all possible parings of all videos with the male and female speakers both with and without disclosure statements. Immediately after viewing two videos, participants completed a two-part survey consisting of the speaker personality traits (e.g., friendly, outgoing, intelligent, confident, distracted). Response options to the questions were Tape 1, Tape 2, and no difference. The second part of the survey consisted of a series of 13 questions concerning the participants' experience with people who stutter and comments about the speaker and the speaker's

CLINICAL INSIGHT

The following is the acknowledgment of stuttering by a college senior. Following a group therapy meeting where avoidance and risk-taking were discussed, he decided to email all the members of his class with the following comments:

Good morning everybody.

As you all know, the presentation on Russia's human rights is Friday. My group and I are looking forward to it, but I wanted to inform those who may not be aware that I have a speech impediment known as stuttering, which is a communication disorder where the flow of speech is disrupted by a series of either blocks, prolongation of sounds, or repetition of sounds. For the first time as an adult, I have gotten back into speech therapy, and I have 9 months of progress under my belt, and I am ready to face my fear of public speaking. In the past, I would drop any class that required any form of oral communication in front of the class or I would do any such assignment in private. This is my last semester and I will be doing all my oral presentations as they are meant to be done. All of my professors are "on board" with what I am trying to achieve for myself, and I just wanted to take this opportunity to give everyone a heads-up on what to expect Friday. If anyone has questions about stuttering or about Russia after Friday, I am more than happy to answer them in person or by email. I appreciate everyone for taking the time to read this, and I hope everyone has had an opportunity to catch up on rest and relax over the break.

Best regards, Trevor

Note: As it turned out, he took the risk, stuttered somewhat at the outset of his presentation (including some voluntary stuttering), and received a warm reception by the class after concluding a successful presentation.

communication in Tape 1 or Tape 2 along with any additional comments.

The results indicated that the speakers who self-disclosed their stuttering were significantly more likely to be designated as friendly, outgoing, and confident. Observers rated the male speaker more positively than the female whether there was a self-disclosure statement or not. In comparison to the male speakers, observers were also less likely to choose the female speaker as friendly, outgoing, and confident, a bias that the authors pointed out has been documented in many disciplines (see Coleman et al., 2015). In addition, observers were more likely to identify the female speaker as unfriendly, shy, unintelligent, insecure, and more distractible during the videos. The authors advised that this being the case, females who stutter are especially likely to be vulnerable to being stigmatized.

COGNITIVE RESTRUCTURING

Regardless of the overall treatment strategy, in order for speakers to achieve success, they must eventually develop fresh ways of thinking about themself and their problem. Discovering that there are alternative ways of considering one's situation facilitates the development of an agentic lifestyle. As we described in Chapter 8, a primary goal of counseling focuses on assisting the client in experimenting with new ways of creating meaning and developing independent problem-solving responses, change that is necessary for long-term success. This aspect of treatment does not always need to be dealt with directly with all individuals in order for cognitive change to occur. If the clinician targets behavioral change and the elaboration of fluency rather than also focusing on cognitive change, the speaker could nevertheless experience constructive changes in his or her self-concept and ability to communicate.

It is good to remember that it will take some time for the speaker to adjust to and incorporate the new cognitive changes. As described earlier in this chapter, the new ways of speaking and thinking will sound and feel unfamiliar. Adolescents and adults who stutter have spent many years adjusting to their speech and coping with the problems presented by their attempts to communicate. Even though the speaker's new responses are desirable, it will take some time to integrate these changes into everyday life. The client who retains self-defeating mental images and negative thoughts and beliefs about speech and his or her ability to manage it is much less apt to succeed once he or she is on his or her own.

Applying Personal Construct Theory With Adolescents and Adults

In Chapters 7 and 8, we introduced the basic tenets of personal construct theory (PCT) as it relates to principles of counseling. We now present some of the findings of applied research with this theoretical perspective. The first to apply PCT to individuals who stutter, Fransella (1972) hypothesized that a person stutters "because it is in this way that he can anticipate the greatest number of events; it is by behaving in this way that life is most meaningful to him" (p. 58). Although this might sound illogical and even offensive to some individuals who stutter, from a personal construct perspective it simply means that when the speaker stutters in a situation, it is in line with what he or she would predict.

Fransella (1972) attempted to increase the meaningfulness of the fluent speaker role for individuals who stuttered using a technique called "controlled elaboration." That is, Fransella used behavioral experiments (using repertory and implications grids) to assist each of the 16 participants in the study to examine the validity of the construct system and to focus on occasions where he or she had experienced fluency. The treatment focused on assisting the participants to develop a more meaningful construction of the experiences with fluent speech, and no attempt was made to directly alter the behavioral features of speech. Fransella found that stuttering decreased as the meaningfulness of the fluent speaker role increased. Follow-up with 9 of the 16 participants at both 3 months and 1 year indicated that one participant had regressed and eight had maintained or improved their level of fluent speech. Fransella (2003) suggested that the "crucial question" when using behavioral experiments to elaborate how the speaker is construing his or her fluency is, "Did you predict you would be fluent?" As clients learn to be more aware of their fluent speech, predictions of fluency become more frequent, and they are able to attribute their fluency to themselves rather than to some "fluke" or external source; that is, their fluency becomes more *meaningful* to them.

Manning and DiLollo (2007) suggested that, along with questioning the speaker about their occurrences of fluent speech, there might be other ways to help the speaker to reconstrue the meaningfulness of their fluency. As Kelly (1955a, 1955b) described, controlled elaboration can also take nonverbal forms. For example, as speakers practice their fluency-enhancing abilities in hierarchies of increasing communicative difficulty, they can be asked to consider their thoughts and feelings and predict the outcome *before* going into the situation. After completing the "experiment," they can then consider the accuracy of their predictions, including their fluency, their feelings, and listener responses. As the speaker, along with the clinician, assesses the outcome of the experiment by contrasting predictions with the actual outcomes, a deconstruction of the speaker's stuttering role can begin. With continued progress in the achievement of fluency—and increasing predictions of fluency that are confirmed by further experiments—elaboration of the fluent speaker role is more likely to occur.

DiLollo et al. (2003) conducted a systematic content analytic study that examined the cognitive anxiety (Viney & Westbrook, 1976) of persons who stuttered and fluent speakers with respect to "fluent" and "stutterer" speaker roles. Viney and Westbrook (1976) defined cognitive anxiety as the awareness that one's construct systems are inadequate to allow full and meaningful construing (and, therefore, prediction) of the events with which one is confronted. In their study, DiLollo et al. (2003) determined the cognitive anxiety of 29 adults who stuttered (21 males, 8 females, average age of 30.0 years) and a matched group of fluent speakers (21 males, 8 females, mean age of 29.1 years). The two groups were interviewed and asked identical open-ended questions regarding what life was like (a) as a person who stutters, and (b) as a fluent speaker. Responses to the two questions were transcribed and analyzed using a modified version of Viney and Westbrook's (1976) Cognitive Anxiety Scale. Results indicated that both persons who stutter and fluent speakers demonstrated significantly higher levels of cognitive anxiety related to their "nondominant" speaker role compared to their "dominant" role, as they each dismissed experiences of the nondominant role as meaningless. The authors found that people who stutter tended to protect their "stutterer" self-image by ignoring or discounting episodes of fluent speech, referring to them as "lucky" or "a fluke," and always predicting a return to stuttering. In contrast, fluent speakers made little meaning out of their occasional disfluencies and reasserted their identities as fluent persons.

DiLollo et al. (2005) again examined the meaningfulness of the fluent speaker role for the 29 persons who stuttered from the DiLollo et al. (2003) study but reanalyzed the data applying a measure of cognitive complexity (Bieri, 1955; Crockett, 1965) to the transcripts. According to Crockett (1965), the number of constructs participants use to describe a domain of interest will be a reflection of the complexity of their construct system with respect to that domain. In this study, the number of constructs used by persons who stuttered to describe the domains of their fluent speaker role and their stutterer role were taken to indicate the cognitive complexity—or meaningfulness—of each role. Again, results provided support for constructivist interpretations of stuttering, indicating that the participants in this study demonstrated significantly less complex construct systems related to the fluent speaker role compared to the stutterer role.

Plexico et al. (2005) took a constructivist perspective in attempting to understand the ability of adults who achieved the successful management of their stuttering. Seven participants described their experiences across three temporal stages (past, transitional, and current). Using a phenomenological approach, recurring themes were identified across participants in order to develop an essential structure of the phenomena at each stage. There were five recurring themes associated with past experiences when stuttering was being unsuccessfully managed: (a) gradual awareness, (b) negative reactions of listeners, (c) negative emotions, (d) restrictive lifestyle and avoidance, and (e) inadequate therapy. The ability to make the transition from unsuccessful to successful management of stuttering occurred gradually and was associated with six recurring themes: (a) support from others, (b) successful therapy, (c) self-therapy and behavioral change, (d) cognitive change, (e) utilization of personal experience, and (f) high levels of motivation and determination. The four recurring themes identified for the current situation where stuttering continued to be successfully managed were (a) continued

management, (b) self-acceptance and fear reduction, (c) unrestricted interactions and sense of freedom, and (d) optimism. This study provided information from a constructivist perspective in that it searched for evidence of meaning making in the individual constructions of reality as part of the data collection process. The results of this study suggest that those who are able to successfully manage stuttering are able to reorganize a sense of the self and provide a cognitive and emotional context for the changes in their fluency.

Other PCT-based methods have been used with persons who stutter. Botterill and Cook (1987), for example, discussed the use of a "problem-solving" exercise based on Kelly's (1955b) "circumspection, pre-emption, and control" (CPC) cycle, and a role-playing method based on Kelly's "fixed-role" therapy.

GUIDELINES FOR CLINICIANS

Perry and Doan (1994) provided guidelines for clinicians as they assist their clients to understand and revise their stories. Although there are 12 guidelines, we present five that appear to have the most obvious utility for clinicians assisting individuals who stutter.

Be Curious

Be extremely curious but know little. Do not assume that you know all there is to know and that you fully understand your client's story. Perry and Doan (1994) suggested that if clinicians find themselves becoming bored it is because they have put their curiosity on hold and have begun to assume that they know all they need to know about the person.

Have a Broad Focus

As we noted in Chapter 1 when discussing the effective clinician, Perry and Doan (1994) suggested that we should expand the focus of treatment by looking beyond the basic characteristics of the client's speech and pattern of communication. We need to understand the person we are assisting from a broad social and cultural perspective. This is particularly the case when we are having a difficult time understanding the client's story and the patterns of cognition and behavior we are observing. On occasion, there are powerful influences in the form of the client's gender, culture, religion, family, or ethnic heritage.

Use Resistance

Avoid an oppositional stance and allow yourself to "go with the resistance." That is, in spite of the natural tendency to do so, do not attempt to edit the client's story from the position of an expert. To the extent that we try to revise their story by telling them how to live it, we escalate the person's resistance and possibly invite resentment and defensiveness. By going with clients' resistance, we can provide them with the space to create their own story. As clients describe the ways they have selected to make their decisions and develop their story, we might respond with, "How is that working for you?"

Find Unique Outcomes

As the client describes his or her current situation, listen closely for quality words that provide examples of client strengths.

These examples can provide clues of successful authorship in the emergence of the new narrative. Look also for examples of the sparkling moments or unique outcomes that run counter to the dominance of stuttering in the speaker's life. Listen for examples where the speaker describes solution-focused rather than problem-saturated responses to their experiences. Often these counter themes are found in other areas of their lives and can be used to inform speakers about new responses to their stuttering (Plexico et al., 2005).

Share Responsibility

Although our instinct as members of a helping profession is to do all that we can for those who come to us for assistance, Perry and Doan (1994) cautioned that we should not work harder than our clients in helping them to revise their narratives. These authors suggested that the more the clinician (or parent) works, the less the client (or child) is invited to participate. In other words, the more responsible the clinician is, the less responsible the client is likely to be. As Perry and Doan (1994) suggested, "'Working Harder Than My Clients' is also an excellent title for a book whose final chapter will be titled 'Burned Out'" (p. 127).

ADDITIONAL THERAPY APPROACHES

Assistive Devices

Devices that alter the auditory feedback of the speaker's voice (sometimes referred to as "sidetone") have been shown to passively (versus active behavioral techniques) enhance the fluency of some individuals who stutter. Several explanations have been proposed for the fluency-enhancing effect of such altered or distorted feedback. Although the fluency-enhancing effect of several different forms of auditory feedback distortion results in immediate fluency for some speakers, there is typically little carryover once the device is removed. The altered auditory feedback (AAF) could be achieved by masking the speaker's auditory feedback (MAF), usually with white noise; delayed auditory feedback (DAF) with delays of 75 to 100 milliseconds; and, more recently, frequency-altered feedback (FAF), which shifts the fundamental frequency of the speaker's voice up or down (for a comprehensive review of the current literature see Lincoln et al., 2006). Devices that provided MAF or DAF were popular in the 1960s through the 1980s. More recent devices are considerably more sophisticated, offering combinations of digitally controlled feedback effects, greater miniaturization, and programmable options.

One of the more well-known devices is the SpeechEasy. Some models of the SpeechEasy allow placement behind the speaker's ear or in the ear canal, with the latest offerings including a completely in canal (CIC) option that is labeled "very discreet." They offer programmable combinations of DAF and FAF alterations of the speaker's auditory feedback. Prior to the introduction of the SpeechEasy device in 2001, a number of laboratory studies demonstrated that combinations of DAF (often set at 20–200 milliseconds) and FAF (e.g., 500 Hz above or below the speaker's voice) often resulted in decreased stuttering (Doopdy et al., 1993; Kalinowski et al., 1994; Kalinowski et al.,1996). The authors proposed that speech delay and frequency shifting of the speaker's voice create a "choral reading effect" similar to that experienced as one reads in unison with

another speaker. Group data indicated that speakers experiencing this effect produced significantly less, and in some instances no, stuttering. Stuttering was typically reduced more during reading than conversational speech tasks. However, when individual data were reported, results varied widely, with some speakers showing dramatic reductions in stuttering and others showing little or no decrease in the frequency of stuttering (Armson & Stuart, 1998; Ingham et al., 1997). Aside from some evidence of a reduction in stuttering during telephone calls and public speaking situations (Kalinowski et al., 2004), few studies considered the effect of these devices beyond laboratory or clinic environments. O'Donnell et al. (2008) did find that five of seven adults who reduced their stuttering by at least 30% in laboratory settings also experienced reduced stuttering during daily activities (face-to-face and telephone conversations). However, only three of these five participants experienced stable amounts of stuttering reduction (less than 3 %SS) during long-term use (9–16 weeks). O'Donnell et al. pointed out the difficulty in determining the ameliorative effects of the device based on a speaker's performance in laboratory conditions. Subsequent investigations with the actual SpeechEasy device in clinical settings found similar variability across speakers and speaking tasks (Armson & Kiefte, 2008; Merson, 2003; Molt, 2006a, 2006b; Pollard et al., 2007).

One of the more consistent and interesting findings is the discrepancy between the extent to which the SpeechEasy enables speakers to reduce their stuttering and their satisfaction with the device (Pollard et al., 2009; Ramig et al., 2010). Although many speakers continue to stutter to varying degrees with the device in place, they indicate high levels of satisfaction and would choose to purchase the device again. Conversely, investigators have also found speakers who, despite obvious fluency enhancement when using the device, choose not to purchase it (Pollard et al., 2009; Ramig et al., 2010). Regardless of the fluency-enhancing effect, some speakers reported that the device increased their confidence in the ability to communicate and lessened avoidance and anxiety (Cook & Smith, 2006; Molt, 2006a; O'Donnell et al., 2008; Runyan et al., 2006). Ramig et al. (2010) suggested that these inconsistencies could reflect the complex and variable nature of stuttering across a variety of communicative situations.

There are several additional issues that could help to explain the lack of correspondence between the resulting fluency and the choice to use such a device. At this writing, the four SpeechEasy models cost between $2,500 and $4,500, a cost that is comparable to (or greater than) the cost of more traditional therapy. The initial evaluation (2–3 hours) and audiological fees (a hearing evaluation and ear impression) are approximately $300 to $500 (Ramig et al., 2010). Ramig et al. (2010) also pointed out that although the device can be returned for a 90% refund within 60 days, the total cost to this point is likely to be approximately $1,000. For the majority of speakers, there appears to be little to no carryover of the effect without the device (Molt, 2006b; Pollard et al., 2009; Stuart et al., 2004). There are, however, indications that some speakers are able to wean themselves from the device (see the related comments by Alan Badmington in Chapter 14) and use it only during especially difficult communication situations (Pollard et al. 2009; Ramig et al., 2010). Despite research indicating that binaural delivery of the signal is more effective than a monaural presentation (Stuart et al., 1997), the devices are frequently worn monaurally. As Armson et al. (2006) noted, this monaural arrangement in daily speaking situations allows for the inclusion and distortion of background sounds in noisy environments and the speech of others as well as the speaker's unaltered speech in the other ear. Another issue is the requirement of initiating airflow and voicing during blocking (the device's feedback is voice activated). In order to initiate the altered feedback, speakers are advised to initiate speech by producing the schwa or /m/ (Stuart et al., 2004). Such techniques are contrary to most traditional therapeutic protocols because they can easily result in undesirable associated (secondary) behaviors.

Although the SpeechEasy is designed for both children and adults, clinicians prefer to fit the device with adolescents and adults (Ramig et al., 2010) and little research has taken place with younger speakers. Howell, Sackin, and Williams (1999) found that younger speakers (9–12 years old) decreased their stuttering much less than adults in response to FAF (approximately 3.0% vs. 8.5%, respectively). Because of the documented success of more traditional treatment approaches for younger children, the fitting of such devices with children is especially questionable (Lincoln et al., 2006).

Literature from The Janus Group (SpeechEasy Professional Information Packet, 2006) recommends that the SpeechEasy is most effective when used in conjunction with traditional behavioral techniques that assist the speaker in actively changing patterns of stuttering. Preliminary research supports this recommendation (Molt, 2006a, 2006b; Pollard et al., 2009). Of course, traditional therapy, particularly for adults, requires the active participation of the speaker as well as concerted effort and time to produce both cognitive and behavioral change. The less active role required by devices such as the SpeechEasy could explain their appeal to some individuals. Nevertheless, as discussed by Pollard et al. (2009) and Ramig et al. (2010), because of a variety of logistical, socioeconomic, and scheduling issues, it can be difficult for individuals to attend treatment. Even in those instances where individuals are able to obtain a SpeechEasy, professional help might not be available. Furthermore, it has been suggested that in instances where the speaker has been unable to achieve lasting benefit from other treatment methods, or for individuals with especially severe or chronic stuttering, such devices could be an important adjunct to traditional treatment (Cooper, 1986a; Merson, 2003; Ramig et al., 2010).

The Use of Pharmacological Agents

A comprehensive review of pharmacological agents being trialed with adults who stutter was conducted by Bothe, Davidow, Bramlett, Franic, and Ingham (2006). The authors pointed out that none of the agents were intended to be used by individuals who stutter but rather were designed to treat a variety of psychological and medical problems that have in some way been associated with stuttering. Based on their review of 31 articles published between 1970 and 2005, Bothe et al. concluded that the evidence for using these pharmacological agents was "overwhelmingly negative" (p. 348).

A more recent review of the pharmacologic treatment of stuttering was provided by Maguire et al. (2020). Despite the 14 years between Bothe, Davidow, Bram-

lett, Franic, and Ingham's (2006) review and Maguire's review, little appears to have changed with regard to an effective pharmacologic intervention for stuttering. Maguire et al. stated that although there is currently no FDA-approved medication for the treatment of stuttering, medications with dopamine-blocking activity have shown the most efficacy but tend to be limited by their side-effect profiles. Other agents have been tried with limited efficacy, but they do hold out hope for some newer medications that have shown some promise. Table 12–1 provides a summary of Maguire et al.'s (2020) review.

Mindfulness and Acceptance and Commitment Therapy

As we have mentioned on several occasions in this text, it is clear that the process of approaching stuttering involves the related theme of acceptance or at least acknowledgment of the situation (Plexico et al., 2005; Sheehan & Martyn, 1966, 1970; Wingate, 1964; Yaruss et al., 2012). Yaruss et al. (2012), along with more than 100 colleagues, provided a convincing case that acceptance is an important step in the process of minimizing the adverse impact of stuttering for children. It is important to understand that the term *acceptance* is not being used in a passive sense suggesting that the person is resigned to his or her circumstances. Rather, as others have, we are proposing that by accepting, or perhaps integrating, the experience of stuttering, people achieve the opportunity to become fully engaged with the problem and become desensitized to the extent that they can begin to experiment with creative and alternative responses to their situation. The process is similar to the notion

TABLE 12–1. Summary of Review of Pharmacological Treatments for Stuttering

Drug	Class/action	Effective for stuttering	Side effects
Haloperidol	Dopamine-blocking antipsychotic	Yes	Disabling side effects (e.g., dysphoria, sexual dysfunction, extrapyramidal symptoms, and tardive dyskinesia)
Risperidone	Block dopamine at the D2 receptor	Significantly decreased overall stuttering severity	Lower risk of motor system side effects (e.g., tardive dyskinesia) and generally better tolerated than haloperidol, but side effects include sexual dysfunction, galactorrhea, amenorrhea, and dysphoria
Olanzapine	Block dopamine at the D2 receptor	Yes	Fewer motor symptom side effects, sexual dysfunction, and prolactin elevation, but does have a greater propensity for significant weight gain
Pimozide	Dopamine-blocking antipsychotic	Promising	Extrapyramidal symptoms, tardive dyskinesia, dysphoria, prolactin elevation, and cardiac conduction concerns
Paroxetine	Antidepressant; decreases the reuptake of serotonin	No	
Clomipramine, desipramine		Minimal short-term improvements in fluency	
Ziprasidone		Effective	Well tolerated
Asenapine	Newer dopamine antagonist medication	Effective	Well tolerated; less association with significant weight gain or glucose and lipid increases compared to olanzapine

TABLE 12–1. *continued*

Drug	Class/action	Effective for stuttering	Side effects
Aripiprazole	Partial agonist of D2 and 5HT1a receptors	Yes	Akathisia
Lurasidone	Newer dopamine antagonist	Yes	Less sedation and lower risk of metabolic side effects (including weight gain and lipid elevations)
Pagoclone	Selective GABA-A partial agonist	Limited	
Clonidine	An alpha receptor agonist	No	
Verapamil, Nimodipine	Calcium channel blockers	Limited	
Benzodiazepines, barbiturates		No	
Ecopipam	A D1 antagonist	Significantly improved objective and subjective stuttering symptoms	No reports of Parkinsonian-like extrapyramidal symptoms; no weight gain
Valbenazine, Deutetrabenazine	Vesicular monoamine transporter 2 (VMAT2) inhibitors	No data	Could precipitate symptoms of depression

Source: Maguire et al. (2020).

of *mindfulness*, whereby the person pays attention to an experience as it occurs in the present moment, without judgment. Rather than trying to change the situation or circumstance by struggling against the experience—often in unhelpful ways that result in increased tension and dissatisfaction—such mindfulness invites us to just be with what is occurring (Cheasman, 2007). Paradoxically, such a response often results in more positive and helpful changes in the experience.

As Cheasman (2007) stated, "It seems as though sometimes the best way of getting from A to B is to just allow ourselves to be at A!" (p. 10). Beilby, Byrnes, and Yaruss (2012) were the first to study the effectiveness of acceptance and commitment theory (ACT) for individuals who stutter. In contrast to cognitive behavioral therapy (CBT), where the focus is on thought regulation, suppression, and eradication of negative thoughts and feelings, with ACT frustration is reduced via acceptance and the achievement of valued living. The focus is on six core principles: *self-concept* (developing flexibility in how the person views and defines themselves), *defusion* (promoting behavioral flexibility), *acceptance* (teaching the client to embrace emotional and cognitive events without attempting to change them), *mindfulness* (promoting a perspective on the present rather than thoughts and experience from the past), *client values* (clarifies the client's most meaningful values), and *committed action* (supports the client in following through with those goals that enhance future quality of life priorities).

Beilby, Byrnes, and Yaruss (2012) administered 8 weeks of therapy presented in a group format to 20 adults (10 males, 10 females) who stuttered (as verified by two speech pathologists). Traditional stuttering modification and fluency-shaping skills were tailored for each participant and focused on increasing fluency and speech naturalness, reducing severity of stuttering behaviors, and improving overall communication. Integrated sessions included traditional fluency therapy and mindfulness skills and ACT activities for 2-hour group meetings each week. The ACT activities focused on awareness, acceptance, and understanding of the context of thoughts rather than direct challenges or changes to the content of the thoughts. Along with stuttering frequency (%SS) the researchers administered the Overall Assessment of the Speaker's Experience of Stuttering (OASES), Modified Stages of Change Questionnaire (SOQ), Mindfulness Attention Awareness Scale (MAAS), Kentucky Inventory of Mindfulness Skills (KIMS), and the Acceptance and Action Questionnaire (AAQ-II). These measures were administered pre- and posttherapy as well as 3 months posttreatment. The re-

sults showed significant desirable changes across all measures from pretreatment to posttreatment, including the 3-month follow-up assessment. All participants demonstrated significant lessening of the impact of stuttering in their lives, increased readiness for change, improvement in their mindfulness skills, and a reduction in overall frequency of stuttering (%SS). All gains were maintained for a 3-month period following treatment.

The authors emphasized an especially interesting result in that participants were able to achieve an acceptance of their stuttering while also modifying their speech behaviors and increasing their fluency, indicating that it is possible to achieve both goals simultaneously and that these two goals can complement one another (see Yaruss et al., 2012, for a comprehensive discussion of this issue).

They also suggested that the effectiveness of ACT is a function of the nonconfrontational nature of the approach and the emphasis on acceptance. These same qualities could also improve the therapeutic alliance as well as cognitive restructuring by the speaker resulting in an agentic lifestyle.

Avoidance Reduction Therapy

Many of the concepts relating to spontaneity in the earlier paragraphs coincide with the Avoidance Reduction Therapy for Stuttering (ARTS) program developed by Sisskin at the University of Maryland. Unlike many programs, the primary focus of the protocol is not on techniques or strategies to manage the stuttering at the expense of spontaneity and the enjoyment of communicating. Rather, the focus is on desensitization and reducing speakers' reactions to the stuttering. The process also includes self-acceptance as one who stutters and experiencing minimal life impact due to stuttering.

Much of the rationale for the approach is based on the work of Sheehan and his wife Sisskin. They viewed the daily experience of stuttering as a conflict between the person's desire to speak and the possibility of a negative reaction by the listener. Because of the natural periods of fluency experienced by the speaker, they are attracted to the preferred role of a fluent speaker. This results in a lifestyle of hiding their identity as person who stutters. Of course, when stuttering occurs, role conflict occurs. When stuttering does occur often, accompanied by tension, struggle, and escape behaviors, the problem becomes one of struggle rather than a problem of stuttering.

In order to reconsider ways to respond to stuttering, the ARTS program initially focuses on doing the very behavior the speaker is trying so hard to avoid—stuttering, or more accurately "open or clean stuttering," stuttering without avoidance or escape behaviors. Once this form of stuttering is achieved in less stressful situations, the speaker begins to make choices about how to produce easy, comfortable, forward-moving speech by allowing his or her speech production system to achieve the "normal speaking" parameters proposed by Williams, discussed earlier in this chapter (e.g., airflow, vocalization, timing, and movement of the speech mechanism). Open stuttering also requires desensitization and a tolerance of the ingrained negative feelings about stuttering. The ultimate goal is for the participants to say exactly what they want to say, when they want to say it, comfortably, efficiently, and spontaneously.

THE SPECIAL CASE OF ADOLESCENTS

Although it was probably recognized long before, Van Riper (1971) commented that adolescents can be difficult cases. Daly et al. (1995) suggested that this age group is particularly challenging because the teenage years are often characterized by emotional conflicts, fears, and frustrations. Of course, these characteristics can be compounded by the anxieties and negative consequences of stuttering. In acknowledging the special nature of this population, Blood (1995b) noted that the extensive treatment some adolescents experience during elementary school tends to reduce their motivation to continue working on the problem. Blood also pointed out that an adolescent's many social and school activities might leave little time for treatment. A survey of 287 school-based clinicians by Brisk et al. (1997) found that the clinicians felt that they had fewer successes with adolescents who stutter than with any other age group. Others, including Manning (1991b) and more recently Zebrowski (2002), have pointed out the difficulties often encountered when attempting to convince an adolescent who stutters to enroll in treatment. Achieving success with this population requires understanding at least as much about adolescence as it does about stuttering.

Zebrowski's (2002) discussion of building relationships with teenagers who stutter should be required reading for clinicians working with these clients. Relying on her personal experience as well as an insightful book by Wolf (1991) whose title is worth mentioning—*Get Out of My Life, But First Could You Drive Me and Cheryl to the Mall?*—Zebrowski provided

CLINICAL INSIGHT

A long time ago in a galaxy far away . . . I was a high school student who, when I was unable to avoid using the telephone or a classroom presentation, stuttered at a moderate to severe level. Eventually, I was referred to the speech therapist at the school. Although I was certainly embarrassed by stuttering in front of my peers, I was also embarrassed and somewhat angered by being singled out and asked to report to the speech therapist. I marched across the street to the office where I had been told to report and found not one, but two young men in their early 20s, both of whom were the therapists. With complete fluency I told them that I was asked to report to their office, that I didn't have a problem, and that I wasn't at all interested in receiving any help. My fluency, as well as my agitated state, must have convinced them, for they immediately responded by saying something like, "Well, I guess you're right." Thus ended my first encounter with the field I would enter as a graduate student some 7 years later.

During my 2 years as a speech clinician in the public schools (as well as on other occasions), I had adolescents provide me with their own versions of denial. My response was to engage them long enough to show them that I had an understanding of their situation. If I could interest them enough, I could take the opportunity to tell them about some of the many stories of success I have seen and inform them about organizations such as The Stuttering Home Page, The National Stuttering Association, and The Stuttering Foundation and Friends: The National Association of Young People Who Stutter. As they were running out the door, I would tell them that good help was available when they were ready. (WM)

some suggestions for understanding adolescents and for facilitating treatment for those who stutter. Of course, it is not always the case, but teenagers tend to be intensely self-focused, appear to be immune to the many stresses facing them, strive to be cool and collected in social situations, value relationships with their peers above all else, and tend to see adults as clueless about how adolescents see the world.

The handicapping effects of stuttering often increase as a young person reaches the early adolescent years. Peer pressure becomes a major factor in the social life of middle and high school students, and if they have not already encountered teasing and bullying, these behaviors are likely to increase at this time. It is not unusual for

these inappropriate actions of others to be the catalyst that drives an adolescent or teenager to seek help. Not surprisingly, teenagers who stutter might respond to these pressures by expanding their tendencies of avoidance and denial, and coping strategies can become further refined and sophisticated. Despite all of the difficulties presented by stuttering during the years of adolescence, there are many reasons why these individuals are likely to resist treatment.

■ Priorities during the adolescent years make it difficult to convince those who stutter about the advantages of treatment. Although stuttering might be seen as a problem, it is not usually seen as the most pressing one. Other issues take higher priority, including social activities, sports, and part-time work.

■ Many teenagers harbor the hope that, with time and maturity, they will "outgrow" stuttering and that, at least for now, facing the problem can be postponed.

■ In some instances, adolescents who are willing to give treatment a try soon find it difficult to take responsibility for practicing and committing to the tasks necessary for change. Although they might be willing to come to the treatment sessions, they are unlikely to use behavioral techniques in daily speaking situations socially or at school.

■ Many of the activities and techniques associated with treatment strategies tend to highlight the speaker and set him or her apart from peers, a crucial issue for teenagers.

■ Adolescents are especially sensitive to overstatements by adults who are attempting to make a point (Zebrowski, 2002) or to the perception of being talked down to (Haig, 1986).

These issues could be exacerbated if clinicians are unable to communicate that they understand the experience of stuttering. Because adolescents are unlikely to credit adults with great understanding and wisdom about the things that are important to them, it is all too easy for clinicians to show them that stuttering is simply another thing that adults are clueless about. Zebrowski (2002) pointed out that adolescents are not likely to tell you this. They are more likely to demonstrate their displeasure in a passive-aggressive manner by refusing to communicate, not showing up for an appointment, or by failing to do the activities that have been agreed upon.

■ Some teenagers are not particularly good at confronting emotions, often assigning responsibility or blame to others, including clinicians, parents, and teachers.

■ As a function of their desire for independence, teenagers are sometimes less likely to enter into a trusting clinical relationship with adults. Given the importance of the clinical alliance described in earlier chapters, this could impede therapeutic progress.

■ Particularly aversive for some adolescents is the fact that successful therapy requires the involvement of their family.

Many teenagers are characteristically striving on many levels to become independent of adults (often with limited success). However, the involvement of the parents is often critical because they often have insight about their children and know what they are capable of accomplishing. Accordingly, parents, who are sometimes able to push their child harder than we can, come up with problem-solving strategies, and help set up contingencies that will enable their child to modify their behavior and their attitudes. The fact that a child's parents are willing to take an active part in therapy demonstrates their sincerity and commitment. Of course, having other family members or friends involved in the therapy process can be important for understanding, support, disclosure, and activities related to transfer and maintenance.

Finally, there are also some interesting gender issues that could hinder the therapy process with adolescents. For example, adolescent males who stutter—and of course there are more males who do—might have some hesitancy about being seen by a female clinician. For a teenage boy to be forthright and honest about his stuttering behavior as well as his feelings of anxiety, helplessness, loss of control, and shame with a female clinician is not something that necessarily happens naturally or spontaneously. Curiously, this has not been a topic of discussion or research in the literature on stuttering treatment.

Treatment is more likely to be successful for adolescents if they are able to locate a clinician who specializes in stuttering. Several websites provide lists of specialists including the American Board of Fluency and Fluency Disorders, the Special Interest Division 4 of the American Speech-Language-Hearing Association, and groups such as the National Stuttering Association, Friends, and the Stuttering Foundation of America (see Appendix A). Most of these groups also provide important sources of information and support including newsletters, informative pamphlets, and videos. Furthermore, in the security and privacy of their own rooms, adolescents can make contact with others around the country and the world via the Internet. Such contacts allow like minds to share information in a nonthreatening way. The isolation of being a person who stutters can be dramatically lessened by contact with other people who are likely to have many shared experiences. Each of these options enables the adolescent to understand that he or she is not alone and is, in fact, far from being the only person with this problem. This information can help to inform, desensitize, and encourage the adolescent so that he or she can find effective help.

Adolescents are often ideal examples to demonstrate that, as clinicians, we "can-

not push the river" (Zinker, 1977) and that it is usually best to show that we are willing to follow their lead. Zebrowski (2002) stressed the importance of placing teenage clients in the role of the expert about their own stuttering and emphasizing that the therapeutic alliance with the clinician is one of mutual dependence. This is especially important given that a teenage client is likely to be carefully scanning for efforts by the clinician to direct or monopolize the therapeutic narrative. By following the client's lead, the clinician can elaborate the client's understanding of his or her problem. This strategy also facilitates the clinician's ability to explain the nature of therapy based on the speaker's interests and to demonstrate the knowledge and genuineness of the clinician. Several therapy suggestions provided by Zebrowski include the use of humor for strengthening the therapeutic relationship, writing activities by the client for developing responsibility and expanding insight and coping responses, developing positive self-talk, imagery, motor and mental focus (as used with athletes), and cognitive restructuring for altering core beliefs about themselves and their interactions with others. She also stressed the importance of developing the teenager's ability to effectively communicate with his or her parents about his or her experience with stuttering.

Motivational Interviewing

Zebrowski's experience at the University of Iowa summer program for adolescents led to the development of motivational interviewing (MI) to promote engagement in therapy. She found that many teenagers come to the program with vague notions about stuttering and what they want to change. They are still in the *contemplating stage of change* as described in Chapter 7. Zebrowski found that in many instances they are less interested in changing their speech than they are about changing how they *feel* about their speech. For treatment to be effective, these clients needed to be clear about what they wanted to change. When the speakers were able to participate in making decisions about therapeutic goals, they were more engaged and motivated to take part in therapy. Zebrowski and her clinicians found that MI (Behrman, 2006; Rollnick & Miller, 1995) helped the clients to explore and resolve ambivalence about taking part in therapy. The process is a collaborative style of interaction that is similar to *empathic listening* discussed in Chapter 8. Four principles help to guide the clinician during the interaction: expressing empathy, developing discrepancy (helping the client to verbalize the inconsistencies of their rationales and behavior), allowing and rolling with the client's resistance (which is associated with the client's ambivalence), and fostering self-efficacy. Five dialogue strategies are used to facilitate the therapeutic interaction: asking open-ended questions, affirming, reflective listening, summarizing, and eliciting change talk. The clinician honors the client's autonomy and facilitates the client's determination of "what is right for him" by having the client determine what it is he or she wants to achieve, what is possible, what are the benefits, and how important is it to make the change. The client's "decisional balance" is explored as the person considers the pros and cons of making a change given its consequences. Based on interviews and focus groups with the teenagers, Zebrowski created a staging

algorithm for moving from the precontemplation stage to the action stage.

1. The best way for a teenager who stutters to do something to help with stuttering is to learn and use speech strategies or techniques for speaking more fluently or stuttering with less tension and struggle; change negative thoughts about stuttering and say what you want to say without avoiding sounds, words, or situations. It is important to pay attention to all three of these things because focusing on one is not enough to make long-lasting changes in the way you talk. For any of these things to become automatic, you will need help and regular practice for up to 1 year or more.

2. Thinking about the three things just mentioned (learning and using speech strategies, changing negative thoughts, and speaking without avoiding), how ready are you to do something about your stuttering?

   - ■ I am not thinking about doing any of these things in the next 6 months (precontemplation).
   - ■ I am thinking about doing one or more of these things in the next 6 months (contemplation).
   - ■ I am planning to do one or more of these things in the next month (preparation).
   - ■ I have been doing one or more of these things for less than 6 months (action).
   - ■ I have been doing one or more of these things for more than 6 months (maintenance).

The clients then use a scale ranging from 1 (*not important*) to 5 (*extremely important*) to rate the pros and cons for working through the stages of change. They also rate their self-efficacy on a scale ranging from 1 (*not at all confident*) to 5 (*extremely confident*) for effectively managing their stuttering in a series of speaking situations (e.g., You are giving an oral presentation in your class at school. You are meeting new people. You are answering a question in class).

Given the potentially exasperating aspects of working with adolescents, it should also be said that spending time with them can be enjoyable. It is fun to hear about the many activities adolescents are energetically participating in at this stage of their lives. They often display high levels of enthusiasm, and they generally appreciate an occasional enlightened or even humorous perspective about the difficult speech situations (as well as other social predicaments) they find themselves in. Such moments could provide the opportunity for the clinician to reveal embarrassing or uncomfortable occurrences in his or her own life. Timely and spontaneous humor has been suggested as a way to prevent talking down to adolescents and to lessen the problem as we talk playfully and informally about their stuttering (Haig, 1986). Metaphors about such sports or related activities could promote a shared understanding of the experience of stuttering, and the progress that is being made in and beyond the therapy setting also can be beneficial (Manning, 1991b). Young people, for example, might appreciate how the persistence and hard work necessary for success on an athletic team (or other school or club activity) easily translates to their experiences with changing their stuttering.

It should also be said that a realistic option for the adolescent is to decline therapy, and we might want to take the lead in presenting the possibility of doing just that. We can acknowledge that the decision for taking the therapeutic journey is largely theirs. It makes little sense to be dragging them along on a trip only their parents, their teachers, or their potential clinician want to take. Nevertheless, although we might be unsuccessful in convincing some teenage clients to pursue treatment at this stage of their life, we can leave them with two take-home messages:

- It is possible to have a happy and productive life even though you stutter. Many things tend to improve with age, particularly as one develops a variety of skills and achieves different forms of success. With a broader understanding of relationships, social skills, and life in general, individuals often develop greater insight and confidence, even if they happen to stutter.
- There are qualified professionals who enjoy working with people who stutter who will be willing to help when you are ready.

A few years ago at a National Stuttering Association Meeting, we met a teenager who demonstrated remarkable insight when he wrote an article describing the common themes he noted as he simultaneously learned to rock climb and to work through treatment for his stuttering. His words are likely to resonate with others of his age. His name is Brad Sara, and he was 14 years old when he wrote the following article that appeared in the National Stuttering Association Newsletter *Letting GO* in April 1999 (see also the NSA website). Brad's insight might well resonate with others of his age.

LESSONS I LEARNED WHILE ROCK CLIMBING

My name is Brad Sara, and I am a 14-year-old eighth-grade student who stutters. Last year I attended a monthly "speech group." I have also been learning to rock climb. In indoor rock climbing, there are two people: one who is climbing while the other is holding the rope that is connected to the ceiling. So, if you fall, that person will catch you. The lessons I learned about rock climbing were many, but they also taught me about speech. Here's how they are similar.

You have to learn and then practice. In rock climbing, we had to practice over and over before we could even get on the wall. This is just like in speech, where you have to practice speech tools in order to get better at them.

You have to take on more responsibility. As we paired up for climbing, I remember thinking that I had not expected to be in charge of another person's safety. This meant that I had to be really responsible. This reminded me of how I used to feel about working on speech. I have learned that dealing with stuttering is my responsibility, and I have to accept more and more of it as I get older.

You have to trust the other person. While climbing, I needed to trust that my partner would not drop me. With stuttering, you have to trust listeners, teachers, friends, your speech therapist, and your parents that they will listen to you and say positive messages. You also have to trust yourself to follow through on your goals.

Effective communication is essential. When people are rock climbing, they have to talk to each other for safety. In speech, the most important thing is to get your point across, whether you stutter or not. The message is more important than how you say it.

You have to conquer your fear. When we started up the wall, I think we were all afraid at first. But we faced it because we trusted the person hanging onto our rope. I also had trust in my training and got less afraid by watching others being successful. So, I went up and climbed, too. When I speak in front of a large group, I get afraid. Fear has a big deal to do with speech. If you don't face it, you will hold yourself back. If you conquer your fear, you will learn to be less afraid each time.

It's OK to make mistakes. One thing is very obvious to me. It's OK to make mistakes. Because if we felt we had to climb perfectly all the time, we were most likely to do worse. If you stutter, it's not the end of the world. If you say it's not OK, you're putting too much pressure on your speech to be perfect, and then if you do make a mistake, you will discourage yourself.

It's OK to get frustrated; eventually you will get it. There were many times while climbing that we got frustrated. Just like in speech, you keep on trying and you are going to "get it" someday. Have faith in yourself.

continues

It's OK if you fall. You catch yourself and start from there. Sometimes on the wall, I would slip and then catch myself. I just started again from where I was. If you stutter, it's OK and you can pick up your message from where you left off.

If you fall all the way down, start over again. When I fell a long way down while climbing, I started from the bottom, but knew I had learned the skills I needed to begin again. We have bad spells in our speech, sometimes. It's OK. We have learned what to do, and can start again.

Remain calm. I thought of this because one of our speech teachers is afraid of heights. When she got to the top, she was very scared to start down again, and we all talked to her to help her remain calm. In dealing with stuttering, I have had to learn how to deal with fear and to calm myself down when I am nervous so that I can manage my speech better.

When you're facing the edge, have faith in your support. When we got to the top of the wall, we had to stand on a ledge and then lean out to start going down again. We had to really have faith in the person who was supporting us. When I am real anxious and nervous about my speech, I have faith in the people who are behind me and who support me in whatever I do or say.

You just have to find the right rocks. When I was climbing, my partner and I were giving each other advice about which way to go, and which rock might be the best one to go to next. In learning to manage my stuttering, I have found that I need to find the things that work for me. I need to use my own best words to express myself, find my best chances or opportunities to talk, and discover which tools work best for me. Other people can guide me, but I have to find my own "right rocks."

Source: "Lessons I Learned While Rock Climbing," National Stuttering Association Newsletter, *Letting GO,* April 1999. Reprinted with permission.

GROUP TREATMENT

One of the earliest applications of group treatment in the field of communication disorders was the work of Backus (1947), who advocated the use of speech in social situations beyond the usual speech-production drills popular at the time (Backus, 1957). The popularity of group treatment for adults increased as a result of World War II. The many men in need of treatment for psychological and medical problems, in combination with the relative shortage of therapists and counselors, resulted in group meetings replacing individual treatment. In more recent years group treatment became less prevalent. Conture (2001) suggested two trends that contributed to a decrease in the use of group therapy for individuals who stutter: the increased application in the 1970s of behavioral modification procedures necessitating prescribed individual therapy protocols, and a more recent emphasis on a "bottom line mentality" (p. 289) emphasizing the time and cost of treatment.

Luterman (2017) suggested that there are two basic types of groups: *therapy groups* and *counseling groups*. Group meetings for clients with fluency disorders typically serve both functions. The group setting provides opportunities for enhancing as well as maintaining change in both the surface and intrinsic aspects of the problem. The group provides a social setting where the client appreciates that he or she is not alone and has the opportunity to address his or her problem openly. As the client adjusts to the roles and expectations of the group setting, he or she is more likely to become desensitized to stuttering in general as well as his or her own stuttering in particular.

Advantages of Group Therapy

Nearly anyone who has taken part in group therapy experiences as a clinician or participant knows that the opportunities provided by group interaction are a valuable part of a comprehensive treatment program. The activities that are possible in a group are a natural extension of the individual treatment session. The social environment permits a greater variety of activities as well as a more comprehensive treatment approach than would be possible with individual treatment alone (Levy, 1987a, 1987b). The group provides an ideal setting for "divergent thinking" as members have the opportunity to observe how others have dealt with similar problems. Of course, as Egan (2007) pointed out, divergent thinking (e.g., "lateral thinking," "thinking outside

the box") is uncomfortable for individuals who are bound to the idea that there is a single "correct way to approach issues or problems" (pp. 228–231). Participants begin to develop a broader view of their problem. It is not unusual to hear members of the group volunteer comments such as, "I had the same thing happen to me," "I often do that too," or "I felt just like that," as they begin to realize they are not alone. Perhaps most important, the support in terms of understanding, motivation, and courage provided by the members of the group to each individual can hardly be underestimated. These are powerful effects that are difficult to explain to someone who has never had the experience.

Depending on the therapeutic philosophy of the clinician(s) who organized the group, there are many other potential benefits of the group therapy experience. The group meeting is likely to be the only place in the community where a person who stutters can feel safe, and the only place he or she will not be penalized for stuttering—and rewarded for "good stuttering." The structure provided by a group setting provides the client with the opportunity to practice the techniques learned during individual treatment sessions. Conture (2001) pointed out that in some instances, group meetings can also provide social and speaking opportunities for people who might otherwise go for days or weeks without communicating with others. The group provides an audience for gaining confidence during many activities such as public speaking, making introductions, role-playing, discussion, and even debate.

Group interaction also provides the clinician with the opportunity to monitor the client's progress in a social context (Conture, 2001). When the treatment is taking place in an academic program, the group setting provides an opportunity for student clinicians to observe a broad range of behavior and to note the dynamics of progress in other clients. Group sessions also provide an ideal way for clients to gradually phase out of individual treatment schedules and facilitate the transition to communication experiences beyond the treatment environment. Following the conclusion of formal treatment, clients can readily return again to the group meetings if they desire continued support or begin to experience signs of relapse (Levy, 2018). Luterman (2017) also indicated several characteristics of group treatment that are beneficial:

The instillation of hope: As other members of the group are able to make positive changes in their speech and ways of interpreting their situation, the client can increase his or her belief that he or she is also capable of such success. The client can often gain momentum from others in the group who are becoming more assertive and taking risks. Much like being a member of an athletic team, group participation often motivates a client to extend himself or herself beyond his or her original notions of what is possible.

The promotion of universality: By being a member of a group of individuals who share a common problem, the client comes to recognize that he or she is not alone. The group provides a means for coping with feelings of isolation and loneliness. The group setting also provides the client with the opportunity to practice recently learned modification techniques in a more realistic setting than alone with the clinician. For

most speakers, publicly speaking in a group situation is a good initial step in generalizing newly acquired behavioral techniques to a social situation; successfully using the techniques in a group setting helps to reduce the client's dependence on his or her clinician.

The imparting of information: Information is provided not only by the group leader, as in individual treatment, but also by the other group members and, in some cases, other clinicians. All members of the group, whether or not they stutter, are able to provide examples and advice based on their own, unique problem-solving experiences. The inclusion of other clinicians, spouses, or friends provides the opportunity for individuals who stutter to understand, many for the first time, that nonstuttering speakers share many of the same fears about speaking in public or about risk-taking in general. Sheehan and Sisskin (2001) suggested the inclusion of a person who has recovered from stuttering or someone advanced in the therapy process to enact the role of a "big brother" or "big sister." They have found that their clients are more likely to take risks and experiment with their stuttering when they observe the rewards achieved by others.

The provision of altruism: Each group member provides not only information to other members, but also support, reassurance, and insight. Furthermore, as the group members are helping others, they also tend to experience an increase in their own self-esteem.

The enhancement of group cohesiveness: As with most small groups, the treatment group develops its own history and evolves through the stages of "forming," "storming," "norming," and "performing" (Tuckman, 1965). That is, group members learn to adjust to the group protocol, discover how to identify roles and resolve conflicts, become committed to working with each other, and eventually focus on group objectives and goals. As this process occurs, the group becomes more self-directed, and individual members experience an increased desire to maintain their role in the group and look forward to group meetings. As group unity increases, group activities will be more likely to facilitate growth and change of individual members.

The possibility of catharsis: As the group provides a safe place for individual members to release and share feelings concerning their own problems, there is often a release from the control these feelings have had over the individual. This can be especially obvious as members become desensitized to their long history of fear associated with fluency failure and begin to achieve increased agency in daily communication situations. The group provides a safe place to ventilate feelings of embarrassment, shame, and social failure associated with previous stuttering experiences. Participants are often able to revise their interpretation of these past experiences. With greater distance, objectivity, and understanding of these events, the possibility of a humorous interpretation often occurs.

The development of existential issues: The group can provide the opportunity for individual clients and clinicians to deal with questions concerning anxiety associated with daily living, such as feelings of loneliness, dependency, and meaninglessness. The discussions can help reduce anxiety and allow the members to improve the quality of their decision making, including the many interpersonal aspects of their lives.

Determining Group Membership

The selection of those who will participate is an important part of assuring the success of the group. Each individual participant must be committed, motivated, and willing to contribute to the group process. It is also good to keep in mind that once an individual is included, it will be difficult to remove him or her. As Luterman (1979) suggested, individuals must have "a willingness to examine their lives and to share their insights with the group" (p. 199). Furthermore, the group will be more likely to be dynamic and self-directed if the members are motivated and share a common interest for introspection and contributing to the success of others in attendance (Luterman, 1979). Individuals who tend to be argumentative, who consistently dominate group discussions, or who consistently withdraw from participation are generally not good candidates for group sessions.

Group participation is not appealing to all clients, and it can be difficult to get adults who stutter to commit to a group setting. Silverman and Zimmer (1982) found, for example, that women who seek treatment for stuttering tend to prefer individual rather than group settings. On occasion, some individuals will express the fear that their problem will become more severe by being exposed to others who stutter (Conture, 2001). For those with a long history of stuttering, even an informal group can be intimidating and carry with it the threat of social penalty. Some individuals might need to become desensitized somewhat before engaging in a group session. Thus, simply getting a client to attend his or her first group meeting can be a major success. Telling the reluctant individual that it is all right for him or her to observe and not take part in the discussions for several sessions usually increases the possibility of participation. Most people are attracted by the interest, support, and energy provided by the participants.

The Group Leader

As in individual treatment, the group leader is likely to be somewhat more directive during the initial meetings. At the outset, the effective clinician will need to establish credibility by demonstrating both knowledge of stuttering and people who stutter as well as a genuine interest in the members of the group. Just as the characteristics discussed in Chapter 1 describe the actions of an ideal clinician during individual treatment, these same features of empathy, warmth, and genuineness are necessary requirements of an effective group leader. Furthermore, the leader should be flexible and not only be able to sufficiently structure the group so that the participants have a sense of direction, but also to discard prearranged plans when necessary. One of the most difficult aspects of group therapy is striking a balance between the concerns of the individual members and group issues and goals. Another concern is finding a balance

between a focus on the use of behavioral techniques that enhance fluency and issues of cognitive and affective change. As Conture (2001) pointed out in a commentary on the dynamic nature of group meetings, the meeting "is no place for those who have a low tolerance for ambiguity" (p. 292). Once the norms of the group become established and the goals and direction of the group have been defined, the group leader will be less instructive, creating increased opportunity for the members to be self-directive and interact with one another (Luterman, 1991). Of course, the group is more likely to become self-directed if group attendance remains consistent over several weeks. If the membership of the group is constantly changing, it will be more difficult for the group members to assume their own direction and develop their own norms.

Establishing Group Norms

Because a primary goal of group therapy is to create an environment where the individual members will interact with one another, it is usually unhelpful for the group leader to assume the role of asking and responding to questions from the group. In order for the group to become self-directive, the leader must promote the primary goal of members taking responsibility for the activities and topics. Another norm or characteristic of the group is one of self-disclosure. As the leader and other clinicians model disclosure of their experiences and attitudes, the group members are likely to become more comfortable about revealing their own feelings, beliefs, and attitudes. However, group members should not feel pressure to self-disclose before they are ready. A good guideline is that no one has to talk unless he or she wants to, and no question has to be answered. The goal is to encourage participation without eliciting judgmental statements by other members. A basic guideline used in many support groups is for the participants to describe their experiences and responses that were helpful to them while refraining from telling others what they should think or do. Finally, members must be reassured of the confidentiality of the group's discussions (Luterman, 2017).

Possible Complications

As might be expected, there are apt to be a variety of problems with attendance and schedules. In some settings it can be a major hurdle simply to find a time and a place to meet. It might be necessary for some participants to arrive somewhat after the starting time or leave prior to the end of the session in order to maintain consistent participation. It might be difficult to gather enough people in order to reach a critical and consistent mass of participants. The number of people in groups varies widely. Most authors suggest a group size of around seven members, with a range of six to ten (e.g., Conture, 2001; Van Riper, 1973). Luterman (2017) suggested an upper limit of 8 to 15 members. A general rule might be that the group should be large enough for a variety of interactions but small enough that members have the opportunity to get to contribute, know, and trust one another. If clinicians are included (something that is highly recommended for student clinicians), the group can easily become too large. One solution is to break up the larger group into smaller subsets so that all members have the opportunity to participate. At the conclusion of the session, all members can gather together for summary comments.

Achieving diversity among the members is desirable for promoting divergent thinking as described at the outset of this section. In most instances, clients will have been in treatment for varying lengths of time or will be at different stages of change. It has been our experience over the years that it is often possible to achieve a wide range of diversity in terms of age, social, cultural, educational, and occupational background. Of course, group members will bring a variety of personalities and experiences to the meetings, and as Sheehan (1970) suggested, a group is only as good as its membership. On occasion, a participant might impart inaccurate and unhealthy information or provide feedback to others that is less than constructive. In a few cases, members might fail to demonstrate any efforts at self-improvement, being content to use the group as their basic means of socializing (Levy, 1987a, 1987b).

Suggestions for Group Activities

Ideally, group meetings should be held in an adequately sized room with comfortable seating. A degree of privacy is preferred (Levy, 1987a, 1987b), and if relaxation and imagery activities are to be conducted, the area must be quiet. It is also useful if the room (or adjacent rooms) is large enough for public speaking activities and can be divided into areas for small group discussion or role-playing. Some availability of outside speaking situations is ideal so that group members (usually in pairs) can leave the building, conduct brief speaking assignments, and return to evaluate and discuss their experiences. Of course, arranging the participants in a circle is useful for enhancing conversation as well as for promoting eye contact and allowing the clinicians and clients to read each other's body language (Luterman, 1991). Once the group's structural and procedural norms have been established, the group culture will begin to evolve, and a variety of activities can be considered.

Relaxation-Imagery Exercises

Many of the activities that are done in group meetings for fluency disorders are useful for all members, regardless of the quality of their speech (Kirby et al., 1992). It is not necessary or even desirable to be extremely relaxed in order to produce fluent speech. However, being able to relax in the midst of life's many anxiety-producing stimuli is a valuable skill for anyone. The process can be done at any time during the meeting, but often it works well to begin the meeting with these activities. Assuming the meeting is taking place in a reasonably quiet room with comfortable seating, the lights are dimmed. Playing quiet, relaxing music designed for such activities is helpful. Each group member closes his or her eyes and gradually focuses his or her thoughts on the instructions being delivered by a member of the group. The instructions direct each participant to progressively relax groups of his or her skeletal muscles, eventually focusing on the muscles of respiration, phonation, and articulation. The emphasis is on slowing and smoothing one's breathing, as well as visualizing an open vocal tract with cool air smoothly flowing through and out of the oral cavity. Participants are asked to imagine themselves in a serene and natural setting. Once relaxed, they are led through images of success, which include speaking activities. They are asked to remember the positive feelings associated with each success. The process usually lasts approximately 10 minutes. Often, a relaxed state is cre-

ated that carries over into the remainder of the group session. Initially, the responsibility of leading this portion of the session can fall to the clinician. However, the instructions, which are delivered slowly and smoothly, provide an ideal speaking situation for speakers who have limited experience speaking in front of a group.

Relaxation has been advocated as a way of promoting fluency for many years. In and of itself, relaxation is not a comprehensive solution to the problem of stuttering. Such techniques can, however, contribute to the learning that takes place during treatment. The goal is not to promote fluency per se but to teach the client better ways of responding to stress-producing situations, whether giving a presentation to a large audience, flying in turbulent weather, or undergoing dental work. Some members of the group will respond more readily to this experience than others, and some will be better able than others to make use of the relaxation and imagery skills in everyday situations. Of course, it takes consistent practice for these skills to be available when needed. These activities also work well with the goals of mindfulness activities described earlier.

Role-Playing

The acting out of real-life situations is facilitated by group treatment sessions. The exercises can be useful in helping the speaker reconsider especially negative experiences associated with past fluency failure and experiment with various coping responses for future anxiety-provoking situations. Such situations could include ordering food at a restaurant or drive-through window, taking an oral exam, giving an oral presentation, exchanging marriage vows, or dealing with threatening or confrontational situations at home, work, or school. Role-playing activities by the group lend themselves to creative and often humorous responses to the situation. Participants are free to experiment with role reversals, alternately taking on the personality of different characters in the exchanges. Observers can analyze the interpersonal aspects of the situation and offer constructive feedback and alternative ways of responding to a situation.

Public Speaking

Public speaking has been consistently shown to be a highly threatening situation for nearly everyone. For many individuals who stutter, the therapy group is likely to be the only opportunity they will have had to assume such a role before an audience. Group members have the opportunity to experience the preparation of different types of presentations (informative, demonstration, storytelling, extemporaneous) and to practice responding to questions from the audience. Members can practice upcoming presentations at school or work. Although the speakers have the opportunity to practice their fluency-enhancing techniques, it is important to also stress basic communication skills (e.g., eye contact with all members of the group, clarity, organization and sequencing of ideas, appropriate rate and timing of speech). Public speaking can be done in the same room where the group session normally takes place or (eventually) in a more formal setting such as a classroom or auditorium, sometimes making use of a microphone and amplification system. During the final stages of preparing for a speech at work or school, the speaker and members of the group can meet at the site where the presentation will take place. When it comes time for the actual presentation, the group members can share in the success of the event

by being there or by viewing a recorded version of the presentation. A particularly interesting possibility for achieving success in a variety of progressively more challenging communication situations is the use of virtual reality environments (Brundage, Graap, et al., 2006) described in Chapter 14. Used in a controlled, clinical setting, the procedure enables the clinician to evaluate the ability of the client to generalize his or her new capabilities to beyond-treatment speaking situations in a controlled and repeatable manner.

Demonstration of Client Skills and Progress

During the group meeting, each participant has the opportunity to demonstrate techniques being worked on during the individual treatment sessions. For example, each group member can explain, demonstrate, and respond to questions about the rationale and effectiveness of different techniques. Voluntary stuttering is a good example of such an activity. Other activities involve demonstrating examples of decreased avoidance behavior, risk-taking activities, and humorous situations that have occurred as a result of potential or real stuttering.

However, it is also important to recognize that superb outcomes can occur for individuals with whom we had relatively little contact. One year just prior to January 1, a card arrived from China. The clinician and this individual never met and nothing resembling therapy had taken place. The clinician and the person had exchanged email correspondence over several months.

Dear Professor,

I always think you are the person who change my life. It's your letters, books that open a door for me. I still remember the day when I saw your

CLINICAL INSIGHT

Over the years, the best of clinicians will experience what they consider to be failure. Many variables that we have mentioned must come together in order to create a successful therapy outcome, including the motivation of the client, experience and expertise of the clinician, and timing and quality of the developing therapeutic alliance. In spite of our best efforts, perhaps over many months, the client will drop out of therapy or fail to achieve what we believed he or she was capable of achieving.

By all accounts, Dean Williams was the embodiment of the expert clinician. His description of one of his "clinical failures" provides a comment on the principle of following the client's lead in the clinical process. Upon analysis of this case, Williams felt that this person was "help-able" but that he was unable to help her (Susan) because of his own errors in judgment. Here is his description of one such error:

> Unfortunately, I began therapy with the preconceived idea of what it was I wanted her to accomplish. There was no attempt to first find out what she considered to be her problems and then to begin at this point. In other words, I did not bother to listen to what she was trying to tell me. I was too busy explaining the "stuttering problem" and the therapy procedures she was to follow. (p. 131)

Source: Williams, D. E. (1995). A clinical failure: Susan. In *Stuttering: Successes and failures in therapy* (pp. 130-131). Stuttering Foundation. © Stuttering Foundation. See also *The Genius of Dean Williams* (2004) (pp. 71–76). Stuttering Foundation. © Stuttering Foundation. http://www.stutteringhelp.org

paper on the net. Indeed, I'm most appreciative of all you have done for me. In Chinese tradition, red is the badge of happiness and beatitude. I hope this red card can fully express my blessing for you. Best wishes for you. Happy New Year!

CONCLUSION

For the clinician who understands the surface behaviors as well as the underlying cognitive and affective components of stuttering as they are manifested in a particular individual, the fundamental treatment decisions become reasonably obvious.

The creative challenges for the clinician center on how we can assist the speaker to achieve the goals of enhanced fluency, improved communication abilities, and especially a more agentic lifestyle. In contrast to the young person who stutters, the adolescent or adult client typically enters treatment with well-developed and sometimes subtle coping responses—responses that have helped the speaker to negotiate within the fluent culture. Because the person has learned to survive with his or her problem and because the coping responses are ingrained and tightly bound together with anxiety and fear, treatment for older speakers is typically more complex and requires more effort and time. The many subtle adjustments for coping behaviors, some of which the speaker might be unaware of, could take even the most experienced clinician time to detect. Working together, the client and the clinician can begin the process of identifying and varying the behavioral and cognitive patterns that have for so long informed the person's choices about communicating with others. The experienced clinician recognizes that, in many ways, it is the client who will lead the way throughout the process of therapeutic change. What is possible during treatment is often determined by treatment variables such as the availability, setting, and cost of services. At the outset of treatment, the clinician, although being realistic about the level of fluency that the speaker could eventually achieve, should include spontaneous and natural fluency as a real possibility. For some adult speakers, however, controlled or acceptable fluency is the more likely outcome. Nevertheless, regardless of the eventual level of the person's overt fluency, it is possible to greatly reduce the limiting effects of the problem and enable the speaker to improve his or her quality of life.

Treatment for adults typically includes many features of both stuttering and fluency-modification strategies. Fluency-modification techniques can help adult clients learn how to use their speech production mechanism more effectively and produce stable fluency in progressively more challenging speaking situations. However, most adult speakers who are able to achieve controlled or acceptable fluency also need to be able to confidently use stuttering-modification techniques that will enable them to repair the fluency breaks that do occur. Following the client's lead, the clinician can determine how to sequence and blend the variety of strategies and techniques for altering the behavioral features of the person's speech. Both stuttering and fluency-modification protocols can result in the achievement of spontaneous fluency for some speakers. Regardless of the treatment protocol, the support and understanding provided within the therapeutic alliance facilitate all-important cognitive changes that provide the scaffolding for behavioral change. Group meetings often serve as an essential part of treatment, providing information, support, and insight that are otherwise unavailable. The activities of the group provide the members with an opportunity to practice skills learned during individual meetings, try out new speaking roles, and test new perceptions with others who share the same problem. The group experience reinforces the basic ideas that the speaker is not alone and that they do have choices about communicating and how they want to live their lives.

❓ TOPICS FOR DISCUSSION

1. What are several indicators to the clinician that the client is not yet desensitized enough to move to the variation or modification stages of stuttering modification?

2. During the next week take part in three activities (ideally communication situations) that you typically avoid. Journal a description and your reaction to each experience.

3. Use Brad Sara's description of rock climbing to create a similar set of guidelines in preparing for a challenging activity of your own.

4. Given the potential problems in getting an adolescent to give therapy a

try, describe the basic take-home messages you would choose to impart during a 30-minute meeting.

5. Describe your response to an adult who has been stuttering for many years when he or she asks you, "What are my chances of success?"

6. What are some common misconceptions that clinicians typically have about stuttering modification techniques?

7. Write a short paragraph describing your use of negative self-talk about an upcoming event. Indicate whether or not you were able to change your negative self-talk to neutral or more positive self-talk.

8. Describe the possible benefits of group treatment meetings to a potential participant.

9. Describe the most important characteristics of an effective group therapy leader.

10. Given the discussions in Chapters 7, 8, and 10, prepare a short paper describing your philosophy about the therapeutic process that you would be willing to give to a potential client.

RECOMMENDED READINGS

DiLollo, A., & Neimeyer, R. (2008). Talking back to stuttering: Constructivist contributions to stuttering treatment. In J. D. Raskin & S. K. Bridges (Eds.), *Studies in meaning 3: Constructivist psychotherapy in the real world* (pp. 165–182). Pace University Press.

DiLollo, A., & Neimeyer, R. A. (2022). *Counseling in speech-language pathology and audiology: Reconstructing personal narratives* (2nd ed.). Plural Publishing.

Drewery, W., Winslade, J., & Monk, G. (2000). Resisting the dominating story: Toward a deeper understanding of narrative therapy. In R. Neimeyer & J. Raskin (Eds.), *Constructions of disorder: Meaning-making frameworks for psychotherapy* (pp. 243–263). American Psychological Association.

Fransella, F. (2003). From theory to research to change. In F. Fransella (Ed.), *International handbook of personal construct psychology* (pp. 211–222). Wiley.

Ramig, P. R., Ellis, J. B., & Pollard, R., (2010). Application of the SpeechEasy to stuttering treatment: Introduction, background, and preliminary observations. In B. Guitar & R. McCauley (Eds.), *Treatment of stuttering: Traditional and emerging approaches* pp. 312–328). Lippincott Williams & Wilkins.

Assessment and Management of Atypical Fluency Disorders

CHAPTER OBJECTIVES

- To describe assessment procedures that enable the clinician to differentiate between child-onset stuttering and other, less common forms of fluency problems
- To discuss treatment protocols and procedures that have been found to be useful for promoting fluency and improving the ability of these speakers to communicate

As the title of this chapter suggests, humans experience fluency problems other than the more common form of child-onset stuttering that we have focused on up to this point. Although less common than child-onset stuttering, it is not unusual for clinicians who specialize in fluency disorders to encounter individuals with fluency problems associated with cluttering, neurogenic stuttering, and psychogenic stuttering.

We begin this chapter by discussing the assessment and treatment of cluttering, the most common of these fluency problems. Another rationale for discussing cluttering at the outset is that it is not unusual for speakers with child-onset stuttering to also possess some characteristics of cluttering. Most individuals who clutter also stutter, a combination that occurs most often in children (Bloodstein, 1987; Daly, 1986; St. Louis & Hinzman, 1986). Weiss (1964) suggested that stuttering often is the result of the child's attempts to cope with cluttering, although the onset of cluttering usually occurs somewhat later than child-onset stuttering. Fluency problems of neurogenic and psychogenic origins tend to occur later in life, often in the middle years of adulthood, typically in individuals without a history of stuttering.

CLUTTERING

In their historical overview of cluttering, Duchan and Felsenfeld (2021) described the first known use of the English term *cluttering* in a 1762 paper written by Thomas Sheridan. They quoted Sheridan, who described the condition as:

> To this hasty delivery, which drops some letters and pronounces others too faintly; which runs syllables into each other, and *clutters words together*; is owing that thick, mumbling, *cluttering utterance*, of which we have too many examples. (p. 33, emphasis added)

As so eloquently described by Sheridan, cluttered speech appears to be just that, cluttered and chaotic. The most prominent feature of speech is a rapid rate and often uneven rate. An already rapid rate of speaking often accelerates as the speaker produces longer sentences (Daly, 1986). The speaker appears to be in a hurry, even driven, sometimes displaying a compulsive and tense demeanor. Sounds and syllables are omitted, and there are few, if any, gaps between words or sentences. The speaker can pause only long enough to take a breath before continuing. Words are often poorly articulated and produced at a rate that might be unintelligible. During both speaking and writing, the person seems to lack the ability to attend to the details of the task. The speaker appears to take a gestalt view of communication and only with concentrated effort is he or she able to attend to the individual words or the punctuation on a page of text. Oral reading sounds as though the person is demonstrating speed-reading aloud and

is attempting to produce the entire page of text in a single utterance. The speech is frequently unorganized, and the speaker might have difficulty describing the details of an activity or event. There are apt to be many false starts and irrelevant or meaningless words. Although disfluencies occur, they seem to be the result of the speaker's attempts to rapidly formulate and produce the utterance. Complicating the problem is the speaker's lack of awareness concerning his or her ineffective communication.

Cluttering is unlikely to be detected until a young child begins to produce longer and more complex utterances (St. Louis et al., 2007). Thus, onset is not usually recognized until about age 7, later than the 33-month average for child-onset stuttering. The 2007 review of the literature by St. Louis et al. indicates that little is known about the possibility of recovery or therapeutic outcome.

Although cluttering has been described in the European literature for several decades (e.g., Weiss, 1964), until the 1980s few authors in the United States showed much interest in the problem. Because we tend to find what we are looking for, and because few clinicians or researchers were looking for speakers who cluttered, few were identified. This began to change with the work of authors such as Daly (1992, 1993), Myers (1992, 1996), St. Louis (1986, 1992), and St. Louis and Myers (1995). Recent investigations by these and other authors have resulted in an increasing understanding of the occurrence of cluttering both in its "classic" or "pure" form and as cluttering co-occurs with stuttering. St. Louis et al. (2007) indicated that cluttering could occur in conjunction with stuttering approximately 22% to 32% of the time. Daly (1992, 1996) estimated the occurrence of this combination at 40% based on the clients he had seen over 20 years. Both St. Louis et al. (2007) and Daly (1996) estimated that approximately 5% of these speakers demonstrate a pure form of cluttering. St. Louis et al. (2007) indicated that these figures might be underestimates because few individuals who clutter recognize their problem and ask for assistance. These authors also suggested that an absence of a working definition of the problem, as well as a lack of knowledge about cluttering by many clinicians could have contributed to underestimates of the problem.

The various definitions emphasize the complexity of cluttering and highlight the many etiological and behavioral characteristics of the problem. Most authors agree that cluttering involves aspects of perception, learning, and expression (both verbal and written). Extensive lists of the features associated with cluttering are provided by many authors, with St. Louis and Hinzman (1986) developing a list of 65 different characteristics. Weiss (1964, 1967) considered cluttering to be the consequence of a central language imbalance that affected all language modalities. Luchsinger and Arnold (1965) described cluttering as an inability to formulate language, with associated organic, familial, and aphasic-like symptoms. St. Louis and Rustin (1992) described the problem as a speech-language disorder, characterized by abnormal fluency that is not characteristic of child-onset stuttering and a speech rate that is rapid, irregular, or both. The American Psychiatric Association's (2022) *Diagnostic and Statistical Manual of Mental Disorders* (5th ed., Text revision; *DSM-5-TR*) no longer has the "Expressive Language Disorder" (DSM 315.31) category that cluttering was classified in with

DSM-IV. It is unclear where cluttering fits in the new categories—either "language disorder" or "social (pragmatic) communication disorder."

Daly (1996) provided a behavioral description that includes what he felt to be the primary features of the problem: "Cluttering is a disorder of speech and language processing resulting in rapid, dysrhythmic, sporadic, unorganized, and frequently unintelligible speech. Accelerated speech is not always present, but impairment in formulating language almost always is." (p. 107)

Distinguishing Cluttering From Stuttering

For the relatively few individuals (approximately 5–7%) who produce purely cluttered speech, the nature of the problem is usually obvious. Because the majority of individuals with cluttering characteristics also stutter, though, distinguishing the two patterns of fluency problems is useful. For example, the lack of self-awareness of speakers who clutter makes both assessment and, especially, treatment difficult. Whereas individuals who stutter typically have more fluency breaks when asked to monitor their speech, people who clutter often show an immediate improvement in rate, intelligibility, and naturalness. To the extent that these speakers are able to continue monitoring their speech, they are able to speak at a consistent rate and without fluency breaks, even when under communicative pressure. However, their ability to monitor their production is short-lived. Although treatment includes increasing self-awareness and monitoring skills, for the person who stutters that is only a part of the challenge. Individuals who stutter must also become adept at modifying behavior.

Another difference between individuals who clutter and those who stutter has to do with formulating and organizing language. For those who clutter, the disorganized flow of information, false starts, interjections, and phrase repetitions suggest that the speaker is having difficulty selecting the word he or she wants to use. In addition, Daly and Burnett (1999) provided examples of transpositions by speakers who clutter such as "at this plant in time/at this point in time" and "taking/talking." Much the same thing might seem to be occurring for the person who stutters when he or she approaches and hesitates to attempt a word due to the fear of stuttering. The person who stutters usually knows the word he or she wants to say but might avoid, substitute, or use circumlocution to conceal the stuttering. St. Louis et al. (2007) provided an interesting sentence that explains the situation: "Stutterers know what they want to say but are interfered in their attempt to produce various words, whereas clutterers do not necessarily know all of what they want to say—or how—but say it anyway" (p. 304).

The Assessment of Cluttering

Cluttering as a Rate-Regulatory Problem

St. Louis et al. (2007) constructed a working definition that includes cluttering within the realm of fluency disorders. These authors viewed cluttering as a fluency problem that is distinctly different from stuttering. In fact, as the authors explained, some speakers who clutter do not produce excessive disfluencies. The definition, somewhat different from that of

Daly's presented earlier, emphasizes the central issue of rate—a speaking rate that is too rapid and too irregular and that hinders the speaker's ability to produce clear and intelligible speech. St. Louis et al. included in the definition only those features that they believe are essential features of cluttering, not those that often co-occurred (e.g., disfluencies, language component, lack of awareness). Accordingly, their definition indicates that:

Cluttering is a fluency disorder characterized by a rate that is perceived to be abnormally rapid, irregular, or both for the speaker (although measured syllable rates may not exceed normal limits). These rate abnormalities further are manifest in one or more of the following symptoms: (a) an excessive number of disfluencies, the majority of which are not typical of people who stutter; (b) the frequent placement of pauses and use of prosodic patterns that do not conform to syntactic and semantic constraints; and (c) inappropriate (usually excessive) degrees of coarticulation among sounds, especially in multisyllabic words. (St. Louis et al., 2007, p. 299)

The authors explained an important distinction in that the term *manifest* in the second sentence of the definition indicates that the rate alterations *cause* many of the other coexisting symptoms often found with cluttering. The best example of this cause-and-effect relationship is seen in the deletion and neutralization of sounds and syllables, particularly during the production of multisyllabic words. Acoustic analysis of cluttered speech by Martin et al. (1983) indicated a lack of distinct vowel formant structure, release of energy for stop bursts, and aperiodic fricative energy. Substitutions and distortions of phonemes such as /s/, /r/, or /l/ were also noted by Daly and Burnett (1999).

An investigation employing spectrographic analysis of cluttered speech by Bakker et al. (2011) indicated that although listeners perceived the rate of cluttered speech as extremely fast, spectrographic analysis of the speech samples indicated that the number of syllables per second fell within the normal range. The perception of a rapid rate of speech was the result of the speaker's omission of many sounds and syllables. When the authors considered the number of omitted or "intended" syllables that could have been tabulated (and that listeners were undoubtedly processing), the "perceived rate" was indeed much higher than normal. Research (Raphael et al., 2004; Raphael et al., 2005) comparing speakers who clutter with matched normal-speaking controls indicated that the individuals who cluttered self-selected comfortable speaking rates when performing diadochokinetic (DDK) tasks (e.g., "pattycake, pattycake") and pronouncing analogous real words that were somewhat slower than the matched controls. Raphael and colleagues suggested that a possible interpretation of this result is that individuals who clutter produce conversational speech at a rate faster than their systems can handle. For such nonconversational DDK tasks in which clutterers can concentrate on articulation but do not have to formulate speech to convey a message, they are more likely to select a rate they can handle.

Also included in the definition by St. Louis et al. (2007) is that the fluency breaks are not those typically produced by individuals who stutter (part-word repetitions, monosyllabic word repetition, and dysrhythmic phonations). Rather, the disfluencies take the form of interjections, unfinished words, revisions, and repetitions—especially one-syllable words and phrases. Also unlike those who stutter, the person who clutters is not likely to associate fear or avoidance with specific sounds or words. Accordingly, clutterers rarely show the accessory or secondary coping behaviors often seen with speakers who stutter. The person who clutters might, however, indicate concern about certain speaking situations. The intrinsic features of the person who stutters—loss of control, helplessness, and fear—do not appear to be operating here. In fact, in some speakers, especially with those considered to be pure clutterers, there might be no awareness that there is any problem at all with their speech.

Finally, there are several other features, that although they are commonly found with people who clutter, are viewed as nonobligatory characteristics. Although this differs from the views of Weiss (1964, 1967) and Daly (1992, 1996), who viewed problems with language processing as a core aspect of cluttering, St. Louis et al. (2007) viewed language problems as coexisting rather than central or essential features of their definition. Likewise, maze activity (Loban, 1976) consisting of false starts, disfluent speech, and words irrelevant to the message is common. As a result of this activity, individuals who clutter are often unable to communicate in a coherent manner, resulting in pragmatic issues and an inability to consider the listener's perspective. Clutterers are also often reported to possess attention deficit hyperactivity disorders (ADHDs), resulting in distractibility, an inability to attend to details, and a lack of follow-through with activities. Specific learning disabilities (LDs) are also common, as well as poor handwriting and musical ability. Apraxia is another common characteristic of individuals who clutter, with the effects being more pronounced during the production of longer and more complex words. Speakers will often make several attempts before producing the word correctly.

Efforts to explain the etiology of cluttering reflect the many, widely varying characteristics of the problem and are well summarized by St. Louis et al. (2007). Models include cognitive and linguistic processing problems (e.g., Daly, 1986, 1992; Daly & Burnett, 1999; Molt, 1996; Myers, 1992; St. Louis & Hinzman, 1986; Tiger et al., 1980; Weiss, 1964), genetic models suggesting a predisposition for disfluent speech (Arnold, 1960; Daly & Burnett, 1999; St. Louis & Myers, 1995; Weiss, 1964), and models suggesting that the central nervous system might contain lesions in the region of the basal ganglia that impede the "executive functions" of the brain (Myers et al., 2002a, 2002b). Such individuals tend to experience problems with behavioral regulation, initiation of action, organization and planning, monitoring, responding to feedback, and self-motoring. Myers et al. pointed out that there are several other disorders that manifest such characteristics, including Tourette's syndrome, autism, Asperger's syndrome, pervasive developmental delay, obsessive-compulsive disorders (OCD), learning disabilities, and ADHD.

The many core and accompanying characteristics that are often associated with individuals who clutter require that the assessment process be multidimensional—even more so than is often the case for speakers who stutter. An example of such a multifaceted approach is illustrated by the work of St. Louis et al. (2004). Two groups of 48 listeners (a group from New York and a group from West Virginia) rated two young male speakers who cluttered across five attributes: naturalness, articulation, language, disfluency, and rate. Listeners used 9-point equal-appearing interval scales similar to the naturalness scale of Martin et al. (1984). Scores of 1 represented *highly natural* or *excellent*, and scores of 9 represented *highly unnatural* or *very poor*, depending on the attribute being considered. Listeners found the attributes of rate and naturalness to be least acceptable, followed by the speaker's articulation. The results supported the concept that an essential characteristic of cluttered speech is the rapid and irregular rate of speech. The attributes of disfluency and language were rated most acceptable. In fact, disfluencies were not seen to be a prominent characteristic of cluttered speech, even when the rate of speech was moderately high. The authors felt that the global measure attribute of naturalness best captured the most important aspects of all five attributes.

St. Louis et al. (2007) suggested the use of an experimental Cluttering Assessment Program (Bakker, 2005). This program can be found on The Stuttering Home Page (http://www.mnsu.edu/comdis/kuster/stutter.html) or at http://www.mnsu.edu/comdis/isad8/papers/bakker8/bakker8.html

Designed to provide a molar or perceptual rather than a molecular or behavioral approach, this computer-based tool consists of two tracks for indicating severity. The first track provides a computation of the percentage of talking time from individual or cumulative samples that is cluttered or noncluttered. The second track provides a visual-analog scaling procedure for the listener to rate the perceptual effects of nine features associated with cluttered speech: speaking rate, rate

TABLE 13-1. Self-Awareness of Speech Index (SASI).

Name   **Date**

Instructions: Please check (✓) the appropriate box for each question. Work rapidly and do not look back or change your answers.

		Never	Rarely	Usually	Always
1	I notice differences in the way I say words as compared with the way other people say words.	❏	❏	❏	❏
2	I notice when other people use fillers when they talk, such as "uh," "ya know," and "um."	❏	❏	❏	❏
3	I try to copy the way other people say certain words.	❏	❏	❏	❏
4	I listen to whether someone else's voice is high pitched or low pitched.	❏	❏	❏	❏
5	I am aware of other people's accents as they talk.	❏	❏	❏	❏
6	I know when I repeat a sound, word, or phrase.	❏	❏	❏	❏
7	I notice pitch changes in my own voice.	❏	❏	❏	❏
8	I pay attention to how fast other people talk.	❏	❏	❏	❏
9	I notice repetitions of sounds, words, or phrases when other people talk.	❏	❏	❏	❏
10	I am aware of how other people say words.	❏	❏	❏	❏
11	I pay attention to how fast I talk.	❏	❏	❏	❏
12	I notice when I stumble over words.	❏	❏	❏	❏
13	I notice my own accent.	❏	❏	❏	❏
14	I am aware when I use fillers when I talk, such as "uh," "ya know," and "um."	❏	❏	❏	❏

Summary Form

Instructions: Count the number of checks in each of the four columns of the completed SASI form. Write the totals in the boxes in the first row. Multiply these numbers by the weights provided in the second row and write Weighted Totals in the boxes in the third row. Write the sum of these four numbers in the Grand Total box in the fourth row. On the line below, divide the Grand Total by 14 to determine the Average SASI Score. Round the Average SASI Score to the nearest tenth, e.g., 2.4.

	Never	Rarely	Usually	Always
Total Checks in Each Category	❏	❏	❏	❏
Weights (Multipliers)	×1	×2	×3	×4
Weighted Totals	❏	❏	❏	❏
Grand Total			❏	

Average *SASI* Score: _____ /14 = _____
                                  Grand Total

Source: Reprinted with permission of St. Louis and Atkins (authors) (2005). Morgantown, WV: Populore.

regularity, disfluency, syllable-production integrity, overall articulation accuracy, naturalness, pragmatic language appropriateness, language coherence, and thought organization.

Because of the lack of self-awareness for many people who clutter, St. Louis et al. (2007) recommended using a variety of assessment measures typically used for individuals who stutter (see Chapters 5 and 6) in order to determine the level of the speaker's self-awareness associated with speech and communication. In addition, they suggest using the Self-Awareness of Speech Index (SASI; St. Louis & Atkins, 2006), a 14-item measure that provides a criterion-referenced indication of a speaker's lack of awareness of his or her own speech characteristics (Table 13–1). In addition, St. Louis et al. (2007) also recommended the use of several diagnostic measures that provide information about a wide variety of difficulties, including oral motor problems and general coordination, handwriting, central auditory problems, reading comprehension, spelling, and mathematical skills. Testing for LD and ADHD might also be warranted based on school reports and related therapeutic history.

Cluttering as a Cognitive-Linguistic Problem

Another group of clinicians who have considerable experience with speakers who clutter is Daly and his associates. Although there is considerable overlap in the characteristics of cluttering as described by St. Louis et al. and Daly et al., Daly takes more of a cognitive-linguistic perspective and deemphasizes the importance of a rapid speech rate. Daly and Burnett (1999) stated that they have yet to

evaluate a person who clutters who did not exhibit at least one disturbance in each of the following five dimensions:

1. *Cognitive*—People who clutter demonstrate a near-total lack of awareness of their inability to communicate. They characteristically have poor self-monitoring abilities, inadequate thought organization, poor attention span, verbal and nonverbal impulsivity, and show signs of perceptual deficits (auditory or visual processing or poor auditory memory).

2. *Language*—These individuals show some form of language difficulties that are expressive, receptive, or both. This could be related to their poor auditory memory, attention deficits, and inability to concentrate. They are often poor readers and show little interest in music and literature. Daly and Burnett (1999) also reported the occurrence of transpositions such as "The Lord is a shoving leopard."

3. *Pragmatics*—Clutterers are notoriously poor at turn-taking as well as the introduction, maintenance, and termination of topics. They fail to recognize subtle nonverbal signs indicating turn-taking, and show a lack of interest or attention in the conversation.

4. *Speech*—The fluency breaks of people who clutter are characterized by irregular rate, accelerations, sporadic bursts of speech, variable intensity, and overall poor rhythm. Some fluency breaks are typical of stuttering.

5. *Motor*—People who clutter tend to be clumsy and uncoordinated and demonstrate impulsive motor movements. The client might appear to be physically immature. Lack of coordination also could be reflected in the poor legibility of handwriting, which

Cluttering

Cognition	Language	Pragmatics	Speech	Motor
Awareness - listener perspective - self-monitoring Attention span Thought organization - sequencing - categorization Memory Impulsivity	Receptive - listening/directions - reading disorder Expressive – Verbal - thought organization - poor sequence of ideas - poor story telling - language formulation - revisions and repetitions - improper linguistic structure - syllabic or verbal transpositions - improper pronoun use - dysnomia/word finding - filler words, empty words Expressive—Written - run-on sentences - omissions and transpositions of letters, syllables, and words - sentence fragments	Inappropriate topic introduction, maintenance, termination Inappropriate turn-taking Poor listening skills; impulsive responses Lack of consideration of listener perspective Inadequate processing of non-verbal signals Verbose or tangential Poor eye contact	Speech disfluency - excessive repetition of words/phrases Syllabic or verbal transpositions Prosody of speech - rate (rapid or irregular) - poor rhythm - loud, trail off - lacks pauses between words - vocal monotony Slurred articulation - omit sound(s) - omit syllable(s) - /r/ and /l/ Dysrhythmic breathing Silent gaps/hesitations	Poor motor control Slurred articulation Dysrhythmic breathing Speech disfluencies, - excessive repetitions of sounds or words Silent gaps, hesitations Prosody problems - rate (rapid or irregular) - poor rhythm Clumsy, uncoordinated Poor penmanship Impulsivity

FIGURE 13–1. The linguistic disfluency model for individuals who clutter, indicating possible impairments across five broad communicative dimensions. *Source:* Used with permission of Thieme Medical, from Daly, D. A., and Burnett, M. L. (1997). Cluttering: Traditional views and new perspectives. In R. Curlee (Ed.). *Stuttering and related disorders of fluency* (2nd ed., pp. 222–254). Permission conveyed through Copyright Clearance Center, Inc.

tends to disintegrate during the writing of a paragraph. There is often a lack of ability to imitate a simple rhythm or to sing.

These characteristics are presented as the major components of a "linguistic disfluency model" provided in Figure 13–1. Linguistic disfluency is characterized by Daly and Burnett (1999) as "frequent verbal revisions and interjections, excessive repetitions of words or phrases, poorly organized thoughts, lack of cohesion in discourse, and prosodic irregularities" (p. 226).

Given the perspective by Daly and colleagues that cluttering involves the inability to formulate language, it is not surprising that the writing of people who clutter also tends to be disorganized and often illegible. Daly (1986, 1992) recommended procedures for obtaining writing samples. In many ways, handwriting vividly illustrates many of the features

of cluttering. Williams and Wener (1996) described the handwriting of a young man in his 20s who was diagnosed with both stuttering and cluttering behaviors. His writing was composed of simple declarative sentences with short, simple words. Of 148 words, 54 were stricken due to grammatical errors or misspellings. Legibility was poor, and there were many punctuation errors, particularly misused commas. Figure 13–2 is an example of handwriting by a 16-year-old male who possessed virtually all of the classic characteristics of cluttering. Figure 13–3 provides an example of unguarded typing (Meyers & Kissagizlis, 2007).

Daly (2006) provided an updated version of a series of checklists originally created by Daly and Burnett (1996, 1999). Based on the responses of 60 clinicians and researchers experienced in fluency problems who rated the factors they felt to be most important for identifying cluttering, Daly (2006) developed a 33-item

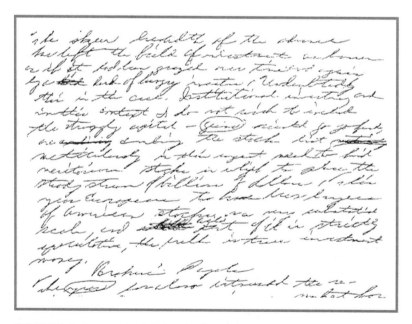

FIGURE 13–2. An example of cluttered writing.

After years of feeling insecure, different, isolated and excluded, I know Kknow the comndition I have, which is clutteroimng, although it is not cured and nebver can be as fra as I am aware, at lwast I am aware of the conditini aadn people wil learn from tihs, and poepke who sufer as I do wil be able t undrestand what they ahve, the amin thinsg is, peiopokle worlkd wide awil be able to reecognise the condition and maybe the ptofessionals can impement a suitable treainhg/teacjhing athen evebntaualy a treatment regime. Meyers & Kissagizlis, (2007)

FIGURE 13–3. An example of "unguarded" cluttered typing.

Predictive Cluttering Inventory (PCI; Figure 13–4). The inventory includes four categories or speaker characteristics (pragmatics, 10 statements; speech-motor, 10 items; language-cognition, 8 items; and motor coordination-writing problems, 5 items). Listeners indicate the frequency of occurrence of the characteristics using a 7-point scale from 6 (*always*) to 0 (*never*). The two items that clinicians ranked as the most frequent characteristics of cluttering were "omits, transposes sounds and syllables" (Item 30) and "lack of effective, sufficient self-monitoring skills" (Item 1). A total score of 120 or greater is indicative of a "pure clutterer," which, according to Daly, rarely occurs. Scores ranging from 80 to 120 are more typical and indicate the more common classification of "clutterer-stutterer."

Treatment Options for Individuals Who Clutter

There are a variety of factors, such as the speaker's lack of awareness of speech rate and the inability to effectively communicate with others, that make treatment for cluttering difficult. To the degree that a person who clutters becomes aware of these problems, he or she might deny that they occur. This response, along with other personality characteristics such as compulsivity, poor concentration, and a host of pragmatic issues, can make these individuals particularly difficult to interact with and assist. Individuals who clutter tend to be intolerant of interruptions (Van Riper, 1992) and are particularly resistant to suggestions to monitor the details of their speech. The prognosis for success is not particularly good, but, as always, the prognosis for a successful treatment outcome is better for children than adults (Daly, 1986, 1993; Luchsinger & Arnold, 1965; Myers & St. Louis, 1992; Silverman, 1996; Weiss, 1964).

In more extreme cases, individuals who clutter might display immature responses, a short temper, and a history of emotional problems. On occasion, such individuals can appear defensive and even antagonistic, characteristics that make it difficult to develop a successful therapeutic alliance. Daly has often pointed out that individuals who clutter can provide a challenge to our ability and especially our patience. In addition, the person often finds it difficult to tolerate speaking

PREDICTIVE CLUTTERING INVENTORY (PCI)
David A. Daly (2006)

INSTRUCTIONS: Please respond to each description section below. Circle the number you believe is most descriptive of this person's cluttering.

Descriptive Statement	Always	Almost Always	Frequently	Sometimes	Infrequently	Almost Never	Never
PRAGMATICS							
1. Lack of effective self-monitoring skills	6	5	4	3	2	1	0
2. Lack of awareness of own communication errors or problems	6	5	4	3	2	1	0
3. Compulsive talker; verbose; tangential; word-finding problems	6	5	4	3	2	1	0
4. Poor planning skills; mis-judges effective use of time	6	5	4	3	2	1	0
5. Poor social communication skills; inappropriate turn-taking; interruptions	6	5	4	3	2	1	0
6. Does not recognize or respond to listener's visual or verbal feedback	6	5	4	3	2	1	0
7. Does not repair or correct communication breakdowns	6	5	4	3	2	1	0
8. Little or no excessive effort observed during disfluencies	6	5	4	3	2	1	0
9. Little or no anxiety regarding speaking; unconcerned	6	5	4	3	2	1	0
10. Speech better under pressure (improves short-term with concentration)	6	5	4	3	2	1	0

FIGURE 13–4. Predictive Cluttering Inventory (PCI). *Source:* Daly, D. [2006]. Copyright © David Daly. Reprinted with permission. *continues*

	SPEECH-MOTOR							
11.	Articulation errors	6	5	4	3	2	1	0
12.	Irregular speech rate; speaks in spurts or bursts	6	5	4	3	2	1	0
13.	Telescopes or condenses words	6	5	4	3	2	1	0
14.	Rapid rate (tachylalia)	6	5	4	3	2	1	0
15.	Speech rate progressively increases (festinating)	6	5	4	3	2	1	0
16.	Variable prosody; irregular melody or stress pattern	6	5	4	3	2	1	0
17.	Initial loud voice trailing off to unintelligible murmur	6	5	4	3	2	1	0
18.	Lack of pauses between words and phrases	6	5	4	3	2	1	0
19.	Repetition of multi-syllablic words and phrases	6	5	4	3	2	1	0
20.	Co-existence of excessive disfluencies and stuttering	6	5	4	3	2	1	0
	LANGUAGE-COGNITION							
21.	Language is disorganized; confused wording; word-finding problems	6	5	4	3	2	1	0
22.	Poor language formulation; poor story-telling; sequencing problems	6	5	4	3	2	1	0
23.	Disorganized language increases as topic becomes more complex	6	5	4	3	2	1	0
24.	Many revisions; interjections; filler words	6	5	4	3	2	1	0
25.	Seems to verbalize before adequate thought formulation	6	5	4	3	2	1	0

FIGURE 13–4. *continues*

26.	Inappropriate topic introduction, maintenance, or termination	6	5	4	3	2	1	0
27.	Improper linguistic structure; poor grammar; syntax errors	6	5	4	3	2	1	0
28.	Distractible; poor concentration; attention span problems	6	5	4	3	2	1	0
	MOTOR COORDINATION-WRITING PROBLEMS						
29.	Poor motor control for writing (messy)	6	5	4	3	2	1	0
30.	Writing includes omission or transposition of letters, syllables, or words	6	5	4	3	2	1	0
31.	Oral diadochokinetic coordination below expected normed levels	6	5	4	3	2	1	0
32.	Respiratory dysrhythmia; jerky breathing pattern	6	5	4	3	2	1	0
33.	Clumsy and uncoordinated; motor activities accelerated or impulsive	6	5	4	3	2	1	0

TOTAL SCORE: _____

COMMENTS:

FIGURE 13–4. *continued*

at what seems to him or her an exceedingly slow rate. The "driven" quality of these clients becomes obvious after even a brief period of attempting to speak at a slower rate. Because these speakers are often oblivious to their communication problem, to the extent that they are able to develop the ability to monitor their speech, intelligibility and fluency can be dramatically improved. As the person becomes aware of his or her irregular and rapid speech, appropriate alterations in production are likely to occur, even without specific instruction.

As with the assessment of cluttering, the multidimensional characteristics of these speakers also require a wide-ranging approach to treatment. It is likely that the clinician will want to consult with a variety of other professionals (psychologists, mental health specialists, neurologists, and specialists in LD or ADHD). In fact, during the initial contact with the speech-language pathologist, it is not unusual for adults to report that they have seen or are currently seeing one or more of these professionals. The focus of treatment will vary somewhat depending on whether the speaker manifests the relatively infrequent pure form of cluttering or the more commonly occurring combination of stuttering-cluttering. Following the primary assumption of St. Louis et al.'s (2007) definition of cluttering, that individuals who clutter are attempting to speak at a rate that they are unable to manage, these authors recommended a synergistic therapy approach (Myers, 1992; St. Louis & Myers, 1995). That is, the underlying goal of treatment is to help the speaker to enhance the synchrony of language formulation and the rate of speech production. Primary emphasis is on enhancing the coordination of the linguistic and articulatory levels in order to prevent "derailment" of the speech sequence at

either of these levels. Another key element is increased awareness by the speaker of the excessive rate, or "haste," during both linguistic organization and motoric and articulatory production. With these principles as a guide, the clinician can experiment with the variety of techniques that clinicians have found to have clinical utility for individuals who clutter. A detailed compendium of techniques from which the client and the clinician can select is found in both St. Louis and Myers (1995) and St. Louis et al. (2007). These authors suggested that a focus on these principles often results in improvement in articulation and intelligibility as well as fluency. These principles are nearly identical to those suggested by Daly and Burnett (1999), who suggested three basic principles of intervention:

1. Because speakers are usually unaware of their communication behavior as well as listener reactions, the frequent repetition of therapy goals and rationale will be necessary.
2. Because of the speaker's lack of awareness, the clinician should provide immediate and direct feedback.
3. Parents and significant others should play a major part in providing feedback, correction, and reinforcement. Regardless of the techniques that are selected, all authors stress the importance of daily practice as well as the understanding and encouragement of family, friends, and support groups.

Even for those individuals with a pure form of cluttering, several stuttering-modification and particularly fluency-shaping techniques used with individuals who stutter could also be used to heighten awareness and facilitate changes in rate and fluency. Readers will find it especially useful to consult the list of techniques designed for individuals who clutter provided by such authors as Daly (1996), St. Louis and Myers (1995, 1997), St. Louis et al. (2007), and Van Riper (1973). The following are examples of such techniques that can be employed by the clinician or by the client (in some cases with the assistance of family or friends), organized according to categories suggested by St. Louis et al. (2007). Of course, many of these activities, particularly when done in written or verbal form, can serve a variety of functions across several categories.

Awareness and Self-Monitoring Skills

- Play back audio and video recordings to identify and monitor speech.
- Vary the rate of nonspeech (e.g., hand) movements prior to speech movements.
- Heighten awareness of listener indicators of unintelligible speech.
- Increase proprioceptive and kinesthetic feedback associated with the articulatory movements (possibly using altered feedback devices).
- Purposely vary the rate of speech from extremely slow through very fast.

Rate, Articulation, and Intelligibility

- Read in unison, beginning with a fast rate, and systematically change speed while the client shadows the clinician's rate changes.
- Imitate and vary rhythmic patterns by tapping a finger or other object; perform verbally with numbers or word sequences.
- Use a window-card so that one or a few words are visible to the client.
- Read a passage backward one word at a time in order to increase tolerance for a slower rate.

- Repeat phrases using different tempos, altering the stress placed on different words or syllables.
- Say words as they are written or produced on a keyboard.
- Slow speech rate during reading by using the natural pauses afforded by punctuation and clause boundaries.
- Heighten the awareness of final sounds and syllables.
- Shadow the speech of the clinician (and others).

Linguistic and Narrative Skills

- Write down the words of a sentence prior to speaking.
- Heighten turn-taking ability during conversation to decrease overtalking.
- Describe sequencing of steps for a moderately complex task.
- Practice selecting one of several thoughts or words that occur at once.
- Organize the sequence of a story in writing, then verbally.
- Practice telling jokes requiring precise sequencing and timing.

Fluency

- Analyze recorded speech samples for repetitions, misarticulations, revisions, and interjections.
- Use rate-altering techniques and fluency-shaping targets of respiration, phonation, and articulation (Chapter 10) to enhance fluency.

Ability to Understand and Describe the Characteristics of Cluttered Speech

- Contrast the proprioceptive feedback associated with slow, fast, and irregular speech rates.
- Contrast the nature of the emotions (e.g., anxiety, sense of urgency) and

behaviors (avoidance, anticipation, types of fluency breaks) associated with stuttering and cluttering.

- Contrast the influence on communication of helpful and poor pragmatic skills.
- Role-play nonverbal and verbal cues of listener confusion.

Phonatory, Respiratory, and Motor Skills

- Practice fluency-shaping targets of respiration, phonation, and articulation; begin with shorter, and then longer, breath groups.
- Prolong vowels during progressively longer utterances.
- Engage in oral-motor skills training.
- Practice writing or printing skills using graph paper.

Family, Friend, and Employer Support

- Request feedback of clear and poor communication from family and friends; role-play in clinic environment.
- Interact with others who have similar communication problems (e.g., local chapters of the National Stuttering Association, cluttering@yahoo.com).
- Consider involvement in group-speaking activities socially or at school or work.

A comprehensive treatment approach is also provided by Daly (2006), who described a strategy for treatment called the Cluttering Treatment Profile Analysis (Figure 13–5). Information obtained on the PCI is converted to this profile. Rather than focusing on rate alone, treatment can focus on other commonly occurring characteristics, such as #17 (Initial loud voice trailing off to unintelligible murmur) and #2 (Lack of awareness of own commu-

nication errors or problems). The profile analysis is intended to facilitate individualized treatment according to the areas where the speaker is in particular need of assistance.

The International Cluttering Association

The International Cluttering Association (ICA) was initially formed in 2007. The primary goal of the association is to increase awareness and understanding of cluttering, and to improve treatment and quality of life for people who clutter. The website provides information to the public about what cluttering is, how it is diagnosed and treated, and where consumers and their families can go to get information, help, and support. The ICA intends to develop a forum for experts in cluttering to share their work and to provide resources for learning and teaching about this communication disorder (see http://associations.missouristate.edu/ica/).

ACQUIRED STUTTERING

The next two fluency problems have been referred to as "acquired stuttering" because they tend to occur for the first time in adults, long after the onset of child-onset stuttering in childhood and after many years of fluent speech. With adult onset of stuttering, it is possible that we could be observing the result of a relapse following previously successful therapy or the occurrence of overt stuttering characteristics for speakers who have been able to manage their stuttering in a covert or "interiorized" manner (Deal, 1982; Van Riper, 1971). Although child-onset stuttering could have a rapid onset, this is more likely to be the case for older speakers with neurogenic and psychogenic

CLUTTERING TREATMENT PROFILE ANALYSIS
David A. Daly (2006)

NAME _____

INSTRUCTIONS: Transfer the scores from the PCI, and then connect the scores. Higher scores indicate more severe deficit areas. For best results, clinicians should focus on at least two deficit areas, in additon to "rapid rate."

CLUTTERING CHARACTERISTICS	Very Severe	Severe	Moderate	Mild	Very Mild	Inconsistent	Not a Problem
PRAGMATICS							
1. Lack of effective self-monitoring skills	6	5	4	3	2	1	0
2. Lack of awareness of own communication errors or problems	6	5	4	3	2	1	0
3. Compulsive talker; verbose; tangential	6	5	4	3	2	1	0
4. Poor planning skills; misjudges effective use of time	6	5	4	3	2	1	0
5. Poor social communication skills; inappropriate turn-taking; interruptions	6	5	4	3	2	1	0
6. Does not recognize or respond to listener's visual or verbal feedback	6	5	4	3	2	1	0
7. Does not repair or correct communication breakdowns	6	5	4	3	2	1	0
8. Little or no excessive effort observed during disfluencies	6	5	4	3	2	1	0
9. Little or no anxiety regarding speaking; unconcerned	6	5	4	3	2	1	0
10. Speech better under pressure (improves short-term with concentration	6	5	4	3	2	1	0

FIGURE 13–5. Profile analysis for planning treatment with cluttering clients. *Source:* Copyright © David Daly. Reprinted with permission.

	SPEECH-MOTOR							
11.	Articulation errors	6	5	4	3	2	1	0
12.	Irregular speech rate; speaks in spurts or bursts	6	5	4	3	2	1	0
13.	Telescopes or condenses words	6	5	4	3	2	1	0
14.	Rapid rate (tachylalia)	6	5	4	3	2	1	0
15.	Speech rate progressively increases (festinating)	6	5	4	3	2	1	0
16.	Variable prosody; irregular melody or stress pattern	6	5	4	3	2	1	0
17.	Initial loud voice trailing off to unintelligible murmur	6	5	4	3	2	1	0
18.	Lack of pauses between words and phrases	6	5	4	3	2	1	0
19.	Repetition of multi-syllabic words and phrases	6	5	4	3	2	1	0
20.	Co-existence of excessive disfluencies and stuttering	6	5	4	3	2	1	0
	LANGUAGE-COGNITION							
21.	Language is disorganized; confused wording; word-finding problems	6	5	4	3	2	1	0
22.	Poor language formulation; poor story-telling; sequencing problems	6	5	4	3	2	1	0
23.	Disorganized language increases as topic becomes more complex	6	5	4	3	2	1	0
24.	Many revisions; interjections; filler words	6	5	4	3	2	1	0
25.	Seems to verbalize before adequate thought formulation	6	5	4	3	2	1	0
26.	Inappropriate topic introduction, maintenance, or termination	6	5	4	3	2	1	0
27.	Improper linguistic structure; poor grammar; syntax errors	6	5	4	3	2	1	0
28.	Distractible; poor concentration; attention span problems	6	5	4	3	2	1	0

FIGURE 13–5. *continues*

	MOTOR COORDINATION-WRITING PROBLEMS							
29.	Poor motor control for writing (messy)	6	5	4	3	2	1	0
30.	Writing includes omission or transposition of letters, syllables or words	6	5	4	3	2	1	0
31.	Oral diadochokinetic coordination below expected normed levels	6	5	4	3	2	1	0
32.	Respiratory dysrhythmia; jerky breathing pattern	6	5	4	3	2	1	0
33.	Clumsy and uncoordinated; motor activities accelerated or impulsive	6	5	4	3	2	1	0
	Totals							

Grand Total _____   Diagnosis _____

FIGURE 13–5. *continued*

stuttering. Although far less common than both child-onset stuttering and cluttering, more recent reports suggest that acquired neurogenic and psychogenic stuttering occur more often than previous literature suggests. As with cluttering, there have been relatively few reports and nearly all in the form of case studies. De Nil et al. (2007) stressed the need for continuing systemic literature reviews, meta-analysis, and prospective investigations in order to develop a better understanding of these speakers.

The differential diagnosis of these forms of acquired stuttering can be difficult, not only because these speakers are seen relatively infrequently in most clinical locations (with the exception of large medical centers), but also because they can occur together—particularly with neuropathologies related to closed head injuries and medications. In the following paragraphs we discuss the characteristics of these forms of acquired stuttering, as well as the speaker characteristics that assist the clinician in distinguishing between the two. Because speech and language characteristics can reflect the overall health of a person, speech-language pathologists are often able to play a vital role in the diagnostic process. Based on the speaker's characteristics and the results of trial therapy, the clinician might be able to detect the presence of neuropathology, including possible sites of lesion (Baumgartner, 1999).

Characteristics of Neurogenic Stuttering

Neurogenic stuttering is likely to occur postpuberty, characteristically occurring in the decade of the 40s (Jokel & De Nil, 2003; Market et al., 1990; Mazzucchi et al., 1981; Stewart & Rowley, 1996). As with most fluency difficulties, the majority of individuals presenting with neurogenic stuttering are males (De Nil et al., 2007; Market et al., 1990; Stewart & Rowley, 1996). Clinicians who specialize in fluency disorders will eventually encounter these speakers, particularly if they work in large clinic or medical environments. Estimates of occurrence are complicated by a number of factors, including the multiple linguistic, cognitive, and motor problems that often accompany and sometimes mask the speaker's disfluency as well as the sometimes transient nature of the problem (Helm et al., 1980; Helm-Estabrooks, 1993; Rosenbek et al., 1978).

As others have done, we have chosen to use the term *neurogenic stuttering* (Helm et al., 1980; Silverman, 1996). However, many other terms have been used to describe this form of acquired disfluency, including *late* or *adult-onset stuttering*, *cortical stuttering* (Rosenbek et al., 1978), *organic stuttering* (Van Riper, 1982), and *stuttering associated with acquired neurological disorders* (SAAND; Helm-Estabrooks, 1999). The variety of terms is a result of the many etiologies and resulting subgroups of individuals who experience forms of acquired fluency problems. These include onset as a result of stroke, head trauma, extrapyramidal disease, tumor, dementia, and drug usage (Helm-Estabrooks et al., 1986). Recently, cases of neurogenic stuttering resulting from SARS-CoV-2 infection (long COVID-19) have also been reported (Furlanis et al., 2023; Morrison et al., 2020).

Accordingly, neurogenic stuttering does not appear to be associated with a particular site of lesion. One or both hemispheres could be involved, although Rosenbek et al. (1978) indicated that the left hemisphere is more likely to be implicated. De Nil et al. (2007) described the onset of neurogenic stuttering associated with many sites for head injury patients, including the internal and external capsule, low frontal white matter tracts, and the caudate and lentiform nuclei, and for stroke patients the thalamus and brain stem, basal ganglia, and cerebellum. The work of Alm (2004) indicates that the basal ganglia circuits are often involved. Certainly the wide variety of sites of anomalous brain function noted by many researchers and authors provides support for a multifocal view of stuttering etiology in which one, and perhaps several, regions of the brain associated with (at the minimum) linguistic and motor planning are involved. Researchers have suggested that a more thorough understanding of neurogenic stuttering is likely to inform our understanding about the onset of child-onset stuttering (De Nil et al., 2007).

In some instances, the onset of neurogenic stuttering is unquestionably associated with head trauma, stroke, cryosurgery, drug usage, infection, or anoxia. In other cases, when the speaker's fluency is slowly degraded, as with degenerative disorders, vascular disease, dementia, viral meningitis, or dialysis dementia (the effects of long-term dialysis procedures), the association between neurological damage and fluency is less obvious (Helm et al., 1980; Helm-Estabrooks, 1986). In other cases, a speaker's fluency could deteriorate as the result of a reoccurring medical condition (De Nil et al., 2007; Helm-Estabrooks, 1999). Fluency problems could also be observed as an early sign of what turns out to be a gradually evolving and yet-to-be discovered medical condition. Complicating the diagnostic situation still further are other problems, including dysarthria, apraxia, and aphasia, that tend to accompany neurogenic stuttering.

Assessment Procedures

Individuals with neurogenic stuttering tend to have some unique speech and fluency characteristics. However, Van Borsel (1997) cautioned that the speaker's clinical symptoms alone do not provide adequate information for distinguishing neurogenic from child-onset stuttering. Likewise, De Nil et al. (2007) commented that generalized criteria do not provide the necessary specificity for individual speakers who have acquired fluency problems as a result of central nervous system insults or disease processes. Furthermore, De Nil and colleagues also pointed out exceptions to some of the fluency characteristics that have been used in the past to identify neurogenic fluency problems.

For example, Canter (1971) and Helm-Estabrooks (1993) provided a list of six criteria that have traditionally been associated with neurogenic stuttering:

1. Fluency breaks are produced on grammatical (function) as well as substantive (content) words. Compared to individuals with child-onset stuttering who are more likely to have fluency breaks on content words, those with neurogenic stuttering are equally likely to stutter on function and content words.
2. The speaker might appear annoyed but does not appear anxious about the stuttering.
3. Repetitions, prolongations, and blocks are not restricted to the initial syllables. Unlike child-onset stuttering, fluency breaks occur not only on initial sounds and syllables, but also in medial

and final positions of words, for example, "gre-e-en" and "sto-o-o-ore."
4. Secondary symptoms such as facial grimacing, eye blinking, and fist clenching are rarely associated with the fluency breaks.
5. Fluency does not improve with repeated readings of a passage (the adaptation effect).
6. The speaker stutters regardless of the nature of the speech task.

De Nil et al. (2007) suggested that an appreciation of the wide variety of problems that accompany neurogenic stuttering calls for a modification of the traditional diagnostic characteristics recommended by Canter (1971) and Helm-Estabrooks (1993). For example, in spite of the tendency for disfluencies to occur on medial and final positions of words, in their work with six stroke patients, Jokel and De Nil (2003) and Jokel et al. (2007) found that 93% to 95% of disfluencies occurred in the initial position. The lack of an adaptation effect (a reduction in disfluency with repeated readings of the same passage) has often been offered as diagnostic criteria for neurogenic stuttering. Again, exceptions to this have been noted by Jokel and De Nil (2003) and Jokel et al. (2007), who found as much as a 30% reduction in disfluencies with successive readings for some stroke patients (adaptation was less likely to occur with patients with head injury). Clinicians have also been advised that neurogenic stuttering tends to be consistent regardless of such factors as the speaking situation, time pressure, and grammatical complexity (Rao, 1991). Exceptions to this trend have been noted by Abe et al. (1993), who found a greater number of repetitions occurring during spontaneous speech than during reading and, by Jokel et al. (2007), who noted more disfluencies during monologue than in conversation as well as less stuttering with more complex reading material.

Two additional related characteristics have often been attributed to speakers with neurogenic stuttering: a lack of both secondary behaviors and anxiety or emotion associated with the disfluencies. As De Nil et al. (2007) pointed out, because of the variety and the difficulty in identifying and describing secondary behaviors, relatively little is known about them. Jokel and De Nil (2003) and Jokel et al. (2007) noted the occurrence of eye blinking, facial grimacing, head bending, foot tapping, and limb or head movements associated with occurrences of stuttering. De Nil et al. (2007) pointed out that Rosenbek et al. (1978) also reported accessory features in half of the 57 patients they studied, particularly in the most severe patients. De Nil et al. (2007) suggested that the more time that elapses between the lesion or disease and the onset of disfluencies and the formal assessment, the more likely speakers are to develop accessory or coping responses. Likewise, it has been suggested that speakers experiencing neurogenic stuttering are likely to indicate annoyance rather than a high level of anxiety about their lack of fluency. It could be, of course, that such individuals have many emotions associated with their fluency problems but lack the ability to fully express themselves about their condition. Furthermore, although speakers might simply be annoyed about their ability to communicate at the outset, their emotions are more likely to become more elaborate after suffering the prolonged effects of disfluency. Jokel and De Nil (2003) and Jokel et al. (2007) found that six speakers with stroke-induced neurogenic stuttering scored an average of 18.3 on the S-24 Communication Attitudes Inventory,

a score comparable to the average of 19.22 reported for individuals with child-onset stuttering and significantly greater than the S-24 average (9.42) for fluent speakers (Andrews & Cutler, 1974). De Nil reported observing patterns of people withdrawing from social and professional situations as a result of their disfluencies. It has also been suggested (Grant et al., 1999) that behavioral and emotional reactions to acquired, neurogenic stuttering are especially likely to occur in cases where a neurological problem triggers preexisting stuttering.

Two characteristics that appear to be uniquely associated with neurogenic stuttering are (a) the relative ineffectiveness of fluency-enhancing techniques that tend to immediately eliminate stuttering for most individuals with child-onset stuttering (e.g., choral speaking, rhythmic speech, singing, prolonged speech, whispering, and silent speech; Andrews et al., 1983; Bloodstein, 1949; e.g., Perkins [1973] noted that of more than 100 people who stuttered, the only person who did not show a reduction in stuttering under such conditions was a woman who was later diagnosed as having a neurological disorder); and (b) people with neurogenic stuttering are more likely than those with child-onset stuttering to produce disfluencies during the production of automatic speech tasks such as counting, naming days of the week, and so on (Helm-Estabrooks, 1993; Helm-Estabrooks et al., 1986).

Given the multiple etiologies and resulting varieties of neurogenic stuttering, it is clear that the assessment process needs to be both thorough and individualized. De Nil et al. (2007) suggested a battery of assessment procedures (Assessment Battery for Acquired Stuttering in Adults [ABASA]; Table 13–2) for obtaining case history, general communication

TABLE 13–2. A Summary of Characteristics That Help to Differentiate Neurogenic and Psychogenic Stuttering From Child-Onset Stuttering

Child-Onset Stuttering	Neurogenic Stuttering	Psychogenic Stuttering
Gradual onset usually 2–4 years of age during rapid period of speech and language development	Sudden onset in adults, triggered by neurologic event: stroke, TBI, epilepsy, degenerative disease; medication effect (tardive dyskinesia)	Sudden onset in adults; triggered by somatization (unusual reaction to stress), prolonged stress, or trauma, conversion disorder
Can occur with speech and language delays, disorders	Can occur concomitant to aphasia, apraxia, dysarthria, or in isolation	Can occur with neurologic disease or present with suspected neurologic disease
Repetitions, prolongations, and blocks of initial sounds and syllables; differs from cluttering	Similar core behaviors but not restricted to initial sounds or syllables	Similar core behaviors but not restricted to initial syllables; excessive repetitions on every phoneme
Likely to occur on function words for children, content words for adults	May occur on function words as well as content words	Can occur anywhere in speech; unusual secondary behaviors that can occur independently or core behaviors
Adaptation effect present	Consistent across speech tasks	No adaptation effect
Responds to fluency-inducing conditions	No adaptation effect	May respond to fluency-inducing conditions
Awareness, anxiety, fear and avoidance, tension, struggle increase over time	Does not respond to fluency-inducing conditions	Unusual grammatical constructions; telegraphic

Source: The above table was presented by Drs. Joseph R. Duffy, R. Kevin Manning, and Carole R. Roth at the American Speech-Language and Hearing Association, San Diego, CA, 2009.

functions (language, speech, and cognition), speech fluency assessments, and speaker self-assessment of attitudes (S-24, LCB).

The guidelines provided by Canter (1971) and Helm-Estabrooks (1993) appear to be useful in identifying the occurrence of neurogenic stuttering. As we have seen, though, particularly depending on the nature of the insult to the speaker's neurological system and the duration of the disrupted fluency, there are excep-

tions to these characteristics. Continuing research with these individuals suggests that there is likely to be individual variability associated with what might be too readily thought of as stereotypical behavioral characteristics for this population. It might be best to consider the list in the following Clinical Decision Making box as characteristics that could accompany the various forms of neurogenic stuttering and that can help the clinician to distinguish these individuals from those with child-onset stuttering.

Treatment Procedures

An interesting aspect of treatment for individuals with the various forms of neurogenic stuttering is that not all speakers will require therapy. In some cases, the neurological problem will be transient and as the person recovers over a period of weeks or months, the fluency problem subsides. This is most likely to be the case for stroke patients (Helm-Estabrooks, 1999). For patients with closed head injuries associated with seizure activity, resolution of the seizures could result in improved fluency. Particularly interesting are the reports of clinicians who describe an improvement of fluency in clients with neurogenic stuttering who have suffered further damage to their central nervous system (Helm-Estabrooks et al., 1986;

Jones, 1966; Manders & Bastijns, 1988; Van Riper, 1982). The additional trauma apparently resulted in further neurological change that facilitated speech fluency.

Because acquired neurological stuttering is far from a unitary disorder, no single therapeutic approach is preferred, and it is not possible to predict a particular speaker's response to intervention. For example, Helm-Estabrooks (1993) found that Parkinson's patients tend to respond well to a variety of therapeutic approaches, whereas stroke patients tend to be less responsive. The treatment strategies and associated techniques described in Chapter 11 for speakers with child-onset stuttering are routinely used for those with neurogenic stuttering. Clinicians experienced with this population indicate that the behavioral changes and cognitive restructuring promoted in stuttering-modification techniques and fluency-shaping techniques that facilitate easy,

CLINICAL DECISION MAKING

Characteristics that *might* occur for speakers with neurogenic stuttering are as follows:

1. No reported history of previous fluency problems.
2. Evidence of sudden or progressive degrading of the speaker's central nervous system.
3. Fluency-enhancing techniques do not result in significantly improved fluency.
4. Fluency does not improve during automatic speech tasks.
5. There is a tendency for stuttering to occur on medial and final syllables of words.
6. Compared to individuals with child-onset stuttering, there is less of a tendency for speakers to demonstrate
   - improved fluency with repeated readings of a passage (adaptation effect);
   - variability in fluency across speech tasks or speaking situations;
   - struggle behavior and secondary behaviors, particularly at the onset of the problem; and
   - emotional reactions associated with their disrupted fluency, particularly at the outset of the problem.

slowed, and relaxed speech production can be successfully employed with these speakers (De Nil et al., 2007; Helm-Estabrooks, 1999; Market et al., 1990; Meyers, Hall, & Aram, 1990; Rousey et al., 1986). In addition, because word finding is a common problem in neurogenic fluency disorders and can contribute to fluency breaks (Brown & Cullinan, 1981; Meyers, Hall, & Aram, 1990), a slow rate of speech production could also assist the speaker by providing more time for retrieval. Helm-Estabrooks (1986) suggested that for all forms of fluency disorders encountered, pharmacological treatment might be the most beneficial, although she also noted that undesirable side effects are possible.

Characteristics of Psychogenic Stuttering

As we discussed in Chapter 3, the vast majority of people with fluency problems do not differ from a matched group of normally fluent speakers in terms of personality and psychological characteristics (Goodstein, 1958; Manning & Beck, 2013a; Sheehan, 1958). However, in any randomly selected group of people there will be some individuals with emotional problems. Van Riper (1979) indicated that only a handful of people who come to us with the complaint of stuttering are emotionally ill. To be sure, many of the people we will see are deeply troubled by what they correctly perceive as an extremely frustrating and sometimes devastating communication problem. For some people, the coping responses are far from normal and could take on the characteristics of extreme anxiety as well as neurotic and compulsive behavior. However, as Van Riper (1982) suggested, these behaviors are best interpreted as a result rather than

a cause of stuttering. The behaviors are rarely the symptoms of some deep-seated emotional conflict. Rather, the behaviors are learned and, in some cases, maladaptive coping responses to the fear and helplessness of stuttering.

On occasion, however, clinicians might encounter people with more pronounced emotional problems resulting in stuttering. Acquired psychogenic stuttering occurs with roughly equal frequency in men and women (Baumgartner & Duffy, 1997). In some instances, the client will have a history of emotional problems and might be currently receiving professional help for his or her condition. Even in the absence of a serious or long-standing emotional problem, some people react strongly to the common stresses of life, and disrupted fluency is a result.

Baumgartner (1999) suggested that psychopathology is not always present in psychogenic stuttering; the symptoms could be a natural response to either the anticipation or the experience of life events. As one with considerable experience with acquired psychogenic stuttering, Baumgartner (1999) disagreed with the suggestion that the term "psychogenic stuttering" should apply only to individuals who have been diagnosed with a psychopathology. He provided a convincing argument that, at least in many cases, such a diagnosis is not necessary for the speech-language pathologist to determine that a fluency problem is psychogenic in nature. Furthermore, Baumgartner suggested that waiting to begin therapeutic intervention until a formal psychiatric diagnosis is forthcoming negates the valuable information that could be gained through trial therapy.

As with neurogenic stuttering, the onset of disfluent behavior is likely to be relatively sudden, and the person might have no previous history of fluency problems. There could be, however, a history of psychological problems, neurological problems, or both (Baumgartner, 1999). As Aronson (1992) suggested, speech and voice disorders could be caused by distress or "psychologic disequilibrium." Baumgartner and Duffy (1997) found that when a diagnosis of psychopathology does take place, the most common classifications are conversion reaction (Mahr & Leith, 1992), anxiety, and depression. Other possible diagnostic categories are reactive depression, personality disorder, drug dependence, and posttraumatic neurosis, with some individuals being placed into more than one category. For some people, there could be an interaction of psychogenic and neurological problems as a result of psychological reactions to a medical condition. As several authors have indicated, a person's awareness of a serious neurological disease might quite naturally precipitate a psychological reaction, resulting in psychogenic stuttering (Baumgartner & Duffy, 1997; De Nil et al., 2007; Helm-Estabrooks & Hotz, 1998; Van Borsel, 1997).

Assessment Procedures

One of the more striking aspects of this form of disfluency is the stereotypical nature of the fluency breaks. Some people with psychogenic stuttering might give the impression of "holding onto" their stuttering, in the sense that both the frequency and the form show little change. The listener might get the sense that it is as though the speaker has chosen a particular "brand" of stuttering and for a time, at least, that is the way he or she is choosing to speak. In some cases, speakers will stutter on nearly every word, show little adaptation during multiple readings, continue to stutter during fluency-enhancing activities, and produce stuttering-like movements during miming—mouthing words without voicing (Deal, 1982). Another characteristic of both neurogenic and psychogenic stuttering is the lack of an adaptation effect. In fact, if stuttering becomes *more* severe with successive readings of a passage, it is a strong indicator of psychogenic stuttering (Baumgartner & Duffy, 1997).

Distinguishing Between Neurogenic and Psychogenic Stuttering

Distinguishing among possible neurological and psychological etiological factors presents one of the most difficult aspects of assessment. In a retrospective study of 69 patients diagnosed at the Mayo Clinic for psychogenic stuttering, 20 patients were found to have confirmed neurologic disease. Baumgartner and Duffy (1997) noted the considerable overlap between the characteristics of both etiologies, and the two forms of acquired stuttering cannot be distinguished solely on the nature of the disfluencies (Baumgartner, 1999; Helm-Estabrooks, 1999). One potentially helpful fact is that many more cases of neurogenic stuttering are reported in the literature than psychogenic stuttering (Helm-Estabrooks & Hotz, 1998).

Information obtained in the speaker's case history is particularly important in the assessment of acquired stuttering. Baumgartner (1999) recommended a careful and systematic "psychologic interview" process in order to determine events that could indicate a temporal relationship between the patient's speech problems, evidence of central nervous system impairment, and possible sources of emotional stress in the person's life. Baumgartner suggested that the clinician look for patterns of unexplained problems and communication difficulties in the near or distant past. In order to achieve this goal, it is critical that the clinician approach this interview by creating a setting that allows the client to describe these events, as well as his or her reaction to them. As Baumgartner (1999) described:

> The skilled interviewer creates an atmosphere that encourages and supports discussions of feelings, fears, and information not previously disclosed (very possibly to anyone). It is not enough to find out what has happened in an individual's life. The truly successful interview explores how people feel about these things, how they have dealt with them, and whether they would "really like" to do something else about them. (p. 272)

If the clinician is able to facilitate such an exchange of information and the speaker is, in fact, experiencing acquired psychogenic stuttering, speech fluency is likely to show an immediate change, either by becoming more or less severe. In some cases, stuttering could disappear completely (Baumgartner, 1999). This can be taken as a clear diagnostic sign: "Symptom resolution, a marked disclosure of emotionally sensitive information, is powerful evidence in support of psychogenicity and argues strongly against organicity" (Baumgartner, 1999, p. 272).

Baumgartner (1999) also suggested a series of tasks to further define the nature of the problem with these speakers and to rule out the possibility of coexisting neurogenic communication disorders. The quantity and form of the stuttering might have little etiological value, as these might closely parallel those in speakers with child-onset stuttering. Although disfluen-

cies are more variable than those of neurogenic speakers, a pattern of worsening of symptoms during the performance of less difficult speaking tasks is a clear sign of psychogenicity. Bizarre movements (e.g., of the head and eyes) that are unrelated to speech production and unusual speech patterns are also a sign of psychogenicity. Considering the suggestions of Baumgartner and Duffy (1997) and Mahr and Leith (1992) for identifying psychogenic stuttering, as well as the research presented in the previous paragraphs, the next Clinical Decision Making box provides a list of 10 characteristics that could assist the clinician in identifying speakers experiencing this acquired fluency problem. Because of the similarities of psychogenic and neurogenic stuttering, a good first step is to rule out evidence of central nervous system impairment. As mentioned, it is also useful to consider that there are many more reported instances of neurogenic than psychogenic stuttering.

Treatment Procedures

Because of the relatively small number of speakers with acquired psychogenic stuttering, there are few empirical studies documenting treatment strategies and the nature of recovery for this population, especially over the long term. Roth et al. (1989) recommended "traditional fluency treatment" in combination with counseling from a psychologist or psychiatrist. According to Roth et al., these patients are receptive to both stuttering and fluency modification procedures. These authors stressed the importance of encouragement and optimism concerning a successful outcome on the part of the clinician. Psychiatric referral is not typically the treatment of choice (Baumgartner, 1999). However, in cases where the patient con-

CLINICAL DECISION MAKING

Characteristics that might occur for speakers with psychogenic stuttering include the following.

1. Case history information indicates a history of emotional problems such as personality disorder, posttraumatic stress, drug dependence, acute anxiety, or depression. (A diagnosis of psychopathology is not necessary.)
2. The speaker gives the impression of "holding onto" stuttering, and continues to stutter during fluency-enhancing activities, including miming.
3. A rapid improvement in fluency occurs following the disclosure of emotionally sensitive information.
4. The speaker shows a rapid and favorable response to a brief period of trial therapy.
5. The speaker shows a pattern of worsening symptoms during the performance of less difficult speaking tasks.
6. Stuttering becomes more severe with successive readings of a passage.
7. The speaker demonstrates bizarre struggle behaviors and signs of anxiety that are not associated with breaks in fluency.
8. The speaker produces unusual grammatical constructions (e.g., "Me get sick").
9. The speaker shows unusual forms of fluency disruptions such as multiple repetitions of nearly all phonemes with simultaneous head bobbing, facial grimaces, and tremor-like movements.
10. There are intermittent or situation-specific episodes of stuttering.

tinues to be affected by environmental stress or if there is little change in the patient's fluency following several sessions, such referrals are in order.

Baumgartner (1999) indicated that because behaviors vary so much across patients and because even the initial assessment procedures could be highly therapeutic, treatment goals should be open ended. The initial goals of treatment, which can occur during the first (diagnostic) session, are to provide the client with an explanation of the evaluation and the development of an atmosphere whereby "the patient becomes receptive to the idea that these findings are good news and indicate that a total resolution of symptoms is possible" (p. 279). Because many

patients with acquired psychogenic stuttering believe that the problem is organic in nature, it is important for the patient to have a positive reaction to the news that no organicity is present and that this an unsurprising result of the evaluation. As Baumgartner (1999) explained:

A "cognitive set" must be achieved so that the lack of the lack of organicity is perceived in a positive light by the patient, as is the clinician's belief that this is a reasonable, not unexpected finding. If this is not achieved, a patient may have received indirectly the message that the clinician is surprised or that the findings are somehow mysterious. Worse yet would be the message that a lack of organicity indicates that there is not a real problem. In my opinion, a prerequisite for patients achieving such a cognitive set is the clinician's belief that psychogenicity is a valid concept and that the findings pointing to such a diagnosis are reasonable and not uncommon. (p. 279)

Treatment should proceed with the same confidence on the part of the clinician about the possibility of achieving normally fluent speech. According to Baumgartner (1999) and Duffy (2016), it is not unusual to achieve much improved fluency during the first treatment session. If improvement occurs, the patient should be informed that this is a positive sign. On those occasions when this is not the case, the clinician can focus on helping the speaker to reduce struggle behavior associated with abnormal movements that are unrelated to speech production (e.g., movements of the limbs or torso or bizarre movements of the eyes) and to alter such aberrant behaviors as speaking only when lying down or when grasping an object. Baumgartner (1999) recommended that it is often helpful to focus treatment activities on the area of the body that is associated with excessive effort or tension. He found that touching or manipulating of these areas by the clinician is particularly effective in reducing musculoskeletal tension (see Baumgartner, 1999, pp. 284–285, for a description of this technique). Duffy (2016) provided principles and guidelines as well as specific treatment techniques for assisting adults with psychogenic stuttering.

Baumgartner stressed that it is important not to "rush" the speaker with these therapeutic activities, but rather to emphasize the fact that the speaker's improving fluency represents a good prognosis. He argued that it is more essential to change the patient's "belief system" than to elicit fluent speech or practice speech-related movements. As these measures are successful, the clinician can then show the speaker how to expand his or her fluency. In contrast to the prognosis for persons with acquired neurogenic stuttering, individuals with acquired psychogenic stuttering are more likely to demonstrate a rapid achievement of fluency. For example, Baumgartner and Duffy (1997) reported that more than 50% of their patients improved to normal or near-normal fluency following one or two sessions of symptomatic treatment.

ACQUIRED STUTTERING AS A RESULT OF COVID-19

COVID-19 was designated as a global pandemic by the World Health Organization (WHO) on March 11, 2020. The disease found its way to all corners of the globe, bringing the world to a standstill, with a death toll in the millions. Initially described as a respiratory virus, additional residual effects of the disease have been emerging as people live with lingering symptoms. Recently, cases of neurogenic stuttering have been reported in relation to COVID-19 infection.

Furlanis et al. (2023) reported on two patients who developed neurogenic stuttering after long COVID-19 related to SARS-CoV-2 infection. Both patients reported physical and cognitive difficulties, which included impaired attention, lexical retrieval, and memory. In addition, both patients demonstrated new-onset stuttering-like speech disfluencies characterized by blocks and repetitions at the initial part of words and sentences. These disfluencies were sometimes accompanied by effortful facial grimaces and orofacial movements. Neuropsychological evaluations and electroencephalography indicated cognitive impairments and the presence of "slowed" patterns of brain activity. The neurogenic stuttering and cognitive difficulties persisted for 4 to 5 months after the patients tested negative for the SARS-CoV-2 virus, with gradual improvement and near-to-complete recovery.

Similarly, Morrison et al. (2020) reported on a single case of a 53-year-old woman who visited the emergency department (ED) with COVID-19 symptoms. On her second ED visit, the woman complained of new-onset stuttering and word-finding difficulties. This patient reported that her speech symptoms persisted for at least 7 days after discharge from the ED.

These cases demonstrate that SARS-CoV-2 infection can significantly involve the central nervous system, potentially resulting in severe and long-term consequences, with new-onset stuttering one of the symptoms. In all three cases, the neurogenic stuttering resolved, although in two cases it persisted for months after the patients tested negative for the virus.

FLUENCY PROBLEMS AS A RESULT OF COMBAT-RELATED TBI AND PTSD

In recent decades, a related form of adult-onset stuttering has significantly increased as a result of both physical and emotional trauma during combat. In contrast to earlier conflicts, improved body armor and advances in medical care have resulted in higher survival rates. Higher survival rates, in turn, have increased the occurrence of issues with traumatic brain injury (TBI) and posttraumatic stress disorder (PTSD; Duffy et al., 2009). Many individuals with PTSD have also experienced TBI. Clinicians who work in Veterans Administration hospitals as well as those who work in geographic areas where there are large numbers of military personal have experienced an increase in clients with speech and language-related problems, including fluency.

The diagnostic criteria for PTSD have changed somewhat since the presentation by Duffy et al. (2009). PTSD is no longer listed as an anxiety disorder. The current criteria specify the onset of PTSD as exposure to actual or threatened death, serious injury, or sexual violation. The exposure must result from one or more of the following where the individual:

- directly experiences the traumatic event;
- witnesses the traumatic event in person;
- learns that the traumatic event occurred to a close family member or close friend (with the actual or threatened death being either violent or accidental; or
- experiences firsthand repeated or extreme exposure to aversive details of the traumatic event (not through media, pictures, television, or movies unless work related).

Behaviors that could occur include a persistent and distorted sense of blame of self or others, estrangement from others or markedly diminished interest in activities, avoidance of thoughts, or an inability to remember key aspects of the event. Individuals might become aggressive, self-destructive, or hypervigilant; experience "flight-or-fight" reactions; or have sleep disturbances.

As a result of the combinations of PTSD and TBI, the veterans are likely to have short-term memory, attention, and concentration problems, resulting in difficulty with word retrieval. They might also have receptive language problems. Duffy et al. (2009) stated at the time of their presentation that there are no data regarding the incidence of sudden-onset, adult stuttering related to TBI. The combination of problems resulting from combat-related brain injury with co-occurring PTSD obviously presents a challenge for the clinician. The many symptoms of PTSD and TBI are amplified by the co-occurrence of each (Bryant & Allison, 1999). Duffy et al. (2009) indicated that the following characteristics could be present:

- False starts, hesitations, or blocks before initial sounds
- Repetitions of a whole utterance, word, and initial syllable
- Posturing with the jaw, lips, or tongue before initiating speech
- Attention and slow information processing contributing to disfluencies
- Tension: facial grimace, jar tremors
- Whispering (reauditorizing) prior to initiating speech
- Secondary characteristics
  - Blepharospasms (a neurological condition resulting in forcible closure of the eyelids)
  - Le Belle indifference (an inappropriate lack of emotion or concern for one's disability)

Recommendations for Assessment

The assessment of these individuals overlaps considerably with the earlier comments about psychogenic stuttering and includes obtaining case history and background information and cognitive, language, and speech assessments. It is also recommended that the clinician observe the speaker during various speaking conditions including conversation; choral reading; whispered, shouted, and lipped speech; imitation of words, phrases, and sentences; experimenting with automatized speech such as days of the week; counting (e.g., from 1 to 20); and checking for the adaptation effect. Finally, it is suggested that the clinician experiment with therapeutic probes to see if fluency-enhancing techniques would improve fluency.

Recommendations for Treatment

The treatment protocols and techniques for these individuals are similar in many ways to those used with childhood-onset stuttering. Mattingly and Roth (2022) recommended the use of rate reduction, self-monitoring, biofeedback, relaxation, and speech pacing techniques. Although there might be many forms of fluency breaks, they recommended selecting a frequently occurring disfluency as a good place to start. They suggested observation and reduction of musculoskeletal tension via palpitation of the neck and related areas and telling the client that the dysfluencies are partially the result of the increased tension. They also recommended experimenting with such fluency-inducing activities as production of single vowel sounds, single words, and prolonged speech. Once disfluencies are reduced, the clinician can begin moving toward developing more natural rate and inflection.

THE POSSIBILITY OF MALINGERING

There exists another—perhaps the least likely—possibility for explaining the sudden onset of stuttering in adults. It could be that the speaker is malingering in an effort to gain some advantage by posing as a person who stutters. Based on diagnostic criteria described by Morrison (1995), Seery (2005) described two levels of malingering. Pure malingering involves intentional faking all of the symptoms of a physical or mental disorder. Partial malingering is the exaggeration of existing symptoms. Both forms of malingering are motivated by the intention of achieving some form of gain or advantage (e.g., money or avoidance of responsibility). Seery noted cases of malingered stuttering found in the literature (Bloodstein, 1988; Culatta & Goldberg, 1995; Shapiro, 1999) that involved partial malingering, the exaggeration of true stuttering.

The few documented instances of this behavior are forensic cases, whereby individuals are attempting to demonstrate their innocence (Bloodstein, 1987; Seery, 2005). Seery (2005) provided an especially interesting example of a man accused of armed robbery. Part of his attorney's defense was that his client's severe stuttering would have prevented his complete fluency when uttering a statement made during the robbery. When asked to consult on the case, Seery adapted procedures by Resnick (1993) for detecting malingering for psychosis. Her assessment protocol included elements of speech sampling under multiple speaking conditions, a thorough examination of case history information, and indirect tests of malingering. Although some indicators suggested developmental, psychogenic, and neurological stuttering, Seery (2005) found the strongest evidence supporting partial malingering. Specifically, she found little variability from a consistently high frequency of stuttering across speaking tasks, little or no decrease in stuttering frequency with multiple readings, a lack of consistency of stuttering on specific words during multiple readings, direct and relaxed eye contact with the examiner during even the most severe stuttering events, a lack of secondary or struggle behavior during stuttering events, stuttering on the last rather than the first words of a statement, and reports of "islands of fluency" by witnesses in spite of the speaker's report of consistent stuttering during all communication situations. Perhaps most revealing was the speaker's maintenance of consistently severe stuttering during conditions that often elicit enhanced fluency (automatic speech tasks, finger tapping while talking, prolonged speech, as well as both lipped and unison speech). It was apparent that this speaker was able to make use of his history of child-onset stuttering in order to call attention to and magnify his stuttering.

CLINICAL INSIGHT

Several years ago, I had the opportunity to interview a woman in her early 30s who complained of a sudden onset of severe stuttering. Approximately 3 weeks prior to our assessment, she had been sexually assaulted. One week following the attack, she lost her ability to speak, and when she began speaking again, approximately 3 days later, she demonstrated well-developed stuttering. She reported no personal or family history of stuttering. At the time of the assessment interview, she was stuttering on nearly

continues

every word and showed a high level of anxiety. The frequency of her fluency breaks was uniform throughout the interview and consisted almost entirely of tense prolongations of whole words. We were unable to elicit any periods of fluent speech through using a variety of fluency-enhancing activities.

We also had the opportunity to interview a 41-year-old man who complained of a sudden onset of stuttering. As was the case with the woman described earlier, this man also had no previous history of fluency disorders. In this instance, however, there appeared to be no indication of a traumatic event preceding the onset of his disrupted fluency. During the evaluation and for many years following this interview, I had conceived of this speaker as an example of psychogenic stuttering but now believe there was a good chance that he was malingering. For several years he had been receiving ongoing inpatient treatment in the psychiatric ward at a local Veterans Administration hospital for an undisclosed emotional disorder. As with the woman described earlier, we were also unable to elicit moments of fluent speech using fluency-enhancing activities. The frequency of his stuttering was consistent throughout the entire 2-hour assessment interview. His fluency breaks consisted of relatively easy one- and two-unit repetitions produced at the same rate as the rest of his speech, rather than at a relatively more rapid pace characteristic of stuttering. Although he explained that he was very concerned about his fluency problem, he showed no struggle or tension during his fluency breaks, nor did he report any avoidances or fear associated with this problem. Perhaps the most interesting aspect of his stuttering was the way he watched listeners as he stuttered. He constantly maintained eye contact, and although we cannot say for sure that he "enjoyed" intently observing his listeners for their reactions, he clearly did not appear embarrassed or upset by his disfluencies. He appeared to remain detached from his stuttering—sometimes smiling as he closely watched the interviewer while stuttering. As with the woman, it was apparent to us that stuttering was not his most important problem—a characteristic response that the clinician is likely to have when interviewing such clients. However, whereas the woman's speech displayed a profound emotional reaction to a specific and documented trauma, this man's speech appeared to be contrived and manipulative. (WM)

CONCLUSION

The increasing interest in the less common forms of disrupted fluency has resulted in an appreciation of the complexities as well as the possible etiological and epidemiological characteristics of these problems. Of these less typical fluency problems, cluttering is by far the most prevalent either in a pure form or, more frequently, co-occurring with stuttering.

The combination of stuttering and cluttering will dramatically influence the plan of treatment, possibly making treatment more complex, in large part because of speakers' difficulty in self-monitoring the rate and quality of their speech. Although individuals who stutter occasionally have problems formulating language and coordinating speech production, these are especially important issues for those who clutter. Fortunately, many of the fluency and stuttering-modification techniques employed with individuals who stutter are helpful for enhancing the fluent speech of those who clutter. However, a multifaceted approach is necessary that also includes activities that assist the individual to develop self-monitoring, linguistic, rate-control, and motor skills.

Even less common are those persons who, often in the middle years of adulthood, experience the onset of an acquired fluency problem in the form of neurogenic or psychogenic stuttering. It can be difficult to distinguish these two forms of acquired stuttering from one another, for although there are many important behavioral and cognitive-affective differences, there is also considerable overlap, including the possibility of coexisting neurological damage. Both assessment and treatment for acquired fluency disorders will depend on the nature and extent of the insult to the person's neurological system. It is not possible to distinguish forms of neurogenic stuttering based solely on the speaker's clinical symptoms. The greater occurrence of neurogenic stuttering than psychogenic stuttering is of some help in differentiating between the two forms of acquired stuttering.

Although a diagnosis of a psychopathology might not be necessary for individuals with psychogenic stuttering, case history is likely to provide important information for an accurate diagnosis. The unique speech and behavioral characteristics of individuals presenting with what could be psychogenic stuttering during assessment procedures, as well as the often positive response to intervention, provide key indicators for making an appropriate diagnosis. In some cases, the initial assessment and trial therapy procedures could be therapeutic. Recommended therapeutic strategies emphasize enhancing the speaker's belief that improved fluency is highly likely rather than improving the individual's fluency. In rare instances of adult onset of stuttering—sometimes having to do with forensic matters—it might also be necessary to consider the possibility of malingering.

All of these problems that humans confront as they attempt to communicate fluently present clinicians with unique challenges. They could also provide exciting opportunities to operate for a time "on the edge of our incompetence."

TOPICS FOR DISCUSSION

1. In what ways would your diagnostic and treatment choices differ for speakers who present with characteristics of stuttering versus speakers with both stuttering and cluttering?

2. What are the core and accessory characteristics of cluttering as described by St. Louis et al. (2007)? How does this view of cluttering differ from that of Daly and colleagues?

3. What differences can be noted in the disfluencies of speakers with child-onset stuttering, speakers who clutter, and speakers with acquired neurogenic stuttering?

4. Describe the characteristics of individuals who have suffered from symptoms of PTSD and TBI.

5. According to St. Louis and colleagues, what are the primary goals of treatment for cluttering?

6. What are the speech, fluency, linguistic, and emotional characteristics of individuals presenting with neurogenic stuttering?

7. Why is it appropriate to consider a variety of treatment options for speakers with neurogenic stuttering?

8. What are the speech, fluency, linguistic, and emotional characteristics of psychogenic stuttering?

9. What would you say are the primary considerations when developing a therapeutic strategy for a speaker with psychogenic stuttering?

10. Differentiate between pure and partial malingering. What activities would you consider in order to identify the possibility of malingering?

RECOMMENDED READINGS

Baumgartner, J. M. (1999). Acquired psychogenic stuttering. In R. Curlee (Ed.), *Stuttering and related disorders of fluency* (2nd ed., pp. 269–288). Thieme Medical.

Daly, D. A. (1996). *The source for stuttering and cluttering*. LinguiSystems.

De Nil., L. F., Jokel, R., & Rochon, E. (2007). Etiology symptomatology, and treatment of neurogenic stuttering. In E. Conture & R. Curlee (Eds.), *Stuttering and related disorders of fluency* (3rd ed., pp. 326–343). Thieme Medical.

Duffy, J. R. (2013). *Motor speech disorders: Substrates, differential diagnosis, and management* (3rd ed.). Elsevier.

Seery, C. H. (2005). Differential diagnosis of stuttering for forensic purposes. *American Journal of Speech-Language Pathology, 14,* 284–297.

St. Louis, K. O., Myers, F. L., Bakker, K., & Raphael, L. J. (2007). Understanding and treating cluttering. In E. Conture & R. Curlee (Eds.), *Stuttering and related disorders of fluency* (3rd ed., pp. 297–325). Thieme Medical.

If you want something you have never had you must be willing to do something you have never done.

—Thomas Jefferson

Indicators of Successful Change During Treatment

CHAPTER OBJECTIVES

- To describe the multidimensional nature of therapeutic change
- To examine the variables that influence progress
- To define indicators of progress
- To describe constructs that indicate a person's ability to promote change
- To describe additional indicators of desirable change

Traditionally successful therapeutic change has most often been informed by the clinician's observation and interpretation of data, which appear to indicate the speaker's progress. More recently there is growing appreciation of the importance of locating these data in the context of the unique lived experience of the speaker, giving value to the specific knowledge of the individual experiencing the phenom-

enon. From the outset of therapy, there will be many opportunities for speakers to inform the clinician about the goals that are important to them in their journey from being dominated by stuttering to the achievement of successful management and an improved quality of life. This philosophical position is consistent with the key principle of evidence-based practice as well as recommendations by clinicians to focus on individual, rather than group, data as a means for assessing treatment efficacy. For example, Starkweather (1999) and Quesal (1989) suggested that a primary reason for our lack of success in understanding and combating relapse following initially successful therapy is a tendency to study the commonalities of group studies rather than considering patterns of individual change. It is apparent that many clinicians and clients understand the nature of successful therapy in very different ways (Bothe, 2004; Finn, 2003; Krauss-Lehrman & Reeves, 1989; Reeves, 2006; St. Louis, 2006; Yaruss & Quesal, 2002; Yaruss, Quesal, & Murphy, 2002). For example, Krauss-Lehrman and Reeves (1989) found that 75% of National Stuttering Association members surveyed felt that their therapy had been mildly or very successful even though many continued to display varying degrees of stuttering. It is unlikely that some individuals who describe a successful therapy experience or self-report recovery from stuttering would meet the threshold of fluency that some professional clinicians or researchers would judge as acceptable (see Ryan, 2001, particularly Chapter 11). Nonetheless, many of these former clients indicate a clear sense of accomplishment and genuinely feel that their lives are unrestricted by the occasional occurrence (or the possibility) of stuttering.

On occasion, clients as well as clinicians are confused by information, particularly on the Internet and even in professional journals, describing impressive levels of success for individuals undergoing treatment using unique treatment techniques or devices. Often closer examination of these reports indicates a variety of factors accounting for "success" such as a highly restrictive selection process for those enrolled in treatment (e.g., the only individuals who took part in treatment were highly motivated, could afford the time and expense of treatment, were responsive to the diagnostic tasks, and had few or no concomitant learning or communication problems). In addition, it is not unusual for individuals who decline or drop out of a treatment protocol to be excluded from the experimental cohort, resulting in an inflated sense of treatment effectiveness. It could also be that the criteria for success include only an overt measure of percentage of syllables stuttered within the clinic environment.

THE MULTIDIMENSIONAL NATURE OF THERAPEUTIC CHANGE

Therapeutic progress goes far beyond the changes that take place during the time the client is occupied in formal treatment. Formal treatment can be thought of as that time when the client is receiving and in all likelihood paying for the services of a professional clinician. It is important, however, to view the speaker's long-term progress as a continuum of both formal and informal treatment. As discussed in the next chapter, informal, self-treatment can be regarded as the much longer time following formal treatment during which the client is fully independent of the clinician. In many important ways this latter stage of treatment is the most critical part of the process and provides the true measure of treatment efficacy. Treatment can be regarded as a success to the extent that the speaker is able to elaborate his or her understanding of the stuttering and make choices that alter his or her relationship with stuttering. Will the person take the time to develop his or her ability to monitor and modify the quality of his or her fluency in increasingly challenging situations? Will the person be able to muster the energy necessary to cultivate the cognitive and affective changes necessary to reduce the influence of stuttering? Or will relapse—to a greater or lesser degree—dictate additional periods of formal intervention?

Van Riper (1973, pp. 178–199) provided a comprehensive overview of ways to consider progress during treatment. His fundamental point is that any view of progress should be comprehensive and consider multiple factors. That is, along with several overt or surface characteristics, more subtle, intrinsic features of the problem must be taken into account. Otherwise, success will be either overstated or unrecognized. As Sheehan (1980) pointed out, the more trivial the criteria for improvement, the greater the likelihood of success.

The changes in the surface behavior of the client often occur relatively early in the treatment process. The frequency and effort of stuttering might begin to lessen. Alternatively, cognitive changes are reflected in the quality of the client's self-management and patterns of decision making, aspects of change that generally take longer (Emerick, 1988; Manning, 1991a). Experienced clinicians have suggested what seems intuitively correct— that desired changes in the surface behaviors will be more likely to be permanent if changes in the cognitive features also occur (Emerick, 1988; Guitar, 1976; Guitar & Bass, 1978; Maxwell, 1982).

Some speakers are likely to begin making important changes prior to the initiation of formal treatment (Andrews & Harvey, 1981; Bordeau & Jeffrey, 1973; Gregory, 1972; Ingham et al., 1972; Ost et al., 1976; Peins et al., 1972; Webster, 1979). For example, Andrews and Harvey (1981) obtained data on 132 adults who were placed on a list awaiting treatment. A variety of measures were taken approximately 8 months prior to treatment and again immediately before treatment. The speakers showed significant decreases in the percentage of syllables stuttered (18.2%–14.4%) and a significant increase in the rate of speech in syllables per minute (91.5–129.8), changes that became evident after the first 3 months on the waiting list. However, no significant change was found in the speakers' attitude about speech communication as measured by the S-24 Scale (Andrews & Cutler, 1974). In addition, no significant changes were found in two of the three measures (perceived avoidance

CLINICAL INSIGHT: ALTERING THE RELATIONSHIP WITH STUTTERING

Some time ago, I was working with a young man who was a graduate student in a speech pathology program. He was doing a clinical placement in a school at a time when he had been experiencing a significant period of control over his stuttering. One day, he came to see me and was clearly distressed. He related an experience in an Individualized Education Program (IEP) meeting in which he failed to control his stuttering. He talked about how this lack of control was unexpected and surprised him. As we discussed this, I asked him what he thought this said about him and his progress. He responded that it seemed that he still had a long way to go and clearly needed to increase his practice, as he might have become a bit lazy with that aspect. Although not disagreeing with him, I asked him to think about the fact that his failure to control his stuttering "surprised" him. As we discussed this further, he came to the "epiphany" that he would never have been surprised by stuttering in the past—he always expected to stutter—and that him not expecting to stutter signaled a change in his relationship with stuttering. A number of years later, this client commented to me that this conversation had a profound impact on his journey toward managing his stuttering. (AD) and severity of stuttering) indicated by the Stutterers Self Rating of Reactions to Speaking Situations (Johnson et al., 1963). If, as suggested in Chapter 6, adults are apt to seek treatment when their problem is the greatest, this regression toward the mean is not surprising. Furthermore, the process of seeking professional help and asking for assistance indicates that an individual is in the preparation stage of change (see Chapter 7). Even though formal intervention has not yet taken place, the speaker has demonstrated some degree of assertiveness. In addition, being selected for a waiting list is likely to provide a measure of support.

Certainly, clinicians will interpret progress differently, depending on the overall treatment strategy and the associated techniques. An indicator of progress for a speaker taking part in a treatment program emphasizing fluency enhancement will not necessarily be thought of as progress for another client who is taking part in a program where stuttering modification is the major goal. Regardless of the therapeutic protocol, clinicians need to be looking for what might seem to be small victories that reflect increased resilience, self-esteem, self-efficacy, and agency. The seemingly small successes often open the door for greater changes in the future. Conture and Guitar (1993) suggested that treatment can be considered successful if a child begins to communicate easily whenever and to whomever he or she chooses. This also seems to be a reasonable approach to take with adults.

The Variability of Change

Just as speech fluency itself can be highly variable, change resulting from treatment is far from linear. As our comments in earlier chapters on the nature of the counseling and therapeutic processes suggest, although successful change is apt to be the result of good and timely treatment, we cannot force the process. The pace and direction of change are often dictated by the speaker. In addition, at different times and for different people, fluctuations in some features of stuttering are better indicators of change than others. For example, although treatment might focus on decreasing stuttering and avoidance behavior, it is often the case (particularly early in treatment) that decreased avoidance results in greater frequency of stuttering. Increased stuttering might be desirable as speakers become more assertive about communicating and entering into the more challenging speaking situations that they have avoided for years. The nature and rate of change are influenced not only by the primary focus of a particular treatment strategy but also by many other factors, including the treatment schedule, the quality of the therapeutic alliance, the person's increasingly agentic nature, and the support available from family, friends, and colleagues.

As we have described in earlier chapters, children, especially those of preschool age, typically enjoy good success rates as a result of treatment (again, partly because some of them would have spontaneously recovered). For adolescent and adult speakers, however, regardless of the treatment strategy, clinicians who have studied these populations seem to follow what could be called the "one-third rule." That is, regardless of the overall treatment strategy, and everything else being equal in terms of client motivation and intelligence, clinician experience, and the timing of intervention, approximately one third of clients will make good progress; one third, moderate progress; and one third

Shortly after arriving for the therapy session, the woman informed the clinician that earlier that day she did something she had never done before. With obvious pride she said, "I asked for a towel today." Of course, the confused clinician asked what she meant. She explained that, after years of getting out of the pool at the gym and meekly standing by the window waiting for one of the attendants to hand her a towel, she asked for one. "Of course I stuttered some but I asked for a towel!" This seemingly small victory opened the door for future significant changes. (WM)

(often because they prematurely drop out of treatment) little or no progress.

Of those speakers who make good progress, there are some who do extremely well and conclude formal treatment exhibiting little or no stuttering behavior. Some also demonstrate cognitive changes, suggesting a reinterpretation of their situation that results in a greatly improved quality of life. Should these speakers experience a break in their fluency, they are unlikely to panic. Rather than avoid as they have in the past, they are able to analyze what it is they are doing as they speak and vigorously employ fluency or stuttering-modification techniques. They are gradually more assertive and able to assess the circumstances and adjust to the situation in an ever-widening array of communication situations. Other individuals, although not showing such marked change, make good progress. As they move away from the security and support provided by the clinician and the clinic environment, the quantity and quality of their fluency might regress to a degree. Still, they are able to maintain many of their new coping responses and stutter with considerably less frequency and struggle. The fact that they are people who stutter incrementally plays a smaller role in their lives.

Then there is the perplexing final third of all clients, those who make little progress or fail to maintain the gains they achieve within the supportive therapy environment. Every clinician has seen these people. They range from people who stutter in extremely overt to extremely covert ways—although the latter are unlikely to seek our help to begin with. Our chance to interact with these people might be fleeting, and we might be able to have contact with them only during an initial diagnostic meeting or perhaps one or two treatment sessions. As we help them approach and begin to unpack their situation, they begin to realize the full nature of their stuttering and the importance of their role in the process of change. For some, motivation quickly fades, attendance becomes inconsistent, and eventually it ceases. When we suspect that we are with people who will respond in this manner, it would seem that we should attempt to do what we can for them while we have the chance. It could be our only opportunity to provide them with encouragement and hope by showing them a few techniques that will provide them with immediate, if temporary, fluency. We can provide them with sources of information about support groups and useful websites so that they might acquire greater understanding and some new insights, including the realization that they are not alone. As they learn more about support groups, they might realize that, when they are ready, good, professional help is available.

Nevertheless, often for reasons unknown to us, they eventually fail to show up for their sessions. It could be that they found our information and suggestions helpful and they feel that they have made enough progress for now. They might feel that the cost of additional change, at least at this point, is not worth the time and effort. Or maybe the timing and the quality of the therapeutic alliance were not satisfactory.

Several clinical investigations support the notion of the one-third rule. In a review of 13 clinicians and their associates, Martin (1981) determined that one third of the clients achieved and maintained satisfactory fluency, one third achieved fluency during therapy but regressed over time, and one third either failed to complete treatment programs or were unavailable for follow-up assessment. Martin stressed that a major problem preventing a complete interpretation of the data was the fact that many clients left treatment prior to completion of the therapy program. Prins (1970) found comparable results, noting that 67% of 94 male clients taking part in an intensive residential program completed questionnaires indicating "much or complete" improvement. Interestingly, 65% of the subjects indicated that little or no posttreatment regression had occurred in terms of morale. In addition, Prins noted that once they occurred, interpersonal changes were more durable than the level of fluency or decreased avoidance of words. Even speakers who are fortunate enough to take part in an intensive, comprehensive, and elaborately constructed treatment program with repeatedly documented success, such as the ISTAR Comprehensive Stuttering Program (Boberg & Kully, 1985), are not always able to maintain behavioral and cognitive changes following treatment. Langevin et al. (2006) found that as many as 28% of such individuals are unable to maintain clinically

meaningful speech gains, results that were comparable to earlier investigations of the ISTAR program (Boberg & Kully, 1994; Franken et al., 1997).

Chronic Stuttering

There is one other distinct category of clients that can be included in a discussion of therapeutic progress. These people would most likely fall into the second or third of the three groups discussed in the previous section. Cooper (1986a, 1987) proposed that there is a significant group of individuals for whom fluent speech is an unrealistic goal. Any clinician who has worked for several years in the area of fluency disorders will recognize their patterns of behavior. Cooper described this group as manifesting *chronic perseverative stuttering* (CPS). These speakers are adolescents or adults who have stuttered for several (at least 10) years. They typically respond to treatment with increased fluency, only to experience profound levels of relapse shortly after completing treatment. Their predominant self-perception and core constructs (Chapter 7) are those of a person who stutters. They demonstrate some degree of obsessive striving for completely fluent speech as well as a deep fear of fluency loss, even though such loss might occur infrequently.

Cooper (1986a, 1987) suggested that if clinicians are unwilling to recognize that fluent speech is not a realistic possibility for these people, they are likely to create and perpetuate unwarranted feelings of guilt on behalf of their clients. Based on the feedback he received from such individuals, Cooper found that an acknowledgment of this pattern of stuttering by clinicians results in a profound relief for clients who see themselves as chronic stutterers. Whether this view would predispose a client to failure is debatable. It could be that accepting the fact that some people who stutter will always have a chronic problem is simply being realistic. Still, it is important to point out that although these speakers might always have a degree of obvious stuttering present in their speech, they might be able to decrease their avoidance and alter their stuttering to the degree that they can communicate more effectively and improve the quality of their life. These speakers could also be ideal candidates for fluency-enhancing devices to supplement more traditional treatment.

VARIABLES INFLUENCING PROGRESS

It would be comforting to think that our understanding of the cause-and-effect relationships we attend to during treatment can be explained by our theoretical understanding about the nature of stuttering and the empirical and experiential evidence we accumulate. Whatever the level of understanding, it appears that clinicians most often choose strategies and techniques because they believe they work (Apel, 1999; Fey & Johnson, 1998; Kamhi, 1999). But just as individuals have widely varied reactions to identical levels of medications (not to mention the effects of drug interactions), people respond to behavioral intervention in diverse and unpredictable ways. The variables that influence such diverse responses are probably too numerable to mention, but we suggest some of the more obvious ones that are likely to influence therapeutic success for individuals who stutter.

Age of the Speaker

The major focus for much of this chapter has been on adolescents and young adults who stutter. Of course, there are similar indicators of progress among all people who stutter. However, there are at least three age groups that are distinct enough in their response to treatment that they should be considered further: young (particularly preschool) children, adolescents, and older speakers.

Young children often have good success during both direct and indirect intervention for fluency disorders (de Sonneville-Koedoot et al., 2015; Franken et al., 2005). They are relatively easy to work with, and the behavioral, attitudinal, and cognitive aspects of their stuttering tend to be responsive to intervention. Therapeutic progress with these speakers can be measured in the frequency of stuttering, increased rate of speech, lessening of speaking effort, and increased spontaneity and enjoyment of communication.

As described in Chapter 12, adolescents present an entirely different set of circumstances. Van Riper (1982) stated that adolescents are some of the clinician's most difficult cases. Motivation for change is relatively rare in adolescents. Daly et al. (1995) explained that it is often extremely difficult to get adolescents to even take part in treatment: "Many adolescents drop out of therapy, skip sessions, or attend begrudgingly. [They may] downplay the effects of their stuttering on their communication and social interactions. . . . Student rationalizations for poor attendance or for not practicing are common" (p. 163).

As Daly et al. (1995) described, adolescents are apt to be highly sensitive and find great difficulty confronting their problem. They strongly resist being singled out for anything that carries the potential of social stigma. To complicate matters even further, adolescents often challenge the clinician's qualifications, clinical experience, and overall expertise (Daly et al., 1995). Consequently, progress can be measured by the consistency of attendance for treatment sessions, the level of interaction with the clinician, interest shown in the topics and techniques, and even a minimal decrease in avoidance behavior. If the clinician is unable to achieve great change in the way of modification, he or she can begin to demystify the problem, explain some of the cause-and-effect relationships of the stuttering, and sow some seeds of knowledge and understanding that another clinician can someday harvest.

The third group of speakers consists of older stutterers who have been coping with their lack of fluency for decades. Clients over the age of 50 are rarely seen in treatment or included in research reports (Manning, Dailey, & Wallace, 1984; Manning & Monte, 1981; Manning & Shirkey, 1981; Yaruss, Quesal, Reeves, et al., 2002). This is unfortunate, because to fully understand a fluency disorder, it would appear to be essential to follow the development of stuttering throughout the life cycle. A review of the literature indicates that this subgroup of stuttering adults has received almost no investigation. According to the U.S. Census Bureau, as of 2016 there were 40.3 million adults over the age of 65 (13% of the population). Assuming a prevalence of stuttering of 0.7%, there are approximately 2.8 million people in the United States over the age of 65 who stutter.

Anecdotal reports have indicated that stuttering is less of a problem for older individuals. The few data available indicate some support for this argument. Manning, Dailey, and Wallace (1984) obtained attitude and personality information from 29 adults ages 52 to 82 years old who were members of two national self-help groups, the National Stuttering Project and the National Council of Stutterers. Scores on six self-assessment stuttering severity measures indicated that the scores of older stuttering individuals were similar

(slightly lower or higher) than the typical scores for young adults who were about to enter treatment. Scores on the Perceptions of Stuttering Inventory (PSI; Woolf, 1967) averaged 20.3 ($SD = 12$) for the older subjects, in contrast to pretreatment scores for young adults who stutter of 21.1 (Manning & Cooper, 1969) and 27.2 (Ornstein & Manning, 1985). Responses to the S-24 Scale (Andrews & Cutler, 1974; Erickson, 1969) for the older speakers averaged 16.0, in contrast to mean pretreatment scores for younger speakers of 19.4 (Howie, 1981), 20.0 (Guitar & Bass, 1978), and 15.6 (Ornstein & Manning, 1985). Scores on the Self-Efficacy Scale for Adult Stutterers (SESAS; Ornstein & Manning, 1985) averaged 70.5% for approach items and 60.5% on the performance items, in contrast to 66.2% and 55.8% for young adults who stutter (Ornstein & Manning, 1985). In addition, the older participants ranked the approach tasks significantly higher than the performance tasks, just as the younger subjects had done ($p < .05$; Ornstein & Manning, 1985). Finally, responses to a 25-item bipolar-adjective scale (Woods & Williams, 1976) designed to describe the personality characteristics of individuals who stutter indicated no significant differences between the 29 individuals who stuttered and the matched group of 13 nonstuttering individuals.

When asked to indicate whether the handicap associated with stuttering had lessened over the years, a large majority of the subjects agreed that this had been the case. Using a 7-point, equal-appearing interval scale to rank their perceived severity as young adults and at the present time, subjects scored their current severity as significantly less ($p < .005$). Furthermore, in response to open-ended queries concerning past and current perceived severity, subjects responded with statements such as these: "Stuttering is less of a problem now [since] there is not so much competition," "I accept myself more now than when I was younger," "I've become more insightful about personal problems as I grow older," and "Stuttering has less of an all-consuming hold on me than when I was younger." Because of the way the subjects were selected, this group of older individuals who stutter best represents those older individuals who are actively involved in self-help groups. Nevertheless, the results suggest that although the severity of stuttering in older speakers is similar to or slightly less than their younger counterparts, they consider themselves significantly less handicapped by the problem. The lessening of the perceived handicapping effect of stuttering on these participants could be the result of their participation in a support group for adults who stutter.

Katz et al. (2006) analyzed 10-minute speech samples of 12 men and 4 women over the age of 55 (mean age of 70.4 years) who had stuttered since childhood. Analysis of conversational speech, reading, and telephone conversations with a stranger indicated frequencies of stuttering similar to those of younger speakers. Subsequent studies by Bricker-Katz and her colleagues indicated somewhat less optimistic results for older adults who stutter. Bricker-Katz et al. (2009) found evidence that a lifetime of stuttering can result in continued limited communication and restricted participation in daily activities as indicated by OASES impact scores. In comparison to 14 fluent peers (3 women, 11 men; average age of 69.1), 12 adults who stuttered (3 women, 9 men; average age of 68.8) scored significantly higher ($p = .0029$) on the Fear of Negative Evaluation Scale (FNES), the social evaluative anxiety ($p = .02$) and physical danger ($p = .0008$) domains of the Ender Multidimensional Anxiety Scales-Trait (EMAS-T)

and the satisfaction with health domain of the Australian Personal Wellbeing Index (PWA-I). The authors did note that although the OASES impact scores indicated that the older adults who stuttered reacted to stuttering in the moderate to severe range, the OASES quality of life section indicated that they felt that stuttering impacted less negatively on their overall sense of well-being.

Bricker-Katz et al. (2010) also conducted a qualitative study with focus groups of 11 participants (8 men, 3 women, average age of 70; range = 57.2–83.8). Participant descriptions about their limitations due to stuttering were similar to those of younger adults who stutter. This was especially the case for participants who had continued to work. The participants also reported difficulty in living independently and maintaining their connections to a variety of health-related services. Some of the participants did indicate that they felt that stuttering had impacted them to a greater degree when they were younger and that their acceptance of stuttering helped them to lessen their limitations as they became less fearful of the consequences of their stuttering. Another theme expressed by the participants was their disappointment with their previous therapy experiences, especially with those clinicians who were uncertain and lacked understanding and expertise about stuttering. Others indicated they would consider additional therapy if it was "short-term and effective" (Bricker-Katz et al., 2010, p. 28).

Treatment Strategy and Intensity

If a fluency-enhancement approach (e.g., Onslow et al., 2003; O'Brian et al., 2003; Ryan & Van Kirk Ryan, 1995; Webster, 1975) is the primary therapeutic strategy, a reduction in the frequency of stuttering would, of course, be considered the indicator of progress. However, if stuttering modification is the primary focus of treatment, a decrease in stuttered moments (particularly early on in treatment) is not necessarily desirable and will, in fact, prevent speakers from having the opportunity to identify, become desensitized to, and modify their stuttering. Furthermore, if a decrease in avoidance behavior is also a primary goal of treatment (which it often is), increases in the frequency of stuttering are likely to occur as a result of increased assertiveness and participation in speaking opportunities.

Intensive treatment is often desirable for many behavioral problems. For many people, becoming totally immersed in the treatment process increases the possibility of desirable changes in the behaviors and attitudes that have persisted for many years (Gregory, 1983; Ingham, 1984; Shames & Florance, 1980; Webster, 1975, 1986). Azrin et al. (1979) and Webster (1975) advocated short-term, intensive approaches on the grounds that it takes a big push for speakers to alter their habitual responses of coping with stuttering and begin moving in a new direction. The support, energy, and challenges provided by intensive programs can provide such a push. The commitment of time, effort, and money required for such programs suggests a readiness for change that might not be the case for individuals taking part in a therapeutic experience 1 or 2 hours a week.

However, as described in Chapter 12, many people are unable to attend intensive programs. Intensive treatment often presents logistical problems. Some people are unable to leave their work for weeks at a time or cannot commute to and from the treatment site. Potential clients cannot always afford the cost of intensive treatment. Moreover, although intensive programs can result in rapid behavioral change, treatment is sometimes followed by dramatic relapses (Kuhr & Rustin, 1985; Prins, 1970). An intensive program, especially if it requires the person to live apart from his or her typical environment, could yield rapid behavioral and cognitive changes. However, the transition back to the daily world can be traumatic, especially if it is not well thought out and approached in a systematic manner. The old discriminative stimuli and expectations, on the part of the speaker as well as the listener, are powerful and usually still operating. Therefore, relapse is sometimes the case, even for those who practice diligently and attend follow-up or "booster" sessions. Perhaps the suggestion by Cooper (1979a) provides the ideal situation. He suggested a period of intensive treatment to modify the surface behaviors followed by less intensive maintenance sessions in the person's typical environment to allow for the necessary changes of the speaker's cognitive and affective features.

Related Problems

As we discussed in earlier chapters, clients come to us with a wide range of communication skills, sometimes involving language, learning, phonological, and cluttering problems. Some have difficulties with school performance, social interaction, general physical and emotional health, and in some instances, alcohol and various drugs. Anything that makes learning, formulating, and producing language and speech difficult is likely to make therapeutic change more challenging. As several authors have noted, when a fluency problem is complicated by other difficulties such as excessive anxiety, psychological or social issues, or articulation or language disabilities, individually tailored therapy becomes mandatory (Gregory, 1984; Riley & Riley, 1983, 1984, 2000; St. Louis, 1986; Van Riper, 1973). Children and adults who have some of the characteristics mentioned throughout this book (resilience, self-esteem, self-efficacy, and agency) along with support from parents and family members are more likely to experience therapeutic success.

Denial and Avoidance

There are, of course, extreme examples of avoidance and denial regarding stuttering. On the rare occasion when we are able to see these individuals in the clinic, they might refuse to consider that the problem they are facing is stuttering. Denial has served as a primary coping response, and any suggestion that it might be better to approach and discuss stuttering is likely to be met with resistance. The speaker could refer to what clearly seems to the clinician to be stuttering as a "communication prob-lem," "stammering," or as in the case of the young woman described in Chapter 2, a "social anxiety disorder." These people could need our help as much or more than any others we have the opportunity to see. Because their primary response is to run from the problem, getting such individuals to attend even a few therapy sessions requires an artful interaction on our part as well as support from others.

Most of the people who seek our help have begun to move beyond such extreme levels of denial and are able to tolerate some degree of discussion of the stuttering experience. Often we need to metaphorically take the person by the shoulders and slowly turn him or her around to face the problem, initially with more of a side glance and eventually facing full on. In some cases, we have to be extremely sensitive to the fear and stigma the person is attaching to the problem. As the individual is able to stay in the moment and experience some success at approaching and possibly modifying even a small aspect of the stuttering, the likelihood of additional change is increased. With modeling, support, and

---

CLINICAL INSIGHT: DENIAL OR JUST A DIFFERENT STORY?

I often tell my students, "Denial is a river in Egypt, not something that your clients do!" Recall in Chapter 8 we discussed the concept of personal narratives and the impact that these have on our behavior and emotional reactions. One way for clinicians to attempt to better understand individuals who appear to be in "denial" is to consider their story. What is the story that they are telling themselves and/or that others are telling about them that has led them to not recognize or accept that they are stuttering? How does that story benefit them or support them emotionally? Is it linked to other stories about them? By clinicians taking a "credulous approach" (see Chapter 8) and accepting the client's story as true (at least for the client in his or her present circumstances), clinicians can engage with the client and begin searching for clues to alternative stories that he or she is currently ignoring—stories that might include recognition of stuttering as a problem to be accepted and worked on. (AD)

some initial victories, the person might begin to believe that it is possible for him or her to achieve at least a tiny grasp on the wall that seems to be blocking progress. These can be the cathartic moments we have all experienced as we accomplish for the first time something we have never done before and did not believe was possible.

Increasing Approach Behavior

Patterns of denial and avoidance are natural coping responses to situations with high levels of stress that the individual feels powerless to change. Speakers come to us with various levels of this coping pattern, and virtually all adolescent and adult speakers manifest some of these responses to stuttering. Patterns of avoidance and escape are deeply embedded and involve more than the simple act of substituting one word for another or avoiding particular speaking situations. Accordingly, altering what have become reflexive avoidance responses and slowly developing and expanding forms of approach behavior takes considerable effort and persistence. This is often a major component of therapeutic change and the modeling of approach behaviors and support by the clinician (and perhaps other clients) as well as the speaker's family and friends play a critical role.

The Speaker's Ability to Self-Monitor

Another primary indicator of progress is the speakers' ability to accurately monitor what they are doing when they stutter. Even if the speaker is not yet able to modify the way he or she is producing speech, the speaker might be able to analyze what

he or she is doing to make it so difficult to move through the desired sequence of sounds and words during a moment of stuttering. This is often especially difficult for individuals with high levels of anxiety associated with their stuttering. Staying in the moment and accurately self-monitoring any behavior or thought process is a requisite step in taking responsibility and transforming the event. Martin and Haroldson (1982) demonstrated the value of self-monitoring in generalizing the reduction of stuttering. Ingham (1982) found self-evaluation training to be associated with substantially reduced stuttering for up to 6 months posttreatment.

One place to begin monitoring is to identify listener responses to stuttering. The process of identifying and distancing from the stress and fear of listener responses can have an empowering effect on the speaker and begin to facilitate a conceptual shift concerning the communication process. What are the subtle and more obvious responses of individual listeners as they observe stuttering? By scrutinizing individuals before approaching them, it is sometimes possible to predict (or even create) particular responses from them in terms of body language and verbal reactions. Role-playing can be a particularly helpful desensitizing activity as both client and clinician take turns portraying typical listener responses observed in daily speaking situations. Progress is seen in the ability of the speaker to identify progressively more subtle aspects of their stuttering. The process of discovering the various behaviors and emotional reactions can be interesting and exciting, and it also sets the stage for subsequent changes. Eventually, the client will be able to monitor his or her own speech production via both auditory and, more important, proprioceptive feedback. Auditory feedback

Van Riper (1978) reported that his stuttering increased in frequency (although not, he felt, in severity) after an initial heart attack at age 65. He described "little sluggish prolongations" that mostly disappeared after his recovery. Following his retirement, he again noticed an increase in the frequency and, occasionally, the severity of his stuttering. He found that he was experiencing more frequent and longer tremors as well as some laryngeal blocks. Because these fluency breaks were surprising, he thought that these changes were probably due to his lack of monitoring of his speech. He speculated that the hard work of closely monitoring his speech and "stuttering fluently" was no longer worth the effort.

provides an indication of the nature and quality of fluent speech, but proprioceptive feedback provides a more immediate and direct indication of the status of the vocal tract and ease of movement. Auditory feedback allows little or no opportunity to alter the motoric aspects of speech production. Proprioceptive feedback, alternatively, provides an instantaneous way to monitor the quality of fluency and the extent to which speech is being produced in an open, flowing, and effortless manner. Self-monitoring will continue to be a critical element of long-term success.

The Self-Discipline of Practice

As suggested in Chapter 12, an important characteristic of effective clinicians is the ability to motivate their client to practice between therapy sessions. The achievement of any moderately complex behavior requires repetition and persistence in order to obtain a degree of mastery. This is especially the case when stressful elements such as time pressure and social stigma are involved. Most individuals understand that some practice is necessary, but few fully appreciate the extent that is required for consistent and depend-able performance in the many communication situations where fluency failure has been both the expectation and often the reality. For the adolescent, and particularly for the adult who has been stuttering for many years, practice must take place for many months and years before the techniques will begin to become functional and an integrated part of the speaker's ability to manage his or her stuttering. Of course, it is one thing to practice and develop confidence in using new responses to stuttering within the clinical environment and quite another to make the transition to the variety of everyday speaking situations in which the support provided by that environment is absent.

As the speaker progresses from the security of the treatment setting to beyond-treatment environments, successful management will help to prevent plateaus or regression. The self-motivated requirement of continued practice could be the hardest lesson that many speakers have to learn. Each individual has a choice to make about the price he or she wants to pay for enhanced fluency and communicative facility. The good news is that highly successful management of stuttering is possible, and that, over time, the work becomes easier.

CLINICAL INSIGHT

One of our teenage clients who was beginning to realize how much he was going to have to practice his treatment techniques brought this story back from a skiing trip to Colorado. He had been watching people learning to negotiate a hill with a series of moguls and wondered out loud to a nearby instructor how long it would take to master such a difficult section. After considering the question for a moment, the instructor responded by saying, "Well, if you practiced every day for about 6 hours and you did that for about 6 months you would be pretty good. But you still wouldn't master it." Only after hearing that description did the young man fully appreciate how much he was going to have to practice so that he would become "pretty good" at using his therapy techniques during more difficult speaking situations.

A series of investigations by Brundage and her colleagues in the use of virtual reality environments (VREs) provides a unique way to help speakers to make this transition. The control and options provided by this technology help individuals to reduce their anxiety as they transition to gradually more difficult situations beyond the clinical environment (Brundage, 2007). The technology creates a realistic, three-dimensional immersion in an environment that has been found to be comparable to live experiences in terms of the physiologic, cognitive, emotional, and behavioral responses (Brundage, 2007; Brundage & Graap, 2004; Brundage, Hancock, et al., 2006) including the amount of stuttering and communication apprehension (Brundage, Graap, et al., 2006).

The system makes use of a head-mounted display, combined with headphones for auditory input, as well as a tracking system that provides for changing views that correspond to the speaker's head movements. It is possible to develop a variety of virtual situations that occur in the person's everyday experiences at school, work, or social activities. Importantly, these situations can be controlled for extraneous distractions that tend to occur in real-world situations, allowing the speaker to focus on events and stimuli that have particular meaning for them. Experiences can be organized in a hierarchical manner and repeated as often as necessary in order for the individual to achieve desensitization and to explore a variety of responses to the situation. For example, an individual can enter a virtual classroom to find one of several different groups of people in the audience. Along with the size of the audience, the response of the individuals in the room can be altered according to such factors as the attentiveness of the listeners, their response to the speaker, background noise, and time pressure. As Brundage and colleagues described (Brundage, 2007; Brundage & Graap, 2004; Brundage, Graap, et al., 2006), the virtual environment provides a realistic experience for practice and exploration but without the risks inherent in live performances. Speakers have the opportunity to develop a sense of empowerment in speaking experiences that they would otherwise avoid.

More recently, studies by Brundage and Hancock (2015) and Brundage et al.

CLINICAL INSIGHT

Another example about the degree of practice and overlearning that must occur in order to master difficult and complex activities was related to me (WM) by friend and colleague, David Daly. He described how every spring he and his friends charter a sailboat and spend a week on the Chesapeake Bay. One year one of the friends wasn't able to attend and another person took his place. The new fellow happened to be a professional oboe player. Each morning he would come up on deck and practice his oboe. His playing was enjoyable for everyone but eventually one of the crew members asked him why he continued to practice even though he was on a vacation. He responded by saying, "If I didn't practice for one day, I would know it. If I didn't practice for two days, the oboe section would know it. And if I didn't practice for three days, the entire orchestra would know it."

(2016) found that that VRE experiences that represent daily activities provide a valid indication of speaker affective, cognitive, and behavioral experience and can provide an indication of subjective (rather than objective) measures of distress and arousal.

Another method for maintaining or recovering successful treatment outcomes is the use of video self-modeling (VSM). Following successful therapy, videos of the upper body are made as the speaker successfully uses behavioral fluency-enhancing or stuttering-modification techniques in a variety of communication situations. In order to maintain their fluency-enhancing ability and reinforce their belief in their ability to alter their speech, the speakers are asked to view the videos and self-model their earlier performance one or more times a week. The activity reinforces the speaker's ability to effectively employ the techniques (e.g., Cream et al. 2010; Cream et al., 2009; Harasym et al., 2015). Although the results of the studies indicate considerable variability across participants in using this method, particularly for decreasing

the frequency of stuttering, participants self-report increased motivation, fewer avoidance behaviors, greater satisfaction with their fluency, improved self-efficacy, and improved quality of life. As Cream et al. (2010) pointed out, this procedure requires minimal clinician and speaker time and could assist the speaker in integrating these desirable changes into his or her self-concept.

Available Support

The appraisal by speakers of their situation involves self-assessment of their competence and available resources for problem solving (Plexico et al., 2009a, 2009b). The availability of resources such as money, individual skills, physical health, energy, and a general sense of optimism are likely to be important components of a successful problem-solving approach. Social resources include the availability of social networks for providing informational and emotional support (Compas et al., 1992). Of course, regardless of the speaker's age, the consistent involvement of family and friends can provide invaluable support for promoting and providing a historical context for successful change.

In some instances, the clinician might be unable to alter these and other factors that influence the chance of success for an individual speaker. However, if the time is right and the client is ready, significant progress can take place. Moreover, when important changes occur, it is critical for the clinician to recognize the presence and nature of the breakthroughs. He or she must recognize the victories when they occur, even though they might be small ones. If the clinician is unable to identify success—the sometimes small victories that nevertheless signal progress in the desired direction—it will go unrecognized and unrewarded. The following section describes the nature of such victories by describing several indicators of progress.

INDICATORS OF PROGRESS

Clues From the Speaker: Listening to the Client

It is helpful to keep in mind that even the most comprehensive assessment measures do not always provide a clear picture of the extent and nature of therapeutic change. Although these measures provide ways of estimating change and progress, there is also the possibility of obtaining information directly from the source, the person we are assisting. Listening closely to our clients when they respond to a simple question such as, "How are you doing?" can yield a wealth of information.

Speakers provide both verbal and nonverbal clues as they describe themselves and their circumstances, clues that reflect their condition and whether or not progress is taking place. Clinicians might find it useful to consider the client's self-talk, journal entries, and email communications for indicators of change. The language people use to describe their situation provides important clues about who they are and where they are going. The way a person depicts his or her situation or problem often indicates important signs of progress during treatment. Moreover, as described in our earlier discussions of cognitive restructuring approaches to counseling and treatment, by changing the way we describe a problem, we can often change the problem itself (Curlee, 1984; Fransella, 1972; Hayhow & Levy, 1989; Johnson, 1946; Kuhr & Rustin, 1985; Williams, 1979; R. Williams, 1995).

Early on in treatment the client typically feels helpless and his or her language could reflect his or her level of "stuckness." The client might well believe that he or she is unable to do much to change his or her speech or himself or herself. There is often a high degree of mystery associated with stuttering. The client might say such things as, "When it happens I feel helpless," "When I'm in a block I feel lost and I don't know what to do," or "That is a word that I can't say." As treatment progresses, the speaker slowly begins to develop the "language of fluency" (Blodgett & Cooper, 1988; Cooper & Cooper, 1985b), as well as use more appropriate self-talk (Daly, 1986; Emerick, 1988; Maxwell, 1982). As speakers begin to successfully change their previously uncontrollable behavior, they will begin to change the way they interpret themselves and their ability to produce fluent speech. Moreover, they will begin to describe their behavior and actions in more objective, specific, and realistic ways. They will begin to interpret stuttering as something that they are doing rather than something that is happening to them. They will begin to say such things as, "When I stutter, sometimes I hold my breath or stop the airflow at the

CLINICAL INSIGHT

One of the events that motivated the writing of the first edition of this text was a presentation I attended at the annual meeting of the American Speech-Language-Hearing Association. The six presenters were experienced researchers and clinicians in the area of fluency disorders. The panel members were charged with discussing criteria for determining successful treatment. After listening for most of the 1.5-hour session, I found myself becoming progressively frustrated. I suspected that, with the possible exception of one presenter, the speakers had managed to alienate a large portion of the approximately 100 clinicians in attendance about the experience of assisting those with fluency disorders. The speakers managed to describe their frustration with the inconsistency of the research data concerning the efficacy of different treatment strategies. The emphasis was group data: the lack of data, inaccurate data, and conflicting data. There was no recognition of the many important indicators of success that take place during treatment—including those that are seemingly small at the time. There was no enthusiasm concerning the exciting process of therapeutic change. It was a fine example of being unable to see the people for the data.

Near the end of the session there was a glimmer of hope. One of the panel members (Dr. Eugene Cooper) who was also clearly frustrated with the discussion made the suggestion that perhaps the most useful data are sitting right in front of us during treatment. "If you want data," he suggested, "try asking the client. That person might have some good information for you about what is helpful and what is not. He might be able to inform you about whether the therapy is successful or not." (WM)

vocal folds," "I was able to change the way I repeated that syllable into a smoother and easier way of stuttering," and "Even though that was a difficult telephone call, I was able to make it and successfully achieve most of my fluency targets." They are also changing their core constructs as discussed in Chapters 7 and 15.

On occasion, the clinician can take an active role and point out to clients how they are describing themselves and their problem. They might begin talking about their problem in a different way and, in turn, facilitate new and better ways of thinking about themselves and their speech (Daly, 1986; Emerick, 1988; Maxwell, 1982). As a result of a successful therapy experience, speakers' language will begin to reflect some degree of lib-

eration from their problem. One adult female client related how she gathered the courage to enter a feared daily speaking situation she had always avoided. As she later related to her clinician, "You know, I believe that I stuttered as much as I always have in that situation, but this time when I walked away I didn't feel ashamed."

CONSTRUCTS THAT INDICATE A PERSON'S ABILITY TO PROMOTE CHANGE

Underlying successful change for many human conditions is a reconceptualization of both the nature of the problem and one's ability to cope with the problem (Plexico et al., 2009a, 2009b). There are many constructs that have been suggested for explaining how humans self-perceive their capabilities and develop a more agentic lifestyle. The following constructs have been considered as meaningful measures of cognitive change.

Self-Efficacy

Self-efficacy is a one-dimensional construct that refers to one's sense of competence regarding environmental demands and life stressors. It was originally developed by Albert Bandura, who developed a self-scaling technique that indicates one's capability level and the strength of that belief (Bandura, 1977; Bandura et al., 1977). Bandura (1977) distinguished between confidence (a general belief in one's ability) and self-efficacy, which is more focused on one's certainty to produce particular levels of attainment. Several studies have demonstrated strong associations between greater self-efficacy scores and subsequent performance in assertive behavior (Kazdin, 1980). Those with higher levels of self-efficacy are more likely to take a broader view of a task and actively persist in order to complete a task.

The Self-Efficacy Scale (SESAS)

Blood (1995a) noted a clear improvement in SESAS scores during and following a successful cognitive-behavioral treatment program for three high school clients. Treatment consisted of 25 hours of intensive work on changing speech (a modified version of the Shames & Florance [1980] fluency-shaping program), 50 hours of relapse prevention, and two follow-up phases (6 and 12 months posttreatment). All three clients showed gradual improvements in overall (Approach plus Performance) scores, which averaged 56.3% (baseline), 77.6% (posttreatment), 87.3% (postrelapse management), 89.7% (6-month follow-up), and 86.7% (12-month follow-up).

Hillis (1993) pointed out that the pragmatic nature of the SESAS Approach scale can be interpreted as an indication of the scale's content validity. In addition, the construct validity of the SESAS Approach scale is supported by a 28-point difference found on the 100-point SESAS Approach between 20 subjects who stuttered and the 20 who did not. The construct validity of the SESAS Performance scale is supported by a 42-point difference between means on the 100-point scale between the 20 subjects who stuttered and the 20 who did not.

In order to decrease the uncontrolled variance resulting from the different levels of fluency selected by clients, Hillis (1993) modified the instructions for the Performance section of the SESAS. Rather than using the original (Ornstein & Manning, 1985) instructions that had the client determine a "level of fluency" based on his or her stage of treatment when scoring this section, Hillis (1993) asked the client to define fluent speech as "speech [that] would be so fluent in a given situation that, in the client's opinion, a listener would not recognize that the client had a history of stuttering" (p. 28).

Hillis (1993) also provided data on a variety of measures, including the SESAS for an adult male stuttering client (Figure 14–1). Despite two relapses during which the client's pauses per minute and stuttered syllables per minute increased (to less than pretreatment levels), there was continued progress in that the client was judged by himself, the clinician, and an independent observer to be speaking in a natural and fluent manner. Because

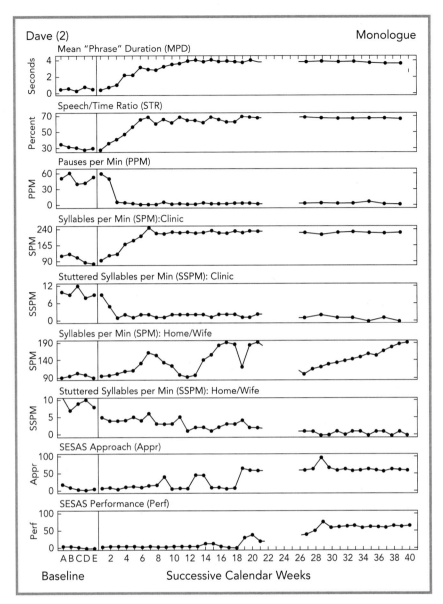

FIGURE 14–1. Baseline and treatment effects for an adult man on nine measurement parameters across a baseline period and 45 calendar weeks of treatment. *Note:* APPR = SESAS Approach; MPD = mean phrase duration in seconds; PERF = SESAS Performance; PPM = pauses per minute; SPM = syllables per minute; SSPM = stuttered syllables per minute; STR = speech-time ratio. *Source:* Used with permission of the American Speech-Language-Hearing Association, from Hillis, J.W. (1993). Ongoing assessment in the management of stuttering: A clinical perspective. *American Journal of Speech-Language Pathology, 2*(1), 24–37; permission conveyed through Copyright Clearance Center, Inc.

this was not the case in speaking situations outside the clinic, this fluency was termed "clinical fluency." At the end of treatment, the client was maintaining a high level of fluency, both in the treatment environment and in selected beyond-treatment situations. Nevertheless, Hillis pointed out that the SESAS Approach score remained less than 70 and SESAS Performance score less than 80 at the end of treatment—lower than the scores of typically fluent speakers of 94 and 96, respectively. Hillis noted that even successfully treated clients rarely score much above 80 on the modified SESAS Performance scale. This is still within the range of normal speakers reported by Ornstein and Manning (1985) of 74 to 100, but well less than one standard deviation (8) of 86.2. Thus, it is likely that clients can demonstrate high levels of fluent behavior but nevertheless be lagging behind in terms of cognitive change (SESAS Approach) and speech performance in extra-treatment performance (SESAS Performance).

Locus of Control

Locus of control refers to the extent that individuals believe they can control their environment and events that affect them. Rather than being associated with specific situations or abilities as with self-efficacy, locus of control relates to general, cross-situational beliefs about internal versus external control (Lefcourt, 1976; Rotter, 1954, 1966). Rotter viewed locus of control as a single construct with internality and externality representing two ends of a continuum (Rotter, 1966). Individuals with an internal locus of control believe the outcomes of their actions are the result of their own abilities and have lower scores indicating greater internality. Individuals who attribute the outcome of events to external circumstances or chance score higher, indicating greater externality.

Locus of Causality

Locus of causality is a two-dimensional construct developed by DeCharms (1968, 1971). DeCharms viewed human behaviors as being motivated by an individual's basic nature and temperament rather than responses to external stimuli. He also took into account that behaviors are influenced by an individual's social environment. That is, a person could choose to behave in a certain manner because the person "wants to" or "has to" depending on the circumstances. DeCharms termed these choices "origins" or "pawns," respectively. DeCharms (1971) indicated that origin and pawn and locus of control can be viewed as different constructs with different underlying theoretical perspectives. Groat and Allen (2011) described it as exercising autonomy or agency and taking responsibility. Monk et al. (1997) described agency as "the ability to live life and achieve a voice in a literal as well as a metaphorical sense; or you could think of it has having a lifestyle where the person can act for themselves and speak on their own behalf" (p. 301).

Resilience

Resilience facilitates a person's ability to respond to physical and mental adversity. Individuals who possess greater resilience are likely to have a positive attitude, optimism, and the ability to regulate their emotions. Resilience has also been described as the ability to become successful following failure or a hardship. Those with resilience tend to respond to stress in adaptive ways that can promote growth. Individuals who have experienced a stable, supportive relationship with a parent, caregiver, or mentor are more likely to be resilient. Resilience is also promoted by exercise, stress-reduction practices, and activities that promote self-regulation skills.

Self-Concept and Self-Esteem

Self-concept and self-esteem have been described as the cornerstone of psychological change (Peck, 1978). As the behavioral and cognitive changes evolve as a function of the support and encouragement provided by the therapy experience, the speaker is likely to undergo changes to his or her core structure as described in Chapter 7. Self-concept and self-esteem have been referred to many times in the literature on fluency disorders. Although persons who stutter have not been found to have a unique self-concept or to be lacking in self-esteem, this concept has frequently been mentioned as an important aspect of treatment programs (Van Riper, 1973, pp. 364–367).

Self-esteem is not something that can be given to you. Nonetheless, the stage can be set by supportive parents and friends as well as the clinician. The clinician is capable of providing a secure and stable therapeutic environment where growth and change will be likely to occur. As the speaker experiences the successful management of the behavioral and cognitive features of stuttering, self-esteem and self-concept are likely to begin shifting in a more favorable direction. This is certainly the case with preschool and early school-age children and a major reason why intervention for stuttering is much more likely to result in long-term success with these young speakers than with older individuals (Bothe, Davidow, Bramlett, & Ingham, 2006). The drawings by Brad,

age 10, provide a clear description of how he interprets his stuttering (Figure 14–2) and the treatment process (Figure 14–3). Carol, age 6, is able to indicate her feelings about herself before and after 3 months of

FIGURE 14–2. Brad's picture of the "stuttering monster."

FIGURE 14–3. Brad's picture of treatment for stuttering.

FIGURE 14–4. Carol's self-drawing before and after 3 months of treatment.

successful therapy, including how to deal with teasing (Figure 14–4).

Importantly, adults are able to redefine themselves and create an altered paradigm of their lives. In his book *Social Intelligence*, Goleman (2006) described how the brain is capable of reorganizing itself in response to new experiences. Although stem cells produce new neurons at a much higher rate for children, the process continues, even in older adults. Given the number of connections in a limited space, those that are unused or unneeded are pruned, and new

ones are formed and integrated through constant use ("cells that fire together wire together"). Therapeutic procedures have long made use of what neuroscientists are now beginning to understand: Memory retrieval allows for the reconstruction of past events through a process of "reconsolidation" at the cellular level. The retrieved memory will be "slightly altered chemically by a new protein synthesis that will help store it anew after being updated" (Goleman, 2006, p. 78). This allows, for example, a reduction of the fear associated with a recalled event according to how it is reprogrammed in the neurons and associated neural connections. Such changes can be quantified by self-reports during individual and group treatment sessions as well as by measures such as the locus of control (Kuhr & Rustin, 1985). The information described in Chapter 3 concerning the plasticity of the human brain provides direct support for the many cognitive and behavioral changes observed by clinicians.

Figures 14–5, 14–6, and 14–7 indicate the changes for an adult woman

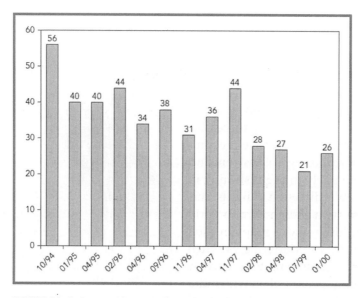

FIGURE 14–5. Locus of Control of Behavior (LCB) scores for an adult female with severe stuttering over 6 years of treatment.

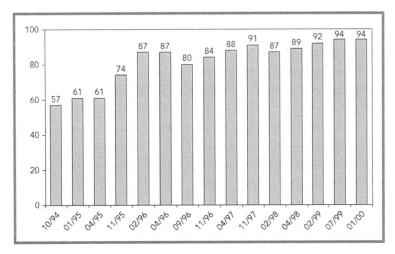

FIGURE 14-6. Approach scores for the Self-Efficacy Scale for Adult Stutterers for an adult female with severe stuttering over 6 years of treatment.

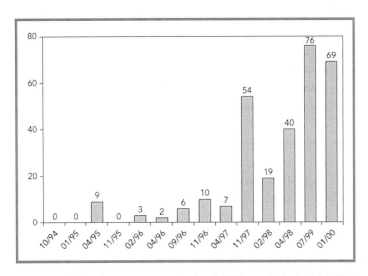

FIGURE 14-7. Performance scores for the Self-Efficacy Scale for Adult Stutterers for an adult female with severe stuttering over 6 years of treatment.

(SSI score of very severe) over a period of 6 years for the 17-item Locus of Control of Behavior Scale (Figure 14–5), and Approach (Figure 14–6) and Performance (Figure 14–7) portions of the SESAS. This person was seen once a week for both individual and group therapy. Figure 14–5 indicates extremely high LCB scores at the outset of treatment (the highest we have ever recorded) with scores progressively decreasing (indicating greater internality). With absences from treatment, scores would often increase in the direction of greater externality. After some 2 years of treatment, scores began to reach the range expected for fluent speakers.

Figure 14–6 indicates gradually increasing SESAS Approach scores, and Figure 14–7 shows SESAS Performance scores lagging behind, as noted by Hillis (1993).

It took some 5 years for this speaker with very severe stuttering to begin to achieve a level of fluency where she believed listeners would not be aware that she had a history of stuttering. Near the end of the fifth year of treatment, periods of spontaneous and natural fluency began to be observed.

Agency

Coinciding with the speaker's ability to approach rather than avoid the stuttering experience is the increasing ability to make choices about communicating that are based on information beyond the possibility of stuttering. As explained in Chapter 12, a person living an agentic lifestyle is able to act and speak on his or her own behalf (Monk et al., 1997), and the ability to live an autonomous and healthy life has more to do with the person's capacity for agency than the absence of the problem (Drewery et al., 2000).

With increasing agency the speaker will also be likely to alter other related interpersonal characteristics. Greater levels of speech assertiveness are likely to translate into increased assertiveness in general. For example, a distinct indicator of progress takes place when the speaker begins to decrease reflexive self-censorship and starts to consider entering into speaking situations once seen as daunting or even unimaginable. This is not to say that the person will now take part in these situations with ease or idyllic fluency. However, the choice to take part, in and of itself, is a significant measure of progress. Each time speakers extend themselves into communication situations that involve factors such as competition, time pressure, and responsibility, they are expanding their world. It is worth considering that many of these experiences are not only challenging but can also be exciting.

CLINICAL INSIGHT

Even in the absence of formal therapy, change can be noted in the transcripts of conversations or written documents by the speaker. Making use of the Origin and Pawn scales described in Chapter 12, we (Manning et al., 2005) analyzed correspondence from a young man over a 5-year period. Mickey first wrote to me in the fall of 2002. At the time, he was a 21-year-old college student living in Sarajevo, the capital of Bosnia-Herzegovina. He had come across something on the Stuttering Home Page that I had written a few years earlier for one of the International Stuttering Awareness Day (ISAD) conferences. My comments resonated with him, and he contacted me with some general questions about stuttering. Mickey's Internet searches had identified several sources of information, some good, some not so useful. Although I commented on some of the sites and the information he had discovered, my primary role in our subsequent correspondence was that of providing understanding, support, and feedback. I also offered encouragement and acknowledgment of his successes. We spent some time discussing possibilities for problem-solving issues that were unique to his situation. We were not conducting treatment in any formal sense in this long-distance relationship. Mickey viewed our exchanges that took place every 2 or 3 months as self-therapy.

As Mickey and I continued our correspondence, it became clear that he was making important, often dramatic, changes in how he viewed himself and his ability to communicate. We began analyzing his email letters using the Origin and Pawn scales. Although the majority of Mickey's communications had to do with his experience with stuttering, the entire contents of the letters were included in the scoring process. For that reason, our analysis of his narratives also included topics such as politics, travel, weather, and family and social interactions. We analyzed a total of 22 letters from Mickey, which he sent from the fall of 2002 through the spring of 2007. Two judges independently identified Origin and Pawn statements and then compared their decisions. Item-for-item judgments matched an average of 85% of the time.

Examples from Mickey's letters during the first 4 years provide a sense of his progress, and this analysis helped to document the nature and extent of these changes. Two brief passages provide vivid examples of how Mickey was reinterpreting himself and his situation.

Examples of Pawn Statements (P) October 2003 . . . but sometimes it looks like progress is coming too slow and that demoralize me totally from time to time. (P) I am 22 years old now, and I don't know how much time I have left for overcoming stuttering in order to achieve normal life. (P) I feel like I'm spending best years of my life in the "mud," (P) not using all the available opportunities out there. (P) Despite the fact that I understand stuttering better now, some emerging fears are making progress difficult: (P) If I don't succeed in time I don't know how my life is gonna turn out. (P)

Examples of Origin Statements (O): December 2004. But I am trying to enter them (stuttering blocks) without avoiding and using tricks. (O) But I am gaining more and more self-confidence, (O) and I think it is the most important thing in all this. Also I feel much more freedom (O) as I am accepting my stuttering (O) and decreasing emotional attachment and sensibility to it. I am now in position to feel and to see the full potential of the struggle free life (O) that I can achieve (O) if I put enough effort in this process of change. (O) Generally speaking I am now focusing more on reducing fear and emotional tension, (O) on improving the quality of my life, (O) than on techniques for improving fluency. I think it will be much easier to use those techniques (O) when I substantially improve my self-confidence and psychological health or life quality in general. I already achieved that in some extent (O) through facing feared situations, voluntary stuttering and changing negative attitudes, (O) but there is still a lot to be done in the coming weeks, months and years. (O) Also I am trying to increase physical activities (O) and to engage in some sport, (O) because I noticed such activities are contributing significantly to increasing my self-confidence. (O)

The results of the Origin and Pawns analysis (Figure 14–8) during the first four years (2002–2005) of our correspondence indicate a clear reduction in pawn statements and a corresponding increase in origin statements. There was a significant interaction of the

continues

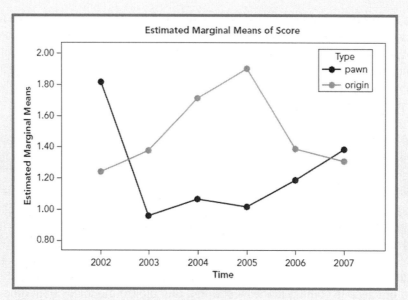

FIGURE 14–8. Pawns and Origins scores for Mickey over a 6-year period.

sets of scores, with Pawn scores showing a significant decrease in 2003 and Origin scores significantly increasing through 2005. However, during the last 18 months, in 2006 and 2007, although not returning to the clear dominance of Pawn over Origin scores found in 2002, there was no significant difference between the two sets of scores. The Pawn and Origin scores during the final 2 years suggest a degree of relapse or possibly regression to the mean. According to Mickey, these values could also reflect his general dissatisfaction and frustration with other personal, social, and economic aspects of his circumstances at the time. The most recent letter we received from Mickey was in 2012. The letter contained some 19 clauses identified as Origin and zero identified as a Pawn. (WM)

ADDITIONAL INDICATORS OF DESIRABLE CHANGE

Changing Attitudes About Communication: The S-24

Guitar and Bass (1978) studied 20 adults who underwent a 3-week intensive fluency-shaping program. The study has been frequently cited for two reasons: (a) it provided support for the idea that the failure to change communication attitudes (as measured by the S-24) might be predictive of relapse within 12 to 18 months, and (b) it questioned the desirability of an entirely operant view of therapy (a popular approach at the time). Young (1981) used a combination of regression analysis and causal modeling to reconsider the results of the Guitar and Bass study. He found that pretreatment S-24 scores were unrelated to either pre- or posttreatment %SS or to posttreatment S-24 scores. Although the causal modeling technique did indicate that posttreatment S-24 scores were moderately predictive of posttreatment %SS, Young questioned how much communication attitudes might change during a 3-week treatment program that was not intended to focus on attitude change. He concluded that to the degree that the S-24 is capable of measuring such attitudes, the results of Guitar and Bass did support the notion that treatment programs (including behavior modification) should consider such aspects of change. Finally, the results of a study by Andrews and Craig (1988) also found a relationship between attitude change as indicated by the S-24 and long-term success.

The Frequency of Stuttering

Just as the frequency of stuttering is the dependent variable, sometimes the only one, in research concerning treatment, many clinicians look to the frequency of stuttering as a primary measure of change or progress—and to some degree this makes sense. For example, for young children who stutter and older clients who clutter or exhibit a combination of stuttering and cluttering characteristics, the frequency of the fluency breaks could provide a reasonably straightforward indication of progress. In most instances, these are speakers who are less adept or interested in concealing their stuttering. Younger children, especially those who are in the early stages of child-onset stuttering, usually have not yet developed sophisticated methods of hiding or avoiding their stuttering. The percentage of stuttered moments could also provide a relatively unencumbered picture of the situation for speakers with a psychogenic or neurogenic etiology. Moreover, there is also some indication that the surface behavior in the form of stuttering frequency might more clearly reflect progress for the developmentally delayed individual who stutters. Despite the fact that developmentally delayed individuals who stutter typically demonstrate high levels of stuttering frequency (Cooper, 1986b), these speakers often appear generally unconcerned about their fluency (Bonfanti & Culatta, 1977; Cabanas, 1954). These speakers also tend to use fewer avoidance and postponement behaviors and indicate less anxiety associated with stuttering. However, for the more common case of child-onset stuttering, the frequency of stuttering is only one of many features of the problem, and by itself typically fails to provide an accurate picture of the speaker's status.

A decrease in the frequency of stuttering obviously indicates change, and such change could indicate progress. Many others, however, argue that the intrinsic aspects of the problem, the attitude and cognitive features, are at least as important (and possibly more so) for determining long-term progress (e.g., Cooper & Cooper, 1985b; Rubin, 1986; Sheehan, 1970; Starkweather, 1999; Van Riper, 1973). In addition, studies on the quality of fluent speech (also referred to as speech naturalness) following both stuttering modification as well as fluency-modification strategies, indicate that the absence of stuttering, in and of itself, is not necessarily an indicator of successful treatment (Onslow & Ingham, 1987). Fortunately, the tendency of considering the frequency of stuttering as the sole indicator of success has decreased in recent years, in part because of increased appreciation of the importance of the cognitive features of the stuttering experience and the development of procedures for obtaining this information.

The Relationship of Formulative and Motoric Fluency Breaks

Nearly all clinicians would agree that progress during treatment is reflected by decreases in the occurrence of motoric fluency breaks. However, as Goldman-Eisler (1961) and Starkweather (1987) have indicated, fluency breaks are an important aspect of normal speech formulation. Preliminary findings by Manning and Monte (1981) suggest that adults who stutter, although they obviously produce more motoric fluency breaks than nonstutterers, also demonstrate significantly fewer formulative fluency breaks. If speech is to be normalized for people who stutter, one important aspect of that process, aside from a decrease in motoric breaks, could well be an increase to near-normal levels of formulative fluency breaks (Manning & Monte, 1981).

As the speaker produces fewer motoric fluency breaks as a result of treatment, there are fewer opportunities to formulate the content of the message. As with typically fluent individuals, the speaker could choose to include some fluency breaks (typically pauses or interjections) in order to consider alternative ways of formulating a message. Some speakers who stutter will be unwilling to voluntarily stop and use a formulative fluency break for fear of being unable to initiate speech again. Accordingly, with successful treatment the speaker might be less concerned about the ability to continue once the formulative break has provided the opportunity to organize his or her thoughts. Yairi (1993) found that children who recovered from stuttering continued to produce (or even increased their production of) other types of fluency breaks (revisions, interjections, phrase repetitions, and other between-word or formulative fluency breaks).

During the later stages of treatment it might be helpful for some speakers to engage in spontaneous monologues in order to practice sequencing and branching their thoughts. The process provides an opportunity for the person to speak "without putting on the brakes" and to free-associate out loud. Progress is seen as individuals are able to gradually free themselves from the practice of scanning ahead for feared words and "pretasting" feared sounds. Following a lifetime of speaking in a careful, cautious, or inhibited manner, some individuals are able to achieve remarkable levels of fluency and communicative competence.

The Naturalness of Speech

The impetus for studying the speech naturalness of individuals treated for stuttering came from observations that many people who had undergone successful treatment continued to sound unnatural (Onslow & Ingham, 1987; Runyan et al., 1982; Sacco et al., 1992). Their speech was perceived as effortful, uncomfortable to listen to, and contained auditory or visual features that prevented the listener from fully attending to the content of the message. Despite an otherwise successful treatment experience, many speakers found that they were still unsatisfied with their speech and were still regarded by others as having a problem (Schiavetti & Metz, 1997). Tasko et al. (2007) found, for example, that of 35 adults who reduced their stuttering severity during an intensive fluency-shaping program (mean SSI-3 score reductions of 26.0 to 9.3), the speakers who showed the greatest success in decreasing the severity of their stuttering were also determined to be the most unnatural sounding. Tasko et al. suggested that decreased naturalness ratings might have resulted from the effort the successful participants had to put forth in order to execute the behavioral therapeutic targets (e.g., increased abdominal breathing, continuity of airflow, prevoiced exhalation, easy articulatory and phonatory onset, and continuous phonation). Although the strongest speech-motor correlate of the reduced speech naturalness was a reduced syllable rate ($r = -.40$), the authors also acknowledged that the increased inspiration and monitoring of speech movements required of the speakers could have also contributed to decreased speech naturalness.

Martin et al. (1984) began the development of a reliable scale for rating speech naturalness. The scale consisted of a 9-point Likert scale, with 1 equivalent to highly natural-sounding speech and 9 equivalent to highly unnatural-sounding speech. This scale was subsequently used in many investigations of speech naturalness. Martin et al. found that mean naturalness ratings for the speakers who stuttered was 6.52, whereas normally fluent adult speakers averaged 2.12.

The naturalness of speech is recognized as an important consideration in determining the success of treatment. The scale developed by Martin et al. (1984) appears to be reliable for either oral reading or spontaneous speech. Some (but not all) clients improve their speech naturalness as a result of treatment, and listeners tend to judge treated clients' speech as being significantly less natural than that of normally fluent speakers (Franken et al., 1992; Kalinowski et al., 1994;

Runyan et al., 1990). Runyan et al. (1990) found posttreatment naturalness ratings of 4.26 for speakers judged to be mild, 3.82 for speakers judged to be moderate, and 3.68 for speakers judged to be severe. These findings coincide with Starkweather's (1992) observation that even with increased fluency, some therapy procedures often tend to diminish the quality of a person's speech. Speakers who differ on naturalness ratings at the outset of treatment might be rated much the same after treatment, although pre- and posttreatment severity ratings influence judgments of naturalness. Moreover, feedback appears to enhance the speaker's ability to improve naturalness (Ingham et al., 1985; Ingham & Onslow, 1985). It also appears that listeners and speakers might have different criteria for determining naturalness. Listeners tend to evaluate an audio recording of a speaker as being more natural than when both audio and visual signals are presented (Martin & Haroldson, 1992). Last, voice-onset time and sentence duration have been suggested as important acoustic features of speech naturalness (Metz et al., 1990).

The research on speech naturalness indicates that the goal of treatment is considerably more complex than assisting clients to decrease the frequency of their stuttering. Some moments of stuttering are not likely to detract from a speaker's naturalness and spontaneity, particularly if these breaks are brief and relatively effortless. Clinicians who understand the importance of these effortless and smooth fluency breaks are most likely to appreciate this change. However, the research suggests that even naïve listeners might prefer speech with fluency breaks to unnatural-sounding and highly controlled speech devoid of all fluency disruptions. Fluency without ease of production represents something short of an ideal therapeutic success. If the client's speech sounds unnatural and the fluency is tenuous, it could foreshadow the possibility of relapse. If clients' fluent but unnatural speech elicits a negative response from listeners, it could be that they will soon grow tired of the practice necessary to maintain their new and unnatural speech and will return to their original and familiar form of stuttering. Adams and Runyan (1981) stated that the client who is ready for dismissal should have speech that is objectively and perceptively indistinguishable from that of normal speakers. The client's speech should not only be free of stuttering but should be produced at an acceptable rate, sound natural, and be free of perceptible signs of tenuous fluency. Some speakers, after several years of experience, might be able to achieve spontaneous fluency. However, as suggested earlier in this chapter, although this might be possible for younger speakers, these are lofty and perhaps unrealistic goals for many adults who stutter. Nonetheless, increases in speech naturalness and spontaneity should certainly be viewed as important signs of progress.

Success also can be observed through the reports of others in the speaker's environment, such as teachers, parents, a spouse, or friends, who indicate to the client or the clinician the desirable changes both in fluency and daily participation in activities. For example, Conture (1990) indicated that early signs of improvement often take the form of others reporting that they are noticing an improvement in speech or related behavior. These reports could appear spontaneously or might be elicited from those in the client's environment who are able to provide candid feedback. Such feedback should be taken seriously and regarded as an important indicator of success.

Developing a New Perspective Through Humor

As the speaker is able to achieve success in the management of his or her stuttering, many associated cognitive changes are reflected by the presence and acknowledgment of humor. As we suggested in Chapter 1, the clinician can lead the way in identifying and appreciating the humorous aspects of a situation by providing "new eyes" for viewing the old problem. As the speaker is able to externalize and achieve some distance from his or her relationship with stuttering, the clinician can be on the lookout for indicators of the client's ability to provide a humorous interpretation of events. Such opportunities occur frequently during group sessions, where a humorous story by one client often leads to a change in perspective by others in the group. With the distance afforded by the passage of time, behavioral mastery, and cognitive changes in perspective resulting from therapeutic success, the client is able to release the damaging effects of the experience and see his or her previous experiences with new eyes. Listener reactions from the past, from mildly inappropriate to obviously patronizing, as painful as they might have been when first experienced, lose some of their bite when distance and objectivity are applied to the wound. The entire group can share the experience and participate in a new interpretation of an old predicament. Along with the examples found in Chapter 1, we provide two additional examples of the many stories people have provided over the years.

CLINICAL INSIGHT

James, a middle-aged man, had attended therapy for only a short time but was already considerably desensitized to his stuttering. One day during group therapy, he related how, during his college years, he had eventually worked up the courage to call a young woman he had noticed in one of his classes for a date. He rarely used the telephone and never had telephoned a woman's dormitory before. [Note: Although it might be difficult for some of today's readers to appreciate, in those days there was only a single telephone located in the hallway of each floor of the woman's dorm.] The coed James wanted to call was named Harriet, and rather than risk saying an entire sentence such as, "May I speak to Harriet?" he decided to simply say "Harriet?" to whoever happened to answer the telephone. With great trepidation James dialed the dormitory and the telephone began ringing. After a few moments, a woman came to the phone and answered it. James froze, and the very best he could do was produce a series of breathy sounds as he kept repeating the initial "H" of Harriet's name. After this went on for several seconds, he heard the coed partially cover the phone and announce to the other women in the hall, "It's him again!"

CLINICAL INSIGHT

Walt had recently graduated from college and had enrolled himself in an intensive treatment program at a local university. As part of a group assignment, clients were to pair up and walk across campus to the streets of the college town and keep a record of listener reactions as they asked for directions from strangers. Walt and his partner decided they would ask for the location of the police station. Still in the early stages of treatment and clearly stuttering, he saw the task as a daunting one. He attempted to find a listener who posed the least possible threat. Entering the first street adjacent to the campus, he spied the best of all possible targets. Coming around the corner and approaching him on the street was an elderly woman. As he approached her, he positioned himself so that even if he stuttered, she would have no alternative but to stop. She was the prototypical grandmother. She wore a cloth coat and a hat with a veil. She was carrying a shopping bag in each hand, along with an umbrella. As Walt began to ask his question, she stopped. She looked up at him and placed both shopping bags on the sidewalk. Walt continued stuttering his way through his required question, asking about the location of the police station. As he completed his sentence, she responded. Yes, she did know the location of the police station. She spoke very slowly, a fact that was enhanced by her lipstick-red mouth as well as the veil attached to the front of her hat. "See the ... big ... red ... light?" she asked, as she turned and pointed to the stoplight one block behind her. She continued, even slower now, "When you get to that big ...

continues

red … light … turn … (and she paused even longer here as she took the elbow of his right arm) … left." At that same moment, to emphasize her instructions, she spun him around to his left. Somewhat wide-eyed and mortified for the moment, he pondered these events as he made his way back to the group meeting. As he shared his experience with the other group members, everyone, including the clinician, appreciated the humorous telling of his experience. There was genuine empathy and laughter all around as each member of the group shared similar experiences with well-meaning but overly patronizing listeners. (WM)

CONSIDERATIONS FOR CONCLUDING FORMAL TREATMENT

For children, the decision of terminating formal therapy is reasonably straightforward. As described in Chapter 11, once the child is able to maintain easy, fluent speech in a variety of situations at home and in school for several weeks or months, the decision to conclude treatment becomes obvious. The Stage 2 criteria of the Lidcombe Program described in Chapter 11 provide a reasonable approach for phasing out weekly therapy meetings (e.g., home severity ratings [SR] of less than 2 and 1 %SS during clinic visits for several weeks). Some monitoring in the form of meetings, telephone calls, and emails—perhaps as long as 2 years following the conclusion of formal treatment—is frequently recommended.

For adults, the issue is usually a little more complex because, as we have described, patterns of coping with stuttering have been well established and are usually more difficult to change. For those who take part in intensive treatment programs that are organized over a period of weeks, the participants are enrolled for a set period, and follow-up sessions and support are typically provided. Many individuals are unable to take part in intensive programs and choose, instead, to attend treatment on a once- or twice-a-week basis.

In this situation there is often no preset determination or discussion about when treatment is likely to be concluded. As discussed at the outset of this chapter, it is probably reasonable to conceive of the process as a period of formal or professional assistance followed by a longer period of informal or self-therapy. Still, there are no uniform criteria that have been recommended for terminating formal treatment.

Van Riper (1973) suggested that if the speaker becomes bored and unenthused about treatment or even about maintaining fluency, it could be time to terminate formal treatment. Certainly it is better to anticipate the end of treatment and to schedule a final exit meeting or two than to have the client simply cease attending. Apart from the effect on the client, such lack of closure provides the clinician with less opportunity to learn from the therapeutic encounter. Like Adams and Runyan (1981), who suggested that dismissal can take place when the client's speech is indistinguishable from typically fluent speakers, Bloodstein (1987) suggested that successful treatment should result in speech that sounds not only natural but also spontaneous, and that the speaker should be free of the need to monitor his or her speech. St. Louis and Westbrook (1987) proposed that clients should be free from stuttering before being dismissed from treatment. Whether it is realistic to expect adults who have stuttered for most of their lives to be able to achieve such goals before being dismissed from formal treatment is questionable. Although it is possible that a high level of spontaneous and natural-sounding fluency might be a realistic goal for some speakers, it is not likely to be the case for many adults. Obviously, there should be a clinically significant reduction in stuttering as formal treatment is concluded, but there are still likely to be occasions where some form of stuttering will take place. Patterns of avoidance and stress reactions during particularly difficult communication situations are likely to persist, depending on the extent to which speakers challenge themselves in expanding their speaking experiences and confidence.

Discussing the criteria for termination with the speaker at or near the outset of treatment is one possible solution to this problem. It is probably never too soon for the clinician to begin asking the client to address the issue of terminating or phasing out formal treatment. A request to the speaker to consider some operational definitions about when he or she will be able to be on his or her own is a valid issue from the outset or shortly thereafter. Often the client will respond with, "You're the expert, you tell me." Of course, the clinician is the expert about fluency disorders in a generic sense, but as we indicate throughout this book, the client must become the authority concerning his or her own situation and therapeutic goals. Certainly, we can obtain several measures of the speaker's progress that will be helpful in making the decision to end formal treatment. In a high-quality therapeutic alliance, though, our client will be likely to tell us when he or she is ready.

Continued treatment beyond what is necessary could serve to reinforce the client's dependency. In addition, there is a law of diminishing returns whereby, at a certain point, the cost of treatment, financial or otherwise, is no longer worth the effect. If the client has reached a plateau and little progress is noted for several weeks, such leveling-off could suggest that the client—not to mention the clinician—needs a break. A break from treatment also might be indicated if the client becomes bored or other issues such as financial constraints or the logistics of attending treatment become preeminent. Just as in the case of attending graduate school or beginning a period of arduous athletic training, pushing ahead at full speed is not always the best strategy. Sometimes "less is more," and it might be best to back away for a while. A break could provide the opportunity to reassess priorities and evaluate and regain motivation. It might be that a vacation from treatment is the best investment for future growth. Temporary dismissal from treatment might not be an easy decision, for there is the chance that we will lose contact with the person and progress could cease. Nonetheless, forgoing treatment for a time can be an essential step in the overall process. When termination of treatment is discussed, the clinician can make it clear that group treatment or consultation on a less formal basis is available. If the speaker has not already done so, joining a support group can serve to keep his or her momentum going and foster desensitization and an assertive approach concerning the achievement of fluency.

CONCLUSION

The consistent findings from in-depth studies of the experiences provided by people who stutter indicate themes of suffering, struggle, helplessness, anxiety, low self-worth, and highly restricted lives

(Anderson & Felsenfeld, 2003; Corcoran & Stewart, 1998; Crichton-Smith, 2002; Finn, 1996; Plexico et al., 2005). The descriptions are dominated by the individuals' overall response to their global life experience and their self-interpretation as communicators and as human beings. From the speaker's perspective, the experience of stuttering is represented by these intrinsic features as much or more than it is by the more obvious surface behaviors. These findings strongly indicate that a successful therapeutic outcome should include validation by the client of changes in the intrinsic features of the problem (see also Conture, 1996). Findings by Langevin et al. (2006) also provide convincing support for a model of treatment effectiveness that incorporates input from clients and significant others as well as clinicians and researchers.

The process of change both within and beyond the therapeutic environment is most often indicated in the form of small victories. Change often begins once the speaker begins to recognize the need for help and begins to take action for obtaining assistance. For most speakers, multiple factors must be considered when tracking successful change for a multidimensional problem such as stuttering. Trivial criteria are likely to yield convincing but inaccurate views of success. The surface features of the problem in the form of less frequent, easier, and more open stuttering clearly indicate success. Alterations in cognitive and affective responses also indicate important, sometimes substantial, changes as speakers develop more insightful, less reflexive, and fearful responses to the possibility as well as the reality of their stuttering. The speaker brings to the therapeutic experience a history of abilities and speech-related problems that will interact with the therapeutic alliance

and the particular treatment strategy. It is not surprising that success will look and sound somewhat different for each individual given the interplay of these factors. Regardless of the therapeutic program, speakers achieve excellent, modest, or—particularly if they terminate the program prematurely—little success.

Peck (1978), in a discussion of the psychotherapeutic process, indicated that "the majority of patients, even in the hands of the most skilled and loving therapists, will terminate their therapy at some point far short of completely fulfilling their potential" (p. 180). Early termination is also sometimes characteristic of intervention for fluency disorders. Not all clients make as much progress as we would like, at least during the time that we share with them, but nearly any person who is ready and motivated enough to approach rather than avoid the problem is likely to make progress. As clients meet with an experienced clinician, they begin to learn something about themselves and their communication problems. They are likely to become desensitized to the problem over time. As they develop a more accurate and broader view of their situation, they are more likely to begin coping in ways that are more agentic and less influenced by the habitual and typically less efficient responses.

As treatment progresses, it becomes increasingly important for indicators of change to accurately reflect the speaker's ability to enter into and successfully communicate in speaking situations beyond the therapy setting. Many individuals quickly adapt to and become fluent within the supportive therapeutic environment. Clues to successful change in daily speaking situations can be indicated by self-report devices and, of course, by clinician observation. Perhaps the most salient clues are provided by the speaker's written or verbal descriptions of their experiences. All of these sources provide information about clients' ability to accomplish improved levels of self-monitoring, practice and self-discipline, approach behavior, open and effortless speech, self-confidence and self-esteem, and a new and often humorous perspective of themselves and their situation. As a result of these accomplishments, the individual is able to elaborate an increasingly agentic lifestyle.

Ideally, the decision to gradually phase out of and terminate the formal support provided by the clinician and the therapy program should be made by the speaker. It can be difficult for the clinician to see some clients leave, for the therapeutic alliance is often a positive experience for everyone involved. Therapy that is unnecessary, beyond the obvious ethical issues, could serve to reinforce the client's dependency. As we discuss in the final chapter, some speakers will need additional contact with the clinician in one form or another. Should additional individual or group treatment become necessary, it is helpful for the speaker to interpret the decision as an opportunity for continued growth and support rather than dependency.

? TOPICS FOR DISCUSSION

1. How would you explain what you consider to be the primary principles of therapeutic change to an adult who stutters?

2. Describe the factors that are likely to facilitate or detract from the possibility of therapeutic success.

3. How would you document attitudinal, behavioral, and cognitive indica-

tors of successful therapeutic change for (a) children and (b) adults who stutter?

4. What are examples of the "little victories" that are demonstrated by a speaker whom you are particularly interested in highlighting and rewarding?

5. Using a 3-minute sample of spontaneous speech, rate five nonstuttering adult speakers using the 9-point naturalness rating scale described in this chapter. Also rate recorded samples of speakers who are approaching the conclusion of treatment.

6. Explain your criteria for considering the termination of formal treatment for an adolescent or adult who has been coming to you for treatment.

📖 RECOMMENDED READINGS

Hillis, J. W. (1993). Ongoing assessment in the management of stuttering: A clinical perspective. *American Journal of Speech-Language Pathology, 2*(1), 24–37.

Langevin, M., Hunick, W. J., Kully, D., Peters, H. F. M., Lomheim, H., & Tellers, M. (2006). A cross-cultural, long-term outcome evaluation of the ISTAR Comprehensive Stuttering Program across Dutch and Canadian adults who stutter. *Journal of Fluency Disorders, 31,* 229–256.

Manning, W. H. (1999). Progress under the surface and over time. In N. B. Ratner & E. C. Healey (Eds.), *Stuttering research and practice: Bridging the gap* (pp. 123–129). Erlbaum.

Starkweather, C. W. (1999). The effectiveness of stuttering therapy: An issue for science? In N. B. Ratner & E. C. Healey (Eds.), *Stuttering research and practice: Bridging the gap* (pp. 231–244). Erlbaum.

Indicators of Successful Change Following Treatment

CHAPTER OBJECTIVES

■ To consider the issues associated with maintaining the changes that have taken place during formal therapy

■ To examine the various responses to the possibility of relapse

■ To describe ways of predicting a relapse or, conversely, the likelihood of long-term enhancement of the desirable behavioral skills and the coping abilities that have been realized

■ To describe a variety of maintenance activities

■ To explore the empowering effect of support groups

RECOVERY OR SUCCESSFUL MANAGEMENT?

While young children are more likely to recover with little or no memory of having stuttered, it might be more realistic to think of older speakers as undergoing an evolving process of successful management, as is often the case with other complex human problems. Although investigators of treatment efficacy and relapse have found that substantial changes take place during treatment for the majority of people, a review of this literature suggests that, with many important exceptions, relatively few people who stutter into adulthood become completely spontaneous and fluent speakers. Having stuttered for decades, the evolution of new ways of speaking and thinking are going to take practice and adjustment (and as discussed in Chapter 3, time to reorganize cortical and subcortical neural functioning). Even for individuals who attain fluent speech, for some time at least, there are likely to be some residual effects in the form of avoidance and anxiety associated with communicating, particularly in more challenging situations. Nearly all autobiographical accounts written by people who have undergone successful treatment contain descriptions of the long-term effects of being a person who stutters (e.g., Chmela, 1998; Johnson, 1930; Krall, 1998; Logan et al., 2016; Manning, 1991a, 1998, 1999b; Murray & Edwards, 1980; Quesal, 1998; Ramig, 1998). These accounts also document that these effects can be diminished with vigilance, practice, support, and continued development of fluency and communication skills. As described at the end of this chapter, it is also important to emphasize that many speakers report a variety of positive effects from being someone who has spent several years journeying through life as a person who stutters. These speakers genuinely appreciate the fluency they have earned and enjoy their enhanced ability to communicate with others *even if some stuttering remains*. The lessons learned from successfully coping with adversity are applied to other aspects of their lives, helping them to become more empathetic and resilient. There are also many individuals who, having stuttered during the earlier decades of their lives, have been able to become highly effective communicators and successful public speakers.

The ability to successfully manage stuttering is similar to other areas of clinical intervention where relapse is a common phenomenon such as drug addiction, alcoholism, weight reduction, smoking cessation, and marital problems (Lefcourt, 1976). For example, 1-year success rates for intensive smoking cessation programs range from 20% to 40%. For nonintensive interventions, success rates range from 10% to 20% (DiClemente, 1993). On a somewhat more optimistic note, a review of the relapse literature by Craig (1998)

indicates that relapse rates for individuals with addictive disorders have decreased from 70% by 12 months postintervention in the 1960s and 1970s to 12-month rates of 40% to 60% in the 1990s. This improvement has been attributed to the incorporation of antirelapse programs, including follow-up programs, enhancement of self-efficacy, and active participation with self-help support groups.

After formal treatment is concluded, the process of change becomes self-directed. This informal or maintenance phase of the process for the adult who stutters can continue to some extent for the rest of the speaker's life. The person who stutters must be ready to accept full responsibility for self-management, a role that should be considered as early as possible during formal treatment. Because subsequent self-directed maintenance is by far the longest stage in the therapeutic process—typically with little or no contact with a clinician or researcher—it is the part of the process that is least understood. The emphasis for the speaker is on consolidating the gains of therapy, perhaps coping with relapse, and continuing the evolution of the individual's ability to live an increasingly agentic lifestyle.

OUR LIMITED VIEW OF CHANGE

As discussed in Chapter 1, student clinicians rarely have the opportunity to observe speakers for more than one or two semesters. As a result, students are apt to see only a small window of the affective, behavioral, and cognitive changes that are taking place for the speaker. Professional clinicians also see a relatively small window of change if they have little or no contact with the individual following the termination of treatment, a time when significant lifestyle changes are likely to occur. Certainly, some people do maintain contact with their clinician, but usually—as Van Riper (1973) pointed out—these are clients who need additional help. The majority go off on their own, leaving the clinician with no idea about their progress over the years. Boberg (1981, 1986) was one of the first clinical researchers to recognize this issue and suggested that comprehensive clinical programs should have a system for assisting the client in the maintenance of clinical gains as well as providing refresher programs emphasizing client self-management of cognitive and attitudinal changes.

Relapse is likely to occur during the first few months or years following the termination of formal intervention. It is during this time when the ability of the speaker to perform self-directed change determines the ultimate effectiveness of the formal therapy experience. To the listener, relapse is likely to be first observed in the surface features of the problem in terms of the quantity and quality of the speaker's fluency. For the speaker, however, relapse begins earlier with the return of the old and ingrained responses of fear and avoidance. Thus, just as the assessment of stuttering is multidimensional, the determination of the speaker's ability to maintain change must be multidimensional as well. Concentration on a single feature such as the frequency of stuttering tends to exclude the important affective and cognitive features of the problem, features that those who stutter perceive as vital (Krauss-Lehrman & Reeves, 1989; Reeves, 2006; St. Louis, 2006; Yaruss, Quesal, & Murphy, 2002; Yaruss, Quesal, Reeves, et al., 2002). Maintenance of the many changes that take place during for-

mal treatment is apt to be somewhat more difficult when the client is on his or her own doing battle against the inertia of a long history of stuttering and the well-learned coping techniques that have been relied on for years to conceal the problem.

TRANSFER AND MAINTENANCE

Of the three basic stages of treatment—establishment of fluency, transference of new abilities to beyond-treatment speaking situations, and maintenance of the new abilities following formal treatment—maintenance is typically regarded as the most challenging aspect of the treatment process (Boberg, 1981). Maintenance is burdensome for the client, for he or she is working against many forces that are pulling in the direction of pretreatment performance and cognition.

Maintenance is often enigmatic for the clinician because it is often difficult to maintain contact with the client. Even when some form of contact is maintained, there are practical and ethical issues that make it difficult to obtain accurate data concerning posttreatment performance. Maintenance of the changes achieved during informal treatment will be more likely to occur if, during the period of formal treatment, the clinician has provided opportunities that enable the client to focus on the transfer of cognitive, affective, and behavioral changes to a variety of speaking experiences beyond the treatment setting. As Gregory (1995) pointed out, "The essence of effective therapy is transfer" (p. 199). It is unnecessary to wait until the speaker achieves partial or complete fluency in the treatment environment before taking the speech to the street. Most people can benefit from these activities from the outset of treatment. Early on, the speaker can gradually begin the process of becoming desensitized to a wide variety of environmental stimuli that have elicited habitual coping patterns of avoidance and fear. The clinician can help the speaker to successfully predict and identify listener reactions. Experiences in speaking situations beyond the immediate therapy environment can help the speaker to self-monitor and eventually vary and experiment with the characteristic behavioral patterns of their stuttering. Something as basic as an audio or video recording can function as a stimulus for achieving success in extra-treatment speaking situations (Howie et al., 1982). Of course, a most powerful stimulus for providing the speaker with cues and support in daily speaking situations is the participation of the clinician. Objects (books, games, work-related items) and individuals (family members, friends, colleagues) that are brought to the treatment setting can serve as powerful discriminative stimuli that help to cue the client for achieving success when he or she ventures beyond the treatment room.

As discussed in earlier chapters, the lack of homogeneity among clients is a major variable that contributes to the capricious effects of treatment. This lack of client, as well as environmental, homogeneity could also help to explain the difficulty of successful speaker maintenance following treatment. For example, Boberg (1986) proposed that differences in long-term progress are as likely to be due to personality factors and the ability of the clients as they are to the nature of the treatment program or even the quality of the clinician. Huinck et al. (2006) provided support for this proposal with an investigation of 25 adults who underwent intensive treatment in the Comprehensive Stuttering Program (CPS; Boberg & Kully, 1985). They classified speakers as severe or mild based on the SSI (Riley, 1972) and three measures of emotional and cognitive reactions to their stuttering. Although the speakers rated as severe made larger treatment gains than speakers who were classified as mild, they also demonstrated higher levels of regression during follow-up 1 and 2 years later. These results suggest that individuals with mild stuttering are likely to profit most from treatment that helps them put their stuttering into perspective and decreases negative emotions and cognitions, whereas those with more severe profiles might first need to focus on reducing stuttering.

THE NATURE OF REGRESSION AND RELAPSE

By discussing the nature of relapse with the client and preparing him or her for the possibility of regression, is the clinician creating a self-fulfilling prophecy? If the topic of regression is never mentioned, is relapse less apt to occur? Or does the clinician have an obligation to prepare the client for something that, in some form at least, is likely to happen? The literature consistently indicates that for adult speakers, some degree of relapse is a possibility following successful treatment and that the clinician is responsible for preparing the client to respond to it if it occurs. Many authors have recognized relapse as a common event following treatment for adults who stutter (Bloodstein & Bernstein Ratner, 2008; Craig, 1998; Kuhr & Rustin, 1985; Martin, 1981; Perkins, 1979; Silverman, 1981; Van Riper, 1973). Prins (1970) found that about 40% of clients taking part in an intensive residential program experienced some regression following treatment. Although Prins noted that clients believed that maximum regression occurred within 6 months after the termination of formal treatment, other writers have suggested that clients should be followed for at least 2 to 5 years following formal treatment (Bloodstein & Bernstein Ratner, 2008; Conture & Guitar, 1993; Young, 1975). Martin (1981) reviewed the literature and estimated relapse at approximately 30%. Craig and Hancock (1995) found that 71.7% of 152 adults surveyed experienced relapse but that the majority found that they subsequently regained fluency. Craig and Hancock also noted that relapse tended to be cyclical, occurring up to three times in a year.

Cooper (1977) viewed relapse as part of the human condition. Silverman (1981) suggested that relapse is likely to occur with a 40% to 90% probability. A survey of members of the National Stuttering Association support group by Yaruss, Quesal, Reeves, et al. (2002) found that 40 of the 67 respondents (59.7%) indicated that they did not maintain their fluency after treatment (regardless of the treatment approach) and that 35 (52.2%) stated that they were not able to achieve the same fluency in daily life as they did in the treatment environment. Van Riper (1973) indicated that, "Relapses and remissions are the rule, not the exception, for the adult stutterer if long-term follow-up investigations are conducted" (p. 178). St. Louis and Westbrook (1987) reported that "relapse is a ubiquitous and familiar problem in stuttering therapy" (252). Perkins (1979) stated that "maintenance of fluency is the perennial weak link in the therapeutic chain" (p. 119) of stuttering treatment. Finally, as Bloodstein (1995) maintained, although we are adept at making people who stutter fluent, we know little about how to keep them that way.

Thus for most clients, some type of follow-up is necessary. The learning curve is long, and as Van Riper was fond of saying, our old habits are always the strongest. Clients should at least have the option of continuing treatment in some form for as long as they feel that it is necessary. This, of course, is not likely to happen if coming back to the clinic is viewed by the clinician or the client as an indication of failure. If learning how to successfully manage stuttering is viewed as a long-term process—which in the majority of cases it surely is—then the client returning for follow-up sessions is not a sign of failure. Rather, it is a natural and acceptable part of the process of change. Additional treatment, more than anything else, simply means that those involved are wise enough to recognize that they are likely to benefit from further support, effort, and growth. Fortunately, many clients do not require a return to intensive individual treatment. Often, group treatment sessions or support group meetings once or twice a month (or as necessary) will enable many clients to get back on track and continue making progress.

Somewhat less is known about relapse for children or adolescents. Craig et al. (1996) followed 97 children (ages 9–14) for 1 year posttreatment and found that 3 of 10 children experienced relapse, defined as 2% SS. In a subsequent study, Hancock and Craig (1998) followed 77 of these same children in order to identify possible predictors of relapse (2% SS). Regression analysis indicated that only pretreatment %SS and immediate posttreatment trait anxiety were significant predictors (accounting for 14.4% and 8.0% of the variance, respectively). That is, children who stuttered to a greater degree prior to treatment were more likely to relapse, a finding similar to a study by

Huinck et al. (2006) with adults. Surprisingly, the children who indicated higher immediate posttreatment measures of trait anxiety (within the normal range) were less likely to relapse. The authors considered that perhaps the normal but heightened anxiety resulted in the children being more willing to work on their fluency skills. A variety of other variables (age and sex of the children, number of years stuttered, family history of stuttering) had little predictive value.

Defining Relapse

Defining relapse following formal treatment is nearly as difficult as determining the severity of the stuttering at the outset. As Craig (1998) pointed out, a medical definition that defines relapse using an all-or-none criterion (the presence or absence of a disease) clearly does not work well for stuttering. An all-or-none criterion might be used for some addictive behaviors (e.g., setting a threshold of total abstinence for the use of alcohol or cigarettes). However, it is clear that following therapy, at least initially, most people who stutter will have residual attitudes and behaviors following treatment, and zero stuttering is not likely to be the case.

Many investigators who have studied relapse in stuttering have used the presence of overt stuttering as the one—and often the only—measure of relapse. Some investigators have considered the percentage of syllables stuttered and have used a relapse criteria of 2% SS (Craig et al., 1984; Evesham & Fransella, 1985) or 4 %SS (Boberg, 1981). Blood (1995a, 1995b) and Ladouceur et al. (1989) used 3% SS to define treatment success. If the focus of change is going to be the frequency of stuttering, perhaps a better approach is to consider follow-up fluency levels in terms of both pre- and immediate posttreatment fluency levels (adding 3% to follow-up percentages to account for expected regression) as suggested by Langevin et al. (2006) in Chapter 14.

As we have suggested, the frequency of stuttering is usually not the initial or only indicator of regression. Van Riper (1973) stated, "Stuttering does not mean relapse. Another moment of fear is no catastrophe" (p. 209). Changes in the attitudinal and cognitive aspects of the problem, often in the form of negative self-talk, are more likely to take the lead in the progression of relapse. As an example, Craig and Hancock (1995) found that adults with significantly raised levels of trait anxiety were three times more likely to experience relapse. When elements of avoidance and fear begin to multiply and increasingly influence the speaker's decision making, overt stuttering will not be far behind. Recognizing the great variability of stuttering frequency and the variability of fluency across different speaking situations, Craig and Calver (1991) defined relapse as "stuttering to a degree which was not acceptable to yourself for at least a period of one week" (p. 283), a definition that seems to be more realistic and functional than many others.

Relapses can take many forms and can range from brief periods that are mildly irritating to long episodes that are extremely handicapping. The clinician might be able to determine that the client has reached the threshold of a relapse based on observable affective, behavioral, and cognitive aspects of the problem. However, the presence and degree of relapse are probably best determined by the speaker. When speakers get to the point where they believe they are no longer confident of managing their speech on their own or their decisions are increasingly based on the possibility of stuttering, relapse has reached a clinical level. At that point, it is both reasonable and desirable to seek additional professional help.

Possible Causes of Relapse

While describing the shadow side of implementing change, Egan (2007) briefly discussed the idea of "entropy," the tendency of things—lacking frequent maintenance—to break down or fall apart. Applied to humans who are attempting therapeutic or self-directed change, this might be thought of as the tendency to give up on a course of action that has been initiated, something we have all experienced. We intend to lose some weight, we get in a little better shape, and then we fall back a bit . . . or maybe a lot. As we begin a process of learning and change, the actions we are taking seem reasonable, often exciting as we hope for success in the endeavor. However, with the routine requirements of hard work, enthusiasm fades and a lack of time and other priorities soon interfere. As Egan described, we are distracted or become discouraged and flounder. Citing Brownell et al. (1986), Egan made the important distinction between the clinician preparing clients for the mistakes they might make and "giving them permission" to make mistakes and implying that they are inescapable. Perhaps even more important, he suggested the critical distinction between a "lapse" (a slip or a mistake) and a "relapse" (a complete cessation of a program of change). A minor regression of confidence and performance does not need to result in a relapse. Finally, Egan (2007) commented that accepting that entropy is common and expected is not a defeatist attitude—it is realism: "At-

trition, noncompliance, and relapse are the name of the game" (p. 352), and as clinicians, we should recognize this. Moreover, despite a lapse or even a relapse, the individual, with the assistance of the clinician, can choose to do what is necessary to keep moving in the desired direction.

Silverman (1981) suggested a number of possible reasons for relapse. Clients who are especially likely to relapse are those who, following treatment, believe themselves to be cured. Believing they have experienced a cure, they are less likely to continue the process of self-management. Other clients might regress as they lose confidence in the treatment program, something that is apt to occur if they have experienced relapse following previous treatment. As Silverman suggested, people tend to expect events to replicate themselves.

Another possible reason for relapse could be that the clinician and the client have thresholds for fluency breaks that are too liberal. In this case, small fluency breaks are accepted and left unchanged. Relapse is also more likely to occur if clients are released from treatment too soon, although just how soon is "too soon" is difficult to determine. It might be worthwhile seeing the client through at least one period of relapse while the support of the clinician is still available. For some speakers, the return of stuttering at some level might be acceptable if it has been the norm for decades. For some people, the presence of stuttering could provide an escape from responsibilities, including work. This probably does not occur enough to explain relapse in most people, but, no doubt, it is one force that can nudge the client back into old, habitual coping patterns. Disruptive life events could sap the motivation and strength for continued self-management. Daly et al. (1995) suggested that this might be especially true for adolescents where an emotional crisis precipitates the loss of self-esteem and negatively impacts fluency. As Daly et al. indicated, adolescent clients are likely to see many negative events, be they social, academic, or treatment related, as catastrophic.

Neurophysiological Loading

For many years, researchers who have studied the etiology, spontaneous recovery, and relapse for subjects with fluency disorders have suggested that some of these speakers possess an underlying physiological or neurophysiological condition (Boberg, 1986; Moore & Haynes, 1980; Perkins et al., 1990; Zimmerman, 1980, 1981). Findings from the neuroimaging studies described in Chapter 3 provide examples of anatomical and physiological alterations in adults as well as some children who stutter. Although the implications of these findings are not always certain, they indicate that at least some individuals who stutter might be working with cortical and subcortical systems that do not readily facilitate speech fluency. The possibilities of such differences might be especially likely for clients who have a clear family history of stuttering. Longitudinal studies by Yairi and Ambrose (2005) have supported earlier suggestions by perceptive clinicians concerning the likelihood of genetic factors in the recovery from or the persistence of stuttering (Boberg, 1986; Sheehan & Martyn, 1966). It could also be that some speakers are genetically predisposed to relapse (Cooper, 1972; Neaves, 1970).

The Natural Variability of Fluency

In earlier chapters, we discussed how the variability of fluency might make it difficult to diagnose stuttering and to predict future levels of fluency. Kamhi (1982) pointed out that some people who stutter must expend considerably more effort than others to achieve and maintain fluency, due to the natural variability of their speech production systems. For some speakers, such variability (including relapses) is more common and perhaps more severe. A related theme is the levels of pretreatment severity estimates. Regardless of how such estimates are made—whether simply estimates of stuttering frequency or indicators of various cognitive and behavioral responses to stuttering—investigators typically find that pretreatment severity is a good predictor of posttreatment regression (Eichstaedt et al., 1998; Huinck et al., 2006).

Speaking in a Nonhabitual Manner

As described in Chapter 14, authors have frequently pointed out that the treatment techniques associated with many treatment protocols result in increased fluency by encouraging the person to speak in a nonhabitual and unnatural manner. Boberg (1981) suggested that, in many ways, the requirements of practicing self-management techniques can be a highly punishing experience that results in a loss of spontaneity. Although altered ways of speaking typically result in rapid increases in fluency, it takes concentration and effort to maintain what are clearly nonhabitual respiratory, phonatory, and articulatory patterns. A review of the research on the measurement of speech naturalness for stuttering speakers by Schiavetti and Metz (1997) suggested that some speakers who achieved stutter-free speech sounded as unnatural after treatment as they had prior to treatment. Over the years, experienced clinicians have suggested that such techniques tend to have only a temporary impact on a speaker's fluency (Bloodstein, 1949, 1950; Boberg, 1981; Van Riper, 1973, 1990). If the only changes that are emphasized during treatment are the client's speech rate and the related improvement in fluency, it could explain the reasonably high occurrence of relapse with this treatment strategy (Silverman, 1981). Moreover, if, following treatment, the client's speech sounds and feels unnatural and lacks spontaneity, the effects of these changes are not likely to last in the long term (Boberg, 1986; Kalinowski et al., 1994; Schiavetti & Metz, 1997).

Starke (1994) further pointed out that the use of artificial speech can also result in prosodic distortion. Although the altered ways of producing speech might promote fluency in a technical sense, they could also result in messages being misperceived. Because of the altered prosody, there is a distinct possibility of a distortion in the speaker's communicative intentions and the relationship between the speaker and the listener, an effect Starke termed "message incompatibility conflict." Although the speaker might no longer be stuttering in his or her typical manner, the pragmatics of human communication might suffer unless the listener is able to understand that speech modification techniques are being used.

Commitment to Ongoing Self-Management

Once formal treatment is concluded, the speaker is likely to feel both internal as well as external pressure to maintain an improved level of fluency. This pressure might be particularly true if the speaker has attended an intensive program away from home and family. Upon returning home, there are apt to be subtle (as well as not-so-subtle) expectations from others for the speaker to consistently display their new and much-improved fluency. The

occurrence of sporadic stuttering could be viewed as a sign of failure by some ("How awful. After all this time, effort, and money and he still stutters!"). Although many individuals can show much-improved fluency, the fear of even a single fluency break can be immense. One good response to the pressure of others to be fluent when they say such things as, "Your speech is wonderful now that you've had therapy. You don't stutter at all any more, do you?" might be to say something like, "Www-well, I'm do-do-doing my b-b-best!" as suggested by Van Riper (1971).

Throughout this text, we have proposed that success in the treatment of stuttering is possible on many levels. Nevertheless, it must also be stated that changing the surface and intrinsic features of stuttering usually takes considerable effort and time. For the treatment process to be effective and functional in the longer term, continuing effort and vigilance must occur. As Cooper (1977) pointed out, it takes a good deal of psychic energy to maintain success. There are many reasons why speakers make the choice not to use techniques introduced during treatment. Crichton-Smith (2002) noted that some speakers feel that the effort that must be expended to modify their speech competes with their ability to focus on what it is they want to communicate. This is especially likely to be the case in the early stages of behavioral variation and modification as well as maintenance of these techniques following therapy. It is not surprising that the additional disruption to the linguistic process required by some of the techniques might not be worth the effort. Crichton-Smith also proposed that many therapeutic techniques (and clinicians) overly emphasize the production of fluency, thereby inadvertently promoting the concealment of stuttering, possibly setting the stage for relapse

(Sheehan, 1982). This might be especially true for programs that emphasize the achievement of fluency without attending to the cognitive and attitudinal aspects of change (Yaruss, Quesal, Reeves, et al., 2002). When surveying a total of 67 individuals about their experiences following treatment, Yaruss, Quesal, Reeves, et al. (2002) found that those who had experienced only fluency-shaping approaches were more likely to report that they had experienced a relapse ($p = .037$) or that treatment was unsuccessful ($p = .045$) than those who had taken part in stuttering modification, avoidance reduction, or combined approaches.

Integrating the New Speaking Role— Altering Core Constructs

Sheehan often commented that for therapy to be successful in the long term, the person must eventually make the adjustment of viewing himself or herself as something other than an individual who stutters. For this to occur, Sheehan (1970) suggested that the speaker must integrate a new and unfamiliar role as a fluent speaker and "wash the stutterer aspect out of the self-concept" (p. 8). This proposal parallels the frequent comments throughout this text about the concept of cognitive restructuring and altering one's core constructs when defining oneself. Separating from a self-concept shaped by many years of living with the experience of stuttering can be a formidable challenge, as described by the late Marty Jezer, author, and a person who stuttered:

> The potential for stuttering, the fact that we might stutter in the next sentence even though the sentence we are speaking is perfectly fluent, is why so many of us who stutter think of our-

selves as stutterers even when we are not stuttering. It would seem, then, that part of our problem lies in how we perceive ourselves as speakers more than in how our listeners react to us when we speak. A stutterer who isn't stuttering may not be a stutterer to the people listening to him, especially if they don't know him. But a stutterer who isn't stuttering often still feels that he is a stutterer, because he knows that fluency is fleeting and stuttering may happen the next time he opens his mouth. (Jezer, 1997, p. 18)

At the heart of many models of therapeutic and self-directed change is the ability of people to evolve and develop new core constructs about themselves and their possibilities (Boberg et al., 1979; Dalton, 1987, 1994; Emerick, 1988; Evesham & Fransella, 1985; Fransella, 1972; Fransella & Dalton, 1990; Hayhow & Levy, 1989). Kuhr and Rustin (1985) noted, for example, that following treatment, those clients who were most satisfied with their fluency also made lifestyle changes at many levels. Of course, it takes some time to change habitual coping responses to many old and powerful stimuli. As Fransella (1972) suggested, the speaker is better able to predict how events will transpire when in the role of a person who stutters and, in many instances, less able to predict events when speaking fluently. As Dalton (1987) explained, at some level, the speaker makes a "choice" to stutter, not because he or she prefers to do so in the usual sense, but because it is what is familiar and consistent with how the speaker understands himself or herself and his or her world. Given the individual's experience and interpretation of events, the choice is not surprising. Adults and adolescents who stutter have learned how to cope and survive in response to emotions such as threat, fear, anxiety, guilt, and hostility. Letting go of such coping responses is daunting. As we have also stressed, it is not likely to happen without the understanding and support of others, including an understanding clinician.

Given these changes in a person's core constructs, it is not unusual for some speakers who have undergone successful treatment to express some anxiety, possibly even vague feelings of guilt, concerning their new fluency. Considering the many changes that are (hopefully) occurring in the speaker's core structures as described in Chapter 7, it is reasonable that the individual could experience fear, anxiety, and even guilt. Kuhr and Rustin (1985) also found evidence of minor depression in several fluent speakers following treatment. Speakers sometimes express surprise that they are not as content as they thought they would be with their fluency. They might indicate that, on occasion, they feel that they are deceiving others or feel that they are not being themselves. Their unaccustomed fluency and the responsibility for self-management have changed the self they grew up with. Even though the speaker enjoys being fluent and feels that the fluency is earned, there could be the sensation of waiting for the other shoe to fall and the tendency to wonder, "Yes, I am fluent now but what if I lose it?"

The "meaningfulness" of these changes to an individual's core constructs is illustrated by the following quote:

My hands were trembling as I began. . . . I felt very much alone. So great was my fear that I seemed to go into a trance. It was a kind of out-of-body experience: a fluent person seemed to be speaking out of my mouth. I heard his words, but they did not come from me. When I was finished, the teacher complimented me for my fluency and for my courage. I think the class may even have applauded—not in sarcasm but in appreciation for my triumph and also, I imagine, in relief. (Jezer, 1997, p. 108)

Although the new fluency might be enjoyable to the listener, it will not always feel comfortable to the speaker, at least not immediately. As R. Williams (1995) explained from the perspective of personal construct theory, even when fluent, speakers are attempting to gain evidence of support for their new construct of themselves and their world. Individuals are now acting in ways that are not congruent with their long-held understanding of themselves. It will take some time for the speaker, as well as others in their environment, to adjust to the speaker's new way of communicating and interacting with others.

Kelly's (1955a, 1955b) theory of personal constructs proposes that cognitive anxiety results from a person's awareness that the events he or she is experiencing are beyond the comfort level of his or her system of personal constructs. Consequently, the person is unable to meaningfully integrate and predict the course of events. Recall that DiLollo and colleagues (DiLollo et al., 2003, 2005) found support for Fransella's perspective and the importance of altering the meaningfulness of the fluent-speaker role. In their studies, measures of cognitive anxiety and cognitive complexity indicated that both the stuttering and fluent speaker groups had integrated the dominant speaker role as a "core construct" and that those speaking experiences that ran counter to this role were ignored or discounted. For example, much like the earlier passage by Jezer (1997), the speakers who stuttered typically expressed the view that periods of fluent speech were an "accident" or a "fluke." Two examples from DiLollo et al. (2003) provided examples of such interpretations from individuals who stutter in their descriptions of fluent speech:

> Okay, so when is this gonna all come falling down on me? Okay, when am I gonna? I always knew that my speech pattern would get worse and would, you know, begin to struggle again eventually. So I was sort of waiting for, you know. I still have the fears. Let's just say that. I have the fear of speaking and all that. Because I knew eventually that my fluent day or my fluent time of speaking was going to be over soon. (p. 179)

> "Well once again, I'm not fluent. However, I think the way I react to people or the way I did when I had my fluent, my lucky fluency, I kinda felt like I was one of them and I guess, and it was kinda interesting to be able to talk amongst them without having any difficulty." In this example, the speaker specifically stopped and revised his utterance to include the defensive term "lucky fluency." (p. 179)

The results of DiLollo et al. (2003) indicate the importance of addressing the meaningfulness of the "dominant" speaker role during therapy for people who stutter. Accordingly, an important goal of treatment for individuals who stutter is to assist them in "deconstructing" the dominant role of a stuttering speaker in order to begin meaningful integration of fluent speaking experiences

and the nondominant fluent speaker role into their construct systems. Indications of speakers' reconstruction of their core constructs can be noted by a reduction of statements that defend or protect their stuttering speaker role. As suggested by the results of DiLollo et al. (2003) and R. Williams (1995), individuals who stutter might be attempting to validate their stuttering predictions, even when experiencing considerable success in producing fluent speech.

A hallmark of individuals who have achieved successful management of their stuttering is a change from concerns about protecting the self and others (especially listeners) to more agentic and approach-oriented strategies. Using a grounded theory procedure, Plexico et al. (2009a, 2009b) drew on the literature on human coping response to stressors in order to investigate patterns of coping for nine adults who stuttered. Speakers who regarded stuttering as an uncontrollable and shameful attribute adopted emotion-based coping responses designed to protect the self and assuage the listener from the stress and discomfort associated with stuttering. Due to fear of listener response, these individuals employed avoidant strategies in order to prevent and escape from stuttering. Although providing momentary relief, this coping strategy resulted in a restricted and reduced quality of life. In contrast, the speakers who employed cognitive-based coping patterns that were self- and problem focused were able to (a) create a broader perspective about themselves and the experience of stuttering, and (b) focus on their own goals resulting in increased agency and self-confidence. As participants moved from emotion-based avoidant patterns and put aside self-protection and concern about possible listener reactions, they began to focus on their own personal goals resulting in many positive social, physical, cognitive, and affective results.

A good example of an individual's evolving core constructs are the comments of Alan Badmington and his response to questions about his paper on the 2006 International Stuttering Awareness Day (ISAD) Interactive Computer Conference. The title of his paper was "Technology: A Friend or Foe of Someone Who Stutters." In response to a question from one of the conference participants, Badmington, a retired policeman from Wales, United Kingdom, and now a highly successful public speaker, described how, in his 50s he began to change his approach to managing his stuttering.

Listener Adjustment to the New Speaker

Because successful stuttering management also impacts the listener, it might be necessary for those in the client's daily environment to shift their perspective in order to establish a new equilibrium in the relationship. There will be changes in roles as the speaker no longer sees himself or herself in the primary role of a person who stutters (Sheehan, 1970). On occasion, others might be resistant to change. It is on such occasions that their participation in treatment is especially important for, as we have emphasized, successful therapy results in many changes beyond enhanced fluency. Kuhr and Rustin (1985) provided an example of just such a response. They

---

CLINICAL INSIGHT

What influenced me to abandon the Edinburgh Masker [a voice-activated device that provided white noise to both ears of the speaker] and cease avoidances? It's no secret that I knew virtually nothing about stuttering until relatively recent times. Although I had stuttered from childhood, I had absolutely no INSIGHT into what was happening. No one told me. Prior to the advent of the Internet, dissemination of information was relatively sparse.

On April 1, 2000, I witnessed a group of PWS speaking, before an audience, about how they were dealing with their respective stuttering problems. The positive manner in which they spoke had a huge impact upon me (so much so, that I even remember the date). One, in particular, had developed into a successful public speaker. At the time, strange as it may seem, I was not aware of the existence of stuttering associations and had long given up on my stuttering. I was resigned to the fact that it would remain a problem for the rest of my days. Everything changed when I heard him speaking. When he addressed the audience, he was so assured, so confident, and so in control of the situation. When he made reference to his public speaking activities and successes, I became even more interested. I wanted to be like him—I wanted to become a public speaker. He became my role model. For the very first time in my life, I believed that it was possible to deal with my stuttering difficulties. He was living proof of that "dream." When British athlete, Roger Bannister, ran the mile in less than 4 minutes back in the 1950s, the beliefs of other athletes changed overnight. Prior to his record-breaking

continues

performance, everyone considered it impossible to break the "4-minute mile" barrier. He proved it could be done. Within a relatively short period, many other athletes were regularly achieving the same feat. Within a year, I understand that over 100 had, amazingly, achieved that "impossible" goal. The person I heard speaking became MY Roger Bannister and I shall be, forever, grateful to him for showing me what was possible. He was hugely instrumental in changing the direction of my life. On May 4, 2000 (that date is also indelibly imprinted upon my memory), I joined a particular program that encouraged nonavoidance and expansion of comfort zones. It provided me with a new speaking technique and tools to deal with words that attracted an emotional charge, while also introducing me to the stuttering hexagon concept. This, together with a 24-hour support network, gave me the confidence to discard the mechanical crutch that had been an integral part of my life for more than 20 years. I felt that it was time to walk unaided. The rest is history, as they say—I have not looked back since. Somehow, the successes that I have attained after ceasing to use the Masker have tasted a little sweeter. I valued its assistance for *two* decades—without it, my life would have embraced so many more avoidance strategies. But, it was great to stand on my own two feet after such a lengthy time. When you achieve something that you, hitherto, considered impossible, it causes you to challenge your self-limiting beliefs. If we conquer something that has challenged our advancement, we grow in stature. That's exactly what I have done during the past 6 years.

Cited October 11, 2006. Reprinted with permission of Alan Badmington. © Alan Badmington 2006.

described a wife who felt uncomfortable when her husband returned home with fluent speech, following successful treatment. His wife's reaction was a negative one, accusing the clinician by stating, "You took him away and made him fluent!" (p. 234). To the extent that others in the client's life fail to understand and recognize the nature of changes that are occurring, they will be less likely to understand, appreciate, and reinforce these changes. Near the end of and especially following treatment, the responsibility for informing others about these important changes will most likely fall to the speaker. If the speaker is desensitized, no longer anxious about stuttering, and comfortable in his or her evolving role as an effective communicator, this information will be delivered in a forthright and effective manner.

There are often many examples of successful adjustment by others in the client's life that contribute much to the continued pattern of growth. In the following example, the client is a middle-aged woman who has stuttered severely for most of her life and only recently began to make even the most routine telephone calls.

Clinician: You say you are beginning to make some of your own telephone calls now?

Client: Oh yes, sometimes I would answer calls when I was at home but I would never place calls. If there was a call that I felt I had to make I would ask my husband to do it.

Clinician: Are you finding that making the calls is becoming less anxiety producing?

Client: Yes, at least some of them. The other thing that I've begun to do is make some of my husband's calls. You know . . . for things related to his business and our personal travel, airlines reservations and things like that.

Clinician: Wow, that's great. How does he like that?

Client: He thinks it great, too. He's busy with his new job and he really appreciates it.

PREDICTING LONG-TERM SUCCESS

Researchers have found it difficult to predict long-term success following treatment, and there are many behavioral, cognitive, and environmental variables to consider. As discussed earlier, speakers who, based on several behavioral and cognitive indicators, are determined to be more severe prior to treatment show higher levels of regression 1 and 2 years later (Huinck et al., 2006). Given the many variables that influence long-term change and the unique combination of factors for each speaker, the best approach to this issue is likely to be a multidimensional one. Andrews and Craig (1985, 1988), using a combination of three factors, found that 97% of the subjects who maintained

high skill mastery (0% syllables stuttered), normal speech attitudes as indicated by such measures as the Modified Erickson Scale of Communication Attitudes (S-24; Andrews & Cutler, 1974), and an internal locus of control as indicated by the Locus of Control of Behavior Scale (LCB; Craig et al., 1984) were able to maintain success. In fact, no speaker who failed to achieve any of these goals was able to maintain his or her posttreatment fluency level. Langevin et al. (2006) found that at 2 years posttreatment, the speakers classified as maintainers consistently had better scores on the S-24; the approach scale of the SESAS; and the struggle, avoidance, and expectancy subscales of the PSI than nonmaintainers.

Using a correlation approach, Craig (1998) considered the relationship between %SS at 10 and 18 months following treatment (an intensive fluency-shaping approach) and numerous pretreatment variables, including subject demographics (age, sex, and social status), stuttering severity (%SS), speech rate as measured in syllables per minute (SPM), health perceptions, self-reported avoidance and reaction to stuttering, neuroticism and extroversion, locus of control, formal practice, and attendance at self-help meetings, there were small to moderate correlations between follow-up %SS and pretreatment severity, %SS ($r = .424$), and SPM ($r = .515$). That is, those with greater stuttering and slower speech rates were more likely to stutter at follow-up. Finally, there was no single predictor variable that showed a strong correlation across the participants. In summarizing suggestions for preventing relapse and achieving long-term success following treatment, Craig suggested that success involves such things as practice of treatment activities and objectives that are achievable, using positive self-reinforcement, practicing self-monitoring skills, scheduling follow-up treatment, and emphasizing self-responsibility.

The LCB (Craig et al., 1984) has been considered as a predictor of speakers' ability to maintain the success achieved during formal treatment. Using such a measure is intuitively appealing. Early in treatment, clients typically indicate that stuttering is something over which they have no control (Van Riper, 1982). As treatment programs assist the speaker in the self-management of speech behavior and a cognitive reinterpretation of his or her circumstances (Adams, 1983; Kuhr & Rustin, 1985), the person begins to internalize these changes (Boberg et al., 1979). Craig et al. (1984) as well as Craig and Andrews (1985) demonstrated that changes in speakers' LCB scores toward more internal control during treatment are related to the long-term treatment outcome. In a related investigation, Madison et al. (1986) found that pretreatment locus of control (LOC) measures corresponded to the degree of change in stuttering following treatment for a group of 7- to 16-year-old children. That is, those children who had a more internal LOC prior to intervention tended to achieve more fluent speech during treatment. However, no significant relationship was found between pretreatment LOC scores and fluency levels during evaluations conducted at both 2 and 6 months following treatment. Alternatively, Ladouceur et al. (1989) found no relationship between LCB scores and fluency improvement in nine adults. Surprisingly, they found that some clients became more externally oriented during treatment while also acquiring increased fluency. Ladouceur et al. suggested that the changes in fluency and

internal control—at least as gauged by the LCB and behavior—might have had to do with the treatment protocol used and whether or not cognitive changes were a focus of therapy.

Another attempt to predict long-term success using the LCB scale was conducted by De Nil and Kroll (1995). They considered to what extent adult stutterers' scores on the LCB scale (Craig et al., 1984) are predictive of their ability to maintain speech fluency both immediately following intensive treatment and approximately 2 years later. Twenty-one subjects participated in a 3-week intensive treatment program based on the Precision Fluency Shaping Program (Webster, 1975). Thirteen subjects who were contacted again 2 years later participated in a follow-up evaluation, which consisted of the administration of several scales, the reading of a brief passage, and a conversation with a research assistant. All participants were seen by an unfamiliar assistant who was unaware of their previous performance. Furthermore, the assessment took place in a new and unfamiliar location. Although the participants showed a significant long-term improvement in fluency, no predictive relationship was found between scores on the LCB scale and level of fluency, as measured in percent words stuttered, during either posttreatment or follow-up. LCB scores were, however, found to be predictive of the subjects' fluency self-evaluation measured posttreatment and at follow-up. The results of the investigation suggest that although the LCB might contribute to the prediction of the long-term treatment outcome, particularly as perceived by the client, other client and process variables also need to be considered. Although it remains to be seen, the individualized narrative analysis provided by the Origins and Pawns scales (Westbrook & Viney, 1980) and the Origins and Paws calculator (OPC) discussed in Chapter 12 might provide a more accurate prediction of long-term success.

THE IMPORTANCE OF SUPPORT GROUPS

One of the more important influences on the long-term maintenance of treatment gains could be the client's involvement in self-help groups. Whether these groups are referred to as self-help, support, or advocacy groups, they all provide helpful sources of information and motivation for those who stutter as well as their families and friends. For speakers who have isolated themselves as a result of their stuttering, support groups are likely to be particularly valuable (see Crowe, 1997c). For the first time, the person finds that he or she is among others who share a common problem. The speaker finds that he or she is not alone and that this unique characteristic called stuttering that has, for so long, set him or her apart now provides a way to connect and bond with others. Although an empathetic clinician and successful treatment might promote dramatic decreases in isolation for a client, there is probably nothing as effective as a good support group for increasing people's ability to communicate and expand their world.

The meetings of the local support group chapters also furnish important opportunities to practice techniques and stabilize cognitive changes following formal treatment. The encouragement and support of the other members is difficult to overestimate and often results in enhanced motivation and assertiveness.

Group membership can also provide an important social function for some of the members, fostering interaction in an accepting, penalty-free environment. It is a place where members can continue the process of coming to terms with the problem. Through newsletters, Internet discussions, and meetings, the groups meet a variety of members' needs, including the facilitation of personal change, fostering of personal responsibility by members, provision of information and advice, discussion of alternative treatments, fundraising, and political activities relating to the goals of the group. Coming together with other people who have similar problems and goals is an empowering and exciting experience, and empathy and support from fellow travelers is all but assured. Importantly, this form of help can be obtained at relatively little cost. For all these reasons, Egan (1998) observed that self-help groups are one of the most popular sources of help for people with a variety of problems, and this is certainly the case for those who stutter.

It is important for clinicians who are serious about assisting those who stutter to have the experience of attending at least one (and hopefully many more) of the national meetings of the support groups (see Appendix A) that meet in various cities around the country. The largest of these groups in the United States are the National Stuttering Association and Friends. You will find that the experience is unique and distinctly different from professional meetings you have attended. The primary goal is to provide support by being with others—to observe people as they "let go" of hiding and avoiding and to witness magnificent acts of courage. The Clinical Insight that follows provides two examples.

CLINICAL INSIGHT

At a national meeting of Friends: The National Association of Young People Who Stutter, I wandered into an evening "jam session" where three talented members were playing guitars and inviting others to sing along. After an hour or so of singing, a young girl about 10 years old volunteered to sing a song. She slowly walked up to the front of the room and climbed up onto a stool. As she attempted to begin singing, she found herself blocking severely, unable to achieve any airflow or voicing. She was determined to sing her song and attempted to begin several times as the audience patiently waited. Recognizing her plight, another young girl, who appeared to be about the same age, came up from the audience and sat next to her on another stool. They whispered to each other for a moment and then, together, they faced the audience. The second girl began singing the song and was immediately joined by the first girl, and they sang the song together. It was a wonderful moment and the audience gave them a prolonged standing ovation as they finished.

In the same city some 17 years earlier I attended my first national meeting of the National Stuttering Association. One of the traditional and well-attended events is an "open mic" session. A microphone on a stand is placed in the middle of a large room and people are invited to say whatever they would like. In this instance there were approximately 300 people in the room. Of course, courage is required for most any speaker in accepting such a challenge, but particularly for those who stutter. A few people lined up to take a turn speaking before the large audience, most of them for the first time in their lives. A young woman at the end of the line eventually moved forward to take her turn. She attempted to speak but was able to say only the initial portion of the first word. The audience remained completely silent. Again and again she continued to block on the initial syllable. More than a minute passed before she gradually turned around and with tears streaming down her face, began to walk back to her seat. From somewhere in the audience someone quietly said, "Go ahead," once, twice, and then again. Others quickly joined in and soon the entire audience was repeating, "Go ahead!" The woman stopped, gradually turned around, and slowly approached the microphone again. After several more attempts she eventually said her name, explained how happy she was to be attending the meeting, and thanked everyone for their support. She also received a standing ovation from the entire audience, many of whom happily displayed their own tears. (WM)

In order to appreciate the nature of such groups, a brief history of two of them is provided here based on a description by Hunt (1987). The British Stammering Association (BSA) was founded in 1968. It is often the case in such groups that the initial development results from the efforts of one person (in this case, Robin Harrison) who is willing to dedicate many years of administrative, public relations, and fundraising activities in order to get the group organized and functional. The age range of the membership in the BSA was generally from 25 to 40 years, with few teenagers.

The average age of people in these groups is greater than those taking part in formal treatment tends to be, where few clients over the age of 50 are typically found. The size of most local groups was 4 to 6 members, ranging from as small as 2 to a rarely exceeded upper limit of 12. The most common goal reported by individual chapters was to transfer and maintain techniques learned in formal treatment. Although group members often practiced treatment techniques during the meetings, much of the discussion centered on adjusting to the cognitive aspects of being a person who stutters, including fears, anxieties, and feelings of inferiority, powerlessness, and frustration. Hunt (1987) reported that this was especially true for groups with "more mature members" who had achieved success in managing their speech.

Most of the local chapters tended to be short-lived, lasting for only 1 or 2 years. In order for a local group to continue for any length of time, strong leadership is essential. In addition, from time to time, the group needs to elicit the support of local speech-language pathologists for referrals as well as advice. Finally, as Hunt suggested, the group must discipline itself so that it will be more than a social group. It must have specific guidelines and objectives that focus on the self-management of communication and stuttering.

The largest self-help and mutual aid group in the United States is the National Stuttering Association (NSA). Originally founded by Michael Sugarman and Bob Goldman in 1977, it was known for more than 20 years as the National Stuttering Project (NSP). The purpose of this group is to provide information and support to children, adolescents, and adults who stutter; their families; and professional clinicians based on their guiding principle, *If You Stutter, You're Not Alone.*

The NSA operates a network of more than 125 local chapters for NSAKids, TWST (Teens Who STutter), and adults across the United States, as well as regional workshops, continuing education events, family fun days, and other local community activities. The NSA also produces *Letting Go*, a newsletter providing information and support in the form of uplifting articles, letters, stories, and reflections written by members. An informative website provides a wide variety of information on stuttering, community, research, and upcoming events, as well as links to related organizations. All these activities, as well as the Annual NSA Conference of more than 900 adults, adolescents, and children who stutter, their families, and speech professionals, are designed to educate, advocate, and instill a sense of solidarity and confidence in the members.

The specific goals of NSA are to provide an opportunity for members to share with others their fears, frustrations, and triumphs; practice therapeutic techniques in a safe and supportive environment; take part in speaking experiences they would otherwise be likely to avoid; develop positive cognitive and affective strategies for managing their fluency disorder; and assist members in achieving these goals.

Undoubtedly, the greatest virtue of support groups is the ability to provide members with a sense of relief from the feelings of isolation and establishment of contact with others who understand their distress and frustration (Hunt, 1987; Reeves, 2006). A survey conducted by Krauss-Lehrman and Reeves (1989) of 600 NSP members (142 questionnaires returned) indicated that the *least* important focus of the groups was to provide an adjunct to formal treatment. Ramig

(1993a) surveyed 62 support group participants, finding that 49 indicated that their fluency had improved "at least somewhat" as a direct result of their involvement in such groups. More important, 55 of the 62 respondents indicated that their participation in support groups had an "at least somewhat positive" or a "very positive" impact on their daily life. The results also suggested that members had to attend something approaching 20 meetings for these changes to take place.

Individuals who stutter and are active members of the NSA are somewhat unique among the many individuals who stutter. This is likely to be especially true for those who are able to attend the annual meeting of NSA. It could well be that these people have greater levels of motivation, time, and the financial ability to travel to and attend such meetings. Nevertheless, a survey of 71 individuals who participated in the 1999 annual meeting by Yaruss, Quesal, Reeves, et al. (2002) indicated that participation had "very positively" affected their self-image and acceptance of themselves. Only 6.1% of the participants indicated no effect, and no respondent indicated a negative impact.

There are a variety of interesting and important issues concerning the functioning of support groups and particularly their interaction with the professional community. For example, a description of self-help groups for individuals who stutter by Reeves (2006) describes a history of hostility regarding professional clinicians by some members. Some members felt (and in some instances rightly so) that they had received poor assistance from clinicians demonstrating a lack of knowledge and understanding about the nature of the stuttering experience. In

turn, some professional clinicians have been leery of self-help groups and the possibility of some members spreading inaccurate, uninformed, or counterproductive attitudes, information, and techniques. However, Cooper (1987), Silverman (1996), and Ramig (1993a) pointed out that the reason some clinicians tend to have a skeptical view of support groups is because they fail to understand the many positive aspects of group membership. Many clinicians recognize that support groups play an important, often critical role, in providing individuals with the support and encouragement essential for success both during and following treatment. It should also be pointed out that, as consumers of treatment services, self-help organizations provide a powerful and effective message to both professional and legislative groups for improved training and service delivery. In recent years there has been a positive and synergistic interaction of the major self-help groups in this country (NSA and Friends) and the professional community. Groups such as the International Stuttering Association (a self-help organization) and the International Fluency Association (a professional organization) have done much to bring together the two communities.

As a speech-language pathologist, it is good to keep in mind some suggestions about the experience of attending a national meeting of a support group. As Reeves (2006) put it, "The key factor is whether the focus is on the sharing of experiential knowledge and support rather than professional directed therapy" (p. 260). He further suggested that professional clinicians should focus less on "fixing" or "curing" the person who stutters by eradicating all occurrences of stuttering (which he viewed as an erroneous expectation for both parties) and think more in terms of providing the opportunity for the person to heal.

The McGuire program (David McGuire) is an international program run by individuals who are recovering or have recovered from stuttering. Along with being a support group, the program provides a rationale and techniques for therapy provided by the members. Because the members are not professional speech-language clinicians, the philosophy and associated techniques have received little study and, thus, lack empirical support. However, the program incorporates many of the therapeutic goals (increased fluency, improved communication, and greater autonomy and agency) described in Chapter 10. The activities and techniques of the program not only address speech and the achievement of fluency but also alter the many cognitive and affective aspects of the stuttering experience. Intended for persons age 16 or older, attendees of the 4-day intensive workshops are offered a holistic approach that emphasizes effective communication and a lifestyle of assertiveness. The therapeutic principles discussed in Chapter 12 (moving toward the problem, assuming responsibility for action, restructuring the cognitive understanding of the self and the problem, and recruiting the support of others) are addressed in a variety of ways. There is also an appreciation of the role of humor when experimenting with new techniques in different settings. To combat the problem of relapse and in recognition that continual practice is necessary, the program includes a support system available to all participants. Comprehensive support in the form of a primary coach is provided for the 12 months following the intensive workshop. In addition, support

is provided for the life of the individual and is international in scope, achieved via landline telephone, email, and Skype communications software. Individuals are encouraged to attend follow-up workshops in order to consolidate skills and enhance their understanding of techniques, as well as to assist others. Graduates of the program carry cards with a checklist of principles emphasizing effort and perseverance and related techniques such as "do not use tricks and cancel violations; do not avoid words, sounds, or situations; resist time pressure; establish eye contact; create air flow; coordinate breathing and articulation with forward movement and no holding back." Few programs have such an extensive system of member support, and this undoubtedly contributes to the enthusiastic participation in the McGuire Program.

MAINTENANCE ACTIVITIES

A basic theme in therapeutic or self-directed change is the requirement that the speaker gradually take the major responsibility for identifying and modifying his or her behaviors and choices concerning his or her situation (DiClemente, 1993; Egan, 2007). In the case of fluency disorders, the client must become increasingly knowledgeable about stuttering in general, and about his or her own stuttering in particular. The speaker must be able to recognize his or her choices and design responses for problem solving and effectively coping with his or her situation. Moreover, in order for ongoing change to occur, the speaker must do the majority of his or her practice outside the context of the treatment setting. To the degree that a person does well beyond the treatment environment during formal treatment, he or she will be likely to do well in those same situations during the months and years of informal treatment.

The following is a compilation of comments and suggestions for maintaining the changes accomplished during successful therapy. Many of these paraphrased suggestions are those by St. Louis and Westbrook (1987) along with recommendations by Van Riper (1958, 1973), Boberg (1983), Boberg and Kully (1984), Boberg and Sawyer (1977), Ryan (1979, 1980), Daly (1987), Dell (1970), Shames and Florance (1980), Howie et al. (1981), St. Louis (1982), Williams (1983), Craig (1998), and the authors of this text.

- Clinicians should not be surprised when a client experiences a relapse.
- The clinician can stress that it is natural and expected for the client's quantity and quality of his or her fluency to swing from greater to lesser amounts and that this does not need to be interpreted as a disastrous event. Speakers can think of a relapse as a temporary "lapse" and an opportunity to recommit to using cognitive and behavioral techniques.
- The clinician can make it clear to the client that continued consultation and support are available following the termination of formal treatment. Returning to treatment is likely to be an acceptable and wise choice.
- Treatment intensity can vary and decrease slowly, with individual sessions gradually occurring less often. Individual treatment sessions can be supplemented or replaced by attendance at group meetings.
- Treatment can be transformed from face-to-face meetings to contact via the telephone, the Internet, and video and audio recordings.
- Recordings made during treatment by the speaker can be used to engender practice and encouragement in the person's home environment.
- Prior to dismissal from formal treatment, the clinician and client can consider the reasons for and indications of relapse and design specific coping responses.
- The speaker can join and become an active member of a national support group for children and adults who stutter, possibly assuming a leadership role.
- Following treatment, the speaker can assertively seek new and challenging speaking situations where the envelope of comfort can gradually be expanded. If professional or social contacts do not provide such opportunities, the client could join groups such as Toastmasters or Dale Carnegie.
- The speaker can contact local groups and organizations to talk about his or her interests, therapy experiences, and professional skills. Libraries are often interested in finding such speakers.
- The speaker could consider contacting local agencies that need volunteers to read newspapers or books on tape to older people who cannot read or to the blind.
- The speaker can expand his or her assertive and risk-taking behaviors for both speech and nonspeech activities, expanding and cultivating other talents and interests.
- The speaker can continue to reassess opportunities for changes in his or her lifestyle, including possible alteration

of interpersonal, vocational, and social roles.

■ The speaker can continue to improve and expand on a variety of nonspeaking skills that are likely to enhance his or her participation in life and his or her interaction with others.

■ The speaker can continue to monitor and evaluate his positive-negative self-talk, using stopping and positive redirection activities.

■ The speaker can practice the use of positive affirmations on a regular basis.

■ The speaker can take part in cognitive behavioral mindfulness techniques that decrease anxiety and fear of social interactions.

■ Individuals can be taught to identify potentially high-risk situations regarding lifestyle, negative moods, or threatening environments, and develop methods of coping with these situations.

■ The client can volunteer to work in a treatment setting with adults and children who stutter.

■ The client can read selections of the Stuttering Foundation of America's Advice to those who stutter (Publication No. 9) and practice the suggestions contained in the chapters.

CLINICAL INSIGHT

Adult male, age 53: Basically, I want to share that striving for perfection impeded my improvement. I read about William Jennings Bryan (the golden tongued orator), and he was my goal. When I readjusted my sights to become "as fluent as my motor system would allow," then I started to make progress. I had gradual progress over a 3- or 4-year period, with occasional relapses and real breakdowns (like when three people very close to me—one my mother—died within a 2-week period). My speech suffered tremendously, but even then I knew that I was grieving and when I grew strong again, and focused attention to my speech again, that I would regain my fluency. I never doubted that. My belief system remained positive that I would speak fluently again, as fluently as my timing system or motor coordination abilities would allow. But striving for perfection was abandoned as unrealistic, and really as unnecessary for success and happiness.

Also, when I took my stuttering out from under the microscope and saw that disfluencies were only a part of me—that helped. When I saw that other qualities (like being a good friend, listener, and caring person to others) were also a part of who and what I was—then I put speech (stuttered or fluent) in a proper perspective. I worked on using light pressure on my first sounds, sure, but also on improving tennis or sailing skills, too—and becoming a better administrator and writer, etc. Putting disfluencies in perspective helped—I realized that our Creator may have more challenges in store for me other than just becoming a perfect speaker. So I decided to work not only on fluency but on other "talents" I have, too. That thinking seemed to send me in a more positive direction.

CLINICAL INSIGHT

Adult male, age 52: I completed an intensive program of treatment in my mid-20s. During the 20-week period of formal treatment, I learned how to decrease my avoidance and postponement behaviors, major characteristics of my stuttering. I found that I had choices about how I stuttered and began to do so with less effort rather than constantly trying so hard not to stutter. Cognitive and affective change occurred at a much slower pace. For several years I experienced high levels of anxiety prior to and during many speaking situations. When speaking to groups during lectures and other presentations, my focus was at least as much on my fluency and the possibility of stuttering as it was the content of the presentation. The progress wasn't linear but over time I gradually saw that I had the ability to take part in more challenging speaking situations. With continued experience I discovered that I was capable of speaking to audiences of all sizes. Best of all, I realized how much I enjoyed the opportunity of interacting with the audience, something I never imagined I would experience. The threat of stuttering was completely absent, and I became spontaneously fluent. Nonetheless, I am pleased to tell people that I have a history of stuttering. Stuttering is an important and valued part of my history. But it's no longer the dominant theme of my story

THE BENEFITS OF STUTTERING?

Although it is difficult to imagine any advantages associated with being a person who stutters, on several occasions authors (e.g., Montgomery, 2006; Sheehan, 1970; Van Riper 1973) have suggested that children or adults could achieve some secondary gain by being excused from unpleasant or fearful situations or being able to escape responsibilities such as class presentations or receive less than the usual discipline by parents or teachers. "Sure, I get what good I can out of my stuttering. I get out of many responsibilities; I've got a good excuse for not trying" (Van Riper, 1973, p. 227). Of course such "benefits" are not really beneficial as they are likely to encourage the individual to escalate his or her patterns of avoidance, decrease his or her motivation to take part in therapy, and possibly reinforce other undesirable coping strategies.

Nevertheless, it seems worthwhile for us to consider interesting, alternative perspectives about communicating with others while stuttering as offered by Christopher Constantino in a presentation on the 2016 International Stuttering Awareness Day Online Conference. The following are a series of brief excerpts from his paper (https://isad.live/isad-2016/papers-presented-by-2016/stories-and-experiences-with-stuttering-by-pws/stuttering-gain-christopher-constantino/).

Do we gain anything from stuttering? Instead of saying that stuttering is OK, can we bring ourselves to say that stuttering is good or advantageous? What experiences do we have access to that fluent people do not? What would we lose by ceasing to stutter? All our lives society has taught us that stuttering is worse than fluency. Stuttering is defined as a disordered form of fluent speech, speech that fails to achieve some predetermined percentage of fluent syllables. However, this is a false dichotomy. Yes, fluency is more common. Yes, stuttering can be hard. Blocking is tough. Getting stuck is frustrating. Nevertheless, stuttering is so much more than our disfluencies. Stuttering is not merely a less fluent or more disfluent way of communicating. It is an entirely different way of communicating. The difference between stuttering and fluency is not a matter of quantity of disfluency; rather it is in the quality of experience. The experience of stuttering, the effort, the unpredictability, the movement (or lack of movement) of tongue and lips, the flood of memories, the quickening of pulse, this is all so much more than part-word repetition, prolongations, and blocks. The experiences we have while stuttering are something fluent speakers do not have access to, and I am glad to have them. Stuttering adds to our speech.

What strikes me about our stuttering is its ability to disrupt the expected flow of a conversation. Much of human communication is routine and automatic. People often speak without actually communicating anything, they engage in a ritualized exchange of mundane phrases in a rehearsed rhythm that requires little thought. Heuristic phrases and trite clichés turn potentially new and exciting situations into familiar and rehearsed routines.

Stuttering shatters this ritual. The irregular rhythms of our speech allow for open and honest communication. When people speak to us, it breaks them out of their routine. They cannot anticipate our responses. They hear our words more clearly than the words of fluent speakers because they are less

predictable. Our stuttering introduces novelty and excitement into conversations making them instantly more interesting and memorable for our speaking partners. This is something we gain by stuttering.

The unexpectedness of stuttering forces both listener and speaker into a space of trust and vulnerability. They must both give up control of the situation. The person speaking does not know when and for how long he or she will stutter. Likewise, the person listening does not know when to expect a stutter. In order for both people to communicate, they must trust one another. This ability to make normal, everyday conversations intimate and sincere is unavailable to the fluent speaker. While talking about the weather, we bare our souls. While stuttering on our names during a handshake, we change an introduction into an intimate moment of vulnerability—the handshake becomes a hug. Fluent speakers do not have access to that. Just by saying hello, we deeply connect with another person.

Every moment of stuttering is an exercise in trust, a verbal trust fall. We are asking the person we are speaking with to catch us. When that person does, we build trust and strengthen the relationship. Luckily, if they happen to let us fall, we do not hit the ground. We may get embarrassed, but we will not get hurt. Vulnerability does not come without risks. In order to be truly vulnerable we must take a chance. Fortunately, with stuttering the rewards greatly outweigh the risks. The risk of stuttering and not being listened to is a funny look. The reward of stuttering and being heard is a deeply intimate connection with another human being. I encourage us to take this risk.

Our stuttered words carry more weight than our fluent words. Their irregular rhythm makes them memorable. Our pauses, hesitations, and silences carry semantic weight; they are meaningful and purposeful. They say, "I am not perfect." They say, "I take risks." They say, "I trust you." They say, "Uncertainty is ok." The silence of stuttering should not be viewed, "as a lack, an absence, or negation but rather as an important and even vital aspect of the fabric of discourse" (Mazzei, 2007, p. xii). This silence can be both humbling and strong. This silence is not simply what happens when we stop talking. It has a function. There is a beauty in this silence. It is the beauty of words not yet spoken. This silence gives the words we do manage to say more meaning, it acts as the negative space around which our words are shown in stark relief. Our silence is "pregnant with what is to be said but cannot be said, just yet" (Mazzei, 2007, p. 35).

All we have to do to make a profoundly humble and vulnerable connection with someone else is to speak and to stutter. Our stuttering is an open door, an invitation for others to relate to us in ways they would be unable to if we did not stutter. Our stutters allow us to build deeper and more personal connections than we would be able to as fluent speakers.

I have had many deeply personal conversations with other people because my stuttering allowed them to feel comfortable talking with me. They have explicitly told me that my stuttering has made me approachable and relatable. Listening to me share my stutter with them allows them the space to share personal stories of their own with me. People have related my stuttering to their own struggles with race, sexuality, and gender. On a flight, a woman sitting next to me heard me stutter to the flight attendant. She asked me what stuttering was like and then shared with me some of her own tribulations. I have had people share intimate details of their lives without having to prompt or ask them. They hear me stutter and they know it is safe to open up and be vulnerable. I have come to know people better than I ever could have as a fluent speaker.

The conversations I have at conferences and support group meetings change my life in profound ways. I have been to very few places where I have felt the kind of love that I feel around other people who stutter. What we have in our communities is special. It is valuable. My relationships with my stuttering friends make me a better person. Stuttering has given me friendships, it has given me opportunities, and it has brought me to places I never thought I would be.

We must encourage each other to keep on talking in spite of our difficulties. One percent of the population stutters. That is a lot of people. Yet we hear very little stuttering in our everyday lives. That is not because people who stutter are not out there, it is because the people who stutter who are out there are not talking. Every time we stutter, we make it a safer place for those people to talk. Every time we stutter, we show someone else what stuttering sounds like. Every time we stutter, we show someone how smart and funny people who stutter are. Every time we stutter, we make it easy for another person to stutter.

Stuttering pride means demanding recognition for what our voices add to the conversation, not for what they lack. However, only when we come to value stuttering will our stuttering pride position become coherent. Other people will not value our stuttering if we cannot value it ourselves. Every time we stutter with a smile, we help spread our message. This will not be easy. Nevertheless, we assuage some of the difficulty when we are able to define what we gain from stuttering. Our stuttering offers us a richness of experience that we would be missing out on should we speak fluently. Our stuttering allows us to be vulnerable and intimate in ways that fluent people cannot be. It allows us to build relationships and communicate in ways that fluent people cannot communicate. Stuttering impregnates our silences with meaning and makes our words stand out. Stuttering makes our voices unique and one of a kind. Stuttering enhances communication and friendship in ways unavailable to the fluent speaker. What does your stuttering do for you?

CONCLUSION

Throughout this chapter, we have described the importance of activities for transferring and maintaining behavioral techniques and cognitive changes acquired during treatment to communication situations beyond the therapy settings. Most speakers who are beginning therapy have much to learn about themselves and their stuttering, and some will require more time than others to become desensitized to stuttering and make better choices. Transfer activities can and

should begin as early as possible for both children and adults. Performance during daily activities with the stress of time pressure and competition for communication is the true test for building confidence in the ability to employ preferred coping responses. Many of the suggestions for continued progress apply to children as well as older speakers. For younger speakers, of course, parent involvement and understanding of the treatment process are critical for supporting and reinforcing the desired progress at all levels of change.

Although many important victories occur throughout treatment, progress must continue long after formal intervention has been completed. Unfortunately, as is the case with many complex human problems, relapse is not unusual, particularly for adults. Emphasis on transfer and maintenance activities beyond the treatment environment will help decrease the possibility of relapse. Following formal treatment, continued persistence, vigilance, and effort are required for continuing success. It is important for the speaker to understand that a small lapse does not mean that a deep and lengthy relapse is imminent. Fluctuations in fluency as well as the speaker's confidence to make good decisions are to be expected. But as those people who have successfully managed their stuttering have informed us, it is important to understand success in the larger context. These speakers have been able to not only achieve improved fluency but also to enhance their ability to communicate with others and achieve an agentic and satisfying lifestyle.

It is also important to realize that other individuals in the client's environment will need to adjust not only to the speaker's newly acquired fluency but also to reformed relationships and altered roles.

Family members and friends might need to adapt to a speaker who has become considerably more assertive. Membership in one or more support groups both during and following treatment is highly recommended for maintaining both behavioral and attitudinal changes. There is an ever-increasing source of useful information available from the Internet as well as materials provided by support groups. If treatment is successful, the client must gradually assume the responsibility for self-evaluating and systematically altering both the surface and intrinsic features of stuttering. He or she could also begin to enjoy ever-expanding participation in many areas of life he or she has so energetically avoided in the past.

Several years ago in one of the Internet discussion groups, I read and cited (Manning, 1999a) some insightful comments by an adult female who stuttered. She described her ability to successfully manage her stuttering in terms of her freedom to not hide her stuttering, to talk gently, and to be comfortable in speaking situations. Her description of how she manifested this freedom speaks to the central importance of assisting individuals to manage the fear of stuttering and live an agentic lifestyle. Her guidelines included the following:

no longer chasing the fluency god,

obtaining treatment as necessary,

living without constant fear of uncontrolled stuttering,

using the telephone without fear,

speaking without scanning for feared words and situations,

initiating conversations rather than choosing to be silent,

speaking for herself rather than relying on others,

choosing to speak even if she believes she may stutter,

selecting leisure and career options that require talking without worrying about the possibility of stuttering,

stuttering gently without avoidance or shame.

These guidelines nicely summarize the primary goals of both therapeutic and self-directed change for individuals who stutter as described in Chapter 10. Certainly, improving fluency is an obvious goal for people who stutter, but the ability to communicate regardless of the possibility or the reality of stuttering is much more important to many people. Even more important is the ability to achieve a clear decrease in the anxiety and fear associated with the stuttering experience and to fully participate in life as he or she becomes a fully independent and autonomous person.

❓ TOPICS FOR DISCUSSION

1. Describe how a clinician's limited view of the speaker during and following treatment could prevent a full understanding about the overall process of therapeutic change.

2. What are some possible causes of posttreatment relapse?

3. What are some of the initial indicators of relapse?

4. Describe several ways to prepare a speaker for the possibility of a lapse or relapse following successful treatment.

5. What speaker characteristics could help to predict relapse (or long-term success) following treatment?

6. Using sources beyond this text, obtain the names, contact information, and goals of the major self-help groups for individuals who stutter around the world.

7. Describe the history and evolving nature of the relationship between self-help and professional communities.

📖 RECOMMENDED READINGS

Boberg, E. (1983). Behavioral transfer and maintenance programs for adolescent and adult stutterers. In J. Fraser Gruss (Ed.), *Stuttering therapy: Transfer and maintenance* (Publication No. 19, pp. 41–61). Stuttering Foundation of America.

Craig, A. (1998). Relapse following treatment for stuttering: A critical review and correlative data. *Journal of Fluency Disorders, 23,* 1–30.

DiLollo, A., Manning, W. H., & Neimeyer, R. A. (2005). Cognitive complexity as a function of speaker role for adult persons who stutter. *Journal of Constructivist Psychology, 18,* 215–236.

Fransella, F. (1972). *Personal change and reconstruction.* Academic Press.

Hood, S. B. (2003). *Advice to those who stutter* (Publication No. 9). Stuttering Foundation of America.

Manning, W. H. (1999). Progress under the surface and over time. In N. B. Ratner & E. C. Healey (Eds.), *Stuttering research and practice: Bridging the gap* (pp. 123–129). Erlbaum.

Useful Links for Information and Support

AMERICAN BOARD OF FLUENCY AND FLUENCY DISORDERS

http://www.stutteringspecialists.org/

Board Certified Specialists in Fluency are individuals who hold their Certificate of Clinical Competence (CCC) awarded by the American Speech-Language-Hearing Association and have demonstrated a high level of knowledge and clinical expertise in diagnosing and treating individuals with fluency disorders. They are designated as Board Certified Specialists in Fluency (BCS-F). To become a BCS-F, a candidate must meet knowledge and skill standards set by the American Board of Fluency and Fluency Disorders that include a specified number of clinical hours working with persons who stutter of all ages and accrual of a substantial number of continuing education hours in fluency disorders. Maintenance of this certification requires continuing clinical and educational activity.

The American Board of Fluency and Fluency Disorders website provides resources for clinicians and persons who stutter, including a way to search for BCS-F clinicians.

THE STUTTERING FOUNDATION

http://www.stutteringhelp.org/

The Stuttering Foundation is a nonprofit organization for helping people who stutter, with headquarters in Memphis, Tennessee. Their website has a lot of resources, many of which are free, for persons who stutter, clinicians, and parents of children who stutter. They also have sections specifically for kids and teens. The website provides a link to the Stuttering Foundation Podcast, that provides monthly episodes that include clinical discussions, research updates, and personal stories of stuttering.

THE NATIONAL STUTTERING ASSOCIATION

http://www.westutter.org/

The National Stuttering Association (NSA) is a national self-help organization for people who stutter. They help people who stutter get in touch with other people who stutter so they can support each other and make friends. They have support groups all over the country, and they hold a national conference each year where hundreds of people who stutter get together to discuss their experiences and all the latest news about stuttering. The website also includes a lot of information about stuttering and resources for persons who stutter, families, and clinicians.

FRIENDS: THE NATIONAL ASSOCIATION FOR YOUNG PEOPLE WHO STUTTER

https://www.friendswhostutter.org/

FRIENDS is a great organization for young people who stutter. They hold 1-day workshops around the country and also have a larger yearly conference. This is another great way for young persons who stutter

to meet other people their age who stutter. The website has some great resources on stuttering, including their Stuttering 101 page that provides a lot of basic information about stuttering that is easy for young people to read and understand.

STUTTERTALK

http://stuttertalk.com/

StutterTalk is a website that publishes podcasts about stuttering, often featuring people who stutter, as well as clinicians and researchers. There are hundreds of great podcasts to listen to about every topic related to stuttering. You can search their database of podcasts for topics that interest you by entering them in the search bar in the upper right-hand corner of the page.

The Fluency Bank

https://fluency.talkbank.org/

The following information is provided by Nan Bernstein Ratner.

In many fields, it has become clear that establishing open-access repositories of data under careful curation can enable research progress in significant ways, through combining sources of data gathered from additional and different groups of subjects, as well as reanalysis of previously gathered basic research data. The best known example of this type of initiative is CHILDES (the Child Language Data Exchange System), established in the mid-1980s by Brian MacWhinney (Carnegie Mellon University) and Catherine Snow (Harvard). This site, which collects child language development data from typical as well as atypically developing children across dozens of language communities, has fostered literally thousands of novel peer-reviewed research articles since its inception. As the benefits of such community-wide collaboration became clear, CHILDES was followed by AphasiaBank, then by PHON (for the analysis of phonological acquisition and disorder), and finally by Home-Bank (for the analysis of the growing number of LENA recordings [daylong recordings of children and families conducted for a wide array of research questions]). Col-

lectively, these initiatives have been subsumed under the broader, permanent initiative now called TalkBank (http://www.talkbank.org), managed by Brian MacWhinney at Carnegie Mellon University. TalkBank utilities are increasingly being translated from basic research use to everyday clinical use through development of clinician-friendly free bundled computer-assisted analyses.

The field of fluency disorders has recently joined TalkBank with National Institutes of Health (NIH) and National Science Foundation (NSF) support for FluencyBank. Jointly managed by Brian MacWhinney and Nan Bernstein Ratner at the University of Maryland, this site is designed to recruit and curate data from fluency researchers around the world, both past and current. It aspires to preserve data from some of the most important published research in fluency for open-access use. FluencyBank's unique attributes include support for media-linked transcripts (so that users can view and hear research participants), specific dedicated coding for fluency analysis, and fluency analysis routines that can speed and deepen analysis of spoken data collected by fluency researchers. FluencyBank already devotes a segment of its site to a teaching resources area for professors and students.

EPILOGUE

There is no greater joy nor greater reward than to make a fundamental difference in someone's life.

—Mary Rose McGeady

It has been said that the process of writing a book is never really done, it is just that the writer(s) must eventually decide to finish. Of course, the minute you finish, the new information that is constantly becoming available begins the aging process of what you have created. But eventually you must decide to stop and let what you have done represent your best effort.

The experience of reading, understanding, and synthesizing the information you discover is continually fascinating and often paradoxical. Writing can be an isolating, sometimes lonely process, as it must be, in order to be alone with your thoughts about what you are reading, synthesizing, and writing. But you are connecting with others around the world and across time through the words and ideas in their manuscripts. You find out what you know, and you quickly find out what you do not know or clearly understand. Sometimes you are delighted with a section you have written, and often, just hours or days later, you are disillusioned as you reread the same material. You are both challenged and energized by the creative process. But you realize that eventually you will have to let go of what you have crafted.

Throughout the many months of preparing these chapters, we often returned to the primary goal that continued to surface above all the others—the development of enthusiasm in those clinicians who desire to assist children, adolescents, and adults who have difficulty communicating fluently. Enthusiasm can be enhanced by exploration in the form of continued learning and the development of expertise, not because a professional organization mandates continuing education, but because of the enjoyment of continually expanding our understanding about the possibilities for assisting those who stutter. Just as we encourage those we are trying to help to take action and expand their ability to communicate and to enhance the quality of their lives, the professional clinician must continually take action by seeking new information and experiment with alternative strategies and techniques.

With an understanding of the many possibilities and choices of intervention, the experienced and wise clinician is free to focus on the needs of the person who has come to him or her for help. Rather than concentrating on doctrine or techniques, the professional is able to employ critical thinking in order to make clinical decisions based on empirically supported research, years of experience, and eventually the moment-by-moment perception of a client's needs and possibilities. As we come to understand individuals and their stories, we become adept at enabling people to consider and select the options that are best for them. As we have suggested throughout this book, although we might become experts about fluency problems, our clients are the authorities about their own lives.

Clinicians who make the decision to spend a significant portion of their lives assisting people with fluency problems need to know that magnificent changes are possible in the speech and the lives of even the most severely involved individuals. Timely and effective treatment can help the young child who stutters to live a life free of stuttering with no memory of the experience. Adults who have stuttered and suffered for decades can achieve the ability to live a life in which speech is spontaneous and enjoyable. They can learn to appreciate the joys of communicating with their fellow travelers perhaps more than those who were never constrained by stuttering for so many years. They can experience the ability to participate in speaking situations they never imagined possible and achieve goals they never thought achievable.

More than anything, however, for those who choose to come to the assistance of people who stutter—people who are struggling to connect with others and struggling to find fulfillment as human beings—there are many profound connections, rewarding victories, marvelous colleagues, and great adventures to be enjoyed!

REFERENCES

Abe, K., Yokoyama, R., & Yorifuji, S. (1993). Repetitive speech disorder resulting from infarcts in the paramedian thalami and mid brain. *Journal of Neurology, Neurosurgery and Psychiatry, 56*, 1024–1026.

Achenbach, T. M., & Rescorla, L. A. (2000). *Manual for the ASEBA preschool forms & profiles.* University of Vermont Center for Children, Youth, & Families. Ainsworth.

Adams, M. R. (1977a). A clinical strategy for differentiating the normal nonfluent child and the incipient stutterers. *Journal of Fluency Disorders, 2*, 141–148.

Adams, M. R. (1977b). The young stutterer: Diagnosis, treatment and assessment of progress. *Seminars in Speech, Language and Hearing, 1*, 289–299.

Adams, M. R. (1983). Learning from negative outcomes in stuttering therapy: Getting off on the wrong foot. *Journal of Fluency Disorders, 8*, 147–153.

Adams, M. R. (1984). The differential assessment and direct treatment of stuttering. In J. Costello (Ed.), *Speech disorders in children* (pp. 260–295). College-Hill Press.

Adams, M. R. (1990). The Demands And Capacities Model I: Theoretical elaborations. *Journal of Fluency Disorders, 15*, 135–141.

Adams, M. R. (1993). The home environment of children who stutter. *Seminars in Speech and Language, 14*(3), 185–191.

Adams, M. R., & Hayden, P. (1976). The ability of stutterers and nonstutterers to initiate and terminate phonation during production of an isolated vowel. *Journal of Speech and Hearing Disorders, 19*, 290–296.

Adams, M. R., & Runyan, C. (1981). Stuttering and fluency: Exclusive events or points on a continuum? *Journal of Fluency Disorders, 6*, 197–218.

Agnello, J. G. (1975). Voice onset and voice termination features of stutterers. In L. M. Webster & L. C. Furst (Eds.), *Vocal tract dynamics and disfluency* (pp. 40–70). Speech and Hearing Institute.

Ahn, H., & Wampold, B. E. (2001). Where oh where are the specific ingredients? A meta-analysis of component studies in counseling and psychotherapy. *Journal of Counseling Psychology, 48*, 251–257.

Alfonso, P. J., Watson, B. C., & Baer, T. (1987). Measuring stutterers' dynamic vocal tract characteristics by x-ray microbeam pellet tracking. In H. F. M. Peters & W. Hulstijn (Eds.), *Speech motor dynamics in stuttering* (pp. 141–150). Springer-Verlag.

Allen, G. (1975). Speech rhythm: Its relation to performance universals and articulatory timing. *Journal of Phonetics, 3*, 75–86.

Allport, G. W. (1961). *Pattern and growth in personality.* Holt, Rinehart and Winston.

Alm, P. A. (2004). Stuttering and the basal ganglia circuits. *Journal of Communication Disorders, 37*, 325–369.

Ambrose, N. G. (2004). Theoretical perspectives on the cause of stuttering. *Contemporary Issues in Communication Science and Disorders, 31*, 80–91.

Ambrose, N. G., Cox, N., & Yairi, E. (1997). The genetic basis of persistent and recovered stuttering. *Journal of Speech and Hearing Research, 40*, 567–580.

Ambrose, N. G., & Yairi, E. (1994). The development of awareness of stuttering in preschool children. *Journal of Fluency Disorders, 19*, 229–246.

Ambrose, N. G., & Yairi, E. (1999). Normative disfluency data for early childhood stuttering. *Journal of Speech, Language, and Hearing Research, 42*, 895–909.

Ambrose, N. G., & Yairi, E. (2002). The Tudor Study: Data and ethics. *American Journal of Speech-Language Pathology, 11*, 190–204.

Ambrose, N. G., Yairi, E., & Cox, N. (1993). Genetic factors in childhood stuttering. *Journal of Speech and Hearing Research, 36*, 701–706.

Ambrose, N. G., Yairi, E., Loucks, T. M., Seery, C. H., & Throneburg, R. (2015). Relation of motor, linguistic and temperamental factors in epidemiologic subtypes of persistent and recovered stuttering: Initial findings. *Journal of Fluency Disorders, 45*, 12–26.

American Psychiatric Association. (1994). *Diagnostic and statistical manual of mental disorders* (4th ed.).

American Psychiatric Association. (2000). *Diagnostic and statistical manual of mental disorders* (4th ed., Text rev.).

American Psychiatric Association. (2013). *Diagnostic and statistical manual of mental disorders* (5th ed.). https://doi.org/10.1176/appi.books.9780890425596

American Psychiatric Association. (2022). *Diagnostic and statistical manual of mental disorders* (5th ed., Text rev.).

American Psychological Association. (1947). Recommended graduate training program in clinical psychology: Report of the committee on training in clinical psychology. *American Psychologist, 2*, 539–558.

American Psychological Association. (2019). *Publication manual of the American Psychological Association* (7th ed.).

American Speech-Language-Hearing Association. (n.d.). *Cultural responsiveness.* https://www.asha.org/Practice-Portal/Professional-Issues/Cultural-Responsiveness/

American Speech-Language-Hearing Association. (1984). Guidelines for case-load size for speech-language services in the schools. *ASHA, 26*, 53–58.

American Speech-Language-Hearing Association. (1995). Guidelines for practice in stuttering treatment. *ASHA, 37*(Suppl. 14), 26–35.

American Speech-Language-Hearing Association. (2004). *Preferred practice patterns for the profession of speech-language pathology.*

American Speech-Language-Hearing Association. (2005). *Evidence-based practice in communication disorders* [Position statement]. http://www.asha.org/members/deskrefjournals/deskref/default

American Speech-Language-Hearing Association. (2015a). *Guidelines for the clinical doctorate in speech-language pathology.*

American Speech-Language-Hearing Association. (2015b). *The role of undergraduate education in communication sciences and disorders.*

American Speech-Language-Hearing Association. (2015c). *Strategic pathway to excellence.*

American Speech-Language-Hearing Association. (2016). *Scope of practice in speech-language pathology* [Scope of practice]. http://www.asha.org/policy

American Speech-Language-Hearing Association. (2023). *Code of Ethics* [Ethics]. http://www.asha.org/policy

Amman, J. O. C. (1965). *A dissertation on speech.* StechertHafner. (Original work published 1700)

Anderson, J. D. (2008). Age of acquisition and repetition priming effects on picture naming of children who do and do not stutter. *Journal of Fluency Disorders, 33*(2), 135–155.

Anderson, J. D., & Conture, E. G. (2000). Language abilities of children who stutter: A preliminary study. *Journal of Fluency Disorders, 25*, 283–304.

Anderson, J. D., & Conture, E. G. (2004). Sentence-structure priming in young children who do and do not stutter. *Journal of Speech, Language and Hearing Research, 47*, 552–571.

Anderson, J. D., Pellowski, M., & Conture, E. G. (2005). Childhood stuttering and dissociations across linguistic domains. *Journal of Fluency Disorders, 30*, 219–253.

Anderson, J., Pellowski, M., Conture, E., & Kelly E. (2003). Temperament characteristics of young children who stutter. *Journal of Speech, Language and Hearing Research, 46,* 1221–1233.

Anderson, J. D., Wagovich, S. A., & Hall, N. E. (2006). Nonword repetition skills in young children who do and do not stutter. *Journal of Fluency Disorders, 31,* 177–199.

Anderson, S. K., & Handelsman, M. M. (2010). *Ethics for psychotherapists and counselors: A proactive approach.* Wiley Blackwell.

Anderson, T. K., & Felsenfeld, S. (2003). A thematic analysis of late recovery from stuttering. *American Journal of Speech-Language Pathology, 12,* 243–253.

Andrews, G. (1984). Epidemiology of stuttering. In R. F. Curlee & W. H. Perkins (Eds.), *Nature and treatment of stuttering: New directions* (pp. 1–12). College-Hill Press.

Andrews, G., & Craig, A. R. (1985). The prediction and prevention of relapse in stuttering. The value of self-control techniques and locus of control measures. *Behavior Modification, 9,* 427–442.

Andrews, G., & Craig, A. R. (1988). Prediction of outcome after treatment for stuttering. *British Journal of Psychiatry, 153,* 236–240.

Andrews, G., Craig, A., & Feyer, A. M. (1983). Stuttering: A review of research findings and theories circa 1982. *Journal of Speech and Hearing Disorders, 48,* 226–246.

Andrews, G., & Cutler, J. (1974). Stuttering therapy: The relation between changes in symptom level and attitudes. *Journal of Speech and Hearing Disorders, 39,* 312–319.

Andrews, G., Guitar, B., & Howie. P. (1980). Meta-analysis of the effects of stuttering treatment. *Journal of Speech and Hearing Disorders, 45,* 287–307.

Andrews, G., & Harris, M. (1964). *The syndrome of stuttering* (Clinics in Developmental Medicine No. 17). Spastics Society Medical Education and Information Unit, in association with W. Heinemann Medical Books.

Andrews, G., & Harvey, R. (1981). Regression to the mean in pretreatment measures of stuttering. *Journal of Speech and Hearing Disorders, 46,* 204–207.

Andrews, G., & Ingham, R. J. (1971). Stuttering: Considerations in the evaluation of treatment. *British Journal of Disorders of Communication, 6*(2), 129–138. https://doi.org/10.3109/13682827109011538

Andrews, G., & Neilson, M. (1981). *Stuttering: A state of the art seminar* [Paper presentation]. Annual Meeting of the Speech-Hearing Association, Los Angeles, CA.

Andrews, G., Yates-Morris, A., Howie, P., & Martin, N. G. (1991). Genetic factors in stuttering confirmed. *Archives of General Psychiatry, 48*(11), 1034–1035.

Apel, K. (1999). Checks and balances: Keeping the science in our profession. *Language, Speech, and Hearing Services in Schools, 30,* 99–108.

Armson, J., & Kiefte, M. (2008). The effect of SpeechEasy on stuttering frequency, speech rate, and speech naturalness. *Journal of Fluency Disorders, 33,* 120–134.

Armson, J., Kiefte, M., Mason, J., & De Croos, C. (2006). The effect of SpeechEasy on stuttering frequency in laboratory conditions. *Journal of Fluency Disorders, 31,* 137–152.

Armson, J., & Stuart, A. (1998). Effect of extended exposure to frequency-altered feedback on stuttering during reading and monologue. *Journal of Speech, Language, and Hearing Research, 41,* 479–490.

Arnold, G. E. (1960). Studies in tachyphemia: I. Present concepts of etiologic factors. *Logos, 3,* 25–45.

Arnold, H. S., Conture, E. G., Key, A. P. F., & Walden, T. (2011). Emotional reactivity, regulation and childhood stuttering: A behavioral and electrophysiological study. *Journal of Communication Disorders, 44,* 276–293.

Arnold, H. S., MacPherson, M. K., & Smith, A. (2014). Autonomic correlates of speech versus nonspeech tasks in children and adults. *Journal of Speech, Language, and Hearing Research, 27,* 1296–1307.

Arnott, N. (1928). *Elements of physics.* Adams.

Aronson, A. E. (1992). *Clinical voice disorders: An interdisciplinary approach.* Thieme.

Attanasio, J. (1987). The dodo was Lewis Carroll you see: Reflections and speculations. *Journal of Fluency Disorders, 12,* 107–118.

Attanasio, J. (1997). Was Moses a person who stuttered? Perhaps not. *Journal of Fluency Disorders, 22*, 65–68.

Au-Yeung, J., Howell, P., Davis, S., Charles, N., & Sackin, S. (2000, August). *UCL survey on bilingualism and stuttering* [Paper presentation]. Third World Congress on Fluency Disorders, Nyborg, Denmark. http://www.speech.psychol.ucl.ac.uk/survey1/paper/ifapaper.html

Ayre, A., & Wright, L. (2009). WASSP: An international review of its clinical application. *International Journal of Speech-Language Pathology, 11*(1), 83–90.

Azios, M., Rangarathnam, B., Jianyuan, N., Irani, F., Bellon-Ham, M., & Manchaiah, V. (2022). Twitter usage about stuttering. *Perspectives, 7*(6), 1757–1768.

Azrin, N. H., Nunn, R. G., & Frantz, S. E. (1979). Comparison of regulated breathing versus abbreviated desensitization on reported stuttering episodes. *Journal of Speech and Hearing Disorders, 44*, 331–339.

Azul, D., Hancock, A. B., Lundberg, T., Nygren, U., & Dhejne, C. (2022). Supporting well-being in gender-diverse people: A tutorial for implementing conceptual and practical shifts toward culturally responsive, person-centered care in speech-language pathology. *American Journal of Speech-Language Pathology, 31*(4), 1574–1587.

Bachelor, A., & Horvath, A. (1999). The therapeutic relationship. In M. A. Hubble, B. L. Duncan, & S. D. Miller (Eds.), *The heart and soul of change: What works in therapy* (pp. 133–178). APA Press.

Backus, O. (1947). Intensive group therapy in speech rehabilitation. *Journal of Speech Disorders, 12*, 39–60.

Backus, O. (1957). Group structure in speech therapy. In L. E. Travis (Ed.), *Handbook of speech pathology* (pp. 1025–1064). Appleton-Century-Crofts.

Backus, O., & Beasley, J. (1951). *Speech therapy with children*. Houghton Mifflin.

Bakker, K. (1995). Two supplemental scoring procedures for diagnostic evaluations with the Speech Situations Checklist. *Journal of Fluency Disorders, 20*(2), 117–126.

Bakker, K. (2005). Cluttering Assessment Program [Computer software]. http://www.stutteringhomepage.com

Bakker, K., Myers, F. L., Raphael, L. J., & St. Louis, K. O. (2011). A preliminary comparison of speech rate, self-evaluation, and disfluency of people who speak exceptionally fast, clutter, or speak normally. In D. Ward & K. Scaler Scott (Eds.), *Cluttering* (pp. 59–79). Psychology Press.

Bamberg, C., Hanley, J., & Hillenbrand, J. (1990). *Pitch and amplitude perturbation in adult stutterers and nonstutterers* [Paper presentation]. Annual Meeting of the American Speech-Language-Hearing Association, Seattle, WA.

Bandura, A. (1977). Toward a unifying theory of behavior change. *Psychological Review, 1*, 191–215.

Bandura, A., Adams, N. E., & Beyer, J. (1977). Cognitive processes mediating behavioral change. *Journal of Personality and Social Psychology, 35*, 125–139.

Bannister, D. (1966). Psychology as an exercise in paradox. *Bulletin of the British Psychological Society, 19*, 21–26.

Barbara, D. A. (Ed.). (1965). *New directions in stuttering: Theory and practice*. Charles C. Thomas.

Barbara, D. A. (1982). *The psychodynamics of stuttering*. Charles C. Thomas.

Barnes, T. D., Wozniak, D. F., Gutierrez, J., Han, T.-U., Drayna, D., & Holy, T. E. (2016). A mutation associated with stuttering alters mouse pup ultrasonic vocalizations. *Current Biology, 26*, 1009–1018.

Baryshevtsev, M., Zhong, L., Lloyd, R., & McGlone, M. (2020). Trait perspective-taking and need for cognition in the formation of stereotypes about people who stutter. *Journal of Fluency Disorders, 65*, 105778. https://doi.org/10.1016/j.jfludis.2020.105778

Baumgartner, J. M. (1999). Acquired psychogenic stuttering. In R. Curlee (Ed.), *Stuttering and related disorders of fluency* (2nd ed., pp. 269–288). Thieme Medical.

Baumgartner, J., & Duffy, J. (1997). Psychogenic stuttering in adults with and without neurologic disease. *Journal of Medical Speech-Language Pathology, 52*, 75–95.

Beach, M. C., Roter, D., Korthuis, P. T., Epstein, R. M., Sharp, V., Ratanawongsa, N., . . . Moore, R. D. (2013). A multicenter study of physician mindfulness and health care quality. *Annals of Family Medicine, 11*(5), 421–428.

Beck, A. T., Steer, R. A., & Brown, G. K. (1996). *Manual for the BDI-II.* Psychological Corporation.

Beech, H., & Fransella, F. (1968). *Research and experiment in stuttering.* Oxford, UK: Pergamon.

Behrman, A. (2006). Facilitating behavioral change in voice therapy: The relevance of motivational interviewing. *American Journal of Speech-Language Pathology, 15,* 215–225. doi:10.1044/1058-0360(2006/020)

Beilby, J. M. (2014). Psychosocial impact of living with a stuttering disorder: Knowing is not enough. *Seminars in Speech and Language, 35*(2), 132–143.

Beilby, J. M., Byrnes, M. L., Meagher, E. L., & Yaruss, J. S. (2013). The impact of stuttering on adults who stutter and their partners. *Journal of Fluency Disorders, 38*(1), 14–29.

Beilby, J. M., Byrnes, M. L., & Yaruss, J. S. (2012). Acceptance and commitment therapy for adults who stutter: Psychosocial adjustment and speech fluency. *Journal of Fluency Disorders, 37*(4), 289–299.

Beilby, J. M., Byrnes, M. L., & Young, K. N. (2012). The experience of living with a sibling who stutters: A preliminary study. *Journal of Fluency Disorders, 37*(2), 135–148.

Beilock, S. L., Carr, T. H., MacMahon, C., & Starkes, J. L. (2002), When paying attention becomes counterproductive: Impact of divided versus skill-focused attention on novice and experienced performance of sensorimotor skills. *Journal of Experimental Psychology: Applied, 8,* 6–16.

Bell, A. M. (1853). *Observations on defects of speech, the cure of stammering, and the principles of elocution.* Hamilton-Adams.

Belyk, M., Kraft, S. J., & Brown, S. (2014). Stuttering as a trait or state—An ALE meta-analysis of neuroimaging studies. *European Journal of Neuroscience, 41*(2), 275–284. https://doi.org/10.1111/ejn.12765

Benecken, J. (1995). *On the nature and psychological relevance of a stigma: The "stutterer" or what happens, when "Grace falls"* [Paper presentation]. First World Congress on Fluency Disorders, Munchen, Germany.

Bennett, E. M., & Chmela, K. A. (1998). The mask of shame: Treatment strategies for adults who stutter. In E. C. Healey & H. F. M. Peters (Eds.), *Proceedings of the Second World Congress on Fluency Disorders* (pp. 340–342). Nijmegen University Press.

Berkowitz, M., Cook, H., & Haughey, J. (1994). Fluency program developed for the public school setting. *Language, Speech and Hearing Services in Schools, 25,* 94–99.

Berlin, C. I., Lowe-Bell, S. S., Cullen, J. K., Jr., Thompson, C. L., & Loovis, C. F. (1973). Dichotic speech perception: An interpretation of right-ear advantage and temporal offset effects. *Journal of the Acoustical Society of America, 53,* 699–709.

Berliner, D. C. (1994). Expertise: The wonder of exemplary performances, In J. N. Mangieri & C. C. Block (Eds.), *Creating powerful thinking in teachers and students* (pp. 161–186). Holt, Rinehart and Winston.

Berlinsky, S. L. (1955). A comparison of stutterers and non-stutterers in four conditions of induced anxiety [Abstract]. *Speech Monographs, 22,* 197.

Bernard, R., Hofslundsengen, H., & Frazier Norbury, C. (2022). Anxiety and depression symptoms in children and adolescents who stutter: A systematic review and meta-analysis. *Journal of Speech, Language, and Hearing Research, 65*(2), 624–644. https://doi.org/10.1044/2021_jslhr-21-00236

Bernstein Ratner, N. (1993) Parents, children, and stuttering. *Seminars in Speech and Language, 14,* 238–250.

Bernstein Ratner, N. (1997). Stuttering: A psycholinguistic perspective. In R. Curlee & G. Siegel (Eds.), *Nature and treatment of stuttering: New directions* (2nd ed., pp. 99–127). Allyn & Bacon.

Bernstein Ratner, N. (2004). Fluency and stuttering in bilingual children. In B. Goldstein (Ed.), *Bilingual language development and disorders in Spanish-English speakers* (pp. 286–308). Brookes.

Berry, M. F. (1938). Developmental history of stuttering children. *Journal of Pediatrics, 11,* 209–217.

Bhatnagar, S. C. & Andy, O. J. (1995). *Neuroscience for the study of communication disorders.* Williams & Wilkins.

Biener, L., & Abrams, D. B. (1991). The contemplation ladder: Validation of a measure of readiness to consider smoking cessation. *Health Psychology, 10,* 360–365.

Bieri, J. (1955). Cognitive complexity—Simplicity and predictive behavior. *Journal of Abnormal and Social Psychology, 51,* 263–268.

Black, J. W. (1951). The effect of delayed sidetone upon vocal rate and intensity. *Journal of Speech and Hearing Disorders, 16,* 56–60.

Blaine, B. E., & Brenchley, K. J. M. (2020). *Understanding the psychology of diversity.* Sage.

Blanton, S., & Blanton, M. G. (1936). *For stutterers.* Appleton-Century.

Blatt, S. J., Zuroff, D. C., Quinlan, D. M., & Pilkonis, P. A. (1996). Interpersonal factors in brief treatment of depression: Further analyses of the National Institute of Mental Health Treatment of Depression Collaborative Research Program. *Journal of Consulting and Clinical Psychology, 64,* 162–171.

Bloch, E. L., & Goodstein, L. D. (1971). Functional speech disorders and personality: A decade of research. *Journal of Speech and Hearing Disorders, 36,* 295–314.

Blodgett, E. G., & Cooper, E. B. (1988). Talking about it and doing it: Meta linguistic capacity and prosodic control in three to seven year olds. *Journal of Fluency Disorders, 13,* 283–290.

Blood, G. (1995a). A behavioral-cognitive therapy program for adults who stutter: Computers and counseling. *Journal of Communication Disorders, 28,* 165–180.

Blood, G. (1995b). POWER2: Relapse management with adolescents who stutter. *Language, Speech, and Hearing Services in Schools, 26,* 169–179.

Blood, G., & Seider, R. (1981). The concomitant problems of young stutterers. *Journal of Speech and Hearing Disorders, 46,* 31–33.

Blood, G. W., & Blood, I. M. (1982). A tactic for facilitating social interacting with laryngectomees. *Journal of Speech and Hearing Disorders, 47,* 416–419.

Blood, G., W., & Blood, I. M. (2004). Bullying in adolescents who stutter: Communicative competence and self-esteem. *Contemporary Issues in Communication Science and Disorders, 31,* 69–79.

Blood, G. W., & Blood, I. M. (2016). Long-term consequences of childhood bullying in adults who stutter: Social anxiety, fear of negative evaluation, self-esteem, and satisfaction with life. *Journal of Fluency Disorders, 50,* 72–84.

Blood, G. W., Blood, I. M., Bennett, S., Simpson, K. C., & Sussman, E. J. (1994). Subjective anxiety measurements and cortisol responses in adults who stutter. *Journal of Speech and Hearing Research, 37,* 760–768.

Blood, G. W., Blood, I. M., McCarthy, J., Tellis, G., & Gabel, R. (2001). An analysis of verbal response patterns of Charles Van Riper during stuttering modification therapy. *Journal of Fluency Disorders, 26,* 129–149.

Blood, G. W., & Hood, S. B. (1978). Elementary school-age stutterers' disfluencies during oral reading and spontaneous speech. *Journal of Fluency Disorders, 3,* 155–165.

Bloodstein, O. (1949). Conditions under which stuttering is reduced or absent: A review of literature. *Journal of Speech and Hearing Disorders, 14,* 295–302.

Bloodstein, O. (1950). Hypothetical conditions under which stuttering is reduced or absent. *Journal of Speech and Hearing Disorders, 15,* 142–153.

Bloodstein, O. (1958). Stuttering as anticipatory struggle reaction. In J. Eisenson (Ed.), *Stuttering: A symposium* (pp. 1–69). Harper and Row.

Bloodstein, O. (1960). The development of stuttering I: Changes in nine basic features. *Journal of Speech and Hearing Disorders, 25,* 219–237.

Bloodstein, O. (1961). The development of stuttering III: Theoretical and clinical implications. *Journal of Speech and Hearing Disorders, 26*, 67–82.

Bloodstein, O. (1974). The rules of early stuttering. *Journal of Speech and Hearing Disorders, 39*, 379–394.

Bloodstein, O. (1987). *A handbook on stuttering* (4th ed.). National Easter Seal Society.

Bloodstein, O. (1988). Verification of stuttering in a suspected malingerer. *Journal of Fluency Disorders, 13*(2), 83–88.

Bloodstein, O. (1992). Response to Hamre: Part I. *Journal of Fluency Disorders, 17*, 29–32.

Bloodstein, O. (1993). *Stuttering: The search for a cause and cure.* Allyn & Bacon.

Bloodstein, O. (1995). *A handbook on stuttering* (5th ed.). Singular Publishing.

Bloodstein, O. (1999). Opening comments. Sixth Annual Leadership Conference of the ASHA Special Interest Division, San Diego, CA.

Bloodstein, O., & Bernstein Ratner, N. (2008). *A handbook on stuttering* (6th ed.). Thomson Delmar Learning.

Bloodstein, O., Bernstein Ratner, N., & Brundage, S. B. (2021). *A handbook on stuttering* (7th ed.). Plural Publishing.

Bloodstein, O., & Shogun, R. (1972). Some clinical notes on forced stuttering. *Journal of Speech and Hearing Disorders, 37*, 177–186.

Bloom, C., & Cooperman, D. K. (1999). *Synergistic stuttering therapy: A holistic approach.* Butterworth-Heinemann.

Bluemel, C. S. (1932). Primary and secondary stammering. *Quarterly Journal of Speech, 18*, 187–200.

Bluemel, C. S. (1957). *The riddle of stuttering.* Interstate.

Blumgart, E., Tran, Y., & Craig, A. (2010). Social anxiety disorder in adults who stutter. *Depression and Anxiety, 27*, 687–692.

Boberg, E. (1981). Maintenance of fluency: An experimental program. In E. Boberg (Ed.), *Maintenance of fluency: Proceedings of the Banff Conference* (pp. 71–112). Elsevier.

Boberg, E. (1983). Behavioral transfer and maintenance programs for adolescent and adult stutterers. In J. Fraser Gruss (Ed.), *Stuttering therapy: Transfer and maintenance* (Publica-tion No. 19, pp. 41–61). Stuttering Foundation of America.

Boberg. E. (1986). Relapse and outcome. In G. H. Shames & H. Rubin (Eds.), *Stuttering then and now* (pp. 501–513). Merrill.

Boberg, E., Howie, P., & Woods, L. (1979). Maintenance of fluency: A review. *Journal of Fluency Disorders, 4*, 93–116.

Boberg, E., & Kully, D. (1984). Techniques for transferring fluency. In W. H. Perkins (Ed.), *Current therapy of communication disorders: Stuttering disorders* (pp. 178–201). Thieme Medical.

Boberg, E., & Kully, D. (1985). *Comprehensive stuttering program.* College-Hill Press.

Boberg, E., & Kully, D. (1994). Long-term result of an intensive treatment program for adults and adolescents who stutter. *Journal of Speech and Hearing Research, 37*, 1050–1059.

Boberg, E., & Sawyer, L. (1977). The maintenance of fluency following intensive therapy. *Human Communication, 2*, 21–28.

Boberg, E., Yeudall, L. T., Schopflocher, D., & Bo-Lassen, P. (1983). The effect of an intensive behavioral program on the distribution of EEG alpha power in stutterers during the processing of verbal and visuospatial information. *Journal of Fluency Disorders, 8*, 245–263.

Boberg, J. M., & Boberg, E. (1990). The other side of the block: The stutterer's spouse. *Journal of Fluency Disorders, 15*(1), 61–75.

Bobrick, B. (1995). *Knotted tongues.* Simon & Schuster.

Boland, J. L. (1953). A comparison of stutterers and non-stutterers on several measures of anxiety [Abstract]. *Speech Monographs, 20*, 144.

Bolton, J., Cox, B., Clara, I., & Sareen, J. (2006). Use of alcohol and drugs to self-medicate anxiety disorders in a nationally representative sample. *Journal of Nervous and Mental Disease, 194*(11), 818–825.

Bonelli, P., Dixon, M., Bernstein Ratner, N., & Onslow, M. (2000). Child and parent speech and language following the Lidcombe Programme of early stuttering intervention. *Clinical Linguistics and Phonetics, 14*, 427–446.

Bonfanti, B. H., & Culatta, R. (1977). An analysis of the fluency patterns of institutionalized retarded adults. *Journal of Fluency Disorders, 2*, 117–128.

Bordeau, L. A., & Jeffrey, C. H. (1973). Stuttering treated by desensitization. *Journal of Behavior Therapy and Experimental Psychiatry, 4*, 209–212.

Bordin, E. S. (1979). The generalizability of the psychoanalytic concept of the working alliance. *Psychotherapy: Theory, Research and Practice, 16*, 252–260.

Bothe A. K. (2004). Evidence-based, outcomes-focused decisions about stuttering treatment: Clinical recommendations in context. In A. K. Bothe (Ed.), *Evidence-based treatment of stuttering: Empirical bases and clinical applications* (pp. 261–270). Erlbaum.

Bothe, A. K., Davidow, J. H., Bramlett, R. E., Franic, D. M., & Ingham, R. J. (2006). Stuttering treatment research 1970–2005: II. Systematic review incorporating trial quality assessment of pharmacological approaches. *American Journal of Speech-Language Pathology, 15*(4), 342–352.

Bothe, A. K., Davidow, J. H., Bramlett, R. E., & Ingham, R. J. (2006). Stuttering treatment research 1970–2005: I. Systematic review incorporating trial quality assessment of behavioral, cognitive, and related approaches. *American Journal of Speech-Language Pathology, 15*(4), 321–341.

Botterill, W. (2011). Developing the therapeutic relationship: From "expert" professional to "expert" person who stutters. *Journal of Fluency Disorders, 36*(3), 158–173.

Botterill, W., & Cook, F. (1987). Personal construct theory and the treatment of adolescent disfluency. In L. Rustin, H. Purser, & D. Rowley (Eds.), *Progress in the treatment of fluency disorders* (pp. 147–165). Taylor & Francis.

Botterill, W., Kelman, E., & Rustin, L. (1991). Parents and their pre-school stuttering children. In L. Rustin (Ed.), *Parents, families and the stuttering child* (pp. 59–71). Singular Publishing.

Bowers, B. J., Fibich, B., & Jacobsen, N. (2001). Care-as-service, care-as-relating, care-as-comfort: Understanding nursing home residents' definitions of quality. *The Gerontologist, 41*, 539–545.

Boyle, M. P. (2013). Assessment of stigma associated with stuttering: Development and evaluation of the Self-Stigma of Stuttering Scale (4S). *Journal of Speech, Language, and Hearing Research, 56*, 1517–1529.

Boyle, M. P. (2015). Identifying correlates of self-stigma in adults who stutter: Further establishing the construct validity of the Self-Stigma of Stuttering Scale (4S). *Journal of Fluency Disorders, 43*, 17–27. https://doi.org/10.1016/j.jfludis.2014.12.002

Boyle, M. P., & Blood, G. W. (2015). Stigma and stuttering: Conceptualizations, applications, and coping. In K. O. St. Louis (Ed.), *Stuttering meets stereotype, stigma, and discrimination: An overview of attitude research* (pp. 43–70). West Virginia University Press.

Boyle, M. P., Dioguardi, L., & Pate, J. E. (2016). A comparison of three strategies for reducing the public stigma associated with stuttering. *Journal of Fluency Disorders, 50*, 44–58. https://doi.org/10.1016/j.jfludis.2016.09.004

Brady, J. P., & Berson, J. (1975). Stuttering, dichotic listening, and cerebral dominance. *Archives of General Psychiatry, 32*, 1449–1452.

Bray, J., Kowalchuk, A., & Waters, V. (n.d.). *Brief intervention: Stages of change and motivational interviewing.* Baylor School of Medicine, InSight SBIRT Residency Training Program. https://www.bcm.edu/education/programs/sbirt/index.cfm?pmid=25042

Bray, M. A., Kehle, T. J., Lawless, K. A., & Theodore, L. A. (2003). The relationship of self-efficacy and depression to stuttering. *American Journal of Speech-Language Pathology, 12*, 425–431.

Breitenfeldt, D. H., & Lorenz, D. R. (1989). *Successful Stuttering Management Program.* Eastern Washington University.

Breitenfeldt, D. H., & Lorenz, D. R. (1999). *Successful Stuttering Management Program (SSMP)* (2nd ed.). Eastern Washington University Press.

Bricker-Katz, G., Lincoln, M., & McCabe, P. (2009). A life-time of stuttering: How emotional reactions to stuttering impact activities and participation in older people. *Disability and Rehabilitation, 31*, 1742–1752.

Bricker-Katz, G., Lincoln, M., & McCabe, P. (2010). Older people who stutter: Barriers to communication and perceptions of treatment needs. *International Journal of Language and Communication Disorders, 45*, 15–30.

Brignell, A., Krahe, M., Downes, M., Kefalianos, E., Reilly, S., & Morgan, A. (2021). Interventions for children and adolescents who stutter: A systematic review, meta-analysis, and evidence map. *Journal of Fluency Disorders, 70*, 105843. https://doi.org/10.1016/j.jfludis.2021.105843

Brill, A. A. (1923). Speech disturbances in nervous and mental diseases. *Quarterly Journal of Speech, 9*, 129–135.

Brisk, D. J., Healey, E. C., & Hux, K. A. (1997). Clinicians' training and confidence associated with treating school-age children who stutter: A national survey. *Language, Speech, and Hearing Services in Schools, 28*, 164–176.

Brissette, I., Scheier, M. F., & Carver, C. S. (2002). The role of optimism in social network development, coping, and psychological adjustment during life transition. *Journal of Personality and Social Psychology, 82*, 102–111.

Broadbent, D. E., & Gregory, M. (1964). Accuracy of recognition for speech presented to the right and left ears. *Quarterly Journal of Experimental Psychology, 16*, 359–360.

Brocklehurst, P. H. (2008). A review of evidence for the covert repair hypothesis of stuttering. *Contemporary Issues in Communication Science and Disorders, 35*, 25–43.

Bronfenbrenner, U. (1976). Is early intervention effective? In A. Clarke & A. Clarke (Eds.), *Early experience: Myth and evidence* (pp. 247–256). Open Books.

Brown, G., & Cullinan, W. L. (1981). Word-retrieval difficulty and disfluent speech in adult anomic speakers. *Journal of Speech and Hearing Research, 24*, 358–365.

Brown, G. S. (2004, November) *Common factors and therapeutic effects in therapy outcomes* [Seminar presentation]. Annual Meeting of the American Speech-Language-Hearing Association, Philadelphia, PA.

Brown, G. S. (2006). *Common factors and therapist effects in therapy outcome* [Paper presentation]. Annual Meeting of the American Speech-Language-Hearing Association, Miami, FL.

Brown, K. W., & Ryan, R. M. (2003). The benefits of being present: Mindfulness and its role in psychological well-being. *Journal of Personality and Social Psychology, 84*(4), 822.

Browne, M. N., & Keeley, S. M. (2015). *Asking the right questions: A guide to critical thinking* (11th ed.). Pearson.

Brownell, K. D., Marlatt, G. A., Lichtenstein, E., & Wilson, G. T. (1986). Understanding and preventing relapse. *American Psychologist, 41*, 765–782.

Brundage, S. B. (2007). Virtual reality augmentation for functional assessment and treatment of stuttering. *Topics in Language Disorders, 27*, 254–271.

Brundage, S. B., Bernstein Ratner, N., Boyle, M. P., Eggers, K., Everard, R., Franken, M., . . . Yaruss, J. S. (2021). Consensus guidelines for the assessments of individuals who stutter across the lifespan. *American Journal of Speech-Language Pathology, 30*, 2379–2393.

Brundage, S. B., Bothe, A. K., Lengeling, A. N., & Evans, J. J. (2006). Comparing judgments of stuttering made by students, clinicians, and highly experienced judges. *Journal of Fluency Disorders, 31*(4), 271–283.

Brundage, S. B., Brinton, J. M., & Hancock, A. (2016). Utility of virtual reality environments to examine physiological reactivity and subjective distress in adults who stutter. *Journal of Fluency Disorders, 50*, 85–95.

Brundage, S. B., & Graap, K. (2004). Virtual reality: An exciting new tool to enhance stuttering treatment. *Fluency and Fluency Disorders, 14*, 4–8.

Brundage, S., Graap, K., Gibbons, K., Ferrer, M., & Brooks, J. (2006). Frequency of stuttering during challenging and supportive virtual job interviews. *Journal of Fluency Disorders, 31*, 325–339.

Brundage, S. B., & Hancock, A. B. (2015). Real enough: Using virtual public speaking environments to evoke feelings and behaviors targeted in stuttering assessment and treatment. *American Journal of Speech-Language Pathology, 24*, 139–149.

Brundage, S., Hancock, A., Kiselewich, K., & Stallings, L. (2006, November). *Frequency of stuttering during speeches given to virtual and live audiences* [Paper presentation]. Annual Meeting of the American Speech-Language-Hearing Association, Miami, FL.

Brutten, G. (1963). Palmar sweat investigation of disfluency and expectancy adaptation. *Journal of Speech and Hearing Research, 6*, 40–48.

Brutten, G. (1973). Behavior assessment and the strategy of therapy. In Y. Lebrun & R. Hoops (Eds.), *Neurolinguistic approaches to stuttering* (pp. 8–17). Mouton.

Brutten, G. J. (1975). Stuttering: Topography, assessment, and behavior change strategies. In J. Eisenson (Ed.), *Stuttering: A second symposium* (pp. 201–262). Harper & Row.

Brutten, G. J., & Dunham, S. (1989). The Communication Attitude Test: A normative study of grade school children. *Journal of Fluency Disorders, 14*, 371–377.

Brutten, G. J., & Shoemaker, D. J. (1967). *The modification of stuttering.* Prentice Hall.

Brutten, G., & Vanryckeghem, M. (2003). *Behavior Assessment Battery: A multi-dimensional and evidenced-based approach to diagnostic and therapeutic decision making for children who stutter.* Stichting Integratie Gehandicapten and Acco Publishers.

Brutten, G., & Vanryckeghem, M. (2007). *Behavior Assessment Battery for Children Who Stutter.* Plural Publishing.

Bryant, R. A., & Allison, H. G. (1999). Postconcussive symptoms and posttraumatic stress disorder after mild brain injury. *Journal of Nervous and Mental Disease, 187*, 302–305.

Bryngelson, B. (1935). Method of stuttering. *Journal of Abnormal Psychology, 30*, 194–198.

Bryngelson, B. (1938). Prognosis in stuttering. *Journal of Speech Disorders, 3*, 121–123.

Bryngelson, B., Chapman, B., & Hansen, O. (1944). *Know yourself: A guide for those who stutter.* Burgess.

Burns, D., & Nolen-Hoeksema, S. (1992). Therapeutic empathy and recovery from depression in cognitive-behavioral therapy: A structural equation model. *Journal of Consulting and Clinical Psychology, 60*, 441–449.

Byrd, C. (2018). Assessing bilingual children: Are their disfluencies indicative of stuttering or the by-product of navigating two languages? *Seminars in Speech and Language, 39*(4), 324–332. https://doi.org/10.1055/s-0038-1667161

Byrd, C. T., Gkalitsiou, Z., Donaher, J., & Stergiou, E. (2016). The client's perspective on voluntary stuttering. *American Journal of Speech-Language Pathology, 25*, 1–16.

Byrd, C. T., Hoffman, D., & Gunderson, E. (2015). Identification of stuttering in bilingual Spanish-English-speaking children. *Contemporary Issues in Communication Science and Disorders, 42*(Spring), 72–87. https://doi.org/10.1044/cicsd_42_s_72

Byrd, C. T., Logan, K. J., & Gillam, R. B. (2012). Speech disfluency in school-age children's conversational and narrative discourse. *Language, Speech, and Hearing Services in Schools, 43*, 153–163.

Byrd, C. T., McGill, M., Gkalitsiou, Z., & Cappellini, C. (2017). The effects of self-disclosure on male and female perceptions of individuals who stutter. *American Journal of Speech-Language Pathology, 26*(1), 69–80.

Byrd, C. T., Vallely, M., Anderson, J. D., & Sussman, H. (2012). Nonword repetition and phoneme elision in adults who do and do not stutter. *Journal of Fluency Disorders, 37*, 188–201.

Cabanas, R. (1954). Some findings in speech and voice therapy among mentally deficient children. *Folia Phoniatrica, 6*, 34–39.

Calkins, S. D., & Fox, N. A. (1994). Individual differences in the biological aspects of temperament. In J. E. Bates & T. D. Wachs (Eds.), *Temperament: Individual differences at the interface of biology and behavior* (pp. 199–217). American Psychological Association.

Canter, G. J. (1971). Observations on neurogenic stuttering: A contribution to differential diagnosis. *British Journal of Disorders of Communication, 6*, 139–143.

Carlisle, J. A. (1985). *Tangled tongue: Living with a stutter.* University of Toronto Press.

Caruso, A. J. (1988). Childhood stuttering: A review of behavioral, acoustical, and physiological research [Abstract]. *ASHA, 30*, 73.

Caruso, A. J., Abbs, J. H., & Gracco, V. L. (1988). Kinematic analysis of multiple movement coordination during speech in stutterers. *Brain, 111*, 439–456.

Cerf, A., & Prins, D. (1974). *Stutterers' ear preference for dichotic syllables* [Paper presentation]. Annual Meeting of the American Speech Language-Hearing Association, Las Vegas, NV.

Chang, S.-E., Garnett, E. O., Etchell, A., & Chow, H. M. (2019). Functional and neuroanatomical bases of developmental stuttering: Current insights. *The Neuroscientist, 25*(6), 566–582. https://doi.org/10.1177/1073858418803594

Chang, S.-E & Guenther, F. H. (2020). Involvement of the cortico-basal ganglia-thalamocortical loop in developmental stuttering. *Frontiers in Psychology, 10.* https://doi.org/10.3389/fpsyg.2019.03088

Charon, R. (2006). *Narrative medicine: Honoring the stories of illness.* Oxford University Press.

Charon, R. (2007). What to do with stories: The sciences of narrative medicine. *Canadian Family Physician, 53*, 1265–1267.

Cheasman, C. (2007, Spring). Revealing and healing—A mindfulness approach to stammering. *Speaking Out*, 9–10.

Chmela, K. A. (1998). Thoughts on recovery. In E. C. Healey & H. F. M. Peters (Eds.), *Proceedings of the Second World Congress on Fluency Disorders* (pp. 376–378). Nijmegen University Press.

Chmela, K. A., & Reardon, N. A. (2001). *The school-aged child who stutters: Practical ideas for working with feelings and beliefs about stuttering* (Publication No. 5). Stuttering Foundation of America.

Choi, D., Conture, E. G., Walden, T. A., Jones, R. M., & Kim, H. (2016). Emotional diathesis, emotional stress, and childhood stuttering. *Journal of Speech, Language, and Hearing Association, 56*, 616–630.

Choo, A. L., & Smith, S. A. (2020). Bilingual children who stutter: Convergence, gaps and directions for research. *Journal of Fluency Disorders, 63*, 105741. https://doi.org/10.1016/j.jfludis.2019.105741

Chow, H. M., & Chang, S.-E. (2017). White matter developmental trajectories associated with persistence and recovery of childhood stuttering. *Human Brain Mapping, 3*(2), 3345–3359. https://doi.org/10.1002/hbm.23590

Cockburn, J. (2004). Adaptation of evidence into practice—Can change be sustainable? *Medical Journal of Australia, 180*, 66–67.

Cohen, J. (1988). *Statistical power analysis for the behavioral sciences* (2nd ed.). Erlbaum.

Coleman, J. M., Brunell, A. B., & Haugen, I. M. (2015). Multiple forms of prejudice: How gender and disability stereotypes influence judgments of disabled women and men. *Current Psychology, 34*, 177–189.

Collins, C. R., & Blood, G. W. (1990). Acknowledgement and severity of stuttering as factors influencing nonstutterers' perceptions of stutterers. *Journal of Speech and Hearing Disorders, 55*, 75–81.

Coloroso, B. (2003). *The bully, the bullied, and the bystander.* HarperCollins.

Compas, B. E., Malcarne, V. L., & Banez, G. A. (1992). Coping with psychological stress: A developmental perspective. In B. N. Carpenter (Ed.), *Personal coping: Theory, research, and application* (pp. 93–110). Praeger.

Connor, K. M., & Davidson, J. R. T. (2003). Development of a new resilience scale: The Connor-Davidson Resilience Scale (CD-RISC). *Depression and Anxiety, 18*(2), 76–82. https://doi.org/10.1002/da.10113

Connors, G. J., Carroll, K. M., DiClemente, C. C., Longabaugh, R., & Donovan, D. M. (1997). The therapeutic alliance and its relationship to alcoholism treatment participation and outcome. *Journal of Consulting and Clinical Psychology, 65*(4), 588–598.

Constantino, C. D., Eichorn, N., Buder, E. H., Beck, J. G., & Manning, W. H. (2020). The speaker's experience of stuttering: Measuring spontaneity. *Journal of Speech, Language, and Hearing Research, 63*(4), 983–1001. https://doi.org/10.1044/2019_jslhr-19-00068

Constantino, C. D., Leslie, P., Quesal, R. W., & Yaruss, J. S. (2016). A preliminary investigation of daily variability of stuttering adults.

Journal of Communication Disorders, 60, 39–50.

Constantino, C. D., Manning, W., & Nordstrom, S. (2017). Rethinking covert stuttering. *Journal of Fluency Disorders, 53,* 26–40.

Constantino, C. D., Manning, W. H., & Olney, A. (2015, July). *Origin and Pawn calculator: Determining agency to improve treatment outcomes* [Paper presentation]. Eighth World Congress of the International Fluency Association, Lisbon, Portugal.

Conture, E. G. (1990). *Stuttering* (2nd ed.). Prentice Hall.

Conture, E. G. (1996). Treatment efficacy: Stuttering. *Journal of Speech and Hearing Research, 39,* S18–S26.

Conture, E. G. (1997). Evaluating childhood stuttering. In R. Curlee & G. Siegel (Eds.), *Nature and treatment of stuttering, new directions* (2nd ed., pp. 239–256). Allyn & Bacon.

Conture, E. (1999). The best day to rethink our research agenda is between yesterday and tomorrow. In N. B. Ratner & E. C. Healey (Eds.), *Stuttering research and practice: Bridging the gap* (pp. 13–26). Erlbaum.

Conture, E. G. (2001). *Stuttering: Its nature, diagnosis and treatment.* Allyn & Bacon.

Conture, E., & Caruso, A. (1987). Assessment and diagnosis of childhood disfluency. In L. Ruskin, D. Rowley, & H. Purser (Eds.), *Progress in the treatment of fluency disorders* (pp. 57–82). Taylor & Francis.

Conture, E., & Guitar, B. (1993). Evaluating efficacy of treatment of stuttering: School-age children. *Journal of Fluency Disorders, 18,* 253–287.

Conture, E., & Kelly, E. (1991). Young stutterers' non-speech behaviors during stuttering. *Journal of Speech and Hearing Research, 34,* 1041–1056.

Conture, E., Louko, L., & Edwards, M. L. (1993). Simultaneously treating stuttering and disordered phonology in children: Experimental therapy, preliminary findings. *American Journal of Speech-Language Pathology, 2*(3), 72–81.

Conture, E., & Schwartz, H. (1984). Children who stutter: Diagnosis and remediation. *Communication Disorders, 9,* 1–18.

Conture, E. G., Walden T. A., Arnold, H. S., Graham, C. G., Hartfield, K. N., & Karrass, J. (2006). A communication-emotional model of stuttering. In N. Bernstein Ratner & J. Tetnowski (Eds.), *Current issues in stuttering research and practice* (pp. 17–46). Erlbaum.

Cook, F., & Botterill, W. (2010). *Tools for success: A cognitive behavior therapy taster* [DVD]. Stuttering Foundation of America.

Cook, M. J., & Smith, L. M. (2006). *Outcomes for adult males using the SpeechEasy fluency device for one year* [Paper presentation]. Annual Meeting of the American Speech-Language-Hearing Association, Miami, FL.

Cooper, A. (2000). *Sticks and stones.* Times Books.

Cooper, E. B. (1966). Client–clinician relationships and concomitant factors in stuttering therapy. *Journal of Speech and Hearing Disorders, 9,* 194–199.

Cooper, E. B. (1968). A therapy process for the adult stutterer. *Journal of Speech and Hearing Disorders, 33,* 246–260.

Cooper, E. B. (1972). Recovery from stuttering in a junior and senior high school population. *Journal of Speech and Hearing Research, 15,* 632–638.

Cooper, E. B. (1977). Controversies about stuttering therapy. *Journal of Fluency Disorders, 2,* 75–86.

Cooper, E. B. (1979). Intervention procedures for the young stutterer. In H. Gregory (Ed.), *Controversies about stuttering* (pp. 63–96). University Park Press.

Cooper, E. B. (1985). *Cooper Personalized Fluency Control Therapy—Revised.* DLM.

Cooper, E. B. (1986a). The mentally retarded stutterer. In K. O. St. Louis (Ed.), *The atypical stutterer* (pp. 123–154). Academic Press.

Cooper, E. B. (1986b). Treatment of dysfluency: Future trends. *Journal of Fluency Disorders, 11,* 317–327.

Cooper, E. B. (1987). The chronic perseverative stuttering syndrome: Incurable stuttering. *Journal of Fluency Disorders, 12,* 381–388.

Cooper, E. B. (1993). Chronic perseverative stuttering syndrome: A harmful or helpful construct? *American Journal of Speech-Language Pathology, 2*(3), 11–15.

Cooper, E. B., Cady, B. B., & Robbins, C. J. (1970). The effect of the verbal stimulus words wrong, right and tree on the disfluency rates of stutterers and nonstutterers. *Journal of Speech and Hearing Research, 13,* 239–244.

Cooper, E. B., & Cooper, C. S. (1965). Variations in adult stutterer attitudes towards clinicians during therapy. *Journal of Communication Disorders, 2,* 141–153.

Cooper, E. B., & Cooper, C. S. (1985a). Clinician attitudes toward stuttering: A decade of change (1973–1983). *Journal of Fluency Disorders, 10,* 19–23.

Cooper, E. B., & Cooper, C. S. (1985b). The effective clinician. In E. B. Cooper & C. S. Cooper, *Personalized fluency control therapy—Revised* (pp. 21–31). DLM.

Cooper, E. B., & Cooper, C. S. (1985c). *Personalized fluency control therapy—Revised* [Handbook]. DLM.

Cooper, E. B., & Cooper, C. S. (1991). A fluency disorders prevention program for preschoolers and children in the primary grades. *American Journal of Speech-Language Pathology, 1,* 28–31.

Cooper, E. B., & Cooper, C. S. (1996). Clinician attitudes towards stuttering: Two decades of change. *Journal of Fluency Disorders, 21,* 119–135.

Corcoran, J. A., & Stewart, M. (1998). Stories of stuttering: A qualitative analysis of interview narratives. *Journal of Fluency Disorders, 23,* 247–264.

Cordes, A. K., & Ingham, R. J. (1994). Time-interval measurement of stuttering: Effects of training with highly agreed or poorly agreed exemplars. *Journal of Speech and Hearing Research, 37,* 1295–1307.

Cordes, A. K., & Ingham, R. J. (1996). Time-interval measurement of stuttering: Establishing and modifying judgment accuracy. *Journal of Speech and Hearing Research, 39,* 298–310.

Cordes, A. K., & Ingham, R. J. (1998). *Treatment efficacy for stuttering: A search for empirical bases.* Singular Publishing.

Coriat, I. H. (1943). Psychoanalytic concept of stammering. *Nervous Child, 2,* 167–171.

Coronary Drug Project Research Group. (1980). Influence of adherence to treatment and response of cholesterol on mortality in the coronary drug project. *New England Journal of Medicine, 303,* 1038–1041.

Costello, J. M. (1983). Current behavioral treatment of children. In D. Prins & R. J. Ingham (Eds.), *Treatment of stuttering in early childhood: Methods and issues* (pp. 69–112). College-Hill Press.

Coutts, K. & Pillay, M. (2021). Decision making and the bedside assessment: The speech language therapist's thinking when making a diagnosis at the bed. *South African Journal of Communication Disorders, 68*(1), a790. https://doi.org/10.4102/sajcd.v68i1.790

Covey, S. (1989). *The seven habits of highly effective people.* Simon & Schuster.

Cox, J. J., Seider, R. A., & Kidd, K. K. (1984). Some environmental factors and hypotheses for stuttering in families with several stutterers. *Journal of Speech and Hearing Research, 27,* 543–548.

Craig, A. (1990). An investigation into the relationship between anxiety and stuttering. *Journal of Speech and Hearing Disorders, 55,* 290–294.

Craig, A. (1998). Relapse following treatment for stuttering: A critical review and correlative data. *Journal of Fluency Disorders, 23,* 1–30.

Craig, A., & Andrews, G. (1985). The prediction and prevention of relapse in stuttering. The value of self-control techniques and locus of control measures. *Behavior Modification, 9,* 427–442.

Craig, A., & Calver, P. (1991). Following up on treated stutterers: Studies on perceptions of fluency and job status. *Journal of Speech and Hearing Research, 34,* 279–284.

Craig, A., Franklin, J., & Andrews, G. (1984). A scale to measure locus of control of behavior. *British Journal of Medical Psychology, 57,* 173–180.

Craig, A., & Hancock, K. (1995). Self-reported factors related to relapse following treatment for stuttering. *Australian Journal of Human Communication Disorders, 23,* 48–60.

Craig, A., & Hancock, K. (1996). Anxiety in children and young adolescents who stutter.

Australian Journal of Human Communication Disorders, 24, 28–38.

Craig, A., Hancock, K., Chang, E., McCready, C., Shepley, A., McCaul, A., . . . Reilly, K. (1996). A controlled trial for stuttering in persons aged 9 to 14 years. *Journal of Speech, Language and Hearing Research, 39*(4), 808–826.

Craig, A., Hancock, K., Tran, Y., & Craig, M. (2003). Anxiety levels in people who stutter: A randomized population study. *Journal of Speech, Language and Hearing Research, 46,* 1197–1206.

Cream, A., O'Brian, S., Jones, M., Block, S., Harrison, E., Lincoln, M., . . . Onslow, M. (2010). Randomized control trial of video self-monitoring following speech restructuring treatment for stuttering, *Journal of Speech, Language and Hearing Research, 53,* 887–897.

Cream, A., O'Brian, S., Onslow, M., Packman, A., & Menzies, R. (2009). Self-modeling as a relapse intervention following speech restructuring treatment for stuttering. *International Journal of Language and Communication Disorders, 44,* 587–599.

Crichton-Smith, I. (2002). Communicating in the real world: Accounts from people who stammer. *Journal of Fluency Disorders, 27,* 333–352.

Crockett, W. H. (1965). Cognitive complexity and impression formation. In B. A. Maher (Ed.), *Progress in experimental personality research* (Vol. 2, pp. 47–90). Academic Press.

Crosby, B. (1997). *The meanest thing to say.* Scholastic.

Cross, D. E., Shadden, B. B., & Luper, H. L. (1979). Effects of stimulus ear presentation on the voice reaction time of adult stutterers and nonstutterers. *Journal of Fluency Disorders, 4,* 45–58.

Crowe, T. A. (Ed.). (1997a). *Applications of counseling in speech-language pathology and audiology.* Williams & Wilkins.

Crowe, T. A. (1997b). Counseling: Definition, history, rationale. In T. A. Crowe (Ed.), *Applications of counseling in speech-language pathology and audiology* (pp. 3–29). Williams & Wilkins.

Crowe, T. A. (1997c). Emotional aspects of communicative disorders. In T. A. Crowe (Ed.), *Applications of counseling in speech-language pathology and audiology* (pp. 30–47). Williams & Wilkins.

Crowe, T. A., & Walton, J. H. (1981). Teacher attitudes toward stuttering. *Journal of Fluency Disorders, 6,* 163–174.

Crystal, D. (1987). Towards a "bucket" theory of language disability: Taking account of interaction between linguistic levels. *Clinical Linguistics and Phonetics, 1,* 7–22.

Cuadrado, E. M., & Weber-Fox, C. M. (2003). Atypical syntactic processing in individuals who stutter: Evidence from event-related brain potentials and behavioral measures. *Journal of Speech, Language and Hearing Research, 46,* 960–976.

Culatta, R., & Goldberg. S. A. (1995). *Stuttering therapy: An integrated approach to theory and practice.* Allyn & Bacon.

Culpepper, B., Lucks Mendel, L., & McCarthy, P. A. (1994). Counseling experience and training offered by ESB-accredited programs. *ASHA, 36,* 55–58.

Curlee, R. (1984). Counseling with adults who stutter. In W. Perkins (Ed.), *Stuttering disorders* (pp. 37–48). Thieme Medical.

Curlee, R. (2000). Demands-capacities versus demands-performance. *Journal of Fluency Disorders, 25*(4), 329–336.

Curlee, R. (2007). Identification and case selection guidelines for early childhood stuttering In E. G. Conture & R. F. Curlee (Eds.), *Stuttering and related disorders of fluency* (3rd ed., pp. 3–20). Thieme.

Curlee, R., & Yairi, E. (1997). Early intervention with early childhood stuttering: A critical examination of the data. *American Journal of Speech-Language Pathology, 6,* 8–18.

Curry, F., & Gregory, H. (1969). The performance of stutterers on dichotic listening tasks thought to reflect cerebral dominance. *Journal of Speech and Hearing Research, 12,* 73–81.

Curtis, E. K. (2013). Why stories matter: Applying principles of narrative medicine to health care ethics. *Journal of the American College of Dentists, 80,* 45–48.

Dalton, P. (1987). Some developments in personal construct therapy with adults who stutter. In C. Levy (Ed.), *Stuttering therapies: Practical approaches* (pp. 61–70). Croom Helm.

Dalton, P. (1994). A personal construct approach to communication problems. In P. Dalton (Ed.), *Counseling people with communication problems* (pp. 15–27). Sage.

Daly, D. A. (1981). Differentiation of stuttering subgroups with Van Riper's developmental tracks: A preliminary study. *Journal of the American Student Speech and Hearing Association, 9,* 89–101.

Daly, D. A. (1986). The clutterer. In K. O. St. Louis (Ed.), *The atypical stutterer* (pp. 155–192). Academic Press.

Daly, D. (1987). Use of the home VCR to facilitate transfer of fluency. *Journal of Fluency Disorders, 12,* 103–106.

Daly, D. A. (1988). *Freedom of fluency.* LinguiSystems.

Daly, D. A. (1992). Helping the clutterer: Therapy considerations. In F. Myers & K. St. Louis (Eds.), *Cluttering: A clinical perspective* (pp. 27–41). Singular Publishing.

Daly, D. A. (1993). Cluttering: Another fluency syndrome. In R. Curlee (Ed.), *Stuttering and related disorders of fluency* (pp. 151–175). Thieme Medical.

Daly, D. A. (1996). *The source for stuttering and cluttering,* LinguiSystems.

Daly, D. A. (2006). Predictive Cluttering Inventory (PCI). https://ahn.mnsu.edu/global assets/college-of-allied-health-and-nursing/speech-hearing-and-rehabilitation-services/stuttering/professional-education/archive-of-online-conferences/2007/dalycluttering2006r.pdf

Daly, D. A., & Burnett, M. L. (1996). Cluttering: Assessment, treatment planning, and case study illustration. *Journal of Fluency Disorders, 21,* 239–248.

Daly, D. A., & Burnett, M. L. (1999). Cluttering: Traditional views and new perspectives. In R. Curlee (Ed.), *Stuttering and related disorders of fluency* (2nd ed., pp. 222–254). Thieme Medical.

Daly, D. A., & Kimbarow, M. L. (1978). Stuttering as operant behavior: Effects of the verbal stimuli wrong, right, and tree on the disfluency rates of school-age stutterers and nonstutterers. *Journal of Speech and Hearing Research, 21,* 589–597.

Daly, D., Simon, C., & Burnett-Stolnack, M. (1995). Helping adolescents who stutter focus on fluency. *Language, Speech, and Hearing Services in Schools, 26,* 162–168.

Dartnall, T. (2003). *Passing as fluent* [Paper presentation]. International Stuttering Awareness Day Online Conference (ISAD). http://www.mnsu.edu/comdis/isad6/papers/dartnall6.html

Davidson, R. J. (1984). Affect, cognition, and hemispheric specialization. In E. Izard, J. Kagan, & R. Zajonc (Eds.), *Emotion, cognition and behavior* (pp. 320–365). Cambridge University Press.

Davidson, R. J. (1995). Cerebral asymmetry, emotion, and affective style. In R. J. Davidson & K. Hugdahl (Eds.), *Brain asymmetry* (pp. 361–387). MIT Press.

Davis, J. M., & Farina, A. (1970). Appreciation of humor: An experimental and theoretical study. *Journal of Personality and Social Psychology, 15*(2), 175–178.

Deal, J. L. (1982). Sudden onset of stuttering: A case report. *Journal of Speech and Hearing Disorders, 47,* 301–304.

DeCharms, R. (1968). *Personal causation: The internal affective determinants of behavior.* Academic Press.

DeCharms, R. (1971). From pawns to origins: Toward self-motivation. In G. S. Lesser (Ed.), *Psychology and educational practice* (pp. 380–407). Scott, Foresman.

Dell, C. (1970). *Treating the school age stutterer: A guide for clinicians* (Publication No. 14). Speech Foundation of America.

Dell, C. W. (1993). Treating school-stutters. In R. F. Curlee (Ed.), *Stuttering and related disorders of fluency* (pp. 45–67). Thieme Medical.

Del Re, A. C., Flückiger, C., Horvath, A. O., Symonds, D., & Wampold, B. E. (2012). Therapist effects in the therapeutic alliance–outcome relationship: A restricted maximum likelihood meta-analysis. *Clinical Psychology Review, 32*, 642–649.

Denhardt, R. (1890). *Das Stottern: Eine Psychose [The Stuttering: A Psychosis]*. E. Keil's Nachfolger.

De Nil, L. F. (1999). Stuttering: A neurophysiological perspective. In N. B. Ratner & E. C. Healey (Eds.), *Stuttering research and practice: Bridging the gap* (pp. 85–102). Erlbaum.

De Nil, L. F. (2004). Recent developments in brain imaging research in stuttering. In B. Maassen, H. Peters, & R. Kent (Eds.), *Speech motor control in normal and disordered speech* (pp. 113–137). Oxford University Press.

De Nil, L. F., & Abbs, J. H. (1990). Influence of rate on stutterers' articulatory movements: A microbeam study. *ASHA, 32*, 72.

De Nil, L. F., & Brutten, G. J. (1991). Speech associated attitudes of stuttering and nonstuttering children. *Journal of Speech and Hearing Research, 34*, 60–66.

De Nil, L. F., Jokel, R., & Rochon, E. (2007). Etiology symptomatology, and treatment of neurogenic stuttering. In E. Conture & R. Curlee (Eds.), *Stuttering and related disorders of fluency* (3rd ed., pp. 326–343). Thieme Medical.

De Nil, L. F., & Kroll, R. M. (1995). The relationship between locus of control and long-term stuttering treatment outcome in adult stutterers. *Journal of Fluency Disorders, 20*, 345–364.

De Nil, L. F., Kroll, R. M., Kapur, S., & Houle, R. (2000). A positron emission tomography study of silent and oral single word reading in stuttering and nonstuttering adults. *Journal of Speech, Hearing, and Language Research, 43*, 1038–1053.

De Nil, L. F., Kroll, R. M., Lafaille, S. J., & Houle, S. (2003). A positron emission tomography study of short- and long-term treatment effects on functional brain activation in adults who stutter. *Journal of Fluency Disorders, 28*(4), 357–380. https://doi.org/10.1016/j.jfludis.2003.07.002

de Sonneville-Koedoot, C., Stolk, E., Rietveld, T., & Franken, M.-C. (2015). Direct versus indirect treatment for preschool children who stutter: The restart randomized trial. *PLoS ONE, 10*(7). https://doi.org/10.1371/journal.pone.0133758

DeVore, J., Nandur, M., & Manning, W. (1984). Projective drawings and children who stutter. *Journal of Fluency Disorders, 9*, 217–226.

DiClemente, C. C. (1993). Changing addictive behaviors: A process perspective. *Current Directions in Psychological Science, 2*(4), 101–106.

Diener, E. D., Emmons, R. A., Larsen, R. J., & Griffin, S. (1985). The Satisfaction with Life Scale. *Journal of Personality Assessment, 49*(1), 71–75.

DiLollo, A. (2010). Business: The crisis of confidence in professional knowledge: Implications for clinical education in speech-language pathology. *SIG 11 Perspectives on Administration and Supervision, 20*, 85–91.

DiLollo, A., & Favreau, C. (2010). Person centered care and speech and language therapy. *Seminars in Speech and Language, 31*(2), 90–97.

DiLollo, A., & Manning, W. H. (2007). Counseling children who stutter and their parents. In E. Conture & R. Curlee (Eds.), *Stuttering and related disorders of fluency* (3rd ed., pp. 115–130). Thieme Medical.

DiLollo, A., Manning, W. H., & Neimeyer, R. A. (2003). Cognitive anxiety as a function of speaker role for fluent speakers and persons who stutter. *Journal of Fluency Disorders, 28*(3), 167–186.

DiLollo, A., Manning, W. H., & Neimeyer, R. A. (2005). Cognitive complexity as a function of speaker role for adult persons who stutter. *Journal of Constructivist Psychology, 18*, 215–236.

DiLollo, A., & Neimeyer, R. A. (2022). *Counseling in speech-language pathology and audiology: Reconstructing personal narratives (2nd ed.)*. Plural Publishing.

DiLollo, A., & Neimeyer, R. A. (2022). Possible Selves Mapping Interview. In *Counseling in speech-language pathology and audiology: Reconstructing personal narratives* (2nd ed., pp. 325–342). Plural Publishing.

DiLollo, A., Neimeyer, R. A., & Manning, W. H. (2002). A personal construct psychology view of relapse: Indications for a narrative therapy component to stuttering treatment. *Journal of Fluency Disorders, 27*(1), 19–42. https://doi.org/10.1016/s0094-730x(01)00109-7

Doopdy, I., Kalinowski, J., Armson, J., & Stuart A. (1993). Stereotypes of stutterers and nonstutterers in three rural communities in Newfoundland. *Journal of Fluency Disorders, 18*, 363–373.

Dorman, M. F., & Porter, R. J. (1975). Hemispheric lateralization for speech perception in stutterers. *Cortex, 11*, 181–185.

Doud, A. K., Hoepner, J. K., & Holland, A. L. (2020). A survey of counseling curricula among accredited communication sciences and disorders graduate student programs. *American Journal of Speech-Language Pathology, 29*(2), 789–803. https://doi.org/10.1044/2020_ajslp-19-00042

Douglass, E., & Quarrington, B. (1952). The differentiation of interiorized and exteriorized secondary stuttering. *Journal of Speech and Hearing Disorders, 17*, 377–385.

Douglass, J. E. (2011). *An investigation of the transition process from covert stuttering to overt stuttering: An interpretive phenomenological analysis of individuals who stutter* [Unpublished doctoral dissertation]. University of Louisiana, Lafayette.

Douglass, J. E., Constantino, C., Alvarado, J., Verrastro, K., & Smith, K. (2019). Qualitative investigation of the speech-language therapy experiences of individuals who covertly stutter. *Journal of Fluency Disorders, 61*, 105713. https://doi.org/10.1016/j.jfludis.2019.105713

Douglass, J. E., & Tetnowski, J. (2009). *Covert stuttering: The hidden journey* [Paper presentation]. American Speech-Language and Hearing Association Conference, New Orleans, LA.

Drayna, D. (2016, April). *Fluency SC21: Using genetics to understand the causes of stuttering* [Short course presentation]. California Speech-Language-Hearing Association, Anaheim, CA.

Drewery, W., Winslade, J., & Monk, G. (2000). Resisting the dominating story: Toward a deeper understanding of narrative therapy. In R. A. Neimeyer & J. D. Raskin (Eds.), *Constructions of disorder: Meaning-making frameworks for psychotherapy* (pp. 243–263). American Psychological Association.

Dreyfus, H. L., & Dreyfus, S. E. (1986). *Mind over machine*. Free Press.

Duchan, J. F., & Felsenfeld, S. (2021). Cluttering framed: An historical overview. *Advances in Communication and Swallowing, 24*(2), 75–85. https://doi.org/10.3233/acs-210029

Duffy, J. R. (2016). Functional speech disorders: Clinical manifestations, diagnosis, and management. *Handbook of clinical neurology, 139*, 379–388.

Duffy, J. R., Manning, K., & Roth, C. R. (2009, November). [Paper presentation]. American Speech-Language and Hearing Association, San Diego, CA.

Duncan, B. L., Miller, S. D., Wampold, B. E., & Hubble, M. A. (Eds.). (2010). *The heart and soul of change: Delivering what works in therapy* (2nd ed.). American Psychological Association. https://doi.org/10.1037/12075-000

Dunlap, K. (1932). *Habits: Their making and unmaking*. Liveright.

Dworzynski, K., Remington, A., Rijsdijk, F., Howell, P., & Plomin, R. (2007). Genetic etiology in cases of recovered persistent stuttering in an unselected, longitudinal sample of young twins. *American Journal of Speech-Language Pathology, 16*, 169–178.

Dykes, R., & Pindzola, R. (1995). *Racial/ethnic differences in the prevalence of school-aged stutterers* [Paper presentation]. Annual Meeting of the American Speech-Language-Hearing Association, Orlando, FL.

Egan, G. (1990). *The skilled helper: A systematic approach to effective helping* (4th ed.). Brooks/Cole.

Egan, G. (1998). *The skilled helper: A problem management approach to helping* (6th ed.). Brooks/Cole.

Egan, G. (2007). *The skilled helper: A problem management and opportunity development approach to helping* (8th ed.). Thomson Brooks/Cole.

Egan, G. (2013). *The skilled helper: A problem management and opportunity development approach to helping* (10th ed.). Brooks/Cole Cengage Learning.

Eggers, K., De Nil, L. F., & Van den Bergh, B. H. R. (2010). Temperament dimensions in stuttering and typically developing children. *Journal of Fluency Disorders, 35*, 355–372.

Eggers, K., Van Eerdenbrugh, S., & Byrd, C. T. (2020). Speech disfluencies in bilingual Yiddish-Dutch speaking children. *Clinical Linguistics & Phonetics, 34*(6), 576–592. https://doi.org/10.1080/02699206.2019.1678670

Eichorn, N., Marton, K., Schwartz, R. G., Melara, R. D., & Pirutinsky, S. (2016). Does working memory enhance or interfere with speech fluency in adults who do and do not stutter? Evidence from a dual-task paradigm. *Journal of Speech, Language, and Hearing Research, 59*, 415–429.

Eichstaedt, A., Watt, N., & Girson, J. (1998). Evaluation of the efficacy of a stutter modification program with particular reference to two new measures of secondary behaviors and control of stuttering. *Journal of Fluency Disorders, 23*, 231–246.

Eisenson, J., & Ogilvie, M. (1963). *Speech correction in the schools* (2nd ed.). Macmillan.

Ellis, C. M. (2017). Using simulation and critical thinking in speech-language pathology: A university case study. *Journal of Human Services: Training, Research, and Practice, 2*(2), 6.

Embrechts, M., Ebben, H., Franke, P., & van de Poel, C. (2000). Temperament: A comparison between children who stutter and children who do not stutter. In H. G. Bosshardt, J. S. Yaruss, & H. F. M. Peters (Eds.), *Proceedings of the Third World Congress on Fluency Disorders* (pp. 557–562). Nijmegen University.

Emerick, L. L. (1974). Stuttering therapy: Dimensions of interpersonal sensitivity. In L. L. Emerick & S. B. Hood (Eds.), *The client–clinician relationship: Essays on interpersonal sensitivity in the therapeutic transaction* (pp. 92–102). Charles C. Thomas.

Emerick, L. L. (1988). Counseling adults who stutter: A cognitive approach. *Seminars in Speech and Language, 9*(3), 257–267.

Epley, N., Keysar, B., Bovan, L. V., & Gilovick, T. (2004). Perspective taking as anchoring and adjustment. *Journal of Personality and Social Psychology, 87*, 327–339.

Epner, D. E., & Baile, W. F. (2012). Patient-centered care: The key to cultural competence. *Annals of Oncology, 23*, iii33–iii42. https://doi.org/10.1093/annonc/mds086

Epstein, R. M. (2003a). Mindful practice in action (I): Technical competence, evidence-based medicine, and relationship-centered care. *Families, Systems, and Health, 21*(1), 1.

Epstein, R. M. (2003b). Mindful practice in action (II): Cultivating habits of mind. *Families, Systems, and Health, 21*(1), 11.

Epston, D., & White, M. (1990). *Narrative means to therapeutic ends.* Norton.

Erickson, R. L. (1969). Assessing communication attitudes among stutterers. *Journal of Speech and Hearing Research, 12*, 711–724.

Ericsson, A. K., & Smith, J. (1991). Prospects and limits of the empirical study of expertise: An introduction. In A. K. Ericsson & J. Smith (Eds.), *Toward a general theory of expertise: Prospects and limits* (pp. 1–38). Cambridge University Press.

Evans, J., & Williams, R. (2015). Stuttering in film media—Investigation of a stereotype. *Procedia—Social and Behavioral Sciences, 193*, 337. https://doi.org/10.1016/j.sbspro.2015.03.310

Evesham, M., & Fransella, F. (1985). Stuttering relapse: The effect of a combined speech and psychological reconstruction programme. *British Journal of Disorders of Communication, 20*, 237–248.

Ezrati-Vinacour, R., & Levin, I. (2004). The relationship between anxiety and stuttering: A multidimensional approach. *Journal of Fluency Disorders, 29*, 135–148.

Ezrati-Vinacour, R., Platzky, R., & Yairi, E. (2001). The young child's awareness of stuttering-like disfluency. *Journal of Speech, Language, and Hearing Research, 44*, 368–380.

Fairbanks, G. (1954). Systematic research in experimental phonetics—I. A. A theory of the speech mechanism as a servomechanism. *Journal of Speech and Hearing Disorders, 19*, 133–139.

Fairbanks, G. (1960). *Voice and articulation drillbook.* Addison-Wesley Educational Publishers.

Fant, G. (1960). *The acoustic theory of speech production.* Mouton.

Farzan, I., & Tetnowski, J. (2022). *Harmful stuttering myths perpetuated by major media outlets @ASHA.* https://leader.pubs.asha.org/do/10.1044/2022-0511-biden-stuttering-news/full/

Faulkner, R. O. (1962). *A concise dictionary of Middle Egyptian.* Griffith Institute at the University Press.

Feller, C. P., & Cottone, R. R. (2003). The importance of empathy in the therapeutic alliance. *Journal of Humanistic Counseling, 42*, 53–61.

Felsenfeld, S. (1996). Progress and needs in the genetics of stuttering. *Journal of Fluency Disorders, 21*, 77–103.

Felsenfeld, S. (1997). Epidemiology and genetics of stuttering. In R. Curlee & G. Siegel (Eds.), *Nature and treatment of stuttering, new directions* (2nd ed., pp. 3–23). Allyn & Bacon.

Felsenfeld, S., Kirk, K. M., Zhu, G., Statham, D. J., Neale, M. C., & Martin, N. G. (2000). A study of the genetic and environmental etiology of stuttering in a selected twin sample. *Behavior Genetics, 30*, 359–366.

Fenichel, O. (1945). *The psychoanalytic theory of neurosis.* Norton.

Fey, M., & Johnson, B. (1998). Research to practice (and back again) in speech-language intervention. *Topics in Language Disorders, 18*(2), 23–34.

Fibiger, S. (1994). Did Moses and Demosthenes stutter? *Journal of Fluency Disorders: Abstracts of the First World Congress on Fluency Disorders, 19*, 173.

Fine, M., & Asch, A. (1985). Disabled women: Sexism without the pedestal. In M. J. Deegan & N. A. Brooks (Eds.), *Women and disability: The double handicap* (pp. 6–22). Transaction.

Finn, P. (1996). Establishing the validity of recovery from stuttering without formal treatment. *Journal of Speech, Language and Hearing Research, 39*, 1171–1181.

Finn, P. (1997). Adults recovered from stuttering without formal treatment: Perceptual assessment of speech normalcy. *Journal of Speech, Language, and Hearing Research, 40*, 821–831.

Finn, P. (2003). Evidence-based treatment of stuttering: II. Clinical significance of behavioral stuttering treatments. *Journal of Fluency Disorders, 28*, 209–218.

Finn, P. (2011). Critical thinking: Knowledge and skills for evidence-based practice. *Language, Speech, and Hearing Services in Schools, 42*, 69–72.

Finn, P., Ingham, R. J., Ambrose, N., & Yairi, D. (1997). Children recovered from stuttering without formal treatment. *Journal of Speech, Language and Hearing Research, 40*, 867–876.

Fish, J. M. (1995). Does problem behavior just happen? Does it matter? *Behavior and Social Issues, 5*(1), 3–12.

Fitch, J. L., & Batson, E. A. (1989). Hemispheric asymmetry of alpha wave suppression in stutterers and nonstutterers. *Journal of Fluency Disorders, 9*, 47–55.

Flanagan, B., Goldiamond, I., & Azrin, N. (1958). Operant stuttering: The control of stuttering behavior through response-contingent consequences. *Journal of Experimental Analysis of Behavior, 1*, 173–177.

Flanagan, B., Goldiamond, I., & Azrin, N. (1959). Instatement of stuttering in normally fluent individuals through operant procedures. *Science, 130*, 979–981.

Flasher, L., & Fogle, P. (2011). *Counseling skills for the speech-language pathologist and audiologist* (2nd ed.). Delmar Cengage Learning.

Fletcher, J. M. (1914). An experimental study of stuttering. *American Journal of Psychology, 2*, 201–255.

Floyd, J., Zebrowski, P., & Flamme, G. A. (2007). Stages of change and stuttering: A preliminary view. *Journal of Fluency Disorders, 32*, 95–120.

Flynn, T. W., & St. Louis, K. O. (2011). Changing adolescent attitudes toward stuttering, *Journal of Fluency Disorders, 36*, 110–121.

Fosnot, S. (1993). Research design for examining treatment efficacy in fluency disorders, *Journal of Fluency Disorders, 18*, 221–251.

Foucault, M. (1983a). On the genealogy of ethics: An overview of work in progress. In H. L. Dreyfus & P. Rabinow (Eds.), *Michel Foucault: Beyond structuralism and hermeneutics* (2nd ed., pp. 229–252). University of Chicago Press.

Foucault, M. (1983b). The subject and power. In H. L. Dreyfus & P. Rabinow (Eds.), *Michel Foucault: Beyond structuralism and hermeneutics* (2nd ed., pp. 208–226). University of Chicago Press.

Foucault, M. (1988). Technologies of the self. In L. H. Martin, H. Gutman, & P. H. Hutton (Eds.), *Technologies of the self: A seminar with Michel Foucault.* University of Massachusetts Press.

Foucault, M. (1997a). The ethics of the concern of the self as a practice of freedom. In P. Rabinow (Ed.), *Ethics: Subjectivity and truth.* (pp. 281–301). New Press. (Original work published 1984)

Foucault, M. (1997b). *Ethics: Subjectivity and truth* (Vol. 1). New Press.

Foundas, A. L., Bollich, A. M., Corey, D. M., Hurley, M., & Heilman, K. M. (2001). Anomalous anatomy of speech-language areas in adults with developmental stuttering. *Neurology, 57,* 207–215.

Frank, J. D. (1974). *Persuasion and healing.* Shocken.

Franken, M. C., Boves, L., & Peters, H. F. M. (1997). Evaluation of Dutch precision fluency-shaping program. In E. C. Healey & H. F. M. Peters (Eds.), *International Fluency Association, Second World Congress on fluency disorders: Proceedings* (pp. 303–307). Nijmegen University Press.

Franken, M. C., & Laroes, E. (2021). RESTART-DCM method (Rev. ed.). https://restartdcm.nl/wp-content/uploads/2021/05/RestartDCM-Method-2021_online.pdf

Franken, M. C., Van der Schalk, C. J., & Boelens, H. (2005). Experimental treatment of early stuttering: A preliminary study. *Journal of Fluency Disorders, 30,* 189–199.

Fransella, F. (1972). *Personal change and reconstruction.* Academic Press.

Fransella, F. (2003). From theory to research to change. In F. Fransella (Ed.), *International handbook of personal construct psychology* (pp. 211–222). Wiley.

Fransella, F., & Dalton, P. (1990). *Personal construct counseling in action.* Sage.

Freeman, F. J., & Ushijima, T. (1974). Laryngeal activity accompanying the moment of stuttering: A preliminary report of EMG investigations. *Journal of Fluency Disorders, 1,* 36–45.

Freeman, F. J., & Ushijima, T. (1978). Laryngeal muscle activity during stuttering. *Journal of Speech and Hearing Research, 21,* 538–562.

Freud, D., & Amir, O. (2020). Resilience in people who stutter: Association with covert and overt characteristics of stuttering. *Journal of Fluency Disorders, 64,* 105761. https://doi.org/10.1016/j.jfludis.2020.105761

Freud, S. (1928). Humor. *International Journal of Psychoanalysis, 9,* 1–6.

Freund, H. (1934). Über inneres Stottern [About inner stuttering]. *Zeitschrift für die gesamte Neurologie und Psychiatrie, 151*(1), 585–598.

Freund, H. (1966). *Psychopathology and the problems of stuttering.* Charles C. Thomas.

Frigerio-Domingues, C., & Drayna, D. (2017). Genetic contributions to stuttering: The current evidence. *Molecular Genetics & Genomic Medicine, 5*(2), 95–102. https://doi.org/10.1002/mgg3.276

Frigerio-Domingues, C. E., Gkalitsiou, Z., Zezinka, A., Sainz, E., Gutierrez, J., Byrd, C., . . . Drayna, D. (2019). Genetic factors and therapy outcomes in persistent developmental stuttering. *Journal of Communication Disorders, 80,* 11–17. https://doi.org/10.1016/j.jcomdis.2019.03.007

Froeschels, E. (1948). *Twentieth century speech and voice correction.* Philosophical Library.

Furlanis, G., Busan, P., Formaggio, E., Menichelli, A., Lunardelli, A., Ajcevic, M., Pesavento, V., & Manganotti, P. (2023). Stuttering-like dysfluencies as a consequence of long COVID-19. *Journal of Speech, Language, and*

Hearing Research, 66(2), 415–430. https://doi .org/10.1044/2022_jslhr-22-00381

Gahl, S. (2020). Bilingualism as a purported risk factor for stuttering: A close look at a seminal study (Travis et al., 1937). *Journal of Speech, Language, and Hearing Research, 63*(11), 3680–3684. https://doi.org/10.1044/2020 _jslhr-20-00364

Gaines, N., Runyan, C., & Meyers, S. (1991). A comparison of young stutterers' fluent versus stuttered utterances on measures of length and complexity. *Journal of Speech and Hearing Research, 34,* 37–42.

Gambrill, E. D. (2012). *Critical thinking in clinical practice: Improving the quality of judgments and decisions* (3rd ed.). Wiley.

Garnett, E. O., Chow, H. M., Nieto-Castañón, A., Tourville, J. A., Guenther, F. H., & Chang, S.-E. (2018). Anomalous morphology in left hemisphere motor and premotor cortex of children who stutter. *Brain, 141*(9), 2670–2684. https://doi.org/10.1093/brain /awy199

Geller, S. M., Greenberg, L. S., & Watson, J. C. (2010). Therapist and client perceptions of therapeutic presence: The development of a measure. *Psychotherapy Research, 20*(5), 599–610.

Geschwind, N., & Galaburda, A. M. (1985). Cerebral lateralization: Biological mechanisms, associations, and pathology: I. A hypothesis and a program for research. *Archives of Neurology, 42,* Pt. I: 429–459; Pt. II: 534–552; Pt. III: 634–654.

Gillam, R. B., Logan, K. J., & Pearson, N. (2009). *Test of Childhood Stuttering.* Pro-Ed.

Gillespie, S. K., & Cooper, E. B. (1973). Prevalence of speech problems in junior and senior high schools. *Journal of Speech and Hearing Research, 16,* 739–743.

Giraud, A., Neumann, K., Bachoud-Levi, A., von Gudenberg, A., Euler, H., Lanfermann, H., & Preibisch, C. (2008). Severity of dysfluency correlates with basal ganglia activity in persistent developmental stuttering. *Brain and Language, 104,* 190–199.

Glasner, P. J. (1949). Personality characteristics and emotional problems in stutterers under the age of five. *Journal of Speech and Hearing Disorders, 14,* 135–138.

Glasner, P. J., & Rosenthal, D. (1957). Parental diagnosis of stuttering in young children. *Journal of Speech and Hearing Disorders, 22,* 288–295.

Glauber, I. P. (1958). The psychoanalysis of stuttering. In J. Eisenson (Ed.), *Stuttering: A symposium* (pp. 71–119). Harper & Brothers.

Glauber, I. P. (1982). *Stuttering: A psychoanalytic understanding.* Human Sciences Press.

Goldberg, B. (1989). Historic treatment of stuttering: From pebbles to psychoanalysis. *ASHA, 31*(6–7), 71.

Goldman-Eisler, F. (1961). The continuity of speech utterance: Its determinants and its significance. *Language and Speech, 4,* 220–231.

Goleman, D. (2006). *Social intelligence.* Bantam Dell.

Gonçalves, M. M., Mendes, I., Ribeiro, A. P., Angus, L. E., & Greenberg, L. S. (2010). Innovative moments and change in emotion-focused therapy: The case of Lisa. *Journal of Constructivist Psychology, 23*(4), 267–294.

Goodstein, L. D. (1958). Functional speech disorders and personality: A survey of the research. *Journal of Speech and Hearing Research, 1,* 359–376.

Gordon, K. C., Hutchinson, J. M., & Allen, C. S. (1976). An evaluation of selected discourse characteristics in normal geriatric subjects. *Idaho State University Laboratory Research Reports, 1,* 11–21.

Gordon, P. (1991). Language task effects: A comparison of stuttering and nonstuttering children. *Journal of Fluency Disorders, 16,* 275–287.

Gordon, T. (1970). *PET: Parent effectiveness training.* Wyden.

Gottschalk, L. A., & Gleser, G. C. (1969). *The measurement of psychological states through the content analysis of verbal behavior.* University of California Press.

Gottwald, S. R. (1999). Family communication pattern and stuttering development: An analysis of the research literature. In N. B. Ratner & E. C. Healey (Eds.), *Stuttering research and practice: Bridging the gap* (pp. 175–192). Erlbaum.

Gottwald, S. R., & Starkweather, C. W. (1995). Fluency intervention for preschoolers and their families in the public schools. *Language, Speech, and Hearing Services in Schools, 26*, 117–126.

Gottwald, S. R., & Starkweather, C. W. (1999). Stuttering prevention and early intervention: A multi-process approach. In M. Onslow & A. Packman (Eds.), *The handbook of early stuttering intervention* (pp. 53–82). Singular Publishing.

Gould, S. J. (1995). *Dinosaur in a haystack.* Random House.

Gould, S. J. (1997). *Why people believe weird things.* Freeman.

Grant, A. C., Blousse, V., Cook, A. A., & Newman, N. J. (1999). Stroke-associated stuttering. *Archives of Neurology, 56*, 624–627.

Gregory, H. H. (1972). An assessment of the results of stuttering therapy. *Journal of Communication Disorders, 5*, 320–334.

Gregory, H. H. (1983). *The clinician's attitudes in counseling stutterers* (Publication No. 18). Stuttering Foundation of America.

Gregory, H. H. (1984). Prevention of stuttering: Management of the early stages. In R. F. Curlee & W. H. Perkins (Eds.), *Nature and treatment of stuttering: New directions* (pp. 335–356). College-Hill Press.

Gregory, H. H. (1986). *Stuttering: Differential evaluation and therapy.* PRO-ED.

Gregory, H. H. (1989). *Stuttering therapy: A workshop for specialists* [Unpublished manuscript]. Northwestern University.

Gregory, H. H. (1995). Analysis and commentary. *Language, Speech, and Hearing Services in Schools, 26*(2), 196–200.

Gregory, H. H. (2004). *Do you stutter: A guide for teens* (4th ed., Publication No. 0021, 40). The Stuttering Foundation.

Gregory, H. H., & Hill, D. (1980). Stuttering therapy for children. In W. Perkins (Ed.), *Stuttering disorders* (pp. 351–363). Thieme Medical.

Groat, M., & Allen, J. G. (2011). Promoting mentalizing in experimental psychoeducational groups: From agency and author-ity to authorship. *Bulletin of the Menninger Clinic, 75*(4), 315–343.

Groopman, J. (2004). The biology of hope. In J. Groopman (Ed.), *The anatomy of hope: How people prevail in the face of illness* (pp. 161–190). Random House.

Grosjean, F. (2010). *Bilingual: Life and reality.* Harvard University Press.

Grossman, H. (2008). *Voluntary stuttering: A mixed-methods investigation* (UMI No. 3343421). ProQuest Dissertations and Theses.

Guenther, F. H. (2008). Neuroimaging of normal speech production. In R. J. Ingham (Ed.), *Neuroimaging in communication sciences and disorders* (pp. 1–51). Plural Publishing.

Guitar, B. (1976). Pretreatment factors associated with the outcome of stuttering therapy. *Journal of Speech and Hearing Research, 18*, 590–600.

Guitar, B. (1997). Therapy for children's stuttering and emotions. In R. F. Curlee & G. M. Siegel (Eds.), *Nature and treatment of stuttering: New directions* (2nd ed., pp. 280–291). Allyn & Bacon.

Guitar, B. (1998). *Stuttering: An integrated approach to its nature and treatment* (2nd ed.). Lippincott Williams & Wilkins.

Guitar, B. (2006). *Stuttering: An integrated approach to its nature and treatment* (3rd ed.). Lippincott Williams & Wilkins.

Guitar, B. (2014). *Stuttering: An integrated approach to its nature and treatment* (4th ed.). Lippincott Williams & Wilkins.

Guitar, B. (2019). *Stuttering: An integrated approach to its nature and treatment.* Wolters Kluwer.

Guitar, B. E., & Bass, C. (1978). Stuttering therapy: The relation between attitude change and long-term outcome. *Journal of Speech and Hearing Disorders, 43*, 392–400.

Guitar, B., & Grims, S. (1977, November). *Developing a scale to assess communication attitudes in children who stutter* [Paper presentation]. Annual Convention of the American Speech-Language-Hearing Association, Atlanta, GA.

Guitar, G., Kazenski, D., Howard, A., Cousins, S. F., Fader, E., & Haskell, P. (2015). Predicting treatment time and long-term outcome of the Lidcombe Program: A replication and reanalysis. *American Journal of Speech-Language Pathology, 24*, 533–544.

Guitar, B., & Peters, T. J. (1980). *Stuttering: An integration of contemporary therapies* (Publication No. 16). Stuttering Foundation of America.

Guntupalli, V. K., Kalinowski, J., Nanjundeswaran, C., Saltuklaroglu, T., & Everhart, D. E. (2006). Psychophysiological responses of adults who do not stutter while listening to stuttering. *International Journal of Psychophysiology, 62*(1), 1–8.

Gupta, M. (2011). Improved health or improved decision making? The ethical goals of EBM. *Journal of Evaluation in Clinical Practice, 17*, 957–963.

Haig, R. A. (1986). Therapeutic use of humor. *American Journal of Psychotherapy 40*(4), 543–553.

Hakuta, K. (2009). *Encyclopedia of neuroscience.* Elsevier/Academic Press.

Hall, J. W., & Jerger, J. (1978). Central auditory function in stutterers. *Journal of Speech and Hearing Research, 21*, 324–337.

Hall, K. D., Amir, O., & Yairi, E. (1999). A longitudinal investigation of speaking rate in preschool children who stutter. *Journal of Speech, Language, and Hearing Research, 42*, 1367–1377.

Hall, K. D., & Yairi, E. (1992). Fundamental frequency, jitter, and shimmer in preschoolers who stutter. *Journal of Speech, Language, and Hearing Research, 35*, 1002–1008.

Hall, P. K. (1977). The occurrence of disfluencies in language-disordered school-aged children. *Journal of Speech and Hearing Disorders, 42*, 364–369.

Ham, R. E. (1986). *Techniques of stuttering therapy.* Prentice Hall.

Ham, R. E. (1989). What are we measuring? *Journal of Fluency Disorders, 14*, 231–243.

Ham, R. E. (1999). *Clinical management of stuttering in older children and adults.* Aspen.

Hamre, C. (1992). Stuttering prevention I: Primacy of identification. *Journal of Fluency Disorders, 17*, 3–23.

Han, T.-U., Root, J., Reyes, L. D., Huchinson, E. B., du Hoffmann, J., Lee, W.-S., . . .

Drayna, D. (2019). Human GNPTAB stuttering mutations engineered into mice cause vocalization deficits and astrocyte pathology in the corpus callosum. *Proceedings of the National Academy of Sciences, 116*(35), 17515–17524. https://doi.org/10.1073/pnas.1901480116

Hancock, K., & Craig, A. (1998). Predictors of stuttering relapse one year following treatment for children aged 9 to 14 years. *Journal of Fluency Disorders, 23*, 31–48.

Hancock, K., Craig, A., McCready, C., McCaul, A., Costello, D., Campbell, K., & Gilmore, G. (1998). Two-to six-year controlled-trial stuttering outcomes for children and adolescents. *Journal of Speech, Language, and Hearing Research, 41*, 1242–1252.

Harasym, J., Langevin, M., & Kully, D. (2015). Video-self-modeling as a post-treatment fluency recovery strategy for adults. *Journal of Fluency Disorders, 44*, 32–45.

Harris, L. M., Adamson, B. J., Reed, V., & Hunt, A. E. (1998). Impact of curricular change in an undergraduate program for speech pathologists on perceived preparedness for the workplace. *Journal of Allied Health, 27*, 221–227.

Hastorf, A. H., Windfogel, J., & Cassman, T. (1979). Acknowledgement of handicap as a tactic in social interaction. *Journal of Personality and Social Psychology, 37*, 1790–1797.

Hayden, P. A., Scott, D. A., & Addicott, J. (1977). The effects of delayed auditory feedback on the overt behaviors of stutterers. *Journal of Fluency Disorders, 2*, 235–246.

Hayhow, R., & Levy, C. (1989). *Working with stuttering.* Winslow Press.

Healey, E. C. (1982). Speaking fundamental frequency characteristics of stutterers and nonstutterers. *Journal of Communications Disorders, 15*(1), 21–29.

Healey, E. C. (Ed.). (1995, June). *Division 4 Newsletter, 5*(2). American Speech-Language-Hearing Association.

Healey, E. C., Gabel, R. M., Daniels, D. E., & Kawai, N. (2007). The effects of self-disclosure and non self-disclosure of stuttering on listeners' perceptions of a person who stutters. *Journal of Fluency Disorders, 32*(1), 51–69.

Healey, E. C., & Scott, L. A. (1995). Strategies for treating elementary school-age children who stutter: An integrative approach. *Language, Speech, and Hearing Services in Schools, 26*, 151–161.

Heather, N., Smailes, D., & Cassidy, P. (2008). Development of a readiness ruler for use with alcohol brief interventions. *Drug and Alcohol Dependence, 98*, 235–240.

Heelan, M., McAllister, J., & Skinner, J. (2016). Stuttering, alcohol consumption and smoking. *Journal of Fluency Disorders, 48*, 27–34.

Hegde, M. H. (1972). Stuttering, neuroticism and extroversion. *Behavior Research Therapy, 10*, 395–397.

Heifetz, R. A., Grashow, A., & Linsky, M. (2009). *The practice of adaptive leadership.* Harvard Business Press.

Heifetz, R. A., & Laurie, D. L. (1997). The work of leadership. *Harvard Business Review, 75*, 124–134.

Heifetz, R. A., & Linsky, M. (2002). *Leadership on the line.* Harvard Business Press.

Helm, N. A., Butler, R. B., & Canter, G. J. (1980). Neurogenic acquired stuttering. *Journal of Fluency Disorders, 5*, 269–279.

Helm-Estabrooks, N. (1986). Diagnosis and management of neurogenic stuttering in adults. In K. O. St. Louis (Ed.), *The atypical stutterer* (pp. 193–217). Academic Press.

Helm-Estabrooks, N. (1993). Stuttering associated with acquired neurological disorders. In R. Curlee (Ed.), *Stuttering and related disorders of fluency* (pp. 255–268). Thieme Medical.

Helm-Estabrooks, N. (1999). Stuttering associated with acquired neurological disorders. In R. Curlee (Ed.), *Stuttering and related disorders of fluency* (2nd ed., pp. 255–268). Thieme Medical.

Helm-Estabrooks, N., & Hotz, G. (1998). Sudden onset of "stuttering" in an adult: Neurogenic or psychogenic? *Seminars in Speech and Language, 19*(1), 23–29.

Helm-Estabrooks, N. A., Yeo, R., Geschwind, M., Freedman, M., & Wenstein, C. (1986). Stuttering: Disappearance and reappearance with acquired brain lesions. *Neurology, 36*, 1109–1112.

Herder, C., Howard, C., Nye, C., & Vanryckeghem, M., (2006). Effectiveness of behavioral stuttering treatment: A systematic review and meta-analysis. *Contemporary Issues in Communication Science and Disorders, 33*, 61–73.

Hillis, J. W. (1993). Ongoing assessment in the management of stuttering: A clinical perspective. *American Journal of Speech-Language Pathology, 2*(1), 24–37.

Hillis, J., & Manning, W. H. (1996, November). *Extraclinical generalization of speech fluency: A social cognitive approach* [Paper presentation]. Annual Meeting of the American Speech-Language-Hearing Association, Seattle, WA.

Hillman, R. E., & Gilbert, H. R. (1977). Voice onset time for voiceless stop consonants in the fluent reading of stutterers and nonstutterers. *Journal of the Acoustical Society of America, 61*, 610–611.

Hoepfner, T. (1922). Zur klinik und systematik der assoziativen aphasie [On the clinic and systematics of associative aphasia]. *Zeitschrift für die gesamte Neurologie und Psychiatrie, 79*(1), 1–45.

Holland, A. L. (2007). *Counseling in communication disorders: A wellness perspective.* Plural Publishing.

Holland, A. L., & Nelson, R. L. (2018). *Counseling in communication disorders: A wellness perspective* (3rd ed.). Plural Publishing.

Hollis, S., &, Campbell, F. (1999). What is meant by intention to treat analysis? Survey of published randomized controlled trials. *British Medical Journal, 319*, 670–674.

Hood, S. B. (1974). Clients, clinicians and therapy. In L. L. Emerick & S. B. Hood (Eds.), *The client–clinician relationship: Essays on interpersonal sensitivity in the therapeutic transaction* (pp. 45–59). Charles C. Thomas.

Horvath, A. O., & Symonds, B. D. (1991). Relation between working alliance and outcome in psychotherapy: A meta-analysis. *Journal of Counseling Psychology, 38*, 139–149.

Hosseini, R., Walsh, B., Tian, F., & Wang, S. (2018). An fNIRS-based feature learning and classification framework to distinguish hemodynamic patterns in children who stutter. *IEEE Transactions on Neural Systems and Rehabilitation Engineering, 26*(6), 1254–1263. https://doi.org/10.1109/tnsre.2018.28 29083

Howell, P. (2004). Assessment of some contemporary theories of stuttering that apply to spontaneous speech. *Contemporary Issues in Communication Sciences and Disorders, 31*, 123–140.

Howell, P., & Au-Yeung, J. (2002). The EXPLAN theory of fluency control applied to the diagnosis of stuttering. In E. Fava (Ed.), *Pathology and therapy of speech disorders* (pp. 75–94). John Benjamin.

Howell, P., Au-Yeung, J., & Sackin, S. (1999). Exchange of stuttering form function words to content words with age. *Journal of Speech, Language, and Hearing Research, 42*, 345–354.

Howell, P., Davis, S., & Au-Yeung, J. (2003). Syntactic development in fluent children, children who stutter, and children who have English as an additional language. *Child Language Teaching and Therapy, 19*, 311–337.

Howell, P., Sackin, S., & Williams, R. (1999). Differential effects of frequency-shifted feedback between child and adult stutterers. *Journal of Fluency Disorders, 24*, 127–136.

Howie, P. M. (1981). Concordance for stuttering in monozygotic and dizygotic twin pairs. *Journal of Speech and Hearing Research, 24*, 317–321.

Howie, P. M., Tanner, S., & Andrews, G. (1981). Short and long term outcome in an intensive treatment program for adult stutterers. *Journal of Speech and Hearing Disorders, 46*, 104–109.

Howie, P., Woods, C., & Andrews, J. (1982). Relationship between covert and overt speech measures immediately before and immediately after stuttering treatment. *Journal of Speech and Hearing Disorders, 47*, 419–422.

Huang, G. C., Newman, L. R., & Schwartzstein, R. M. (2014). Critical thinking in health professions education: Summary and consensus statements of the Millennium Conference 2011. *Teaching and Learning in Medicine, 26*, 95–102.

Hubble, M. A., Duncan, B. L., & Miller, S. D. (1999). *The heart and soul of change: What works in therapy.* APA Press.

Huinck, W. J., Langevin, M., Kully, D., Graamans, K., Peters, H. F. M., & Hulstijn, W. (2006). The relationship between pretreatment clinical profile and treatment outcome in an integrated stuttering program. *Journal of Fluency Disorders, 31*(1), 43–63.

Huinck, W. J., & Peters, H. F. M. (2004). *Effect of speech therapy on stuttering: Evaluating three therapy programs* [Paper presentation]. IALP Congress, Brisbane, Australia.

Hunt, B. (1987). Self-help for stutterers—Experience in Britain. In L. Rustin, H. Purser, & K. D. Rowley (Eds.), *Progress in the treatment of fluency disorders* (pp. 198–212). Taylor & Francis.

Hunt, H. (1967). *Stammering and stuttering, their nature and treatment.* Hafner. (Original work published 1861)

Hyter, Y. D., & Salas-Provance, M. B. (2019). *Culturally responsive practices in speech, language and hearing sciences.* Plural Publishing.

Ingham, R. J. (1982). The effects of self-evaluation and training and maintenance and generalization during stuttering treatment. *Journal of Speech and Hearing Disorders, 47*, 271–280.

Ingham, R. J. (1984). *Stuttering and behavior therapy: Current status and experimental foundations.* College-Hill Press.

Ingham, R. J. (2004). Emerging controversies, findings, and directions in neuroimaging and developmental stuttering: On avoiding petard hoisting in Athens, Georgia. In A. C. Bothe (Ed.), *Evidenced-based treatment of stuttering: Empirical basis and clinical applications* (pp. 27–64). Erlbaum.

Ingham, R. J., Andrews, G., & Winkler, R. (1972). Stuttering: A comparative evaluation of the short term effectiveness of four treatment techniques. *Journal of Communication Disorders, 5*, 91–117.

Ingham, R. J., & Cordes, A. K. (1992). Inter-clinic differences in stuttering event counts. *Journal of Fluency Disorders, 17*, 171–176.

Ingham, R. J., & Cordes, A. K. (1997). Self-measurement and evaluating treatment efficacy. In R. F. Curlee & G. M. Siegel (Eds.), *Nature and treatment of stuttering: New directions* (pp. 413–438). Allyn & Bacon.

Ingham, R. J., Cordes, A. K., & Gow, M. (1993). Time-interval measurement of stuttering: Modifying interjudge agreement. *Journal of Speech and Hearing Research, 36*, 503–515.

Ingham, R. J., Fox, P. T., & Ingham, J. C. (1994). Brain image investigation of the speech of stutterers and nonstutterers. *ASHA, 36*, 188.

Ingham, R. J., Martin, R. R., Haroldson, S. K., Onslow, M., & Leney, M. (1985). Modification of listener-judged naturalness in the speech of stutterers. *Journal of Speech and Hearing Research, 28*, 495–504.

Ingham, R. J., Moglia, R. A., Frank, P., Ingham, J. C., & Cordes, A. K. (1997). Experimental investigation of the effects of frequency-altered auditory feedback on the speech of adults who stutter. *Journal of Speech, Language and Hearing Research, 40*, 361–372.

Ingham, R. J., & Onslow, M. (1985). Measurement and modification of speech naturalness during stuttering therapy. *Journal of Speech and Hearing Disorders, 50*, 261–281.

Interprofessional Education Collaborative Expert Panel. (2011). *Core competencies for interprofessional collaborative practice: Report of an expert panel.* Interprofessional Education Collaborative.

Iverach, L., Heard, R., Menzies, R., Lowe, R., O'Brian, S., Packman, A., & Onslow, M. (2016). A brief version of the Unhelpful Thoughts and Beliefs About Stuttering scales: The UTBAS-6. *Journal of Speech, Language, and Hearing Research, 59*(5), 964–972. https://doi.org/10.1044/2016_JSLHR-S-15-0167

Iverach, L., Jones, M., O'Brian, S., Block, S., Lincoln, M., Harrison, E., . . . Onslow, M. (2009a). The relationship between mental health disorders and treatment outcomes among adults who stutter. *Journal of Fluency Disorders, 34*, 29–43.

Iverach, L., Jones, M., O'Brian, S., Block, S., Lincoln, M., Harrison, E., . . . Onslow, M. (2010). Mood and substance use disorders among adults seeking speech therapy for stuttering. *Journal of Speech, Language, and Hearing Research, 53*, 1178–1190.

Iverach, L., Menzies, R. G., O'Brian, S., Packman, A., & Onslow, M. (2011). Anxiety and stuttering: Continuing to explore a complex relationship. *American Journal of Speech-Language Pathology, 20*, 221–232.

Jäncke, L., Hänggi, J., & Steinmetz, H. (2004). Morphological brain differences between adult stutterers and non-stutterers. *BMC Neurology, 4*(1). https://doi.org/10.1186/1471-2377-4-23

Jezer, M. (1997). *Stuttering: A life bound up in words.* Basic Books.

Johnson, W. (1930). *Because I stutter.* Appleton-Century-Crofts.

Johnson, W. (1944). The Indians have no word for it: I. Stuttering in children. *Quarterly Journal of Speech, 30*(3), 330–337.

Johnson, W. (1946). *People in quandaries.* Harper Brothers.

Johnson, W. (1958). The six men and the stuttering. In J. Eisenson (Ed.), *Stuttering* (pp. xi–xxiv). Harper & Brothers.

Johnson, W. (1961). Measurement of oral reading and speaking rate and disfluency of adult male and female stutterers and non-stutterers. *Journal of Speech and Hearing Disorders* (Monograph Suppl. 7), 1–20.

Johnson, W. (1962). *An open letter to the mother of a "stuttering" child.* Interstate Printers and Publishers.

Johnson, W., & Associates. (1959). *The onset of stuttering.* University of Minnesota Press.

Johnson, W., Brown, S., Curtis, J., Edney, C., & Keaster, J. (1967). *Speech handicapped school children* (3rd ed.). Harper & Row.

Johnson, W., Darley, F. L., & Spriestersbach, D. C. (1963). *Diagnostic methods in speech pathology.* Harper & Row.

Jokel, R., & De Nil, L. F. (2003). A comprehensive study of acquired stuttering in adults. In K. L. Baker & D. T. Rowley (Eds.), *Proceedings of the Sixth Oxford Dysfluency Conference* (pp. 59–64). Kevin Baker.

Jokel, R., De Nil, L. F., & Sharpe, A. K. (2007). A comparison of speech disfluencies in adults with acquired stuttering associated with stroke and traumatic brain injury. *Journal of Medical Speech-Language Pathology, 15*(3), 243–261.

Jones, J. E., & Niven, P. (1993). *Voices and silences.* Charles Scribner's Sons.

Jones, M., Onslow, M., Packman, A., Williams, S., Ormond, T., Schwartz, I., & Gebski, V. (2005). Randomized controlled trial of the Lidcombe Programme of early stuttering intervention. *British Medical Journal, 331,* 659–661.

Jones, N., Marks, R., Ramirez, R., & Rios-Vargas, M. (2021). *2020 Census illuminates racial and ethnic composition of the country.* https://www.census.gov/library/stories/2021/08/improved-race-ethnicity-measures-reveal-united-states-population-much-more-multiracial.html

Jones, R. (1966). Observations on stammering after localized cerebral injury. *Journal of Neurology, Neurosurgery, and Psychiatry, 29,* 192–195.

Juste, F. S., Sassi, F. C., & de Andrade, C. R. (2012). Exchange of disfluency with age from function to content words in Brazilian Portuguese speakers who do and do not stutter. *Clinical Linguistics and Phonetics, 26,* 946–961.

Kabat-Zinn, J. (2003). Mindfulness-based interventions in context: Past, present, and future. *Clinical Psychology: Science and Practice, 10*(2), 144–156.

Kagan, J., Reznick, J. S., & Snidman, N. (1987). The physiology and psychology of behavioral inhibition in children, *Child Development, 58,* 1459–1473.

Kalinowski, J., Guntupalli, V. K., Stuart, A., & Saltuklaroglu, T. (2004). Self-reported efficacy of an ear-level prosthetic device that delivers altered auditory feedback for the management of stuttering. *International Journal of Rehabilitation Research, 27,* 167–170.

Kalinowski, J., Nobel, S., Armson, J., & Stuart, A. (1994). Pretreatment and post-treatment speech naturalness ratings of adults with mild and severe stuttering. *American Journal of Speech-Language Pathology, 3*(2), 61–66.

Kalinowski, J., Stuart, A., Sark, S., & Armson, J. (1996). Stuttering amelioration at various

auditory delays and speech rates. *European Journal of Disorders of Communication, 31,* 259–269.

Kamhi, A. G. (1982). The problem of relapse in stuttering: Some thoughts on what might cause it and how to deal with it. *Journal of Fluency Disorders, 7,* 459–467.

Kamhi, A. G. (1999). To use or not to use: Factors that influence the selection of new treatment approaches. *Language, Speech, and Hearing Services in Schools, 30,* 92–98.

Kamhi, A. G. (2003). Two paradoxes in stuttering treatment. *Journal of Fluency Disorders, 28,* 187–196.

Kamhi, A. G. (2011). Balancing certainty and uncertainty in clinical practice. *Language, Speech and Hearing Services in Schools, 42,* 59–64.

Kang, C., Riazuddin, S., Mundorff, J., Krasnewich, D., Friedman, P., Mulikin, J. C., & Dranya, D. (2010). Mutations in the lysosomal enzyme-targeting pathway and persistent stuttering. *New England Journal of Medicine, 362,* 677–685.

Kaplan, D. M., Tarvydas, V. M., & Gladding, S. T. (2014). 20/20: A vision for the future of counseling: The new consensus definition of counseling. *Journal of Counseling and Development, 92,* 366–372.

Katz, G., Lincoln, M., & McCabe, P. (2006, November). *Investigating stuttering in people 55 years and older: Do stuttering behaviors persist into older age?* [Paper presentation]. University of Sydney Fifth Health Research Conference, Sydney, Australia.

Kazdin, A. E. (1980). Covert and overt rehearsal and elaboration during treatment in the development of assertive behavior. *Behaviour Research and Therapy, 18,* 191–201.

Kefalianos, E., Onslow, M., Ukoumunne, O., Block, S., & Reilly, S. (2014). Stuttering, temperament, and anxiety: Data from a community cohort ages 2–4 years. *Journal of Speech, Language, and Hearing Research, 57,* 1314–1322.

Kell, C. A., Neumann, K., von Kriegstein, K., Posenenske, C., von Gudenberg, A. W., Euler, H., & Giraud, A.-L. (2009). How the brain repairs stuttering. *Brain, 132*(10),

2747–2760. https://doi.org/10.1093/brain/awp185

Kelly, E. M. (1994). Speech rates and turn-taking behaviors of children who stutter and their fathers. *Journal of Speech and Hearing Research, 37,* 1284–1294.

Kelly, E. M. (2000). Modeling stuttering etiology: Clarifying levels of description and measurement. *Journal of Fluency Disorders, 25*(4), 359–368.

Kelly, E. M., Martin, J. S., Baker, K. I., Rivera, N. J., Bishop, J. E., Kriziske, C. B., . . . Stealy, J. M. (1997). Academic and clinical preparation and practices of school speech-language pathologists with people who stutter. *Language, Speech, and Hearing Services in Schools, 28,* 195–212.

Kelly, G. A. (1955a). *The psychology of personal constructs* (Vol. 1). Norton.

Kelly, G. A. (1955b). *The psychology of personal constructs* (Vol. 2). Norton.

Kelly, G. A. (1991). *The psychology of personal constructs.* Routledge. (Original work published 1955)

Kelman, E., & Nicholas, A. (2020). *Palin Parent Child Interaction Therapy for early childhood stammering.* Routledge.

Kent, R. D. (1983). Facts about stuttering: Neurologic perspectives. *Journal of Speech and Hearing Disorders, 48,* 249–255.

Kent, R. D., & Read, C. (1992). *The acoustic analysis of speech.* Singular Publishing.

Kertesz, A. (1989). Anatomical and physiological correlations and neuroimaging techniques in language disorders. In A. Ardila & F. Ostrosky-Solis (Eds.), *Brain organization of language and cognitive processes* (pp. 37–59). Plenum.

Kfrerer, M., Rudman, D. L., Schermer, J. A., Wedlake, M., Murphy, M., & Marshall, C. A. (2023). Humor in rehabilitation professions: A scoping review. *Disability and Rehabilitation, 45*(5), 911–926. https://doi.org/10.1080/09638288.2022.2048909

Khedr, E., El-Nasser, W. A., Abdel Haleem, E. K., Bakr, M. S., & Trakhan, M. N. (2000). Evoked potentials and electroencephalography in stuttering. *Folia Phoniatrica, 52,* 178–186.

Kidd, K. K. (1977). A genetic perspective on stuttering. *Journal of Fluency Disorders, 2,* 259–269.

Kidd, K. (1984). Stuttering as a genetic disorder. In R. F. Curlee & W. H. Perkins (Eds.), *Nature and treatment of stuttering: New directions* (pp. 149–169). Allyn & Bacon.

Kidd, K. K., Heimbuch, R. C., & Records, M. A. (1981). Vertical transmission of susceptibility to stuttering with sex-modified expression. *Proceedings of the National Academy of Sciences, USA, 78*(1), 606–610.

Kidd, K., Heimbuch, R., Records, M. A., Oehlert, G., & Webster, R. (1980). Familial stuttering patterns are not related to one measure of severity. *Journal of Speech and Hearing Research, 23,* 539–545.

Kidd, K. K., Reich, T., & Kessler, S. (1973). A genetic analysis of stuttering suggesting a single major locus (Abstract). *Genetics, 74* (Pt. 2), s137.

Kimmel, D. C. (1974). *Adulthood and aging.* Wiley.

Kimura, D. (1961). Cerebral dominance and the perception of verbal stimuli. *Canadian Journal of Psychology, 15,* 166–171.

Kimura, D. (1964). Left–right differences in the perception of melodies. *Quarterly Journal of Experimental Psychology, 16,* 355–358.

Kinsbourne, M. (1989). A model of adaptive behavior related to cerebral participation in emotional control. In G. Gianotti & Caltagirone (Eds.), *Emotions and the dual brain* (pp. 248–260). Springer-Verlag.

Kinsbourne, M., & Bemporad, E. (1984). Lateralization of emotion: A model and evidence. In N. A. Fox & R. Davidson (Eds.), *The psychology of affective development* (pp. 259–291). Erlbaum.

Kirby, G., Delgadillo, J., Hillard, S., & Manning, W. (1992, November). *Visual imagery, relaxation, and cognitive restructuring integrated in fluency therapy* [Paper presentation]. Annual Meeting of the American Speech-Language-Hearing Association, San Antonio, TX.

Kleinman, A., Eisenberg, L., & Good, B. (1978). Culture, illness, and care: Clinical lessons from anthropologic and cross-cultural research. *Annals of Internal Medicine, 88*(2), 251–258.

Klich, R. J., & May, G. M. (1982). Spectrographic study of vowels in stutterers' fluent speech. *Journal of Speech and Hearing Research, 25*(3), 364–370.

Kline, M., & Starkweather, C. (1979). Receptive and expressive language performance in young stutterers [Abstract]. *ASHA, 21,* 797.

Kloth, S. A., Kraaimaat, F. W., Janssen, P., & Brutten, G. J. (1999). Persistence and remission of incipient stuttering among high-risk children. *Journal of Fluency Disorders, 24,* 253–265.

Knott, J. R., Correll, R. E., & Shepherd, J. L. (1959). Frequency analysis of electroencephalograms of stutterers and nonstutterers. *Journal of Speech and Hearing Research, 2,* 74–80.

Kolk, H., & Postma, A. (1997). Stuttering as a covert repair phenomenon. In R. Curlee & G. Siegel (Eds.), *Nature and treatment of stuttering: New directions* (2nd ed., pp. 182–203). Allyn & Bacon.

Korzeczek, A., Primaßin, A., Wolff von Gudenberg, A., Dechent, P., Paulus, W., Sommer, M., & Neef, N. E. (2021). Fluency shaping increases integration of the command-to-execution and the auditory-to-motor pathways in persistent developmental stuttering. *NeuroImage, 245,* 118736. https://doi.org/10.1016/j.neuroimage.2021.118736

Korzybski, A. (1941). *Science and sanity: An introduction to non-Aristotelian systems and general semantics* (2nd ed.). International Non-Aristotelian Library.

Kraaimaat, F. W., Janssen, P., & Van Dam-Baggen, R. (1991). Social anxiety and stuttering. *Perceptual and Motor Skills, 72*(3), 766.

Krall, T. (1998). My long term path toward recovery from stuttering. In E. C. Healey & H. F. M. Peters (Eds.), *Proceedings of the Second World Congress on Fluency Disorders* (pp. 388–389). Nijmegen University Press.

Kramer, M. B., Green, D., & Guitar, B. (1987). A comparison of stutterers and nonstutterers on masking level differences and synthetic sentence identification tasks. *Journal of Communication Disorders, 20,* 379–390.

Krasner, M. S., Epstein, R. M., Beckman, H., Suchman, A. L., Chapman, B., Mooney, C. J., & Quill, T. E. (2009). Association of an educational program in mindful communication with burnout, empathy, and attitudes among primary care physicians. *JAMA, 302*(12), 1284–1293.

Krauss-Lehrman, T., & Reeves, L. (1989). Attitudes toward speech-language pathology and support groups: Results of a survey of members of the National Stuttering Project. *Texas Journal of Audiology and Speech Pathology, 15*(1), 22–25.

Kroll, A. (1978). The differentiation of stutterers into interiorized and exteriorized groups. *I.A.L.P. Proceedings Copenhagen 1977* (Special-paedagogisk forlag), 137–157.

Kroll, R. M., De Nil, L. F., Kapur, S., & Houle, S. (1997). A positron emission tomography investigation of post-treatment brain activation in stutterers. In H. F. M. Peters & W. Hulstijn (Eds.), *Proceedings of the Third Speech Motor Production and Fluency Disorders Conference* (pp. 307–320). Elsevier.

Krupnick, J. L., Sotsky, S. M., Simmens, A., Moyer, J., Elkin, I., Watkins, J., & Pilkonis, P. A. (1996). The role of the alliance in psychotherapy and pharmacotherapy outcome: Findings in the National Institute of Mental Health treatment of depression collaborative research program. *Journal of Clinical and Consulting Psychology, 64,* 532–539.

Kübler-Ross, E. (1969). *On death and dying.* Simon & Schuster.

Kuhlman, T. (1984). *Humor and psychotherapy.* Dow Jones-Irwin.

Kuhr, A., & Rustin, L. (1985). The maintenance of fluency after intensive in-patient therapy: Long-term follow-up. *Journal of Fluency Disorders, 10,* 229–236.

Kully, D., & Boberg, E. (1988). An investigation of inter-clinic agreement in the identification of fluent and stuttered syllables. *Journal of Fluency Disorders, 13,* 309–318.

LaBrie, J. W., Quinlan, T., Schiffman, J. E., & Earleywine, M. E. (2005). Performance of alcohol and safer sex change rulers compared with readiness to change questionnaires. *Psychology of Addictive Behaviors, 19*, 112–115.

Ladouceur, R., Caron, C., & Caron, G. (1989). Stuttering severity and treatment outcome. *Journal of Behavior Therapy and Experimental Psychiatry, 20*, 49–56.

Lambert, M. J. (1992). Psychotherapy outcome research: Implications for integrative and eclectic therapists. In J. C. Norcross & M. R. Goldfried (Eds.), *Handbook of psychotherapy integration* (pp. 94–129). Basic Books.

Landfield, A. W., & Leitner, L. M. (1980). Personal construct psychology. In A. W. Landfield & L. M. Leitner (Eds.), *Personal construct psychology* (pp. 3–17). Wiley.

Langevin, M. (2000). *Teasing and bullying: Unacceptable behaviour: The TAB program.* Institute for Stuttering Treatment and Research.

Langevin, M., Huinck, W. J., Kully, D., Peters, H. F. M., Lomheim, H., & Tellers, M. (2006). A cross-cultural, long-term outcome evaluation of the ISTAR Comprehensive Stuttering Program across Dutch and Canadian adults who stutter. *Journal of Fluency Disorders, 31*, 229–256.

Langevin, M., & Kully, D. (2003). Evidence-based practice treatment of stuttering: III. Evidence-based practice in a clinical setting. *Journal of Fluency Disorders, 28*(3), 219–236.

Langevin, M., Kully, D., & Ross-Harold, B. (2007). Treatment of school-age children who stutter: A comprehensive approach with strategies for managing teasing and bullying. In E. Conture & R. Curlee (Eds.), *Stuttering and related disorders of fluency* (3rd ed., pp. 131–150). Thieme Medical.

Langevin, M., Packman, A., & Onslow, M. (2015). Parent perceptions of the impact of stuttering on their preschoolers and themselves. *Journal of Fluency Disorders, 43*, 407–423.

Lanyon, R. I., Goldsworthy, R. J., & Lanyon, B. P. (1978). Dimension of stuttering and relationship to psychopathology. *Journal of Fluency Disorders, 3*, 103–113.

Larson, L. M., & Daniels, J. A. (1998). Review of the counseling self-efficacy literature. *Counseling Psychologist, 26*(2), 179–218.

LaSalle, L. R., & Conture, E. G. (1991). Eye contact between young stutterers and their mothers. *Journal of Fluency Disorders, 16*(4), 173–199.

LaSalle, L. R., & Conture, E. G. (1995). Disfluency clusters of children who stutter: Relation of stutterings to self-repairs. *Journal of Speech and Hearing Research, 38*(5), 965–977.

Laska, K. M., Gurman, A. S., & Wampold, B. E. (2014). Expanding the lens of evidence-based practice in psychotherapy: A common factors perspective. *Psychotherapy, 51*, 467–481.

Lass, N., Ruscello, D. M., Pannbacker, M. D., Schmitt, J., & Everly-Myers, D. (1989). Speech-language pathologists' perceptions of child and adult female and male stutterers. *Journal of Fluency Disorders, 14*, 127–134.

Lass, N. J., Ruscello, D. M., Pannbacker, M. D., Schmitt, J. F., Kiser, A., Mussa, A., & Lockhart, P. (1994). School administrators' perceptions of people who stutter. *Language, Speech, and Hearing Services in Schools, 25*, 90–93.

Lau, S. R., Beilby, J. M., Byrnes, M. L., & Hennessey, N. W. (2012). Parenting styles and attachment in school-aged children who stutter. *Journal of Communication Disorders, 45*(2), 98–110.

LaValley, M. P. (2003, October). *Intent-to-treat analysis of randomized clinical trials* [Paper presentation]. ACR/ARHP Annual Scientific Meeting, Orlando, FL.

Leahy, M. M. (2004). Therapy talk: Analyzing therapeutic discourse. *Language, Speech and Hearing Services in Schools, 35*, 70–81.

Leahy, M. M., O'Dwyer, M., & Ryan, F. (2012). Witnessing stories: Definitional ceremonies in narrative therapy with adults who stutter. *Journal of Fluency Disorders, 37*(4), 234–241. https://doi.org/10.1016/j.jfludis.2012.03.001

Leahy, M. M., & Walsh, I. P. (2010). Paying attention to therapy discourse: Identifying therapy processes and practice in talk about talk. *Seminars in Speech and Language, 31*(2), 98–110.

Leahy, M. M., & Warren, A. (2006). *Making stuttering manageable: The use of narrative therapy* [Paper presentation]. Fifth World Congress on Fluency Disorders, Dublin, Ireland.

LeBlanc, C., Sonnenberg, K. J. M., King, S., & Busari, J. (2020). Medical education leadership: From diversity to inclusivity. *GMS Journal for Medical Education, 37*(2). https://doi.org/https://doi.org/10.3205/zma001311

Lebrun, Y., & Leleux, C. (1985). Acquired stuttering following right-brain damage in dextrals. *Journal of Fluency Disorders, 10*, 137–141.

Leclercq, M. (2002). Theoretical aspects of the main components and functions of attention. In M. Leclercq & P. Zimmerman (Eds.), *Applied neuropsychology of attention: Theory, diagnosis and rehabilitation* (pp. 3–55). Psychology Press.

Lee, B. S. (1951). Artificial stutter. *Journal of Speech and Hearing Disorders, 16*, 53–55.

Lee, K., & Manning, W. H. (2010). Listener responses according to stuttering self-acknowledgment and modification. *Journal of Fluency Disorders, 35*(2), 110–122.

Lee, K., Manning, W., & Herder, C. (2011). Documenting changes in adult speakers' locus of causality during stuttering treatment using Origin and Pawn scaling. *Journal of Fluency Disorders, 36*(3), 231–245.

Lee, K., Manning, W., & Herder, C. (2015). Origin and Pawn scaling for adults who do and do not stutter: A preliminary comparison. *Journal of Fluency Disorders, 45*, 73–81.

Lefcourt, H. M. (1976). *Locus of control: Current trends in theory and research.* Erlbaum.

Lefcourt, H., & Martin, R. (1989). *Humor and life stress: Antidote to adversity.* Springer-Verlag.

Lefcourt, H., Sordoni, C., & Sordoni, C. (1974). Locus of control and the expression of humor. *Journal of Personality, 42*, 130–143.

Levine, J. (1977). Humor as a form of therapy. In A. J. Chapman & H. C. Foot (Eds.), *It's a funny thing, humor* (pp. 127–137). Pergamon.

Levy, C. (1987a). Group therapy with adults. In P. Dalton (Ed.), *Approaches to the treatment of stuttering* (pp. 150–171). Croom Helm.

Levy, C. (2018). Interiorised stuttering: A group therapy approach. In *Stuttering Therapies* (pp. 104–121). Routledge.

Lewis, K. E., & Goldberg, L. L. (1997). Measurements of temperament in the identification of children who stutter. *European Journal of Disorders of Communication, 32*, 441–448.

Lichtheim, M. (1973). *Ancient Egyptian literature, a book of readings: Vol. 1. The old and middle kingdoms.* University of California Press.

Liebetrau, R. M., & Daly, D. A. (1981). Auditory processing and perceptual abilities of "organic" and "functional" stutterers. *Journal of Fluency Disorders, 6*, 219–232.

Lincoln, M. A., Onslow, M., & Reed, V. (1997). Social validity of the treatment outcomes of an early intervention program for stuttering. *American Journal of Speech-Language Pathology, 6*, 77–84.

Lincoln, M., Packman, A., & Onslow. M. (2006). Altered auditory feedback and the treatment of stuttering: A review. *Journal of Fluency Disorders, 31*, 71–89.

Loban, W. (1976). *Language development: Kindergarten through grade twelve.* National Council of Teachers of English.

Logan, J. (2007). From client to consultant: Developing "outsider-witness practices" with adults who stammer. In J. Au-Yeung & M. M. Leahy (Eds.), *Research, treatment and self-help in fluency disorders: New horizons. Proceedings of the Fifth World Congress on Fluency Disorders* (pp. 325–332).

Logan, K., Blomgren, M., Gillam, R., & Manning, W. (2016, November). *The long view: Perspectives on coping with and managing persistent stuttering over the lifespan* [Seminar presentation]. Annual Convention of the American Speech-Language-Hearing Association, Philadelphia, PA.

Logan, K. J., Byrd, C. T., Mazzocchi, E. M., & Gillam, R. B. (2011). Speaking rate characteristics of elementary-school-aged children who do and do not stutter. *Journal of Communication Disorders, 44*(1), 130–147.

Logan, K. J., & Yaruss, J. S. (1999). Helping parents address attitudinal and emotional factors with young children who stutter. *Contemporary Issues in Communication Science and Disorders, 26,* 69–81.

Longenecker, C. O., & Liverpool, P. R. (1987). Counseling the troubled employee. *Mid-American Journal of Business, 2*(2), 7–11.

Louko, L., Edwards, M. E., & Conture, E. (1990). Phonological characteristics of young stutterers and their normally fluent peers: Preliminary observations. *Journal of Fluency Disorders, 15,* 191–210.

Love, L. R., & Jefress, L. A. (1971). Identification of brief pauses in the fluent speech of stutterers and nonstutterers. *Journal of Speech and Hearing Research, 14,* 229–240.

Love, R. E. (2000). *The Bob Love story.* Contemporary Books.

Lowe-Bell, S. S., Cullen, J. K., Jr., Berlin, C. I., Thompson, C. L., & Willett, M. E. (1970). Perceptions of simultaneous dichotic and monotic monosyllables. *Journal of Speech and Hearing Research, 13,* 812–822.

Luborsky, L., Rosenthal, R., Diguer, L., Andrusyna, T. P., Berman, J. S., Levitt, J. T., . . . Krause, E. D. (2002). The dodo bird verdict is alive and well—Mostly. *Clinical Psychology: Science and Practice, 9*(1), 2–12.

Luchsinger, R., & Arnold, G. E. (1965). *Voice-speech-language: Clinical communicology.* Wadsworth.

Luper, H. L., & Mulder, R. L. (1964). *Stuttering therapy for children.* Prentice Hall.

Luterman, D. M. (1979). *Counseling the communicatively disordered and their families.* PRO-ED.

Luterman, D. M. (1991). *Counseling the communicatively disordered and their families* (2nd ed.). PRO-ED.

Luterman, D. M. (2001). *Counseling persons with communication disorders and their families* (4th ed.). PRO-ED.

Luterman, D. (2017). *Counseling persons with communication disorders and their families* (6th ed.). PRO-ED.

Luterman, D. (2020). On teaching counseling: Getting beyond informational counseling. *American Journal of Speech-Language Pathology, 29*(2), 903–908.

MacIntyre, S. (2012). Passing as fluent. In P. Reitzes & D. Reitzes (Eds.), *Stuttering: Inspiring stories and professional wisdom* (pp. 25–38). StutterTalk.

MacKinnon, S. P., Hall, S., & MacIntyre, P. D. (2007). Origins of the stuttering stereotype: Stereotype formation through inference. *Journal of Fluency Disorders, 32,* 297–309.

Madison, L. S., Budd, K. S., & Itzkowitz, J. S. (1986). Changes in stuttering in relation to children's locus of control. *Journal of Genetic Psychology, 147,* 233–240.

Maguire, G. A., Nguyen, D. L., Simonson, K. C., & Kurz, T. L. (2020). The pharmacologic treatment of stuttering and its neuropharmacologic basis. *Frontiers in Neuroscience, 14.* https://doi.org/10.3389/fnins.2020.00158

Mahr, G., & Leith, W. (1992). Psychogenic stuttering of adult onset. *Journal of Speech and Hearing Research, 35,* 283–286.

Maisto, S. A., Krenek, K., Chung, T., Martin, C. S., Clark, D., & Cornelius, J. (2011). A comparison of the concurrent and predictive validity of three measures of readiness to change alcohol use in a clinical sample of adolescents. *Psychological Assessment, 23,* 983–994.

Mallard, A. R., & Westbrook J. B. (1988). Variables affecting stuttering therapy in school settings. *Language, Speech, and Hearing Services in Schools, 19,* 362–370.

Manders, E., & Bastijns, P. (1988). Sudden recovery from stuttering after an epileptic attack: A case report. *Journal of Fluency Disorders, 13,* 421–425.

Manning, W. (1977). In pursuit of fluency. *Journal of Fluency Disorders, 2,* 53–56.

Manning, W. H. (1991a). Making progress during and after treatment. In W. H. Perkins (Ed.), *Seminars in speech and language* (Vol. 12, pp. 349–354). Thieme Medical.

Manning, W. (1991b). Sports analogies in the treatment of stuttering: Taking the field with your client. *Public School Caucus, 10*(2), 1, 10–11.

Manning, W. H. (1994). *The SEA-Scale: Self-Efficacy Scaling For Adolescents Who Stutter* [Paper presentation]. Annual Meeting of the

American Speech-Language-Hearing Association, New Orleans, LA.

Manning, W. H. (1996). *Clinical decision making in the assessment and treatment of fluency disorders.* Delmar.

Manning, W. H. (1998). Long term recovery from stuttering. In E. C. Healey & H. F. M. Peters (Eds.), *Proceedings of the Second World Congress on Fluency Disorders* (pp. 381–383). Nijmegen University Press.

Manning, W. (1999a). Management of adult stuttering. In R. Curlee (Ed.), *Stuttering and related disorders of fluency* (2nd ed., pp. 160–180). Thieme Medical.

Manning, W. H. (1999b). Progress under the surface and over time. In N. B. Ratner & E. C. Healey (Eds.), *Stuttering research and practice: Bridging the gap* (pp. 123–129). Erlbaum.

Manning, W. (2004). "How can you understand? You don't stutter!" *Contemporary Issues in Communication Science and Disorders, 31*, 58–68.

Manning, W. H., & Beachy, T. S. (1995). Humor as a variable in the treatment of fluency disorders. In C. W. Starkweather & H. F. M. Peters (Eds.), *Stuttering: Proceedings of the First World Congress on Fluency Disorders* (Vol. II, pp. 414–416). International Fluency Association.

Manning, W., & Beck, J. G. (2013a). Personality dysfunction in adults who stutter: Another look. *Journal of Fluency Disorders, 38*, 184–192.

Manning, W., & Beck, J. G. (2013b). The role of psychological processes in estimates of stuttering severity. *Journal of Fluency Disorders, 38*, 356–367.

Manning, W., Burlison, A., & Thaxton, D. (1999). Listener response to stuttering modification techniques. *Journal of Fluency Disorders, 24*, 267–280.

Manning, W., & Cooper, E. B. (1969). Variations in attitudes of the adult stutterer toward his clinician related to progress in therapy. *Journal of Communication Disorders, 2*, 154–162.

Manning, W., Dailey, D., & Wallace, S. (1984). Attitude and personality characteristics of older stutterers. *Journal of Fluency Disorders, 9*, 207–215.

Manning, W. H., & DiLollo, A. (2007). Management of stuttering for adolescents and adults: Traditional approaches. In E. Conture & R. Curlee (Eds.), *Stuttering and related disorders of fluency* (3rd ed., pp. 233–255). Thieme Medical.

Manning, W., Emal, K. C., & Jamison, W. (1975). Listener judgments of fluency: The effect of part-word CV repetitions and neutral vowel substitutions. *Journal of Fluency Disorders, 1*(3), 18–23.

Manning, W., Hodak, M., & Plexico, L. (2005, October). *Letters from Sarajevo* [Paper presentation]. International Stuttering Awareness Day Online Conference (ISAD). http://www.mankato.msus.edu/dept/comdis/isad/isadcon.html

Manning, W., & Monte, K. (1981). Fluency breaks in older speakers: Implications for a model of stuttering throughout the life cycle. *Journal of Fluency Disorders, 6*, 35–48.

Manning, W., Perkins, D., Winn, S., & Cole, D. (1984). *Self-efficacy changes during treatment and maintenance for adult stutterers* [Paper presentation]. Annual Meeting of the American Speech-Language-Hearing Association, San Francisco, CA.

Manning, W. H., & Quesal, R. W. (2016). Crystal ball gazing: Research and clinical work in fluency disorders in 2026. *Seminars in Speech and Language, 37*, 145–152.

Manning, W., & Shirkey, E. (1981). Fluency and the aging process In D. S. Beasley & G. Albyn Davis (Eds.), *Aging: Communication processes and disorders* (pp. 175–189). Grune & Stratton.

Manning, W., & Shrum, W. (1973). The concept of control in stuttering therapy: A reappraisal. *Division for Children with Communication Disorders Bulletin, 9*(1), 32–34.

Market, K. E., Montague, J. C., Buffalo, M. D., & Drummond, S. S. (1990). Acquired stuttering: Descriptive data and treatment outcome. *Journal of Fluency Disorders, 15*, 21–34.

Markus, H. (1977). Self-schema and processing information about the self. *Journal of Personality and Social Psychology, 35*, 63–78.

Markus, H., & Nurius, P. (1986). Possible selves. *American Psychologist, 41*, 954–969.

Martin, D. J., Garske, J. P., & Davis, K. M. (2000). Relation of the therapeutic alliance with outcome and other variables: A meta-analytic review. *Journal of Consulting and Clinical Psychology, 68*, 438–450.

Martin, R. A., & Lefcourt, H. (1983). Sense of humor as a moderator of the relation between stressors and moods. *Journal of Personality and Social Psychology, 45*, 1313–1324.

Martin, R. A., & Lefcourt, H. (1984). Situational Humor Response Questionnaire: Quantitative measure of sense of humor. *Journal of Personality and Social Psychology, 47*, 145–155.

Martin, R. E., Kroll, R. M., O'Keefe, B. M., & Painter, C. (1983, November). *Cluttered speech: Spectrographic analysis* [Paper presentation]. Annual Convention of the American Speech-Language-Hearing Association, Cincinnati, OH.

Martin, R. R. (1981). Introduction and perspective: Review of published research. In E. Boberg (Ed.), *Maintenance of fluency* (pp. 1–30). Elsevier.

Martin, R. R., & Haroldson, S. K. (1982). Contingent self-stimulation for stuttering. *Journal of Speech and Hearing Disorders, 47*, 407–413.

Martin, R. R., & Haroldson, S. K. (1986). Stuttering as involuntary loss of speech control: Barking up a new tree. *Journal of Speech and Hearing Disorders, 51*, 187–190.

Martin, R. R., & Haroldson, S. K. (1992). Stuttering and speech naturalness: Audio and audiovisual judgements. *Journal of Speech and Hearing Research, 35*, 521–528.

Martin, R. R., Haroldson, S., & Kuhl, P. (1972a). Disfluencies in child–child and child–mother speaking situations. *Journal of Speech and Hearing Research, 15*, 753–756.

Martin, R. R., Haroldson, S., & Kuhl, P. (1972b). Disfluencies of young children in two speaking situations. *Journal of Speech and Hearing Research, 15*, 831–836.

Martin, R. R., Haroldson, S. K., & Triden, K. A. (1984). Stuttering and speech naturalness. *Journal of Speech and Hearing Disorders, 49*, 53–58.

Martin, R. R., Kuhl, P., & Haroldson, S. (1972). An experimental treatment with two preschool stuttering children. *Journal of Speech and Hearing Research, 15*, 743–752.

Martin, R. R., & Siegel, G. M. (1966a). The effects of response contingent shock on stuttering. *Journal of Speech and Hearing Research, 9*, 340–352.

Martin, R. R., & Siegel, G. M. (1966b). The effects of simultaneously punishing stuttering and rewarding fluency. *Journal of Speech and Hearing Research, 9*, 466–475.

Martin, R., St. Louis, K., Haroldson, S., & Hasbrouck, J. (1975). Punishment and negative reinforcement of stuttering using electric shock. *Journal of Speech and Hearing Research, 18*, 478–490.

Martinez, N. M. (2011). Liminal phases of avatar identity formation in virtual world communities. In A. Peachey & M. Childs (Eds.), *Reinventing ourselves: Contemporary concepts of identity in virtual worlds* (pp. 59–80). Springer.

Maslow, A. (1968). *Towards a psychology of being* (2nd ed.). Van Nostrand.

Masterson, J., & Kamhi, A. (1992). Linguistic trade-offs in school-age children with and without language disorders. *Journal of Speech and Hearing Research, 35*, 1064–1075.

Masuku, K. P., & Mupawose, A. (2022). Student's experiences of using a writing-intense programme to facilitate critical thinking skills on an online clinical training platform: A pilot study. *South African Journal of Communication Disorders, 69*(2). https://doi.org/10.4102/sajcd.v69i2.919

Mattick, R. P., & Clarke, J. C. (1998). Development and validation of measures of social phobia scrutiny fear and social interaction anxiety. *Behaviour Research and Therapy, 36*, 455–470.

Mattingly, E., & Roth, C. R. (2022). Traumatic brain injury in older adults: Epidemiology, etiology, rehabilitation, and outcomes. *Perspectives of the ASHA Special Interest Groups, 7*(4), 1166–1181.

Max, L., Caruso, A. J., & Gracco, V. L. (2003). Kinematic analysis of speech, orofacial non-speech, and finger movements in stuttering individuals. *Journal of Speech, Language, and Hearing Research, 46*, 215–232.

Maxwell, D. (1982). Cognitive and behavioral self-control strategies: Applications for the clinical management of adult stutterers. *Journal of Fluency Disorders, 7*, 403–432.

Mayo, R., Mayo, C. M., & Williams, S. D. (2006, November). *The pseudostuttering project: Affective-behavioral-cognitive experiences of SLP students* [Paper presentation]. Annual Convention of the American Speech-Language-Hearing Association, Miami, FL.

Mazzei, L. A. (2007). *Inhabited silence in qualitative research: Putting poststructural theory to work* (Vol. 318). Peter Lang.

Mazzucchi, A., Moretti, G., Carpeggiani, P., Parma, M., & Paini, P. (1981). Clinical observations on acquired stuttering. *British Journal of Disorders of Communication, 16*, 19–30.

McCabe, A., & Bliss, L. S. (2003). *Patterns of narrative discourse: A multicultural lifespan approach*. Allyn & Bacon.

McCarthy, P., Culpepper, N., & Lucks, L. (1986). Variability in counseling experience and training among ESB accredited programs. *ASHA, 28*, 49–53.

McConnaughy, E. A., Prochaska, J. O., & Velicer, W. F. (1983). Stages of change in psychotherapy: Measurement and sample profiles. *Psychotherapy: Theory Research, and Practice, 29*(3), 368–375.

McDearmon, J. R. (1968). Primary stuttering at the onset of stuttering: A reexamination of data. *Journal of Speech and Hearing Research, 11*, 631–637.

McFarlane, S., & Goldberg, L. (1987). Factors influencing treatment approaches, prognosis and dismissal criteria for stuttering [Abstract]. *ASHA, 29*, 164–165.

McGhee, P. E., & Goldstein, J. H. (1977). *Handbook of humor research: Vol. 1. Basic issues*. Springer-Verlag.

Mehrabian, A., & Reed, H. (1969). Factors influencing judgments of psychopathology. *Psychological Reports, 24*(1), 323–330.

Melnick, K., Conture, E., & Ohde, R. (2003). Phonological priming in picture-naming of young children who stutter. *Journal of Speech, Language, and Hearing Research, 46*, 1428–1444.

Menzies, R. G., Onslow, M., Packman, A., & O'Brian, S. (2009). Cognitive behavior therapy for adults who stutter: A tutorial for speech-language pathologists. *Journal of Fluency Disorders, 34*, 187–200.

Merits-Patterson, R., & Reed, C. G. (1981). Disfluencies in the speech of language-delayed children. *Journal of Speech and Hearing Research, 24*, 55–58.

Merson, R. M. (2003, October). *Auditory sidetone and the management of stuttering: From Wollensack to SpeechEasy* [Paper presentation]. 2003 International Stuttering Awareness Day Conference. http:// www.isastutter.org/what-we-do/isad

Mertz, P. (2009). *Things I learned from therapy* [Paper presentation]. International Stuttering Awareness Day Online Conference (ISAD). http://www.mnsu.edu/comdis/isad12/papers/mertz122.html

Messenger, M., Onslow, M., Packman, A., & Menzies, R., (2004). Social anxiety in stuttering: Measuring negative social expectancies. *Journal of Fluency Disorders, 29*, 201–212.

Metz, D. E., Schiavetti, N., & Sacco P. R. (1990). Acoustic and psychophysical dimensions of the perceived speech naturalness of non-stutterers and post-treatment stutterers. *Journal of Speech and Hearing Disorders, 55*, 516–525.

Meyers, F., & Kissagizlis, P. (2007). *Putting cluttering on the world map: Formation of the International Cluttering Association (ICA)* [Paper presentation]. International Stuttering Awareness Day Online Conference (ISAD). http://www.mnsu.edu/comdis/isad10/ papers/myers10.html

Meyers, S. C., & Freeman, F. J. (1985). Mother and child speech rates as a variable in stuttering and disfluency. *Journal of Speech and Hearing Research, 28*, 436–444.

Meyers, S., Ghatak, L., & Woodford, L. (1990). Case descriptions of nonfluency and loci:

Initial and follow-up conversations with three preschool children. *Journal of Fluency Disorders, 14*, 383–398.

Meyers, S., Hall, N. E., & Aram, D. M. (1990). Fluency and language recovery in a child with a left hemisphere lesion. *Journal of Fluency Disorders, 15*, 159–173.

Millard, S. K., & Davis, S. (2016). The Palin Parent Rating Scales: Parents' perspectives of childhood stuttering and its impact. *Journal of Speech, Language, and Hearing Research, 59*, 1–14.

Millard, S. K., Edwards, S., & Cook, F. M. (2009). Parent–child interaction therapy: Adding to the evidence. *International Journal of Speech-Language Pathology, 11*(1), 61–76. https://doi.org/10.1080/17549500802603895

Millard, S. K., Zebrowski, P., & Kelman, E. (2018). Palin Parent–Child Interaction Therapy: The bigger picture. *American Journal of Speech-Language Pathology, 27*(3, Suppl.), 1211–1223. https://doi.org/10.1044/2018_ajslp-odc11-17-0199

Miller, B., & Guitar, B. (2009). Long-term outcome of the Lidcombe Program for early intervention. *American Journal of Speech-Language Pathology, 18*, 1–8.

Miller, S., & Watson, B. C. (1992). The relationship between communication attitude, anxiety and depression in stutterers and nonstutterers. *Journal of Speech and Hearing Research, 35*, 789–798.

Miller, S. D., Duncan, B. L., & Hubble. M. A. (1997). *Escape from Babel: Toward a unifying language for psychotherapy practice.* Norton.

Miller, W. R., & Tonigan, J. S. (1996). Assessing drinkers' motivation for change: The Stages of Change Readiness and Treatment Eagerness Scale (SOCRATES). *Psychology of Addictive Behaviors, 10*, 81–89.

Mok, C. K., Whitehill, T. L., & Dodd, B. J. (2008). Problem-based learning, critical thinking and concept mapping in speech-language pathology education: A review. *International Journal of Speech-Language Pathology, 10*, 438–448.

Molt, L. (1996). An examination of various aspects of auditory processing in clutterers. *Journal of Fluency Disorders, 21*, 215–225.

Molt, L. (2006a). *SpeechEasy AAF device long-term clinical trial: Attitudinal/perceptual measures* [Paper presentation]. Annual Meeting of the American Speech-Language-Hearing Association, Miami, FL.

Molt, L. (2006b). *SpeechEasy AAF device long-term clinical trial: Speech fluency and naturalness measures* [Paper presentation]. Annual Meeting of the American Speech-Language-Hearing Association, Miami, FL.

Molt, L., & Brading, T. (1994). Hemispheric patterns of auditory event-related potentials to dichotic CV syllables in stutterers and normal speakers. *Journal of Fluency Disorders, 19*(3), 195.

Molt, L. F., & Guilford, A. M. (1979). Auditory processing and anxiety in stutterers. *Journal of Fluency Disorders, 4*, 255–267.

Monk, G. (1997). How narrative therapy works. In G. Monk, J. Winslade, K. Crocket, & D. Epston (Eds.), *Narrative therapy in practice* (pp. 3–31). Jossey-Bass.

Monk, G., Winslade, J., Crocket, K., & Epston, D. (1997). *Narrative therapy in practice.* Jossey-Bass.

Montgomery, C. S. (2006). The treatment of stuttering: From the hub to the spoke. Description and evaluation of an integrated therapy program. In N. Bernstein Ratner & J. Tetnowski (Eds.), *Current issues in stuttering research and practice* (pp. 159–204). Erlbaum.

Moore, S. E., & Perkins, W. (1990). Validity and reliability of judgements of authentic and simulated stuttering. *Journal of Speech and Hearing Disorders, 55*, 383–391.

Moore, W. H., Jr. (1976). Bilateral tachistoscopic word perception of stutterers and normal subjects. *Brain and Language, 3*, 434–442.

Moore, W. H., Jr. (1984). Hemispheric alpha asymmetries during an electromyographic biofeedback procedure for stuttering: A single-subject experimental design. *Journal of Fluency Disorders, 9*(2), 143–162.

Moore, W., & Haynes, W. (1980). Alpha hemispheric asymmetry and stuttering: Some support for a segmentation dysfunction hypothesis. *Journal of Speech and Hearing Research, 23*, 229–247.

Moore, W. H., Jr., & Lang, M. K. (1977). Alpha asymmetry over the right and left hemispheres of stutterers and control subjects preceding massed oral readings: A preliminary investigation. *Perceptual and Motor Skills, 44*(1), 223–230.

Morreall, J. (1982). *Taking laughter seriously.* State University of New York Press.

Morrison, J. R. (1995). *DSM-IV made easy: The clinician's guide to diagnosis.* Guilford.

Morrison, N., Levy, J., Shoshany, T., Dickinson, A., & Whalen, M. (2020). Stuttering and word-finding difficulties in a patient with COVID-19 presenting to the emergency department. *Cureus.* https://doi.org/10.7759/cureus.11774

Mower, D. E. (1998). Analysis of the sudden onset and disappearance of disfluencies in the speech of a 2½ year old boy. *Journal of Fluency Disorders, 23*, 103–118.

Mueller, H. G., & Bright, K. E. (1994). Monosyllabic procedures in central testing. In J. Katz (Ed.), *Handbook of clinical audiology* (4th ed., pp. 222–238). Williams & Wilkins.

Mulcahy, K., Hennessey, N., Beilby, J., & Byrnes, M. (2008). Social anxiety and severity and typography of stuttering in adolescents. *Journal of Fluency Disorders, 33*, 306–319.

Mumy, A. P. S. (2023). Culturally responsive guidelines for serving families of bilingual children who stutter. *Perspectives of the ASHA Special Interest Groups, 8*(1), 164–175. https://doi.org/10.1044/2022_persp-21-00235

Murphy, A. T., & Fitzsimons, R. M. (1960). *Stuttering and personality dynamics.* Ronald Press.

Murphy, W. P. (1998). *The school-age child who stutters: Dealing effectively with shame and guilt* (Videotape No. 86). Stuttering Foundation of America.

Murphy, W. (1999). A preliminary look at shame, guilt, and stuttering. In N. B. Ratner & E. C. Healey (Eds.), *Stuttering research and practice: Bridging the gap* (pp. 131–143). Erlbaum.

Murphy, W. P., Yaruss, J. S., & Quesal, R. W. (2007a). Enhancing treatment for school-age children who stutter I: Reducing negative reactions through desensitization and cognitive restructuring. *Journal of Fluency Disorders, 32*, 121–138.

Murphy, W. P., Yaruss, J. S., & Quesal, R. W. (2007b). Enhancing treatment for school-age children who stutter II: Reducing bullying through role-playing and self-disclosure. *Journal of Fluency Disorders, 32*, 139–162.

Murray, F. P., & Edwards, S. G. (1980). *A stutterer's story.* Interstate Printers and Publishers.

Murray, H. L., & Reed, C. G. (1977). Language abilities of preschool stuttering children. *Journal of Fluency Disorders, 2*, 171–176.

Myers, F. L. (1992). Cluttering: A synergistic framework. In F. L. Myers & K. O. St. Louis (Eds.), *Cluttering: A clinical perspective* (pp. 71–84). Far Communications.

Myers, F. L. (1996). Cluttering: A matter of perspective. *Journal of Fluency Disorders, 21*, 175–186.

Myers, F. L., & St. Louis, K. O. (1992). Cluttering: Issues and controversies. In F. L. Myers & K. O. St. Louis (Eds.), *Cluttering: A clinical perspective* (pp. 11–22). Singular Publishing.

Myers, F. L., St. Louis, K. O., Bakker, K., Raphael, L. J., Wiig, E. K., Katz, J., . . . Kent, R. D. (2002a, November). *Putting cluttering on the map: Looking ahead* [Invited seminar]. Annual Convention of the American Speech-Language-Hearing Association, Atlanta, GA.

Myers, F. L., St. Louis, K. O., Bakker, K., Raphael, L. J., Wiig, E., K., Katz, J., . . . Kent, R. D. (2002b, November). *Putting cluttering on the map: Looking back* [Invited seminar]. Annual Convention of the American Speech-Language-Hearing Association, Atlanta, GA.

Mysak, E. D. (1960). Servo theory and stuttering. *Journal of Speech and Hearing Disorders, 25*, 188–195.

Neaves, A. I. (1970). To establish a basis for prognosis in stammering. *British Journal of Disorders of Communication, 5*(1), 46–58.

Neef, N. E., Anwander, A., Bütfering, C., Schmidt-Samoa, C., Friederici, A. D., Paulus, W., & Sommer, M. (2017). Structural connectivity of right frontal hyperactive areas scales with stuttering severity. *Brain,*

141(1), 191–204. https://doi.org/10.1093/brain/awx316

Neeley, J. N. (1961). A study of the speech behavior of stutterers and nonstutterers under normal and delayed auditory feedback. *Journal of Speech and Hearing Disorders* (Monograph Suppl. No. 7), 63–82.

Neilson, M., & Neilson, P. (1987). Speech motor control and stuttering: A computational model of adaptive sensory-motor processing. *Speech Communications, 6*, 325–333.

Neimeyer, R. A. (2000). *Lessons of loss: A guide to coping.* PsychoEducational Resources.

Neimeyer, R. A., & Raskin, J. D. (2000). *Constructions of disorder: Meaning-making frameworks for psychotherapy.* American Psychological Association.

Neumann, K., Euler, H. A., Kob, M., Wolff von Gudenberg, A., Giraud, A.-L., Weissgerber, T., & Kell, C. A. (2018). Assisted and unassisted recession of functional anomalies associated with dysprosody in adults who stutter. *Journal of Fluency Disorders, 55*, 120–134. https://doi.org/10.1016/j.jfludis.2017.09.003

Neumann, K., Preibisch, C., Euler, H. A., von Gudenberg, A. W., Lanfermann, H., Gall, V., & Giraud, A. L. (2005). Cortical plasticity associated with stuttering therapy. *Journal of Fluency Disorders, 30*, 23–39.

Newman, P. W., Harris, R. W., & Hilton, L. M. (1989). Vocal jitter and shimmer in stuttering. *Journal of Fluency Disorders, 14*, 87–95.

Nezu, A., Nezu, C., & Blissett, S. (1988). Sense of humor as a moderator of the relations between stressful events and psychological distress: A prospective analysis. *Journal of Personality and Social Psychology, 54*, 520–525.

Nicholas, A. (2015). Solution focused brief therapy with children who stutter. *Procedia-Social and Behavioral Sciences, 193*, 209–216. https://doi.org/10.1016/j.sbspro.2015.03.261

Nippold, M. A. (1990). Concomitant speech and language disorders in stuttering children: A critique of the literature. *Journal of Speech and Hearing Disorders, 55*, 51–60.

Nippold, M. A. (2001). Stuttering and language ability in children: Questioning the

connection. *American Journal of Speech-Language Pathology, 21*, 183–196.

Nippold, M., & Rudzinski, M. (1995). Parents' speech and children's stuttering: A critique of the literature. *Journal of Speech and Hearing Research, 38*, 978–989.

O'Brian, S., Onslow, M., Cream, A., & Packman, A. (2003). The Camperdown Program: Outcomes of a new prolonged-speech treatment model. *Journal of Speech, Language, and Hearing Research, 46*, 933–946.

O'Brian, S., Packman, A., & Onslow, M. (2004). Self-Rating of stuttering severity as a clinical tool. *American Journal of Speech-Language Pathology, 13*(3), 219–226. https://doi.org/10.1044/ 1058-0360(2004/023)

O'Connell, E. (2008). Therapeutic relationships in critical care nursing: A reflection on practice. *Nursing in Critical Care, 13*, 138–143.

O'Donnell, J. J., Armson, J., & Kiefte, M. (2008). The effectiveness of SpeechEasy during situations of daily living. *Journal of Fluency Disorders, 33*, 99–119.

Oelke, N. D., Thurston, W. E., & Arthur, N. (2013). Intersections between interprofessional practice, cultural competency and primary healthcare. *Journal of Interprofessional Care, 27*(5), 367–372.

Olish, C. (2009). *Hello my name is Cathy, but you can call me Anne: A story of a covert person who stutters* [Paper presentation]. International Stuttering Awareness Day Online Conference (ISAD). http://www.mnsu.edu/comdis/isad12/ papers/fear12/olish12.html

Olweus, D. (1993). *Bullying at school: What we know and what we can do.* Blackwell.

Onslow, M. (1992). Identification of early stuttering: Issues and suggested strategies. *American Journal of Speech-Language Pathology, 1*(4), 21–27.

Onslow, M., & Ingham, R. J. (1987). Speech quality measurement and the management of stuttering. *Journal of Speech and Hearing Disorders, 52*, 2–17.

Onslow, M., Packman, A., & Harrison, E. (2003). *The Lidcombe Program of early stuttering intervention: A clinician's guide.* PRO-ED.

Onslow, M., Webber, M., Harrison, E., Arnott, S., Bridgman, K., Carey, B., . . . &

Hearne, A. (2023). *The Lidcombe Program Treatment Guide (Version 1.5)*. https://www.lidcombeprogram.org/helpful-resources/helpful-downloads/

Ornstein, A., & Manning, W. (1985). Self-efficacy scaling by adult stutterers. *Journal of Communication Disorders, 18*, 313–320.

Orton, S. T. (1927). Studies in stuttering. *Archives of Neurology and Psychiatry, 18*, 671–672.

Ost, L., Gotestam, K. G., & Melin, L. (1976). A controlled study of two behavioral methods in the treatment of stuttering. *Behavior Therapy, 7*, 587–592.

Otsuki, H. (1958). Study on stuttering: Statistical observations. *Otorhinolaryngology Clinic, 5*, 1150–1151.

Otto, F., & Yairi, E. (1976). A disfluency analysis of Down's syndrome and normal subjects. *Journal of Fluency Disorders, 1*, 26–32.

Oxford Dictionary. (2014). http://www.oxforddictionaries.com/us

Pachankis, J. E., & Goldfried, M. R. (2007). An integrative, principle-based approach to psychotherapy. In S. G. Hoffman & J. Weinberger (Eds.), *The art and science of psychotherapy: An introduction* (pp. 49–68). Routledge/Taylor & Francis.

Paden, E. P. (1970). *A history of the American Speech and Hearing Association 1925–1958*. American Speech and Hearing Association.

Paden, E. P., Yairi, E., & Ambrose, N. G. (1999). Early childhood stuttering II: Initial status of phonological abilities. *Journal of Speech, Language, and Hearing Research, 42*, 1113–1124.

Panagos, J. M., & Bliss, L. S. (1990). Presuppositions for speech therapy lessons. *Journal of Childhood Communication Disorders, 13*(1), 19–28.

Panelli, C., McFarlane, S., & Shipley, K. (1978). Implications of evaluating and interviewing with incipient stutterers. *Journal of Fluency Disorders, 3*, 41–50.

Panico, J., & Healey, E. C. (2009). The influence of text type, topic familiarity, and stuttering frequency on listener recall, comprehension, and mental effort. *Journal of Speech, Language and Hearing Research, 52*, 534–546.

Parry, A., & Doan, R. E. (1994). *Story re-visions: Narrative therapy in the postmodern world*. Guilford.

Paul, R. (1992). Socratic questioning. In R. Paul (Ed.), *Critical thinking: What every person needs to survive in a rapidly changing world* (2nd ed., pp. 360–390). Center for Critical Thinking and Moral Critique.

Pauls, D. L. (1990). A review of the evidence for genetic factors in stuttering. *ASHA Reports Series, 18*, 34–38.

Payne, M. (2006). *Narrative therapy: An introduction for counselors* (2nd ed.). Sage.

Peck, M. S. (1978). *The road less traveled*. Simon & Schuster.

Peins, M., McGough, W. E., & Lee, B. S. (1972). Evaluation of a tape-recorded method of stuttering therapy: Improvement in a speaking task. *Journal of Speech and Hearing Research, 15*, 364–371.

Perkins, W. H. (1973). Replacement of stuttering with normal speech: II. Clinical procedures. *Journal of Speech and Hearing Disorders, 38*, 295–303.

Perkins, W. H. (1979). From psychoanalysis to discoordination. In H. Gregory (Ed.), *Controversies about stuttering therapy* (pp. 97–127). University Park Press.

Perkins, W. H. (1983). The problem of definition: Commentary on stuttering. *Journal of Speech and Hearing Disorders, 48*, 246–249.

Perkins, W. H. (1990). What is stuttering? *Journal of Speech and Hearing Disorders, 55*, 370–382.

Perkins, W., Kent, R. D., & Curlee, R. F. (1990). A theory of neuropsycholinguistic function in stuttering. *Journal of Speech and Hearing Research, 34*, 734–752.

Perry, A., & Doan, R. E. (1994). *Story re-visions: Narrative therapy in the postmodern world*. Guilford.

Peters, H. F. M., & Hulstijn, W. (1984). Stuttering and anxiety: The difference between stutterers and nonstutterers in verbal apprehension and physiologic arousal during anticipation of speech and non-speech tasks. *Journal of Fluency Disorders, 9*, 67–84.

Peters, T. J., & Guitar, B. (1991). *Stuttering: An integrated approach to its nature and treatment*. Williams & Wilkins.

Phillips, D., & Lucks Mendel, L. (2008). Counseling training in communication disorders: A survey of clinical fellows. *Contemporary Issues in Communication Science and Disorders, 35*, 44–53.

Pickett, J. M. (1980). *The sounds of speech communication*. University Park Press.

Pinsky, S. D., & McAdam, D. W. (1980). Electroencephalographic and dichotic indices of cerebral laterality in stutterers. *Brain and Language, 11*, 374–397.

Plexico, L., & Burrus, E. (2012). Coping with a child who stutters: A phenomenological analysis. *Journal of Fluency Disorders, 37*, 275–288.

Plexico, L., Cleary H. J., McAlpine, A., & Plumb, A. (2010). Disfluency characteristics observed in young children with autism spectrum disorders: A preliminary report. *SIG 4 Perspectives on Fluency and Fluency Disorders, 20*, 42–50.

Plexico, L., Manning, W., & DiLollo, A. (2005). A phenomenological understanding of successful stuttering management, *Journal of Fluency Disorders, 30*(1), 1–22.

Plexico, L., Manning, W., & DiLollo, A. (2010). Client perceptions of effective and ineffective therapeutic alliances during treatment for stuttering. *Journal of Fluency Disorders, 35*(4), 333–354.

Plexico, L., Manning, W., & Levitt, H. (2009a). Coping responses by adults who stutter: Part I. Protecting the self and others. *Journal of Fluency Disorders, 34*, 87–107.

Plexico, L., Manning, W., & Levitt, H. (2009b). Coping responses by adults who stutter: Part II. Approaching the problem and achieving agency. *Journal of Fluency Disorders, 34*, 108–126.

Plomin, R., & Crabbe, J. (2002). DNA. *Psychological Bulletin, 126*, 806–828.

Pollard, R., Ellis, J. B., Finan, D., & Ramig, P. R. (2009). Effects of the SpeechEasy on objective and perceived aspects of stuttering: A six-month, Phase I clinical trial in naturalistic environments. *Journal of Speech, Hearing and Language Research, 52*(2), 516–533.

Pollard, R., Ramig, P. R., Ellis, J. B., & Finan, D. (2007, November). *Case study of Speech Easy use combined with traditional stuttering treatment* [Paper presentation]. American Speech-Language-Hearing Association, Boston, MA.

Postma, A., & Kolk, H. (1993). The covert repair hypothesis: Prearticulatory repair processes in normal and stuttered disfluencies. *Journal of Speech and Hearing Research, 36*, 472–487.

Postma, A., Kolk, H., & Povel, D. J. (1990). Speech planning and execution in stutterers. *Journal of Fluency Disorders, 15*, 49–59.

Poulos, M. G., & Webster, W. G. (1991). Family history as a basis for subgrouping people who stutter. *Journal of Speech and Hearing Research, 34*, 5–10.

Preus, A. (1972). Stuttering in Down's syndrome. *Scandinavian Journal of Education Research, 15*, 89–104.

Prins, D. (1970). Improvement and regression in stutterers following short-term intensive therapy. *Journal of Speech and Hearing Disorders, 35*, 123–135.

Prins, D. (1972). Personality, stuttering severity, and age. *Journal of Speech and Hearing Research, 15*, 148–154.

Prins, D., & Hubbard, C. (1988). Response contingent stimuli and stuttering: Issues and implications. *Journal of Speech and Hearing Research, 31*, 696–709.

Prochaska, J. O., & DiClemente, C. C. (1992). Stages of change in the modification of problem behaviors. In M. Herson, R. Eisler, & P. Miller (Eds.), *Progress in behavior modification* (pp. 184–218). Sycamore.

Prochaska, J. O., DiClemente, C. C., & Norcross, J. C. (1992). In search of how people change: Applications to addictive behaviors. *American Psychologist, 47*(9), 1102–1114.

Proctor, A., Duff, M., Patterson, A., & Yairi, E. (2001, November). *Stuttering in African American and European American preschoolers* [Paper presentation]. Annual Meeting of the American Speech-Language-Hearing Association, New Orleans, LA.

Quesal, R. W. (1989). Stuttering research: Have we forgotten the stutterer? *Journal of Fluency Disorders, 14*, 153–164.

Quesal, R. W. (1998). Knowledge, understanding, and acceptance. In E. C. Healey &

H. E. M. Peters (Eds.), *Proceedings of the Second World Congress on Fluency Disorders* (pp. 384–387). Nijmegen University Press.

Quesal, R. W. (2006, February). *Assessing and treating adolescents who stutter in an EBP world* [Invited presentation]. 36th Annual Mid-South Conference on Communicative Disorders, Memphis, TN.

Quesal, R. W. (2010). Empathy: Perhaps the most important E in EBP. *Seminars in Speech and Language, 31*, 217–226.

Rabinowitz, A. (2001). *Beyond the last village: A journey of discovery in Asia's forbidden wilderness*, Island.

Raj, E. X., Daniels, D. E., & Thomson, P. E. (2023). Facebook groups for people who stutter: An extension of and supplement to in-person support groups. *Journal of Communication Disorders, 101*, 106295. https://doi.org/10.1016/j.jcomdis.2022.106295

Ramig, P. R. (1993a). The impact of self-help groups on persons who stutter: A call for research. *Journal of Fluency Disorders, 18*, 351–361.

Ramig, P. R. (1993b). Parent–clinician–child partnership in the therapeutic process of the preschool and elementary-aged child who stutters. *Seminars in Speech and Language, 14*, 226–236.

Ramig, P. R. (1998). My long-term recovery from stuttering. In E. C. Healey & H. F. M. Peters (Eds.), *Proceedings of the Second World Congress on Fluency Disorders* (pp. 390–391). Nijmegen University Press.

Ramig, P., & Bennett, E. (1995). Working with 7- to 12-year-old children who stutter: Ideas for intervention in the public schools. *Language, Speech, and Hearing Services in Schools, 26*, 138–150.

Ramig, P. R., & Dodge, D. M. (2005). *The child and adolescent stuttering treatment and activity resource guide.* Thomson Delmar Learning.

Ramig, P. R., Ellis, J. B., & Pollard, R. (2010). Application of the SpeechEasy to stuttering treatment: Introduction, background, and preliminary observations. In B. Guitar & R. McCauley (Eds.), *Treatment of stuttering: Traditional and emerging approaches* (pp. 312–328). Lippincott Williams & Wilkins.

Rao, P. R. (1991). Neurogenic stuttering as a manifestation of stroke and a mask of dysnomia. *Clinics in Communication Disorders, 1*(1), 31–37.

Raphael, L. J., Bakker, K., Myers, F. L., St. Louis, K. O., Fichtner, V., & Kostel, M. (2005). *An update on diadochokenetic rates of cluttered and normal speech* [Poster presentation]. Annual Convention of the American Speech-Language-Hearing Association, San Diego, CA.

Raphael, L. J., Bakker, K., Myers, F. L., St. Louis, K. O., & MacRoy, M. (2004, November). *Diadochokenetic rates of cluttered and normal speech* [Paper presentation]. Annual Convention of the American Speech-Language-Hearing Association, Philadelphia, PA.

Raskin, J., & Lewandowski, A. (2000) The construction of disorder as human enterprise. In R. A. Neimeyer & J. D. Raskin (Eds.), *Constructions of disorder* (pp. 15–40). American Psychological Association.

Raskin, J. D., & Morano, L. A. (2004). Credulous approach. In *Internet encyclopedia of personal construct psychology.* http://www.pcp-net.org/encyclopaedia/cred-appr.html

Rastatter, M. P., Stuart, A., & Kalinowski, J. (1998). Quantitative electroencephalogram of posterior cortical areas of fluent and stuttering participants during reading with normal and altered auditory feedback. *Perceptual and Motor Skills, 87*(2), 623–633. https://doi.org/10.2466/pms.1998.87.2.623

Ratner, N. B. (1993). Parents, children, and stuttering. *Seminars in Speech and Language, 14*(3), 238–250.

Ratner, N. B. (1995). Treating the child who stutters with concomitant language or phonological impairment. *Language, Speech, and Hearing Services in Schools, 26*, 180–186.

Ratner, N. B. (1997). Stuttering: A psycholinguistic perspective. In R. Curlee & G. Siegel (Eds.), *Nature and treatment of stuttering: New directions* (2nd ed., pp. 99–127). Allyn & Bacon.

Ratner, N. B. (2000). Performance or capacity, the model still requires definitions and boundaries it doesn't have. *Journal of Fluency Disorders, 25*(4), 337–346.

Ratner, N. B. (2005). Evidenced-based practice in stuttering: Some questions to consider. *Journal of Fluency Disorders, 30*(1), 163–188.

Ratner, N. B., & Guitar, B. (2006). Treatment of very early stuttering and parent-administered therapy: The state of the art. In N. B. Ratner & J. Tetnowski (Eds.), *Current issues in stuttering research and practice* (pp. 99– 124). Erlbaum.

Ratner, N. B., & Healey, E. C. (1999). Bridging the gap between stuttering research and practice: An overview. In N. B. Ratner & E. C. Healey (Eds.), *Stuttering research and practice: Bridging the gap* (pp. 1–12). Erlbaum.

Ratner, N., & Sih, C. (1987). The effects of gradual increases in sentence length and complexity on children's dysfluency. *Journal of Speech and Hearing Disorders, 52*, 278–287.

Raza, M. H., Gertz, E. M., Mundorff, J., Lukong, J., Kuster, J., Schäffer, A. A., & Drayna, D. (2013). Linkage analysis of a large African family segregating stuttering suggests polygenic inheritance. *Human Genetics, 132*(4), 385–396. https://doi.org/10.1007/s00439-012-1252-5

Reardon, N. A. (2000). *Working with teachers* [Paper presentation]. Stuttering Foundation of America Conference on Stuttering therapy: Practical ideas for the school clinician, Charleston, SC.

Reardon, N. A., & Yaruss, J. S. (2004). *The source for stuttering: Ages 7–18.* LinguiSystems.

Reeves, L. (2006). The role of self-help/mutual aid in addressing the needs of individuals who stutter. In N. Bernstein Ratner & J. Tetnowski (Eds.), *Current issues in stuttering research and practice* (pp. 255–278). Erlbaum.

Reich, A., Till, J. A., & Goldsmith, H. (1981). Laryngeal and manual reaction times of stuttering and nonstuttering adults. *Journal of Speech and Hearing Research, 24*(2), 192–196.

Reitzes, P. (2006). *50 great activities for children who stutter.* PRO-ED.

Reitzes, P. (2012). His name is Peter Cottontail: My story passing as fluent. In P. Reitzes & C. Reitzes (Eds.), *Stuttering: Inspiring stories and professional wisdom* (pp. 95–122). StutterTalk.

Resnick, P. (1993). Defrocking the fraud: The detection of malingering. *Israel Journal of Psychology and Related Sciences, 30*(2), 93–101.

Reynolds, C. R., & Richmond, B. O. (1994). *Revised Children's Manifest Anxiety Scale.* Western Psychological Services.

Riaz, N., Steinberg, S., Ahmad, J., Pluzhnikov, A., Riazuddin, S., Cox, N. J., & Drayna, D. (2005). Genomewide significant linkage to stuttering on chromosome 12. *American Journal of Human Genetics, 76*, 647–651.

Ribbler, N. (2006, February). When a student stutters: Identifying the adverse educational impact. *Perspectives on Fluency Disorders, 16*(1), 15–17.

Riley, G. D. (1972). A stuttering severity instrument for children and adults. *Journal of Speech and Hearing Disorders, 37*, 314–321.

Riley, G. (1981). *Stuttering Prediction Instrument for Young Children* (Rev. ed.). PRO-ED.

Riley, G. D. (1994). *Stuttering Severity Instrument for Children and Adults—Third edition* (SSI–3). PRO-ED.

Riley, G. D. (2009). *Stuttering Severity Instrument for Children and Adults—Fourth edition* (SSI–4). PRO-ED.

Riley, G., & Riley, J. (1979). A component model for diagnosing and treating children who stutter. *Journal of Fluency Disorders, 4*, 279–293.

Riley, G., & Riley, J. (1983). Evaluation as a basis for intervention. In D. Peins & R. Ingham (Eds.), *Treatment of stuttering in early childhood* (pp. 128–152). College-Hill.

Riley, G., & Riley, J. (1984). A component model for treating stuttering in children. In M. Prins (Ed.), *Contemporary approaches in stuttering therapy* (pp. 123–172). Little, Brown.

Riley, G., & Riley, J. (2000). A revised component model for diagnosing and treating children who stutter. *Contemporary Issues in Communication Sciences and Disorders, 27*, 188–199.

Riley, J., Riley, G., & Maguire, G. (2004). Subjective screening of stuttering severity, locus of control and avoidance: Research edition. *Journal of Fluency Disorders, 29*, 51–62.

Robb, M., & Blomgren, M. (1997). Analysis of F2 transitions in the speech of stutterers and nonstutterers. *Journal of Fluency Disorders, 22,* 1–16.

Robb, M., Blomgren, M., & Chen, Y. (1998). Formant frequency fluctuation in stuttering and nonstuttering adults. *Journal of Fluency Disorders, 23,* 73–84.

Robbins, S. D. (1920). Comparative shock and stammering. *American Journal of Physiology, 52,* 168–181.

Robinson, T. L. (2012). Cultural diversity and fluency disorders. In D. E. Battle (Ed.), *Communication disorders in multicultural and international populations* (pp. 164–173). Mosby.

Robinson, T. L. Jr., & Crowe, T. A. (1998). Culture-based considerations in programming or stuttering intervention with African American clients and their families. *Language Speech and Hearing Services in the Schools, 29,* 172–179.

Rocha, M. S., Yaruss, J. S., & Rato, J. R. (2019). Temperament, executive functioning, and anxiety in school-age children who stutter. *Frontiers in Psychology, 10.* https://doi.org/10.3389/fpsyg.2019.02244

Rogers, C. R. (1951). *Client-centered therapy.* Houghton Mifflin.

Rogers, C. R. (1957). The necessary and sufficient conditions of therapeutic personality change. *Journal of Consulting Psychology, 21*(2), 95.

Rogers, C. R. (1961). *On becoming a person.* Houghton Mifflin.

Rogers, C. R. (1980). *A way of being.* Houghton Mifflin.

Rogers, C. R. (1986). Rogers, Kohut, and Erickson: A personal perspective on some similarities and differences. *Person-Centered Review, 1,* 125–140.

Rollin, W. J. (2000). *Counseling individuals with communication disorders: Psychodynamic and family aspects* (2nd ed.). Butterworth-Heinemann.

Rollnick, S., Heather, N., Gold, R., & Hall, W. (1992). Development of a short "readiness to change" questionnaire for use in brief, opportunistic interventions among excessive drinkers. *British Journal of Addiction, 87,* 743–754.

Rollnick, S., & Miller, W. R. (1995). What is motivational interviewing? *Behavioural and Cognitive Psychotherapy, 23,* 325–334.

Roseman, B. A., & Johnson, K. L. (1998). *Easy does it for fluency.* LinguiSystems/PRO-ED.

Rosenbek, J., Messert, B., Collins, M., & Wertz, T. (1978). Stuttering following brain damage. *Brain and Language, 6,* 82–86.

Rosenbek, J. C. (2016). Tyranny of the randomized clinical trial. *International Journal of Speech-Language Pathology, 18,* 241–249.

Rosenberg, M. (1965). *Society and the adolescent self-image.* Princeton University Press.

Rosenberg, M. (1979). *Conceiving the self.* Basic Books.

Rosenzweig, S. (1936). Some implicit common factors in diverse methods of psychotherapy. *American Journal of Orthopsychiatry, 6,* 412–415.

Roth, C. R., Aronson, A. E., & Davis, L. J., Jr. (1989). Clinical studies in psychogenic stuttering of adult onset. *Journal of Speech and Hearing Disorders, 54,* 634–646.

Rothbart, M. K., Ahadi, S. A., Hershey, K. L., & Fisher, P. (2001). Investigations of temperament at three to seven years: The Children's Behavior Questionnaire. *Child Development, 72,* 1394–1408.

Rotter, J. B. (1954). *Social learning and clinical psychology.* Prentice Hall.

Rotter, J. B. (1966). Generalized expectancies of internal versus external control of reinforcements. *Psychological Monographs, 890,* 609.

Rousey, C. G., Arjunan, K. N., & Rousey, C. L. (1986). Successful treatment of stuttering following closed head injury. *Journal of Fluency Disorders, 11,* 257–261.

Rousseau, D. M., & Gunia, B. C. (2016). Evidence-based practice: The psychology of EBP implementation. *Annual Review of Psychology, 67,* 667–692.

Rubin, H. (1986). Postscript: Cognitive therapy. In G. H. Shames & H. Rubin (Eds.), *Stuttering then and now* (pp. 474–486). Merrill.

Rudolf, S. R., Manning, W. H., & Sewell, W. R. (1983). The use of self-efficacy scaling in training student clinicians: Implications for working with stutterers. *Journal of Fluency Disorders, 8,* 55–75.

Runyan, C. M., Bell, J. N., & Prosek, R. A. (1990). Speech naturalness ratings of treated stutterers. *Journal of Speech and Hearing Disorders, 55*, 434–438.

Runyan, C. M., Hames, P. E., & Proseck, R. A. (1982). A perceptual comparison between paired stimulus and single stimulus methods of presentation of the fluent utterances of stutterers. *Journal of Fluency Disorders, 7*, 71–77.

Runyan, C. M., Runyan, S. E., & Hibbard, S. (2006). *The Speech Easy [sic]device: A three year study* [Paper presentation]. Annual Meeting of the American Speech-Language-Hearing Association, Miami, FL.

Ruscello, D. M., Lass, N. J., Schmitt, J. F., & Panbacker, M. D. (1994). Special educators' perceptions of stutterers. *Journal of Fluency Disorders, 19*, 125–132.

Rusk, T. (1989). *So you want to change: Helping people help themselves* [Presentation]. Twelfth Annual Conference for Trainers, Consultants, and other HRD Professionals, San Francisco, CA.

Rustin, L. (1987). The treatment of childhood dysfluency through active parental involvement. In L. Rustin, H. Purser, & H. Rowley (Eds.), *Progress in the treatment of fluency disorders* (pp. 166–180). Taylor & Francis.

Rustin, L., & Cook, F. (1995). Parental involvement in the treatment of stuttering. *Language, Speech, and Hearing Services in Schools, 26*, 127–137.

Ryan, B. (1979). Stuttering therapy in a framework of operant conditioning and programmed learning. In H. Gregory (Ed.), *Controversies about stuttering therapy* (pp. 129– 174). University Park Press.

Ryan, B. (1980). *Programmed therapy for stuttering children and adults.* Charles C. Thomas.

Ryan, B. (2001). *Programmed therapy for stuttering children and adults* (2nd ed.). Charles C. Thomas.

Ryan, B., & Van Kirk, B. (1974). The establishment, transfer, and maintenance of fluent speech in 50 stutterers using delayed auditory feedback and operant procedures. *Journal of Speech and Hearing Research, 39*, 3–10.

Ryan, B., & Van Kirk Ryan, B. (1995). Programmed stuttering treatment for children: Comparison of two establishment programs through transfer, maintenance, and follow-up. *Journal of Speech and Hearing Research, 38*(1), 61–75.

Sacco, P. R., Metz, D. E., & Schiavetti, N. (1992). *Speech naturalness of nonstutterers and treated stutterers: Acoustical correlates* [Paper presentation]. Annual Meeting of the American Speech-Language-Hearing Association, San Antonio, TX.

Sackett, D. L., Rosenberg, W. M., Gray, J. A., Haynes, R. B., & Richardson, W. S. (1996). Evidence-based medicine: What it is and what it isn't. *British Medical Journal, 312*, 71.

Sackett, D. L., Strauss, S. E., Richardson, W. S., Rosenberg, W., & Hayes, R. B. (2000). *Evidenced-based medicine.* Churchill-Livingston.

Sagan, C. (1996). *The demon-haunted world: Science as a candle in the dark.* Random House.

Salmelin, R., Schnitzler, A., Schmitz, F., & Freund, H.-J. (2000). Single word reading in developmental stutterers and fluent speakers. *Brain, 123*(6), 1184–1202. https://doi.org/10.1093/brain/123.6.1184

Schaeffer, M. L., & Shearer, W. M. (1968). A survey of mentally retarded stutterers. *Mental Retardation, 6*, 44–45.

Schafer, M., Korn, S., Smith, P. K., Hunter, S. C., Mora-Merchan, J. A., Singer, M. M., & Muelen, K. (2004). Lonely in the crowd: Recollections of bullying. *British Journal of Developmental Psychology, 22* (3), 379–394.

Schiavetti, N., & Metz, D. E. (1997). Stuttering and the measurement of speech naturalness. In R. Curlee & G. Siegel (Eds.), *Nature and treatment of stuttering, new directions* (2nd ed., pp. 298–412). Allyn & Bacon.

Schimel, J. (1978). The function of wit and humor in psychoanalysis. *Journal of the American Academy of Psychoanalysis, 6*(3), 369–379.

Schotte, C., & Doncker, D. (1994). *ADP-IV questionnaire.* Belgium University Hospital Antwerp.

Schotte, C., & Doncker, D. (1996). *ADP-IV questionnaire, Manual and norms*. Belgium University Hospital Antwerp.

Schouten, J. W. (1991). Personal rites of passage and the reconstruction of self. *Advances in Consumer Research, 18*, 49–51.

Schwartz, H., & Conture, E. (1988). Subgroupings of young stutterers: Preliminary behavioral observations. *Journal of Speech and Hearing Research, 31*, 62–71.

Schwartz, H. D., Zebrowski, P. M., & Conture, E. G. (1990). Behaviors at the outset of stuttering. *Journal of Fluency Disorders, 15*, 77–86.

Scott, K. S., & Sisskin, V. (2007). *Part II: Speech disfluency in autism spectrum disorders: Clinical problem solving for pervasive developmental disorder, not otherwise specified and Asperger syndrome* [Paper presentation]. International Stuttering Awareness Day Online Conference (ISAD). http://www.mankato.msus .edu/dept/comdis/isad/isadcon.html

Scott Trautman, L., & Keller, K. (2000, November). *Bilingual intervention for stuttering: A case in point* [Paper presentation]. Annual Convention of the American Speech-Language-Hearing Association, Washington, DC.

Scripture, E. W. (1931). *Stuttering, lisping, and correction of the speech of the deaf*. Macmillan.

Seery, C. H. (2005). Differential diagnosis of stuttering for forensic purposes. *American Journal of Speech-Language Pathology, 14*, 284–297.

Shames, G. H. (2006). *Counseling the communicatively disabled and their families: A manual for clinicians*. Erlbaum.

Shames, G., & Florance, C. (1980). *Stutter-free speech: A goal for therapy*. Merrill.

Shames, G. H., & Sherrick, C. E., Jr. (1965). A discussion of nonfluency and stuttering as operant behavior. *Journal of Speech and Hearing Disorders, 28*, 3–18.

Shapiro, D. A. (1999). *Stuttering intervention: A collaborative journey to fluency freedom*. PRO-ED.

Shapiro, D. A. (2011). *Stuttering intervention: A collaborative journey to fluency freedom* (2nd ed.). PRO-ED.

Sharp, M. Y., Reynolds, R. B., & Brooks, K. N. (2013, Summer). Critical thinking skills of allied health science students: A structured inquiry. *Educational Perspectives in Health Informatics and Information Management*, 1–13.

Sheehan, J. (1958). Projective studies of stuttering. *Journal of Speech and Hearing Disorders, 23*, 18–25.

Sheehan, J. (1970). *Stuttering: Research and therapy*. Harper & Row.

Sheehan, J. (1975). Conflict theory and avoidance-reduction therapy. In J. Eisenson (Ed.), *Stuttering, a second symposium* (pp. 97–198). Harper & Row.

Sheehan, J. G. (1980). Problems in the evaluation of progress and outcome. In W. H. Perkins (Ed.), *Seminars in speech, language and hearing* (pp. 389–401). Thieme-Stratton.

Sheehan, J. G. (1982). *Stuttering therapy: Transfer and maintenance* (Publication No. 16). Stuttering Foundation of America.

Sheehan, J. G. (2003). Message to a stutterer. In *Advice to those who stutter* (Publication No. 9, pp. 31–35). Stuttering Foundation of America.

Sheehan, J. G., & Costley, M. S. (1977). A reexamination of the role of heredity in stuttering. *Journal of Speech and Hearing Disorders, 42*, 47–59.

Sheehan, J., & Martyn, M. (1966). Spontaneous recovery from stuttering. *Journal of Speech and Hearing Research, 9*, 121–135.

Sheehan, J. G., & Martyn, M. (1970). Stuttering and its disappearance. *Journal of Speech and Hearing Research, 13*, 279–289.

Sheehan, J. G., & Voas, R. B. (1957). Stuttering as a conflict I. Comparison of therapy techniques involving approach and avoidance. *Journal of Speech and Hearing Disorders, 22*, 714–723.

Sheehan, V. M., & Sisskin, V. (2001). The creative process in avoidance reduction therapy. *Perspectives on Fluency Disorders, 11*, 7–11.

Sheehy, G. (1974). *Passages: Predictable crises of adult life*. Bantam.

Shenker, R. C. (2011). Multilingual children who stutter: Clinical issues. *Journal of Fluency*

Disorders, 36(3), 186–193. https://doi.org/10.1016/j.jfludis.2011.04.001

Shenker, R. C., Conte, A., Gingras, A., Courcey, A., & Polomeno, L. (1998). The impact of bilingualism on developing fluency in a preschool child. In E. C. Healey & H. F. M. Peters (Eds.), *Second World Congress on Fluency Disorders Proceedings* (pp. 200–204). Nijmegen University Press.

Shepard, B., & Marshall, A. (1999). Possible selves mapping: Life-career exploration with young adolescents. *Canadian Journal of Counseling, 33*(1), 37–54.

Shields, D. (1989). *Dead languages.* Knopf.

Shugart, Y. Y., Mundorff, J., Kilshaw, J., Doheny, K., Doan, B., Wanyee, J., . . . Drayna, D. (2004). Results of a genomewide linkage scan for stuttering. *American Journal of Medical Genetics, 124A*(2), 133–135.

Siegel, G. (1970). Punishment, stuttering and disfluency. *Journal of Speech and Hearing Disorders, 13,* 677–714.

Siegel, G. (1993). Research: A natural bridge. *ASHA, 35,* 36–37.

Siegel, G. (2000). "Demands and capacities" or "demands and performance." *Journal of Fluency Disorders, 25*(4), 321–328.

Siegel, G. M., & Martin, R. R. (1966). Punishment of disfluencies in normal speakers. *Journal of Speech and Hearing Research, 9,* 208–218.

Silverman, E., & Zimmer, C. (1982). Demographic characteristics and treatment experiences of women and men who stutter. *Journal of Fluency Disorders, 7,* 273–285.

Silverman, E. M. (2011). Self-reflection in clinical practice. In R. J. Fourie (Ed.), *Therapeutic processes for communication disorders: A guide for clinicians and students* (pp. 183–193). Psychology Press.

Silverman, F. H. (1975). How "typical" is a stutterer's stuttering in a clinical environment? *Perceptual and Motor Skills, 40,* 458.

Silverman, F. H. (1976). Long-term impact of a miniature metronome on stuttering: An interim report. *Perceptual and Motor Skills, 43,* 398.

Silverman, F. H. (1981). Relapse following stuttering therapy. In N. J. Lass (Ed.), *Speech and language, advances in basic research and practice* (Vol. 5, pp. 56–78). Academic Press.

Silverman, F. H. (1988a). Impact of a T-shirt message on stutterer stereotypes. *Journal of Fluency Disorders, 13,* 279–281.

Silverman, F. H. (1988b). The monster study. *Journal of Fluency Disorders, 13,* 225–231.

Silverman, F. H. (1992). *Stuttering and other fluency disorders.* Prentice Hall.

Silverman, F. H. (1996). *Stuttering and other fluency disorders.* Prentice Hall.

Silverman, F. H. (2004). *Stuttering and other fluency disorders.* Waveland Press.

Simmons-Mackie, N., & Damico, J. S. (1999). Social role negotiation in aphasia therapy: Competence, incompetence, and conflict. In D. Kovarsky, J. F. Duchan, & M. Maxell (Eds.), *Constructing (in)competence: Disabling evaluations in clinical and social interaction* (pp. 313–342). Erlbaum.

Simmons-Mackie, N., & Damico, J. S. (2011). Counseling and aphasia treatment: Missed opportunities. *Topics in Language Disorders, 31,* 336–351.

Simmons-Mackie, N., & Schultz, M. (2003). The role of humor in therapy for aphasia. *Aphasiology, 17,* 751–766.

Simon, H. A., & Chase, W. G. (1973). Skill in chess. *American Scientist, 61,* 394–403.

Singer, C. M., Hessling, A., Kelly, E. M., Singer, L., & Jones, R. M. (2020). Clinical characteristics associated with stuttering persistence: A meta-analysis. *Journal of Speech, Language, and Hearing Research, 63*(9), 2995–3018. https://doi.org/10.1044/2020_JSLHR-20-00096

Singer, C. M., Otieno, S., Chang, S.-E., & Jones, R. M. (2022). Predicting persistent developmental stuttering using a cumulative risk approach. *Journal of Speech, Language, and Hearing Research, 65*(1), 70–95. https://doi.org/10.1044/2021_jslhr-21-00162

Sisskin, V., & Wasilus, S. (2014). Lost in the literature, but not the caseload: Working with atypical disfluency from theory to practice. *Seminars in Speech and Language, 35,* 144–152.

Skinner, B. F. (1953). *Science and human behavior.* Macmillan.

Slater, S. C. (1992, August). 1992 omnibus survey: Portrait of the professions. *ASHA, 34,* 61–65.

Smith, A. (1990). Toward a comprehensive theory of stuttering: A commentary. *Journal of Speech and Hearing Disorders, 55,* 398–401.

Smith, A. (1999). Stuttering: A unified approach to a multifactorial, dynamic disorder. In N. B. Ratner & E. C. Healey (Eds.), *Stuttering research and practice: Bridging the gap* (pp. 27–44). Erlbaum.

Smith, A., & Kelly, E. (1997). Stuttering: A dynamic, multifactoral model. In R. F. Curlee & G. M. Siegel (Eds.), *The nature and treatment of stuttering: New directions* (2nd ed., pp. 204–217). Allyn & Bacon.

Smith, A., & Kleinow, J. (2000). Kinematic correlates of speaking rate change in stuttering and normally fluent adults. *Journal of Speech, Language, and Hearing Research, 43,* 521–536.

Smith, A., & Weber, C. (2017). How stuttering develops: The multifactorial dynamic pathways theory. *Journal of Speech, Language, and Hearing Research, 60,* 2483–2505.

Sommers, R. K., Brady, W., & Moore, W. H., Jr. (1975). Dichotic ear preferences of stuttering children and adults. *Perceptual and Motor Skills, 41,* 931–938.

Sønsterud, H., Feragen, K. B., Kirmess, M., Halvorsen, M. S., & Ward, D. (2020). What do people search for in stuttering therapy: Personal goal-setting as a gold standard? *Journal of Communication Disorders, 85,* 105944. https://doi.org/10.1016/j.jcomdis.2019.105944

Specter, M. (2016). DNA revolution. *The National Geographic, August 2016,* pp. 36–55.

SpeechEasy Professional Information Packet. (2006). Janus Development Group.

Spence, S. H. (1998). A measure of anxiety symptoms among children. *Behaviour Research and Therapy, 36*(5), 545–566. https://doi.org/10.1016/S0005-7967(98)00034-5

Spielberger, C. D., Edwards, C. D., Luschene, R. E., Montuori, J., & Platzek, D. (1972). *STAIC preliminary manual.* Consulting Psychologists Press.

Spielberger, C. D., Gorsuch, R., Lushene, R., Vagg, P. R., & Jacobs, G. A. (1983). *STAI manual for the State-Trait Anxiety Inventory.* Consulting Psychologists Press.

Ssikorsky, J. A. (1891). *Uber das Stottern [About Stuttering].* August Hirshwald.

Stansfield, J. (1995). Word-final disfluencies in adults with learning difficulties. *Journal of Fluency Disorders, 20*(1), 1–10.

St. Louis, K. O. (1982, November). *Transfer and maintenance of fluency in stuttering clients* [Short course]. Annual Meeting of the American Speech-Language-Hearing Association, Toronto, Canada.

St. Louis, K. O. (1986). *The atypical stutterer: Principles and practices of rehabilitation.* Orlando, FL: Academic Press.

St. Louis, K. O. (1992). On defining cluttering. In F. L. Myers & K. O. St. Louis (Eds.), *Cluttering: A clinical perspective* (pp. 37–53). Singular Publishing.

St. Louis, K. O. (1999). Person-first labeling and stuttering. *Journal of Fluency Disorders, 24,* 1–24.

St. Louis, K. O. (2006). Measurement issues in fluency disorders. In N. Bernstein Ratner & J. Tetnowski (Eds.), *Current issues in stuttering research and practice* (pp. 61–86). Erlbaum.

St. Louis, K. O., & Atkins, C. P. (2006). *Self-Awareness of Speech Index* (SASI). Populore.

St. Louis, K. O., & Hinzman, A. R. (1986). Studies of cluttering: Perceptions of cluttering by speech-language pathologists and educators. *Journal of Fluency Disorders, 11,* 131–149.

St. Louis, K., Murray, C., & Ashworth, M. (1991). Coexisting communication disorders in a random sample of school-aged stutterers. *Journal of Fluency Disorders, 16,* 13–23.

St. Louis, K. O., & Myers, F. (1995). Clinical management of stuttering. *Language, Speech, and Hearing Services in Schools, 26,* 187–195.

St. Louis, K. O., & Myers, F. (1997). Management of cluttering and related fluency disorders. In R. F. Curlee & G. M. Siegel (Eds.), *Nature and treatment of stuttering: New directions* (2nd ed., pp. 313–332). Allyn & Bacon.

St. Louis, K. O., Myers, F. L., Bakker, K., & Raphael, L. J. (2007). Understanding and treating cluttering, In E. Conture & R. Curlee (Eds.), *Stuttering and related disorders of fluency* (3rd ed., pp. 297–325). Thieme Medical.

St. Louis, K. O., Myers, F. L., Faragasso, K., Townsend, P. S., & Gallaher, A. J. (2004). Perceptual aspects of cluttered speech, *Journal of Fluency Disorders, 29,* 213–235.

St. Louis, K. O., & Rustin, L. (1992). Professional awareness of cluttering. In F. M. Myers & K. O. St. Louis (Eds.), *Cluttering: A clinical perspective* (pp. 23–35). Singular Publishing.

St. Louis, K. O., & Westbrook, J. B. (1987). The effectiveness of treatment for stuttering. In L. Rustin, H. Purser, & D. Rowley (Eds.), *Progress in the treatment of fluency disorders* (pp. 235–257). Taylor & Francis.

Stanhope, V., Ingoglia, C., Schmelter, B., & Marcus, S. C. (2013). Impact of person-centered planning and collaborative documentation on treatment adherence. *Psychiatric Services, 64*(1), 76–79.

Starke, A. (1994). Why do stutterers reject artificial speech? The message incompatibility conflict. In *Proceedings of the 1994 Meeting of the International Fluency Association* (V. II, pp. 445–452). Nijmegen University Press.

Starkweather, C. W. (1987). *Fluency and stuttering.* Prentice Hall.

Starkweather, C. W. (1992). Response and reaction to Hamre, "Stuttering Prevention I." *Journal of Fluency Disorders, 17,* 43–55.

Starkweather, C.W. (1999).The effectiveness of stuttering therapy: An issue for science? In N. B. Ratner & E. C. Healey (Eds.), *Stuttering research and practice: Bridging the gap* (pp. 231–244). Erlbaum.

Starkweather, C. W., & Gottwald, S. R. (1990). The demands and capacities model II: Clinical implications. *Journal of Fluency Disorders, 15,* 143–157.

Starkweather, C. W., & Gottwald, S. R. (2000). The demands and capacities model: Response to Siegel. *Journal of Fluency Disorders, 25*(4), 369–376.

Starkweather, C. W., Gottwald, S. R., & Halfond, M. H. (1990). *Stuttering prevention: A clinical method.* Prentice Hall.

Starkweather, C. W., Hirschmann, P., & Tannenbaum, R. (1976). Latency of vocalization: Stutterers v. nonstutterers. *Journal of Speech and Hearing Research, 19,* 481–492.

Starkweather, C. W., St. Louis, K. O., Blood, G., Peters, T., & Westbrook, J. (1994). Guidelines for practice in stuttering treatment. *ASHA, 37*(Suppl. 14), 26–35.

Stein, L. (1942). *Speech and voice.* Methuen.

Stein-Rubin, C., & Adler, B. (2016). *Counseling in communication disorders: Facilitating the therapeutic relationship.* Slack.

Stern, E. (1948). A preliminary study of bilingualism and stuttering in four Johannesburg schools. *Journal of Logopaedics, 1,* 15–25.

Stetson, R. H. (1951). *Motor phonetics* (2nd ed.). North-Holland.

Stewart, T., & Rowley, D. (1996). Acquired stammering in Great Britain. *European Journal of Disorders of Communication, 31,* 109.

Stocker, B. (1980). *The Stocker Probe technique for diagnosis and treatment of stuttering in young children.* Modern Education Corporation.

Stocker, B., & Gerstman, L. (1983). A comparison of the probe technique and conventional therapy for young stutterers. *Journal of Fluency Disorders, 8,* 331–339.

Stocker, B., & Usprich, C. (1976). Stuttering in young children and level of demand. *Journal of Fluency Disorders, 1,* 116–131.

Stuart, A., Kalinowski, J., & Rastatter, M. P. (1997). Effect of monaural and binaural altered auditory feedback on stuttering frequency. *Journal of the Acoustical Society of America, 101,* 3806–3809.

Stuart, A., Kalinowski, J., Rastatter, M., Saltuklarglu, T., & Dayalu, V. (2004). Investigations of the impact of altered auditory feedback in-the-ear devices on the speech of people who stutter: Initial fitting and 4-month follow-up. *International Journal of Language and Communication Disorders, 39,* 93–119.

Studdert-Kennedy, M., & Shankweiler, D. (1970). Hemispheric specialization for speech perception. *Journal of the Acoustical Society of America, 48,* 579–594.

Sugarman, M. (1980). It's O.K. to stutter: A personal account. *Journal of Fluency Disorders, 5,* 149–157.

Sumsion, T., & Law, M. (2006). A review of evidence on the conceptual elements informing client-centred practice. *Canadian Journal of Occupational Therapy, 73,* 153–162.

Suresh, R., Ambrose, N., Roe, C., Pluzhnikov, A., Wittke-Thompson, J. K., Ng, M. C., . . . Cox, N. J. (2006). New complexities in the genetics of stuttering: Significant sex-specific linkage signals. *American Journal of Human Genetics, 78,* 554–563.

Sussman, H., M., Byrd, C. T., & Guitar, B. (2010). The integrity of anticipatory coarticulation in fluent and non-fluent tokens of adults who stutter. *Clinical Linguistics and Phonetics, 25*(3), 1–18.

Sussman, H. M., MacNeilage, P. F., & Lumbley, J. (1975). Pursuit auditory tracking of dichotically presented tonal amplitudes. *Journal of Speech and Hearing Research, 18,* 74–81.

Tasko, S. M., McClean, M. D., & Runyan, C. M. (2007). Speech motor correlates of treatment-related changes in stuttering severity and speech naturalness. *Journal of Communication Disorders, 40,* 42–65.

Tattum, D. (1989). Bullying—A problem crying out for attention. *Pastoral Care in Education, 7*(2), 21–25.

Thompson, J. (1983). *Assessment of fluency in school-age children* (Resource guide). Interstate Printers and Publishers.

Thorson, J. A., & Powell, F. C., (1993a). Development and validation of a multidimensional sense of humor scale. *Journal of Clinical Psychology, 49*(1), 13–23.

Thorson, J. A., & Powell, F. C., (1993b). Sense of humor and dimensions of personality. *Journal of Clinical Psychology, 49*(6), 799–809.

Throneberg, R. N., & Yairi, E. (1994). Temporal dynamics of repetitions during the early stages of childhood stuttering: An acoustic study. *Journal of Speech and Hearing Research, 37,* 1067–1075.

Throneberg, R. N., Yairi, E., & Paden, E. (1994). Relation between phonologic difficulty and the occurrence of disfluencies in the early stage of stuttering *Journal of Speech and Hearing Research, 37,* 504–509.

Tichenor, S. E., & Yaruss, J. S. (2019). Stuttering as defined by adults who stutter. *Journal of Speech, Language, and Hearing Research, 62*(12), 4356–4369.

Tiger, R. J., Irvine, T. L., & Reiss, R. P. (1980). Cluttering as a complex of learning disabilities. *Language, Speech, and Hearing Services in the Schools, 11,* 3–14.

Toscher, M. M., & Rupp, R. R. (1978). A study of the central auditory processes in stutterers using the Synthetic Sentence Identification (SSI) test battery. *Journal of Speech and Hearing Research, 21,* 779–792.

Tran, Y., Blumgart, E., & Craig, A. (2011). Subjective stress associated with chronic stuttering. *Journal of Fluency Disorders, 6,* 17–26.

Travis, L. E. (1929). Recurrence of stuttering following shift from normal to mirror writing. *Archives of Neurology and Psychiatry, 21*(2), 386–391.

Travis, L. E. (1931). *Speech pathology.* Appleton-Century-Crofts.

Travis, L. E. (1957). The unspeakable feelings of people with special reference to stuttering. In L. E. Travis (Ed.), *Handbook of speech pathology* (pp. 916–946). Appleton-Century-Crofts.

Travis, L. E. (1971). The unspeakable feelings of people with special reference to stuttering. In L. E. Travis (Ed.), *Handbook of speech pathology and audiology* (pp. 1001–1003). Appleton-Century-Crofts.

Travis, L. E., Johnson, W., & Shover, J. (1937). The relation of bilingualism to stuttering. *Journal of Speech Disorders, 2,* 185–189.

Travis, L. E., & Knott, J. R. (1936). Brain potentials for normal speakers and stutterers. *Journal of Psychology, 2,* 137–150.

Travis, L. E., & Knott, J. R. (1937). Bilaterally recorded brain potentials from normal speakers and stutterers. *Journal of Speech Disorders, 2,* 239–241.

Travis, L. E., & Malamud, W. (1937). Brain potentials from normal subjects, stutterers, and schizophrenic patients. *American Journal of Psychiatry, 93,* 929–936.

Travis, L. E., Tuttle, W. W., & Cowan, D. W. (1936). A study of heart rate during stuttering. *Journal of Speech Disorders, 1,* 21–26.

Trichon, M., & Tetnowski, J. (2006). *Perspectives of self-help groups for people who stutter from group leaders* [Paper presentation].

Annual Meeting of the American Speech-Language-Hearing Association, Miami, FL.

Tuckman, B. (1965). Developmental sequence in small groups. *Psychological Bulletin, 63,* 384–399.

Tudor, M. (1939). *An experimental study of the effects of evaluative labeling on speech fluency* [Unpublished master's thesis]. University of Iowa, Iowa City.

Turnbaugh, K. R., Guitar, B. E., & Hoffman, P. R. (1979). Speech clinicians' attribution of personality traits as a function of stuttering severity. *Journal of Speech and Hearing Research, 22,* 37–45.

Turner, V. W. (1969). *The ritual process: Structure and anti-structure.* Aldine.

Turner, V. W. (1974). Liminal to liminoid in play, flow, and ritual: An essay in comparative symbology. *Rice University Studies, 60,* 53–92.

Tversky, A., & Kahneman, D. (1974). Judgment under uncertainty: Heuristics and biases. *Science, 185,* 1124–1131.

U.S. Census Bureau. (2023). *U.S. and world population clock.* https://www.census.gov /popclock/

Usler, E., Smith, A., & Weber, C. (2017). A lag in speech motor coordination during sentence production is associated with stuttering persistence in young children. *Journal of Speech, Language, and Hearing Research, 60*(1), 51–61. https://doi.org/10.1044/2016 _jslhr-s-15-0367

Valiant, G. E. (1977). *Adaptation to life.* Little, Brown.

Van Borsel, J. (1997). Neurogenic stuttering: A review. *Journal of Clinical Speech and Language Studies, 7,* 17–33.

Van Borsel, J. (2011). Review of research on the relationship between bilingualism and stuttering. In P. Howell & J. Van Borsel (Eds.), *Multilingual aspects of fluency disorders* (pp. 247–270). Multilingual Matters. https://doi.org/10.21832/9781847693570-013

Van Borsel, J., Bontinck, C., Coryn, M., Paemeleire, F., & Vandemaele, P. (2007). Acoustic features of palilalia. *Brain and Language, 101,* 90–96.

Van Borsel, J., Geirnaert, E., & Van Coster, R. (2005). Another case of word-final disfluencies. *Folia Phoniatrica and Logopaedica, 57*(3), 148–162.

Van Borsel, J., Maes, E., & Foulon, S. (2001). Stuttering and bilingualism A review. *Journal of Fluency Disorders, 26,* 179–205.

van Gennep, A. (1960). *The rites of passage* (M. B. Vizedom & G. L. Caffee, Trans.). University of Chicago Press.

Van Lieshout, P. H. H. M., Hulstijn, W., & Peters, H. F. M. (1996). From planning to articulation in speech production: What differentiates a person who stutters from a person who does not stutter? *Journal of Speech and Hearing Research, 39,* 546–564.

Van Riper, C. (1937). The preparatory set in stuttering. *Journal of Speech Disorders, 2,* 149–154.

Van Riper, C. (1939). *Speech correction: Principles and methods.* Prentice Hall.

Van Riper, C. (1947). *Speech correction: Principles and methods.* Prentice Hall.

Van Riper, C. (1958). Experiments in stuttering therapy. In J. Eisenson (Ed.), *Stuttering: A symposium.* Harper & Row.

Van Riper, C. (1965). Supervision of clinical practice. *ASHA, 7,* 75–77.

Van Riper, C. (1971). *The nature of stuttering.* Prentice Hall.

Van Riper, C. (1973). *The treatment of stuttering* (2nd ed.). Prentice Hall.

Van Riper, C. (1974). A handful of nuts. *Western Michigan Journal of Speech Therapy, 11*(2), 1–3.

Van Riper, C. (1975). The stutterer's clinician. In J. Eisenson (Ed.), *Stuttering, a second symposium* (pp. 453–492). Harper & Row.

Van Riper, C. (1977). *Adult stuttering therapy: A series of eight video tapes produced at Western Michigan University, Kalamazoo.* Stuttering Foundation of America.

Van Riper, C. (1979). *A career in speech pathology.* Prentice Hall.

Van Riper, C. (1982). *The nature of stuttering* (2nd ed.). Prentice Hall.

Van Riper, C. (1984). Henry Freund: 1896–1982. *Journal of Fluency Disorders, 9,* 93–102.

Van Riper, C. (1990). Final thoughts about stuttering. *Journal of Fluency Disorders, 15*, 317–318.

Van Riper, C. (1992). Stuttering? *Journal of Fluency Disorders, 17*(1–2), 81–84.

Vanryckeghem, M., & Brutten, G. J. (1992). The Communication Attitude Test: A test–retest reliability investigation. *Journal of Fluency Disorders, 17*, 117–190.

Vanryckeghem, M., & Brutten, G. J. (1996). The relationship between communication attitude and fluency failure of stuttering and nonstuttering children. *Journal of Fluency Disorders, 21*, 109–118.

Vanryckeghem, M., & Brutten, G. J. (1997). The speech-associated attitudes of children who do and do not stutter and differential effect of age. *American Journal of Speech-Language Pathology, 6*(4), 67–73.

Vanryckeghem, M., & Brutten, G. J. (2007). Behavior Assessment Battery: Evidence-based approach to the assessment and treatment of children who stutter. In J. Au-Yeung & M. M. Leahy (Eds.) *Proceedings of Fifth World Congress on Fluency Disorders (International Fluency Association): Research, treatment and self-help in fluency disorders: New horizons* (pp. 209–214).

Vanryckeghem, M., & Brutten, G. (2018). *The Behavior Assessment Battery For Adults Who Stutter.* Plural Publishing.

Vanryckeghem, M., Brutten, G. J., & Hernandez, L. M. (2005). A comparative investigation of the speech-associated attitude of preschool and kindergarten children who do and do not stutter. *Journal of Fluency Disorders, 30*, 307–318.

Vanryckeghem, M., Brutten, G. J., Uddin, N., & Van Borsel, J. (2004). A behavior checklist comparative investigation of the speech-associated coping responses of adults who do and do not stutter. *Journal of Fluency Disorders, 29*, 237–250.

Vanryckeghem, M., & Herder, C. (2004). Normative investigation of speech-associated coping behaviors of children who do and do not stutter. *ASHA Leader, 9*, 101.

Vasic, N., & Wijnen, F. (2005). Stuttering as a monitoring deficit. In R. J. Hartsuiker, R. Bastiaanse, A. Postma, & F. Wijnen (Eds.), *Phonological encoding and monitoring in normal and pathological speech* (pp. 226–247). Psychology Press.

Vawter, V. (2013). *Paperboy.* Delacorte Press.

Viney, L L. (1983). The assessment of psychological states through content analysis of verbal communications. *Psychological Bulletin, 94*, 542–563.

Viney, L. L., & Westbrook, M. T. (1976). Cognitive anxiety: A method of content analysis for verbal samples. *Journal of Personality Assessment, 40*, 140–150.

Viswanath, N., Lee, H. S., & Chakraborty, R. (2004). Evidence for a major gene influence on persistent developmental stuttering. *Human Biology, 76*, 401–412.

Wade, C., Tavris, C., & Garry, M. (2014). *Psychology* (11th ed.). Prentice Hall.

Wakaba, Y. (1998). Research on temperament of stuttering children with early onset. In E. C. Healey & H. Peters (Eds.), *Proceedings of the Second World Congress on Fluency Disorders* (pp. 84–87). Nijmegen University Press.

Walden, T. A., Frankel, C. B., Buhr, A. P., Johnson, K. N., Conture, E. G., & Karrass, J. M. (2012). Dual diathesis-stressor model of emotional and linguistic contributions to developmental stuttering. *Journal of Abnormal Child Psychology, 40*(4), 633–644.

Walden, T. A., & Lesner, T. A. (2018). Examining implicit and explicit attitudes toward stuttering. *Journal of Fluency Disorders, 57*, 22–36. https://doi.org/10.1016/j.jfludis.2018.06.001

Wall, M. J. (1980). A comparison of syntax in young stutterers and nonstutterers. *Journal of Fluency Disorders, 5*, 345–352.

Wall, M. J., & Myers, F. L. (1995). *Clinical management of childhood stuttering* (2nd ed.). PRO-ED.

Walle, G. (1975). *The prevention of stuttering, Part 1* (film). Stuttering Foundation of America.

Walsh, B., Christ, S., & Weber, C. (2021). Exploring relationships among risk factors for persistence in early childhood stuttering.

Journal of Speech, Language, and Hearing Research, 64(8), 2909–2927. https://doi.org/10.1044/2021_jslhr-21-00034

Wampold, B. E. (2001). *The great psychotherapy debate: Models, methods, and findings.* Erlbaum.

Wampold, B. (2015). How important are the common factors in psychotherapy? An update. *World Psychiatry, 14,* 270–277.

Wampold, B. E., & Brown, G. S. (2005). Estimating variability in outcomes due to the therapist: A naturalistic study of outcomes in managed care. *Journal of Consulting and Clinical Psychology, 73*(5), 914–923.

Wampold, B. E., & Imel, Z. E. (2015). *The great psychotherapy debate: The research evidence for what works in psychotherapy* (2nd ed.). Routledge.

Wampold, B. E., Mondin, G. W., Moody M., Stich, F., Benson, K., & Ahn, H. (1997). A meta-analysis of outcome studies comparing bona fide psychotherapies: Empirically, "all must have prizes." *Psychological Bulletin, 122,* 203–215.

Watkins, K. E., Smith, S. M., Davis, S., & Howell, P. (2008). Structural and functional abnormalities of the motor system in developmental stuttering. *Brain, 131*(1), 50–59.

Watkins, R. V., Yairi, E., & Ambrose, N. G. (1999). Early childhood stuttering III: Initial status of expressive language abilities. *Journal of Speech, Language, and Hearing Research, 42,* 1025–1135.

Watson, B. C., Freeman, F. J., Devous, M. D., Chapman, S. B., Finitzo, T., & Pool, K. D. (1994). Linguistic performance and regional cerebral blood flow in persons who stutter. *Journal of Speech and Hearing Research, 37,* 1221–1228.

Watson, D., & Friend, R. (1969). Measurement of social-evaluative anxiety. *Journal of Consulting and Clinical Psychology, 33*(4), 448–457.

Watson, J. B. (1988). A comparison of stutterers' and nonstutterers' affective, cognitive, and behavioral self-reports. *Journal of Speech and Hearing Research, 31,* 377–385.

Weber-Fox, C. (2001). Neural systems for sentence processing in stuttering. *Journal of Speech, Language and Hearing Research, 44,* 814–825.

Webster, E. (1966). Parent counseling by speech pathologists and audiologists. *Journal of Speech and Hearing Disorders, 31,* 331–345.

Webster, E. (1968). Procedures for group counseling in speech, pathology and audiology. *Journal of Speech and Hearing Disorders, 33,* 127–131.

Webster, E. (1977). *Counseling with parents of handicapped children.* Grune & Stratton.

Webster, L. M. (1977). A clinical note on psychotherapy for stuttering. *Journal of Fluency Disorders, 2,* 253–255.

Webster, R. L. (1974). A behavioral analysis of stuttering: Treatment and theory. In K. S. Calhoon, H. E. Adams, & K. M. Mitchell (Eds.), *Innovative treatment methods in psychopathology* (pp. 17–61). Wiley.

Webster, R. L. (1975). *Clinicians' program guide: The Precision Fluency Shaping Program.* Communication Development Corp.

Webster, R. L. (1979). Empirical considerations regarding stuttering therapy. In H. H. Gregory (Ed.), *Controversies about stuttering therapy* (pp. 209–239). University Park Press.

Webster, R. L. (1986). Postscript: Stuttering therapy from a technological point of view. In G. H. Shames & H. Rubin (Ed.), *Stuttering then and now* (pp. 407–414). Merrill.

Weiss, A. L. (1993). The pragmatic context of children's disfluency. *Seminars in Speech and Language, 14*(3), 215–224.

Weiss, A. L., & Zebrowski, P. M. (1992). Disfluencies in the conversation of young children who stutter: Some answers about questions. *Journal of Speech and Hearing Research, 35,* 1230–1238.

Weiss, D. A. (1964). *Cluttering.* Prentice Hall.

Weiss, D. A. (1967). Similarities and differences between stuttering and cluttering. *Folia Phoniatrica, 19,* 98–104.

Wesseling, L. (2011). *Riding my bike—From shame to freedom* [Paper presentation]. International Stuttering Awareness Day Online Conference (ISAD). https://www.mnsu.edu/comdis/isad15/ papers/wesseling15.html

West, R., & Ansberry, M. (1968). *The rehabilitation of speech* (4th ed.). Harper & Row.

Westbrook, M. T., & Viney, L. L. (1980). Scales measuring people's perception of themselves as origins and pawns. *Journal of Personality Assessment, 44*, 167–174.

Westen, D., & Morrison, K. (2001). A multidimensional meta-analysis of treatments for depression, panic, and generalized anxiety disorder: An empirical examination of the status of empirically supported therapies. *Journal of Counseling and Clinical Psychology, 69*, 875–899.

Wexler, K. (1982). Developmental disfluency in 2-, 4-, and 6-year-old boys in neutral and stress situations. *Journal of Speech and Hearing Research, 25*, 229–234.

White, E. B. (1960). Some remarks on humor. The second tree from the corner. In J. J. Enck, E. T. Forter, & A. Whitley (Eds.), *The comic in theory and practice* (pp. 102–108). Appleton-Century-Crofts. (Original work published 1954)

White, M. (1989). *Selected papers.* Dulwich Centre Publications.

White, M. (2007). *Maps of narrative practice.* Norton.

White, M., & Epston, D. (1989). *Literate means to therapeutic ends.* Dulwich Centre Publications.

White, M., & Epston, D. (1990). *Narrative means to therapeutic ends.* Norton.

White, P. A., & Collins, S. R. C. (1984). Stereotype formation by inference: A possible explanation for the "stutterer" stereotype. *Journal of Speech and Hearing Research, 27*, 567–570.

Wicklund, R. A., & Gollwitzer, P. M. (1982). *Symbolic self-completion.* Erlbaum.

Willett, J., & Deegan, M. J. (2001). Liminality and disability: Rites of passage and community in hypermodern society. *Disability Studies Quarterly, 21*, 137–152.

Williams, D. E. (1957). A point of view about "stuttering." *Journal of Speech and Hearing Disorders, 22*(3), 390–397.

Williams, D. E. (1971). Stuttering therapy for children. In L. E. Travis (Ed.), *Handbook of speech pathology* (pp. 1073–1093). Appleton-Century-Crofts.

Williams, D. (1979). A perspective on approaches to stuttering therapy. In H. Gregory (Ed.), *Controversies about stuttering therapy* (pp. 241–268). University Park Press.

Williams, D. (1983).Working with children in the school environment. In J. Fraser Gruss (Ed.), *Stuttering therapy: Transfer and maintenance* (Publication No. 19). Memphis, TN: Stuttering Foundation of America.

Williams, D. (1985). Talking with children who stutter. In J. Fraser (Ed.), *Counseling stutterers* (pp. 35–45). Stuttering Foundation of America.

Williams, D. E. (1995). A clinical failure: Susan. In *Stuttering: Successes and failures in therapy* (pp. 130–131). Stuttering Foundation.

Williams, D. E. (2004). *The genius of Dean Williams* (Publication No. 425). Stuttering Foundation.

Williams, D., & Silverman, F. (1968). Note concerning articulation of school-age stutterers. *Perceptual and Motor Skills, 27*, 713–714.

Williams, D. E., Silverman, F. H., & Kools, J. A. (1968). Disfluency behavior of elementary school stutterers and nonstutterers: The adaptation effect. *Journal of Speech and Hearing Research, 11*, 622–630.

Williams, D. F., & Wener, D. L. (1996). Cluttering and stuttering exhibited in a young professional: Post hoc case study (clinical impressions). *Journal of Fluency Disorders, 21*, 1–9.

Williams, J. D., & Martin, R. B. (1974). Immediate versus delayed consequences of stuttering responses. *Journal of Speech and Hearing Research, 17*, 569–575.

Williams, R. (1995). Personal construct theory in use with people who stutter. In M. Fawcus (Ed.), *Stuttering: From theory to practice* (pp. 111–134). Whurr.

Wingate, M. E. (1964). Recovery from stuttering. *Journal of Speech and Hearing Disorders, 29*, 312–321.

Wingate, M. (1968). Research trends in stuttering. *Voice, 17*, 2–6.

Wingate, M. E. (1969). Sound and pattern in "artificial" fluency. *Journal of Speech and Hearing Research, 12*, 677–686.

Wingate, M. E. (1988). *Stuttering: A psycholinguistic analysis.* Springer Verlag.

Winslade, J., & Monk, G. (1999). *Narrative counseling in schools: Powerful and brief.* Corwin Press.

Winslow, M., & Guitar, B. (1994). The effects of structured turn-taking on disfluencies: A case study. *Language, Speech, and Hearing Services in Schools, 25,* 251–257.

Wittke-Thompson, J. K., Ambrose, N., Yairi, E., Roe, C., Cook, E. H., Ober, C., & Cox, N. J. (2007). Genetic studies of stuttering in a founder population. *Journal of Fluency Disorders, 32,* 33–50.

Wolf, A. E. (1991). *Get out of my life, but first could you drive me and Cheryl to the mall? A parent's guide to the new teenager.* Noonday Press.

Wood, F., Stump, D., McKeehan, A., Sheldon, S., & Proctor, J. (1980). Patterns of regional cerebral blood flow during attempted reading aloud by stutterers both on and off Haloperidol medication: Evidence for inadequate left frontal activation during stuttering. *Brain and Language, 9,* 141–144.

Woods, C. L., & Williams, D. E. (1976). Traits attributed to stuttering and normally fluent males. *Journal of Speech and Hearing Research, 19,* 267–278.

Woolf, G. (1967). The assessment of stuttering as struggle, avoidance and expectancy. *British Journal of Disorders of Communication, 2,* 158–171.

World Health Organization. (1977). *Manual of the international statistical classification of diseases, injuries, and causes of death* (Vol. 1).

World Health Organization. (1980). *International classification of impairments, disabilities, and handicaps: A manual of classification of classification relating to the consequences of disease.*

World Health Organization. (2001). *The international classification of functioning, disability and health.*

World Health Organization. (2014). *International classification of functioning, disability and health.* www.who.int/classifications/icf/en/

World Health Organization. (2022). *ICD-11 international classification of diseases for mortality and morbidity statistics.* https://icd.who.int/browse11/l-m/en#/http://id.who.int/icd/entity/654956298

Wright, L., & Ayre, A. (2000). *WASSP: Wright and Ayre Stuttering Self-Rating Profile.* Speechmark.

Wyatt, G. L. (1969). *Language learning and communication disorders in children.* Free Press.

Yairi, E. (1981). Disfluencies of normally speaking two-year-old children. *Journal of Speech and Hearing Research, 24,* 490–495.

Yairi, E. (1982). Longitudinal studies of disfluencies in two-year-old children. *Journal of Speech and Hearing Research, 25,* 155–160.

Yairi, E. (1983). The onset of stuttering in two-and three-year-old children. *Journal of Speech and Hearing Disorders, 48,* 171–177.

Yairi, E. (1993). Epidemiologic and other considerations in treatment efficacy research with preschool-age children who stutter. *Journal of Fluency Disorders, 18*(2–3), 197–219.

Yairi, E. (1997a). Disfluency characteristics of early childhood stuttering. In R. F. Curlee & G. M. Siegel (Eds.), *Nature and treatment of stuttering: New directions* (2nd ed., pp. 49–78). Allyn & Bacon.

Yairi, E. (1997b). Home environment and parent–child interaction in childhood stuttering. In R. F. Curlee & G. M. Siegel (Eds.), *Nature and treatment of stuttering, New directions* (2nd ed., pp. 24–48). Allyn & Bacon.

Yairi, E. (2004). The formative years of stuttering: A changing portrait. *Contemporary Issues in Communication Science and Disorders, 31,* 92–104.

Yairi, E., & Ambrose, N. G. (1992a). A longitudinal study of stuttering in children: A preliminary report. *Journal of Speech and Hearing Research, 35,* 755–760.

Yairi, E., & Ambrose, N. G. (1992b). Onset of stuttering in preschool children: Selected factors. *Journal of Speech and Hearing Research, 35,* 782–788.

Yairi, E., & Ambrose, N. G., (1999). Early childhood stuttering I: Persistency and recovery rates. *Journal of Speech, Language and Hearing Research, 42,* 1097–1112.

Yairi, E., & Ambrose, N. G. (2005). *Early childhood stuttering, for clinicians by clinicians.* PRO-ED.

Yairi, E., Ambrose, N. G., & Niermann, R. (1993). The early months of stuttering: A developmental study. *Journal of Speech and Hearing Research, 36,* 521–528.

Yairi, E., Ambrose, N. G., Paden, E. P., & Throneburg, R. N. (1996). Predictive factors of persistence and recovery: Pathways of childhood stuttering. *Journal of Communication Disorders, 29,* 51–77.

Yairi, E., & Carrico, D. (1992). Pediatricians' attitudes and practices concerning early childhood stuttering. *American Journal of Speech-Language Pathology, 1,* 54–62.

Yairi, E., & Clifton, N. F. (1972). Disfluent speech behavior of preschool children, high school seniors and geriatric persons. *Journal of Speech and Hearing Research, 15,* 714–719.

Yairi, E., & Lewis, B. (1984). Disfluencies at the onset of stuttering. *Journal of Speech and Hearing Research, 27,* 155–159.

Yairi, E., & Seery, C. H. (2023). *Stuttering: Foundations and clinical applications* (3rd ed.). Plural Publishing.

Yalom, I. D. (2002). *The gift of therapy: An open letter to a new generation of therapists and their patients.* HarperCollins.

Yaruss, J. S. (1997a). Clinical measurement of stuttering behaviors. *Contemporary Issues in Communication Science and Disorders, 24,* 33–44.

Yaruss, J. S. (1997b). Improving assessment of children's oral motor development in clinical settings. In W. Hulstijn, H. F. M. Peters, & P. H. H. M. Van Lieshout (Eds.), *Speech production: Motor control, brain research, and fluency disorders* (pp. 565–571). Elsevier Science.

Yaruss, J. S. (2000). The role of performance in the demands and capacities model. *Journal of Fluency Disorders, 25*(4), 347–358.

Yaruss, J. S., Coleman, C. E., & Quesal, R. (2012). Stuttering in school-age children. A comprehensive approach to treatment [Letter to the editor]. *Language, Speech, and Hearing Services in Schools, 43*(4), 536–548.

Yaruss, J. S., & Conture, E. G. (1995). Mother and child speaking rates and utterance lengths in adjacent fluent utterances. *Journal of Fluency Disorders, 20,* 257–278.

Yaruss, J. S., & Conture, E. G. (1996). Stuttering and phonological disorders in children: Examination of the covert repair hypothesis. *Journal of Speech and Hearing Research, 39,* 349–364.

Yaruss, J. S., Murphy, W., Quesal, R. W., & Reardon, N. A. (2004). *Bullying and teasing: Helping children who stutter.* National Stuttering Association.

Yaruss, S., & Quesal, R. (2002). Academic and clinical education in fluency disorders: An update. *Journal of Fluency Disorders, 27,* 43–63.

Yaruss, J. S., & Quesal, R. W. (2004). Stuttering and the *International Classification of Functioning, Disability, and Health* (ICF): An update. *Journal of Communication Disorders, 37,* 35–52.

Yaruss, J. S., & Quesal, R. (2006). Overall Assessment Of The Speaker's Experience Of Stuttering (OASES). *Journal of Fluency Disorders, 31,* 90–115.

Yaruss, J. S., & Quesal, R. W. (2016). *Overall Assessment of the Speaker's Experience of Stuttering.* Stuttering Therapy Resources.

Yaruss, J. S., Quesal, R., & Murphy, W. (2002). National Stuttering Association members' opinions about stuttering treatment. *Journal of Fluency Disorders, 27,* 227–241.

Yaruss, J. S., Quesal, R. W., Reeves, L., Molt, L. F., Kluetz, B., Caruso, A. J., . . . Lewis, F. (2002). Speech treatment and support group experiences of people who participate in the National Stuttering Association. *Journal of Fluency Disorders, 27,* 115–134.

Yates, A. J. (1963). Delayed auditory feedback. *Psychological Bulletin, 60,* 213–232.

Young, M. A. (1975). Onset, prevalence, and recovery from stuttering. *Journal of Speech and Hearing Disorders, 40,* 49–58.

Young, M. A. (1981). A reanalysis of "Stuttering therapy: The relation between attitude change and long-term outcome." *Journal of Speech and Hearing Disorders, 46,* 221–222.

Zebrowski, P. M. (1997). Assisting young children who stutter and their families: Defining the role of the speech-language pathologist. *American Journal of Speech-Language Pathology, 6*(2), 19–28.

Zebrowski, P. M. (2002). Building clinical relationships with teenagers who stutter.

Contemporary Issues in Communication Science and Disorders, 29, 91–100.

Zebrowski, P. M. (2007). Treatment factors that influence therapy outcomes for children who stutter. In E. Conture & R. Curlee (Eds.), *Stuttering and related disorders of fluency* (3rd ed., pp. 23–38). Thieme Medical.

Zebrowski, P. M., & Conture, E. G. (1998). Influence of nontreatment variables on treatment effectiveness for school-age children who stutter. In A. Cordes & R. Ingham (Eds.), *Treatment efficacy for stuttering: A search for empirical bases* (pp. 293–310). Singular Publishing.

Zebrowski, P. M., Conture, E. G., & Cudahy, E. A. (1985). Acoustic analysis of young stutterers' fluency: Preliminary observations. *Journal of Fluency Disorders, 10,* 173–192.

Zengin-Bolatkale, H., Conture, E. G., Walden, T. A., & Jones, R. M. (2018). Sympathetic arousal as a marker of chronicity in childhood stuttering. *Developmental Neuropsychology, 43*(2), 135–151. https://doi.org/10.1080/87565641.2018.1432621

Zimmerman, G. (1980). Stuttering: A disorder of movement. *Journal of Speech and Hearing Research, 23,* 122–136.

Zimmerman, G. (1981). Stuttering: In need of a unifying conceptual framework. *Journal of Speech and Hearing Research, 24,* 25–31.

Zinker, J. (1977). *Creative process in Gestalt therapy.* Random House.

INDEX